More raves for
CALL HER MISS ROSS

"A behind-the-scenes look at the Motown 'family,' suggesting that infighting, possible mob involvement, backstabbing and egos out of control were the norm."

People

"Vividly written ... [The book] does not read as a crass attempt to exploit a star or as the work of an author with a particular ax to grind. ... Taraborrelli brings out the positive side where it exists, debunking some of the more sordid rumors that have circulated around her."

Milwaukee Journal

"The most scathing celebrity tell-all since *His Way*, the 1987 book in which Kitty Kelley revealed that Frank Sinatra ate scrambled eggs off the chest of a call girl."

The Miami Herald

"Immensely entertaining ... Packed with sex, money and ruthless ambition."

The Pittsburgh Press

Also by J. Randy Taraborrelli:

MICHAEL JACKSON: The Magic and the Madness*

Forthcoming from Ballantine Books

CALL
HER
MISS
ROSS

*The Unauthorized Biography
of Diana Ross*

J. Randy Taraborrelli

BALLANTINE BOOKS • NEW YORK

FOR THE FIVE Rs

Library of Congress Catalog Card Number: 89-22131

ISBN 0-345-36925-4

This edition published by arrangement with Carol Publishing Group

Manufactured in the United States of America

First Ballantine Books Edition: July 1991

Cover photo © Albert Ferreira/David McGough Inc.

"You've been watching me since I was a teen-ager. You watched me go crazy. You watched me get big-headed. You watched me spend too much money. You watched me have my family. Then you watched me catch up with myself. And I don't think I'm difficult or unreasonable. I'm sorry, I just don't."

—Diana Ross to J. Randy Taraborrelli
(interview, October 18, 1981)

Private faces in public places
Are wiser and nicer
Than public faces in private places

—W. H. Auden

Author's personal acknowledgments:

There are certain people without whom this project would never have been brought to fruition. Among them are my publisher at Carol Publishing Group, Steven Schragis; associate publisher Carole Stuart; publicists Fern Edison, Jessica Black and Ben Petrone; rights director, Meryl Earl; assistant to Ms. Black, Suzie Hayes; art director, Steve Brower; copy editor, Al Marill; and my attorney Melvin L. Wulf of Beldock, Levine & Hoffman.

Thanks and gratitude to my editor and the president of Birch Lane Press, Hillel Black, for taking this project on, believing in me and pushing me way beyond what I thought were professional limitations.

Without my agent and friend, Bart Andrews, this book would still be just a dream. Bart devoted two years of his life to this work and his contributions to *Call Her Miss Ross* were invaluable. Thanks also to my chief researcher, John Redmann, for a job well done.

I owe a very special debt of gratitude to Paula Agronick Reuben for her perseverance, vision, patience and talent. I would never have been able to complete this work without her assistance and contributions. I feel truly blessed.

Special thanks for the advance word on *Call Her Miss Ross* to: Cindy Adams; Helen Gurley Brown; Betty Liu Ebron; Curtis Kelly; Dick Maurice; Barbara Ormsby (who has been interviewing me for features in the *Daily Times* for the last 15 years); Jeffrey Wilson (a friend for over 20 years who has been invaluable to my work in so many ways); and also to Liz Smith and her staff.

My appreciation to the entire staff of the Margaret Herrick Library of the Academy of Motion Picture Arts and Sciences in Beverly Hills, for their cooperation on so many different levels. Thanks also to the staffs of the Library of the Performing Arts at Lincoln Center in New York City and of the American Film Institute in Los Angeles.

Thanks to Diane Albright for her assistance. Thanks also to John Whyman for sharing memories of his life with "the girls."

Thanks to the staff of Nightmare Records for assisting me in securing interviews with some of the former Motown stars who are now recording again for Nightmare. Thank you, Ian Levine, Rick Gianotos and Carla Marlowe, and best of luck with the careers of the Motown greats you've taken under your wings. Thanks also to make-up man supreme, Rudy Calvo.

Reginald Wilson was instrumental in compiling much of the information for this book in regard to the early Detroit years. His work is very appreciated.

For support in so many ways, thanks to: James Perry, Allen Kramer, Richard Tyler Jordan, Billy Barnes, Linda DiStefano, John Passantino, Maryann McCullough, David Duarte, Val Johns, Edward Jiminez, David Doolittle, Danny Romo, Tom Rachele, Tony Vaughn, Andre Pittmon and Derrick Perrault. And to Cindy Birdsong, thanks for understanding.

My friend Carl Feuerbacher and I started our careers together working for The Supremes almost 20 years ago, and he is still working for Mary Wilson. His dedication is something I have always admired. I appreciate his assistance, always.

All of my books are first read in manuscript form by Wayne Brasler who teaches journalism classes at the University of Chicago. I appreciate his always keeping me on the right track.

Thanks also to Marvin Rothenstein for his keen eye in proofreading this manuscript.

And, to David Bruner, thanks for everything. Finally, special thanks to Rocco and Rose Taraborrelli, Roslyn Taraborrelli, Rocky and Rose Taraborrelli, Nettie Taraborrelli and the rest of my family who have tolerated 25 years of my obsessive interest in Diana Ross and The Supremes.

J. Randy Taraborrelli

❧ Prologue ❧

As soon as she starts to sing "Reach Out and Touch (Some-body's Hand)," the audience leans forward in anticipation. This is why they've come to Caesars Palace. Diana Ross smiles brightly as she glides from the stage, microphone in hand, as though sensing their eagerness and adoration.

"Sing for me," she says to the gray-haired woman sitting close to the stage. "Reach out and . . ." The woman hesitates, overcome with the moment.

"I'll help you," Diana offers. Her smile is gentle now, en-couraging. They sing together, the woman's voice wavering and uncertain, Diana's clear and confident. At the end of the verse, Diana squeezes the woman's hand.

"Thank you," she says.

"Oh, thank *you*. God bless you." There are tears in the wom-an's eyes.

Diana moves two tables to the left. "Now you," she com-mands.

He is young and black and uses his rich baritone to embellish the simple melody. Diana seems delighted. Her smile grows wider. She sings with him, her hand over his as they hold the microphone. "Reach out and touch somebody's hand," they harmonize, the two voices like one.

She moves into the audience.

"Now you."

"Now you."

"Now you."

"Now everyone. Everyone holds hands."

Supple and swaying, she leads the crowd in song. As the spot-lights merge on her, they kindle the red sequined gown. She

1

becomes a beacon, radiating heat, but remaining cool, in control. Night after night, it's always the same. Two thousand people in Las Vegas, 20,000 people somewhere else, a half a million in New York's Central Park, all reaching out, joining hands, touching, arms waving in the air. And all at her command.

Nobody disagrees when it comes to acknowledging her accomplishments. She's come a long way from being ''Diane,'' the kid from the Brewster Projects, and ''Diana,'' the skinny Supreme with the big, brown eyes and the nasally voice.

''Sing,'' she tells them. And they sing.

''Sway,'' she tells them. And they sway.

''Just look at you! You're wonderful!'' she cries. And they are.

It's not easy generating love among a room full of strangers, but for the past eleven minutes Diana Ross seems to have done just that, and she's made it all appear effortless.

To her audience, there is only one Diana, the one they see before them. They are under her spell and the rapport here comes close to magic. But every magician knows the value of illusion.

Things aren't always what they seem.

Chapter

1

Detroit, Friday, February 17, 1976.

"LET ME TELL ya, I was at the funeral for that Temptations guy who shot himself in the head. So I know you gotta get here early if you want a good spot. And at *that* funeral, honey, I saw *all* the Motown stars. They was cryin' and actin' so sad and miserable. Got me some great pictures, too."

The heavy-set woman with the beret pulled over her ears and wearing a bulky green coat checked twice to make sure the film was loaded properly into her Instamatic. She said she had been waiting since seven in the morning; it was now two o'clock, "so you know I'm *serious* 'bout seein' me some stars."

"I went all the way to Philadelphia for that Tammi Terrell funeral a couple years back," she continued, grandly. " 'Course, I had to take a train to get there, but it was worth the trouble because, honey, Mr. Marvin Gaye was there, in person!"

She noticed ears perking up around her. "And I got me a color picture of him cryin' his eyes out. Poor fool. Loved Tammi so much." She shook her head dramatically.

Everyone around her did the same.

"Well, who'd you see at The Temptations funeral?" a young fellow in a suit wanted to know. "Did *you-know-who* show up?"

Looking around, the lady realized that her audience was growing as people gathered around her. "Hell, no, she didn't show up. Too uppity, I guess. Makin' movies now. So grand, ain't she?"

"Sho' is grand," sniffed another woman. "I heard she fired poor Flo from The Supremes."

"That's what *I* heard, too," someone else said. "Kicked her ass right out."

"Sho' is pitiful," the woman in the green coat decided.

3

"Poor Flo."

"And Mary, too. Had to put up with *her* all them years!"" another lady piped in.

"Yeah, poor Mary."

"Poor Flo and poor Mary," everyone agreed.

"Sho' is pitiful."

As a limousine slowly inched its way toward the New Bethel Baptist Church, police officers cleared away people who were peering into its tinted windows and blocking its path.

"Who's in it?" someone asked. "Is it *her*?"

When the car stopped in front of the church, a tuxedoed chauffeur jumped out. The crowd surged forward. A back door opened. Two more men in black suits got out. Finally, one of them opened the remaining door, and a long, black-stockinged, high-heeled leg peeked out, toes pointed demurely.

"It *is* her!"

She looked very small, almost frail, in a black coat trimmed with sable at the collar and cuffs, a matching knit cloche-style hat, and gold hoop earrings. Her face was expertly made up, contoured, blushed and highlighted. Heavy-lashed eyes were properly mournful. She was immediately the center of attention, though she seemed to be oblivious to it all. Flanked by four stone-faced bodyguards, she bowed her head as she walked through the charged crowd. Everyone started taking pictures.

"Look this way."

Click.

"Look over here."

Click.

"Now over here."

Click.

Miss Diana Ross had arrived.

"Well, she certainly has *her* nerve," said the woman who had been waiting since seven in the morning. "Comin' here and all, in a fancy car." She snapped a picture and then elbowed someone in the ribs. "Outta my way, you! Gotta get me an autograph . . . for my daughter."

The woman rushed up to Diana. "Diana, honey, can I have your auto . . . ?"

Ignoring her, the star and her bodyguards rushed by.

People started booing as Diana and her entourage made their way through the huge crowd.

Mary Wilson and her mother Johnnie Mae stood in the long, slow-moving line of people waiting to be seated. Ernestine Ross, Diana's mother, also stood in that line, watching sadly, quietly, with a pained expression on her face. It was obvious to her that her daughter was not welcome at Florence Ballard's funeral.

"Flo, she's the quiet one," Diana had said when she introduced The Supremes during their nightclub act. But she had it all wrong. Maybe it was wishful thinking because in life, Florence Ballard had never been one to keep quiet about much.

In the '60s, Florence Ballard, Mary Wilson and Diana Ross— The Supremes—quickly became the most successful American vocal group of their day. Rising from the Brewster Projects of Detroit to the most prestigious nightclubs and concert halls in the world, they had, by 1965, racked up an enviable string of unforgettable hit records. The leading proponents of Detroit's home-bred music called The Motown Sound, their only logical peers in the pop world were The Beatles and Elvis Presley.

From the start, Diana Ross had that rare star quality, stage presence and unique singing voice that immediately set her apart from the other two. But along with her talent and ambition there was a certain amount of ruthlessness. She was famous and her fans adored her, but she was not popular among her Motown peers, many of whom thought that Berry Gordy helped her rise at their expense. By 1967, she had become the star of the act, much to Mary and Florence's dismay. They thought that the *group* was what mattered, but Diana was never group-oriented. She knew early on that The Supremes were but a stepping-stone on her way to the top. As far as she was concerned, if Mary and Florence couldn't figure out a way to make the group work to *their* advantage, that was their problem, not hers.

"You know, you told me you wouldn't try to stand in Diane's way if she wanted to go out on her own," Berry told Florence one afternoon at the airport in Vancouver, Canada, in 1966. (Though "Diana" is the name on Diana Ross' birth certificate, most of her friends and associates from the early days called her—and still do call her [perhaps not to her face]—"Diane," which is what her parents intended that she be named.) The group was getting ready to board a plane headed back to Detroit. Florence was surprised by Berry's statement. It had been an uneventful trip with none of the usual tantrums, and it seemed that nothing had precipitated the conversation.

"Yeah, that's what I said," Florence once remembered having told him. "If she wants to be on her own, then that's okay with me. But I ain't leaving the group."

"She wants out," Berry said, ignoring her last statement.

"But you're making it tough on her. She told me you're making her feel guilty about it."

Years later, Florence recalled, "That's when I started getting pissed off. I said, 'Look, Berry, she's grown. If she wants to walk all over people to get to the top, then that's her business. I'm not gonna make her feel no better by agreeing with it.'

" 'You're a millionaire,' he told me. 'You can leave the group any time.' But I told him I ain't leaving."

With that, Berry and Florence became locked in the same quarrels about her excessive drinking and weight gain, all of which ended with Florence—tears in her eyes and her voice shaking—threatening Berry once more. "You'll be sorry you messed with me, Berry Gordy," she screamed loud enough for everyone in the terminal to hear. "I know a lot about you, more than you think. And don't you forget it." Then Gordy turned his back and stormed off leaving her to her tears. Diana ran after Berry with a smug look on her face.

Actually, Mary Wilson was "the quiet one," not Florence Ballard. Mary, content to be a Supreme at whatever cost, watched and waited to see what would happen next. But Florence shouted and made threats, claiming to have embarrassing information on Berry Gordy's business practices. She quickly became a threat to Gordy's peace of mind, to the continued success of the group and, maybe even more importantly, to Diana's future career.

On stage, as off, Flo was irrepressible—and audiences loved her for it. During the act, when Diana said, "Thin is in," Flo sassed back, "But honey, *fat* is where it's at." When Diana sang, "Gold won't bring you happiness," during their rendition of "You're Nobody Till Somebody Loves You," Flo would interrupt with, "Give *me* that gold and I'll do my *own* shoppin'." Flo was a crowd pleaser and Diana and Berry couldn't very well ignore that. Though they weren't very fond of her ad-libs, they tolerated them just to keep her "quiet."

But Ballard's smart-aleck remarks on stage hid a lot of pain. Increasingly pushed into the background, she felt cheated. The more successful The Supremes became and the more attention Diana received, the more alienated and bitter Flo seemed. She put on weight and began to show up drunk for performances. She deluded herself into thinking that because she formed the group and chose its name, she was indispensable.

She was wrong. Florence was unceremoniously dumped and quickly replaced. Soon, she found herself without money, without a career, and, worse, without hope.

There are people at Motown who still talk about the last time the three Supremes were seen together. It was in October 1968, over a year after Florence was fired. The scene was a party hosted by Berry at his home in Detroit, the ostentatious Gordy Manor on Boston Avenue. Mary Wilson continued being a cock-eyed optimist despite all that had happened to The Supremes, believing that there should be something shared between them; what exactly, she wasn't sure. Not content to leave well enough alone, she wanted to bring the three original girls together again. She selected this Motown party at Berry's mansion to effect a reconciliation.

When she asked Florence to attend the gathering as her personal guest, Flo refused. "I just don't want to see *her*," Flo said, referring to Diana. Mary couldn't change her mind, so she telephoned Berry's brother Fuller who had always liked Florence. "Yeah, tell her to come," he urged Mary. "We'd all love to see her. We never had a chance to say good-bye."

Florence once claimed that the trouble started when Diana sidled over to her and tugged on the long "fall" wig she was wearing. "I told her don't do it again," she claimed, "and then she ran over to Berry and told him that I was trying to start something." They were acting like spoiled little children; two of the most famous and important figures in pop music history, and this is what it had come to.

Flo was pregnant with twins (she would have the babies prematurely just days after this party) and she had had one can of beer too many. She and Diana exchanged words. The more antagonistic Florence became, the more troublesome Diana proved to be.

"And, bitch, you stop comin' over here and botherin' me," Flo shouted, her speech now slurred.

Diana skulked over to Berry and angrily whispered something in his ear. Berry then went to Florence and told her that she would have to leave the party since she wasn't invited in the first place.

"I ain't goin' nowhere," was Flo's answer. Berry turned away and walked back to Diana's side.

Florence remembered that she was chatting with Fuller Gordy when Berry came back to her and threatened, "If you don't get the hell out of here, I will have you thrown out."

"Nobody tells *me* when to leave a party," Florence snapped back. She looked over Berry's shoulder and directed her loud comment to Diana, who turned away.

Eventually, Mary and Florence were both being ejected from

the party by Berry's beefy bodyguards; Florence defiant and angry, Mary humiliated and in tears.

"No one told you to bring her, Mary," Berry Gordy hollered after them. "And don't you bring her back!" It was the last time Berry would see Florence. He did not attend her funeral. Instead, he sent a floral arrangement with the cryptic message: "Good-bye Flo."

As the battery of news reporters, television cameramen and photographers documented the whole scene, Diana was hurried into the New Bethel Baptist Church ahead of everyone else. Stevie Wonder, The Four Tops, Mary Wilson and other Motown stars, Ballard family members and friends all stood with their mouths agape as the bodyguards elbowed everyone out of the way and spirited the star inside.

Diana did not try to slip anonymously into the church and sit with her own mother, Ernestine, and with Mary Wilson and all of the other mourners who were not family. Rather Diana chose to make a spectacular entrance. She sat in the first pew—reserved for the deceased's immediate family—right next to Florence's grieving mother and husband, Tommy Chapman. She couldn't have been any more conspicuous. One Detroiter observed, "Look at how she's showboatin'. Trying to upstage Florence at her own funeral."

"Be quiet. Sit down and be quiet," shouted Rev. C. L. Franklin, singer Aretha Franklin's father. It was becoming impossible to control the 2,200 people inside the church, some of whom came to pay tribute to Florence but most of whom came to see what was left of The Supremes—Diana Ross and Mary Wilson. People were hanging from the balcony, taking snapshots. "The stars have asked us to ask you not to take pictures of them in the church," said one of the deacons from the pulpit. Diana looked satisfied.

Her eyes were moist and her head bowed. As she held one of Florence's young daughters on her lap, Diana adjusted the yellow bow in the child's hair. Photographs of her holding Florence's child would appear in all of the newspapers the next day.

The services were ruined by pandemonium. Thirty uniformed policemen tried to keep 5,000 fans outside the church from trampling one another while, inside, Rev. Franklin tried to maintain order. The press ran up and down the center aisle snapping photographs of the star who sat in the first row.

"At least have some respect for the dead," Rev. Franklin said to the photographers.

* * *

Toward the end of her life, Florence Ballard lost it all, even self-respect.

In January 1975, Diana was in Rome starring in a glamorous movie titled *Mahogany* about life in the fast lane as a fashion designer.

While Diana rode about in chauffeur-driven limousines in Rome, Florence was bussing it around Detroit. The first time she had to use public transportation, she waited at the bus stop feeling self-conscious, all the while praying that no one would recognize her. She remembered later that to ensure her anonymity she wore large sunglasses and raised the hood on her winter coat. When automobiles would slow down at the intersection to allow for crossing pedestrians, Florence, certain they were slowing down to stare at *her*, would turn her back in shame. Finally, Flo recalled, the bus pulled up to the curb and she got on while rummaging through her purse.

A few seconds later, she got off.

She didn't have exact change for the fare.

Florence walked across the street to a run-down liquor store and politely asked for change of a dollar.

The person at the cash register sized her up and began asking, "Say, ain't you . . . ?"

"No, I ain't . . . ." Florence said, cutting him off.

Then she went back to the bus stop and sat on the bench.

Finally, another bus pulled up. After Florence Ballard got aboard, it drove off in the direction of Detroit's Brewster Projects.

The Reverend called it "the homecoming of Florence Ballard" as he eulogized her. "We have experiences that are not always good, sometimes frustrating and crushing, but positive good grows out of negative situations."

It was an unusually warm winter day and well over 90 degrees inside the overcrowded church. Cardboard fans were the only source of relief. A woman passed out in the back and her husband carried her away. Florence's mother, Lurlee Ballard, fanned herself frantically, eyeing Diana Ross suspiciously at her left, Flo's husband to her right. A heart attack had claimed Lurlee's daughter, Florence, at the age of 32.

Flo still had some unfinished business with Diana. She simply couldn't understand Diana's mercurial behavior—why she did the things she did. The night before she died, Flo asked a friend, "Why did Diane have to act that way?"

Suddenly, after the eulogy, Diana stood up. The noisy crowd hushed for the first time and then everyone began to whisper as she made her way to the altar.

"Could I have the microphone, please?" she asked. Someone handed her one.

"Mary and I would like to have a silent prayer," she announced.

Wilson, wearing a jewel-studded cap and veil and black fur coat, looked horrified by Diana's announcement. She said later that she didn't want to join Diana in any "silent prayer" but, by now, had no choice. She was helped up to the altar and stood near a blue-and-white heart-shaped arrangement of carnations with a ribbon that read: "I love you Blondie—Diana."

As flashbulbs popped all around them, Mary stood beside Diana. The two gazed into the silver-blue casket. Florence wore a light-blue choir robe and matching slippers. Her face looked bloated. Mary wept quietly.

"I believe that nothing disappears and Flo will always be with us," Diana intoned.

Without looking at her, she handed the microphone to Mary. "I loved her very much," Mary barely managed to say. She and Diana didn't speak to each other but the two of them reached out and touched Florence's face, then turned away.

"I could have killed Diane for calling me up there," Mary would say later. "How dare she turn that service into a show! *How dare she!*"

Softly, the organist began to play the recessional hymn, "Someday We'll Be Together."

When Diana left The Supremes, she went on to become a solo recording artist and movie star while Mary went on to try to pick up the pieces of the broken group. Florence went on welfare.

In the years immediately following Florence's dismissal from The Supremes, Diana had no communication with her. Mary kept in touch via an occasional postcard sent from the road. Both women had their own problems and interests. But when Diana heard the news in late 1974 that Florence was about to lose her house on Buena Vista Avenue in Detroit, she was genuinely shocked.

Diana knew how much Florence had depended on the security of her modest house for peace of mind; "If our fame doesn't last and we have nothing else to show for it," Flo had said when she made it big, "at least we'll always have these houses." She decorated hers in Wedgwood blue, white and gold with velvet draperies, brocade furniture and tinted crystal chandeliers. This was her only sanctuary from what she perceived as the cold, cruel world.

"I thought she had at least made provisions for the house," Diana told a friend.

History has painted the picture of Diana Ross' total indifference to Florence Ballard's plight. Certainly many of the people at Ballard's funeral believed that Diana was not only to blame for the former Supreme's downfall, but somehow even planned it. Perhaps Diana could have done more for Florence, but the truth is that even though Florence's plight was widely publicized, all of the Motown artists who had bragged over the years of being "a family" turned their backs on her.

Diana felt that for Florence to lose her house because she owed a few thousand dollars on it was a shame. She couldn't imagine how Flo could let this happen to herself. Apparently, Diana tried to communicate with her, but either Flo refused to return her phone calls or the calls were intercepted by her family because the two women made no contact.

Diana had her business office issue a check for the amount owed on the Buena Vista home and then began making arrangements for the money to be delivered to Florence's estranged husband Tommy Chapman. Tommy became suspicious. Diana had never tried to help Florence before and now he thought that she had ulterior motives for wanting to save the home. He insisted that the check be made payable to him personally.

But Diana didn't trust Chapman. She was uncertain about his relationship with Florence at this point, and why the two separated. Rather than risk him absconding with the money, she insisted that the check be made payable to the bank holding the mortgage. Diana felt that Chapman would allow her to do this favor her way, if he really had his wife's best interests at heart. When he wouldn't—and she couldn't reach Florence—the check was voided. Florence lost the house and had to move herself and her three young children in with one of her sisters. She received $135 every two weeks from welfare. It's not known whether Florence realized what Diana had tried to do.

"If I'd known how it was going to end with Florence, maybe I would have taken more time with her, fought her more, even though she didn't want my help," Diana would later say. "But she got to be a pain in the ass and I said, 'Oh, forget it!' Maybe I should have slapped her face a few times."

Mary Wilson must have known what Diana had tried to do,

but she apparently decided not to write about it when she penned her memoirs in 1986, *Dreamgirl—My Life As a Supreme*. Today, after Mary's book, Ross and Wilson no longer speak to each other. They didn't speak that morning in Detroit either, at Florence's funeral.

Outside the church, the squad of police officers now numbered nearly 50, but it was impossible to control the crowd. When the floral arrangements were being carried from the church, the crowd began tearing them apart one by one. A funeral-home attendant tried to keep people from grabbing the flowers, but soon he gave up and whole arrangements were tossed into the crowds. Fans desperately grabbed bits and pieces while Diana, head still bowed, was rushed into her limousine. The car sped off.

Florence was buried in Detroit Memorial Park later that day. There were no photographers, no intrusive members of the press, no excited fans, and no Diana Ross—just family members and a few friends, including The Four Tops. As the family gathered close to the graveside and the casket was being lowered into the frozen ground, Mary Wilson stood off to the side and cried. It was, by this time, late in the afternoon, the sun was setting and it was getting cold. Mary drew her coat closer to her as she stepped towards the open grave. Shivering, she threw a single red rose onto the coffin.

Later, Mary would remember looking for Diana, hoping that she would appear. But Diana never did. To this day, the two have not discussed Flo's death or the funeral.

Diana Ross and Florence Ballard started out as youngsters from the same government-subsidized housing project in Detroit, both with so much hope and promise. But their lives took such totally different paths: one so glorious, one so sad. Who knows what twists of fate made Diana Ross a star and Florence Ballard a tragic figure?

"Florence was always on a totally negative trip," Diana would say in an interview four months after the funeral. "She *wanted* to be a victim. Then when she left The Supremes and the money stopped coming in, it really messed up her head.

"She was just one of those people you want to grab and shake and yell, 'Get your fucking life together!'"

Chapter

2

IN THE LATE '50s, black music was happening in Detroit. Scores of young people, hoping to make it big, formed groups and rehearsed in basements, apartments and on street corners. They played at school dances, talent contests and tacky nightclubs. Every day, they hung out at 2648 West Grand Boulevard—Hitsville—all the while dreaming of getting the nod and, more important, the contract from Berry Gordy, Jr., that would start them on their road to riches.

Hitsville, Berry Gordy's record company headquarters, was sandwiched between a funeral home and a beauty shop. Once a residence, now newly painted glossy white with blue trim, it bustled with activity. Musicians doubled as producers, arrangers or office workers. For example, Janie Bradford, the teen-ager who wrote the prophetic hit "Money (That's What I Want)" with Berry, worked as receptionist. Berry dubbed the building Hitsville and the record label it housed, Tamla.

As singer Smokey Robinson described it: "Downstairs became headquarters. Kitchen became the control room. Garage became the studio. The living room was bookkeeping. The dining room, sales. Berry stuck a funky sign in the front window—'Hitsville U.S.A.'—and we were in business."

Once the word was out that Berry would sign practically every youngster with a modicum of talent to his record label, hoping that some of them would somehow be magically transformed into stars, Hitsville became a mecca for aspiring black performers. They came with high hopes, singly and in groups. In the summer of 1960, The Primettes—Florence Ballard, Mary Wilson, Betty McGlown and Diana Ross—were in the Hitsville waiting room for their chance to audition. Although it was Flo who founded the group, it was Diana who wrangled the audition through former next-door neighbor, Smokey Robinson. Janie Bradford recalled, "They were four very confident girls in white skirts, matching scarves and bobby socks, acting so sophisticated, as if they were the hottest thing to ever happen."

When the time arrived for their audition, Hitsville talent scout Robert Bateman and record producer Richard Morris ushered the girls into a back room. Standing in a semicircle, The Primettes sang "The Twist" and "Night Time Is the Right Time" a cappella while Berry walked in and out. The girls didn't know who he was, never having met him before. If he was impressed, he didn't show it. He had just signed The Marvelettes, five young girls from Inkster, Michigan, and didn't want any more acts on the label "who had the potential to get pregnant."

"They were okay," Janie Bradford said of The Primettes. "But not outstanding. Just so-so."

As Berry sauntered back into the room, Diana announced that "we have one more song we'd like to do." Her voice was tentative. When he nodded his approval, they began a timid version of The Drifters' song, "There Goes My Baby." The sound seemed a bit weak, but somehow very sincere. Young Ross' lead voice was whiny and untrained but brimming with emotion. Berry, fascinated, stopped and listened for a moment. After they finished, he leaned over to Bateman and whispered in his ear.

"One more time, girls," Bateman commanded.

Diana counted off four and they began again. She sang in high-pitched tones while her partners provided sincere oohs and aahs. After they finished, Berry introduced himself to them.

"You sing through your nose?" he asked Diana.

"Well, I dunno . . ." Diana said, nervously. "If you want me to, I guess I can."

"You already *do*," Berry laughed. "Sit down and we'll talk." Berry motioned to four wooden chairs. The Primettes sat, leaning forward to hear his every word. When he told them they weren't "too bad," the four of them jumped up, squealing in delight. "But you're not too good, either," Berry added. He wanted to know their ages. The girls hesitated. Mary and Diana were 16, Florence was 17 and Betty 18. When they told Berry, he shook his head solemnly.

"No. You, you and you are too young," he said, pointing to Diana, Mary and Florence. For Berry, this was as good an excuse as any. He really was not interested. "Come back when you're through with high school." He started for the door. The meeting was over.

"But, hey! We won the contest," Flo shouted at his retreating back. She was referring to the Detroit/Windsor Freedom Festival, an amateur talent show sponsored annually in Windsor, Ontario, on Independence Day by radio stations on both sides of the Canadian border. The Primettes had won first place. Afterwards, Robert Bateman took Florence aside, identified himself as a talent scout, and suggested that The Primettes audition for his boss, Berry Gordy. But Flo had heard stories about Gordy, and she was not impressed.

"Ain't he that guy who cheats his artists?" she wanted to know. Since Berry had a reputation in the neighborhood for taking financial advantage of the youngsters he signed to the label, Flo didn't think the encounter with Bateman was worth mentioning to her singing partners at that time. But now she was using it as ammunition to break into Hitsville.

"That guy there," she said, pointing to Bateman, "he said for us to come down here, and here we are. Now you're telling us you don't want us? What kind of stuff is that?"

Witnesses recall that Berry turned and sauntered over to Flo. He sized her up and then cut her down with two words: "Get lost!"

"But . . ."

"I'm the boss, girl, and I said good-bye." He opened the door and waved them out.

When Florence looked as though she was going to open her mouth again, Diana dug her fingers into Flo's arms and pulled her along, all the while hissing at her to "shut up. Shut the hell up! You want to ruin our chances forever?"

Once outside, Diana whirled to face Flo. "Why didn't you tell us what happened the day we won?" she demanded. She looked as if she was going to go for Flo's throat.

Diana was wiry and thin, a tomboy if ever there was one. Tall and sassy, Flo was not easily cowed, but this time she seemed to be taken aback. "*I* decide for The Primettes," she managed with a faint show of bravado. She looked to Mary and Betty for support. None came. Diana was infuriated. "Talking to Hitsville, that's too important for you to decide for yourself," she told Florence. "You should've told *me* about this. Why didn't you?"

Flo mumbled that she had forgotten.

"Well, don't you ever forget nothing so important again. Ever. Don't you dare ever forget!"

The four girls then walked back into Hitsville. They couldn't bring themselves to leave. Instead, they just sat in the reception area and gawked at recording artists such as Mary Wells, and producers like Eddie and Brian Holland, who were walking in and out of the building.

Florence later would remember that the next day, Diana made the decision. The Primettes would go back to Hitsville every day until something happened. Berry Gordy would simply have to get used to having them around. "From then on, those girls were always in sight," Janie Bradford recalled. "And talkin' 'bout 'we got things to do,' as if they had some pressing business. 'Things to do,' indeed. They had no business being there, but they were persistent just the same. It didn't matter, though. Berry still wanted nothing to do with them."

Just as 16-year-old Diana had vowed they would, The Primettes started haunting Hitsville and, just as Berry had promised, they were ignored. Soon, Betty McGlown decided she wanted to get married and stop singing. Diana felt that Betty was being foolish. She believed that nothing, even romance, should be more important to any of the girls than their careers, and she decided that Betty was being disloyal. Actually, she never liked this girl.

Betty was a year older than Diana and tried to use her age as justification to influence some of the group's decisions. Whenever Diana wanted to sing lead, Betty would convince Florence and Mary that Flo should be the sole lead singer. Often, Betty would make the initial decisions on what the girls would wear at performances. Hours would be spent trying to determine what costumes would be best, and the meeting would end with all four girls in agreement. Then, when it came time to perform, Diana would show up in something entirely different. An argument would always ensue with Betty accusing Diana of trying to single herself out, which, of course, was exactly what she was trying to do. Still, she didn't like hearing it. So when Betty left, Diana was glad to see her go.

Mary and Florence attended the wedding ceremony alone and began to question the wisdom of having Diana in the group at all. She was certainly proving to be more trouble than they had expected she would be when they recruited her.

The girls were determined that the group should consist of four Primettes and Mary tried to convince Diana that the vacant slot should be filled by a friend named Jackie Burkes. But even though Flo and Mary liked Burkes, Diana didn't, so she never became a Primette. Other girls auditioned, none of whom Diana thought was right, for one reason or another. The more trouble they had replacing Betty, the angrier Diana got. "We wouldn't even be in this mess if she didn't have to go off and get married," she kept complaining.

Finally, they settled on Barbara Martin, a tall, light-skinned girl and fair singer who, it was obvious from the audition, was greatly intimidated by Diana. Diana liked her immediately; she felt comfortable around her because Barbara wouldn't dare tell her what to do. The Primettes then recorded two sides for Lu-Pine, a small record label, and when the single was released, it failed immediately. The company's distributor, suspected of being involved in a payola scam, couldn't market it properly. Then Richard Morris, their producer, disappeared from the scene. Florence discovered that he had been arrested on a parole violation. Things were not going well.

A few months later, Berry Gordy booked studio time for blues singer Mabel John, the first female artist he had signed to the label. Background singers were needed for the session: enter The Primettes. "Let's give them a shot," Berry decided. "What have we got to lose?"

Mabel John stood in a small phone-booth-like cubicle where all the lead vocals to Tamla's hits were recorded. The Primettes were in the same studio but outside the booth, standing behind two microphones next to a black concert grand piano. The four of them, all dressed in neatly ironed white skirts and blouses, stood on clusters of tangled wire cables that seemed to go nowhere and everywhere at the same time.

Mabel John recalled of the session:

"Berry made it clear to them that this was only a test and did not mean they would be signed to the label. Diane was the leader, the in-charge, take-charge type. Mary had the better ear for harmony, but if there was any question it was directed to Diane, not Mary. Oh, Diane was such a little flirt. So young but so attentive to anything Berry wanted. She asked me a lot of questions about Berry, soaking up all of the information. Had the nerve to ask me, 'So what do you really think of him? Is he fair? Is he honest?' as if I was gonna tell her otherwise. She was very direct, a bottom-line kind of girl."

Diana did everything she could to make Berry see that he had made a very serious mistake in not signing the group immediately at the first audition. Their harmonies were tighter than ever, and she made it appear that this was largely the result of her dedication and determination.

After the recording session, the four girls left the studio single file, Diana at the end. Just before they walked out the door, she turned and shot Berry a wink over her shoulder. Then she executed a saucy little hip maneuver.

Berry did a double take.

"Hey. That one on the end. Did she just wink at me?" he asked the recording engineer.

"Yeah, man, the skinny chick is flirtin' with you, Berry."

"Well, shit, man, what do you make of that?"

Later, Mabel John and Berry Gordy sat in the control booth and played back the track. He asked her what she thought about "the girls."

"That Diane," Mabel said with a laugh. "You'd better watch out for her," she warned Berry. "She's somethin' else, and I ain't lyin'."

Recalled Mabel John:

"Berry and I agreed that she was the type of kid who probably knew what she wanted and how she was going to get it. You hear a lot about how Berry thought of the four girls as equals from the beginning. Don't believe it. Diane demanded attention from Berry; from that session on, she was always in his face saying, 'Let's do this!' and 'Please, Berry, let's do that!' Next thing I knew, they were doin' background vocals and handclaps for Marvin Gaye and everyone else at the label. They were becoming part of the family, not because they were greatly talented but because they were *so* determined."

"I think I'm gonna sign that kid Ross to the label," Berry told Mabel John a couple of weeks later.

"And the others?"

"Oh, yeah, them too," Berry responded.

"Now, don't you go breakin' up no group, Berry," Mabel warned him playfully. Berry and Mabel John were close friends. She was one of the only people at the company who could chide Berry and get away with it. "They look like nice girls. Don't mess with them."

"Who, me?" Berry said, widening his eyes innocently.

"Yeah, you."

After that first session, The Primettes continued to go to Hitsville every day: walking, taking the bus, hitchhiking, whatever it took to get there. They had learned that if they spent enough time there, something always came along. There were musical tracks that needed handclaps and, now and then, added background vocals as well. Soon, they were being paid a small salary for their work, but it wasn't always easy to get their money.

Eventually Flo began complaining that she was "tired of workin'" for free." She told her friends, "I warned you 'bout this guy."

One afternoon, Gordy arrived at Hitsville in his beat-up Chevy and, as he walked toward the building, The Primettes jumped out of the bushes like gang members. They surrounded him on all four sides, trying to act threatening in their white pleated skirts and matching blouses. "You owe us money, man," Diana told him. Amused, Berry reached into his pocket and pulled out $2.50, the group's weekly salary. Grinning broadly, he asked how much $2.50 divided by four was.

"Let's just say it ain't much," Flo sniffed.

"Sixty cents should do it," Diana decided in a very serious tone.

With that, Berry pulled out his wallet, offering to make it an even four bucks. Beaming a fatherly smile, he offered them a raise of $1.50 more a week and suggested they use the money for carfare. "We got a lot of stuff that can be done here, and you ladies seem pretty capable," he said, flattering them. "What do you say?"

"Thank you's" turned to giggles when Gordy asked them not to reveal the news to anyone, " 'cause I can't be affordin' no bonuses right now." They turned and walked away. Berry then strutted up to the Hitsville porch where members of The Miracles greeted him warmly, hugging each other as if they were sharing some exciting news. As Mary, Florence and Barbara walked away, Diana trailed behind and stared wonderingly at Berry Gordy and his young protégés.

Many years later, Diana would recall, "I wanted to be a part of that. I wanted to be in. I wanted what they all had. Berry was the most amazing man I, as a kid, had ever seen. So cool, so confident and with such purpose."

Diane was 16. Berry was 31.

A few weeks later, The Primettes got their chance to be "in." Freddie Gorman and Brian Holland, two new company staff writers, had written a dreadful song called "I Want a Guy." Gorman, who was also the Ross family's mailman, remembered, "Diana heard me playing the song one day in the studio and said she wanted to record it. Berry agreed to it. Later, I remember walking into the room where they were rehearsing. Diana was seated at the piano with Brian while the other girls were gathered around her. They had to stand. That's when I knew who was boss."

During rehearsal for "I Want a Guy," Diana whined her way through the song in a nasal, oddly pitched tone. Yet there was something there, Berry felt, and with the right training . . . In a week, he broke the news to The Primettes that he was going to offer them a contract, and then gave Diana a job as his "secretary."

Diana recalled in a 1983 interview, "I was still in high school and I remember I had an art class and I made these cuff links for him. I guess I won him over by being so kind to him, 'cause the truth is, I wasn't his secretary. I couldn't even type or take shorthand."

Though Diana was soon known as "that secretary who thinks she can sing," she knew how to make the best of an opportunity. Anyone who would walk by her desk would inevitably hear phrases like, "Oh, Mr. Gordy, you are so talented!" and "Mr. Gordy, how did you ever get to be so smart?" She never said he was good-looking, though. She was too clever for that. Diana somehow knew that Berry would be more attracted to her if she appealed to his intellect. And, of course, every now and then, just when the timing was right, she would ask when *her* group was to get an opportunity to record their own song. Finally, Berry gave in.

On October 1, 1960, The Primettes were booked into the Hitsville studio and recorded "After All," a tune produced by Smokey Robinson. The song was never released because Berry felt it didn't meet his standards of quality. (In years to come, most of what The Supremes would record would go unreleased for precisely the same reason.) Two months passed. Finally, on December 15, they recorded "I Want a Guy," again with Berry Gordy producing. All of this work, and still without a signed recording contract.

"So, man, what do you think about this?" Berry asked Smokey about "I Want a Guy." "Be honest with me," Gordy insisted. "She sounds kinda whiny, huh? Kinda weird?"

Years later, Smokey would remember that Berry simply could not be sure that Diana actually possessed a singing *voice* and not just an oddly pitched *sound*, especially when he heard rumors at the company that she had recently quit a vocal class in school after discovering that she was going to get a D.

Smokey somehow managed to identify the commercial possibilities of the lead singer, although the muddled arrangement made for one of the most atrocious songs he had ever heard. He told Berry that even though the girl didn't have the best singing voice, she did have "personality" and an interesting sound, "and there ain't nothin' wrong with havin' a sound," he said. "If she catches on, man, watch out!"

Later, Berry offered a deal to Robert Bateman, the man who brought The Primettes to Motown.

"If you want to manage Diane Ross and her group, they are all yours," Berry told him. "And whatever success you have you get a percentage of for the rest of your life."

Did he accept the deal?

"Do I look rich?" Bateman answered years later, deadpan. "No one wanted to get involved with a kid who sings through her nose."

Berry decided to sign the girls to a contract anyway, but first their group name would have to be changed. He said he didn't understand just what a "Primette" was.

"Well, you see, it means . . ." one of them eagerly began.

"Never mind what it means," Berry snapped at her. "We're changing it."

All four girls were stunned by Berry's decision. They had their pride, after all, and had spent the last two years establishing what they thought was a reputation in the Detroit area. Actually, no one knew who they were, or cared.

"By the time I finish with you, *everyone* will know who you are," Berry promised. He then instructed Janie Bradford to come up with a list of names from which the girls would have the "freedom" of choosing their favorite one. Bradford recalled that she was only able to think of three names and, today, can only remember one of them, the one Florence picked: The Supremes. Diana hated the name. She thought it sounded like a male group. The other girls agreed with her and, as they all argued the point, a secretary in an adjoining office typed it into their recording contracts.*

When Diana returned home with the news that she was about to sign a contract with Berry Gordy Enterprises, Fred Ross said, "Daughter, you are not signing any contract with anyone's fly-by-night enterprise." Father and daughter had had years of ar-

---

*In years to come, Mary Wilson would sue Berry Gordy and Motown, claiming that she should have ownership of The Supremes' name because, she claimed, the girls originated it themselves. In her memoirs, *Dreamgirl—My Life as a Supreme*, she doesn't mention that the list of names from which Florence made the choice came from a Motown employee, not from any member of the group.

In any case, this was not the first group to be called The Supremes. The name was first used in 1957 by a male quartet from Columbus, Ohio, who recorded a single on Ace Records called "Just for You and I." They named themselves The Supremes while enjoying a bottle of "Bourbon Supreme." Also, Ruby and the Romantics, the group who recorded the classic pop song "Our Day Will Come," originally called themselves The Supremes.

guments about Diana's show business career, all of which basically boiled down to the fact that he didn't want her to have one. He wanted her to attend college and do something "sensible" with her life, as both he and his wife had done. Academics and practicality had been important parts of the Ross family history, and Fred Ross was determined that his daughter Diane continue the tradition.

Fred Ross was born on Independence Day in 1920 in Bluefield, West Virginia, to Edward and Ida Ross, a middle-class, well-educated couple. His father taught at West Virginia State College; his mother died when Fred was two years old. In 1924, Edward, unable to cope with his job and the responsibility of raising four children, sent them to live with relatives. Fred eventually went to live with an aunt in Detroit, Michigan.

He graduated from Cass Technical High School in 1937. Over six feet tall and weighing 160 pounds, he became a boxer. In the city that produced "The Brown Bomber," Joe Louis, one of the greatest fighters of all time, Fred Ross was considered a comer. He won the middleweight title of the Industrial Championship, the Diamond Belt middleweight crown and got as far as the semifinals of the Golden Gloves competition. Boxing is not a team sport. Although there may be help from trainers, in the end it is the solitary combatant who determines his own success. Fred always felt he was the master of his own fate. Although he was popular with the ladies because of his muscular build and good looks, his peers remember him more for his icy reserve. Always cordial, but never warm, he was a determined, serious young man.

While Fred Ross was jabbing his way through young adulthood, Ernestine Moten had dropped out of Selma University in Alabama to move to Detroit with her sister in 1936. Ernestine, born on January 27, 1916, in Allenville, Alabama, was the youngest of 12 children of Rev. William and Isabel Moten. Her father, pastor of the Bessemer Baptist Church, was as industrious as he was religious. He owned a small produce farm.

Like Fred, Ernestine had a voracious appetite for schoolwork and had been a remarkable student. By the time she was 18, she was a tall, slender woman with chestnut brown skin and flowing black hair that hung fully about her shoulders. Her smile, a family trademark, was bright and full. She had dancing, almond-shaped, light brown eyes. Ernestine enjoyed singing in church and the local clubs, but she never seriously considered a career in show business because such a life seemed frivolous.

Fred and Ernestine met in 1937 and, though both were educated and had a practical outlook on life, they were different in many ways. She was lovable and easygoing, content to leave her studies behind in favor of domesticity. He was distant and aggressive, continuing his boxing as well as his education with almost fanatical determination. He was enrolled in Wayne State College, studying business administration. Soon he secured a trainee position at the American Brass Company, making $60 a week operating heat furnaces. Once employed, he decided to end the two-year engagement to Ernestine and marry her. "I wouldn't marry Ernestine if I thought for a minute we'd have any financial instability," he recalled. "Life is too short to be poor."

They married in March 1941—Fred was 20, Ernestine 23— and moved into a small apartment. Ernestine's sister, Bee, came to live with them.

Their first child, Barbara Jean Ross, was born on June 1, 1942.

Then, on March 26, 1944, Ernestine gave birth to another daughter at Women's Hospital in Detroit. She had intended that this child be named "Diane" but through a clerical error, the name "Diana" appeared on the official certificate. Fred said that he didn't care what name was on the certificate. His daughter's name was Diane and that's what her friends and family would always call her.

With the addition of another child, the Ross' two-bedroom apartment suddenly seemed too small, but Fred and Ernestine realized that they were lucky to have it. Detroit was still trying to regain its balance after a race riot in June 1943, one of the worst the country had ever seen. Strained relations had resulted between the races as poor whites and blacks competed for the same kinds of jobs, and even housing. Fred's job was stable and he and Ernestine were thankful for their good fortune, but then their world was rocked when he was drafted into the Army three months after Diana was born. For the two years he served during and after World War II, Ernestine, who always thought of herself as "a survivor, no matter what," supported her daughters by teaching adult sewing classes one year and kindergarten the next.

By the time the war ended and Fred returned home and to his job at the American Brass Company, Detroit had become one of the right places for blacks to be, a northern Mecca where black people, escaping uncertain futures in the South, could realize financial security working in factories and plants. What used to be middle-class white communities in the heart of Detroit were quickly taken over by impoverished and working-class black people, all competing for jobs on assembly lines. It was in this world that the Rosses settled to raise their two children, both bright, precocious girls who showed signs early in life that they had inherited their parents' intelligence.

From the time young Diana Ross, a skinny five-year-old with long black braids and large questioning eyes, enrolled in Balch Elementary School until she became the lead singer of The Supremes, her life was very different from the portrait of despair and poverty painted over the years. The Motown press department's notions of how "ghetto girls" lived certainly applied to some of their other female artists, but not to Diana Ross. The Rosses had more stable lives and were better off financially than most of their neighbors. Ernestine, remembered by her neighbor Lillian Abbott as "the consummate mother, always at home sewing and cooking," kept her daughters fastidiously clean; their dresses were starched and crisp, and their hair was carefully woven into braids and curls. But even taking into account her family's stability, material possessions and good looks, what really distinguished Diana Ross was her determination at such an early age to make herself the center of attention.

The seed of ambition had already been planted in Diana when she was a small child. Teacher Julia Page recalled that when Diana and her sister Barbara appeared in the school's production of *Hansel and Gretel*, Diana was to hold a flashlight in front of her and sing a children's song. But she insisted on shining the flashlight on her face, "as if it were a spotlight," said Page.

Page remembered that Diana was always the one to set up and inspire class programs because, as the teacher put it, "she had the uncanny ability to organize and include her friends in little productions, even though it was clear that she was the star of the show. She loved school and the excitement it provided." (In 1982, 27 years after leaving Balch Elementary, Diana Ross donated a large sum of money to the school for renovations and other improvements.)

By 1950, Aunt Bee had moved out and Ernestine had given birth to three more children: Margretia, Fred, Jr., and Arthur, nicknamed T-Boy. While the three girls slept in the back bedroom, the dining room had been converted into a sleeping area for the two boys. Fred, still working for the American Brass Company, started moonlighting as a "shade tree mechanic" (rebuilding automobile transmissions) for extra money while he took classes at Wayne State University. His "sensible plan" for raising a family seemed to be working. In 1955, about a year before

Diana entered Dwyer Junior High, the family moved to larger quarters, a new home on Belmont Avenue in Detroit's prosperous end, a former Jewish neighborhood turning black. This was a pleasant community of two-story duplexes and well-trimmed lawns and front porches decorated with flower boxes.

It was at this time that Diana first started singing. As the record player would spin songs like 17-year-old Etta James' "Good Rocking Daddy" and "Dance With Me, Henry," Diana would stand in front of a mirror and mouth the lyrics, "performing" and posing. She entertained at house parties hosted by her parents, an 11-year-old kid with a pigtail on each side of her head and one in the middle, bellowing "Your Cheatin' Heart" and "In the Still of the Night" at the top of her lungs. She'd make a deep curtsy, and the impressed adults would pass the hat. "Once I collected enough money to buy myself a pair of patent leather tap dance shoes," she recalled.

Diana was a rough-and-tumble tomboy and, she's said, "a real close friend to all the bullies. We used to kill chickens in garbage cans. We'd kill rats with bows and arrows. I was the protector of the family." School chums, like McCluster Billups, tell stories of little girl Diana, all skinny arms and wiry legs, rolling through a crowd of school children, over the hedges, and onto the grass in a scuffle. "She didn't like being pushed around and wasn't afraid to do something about it," he said.

Though she played at having boyfriends, her young love was music, and she would stand in front of the ironing board for hours, doing the family's sheets and daydreaming about singing. She would watch curiously as one of her neighbors, a handsome 15-year-old, practiced harmonies and choreography with his friends on their front steps. His name was William Robinson—Smokey—and he would go on to become a prolific Motown songwriter and recording artist.

In December 1955, Ernestine gave birth to another child, Wilbert Alex (nicknamed Chico), and Fred became worried. "There were six kids now, and I wasn't poor but I wasn't rich either," he recalled. "I had heard about these low-income projects that were being built and went to see what they were like. I was impressed, so we moved there. They were called the Brewster Projects." Here, the Rosses could find a suitable three-bedroom apartment for a reasonable monthly rent. On March 26, 1958, Diana's fourteenth birthday, her family moved to 2961 St. Antoine Street in the Brewster Projects.

This is how Diana remembered the Projects for an NBC television special: "Not all of us kids survived the ghetto, but the ones who did were a mighty tough lot. You see, the ghetto will get you ready for anything. The first big fight is just gettin' out. But I didn't know such words as ghetto,'' she concluded. "You see, the ghetto was my home."

Fred Ross disagreed. "The first big fight was getting *in* the Brewster Projects, not out. If you got in, you were one of the lucky ones. The Brewster Projects was a place where large families could afford to live. At that time, a bad stigma hadn't been attached to the projects. The front yards had nice lawns, the housing was decent and there were courtyards. The apartment that we were in had three bedrooms, a full basement, a living room, kitchen and dinette. It wasn't so terrible, believe me."

No matter what they may look like today, in 1958 the Brewster Projects were proof that low-income housing does not have to mean slums. Located on Detroit's east side, within walking distance of downtown, the projects were considered more like a tightknit community than a cutthroat urban jungle. For those who called the Projects home, there wasn't much money for luxuries, but music was always free. As the parents socialized, the youngsters gathered on street corners near their favorite markets, or on the front steps of their houses, to sing and dance to the latest records blaring from radios.

The popularity of black bands and singers had reached an unprecedented level by 1958, not only in Detroit but in the rest of America as well. Artists like Big Maybelle, Chuck Willis and Dinah Washington had already made their marks. However, something fresh and exciting was now changing the face of black music, and all of the local teen-agers were catching the fever. It was a new sound with a more insistent, contagious beat—rock 'n' roll and rhythm and blues—a sound that the kids in the Projects were quick to imitate. They formed their own groups and improvised their own arrangements of songs recorded by Chuck Berry, Little Richard and The Drifters. "It was always rock 'n' roll for me," Diana once said.

Most kids in the neighborhood felt the same way. Three had just arrived from Birmingham, Alabama, and were determined to take their hobby seriously. Young Paul Williams, Eddie Kendricks and Kell Osborne formed a vocal group called The Primes, under the direction of a fast-talking manager named Milton Jenkins. As the oft-told tale has it, after The Primes began to make a local name for themselves, Jenkins decided that they needed a sister group. Jenkins was dating one of the sisters of 15-year-old Florence Ballard. Ballard and Jenkins agreed that she would head up The Primettes.

Florence, nicknamed "Blondie" because of her light skin and auburn hair, recruited another local girl, 14-year-old Mary Wilson, who also lived in the Brewster Projects. Mary, rail-thin with a fair, foggy-sounding voice, thought that Florence, a buxom, shapely girl, was the most dynamic singer this side of Mahalia Jackson. The two girls—Mary shy and reserved, Flo street-wise and loud—began rehearsing with a number of local youngsters trying to find two more group members. They settled on Betty McGlown, and then, finally, Primes member Paul Williams recommended Diana Ross.

When Paul suggested that Diana join the group, she was apprehensive because she had recently lost a chance for the starring role in a school play. Her teacher claimed her voice was too weak and that she sang through her nose. Williams urged her to try, and after he and Eddie Kendricks assured Ernestine that Diana would be home "before the street lights went on," Diana was off to rehearsal. When the four girls blended their voices on "The Night Time Is the Right Time," everyone in the room nodded their heads in agreement. The Primettes had been formed.

Because the girls would be rehearsing at Milton Jenkins' hotel suite on seamy Hastings Avenue, where prostitutes plied their trade, Jenkins thought it best to obtain their mothers' full approval before confirming their memberships in the group. Driving his red Cadillac and dressed in a custom-made sharkskin suit with matching silk handkerchief and tie, Jenkins had one arm in a sling (though no one seemed to know why) and was quite a character. Ernestine regarded him with more than a little skepticism. But he was unfailingly polite and emphasized that the long hours of rehearsal would keep the girls off the streets, out of gangs and away from boys. Ernestine agreed. Jenkins was lucky that he spoke to her and not her husband because as soon as Fred heard about The Primettes, he objected. He thought it would lead to something "impractical."

"I really didn't care so much about her singing," he said, "but I didn't like the fact that she might start coming in late from playing local record hops—or whatever it was those kids used to do. She was still underage. I felt she might not continue her education, and I wanted her to go to Wayne State University one day."

As Fred grew older, he became more implacable. He was determined that his children follow his example and credo: the only path to success is education. Diana felt that she was in a difficult position because her older sister Barbara excelled in academics and thereby won Fred's approval. Diana desperately wanted her father to praise *her* achievements but Fred would recognize no standards except his own. It was a trait Diana would herself display in later years and find justifiable. However, when she was young, she never got the attention and love she felt she needed.

"From her mother, yes, but not from Fred," recalled a friend of the family. "It seemed to Diane that Fred preferred Barbara to her. Anything Diane could do to single herself out, to make herself better in his eyes than Barbara, she would jump at. When Fred didn't encourage her in the group, she assumed it was because he had no faith in her ability as a singer. It was another hole in their relationship. The more Diana felt Fred pushing her away, the more she wanted in. I think it affected her more gravely than she even knew, always trying to make this older man in her life happy but, in her mind anyway, never once succeeding."

Even though Ernestine harbored misgivings about Milton Jenkins' ostentatious style and no apparent source of income, she finally convinced Fred to let Diana have her chance. Ernestine realized Diana's need for acclaim. Besides, she herself had enjoyed a chance in the limelight, entering singing contests when she was young but putting it all behind her when she married. Diana would later say that were it not for her mother's encouragement, she probably would not have become a singer.

Soon, the girls, in letter sweaters, pleated skirts, bobby socks and sneakers, were performing with The Primes and making $15 a show. There were rehearsals almost every day, and Diana would often have to sneak past her father to attend. Since Florence had the biggest, loudest voice, which the girls thought to be "soulful," she sang most of the leads on songs like Ray Charles' "The Night Time Is the Right Time" and Chubby Checker's "The Twist." Mary once said, "Whenever Diana would insist on a lead and then sing it, we would sort of look at each other and try not to laugh. She had this weird little whiny sound."

The girls patterned themselves after the most successful female group at that time, a quartet from the Bronx called The Chantels, so it's easy to understand why they felt Diana's voice was "weird." The Chantels' lead singer, 16-year-old Arlene Smith, had a wailing, gospel-influenced voice. Though Florence had the makings of a similar sound, she didn't have Smith's range but she did have the vocal gusto. Diana's voice was more delicate sounding and usually worked well in the background—when she was able to keep it from being too loud and penetrating. In years to come, Diana's sound would become refined and very precise—even unique—but when she was 14, it was just, as Mary said, "a little whiny sound."

She may not have had the greatest voice, but Diana Ross was a dynamo. Her energy fueled by determination, her drive by competitiveness. No rhinestone, young Diana was a diamond in the rough who in time would become magnificent in her brilliance. Her compelling need to be the center of attention proved particularly galling to Florence who, as founder of The Primettes, considered herself the leader of the group and whenever possible resisted Diana taking the lead.

Mary once remembered the afternoon after a rehearsal when Diana pulled Florence aside and told her that she wanted to sing more leads. "But you ain't a lead singer, Diane," Flo said carefully.

"Well, what makes you think *you* are," Diana challenged. "Just 'cause everybody says so?"

Flo told her that she could sing circles around her "any day of the week" and warned her to "stop messin' with me." The two girls stared each other down. Then, Diana turned and walked away. She and Florence were not off to a good start. But Diana was more concerned with problems at home.

Even though Fred had allowed her to be part of the group, he always had reservations. She would come home late at night after a performance, insert her key in the front door as quietly as possible, and just as she would begin to turn it, the door would swing open and there she would be face to face with her angry father, holding a leather belt. But Diana has never accused Fred of beating her. In fact, as she put it, "He didn't have to whip anybody. He could do it with his voice."

The Detroit/Windsor Freedom Festival—held on Fred's fortieth birthday—became a point of contention between her father and his 16-year-old daughter. "I definitely didn't want her to go to Windsor," he said. "Understand that my main concern was for her education, and I felt she was wasting time with this singing. But she never understood. She felt I was trying to screw up her life." Fred said that he saw his daughter's great ambition being channeled into something he perceived as a worthless venture, and that it was breaking his heart. "I loved her," he said. "I only wanted the best for her."

One morning, in the Ross' small kitchen, Fred told his daughter that her hobby had gotten out of hand. Diana wanted to know why Fred wouldn't support her. "What do I have to do to please you?" she screamed at him. "I'm becoming a success, can't you see that?'' Sobbing, she stormed out of the room. It took visits from Florence and Mary—probably accompanied by what Fred called ''moaning and groaning, which I hated and never allowed in my house''—to get him to change his mind and let her go to the contest.

''Listen, Fred Ross was such a softie,'' Florence recalled. ''Oh, he was tough and stern, but turn on the tears and he'd always bend. Diane never felt she could please him and she had her fights with him. Mary and I never understood what she thought were big problems with her father. We were jealous. At least she *had* a father! [Florence's dad died of cancer when she was 15.] I thought he was the most wonderful man.''

Soon after they auditioned for Berry Gordy at Hitsville, Diana contracted a severe case of the flu. She knew that the show had to go on, even if she felt too sick to be a part of it. What she hadn't counted on was her father suggesting that her older sister, Barbara Jean, the one member of the Ross family with whom Diana was most competitive, be her replacement. Diana couldn't understand how he could suggest such a thing, how her father could do this to her. *''Suppose they like her better.''*

''We always fought because I thought she was so beautiful,'' Diana would later admit when asked about Barbara Jean. ''She had long hair and I thought she got the most attention.''

According to Mary Wilson, Fred had confided to their producer and manager Richard Morris his feeling that Barbara Jean would be a more ideal group member because even though Diana might have been a stronger singer she didn't have a ''group mentality.'' Actually, Fred's observation was almost prophetic. For Richard, this was food for thought. He didn't like Diana's cocky attitude anyway and was looking for an excuse to drop her from the act.

Whether or not Fred was actually trying to undermine her singing career so she would concentrate on academics, Diana certainly thought so. Father and daughter had never been close. This incident caused a rift that would not be easy to repair.

''For Diana, this was the last straw,'' said a family friend. ''She was more hurt than Fred ever realized.''

Fortunately for the family's future tranquility, Barbara Jean had neither the voice nor ambition to pursue a vocal career. She was only too willing to relinquish her temporary spot with The Primettes as soon as Diana recovered.

Back in the group again, Diana's world quickly continued to change. Hitsville every day, that was the focus of her life. Recording sessions, handclaps, oohs and aahs, whatever it took didn't matter because it was all so intoxicating. It was show business, after all, and Diana had quickly embraced it all.

After The Primettes convinced Berry Gordy to sign them to the label, and Diana came home with the recording contract, the argument that ensued was not surprising. Fred didn't trust Berry because he had heard that his artists weren't fairly compensated for their work. When he told Diana that he was afraid Gordy might turn out to be less than reputable, Diana naturally jumped to his defense. She felt that Berry was wonderful, kind and patient and, more important, unlike Fred, that he believed in her talent. "*He* thinks I can sing," she said. "*He* knows I'm going to be successful." After finally rounding out the quartet, now she felt she was facing another obstacle.

"I decided to leave the decision to her mother," Fred remembered. "I was at a loss. I knew this would be the end of her education. She was hostile about it, and I was emotional. I was supposed to co-sign the contract, and I just couldn't."

Fred didn't know it at the time, but Barbara Martin's mother felt exactly the same way. She wanted her daughter out of the group and into a college.

The next day, Diana brought her mother to Hitsville where they were joined by the other Primettes and their mothers. Berry's sister, Esther Edwards, an elegant, articulate, impressive woman, explained the contract to the parents. The lecture Edwards gave regarding growing up at Hitsville was more important to the mothers than any terms of the agreement. Esther explained that they didn't want any troublesome girls cramping their company's efficiency, and that there would be chaperones accompanying them should they be sent out on the road. Diana and Mary were about to turn 17 in March; Flo was already 17 and Barbara 18. Throughout the meeting, a young man in a white angora sweater sat in a corner and listened, but said nothing.

When the meeting was over, Ernestine leaned over and asked her daughter the name of the man in the sweater. "Why, that's Berry Gordy!" Diana answered.

Ernestine sized him up from head to toe and didn't say a word until she and Diana got home. "You aren't signing no contract with no kid like that," she decided.

After the requisite whining, pleading and crying from Diana, she and her mother calmly discussed the problem. When Ernestine realized that Berry was only about ten years younger than her husband, she decided that perhaps he could be trusted. A couple of weeks later, The Primettes and their mothers—who would co-sign their contracts—returned to Hitsville. Though Ernestine had her misgivings and Fred was dead set against the idea, their daughter Diana Ross was signed to Berry Gordy Enterprises and Tamla Records on January 15, 1961.

Chapter

❧ 3 ❧

FRED AND ERNESTINE may have had their own ideas as to how a 16-year-old girl should act, but once their daughter Diana hit those Detroit streets she was just another rowdy teen-ager. As much as they might have wanted to protect her from what was happening out there, there was no holding her back.

Producer and manager Richard Morris began working with the girls, booking them at clubs like the 20 Grand as the opening act for soul stars like Wilson Pickett. However, Morris also sent them to dangerous ghetto establishments. The underage girls were performing illegally. When they sang, drunks threw nickels and quarters onto the stage. Once, Diana jumped down from the performing platform to boogie with a bunch of customers, much to the other girls' horror. When Richard Morris tried to tell her not to take such chances, she told him to go to hell. "Life is too short not to take chances!" she said, echoing her father's sentiment that "Life is too short to be poor," but with a twist. If Fred Ross had known that his teen-aged daughter was performing for rowdy audiences, his punishment of her would surely have been severe.

In just a couple of years, the Brewster Projects had made a transformation for the worse. The streets were rougher, no longer safe. Fred Ross had reason to be concerned, but the girls were young and naïve; nothing had ever happened to them, so why should they worry? But then something did happen.

Florence dropped out of school and stopped showing up for rehearsals. She refused to give anyone an explanation.

"I just don't understand why Flo's being so stand-offish," Mary would say. "This group, we're like sisters."

Two months passed before Florence finally telephoned Mary
and asked that the three meet the next day.

When Florence was late, they were sure she would not appear.
She finally arrived, but the ebullient Flo they had known just
two months earlier had changed dramatically. In her place appeared another Flo with dark circles under her eyes, a young
woman who seemed dazed and unhappy, who would not look
Mary or Diana in the eye as she tried to explain what had happened to her. Slowly, haltingly, the story came out.

One night, she and one of her brothers went to a dance at the
Graystone Ballroom. Flo's mother, Lurlee, felt it was safe since
no liquor was served during the teen-age dances, and she would
be with her brother. But they were separated and, knowing her
mother would be worried if she came home late, she accepted a
ride with someone she knew.

The girls wanted to know the friend's name, but Florence
wouldn't say. Crying, she told her singing partners that the man
had a knife, and that he pulled the car onto a dark, deserted
street. Mary has remembered that Flo could hardly continue her
story; as she sobbed, her language became almost unintelligible.
Diana and Mary were scared, and sick with apprehension over
how Florence was going to end the story. She slowly explained
that her "friend" put the knife to her throat and, threatening her
life, forced her into the back seat. There, he raped her.

After the assault, Flo's oldest brother Cornell insisted that she
stop singing and going to nightclubs. But it was Lurlee who
eventually encouraged Flo to start living her life again, to call
Diana and Mary and "make yourself some singing." Florence
had been complaining of nightmares, and Lurlee thought that
perhaps music might replace the bad dreams.

"That's why I decided to call you," Flo said. "That's why I
came back."

Diana and Mary were too shocked and horrified to know how
to comfort Florence. Rape was such a taboo subject in those
days that newspapers rarely even printed the word. Women were
"assaulted." They seldom spoke of their ordeal even to close
friends. The general opinion was that somehow the victims had
asked for it.

Flo's story was the most brutal Diana and Mary had ever
heard, and for it to happen to someone they knew made it even
more chilling. Mary has said that they both wondered how Florence Ballard, 17 years old, would ever be able to trust anyone
again.

But after this meeting, the girls never again discussed Florence's rape and its emotional aftermath. They did not know how to deal with the subject because of their youth and inexperience. Moreover, they simply weren't close enough to talk about it openly among themselves. Diana and Florence realized that the relationship the three of them shared wasn't of a soul-baring, sisterly nature. They knew that without their music, they would probably not even have been friends because their family backgrounds and personalities were so dissimilar. Mary never understood this. She wondered why the specter of that night always seemed to loom overhead, unresolved. "We're like sisters, aren't we?" she kept asking.

Diana welcomed Flo back so that the group could continue. Although Flo tried to go on with her life and her singing, the nightmares never really ended. Florence Ballard was never the same again.

In March 1961, the month Diana turned 17, "I Want a Guy" was released as The Supremes' first single for Tamla Records. The girls were now earning $10 a week and Berry, going big time, had someone on staff who kept track of the payroll.

"Every Thursday, Diane would come down to the office and collect the money for the other girls," said Taylor Cox, who headed up what Berry called Motown's Multi-Media Management division. "I recall having some problems with her over this $40 because she would always come early to pick it up, and it wouldn't be ready. She had no hit record, we were *giving* her $40 to split four ways, and she was raising hell because the check wasn't there."

"I Want a Guy" was not a success. Florence would have the lead on the follow-up, "Buttered Popcorn." It, too, would be a flop.

"When am I going to get my first hit?" Diana kept whining to Smokey Robinson.

"Soon, Diane. It takes time," he'd always respond.

Smokey Robinson was thin and angular yet athletic looking, light-skinned with wavy black hair worn slicked back. He had luminous green eyes. The first time Diana saw him, years earlier when they were neighbors, she thought he was cute. Now she was 17, he was 21, and Diana felt he was sexy as well. "I have never seen a Negro with green eyes," she told friends. "God, is he adorable."

Florence agreed. She told Diana that she was interested in Smokey but reluctant to do anything about it because she was intimidated by him. After the rape, Florence didn't quite know how to act around men and, sometimes, was even afraid of them. She began to date Joe Shaffner, who was working at Motown as road manager for The Marvelettes. Flo seemed comfortable with him. He was gentle, understanding and, she said, "the kindest man I've known." Still, it was difficult for her not to be fascinated by Smokey Robinson. All the girls were.

Everyone at Motown tried to be as nice to Robinson as possible, mostly because he was Berry's close friend. Berry truly liked Smokey Robinson and often took his advice. People at Hitsville who wanted to get to Berry but didn't know how to approach him, ingratiated themselves with Smokey Robinson. His political clout aside, Smokey's dashing good looks made him attractive to all the girls. Not only did romantic poetry about true and eternal love roll off his lips as easily as simple conversation, he also had a reputation for being something of a stud.

"Smokey was such a womanizer, even back then, and was vulnerable to any overtures," said one of The Vandellas. "There were a lot of cute girls always hanging around him. The word was out that he was real hot in the sack, the best lover at Hitsville, with the best equipment. That was what all the girls talked about constantly—his 'equipment.' "

She remembers clusters of young girls whispering and giggling about Smokey, and then clamming up when they would see him or Berry walking in their direction. The fact that Smokey was married did not dissuade most of the girls.

"He was so romantic, this man," she remembered. "Every young girl at Hitsville wanted to be laid by Smokey Robinson. Honest to God truth. There were some guys at Motown who were also interested. Diane was right on the money when she decided to go after Smokey Robinson. Not only would she have the opportunity we all craved, she would be able to flaunt it in our faces at the same time."

He could also further her career. Not only was he a top producer and writer who could work with her group, but he could keep Gordy interested. Diana loved a good challenge anyway, and Smokey Robinson presented one. He had helped her before by paving the way for the girls to audition for Gordy. At that audition, he stole The Primettes' guitar player, Marv Tarplin (who is still with the Robinson band today). He had also loaned Diana money to enroll in cosmetology school, so she knew he could be generous. He had gone to college, too, so she must have been impressed.

Florence had decided that she was not going to pursue Smokey, out of respect for his young wife, Claudette. She once said that

Smokey's wife mystified her and Diana. They both had to wonder what kind of woman stands by while her husband sleeps
around. But Claudette's loyalty to Smokey was well known.
When Berry Gordy made a pass at Claudette before he knew
that she was Smokey's girl, she turned him down. Later, Berry
signed a glossy photograph of himself for her, with the inscrip-
tion: "To Claudette—The most cutest, the most wonderful, the
most sweetest."

Diana pestered Smokey until they finally started dating. Under
the guise of working on musical material, they began spending
time together.

"Soon, whenever The Miracles were performing around town,
Diana was there backstage," said Gladys Horton of The Marvelettes. "She would throw her arms around him, jump in his
lap, snuggle up next to him, hold his hand, and all in front of
Claudette. She didn't care what Claudette thought. Claudette did
not like Diane one bit because she felt that she flirted too openly
with her husband, that she did not give her the respect that she
deserved as his wife."

Claudette told Smokey that she didn't like the idea of Diana
flirting with him, and, apparently, Smokey shared his wife's feelings with Diana. She did not appreciate being told how to handle
herself in public, and soon she grew to dislike Claudette very
much. Most of the artists at Motown were well aware of her
feelings. Smokey continued seeing Diana, and swore to Claudette that he and Diana were not sexually involved. But it was
difficult for anyone to believe that Diana and Smokey were not
having sex. Still, in his 1988 autobiography, *Smokey*, he would
not admit to it. One friend of his said that since Smokey was a
newlywed when he had the relationship with Diana, he is still
embarrassed by his indiscretion, even today.

Mary has recalled that one afternoon, Diana made an official
announcement to her, Florence and Barbara. "You'll never guess
who I went out with last night. *Mr. Smokey Robinson.*"

The girls reminded Diana that he was a married man. "Besides, you're doing this just to make me feel bad," Florence
added. "You *know* I like Smokey."

Diana just smiled.

Florence continued, "And now you're gonna get us all kicked
out of Hitsville."

With that, Diana turned and walked away.

Smokey and Diana would spend time in the studio together
and, according to one of Smokey's singing partners, late nights
in the apartment of one of the unmarried Miracles. All the while

they were developing what Smokey would later poetically call "an intimacy, a genuine love." Diana would keep her singing partners posted on where she and Smokey would go on their dates, and what kinds of flowers this romantic guy would send her.

Smokey tried to be discreet, but with Diana that wasn't always easy. She was proud of her new conquest and at Hitsville she would try to hold his hand or put her arm around his waist. He would immediately pull away. "Cool it, baby," he would whisper to her urgently. When asked about Smokey, Diana wouldn't say much, certain that the less she said, the more "they" would say. Dating Smokey Robinson was making her the talk of the company.

In December 1961, a month before Diana graduated from high school, The Supremes were scheduled to go into the studio with Smokey to record another song he had written for them. Mary expected the lead and was excited about this opportunity. But when the girls began rehearsing, Smokey handed the lyrics to Diana and gave her a secret, meaningful look. Diana grinned coquettishly as Mary's spirits dropped.

It wasn't long before gossip about her husband and Diana reached Claudette. Claudette knew from the very beginning of her marriage to Smokey that his fidelity was not going to be something she could depend on. She had told him that she would ignore his affairs, as long as he didn't flaunt them and humiliate her—and as long as he didn't impregnate any of his girlfriends. Claudette appeared to be satisfied if her husband came home three or four nights out of the week. Despite her nonchalant façade, she had a long memory when it came to the girls she knew had slept with her husband. Smokey would admit later that it was more difficult for his wife to forgive these girls than it was for her to forgive *him*.

Diana may have been dating Smokey because the association could help her career, and perhaps because she was trying to make Florence envious, but Gladys Horton of The Marvelettes has another theory. "There was only one reason. She was being bitchy. I like Diane, but she did have her ways and we all knew it. She wanted to make Claudette mad. Whatever she could do to get on Claudette's nerves, that's what Diana would do. I don't think she was in love with Smokey, but when she realized that seeing him got such a reaction from Claudette, she liked that. That's the plain, simple truth."

Finally, Claudette could no longer pretend she hadn't heard the stories about her husband and Diana Ross. She told him that everyone was talking about this "friendship," and that the gossip was upsetting her.

"Would it make you feel better if I didn't see Diane so much?" he asked her.

She said it would.

Not only did Smokey stop dating Diana, he also stopped writing and producing for The Supremes.

"See, I told you something like this was going to happen," Florence said to Diana. "Now we don't got no producer."

After the romance with Smokey cooled down, Diana began looking around for a new boyfriend. She wasn't very subtle, and soon she started developing a reputation in the neighborhood as something of a flirt. Any time Mary had a boyfriend, Diana wanted him. At one point, Mary announced her engagement to a young man in the neighborhood and then, immediately, Diana set her sights on the same guy. Whenever Mary and her fiancé were out together and Diana was present, Diana would try to flirt with the fellow and, worse yet, criticize Mary in front of him. Eventually, Mary's engagement was broken off and, even though Diana had nothing to do with the breakup, from that time on Mary would keep a close eye on her where men were concerned. She was reluctant to introduce any of her beaux to Diana because she felt that Diana would try to steal them away.

The streets of Detroit, populated by hot-blooded, unscrupulous young men who were after anything they could get, were often not safe for young girls. Florence could attest to that. Young ladies who were considered flirtatious often found themselves in compromising—even terrifying—situations.

Like the comfort people get when they have money in their pocket, it somehow made Diana feel more secure if she knew she could have any fellow in the projects on whom she set her sights. As gangs with names like The Shakers had started to infiltrate the neighborhood, the time had come to be mindful about who her friends were. Fred and Ernestine tried to shelter all of their children, but the older they got the more difficult that became.

Being with Motown didn't help matters, although Esther Edwards tried to keep her promise that she would watch out for the girls. "If you really want to know the truth, Motown had a sort of swingers' club," said Gladys Horton of The Marvelettes. "They used to have these parties. Holland-Dozier and Holland;*

*Motown's "house" writing-producing team of lyricists Eddie Holland and Lamont Dozier and composer Brian Holland.

Smokey; a couple of the girls, I think; Berry; The Miracles; and Diane was always there. Never The Marvelettes because they thought of us as country girls with no sophistication. Anyway, everyone knew that when Diane was at one of these parties, she'd have the attitude, 'Well, I'm having a good time and nobody's gonna stop me.' She'd get to drinking, start being happy, singing. Her feeling was, 'I don't care who your girlfriend is—you can have who you want in the morning—but let's make *someone* jealous tonight!' She'd get a man piping hot, thinking he was in a relationship with her, then the next morning she'd be talking about some college guy. That was Diane.''

Gladys continued, ''Berry's sister Esther used to tell us, 'Girls, you have got to marry someone out there who is doing something, has a promising career, making money. If you pick a guy who don't have nothing, you're gonna end up the same way.' And it was true. It happened to lots of us. But back then, who cared? The party girls—like Diane—were just out to have fun.''

It was no secret that the Brewster Projects weren't as safe as they used to be, and, says her cousin Barbara Gaines, Diana was ashamed to tell anyone she lived there because the area was becoming so rundown. Diana's cousin said, ''When people found out you lived in the Brewster Projects, they didn't want to socialize with you anymore.''

At this time, Florence had introduced Diana and Mary to a wild crowd that she had started to party with. At one such gathering, which Flo didn't attend, things began to get rough.

One young bully began running his hands over Diana's body. Although she protested, he insisted on continuing. It was hard to take Diana seriously when she batted those big, brown eyes and demurred, ''Stop it . . . *baby.*'' But, soon, she really meant it.

''I told you to let me go,'' she shouted.

Diana's voice was loud enough to attract attention over the music. He spun her around and held her in a bear hug as the other partygoers gathered around. Then, according to witnesses, he crossed one of his arms across her chest to restrain her while pulling at her clothes with the other hand. Everyone laughed as she tried to free herself by jabbing him with her elbows. The harder she struggled and the tighter he gripped her, the more the others seemed to enjoy it. The scene was becoming ugly.

It was all an act to scare Diana and to get a few laughs, but this roughhousing was frightening just the same. Diana was the only one who didn't think it was funny. As he grappled with her, she started to scream for him to let her go. The smell of beer and stale cigarette smoke permeated the air as the party continued.

When Flo had talked about her rape, she had insisted, "He made me do it. It wasn't my fault." Diana was the type of person who couldn't imagine allowing someone to victimize her. If she couldn't sweet talk her way out of a situation, she would revert to being a tomboy and fight back. Now she was trying to do just that, but with little success.

Diana finally broke away, infuriated.

"Oh, we was just kiddin', Diane," one of the guys said. "Don't get so mad."

Mary finally came forward, suppressing a smile. "Game's over. Leave her be. You had your fun."

Everyone laughed again. Mary stood firm. "She's like my sister. You let her be."

Diana stood there, looking wild-eyed at them all. Her hair was a mess, her clothes rumpled and she was crying. Mary put her arm around her shoulder and led her to the door. "Come on, Diana, you best be gettin' home."

Mary Wilson has admitted she became fascinated by these unruly teen-agers. In fact, she and one of the boys at that party soon began dating. The peer pressure to fit in was strong. Mary became one of the crowd. Diana made it very clear that she wanted nothing more to do with this gang, that she was scared of them. It was obvious that she was not as self-confident as she appeared, that she was bossy because she craved attention.

True, Diana would criticize Mary constantly about her figure, her hairstyle and her choice of clothing. Even though all of this was galling to Mary, she could always remind Diana that *she* was the more popular of the two. Mary and the other girls in The Primettes had to put up with Diana because they were bound together by group ambitions. But the others in the neighborhood had no reason to tolerate her and most didn't want to be bothered.

Perhaps in the excitement of being young and having fun, Mary was oblivious to the danger some of her friends posed. Not long after that raucous party, Mary's boyfriend from the gang brought his buddies to her home for an uninvited afternoon visit. Diana was there with Mary, and when she saw that the teen-ager who had roughed her up was among the visitors, she was understandably upset. When Mary decided to go on a joy-ride with these fellows, Diana wanted nothing to do with them.

"Come on, Diane. It'll be fun," Mary said as she and her new boyfriend climbed into the back seat. Diana adamantly refused, especially when she realized that the guy who harassed her at the party was driving. She leaned into the open window on the passenger's side and told them to go ahead without her. Angered by Diana's rejection, the driver slammed his foot on the gas pedal. The car lurched forward. Diana, still holding on to the door handle, was dragged along screaming.

After traveling twenty feet, the car came to a screeching halt. "What are you crazy?" Diana shrieked. By now she was hysterical. The driver began to snicker, as Mary and her new boyfriend jumped out of the back seat to console Diana.

But Diana turned and ran off in tears. She wanted nothing more to do with any of them, Mary included.

Diana graduated from high school in January 1962. These years had not been easy for her. She had decided to go to Cass Technical High School instead of Northeastern High, the school attended by most of the youngsters from the Brewster Projects. Cass, which drew students from all segments of the highly diversified Detroit population, encouraged its pupils to ignore race and economic status. Youngsters in the Projects who weren't smart enough to be accepted considered it a "snob school."

Students at Cass were expected to adhere to higher academic standards than those of any other school in Detroit. A B-average was required for admittance and a C-average had to be maintained in order to continue attending. Mary Wilson once said that she had the opportunity to go to Cass but turned it down "because I didn't want to have to do all of the extra homework I knew I'd get there."

Not only had Diana's father graduated from Cass, but her older sister, Barbara, had been accepted the year before. Always competitive, especially where Barbara was concerned, Diana worked for and achieved the necessary B-average. For once, she did something that made Fred happy. Diana was fascinated by Cass' clothing and design courses since she shared Ernestine's ability to sew and had a flair for style. She knew what suited her and had been interested in fashion ever since she was a small child. Her brother T-Boy recalled her designing an entire wardrobe of doll's clothes for an orphan child who lived in the neighborhood. "All dolls ought to have pretty clothes," she said when the doll's owner told her that *her* doll didn't have any clothes at all.

But Diana had a difficult time fitting in at Cass. Recalled former classmate Doris Jackson, "No one wanted to be her friend because we all thought she was stuck up, but couldn't figure out why she was like that. The school was loaded with snobs who had good reason to be, or at least they thought they did, because of their economic status. But when Diane came in, a nobody acting like a somebody because she thought that *made* her somebody, we laughed at her, looked down our noses at her. She was elite-acting, not very social. Cold is the word."

According to black music historian Nelson George, someone who knew Diana during this time once said of her, "I have to tell you one thing about Diana Ross—I say it in her defense all the time—when she was poor, living in the Projects, she was just as snotty as she is now, so her fame didn't make her snotty."

When Diana became competitive in the school's extracurricular activities, she started becoming more popular because she was good at whatever she set out to do: the girls' swimming team, the Lettergirl Club, a youth club called The Hexagons. "She liked status a lot," said her father. "She would complain about being popular. It's obvious to me now that she was insecure. She needed everyone else's validation in order to feel important."

Once at Cass, Diana became more interested in the social activities than in the academics. "After singing, modeling was becoming my love," she remembered, "because I thought it was the most beautiful business. I was getting taller and very long-legged; I felt it would be just the right thing. I used to love to mess with my hair. I went to beauty school in the evening [which is what Smokey Robinson had loaned her money to do] and on Saturdays to Hudson's department store for modeling classes. They gave me a little hatbox and I felt very grand coming home with that little hatbox in my hand and all the things I had learned in my mind."

There are several Cass instructors who remember her as "Diane, that girl who said she'd be a star."

One of her homeroom teachers, Robert Kraft, recalled, "She wasn't a very good student because she was so certain she would find success in show business. I had her in my English class as well, and many times she would sit in my class and hide behind a book while she painted her fingernails bright colors. When I told her she should work harder on English, she told me she didn't need to, 'because I'm going to make it as a singer without it.' "

Teacher Mary Constance recalled catching Diana staring dreamy-eyed at a newspaper article during study hall. When she demanded to know why Diana wasn't studying, her student became very impatient. "You *know* I'm going to be a singer, *don't* you?'' Diana answered. She handed Constance the article, which she had cut out of the *Detroit News*. It was a story on The Primes. "I know these guys," she boasted. "And *I* sing on weekends, myself."

Constance recalled, "I looked at her and said to myself, 'Oh, you poor child. You'll never make it.' "

When Diana became a recording artist, though, that opinion slowly began to change. She was soon more popular in some circles though still disliked in others. Some students gravitated toward her because she was becoming famous locally. Others were annoyed with her when she started playing her records in millinery class, or when she brought them to school functions and lip-synched to them even if the other Supremes weren't there. Diana was insecure enough to ignore the students who liked her, focus on the ones who didn't and try to figure out why they would not accept her. She would complain to Mary constantly that there were people at school who snubbed her and, even though Mary could certainly understand why, she tried to act sympathetic. But Diana has always been one to keep her eye on the bigger picture. Although she wanted to be accepted by her peers, she was eager to graduate so that she could concentrate on a career far more important to her than school.

While Mary and Florence had taken part-time jobs baby-sitting or working in record stores, Diana was employed by J.L. Hudson's department store. This large 15-floor store that covered a full square block on Woodward Avenue in downtown Detroit was considered the most prestigious in the city. A doorman in full uniform would smile and usher in well-to-do shoppers. Diana had always fantasized about shopping here, but for now her job was to bus tables in one of the emporium's four restaurants. She was said to have been the first black employee at Hudson's allowed outside of the kitchen, a tribute to her poise, sense of style and determination.

"I'd just smile in their faces," she said of the mostly-white customers who shopped at J.L. Hudson's, "and they'd look at me suspiciously as if there was no way I could be so nice and so black at the same time. One woman kept coming up to me and saying, 'Are *you* still here?' I'd say, 'Why, yes, ma'am. You didn't think I would quit, did you?' "

Says Diana's friend Rita Griffin, a journalist in Detroit who was a cub reporter at the time, "She used to call me from Hudson's to tell me what The Supremes would be doing next. As I tried to take notes on their activities, I had to keep asking Diana to talk louder because all I could hear was the clinking and clanging of pots and pans in the background.''

The older Diana got, the more stylish she became. "She wore beautiful clothes; there was always some sort of flair to them,'' said Aimee Kron, the Cass teacher Diana became closest to in her senior year. "A lot of them she made herself. She was inspired by colors and fabrics. There was a regal air about her, though I thought she would have looked better with more weight on her. The thinness emphasized her cheekbones, though. She had fantastic bone structure and played it up to her advantage with the right make-up. Sometimes she looked as if she stepped out of a fashion ad—very sophisticated for her age.

"Also, she was a loner," Kron continued. "She didn't really mix that much with the other youngsters. I hardly ever saw her in a large group of girls. She didn't seem to want to spend her time chattering, gossiping and giggling. She simply wasn't frivolous in that way, though I do think she was lonely.''

When Diana graduated in January 1962, she was voted Best Dressed Girl. She had finally been accepted by her peers, but the victory was an empty, anticlimactic one. It didn't matter as much anymore what the kids at Cass Technical High School thought of her.

Hitsville beckoned.

Chapter

🌱 4 🌱

BERRY GORDY, JR., has been called a maverick, and rightly so. Gordy is a true original who lives by his own rules. Although he started in the recording industry during an era of racial segregation, he believed that white people would be interested in black music from the streets of Detroit—and in the artists who made that music. He also thought that if he surrounded himself with shrewd people, he could control and motivate them to do his bidding and end up a multimillionaire in the process. It worked.

Berry Gordy, Jr., is actually a "third" and not a "junior." His great-grandfather was white slave-owner Jim Gordy whose union with a black slave named Esther Johnson resulted in a mulatto baby boy, Berry, born around 1854. When he was a teen-ager, Berry married Lucy Hellum of black and Indian heritage. During their marriage, Lucy became pregnant 23 times but only nine babies survived, including another boy, Berry II, born in July 1888.

Berry I was an ambitious and clever man. While working for white plantation owners, he squirreled away not only money but knowledge about business as well. By the time he was in his forties, he started farming for himself on 268 acres in Oconee County, Georgia. He also opened a blacksmith shop. All the while, Gordy taught his son, Berry II, the fine art of entrepreneurship. When Berry II was 25 years old, his father was struck by lightning and killed.

Berry II took over the family enterprise and was soon considered one of the shrewdest, most powerful businessmen in the county. Determined to find a proper wife—no poor woman would do—he eventually married Bertha Ida Fuller, a pretty school teacher from a well-to-do Georgia family. When they were wed in 1918, he was 30 and she was 19. Together, Berry and Bertha built a lucrative produce and meat business and eventually moved to Detroit, Michigan, land of better opportunity.

Bertha gave birth to Berry Gordy, Jr., in Detroit on November 28, 1929; Berry joined three older siblings who'd been born in Georgia: Esther, Fuller and George. By this time, his father, "Pops" as he was now known, owned a plastering and carpentry business and was about to open a printing shop. Ambition and family unity had been the hallmark of the Gordy family for decades, and "Pops" and Bertha continued to instill those values in their own family, which would grow with the births of four more children: Gwen, Anna, Louyce and Robert.

Berry's mother, Bertha, continued her education, graduating from the Detroit Institute of Commerce and then becoming one of the founders—and secretary-treasurer—of the Friendship Mutual Life Insurance Company in Detroit. She was also an active member of the Democratic Party, networking with the white political establishment.

Berry Gordy, Jr., decided as a teen-ager that "I'm not going to work on a job for eight hours a day 'cause that ain't where it's at." He quit high school in the eleventh grade at the age of 16 to become a professional featherweight boxer; he had already fought 15 amateur fights.

Though Berry was a decent and powerful boxer by the age of 18, his career in the sport was limited because of his size (5'6", 126 pounds).

He decided to quit fighting one day when he noticed two posters plastered on the wall of a gym: one showed an advertisement for an upcoming fight, the other promoted a "Battle of the Bands" concert. The two fighters on the one poster were 23 years old. In their picture they looked more like 50. On the other poster, the musicians who were at least 50 looked like they were 23. That poster became his inspiration.

He obtained a high school equivalency degree when he was drafted into the Army. Months after his discharge, at the age of 24, Berry married 19-year-old Thelma Louise Coleman. Then he began working in his father's plastering business, more dissatisfying, unfulfilling and backbreaking labor.

However, at night, Berry turned into a "cool cat," frequenting Detroit jazz clubs, befriending and socializing with jazz musicians and vocalists. In 1953, with a $700 loan from "Pops," Berry started his own retail record store, the 3-D Record Mart, which specialized in jazz music. The place went out of business in two years.

Berry recalled, "People kept coming in and asking for The Dominoes and Johnny Ace, rock 'n' roll. I said to myself, 'Hey, you'd better go and get some of that stuff!' Unfortunately, I got the 'stuff' too late to save the business, but I did learn a few valuable lessons about music and the facts of marketing it."

Meanwhile, Berry and Thelma had their first child, Hazel Joy, and another, Terry, was on the way. Desperate to support his growing family, Gordy took a job on the Ford assembly line in April 1955. He earned $86.40 a week attaching chrome strips and nailing upholstery to Lincoln-Mercurys. To Berry, this was demeaning work. He felt certain that the Gordy's upwardly mobile tradition had hit a snag and that he was responsible.

Said a family friend, "Berry was a driven person, but didn't know where to put all his energy. When he worked on the assembly line, he was biding his time, really. He wanted more and, damn it, he was going to find his niche. That's what he used to say constantly, 'One day I'll find my niche.' He'd just learned that word—'niche'—and he used it every day."

After Terry was born in 1956, Berry's marriage began to crumble, and Thelma filed for divorce, claiming that her husband was playing around with other women, had a violent temper and had punched her in the face. (It would be three years before the divorce became final.) "He was a tough lover," said a former girlfriend. "Not romantic in bed, but forceful. He took out his daily frustrations on his women at night, in bed."

During those years. Berry became interested in songwriting and was inspired by Doris Day when he saw her film *I'll See You in My Dreams*. Berry was awed by the precision and clarity of Day's voice.

"You can understand every single word she sings," he said. "And she's sincere in her performance; you really believe her. Man, she made me cry in that movie. When a singer can make you cry, you know she's got the goods, no matter what her color."

He wrote a song for Doris called "You Are You," his first composition. Berry could never figure out how to get the song to Day, but that didn't matter to him because now he had the fever. He wanted to be a songwriter.

Meanwhile, sisters Anna and Gwen—two gorgeous, sophisticated women—became the photography and cigarette concession owners at the Flame Show Bar and introduced their younger brother to the jazz artists who frequented the club. He would peddle his songs with the enthusiasm of a seasoned salesman.

Wrote Peter Benjaminson in *The Story of Motown*, an excellent history of the Gordy empire: "Gordy's first venture into record producing was undistinguished. He bought a secondhand record-making machine and began producing records with anyone who walked in off the street and paid him $100. The fee also bought Gordy's promise to work to get the record played on the radio."

In 1957, Gordy was introduced to entertainment manager Al Greene, who worked for rhythm and blues singer Jackie Wilson. With the aid of Billy Davis, a friend with whom Berry enjoyed collaborating, Berry wrote "Reet Petite" for Wilson, and the song sailed to the Number 11 spot on the rhythm and blues charts at the end of 1957. Finally, he had found his "niche." Two more hits followed, "That Is Why (I Love You So)" and "I'll Be Satisfied," both garnering heavy radio play and chart action.

It quickly became apparent that Berry Gordy was an impressive, even instinctual songwriter. Gordy's sister Gwen and Billy Davis, now involved romantically, were impressed enough by Berry's sudden good fortune in the music industry to start their own record label, Anna Records (named after sister Anna Gordy, a limited partner in the venture). All of the other Gordy family members pitched in to help out by looking for new talent and securing a deal with Chess Records to distribute Anna's product. The Gordys always stuck together, continuing a family tradition that went back generations.

In 1958, Berry met Raynoma Liles, an attractive black woman and talented musician. After his divorce, they married, formed a back-up vocal group called The Rayber Voices, and wrote and produced songs for singer Marv Johnson. Berry met singer/songwriter Smokey Robinson through Jackie Wilson's manager, Al Greene. Greene wasn't interested in Robinson and his group, The Matadors, but they did make an impression on Berry. Gordy took 18-year-old Robinson under his wing, and in 1958, The Matadors became The Miracles and "Got a Job," written and produced by Berry, became their first single on a small New York label, End Records.

However, songwriting and producing instant records failed to make a fortune for Gordy. In early 1959, he claimed a weekly income of $27.20. Berry would have a small taste of success later in the year when he and teen-ager Janie Bradford wrote the prophetic song, "Money (That's What I Want)," recorded by Barrett Strong and leased to his sister's label, Anna Records.

This rocking rhythm and blues number continues to be one of Gordy's most popular songs and was certainly a harbinger of the kind of hard-driving music that would soon be connected to the Gordy name.

"I was broke until the time I wrote 'Money,' " Berry has recalled, "even though I had many hits and there were other writers [I worked with] who had many hits, we just didn't have profits. And coming from a business family, my father and mother always talked about the bottom line, and the bottom line is profit. Are you making money, or not?"

In January 1959, Berry decided to start his own record company rather than continue to lease songs to antagonistic—and cheating—white New York record label executives. Smokey Robinson encouraged him and echoed his own thoughts:

"Why work for the man? Why don't you *be* the man? You're a cat who knows music and people. *You* be the man!"

This was advice for which Berry would always be grateful. Smokey Robinson had earned Berry Gordy's loyalty, and, noted one friend, "Once Berry committed totally to a friend, that commitment was forever."

Gordy started his own record label, Tamla Records (originally named Tammy, after the Debbie Reynolds film, of which Berry was a big fan) with an $800 loan from his family's co-op called Ber-Berry. Berry Gordy, Jr., wanted to live in a world where talent and business acumen, not manual labor, would make him wealthy. The music industry would take him there. He was savvy enough to figure out how the complicated record business worked and sophisticated enough to understand how to finance his new enterprises. None of that would have mattered, however, if he hadn't also developed a keen sensitivity to what people wanted to hear on the radio. Berry Gordy's greatest asset would always be his musical intuition. He knew what it took to make folks want to rock and roll.

By the late '50s, Detroit had the fourth largest black population in America, over half a million. Blacks enjoyed and bought music, and there had been an abundance of black artists—people like Della Reese, Hank Ballard and Little Willie John—whose talents were mined in Detroit but who left to find viable recording companies. Though none of the original roster of young Detroit vocalists and groups Gordy signed ever amounted to much, the momentum for his eventual success had already started.

Berry was so excited about his new ambitions that his enthusiasm became contagious. Soon, all of the Gordy family members were contributing to Berry's dream. In order to allow their brother time to oversee production, sister Esther took over most of the administration tasks while sister Louyce claimed responsibility for accounts receivable. Sisters Gwen and Anna weren't able to make a profit with Anna Records, so Anna went out of business and eventually turned all of her acts over to her brother. The brothers went to work in different executive capacities. "Pops" and a crew of teen-agers undertook the renovation work. All of the family members found something that needed to be done, and then did it.

Berry was already learning how to manipulate others to work for a goal they thought was their own. And in a way, it was. The Gordy credo had always been: "Find success and keep it in the family."

In the summer of 1960, Berry Gordy, Jr.'s income from the record business came to $133 a week. Although he looked impoverished on paper, he owned a $4,800 red Cadillac on which he had paid $1,300. His offices on 2648 West Grand Boulevard were worth $23,000, on which he had paid $3,000. His total assets added up to $32,600, yet he claimed liabilities of $32,500. If Berry's figures are to be believed, his net worth on paper totaled only $100. But that didn't matter to Berry Gordy because he believed that he and his family were standing on the summit of great success.

Many rock 'n' roll music historians have written that the success Berry Gordy had with Diana Ross was an accident, that the two unwittingly stumbled into something magical. Nothing could be further from the truth. When it came to finding a singer to be the company flagship, Berry Gordy always knew exactly what he wanted, and why. As far back as 1960, he was telling his friends that his heart was set on finding a protégée he could mold into the greatest female singer of all time. Berry had diverse musical influences, ranging from the light-hearted but technically precise Doris Day to the earthy and improvised Billie Holiday, from the hardly-can-sing-at-all Debbie Reynolds to the sing-circles-'round-anyone Dinah Washington.

"People like female singers," he said simply. "They can relate to women better than to guys 'cause women, they're more vulnerable."*

---

*Berry also knew that, somehow, white audiences seemed to feel less threatened by women. When Mahalia Jackson started recording her distinctly black-sounding gospel songs, she gave a concert at Carnegie Hall in 1950, which was followed

Gordy wanted a female artist to be the focus of his company, but it would have to be someone whose style could appeal to both black and white audiences. She would be a black woman who would make her race proud because they respected her worldly sophistication. She would also make whites comfortable because they understood her image and finesse.

He certainly had nothing against black music, but Berry realized that it was limited mostly to blacks. He didn't want to accept limitations. Gordy wanted an artist who could cover all bases. He wanted what is known in the record business as a middle-of-the-road singer, a continuation of the Frank Sinatra, big-band style of singing romantic songs in a simple and direct manner.

Doris Day is technically and historically one of the best of the female middle-of-the-road singers, widely admired for her breath control, her great expression of the lyric, the arc she creates with a song—meaning, as Berry would put it, she "always tells a complete story from beginning to end"—and her attention to analyzing and understanding a composition before she sings it. She never casually approached a song nor did she ever sing a song that didn't mean something to her.

When Berry said that Doris made him cry, she touched an emotional chord that is universal. Berry wanted a black singer who had enough of that big-band influence in her technique that whites could relate to her, but also one who would bring a black feeling and sensitivity to the tradition because she has had black life experiences and influences. Lena Horne came to mind but, though she was a proficient big-band singer, Berry thought she was too exotic; a great part of her appeal could be attributed to her being black. He wanted an artist who was more mainstream.*

As he told his receptionist Janie Bradford, "I gotta have me a girl who can be all good things to all people, someone blacks and whites will all spend money on. Then we can really make some money 'round here."

by a European tour. And Berry was very aware of the way whites felt about Billie Holiday, how they were able to relate to her blues and sadness even though they seemed to have nothing in common with her at all. Because they weren't threatened by her, whites allowed her to communicate with them.

*Dinah Shore was another of the middle-of-the-road singers Berry admired. When The Supremes visited Hollywood in 1965, Berry had them kneel reverentially around Dinah's star on the Hollywood Walk of Fame while he took photos of them. One of Gordy's pictures shows Diana touching the star tenderly as if some of its Hollywood magic might rub off on her.

Berry was first interested in Erma Franklin, one of the Rev. C.L. Franklin's three talented daughters; the other two were Carolyn and Aretha. Berry and Billy Davis spent hours with Erma coaching her vocally and teaching her new material, but the Rev. Franklin constantly discouraged Erma in her ambitions, and Berry in his for her.

C.L. Franklin was one of the great father-figures of Detroit, popular because of his ministry, and his decisions were regarded as familial law. Anyone involved with his family had to abide by his wishes. He wanted Erma to enroll in Clark College in Atlanta, and told Berry to put his efforts into daughter Aretha's career instead. Berry did not appreciate being told what to do. He was not interested in Aretha's voice and found her lackadaisical outlook on life and career uninspiring. There ended what could have been a monumental union. If Berry had worked with Erma longer, he would have realized that her bluesy voice really wasn't what he was looking for either.

Gordy then began courting another young singer, Freda Payne. She was about 17 and very interested in working at Hitsville because of the reputation the company was building in Detroit. Freda was exactly what he was looking for. She had a marvelous voice, jazz-influence yet pop enough to be commercial. She was also strikingly beautiful with light skin, sultry bedroom eyes and a shapely, irresistible figure.

"I found Berry dashing, smart and very exciting," Freda once recalled. She was eager to be a part of his company, but her mother, a sharp businesswoman, refused to allow her to sign Gordy's restrictive contract.

It was 1960 when Berry signed his first female artist to the company, blues singer Mabel John, sister of the popular Little Willie John. Mabel John, a small, lovely dark woman with big, luminous eyes, had great ability, but was also much too blues-oriented stylistically to be able to cut it as Gordy's great cross-over artist.

At the end of 1960, Berry signed Mary Wells to the label not only because of her talent but also because of her persistence. He liked persistent people. Mary Wells was a doe-eyed black girl who favored Dynel House of Beauty wigs and tight gowns that fanned out at the knees. Berry was tough on her in the studio, making her record a song 30 times before he finally liked a version. By the thirtieth time, her velvety pop voice was so hoarse and raspy she had a blues-like sound more suitable to rhythm and blues airplay than to pop radio.

By the end of the year, Berry Gordy had established a solid

reputation in the music business. Prior to forming his own company, he had written or co-written 18 Top 100 releases for Jackie Wilson, Marv Johnson, Etta James and others, six of which made it into the Top 20. Now, in December 1960, the Miracles—the group led by Berry's close friend Smokey Robinson—would have their first hit for Tamla, called "Shop Around."

The record sales charts have been compiled in different ways through the years but basically they are popularity lists based on a canvass of retailers who rank the sales of singles (45 RPM) and albums (33⅓ RPM) in their shop on a weekly basis. Radio play figures into the final tally. These charts are compiled by industry publications like *Billboard* and *Cash Box*, which assign the records involved bonus points (one through 100) for placement on the charts.* Records that reached the top of the charts in the early '60s usually sold close to a million copies. Since Gordy's out-of-pocket cost of making a single was relatively small, a runaway hit could be highly profitable.**

There are two kinds of music industry charts by which record sales and radio airplay are evaluated: the black charts and the mainstream, or white, charts. In the '40s and '50s, most records were logged on either one or the other. When an artist's song became popular on *both* charts, and the artist was black, it was said that the song was a "cross-over hit," meaning it had crossed over from black to mainstream charts, which includes all artists. This was always Berry Gordy's goal for his artists.***

"Cross-over, that's where it's at," Berry had said. Gordy started instructing his lyricists to write in the present tense, because "then people can relate." He began to establish a formula—his standards for what would make his company's records

*Within the record business, these charts are anticipated weekly and carry great weight because placement denotes a singer's or group's importance. The higher an artist sails up the charts toward the Number One position, the more popular he or she is becoming.

**Most major record companies are subsidiaries or divisions of publicly owned entertainment companies that give them access to established stars and, more important, capital. Their executives answer to a board of directors and stockholders, not to a single owner like a Berry Gordy. It was—is—difficult for independent companies like Gordy's Motown to achieve and sustain prosperity, so placement on the record charts meant more than popularity for the company's acts. It was also a badge of honor and promised longevity for the company.

***Cross-over happened now and then in the '40s, most notably with artists like Nat "King" Cole, whose "Nature Boy" topped both the black and pop record charts in 1948. After the advent of rock and roll in 1954, "crossing over" became even more commonplace.

cross-over hits. In the next couple of years Hitsville's artists would begin realizing great cross-over success.

By 1962, Diana Ross and Mary Wilson had graduated from high school and Barbara Martin had announced that she was pregnant. Diana felt that Martin's pregnancy would reflect poorly on the group, and she wanted her out. Flo and Mary disagreed and so, for a time, Barbara stayed. Eventually, Diana got her wish. Martin dropped out of the act. "No more fourth girls," Diana decided. "If we can't make it as a trio, then we just won't make it." Mary and Florence didn't have much to say about any of this. The Supremes continued recording and playing local engagements and making local news.

"We try not to be flashy and overdressed," Diana told a reporter. "We keep it very simple; for accents we use white gloves, bows and pearls."

At this time, Gordy switched them from Tamla to Motown which was now considered the home-base label, not that it made any difference. None of their releases was making much of an impact, and all three girls were becoming disconcerted, especially since it seemed that everyone else on the label was doing so well.

Thanks to their Number One record, "Please Mr. Postman," The Marvelettes were the most popular girls at Hitsville.*

With the exception of one member who had just graduated, The Marvelettes were all high school students from Inkster, Michigan, when "Please Mr. Postman" was released. At first, there were five in the group: two lead singers (Wanda Young and Gladys Horton) and three background girls (Georgeanna Tillman, Juanita Cowart and Katherine Anderson). Soon, Cowart dropped out, leaving four.

While the Supremes were still searching for an identifiable sound, The Marvelettes found one immediately with "Postman." Their vocals were often adolescently off-key, yet rich and somehow very appealing. (To demonstrate their importance to the label, when Berry hosted the annual company Christmas

---

*Of all the female groups ever signed to Motown, The Marvelettes are the company's best example of what is known in pop music history as "the girl group phenomenon," a musical trend that peaked and ebbed during a couple of years in the late '50s and early '60s. Music critic Greil Marcus once wrote, "If you were looking for rock and roll between Elvis and The Beatles, girl groups gave you the genuine article." The Shirelles ("Soldier Boy"), The Ronettes ("Be My Baby"), The Dixie Cups ("Chapel of Love") and many other girl groups who specialized in love songs and coquettish deliveries fell into this category.

party in 1962, each of The Marvelettes got a one-third-carat diamond ring. The Supremes were given transistor radios.)

Berry made certain that, despite the fact The Marvelettes were a quintet, there was nothing intricate about the way they harmonized. They were very direct and simple and, as a result, extremely commercial. Everyone at the company was proud of the group's success, everyone, that is, except Diana. Diana's true feelings about The Marvelettes first surfaced when they recorded "Please Mr. Postman."

At that session, many of the company's artists were present to add their own opinions and suggestions as to how to make the song better. Florence even worked with her friend Gladys Horton, lead singer of "Please Mr. Postman," on polishing up her vocals. There was no sense of competition among the artists at this time, just of achievement. Everyone seemed certain that this record would become a hit, and the possibility was truly exciting to them. They all wanted to be a part of it.

Finally, Diana couldn't stand the camaraderie another moment.

"What makes you girls think you're so hot?" she demanded of The Marvelettes.

They looked at her with confused, hurt expressions on their faces.

She continued, directing her comments now to Gladys, who, as lead singer, was getting the most attention. "Think you're real good, huh?" she said. "Well, who do you think you are comin' down here and gettin' a hit record before me? That's what I want to know. You all are gonna go on Dick Clark before me!"

Gladys recalled, " 'American Bandstand' was Diane's dream. She wanted to be on the show more than anything. We all thought, 'Surely she must be joking' and I think we started laughing. But, believe me, she was quite serious."

"I'm next," Diana said. "And don't you all forget it."

Then she turned around and walked off. Mary and Florence were quite embarrassed by her outburst. "Everyone was left with their mouths open," Gladys recalled. "But I thought it was funny. She was telling the truth about how she felt so clearly, so honestly, you had to laugh."

In the spring of 1962, Wanda Rogers, one of The Marvelettes, became pregnant and had to drop out of the group for a time. The group's road manager, Joe Shaffner, had been dating Florence Ballard and suggested that she join the act—just to complete the dates on an upcoming tour. Florence and Diana were alike in the sense that loyalty to their groups only went so far. Singing was the important thing. So Flo jumped at the chance. Everyday, she was at Hitsville rehearsing with The Marvelettes and having a good time, while Diana and Mary sat on the sidelines with nothing to do.

Mary was hurt and disillusioned, not because The Marvelettes were the competition but because "she's *our* sister, not *theirs.*"

Diana, as much as she may have understood Florence's decision—and probably would have done the same thing if she had been asked, and also allowed to sing lead—was outraged by it just the same.

"Oh, she was mad, but who gave a shit?" said Wanda. "Diane was always mad about somethin'. 'If she [Florence] wants to go on and be a Marvelette, then she should just be a goddamn Marvelette for all I care,' was the way Diane felt. No one paid her no mind. That's just the way she was. Pissed off a lot."

On this tour, Florence and Gladys became close friends and, one night, Flo confided to her about the rape. She needed to talk to someone, and she knew that the emotional subject never came up between her and the girls in her own group. Gladys was an orphan who was raised in a series of foster homes. She'd had a difficult life. Flo felt she could understand.

The two girls shared a room on the road and, recalled Gladys, "Florence was a loner. She really liked her privacy, but sometimes she just needed to confide in someone. We got back to the motel after a show, and it all came out. 'No one hardly knows this,' she said, 'but I was raped.' It was a big shock, and I felt so bad for her. I also felt that she didn't want anyone else to know, so I never told a soul. She never asked me not to, but I never even told the girls in my own group."

After the month-long tour was over, Florence returned to The Supremes. By this time, Mary Wells, The Contours and The Miracles were all topping the charts ("The One Who Really Loves You," "Do You Love Me?" and "You've Really Got a Hold on Me," respectively). Marvin Gaye was rolling with "Stubborn Kind of Fellow" and "Hitch Hike." Paul Williams and Eddie Kendricks of The Primes had been joined by three other local singers—Otis Williams, Elbridge Bryant and Melvin Franklin—to become The Temptations.

As Gordy established a number of Motown subsidiaries with names like V.I.P. and Mel-O-dy, he continued to take talented black music makers off the streets—kids entwined with fantasies of fame and fortune as performers, writers and musicians—and built a bridge for them into the world of their dreams. "Give them all an opportunity and see which ones hit," became his motto. Gordy designed his music to be palatable to a much larger audience than any form of black music had ever been before. Just as he had planned, this was "cross-over music," black music that white America could also love. The lyrics told a simple, universally identifiable, first-person story about love or heartbreak. The pulsating rhythm underscoring that story was always contagious and unforgettable.

Many Motown artists were years younger than Berry Gordy. Berry was 33 by the end of 1962. Most of his artists were barely out of their teens. Since many were from broken homes, they were grateful to belong to what was known as "the Motown Family"—a feeling Berry fostered among them because he knew that if they all felt they were working together, he would be better able to control them.

Berry Gordy was rarely idealistic or sentimental. To his way of thinking, each and every artist was a corporate asset. He wanted the best for them—he would be protective, nurture their talents and abilities, try to keep them happy—but he also wanted what was best for himself. Indeed, Berry Gordy, Jr., was nothing if not shrewd. Their opportunities were his opportunities.

Chapter
5

IN NOVEMBER 1962, Berry Gordy, Jr., put together the first
Motor Town Revue. The itinerary of concert dates would cover
much of the South, an area still largely segregated two years
before the passing of federal civil rights legislation.

Berry certainly realized that sending his black groups there
could be risky, but the tour made good business sense because
he had affiliated his company with Supersonic Attractions,
headed by promoter Henry Wynne. Wynne's connections with
theaters in the South were strong and influential. It was not easy
for new record labels like Gordy's to find reputable booking
agencies to arrange concert dates, and the fact that Wynne was
black encouraged Berry. He felt that Wynne would be sympathetic to Motown's needs, that his acts would not be unduly
taken advantage of, and that conditions on the road would not
become too rough—even on the dates in the South.

"Everyone will go out on the tour but the girls," he said,
referring to The Supremes.

When Diana discovered that her group would be excluded from
the tour, she set out to change Berry's mind. Eighteen and with
a will of iron, she was beginning to learn how to get her way
with him: be persistent and, if necessary, difficult. She and her
friends had enjoyed the few engagements they had played out of
town, places like Cleveland and Pittsburgh. Diana spent a lot of
time thinking about the sights she saw and people she met outside of Detroit. To her, the grass *was* greener and she wanted
more.

But Gordy was worried about The Supremes because, to him,
they seemed so vulnerable. He thought of the other women on
the show as being tough and street-wise and knowing how to

defend themselves if necessary. But The Supremes were special; they were "the girls." They had to be protected because they came across as demure and innocent. Actually, Diana Ross was probably every bit as tough in her own way as were any of the guys on the tour. She just didn't look it when she batted those big brown eyes.

Diana pleaded with Berry, telling him that if her group was excluded, "it just won't be fair!" On and on she went until Berry, who was always impressed by her spirit, finally gave in. He told her to be careful and even said he would miss her.

"He thought I was like a baby deer," Diana would recall years later. "Full of energy, vulnerable. I believed there was *nothing* I could not do. I was very cocky. Berry admired these things in me, but he also knew he had to take care of me."

Berry was almost 15 years her senior, but Diana thought he was cute, ambitious and talented. She knew he could certainly help advance her career if they were a team. He was also married, but the three wives in Berry Gordy's life were a colorless bunch compared to women like Diana.

"I'm gonna get him," Diana told her friend. "Just wait and see. That man is *mine*!"

But that was to be years later. Her first priority was the tour.

The original Motor Town Revue featured Mary Wells, The Miracles (with some modifications: Smokey Robinson was laid up with the flu, and Claudette did the leads; and Pete Moore was in the Army and temporarily out of the group), The Marvelettes, Marv Johnson, The Contours, Marvin Gaye (with Martha and The Vandellas as his backup singers), The Supremes and Singing Sammy Ward—practically the entire Motown roster, all of whom thought they were the luckiest young people on the planet. Going out on the road meant only one thing: freedom. Finally, they would be able to leave parental discipline along with the boundaries of home town Detroit for more than a day or two and discover the world at large. Some of their adventures on the road wouldn't be pleasant but, for the young Supremes and the rest of the artists on the tour, the experiences would be life-shaping in many ways.

The atmosphere on the morning of their departure was charged with excitement and apprehension. Forty-five artists and musicians (who had been organized by the house bandleader, Choker Campbell) lined up in front of five cars and a dilapidated bus—with *Motor City Tour* painted on its sides—to pose for photographs together. So many stacks of worn luggage and cosmetic cases were loaded onto the bus that there was barely room for the singers who comprised the bottom of the company's totem pole. These youngsters, including The Supremes, did not rate traveling in the automobiles. The Supremes, all wearing mohair sweaters and clutching brown leatherette purses, would have to squeeze on to the Motown bus with other less successful singers.

Before watching his artists drive off, Berry delivered a fatherly lecture about the virtue of "being good and respectable people" and why they should behave: "Because now you are representing Motown." He warned the fellows, in particular The Contours (known as much for their sexual exploits as they were for "Do You Love Me?") that they had better leave the girls alone. The groups listened attentively, acting as if they had every intention of being obedient on this their first time out of Detroit together. However, autobiographies written by stars who were on those tours have since made it clear that the main question on everyone's mind that morning was simple and direct: who was going to have sex with whom?

There were almost as many romantic entanglements among the kids from Motown as there were hit record collaborations. Understandably, that's what happens when a bunch of hot-blooded youngsters get together to experience the joy of popularity and the euphoria of making music—and love—on long bus tours across the country. Despite Berry's pre-tour warning, some of the fellows couldn't control their sexual appetites for the passions and favors of miscellaneous Vandellas and Marvelettes. They wouldn't dare lay their grubby hands on Berry's Supremes, however, especially on Diana because they feared her connection to Berry. A heavy-set black woman had been hired to keep an eye on the girls and lecture them incessantly about what happened when naughty boys and girls played with each other behind the bus.

When Berry found out that an unruly bunch of singers were caught having a sex party in one of the hotel rooms, he became furious and flew in to straighten matters out. He berated the male singers and suspended a whole group of them from the tour for four nights before allowing them to continue. He warned everyone that if this happened again, there would be no future tours. "He just don't want us to have a good time," one of the girls complained bitterly.

"Oh, please let me drive in the car with you fellows," Diana would repeatedly ask one of The Miracles. The Miracles had their own car. They were stars and didn't have to sit in the bus with the others.

"No way, Diane," he would tell her. "Claudette will kill you. You get back in the bus with your little group."

"But they ain't nobody," she would say. "I want to be *somebody* like you guys."

Diana returned to the stifling bus, where the veteran musicians smoked awful cigars and played card games in the back while the young artists snoozed and watched the scenery pass by them. Sometimes she would venture into the musicians' domain and try to get into a game with the guys. They would always shoo her away. "You're just afraid I'll beat you," she challenged them.

"Oh, just leave us alone, Diane," guitarist Marv Tarplin would tell her.

"Come back up here, girl," Florence would admonish her from the front of the bus. "Your place is up here."

On the tour, Florence was more inclined to be friendly with The Marvelettes than with The Supremes, after having just toured with them, replacing one of the girls during a pregnancy. Mary Wilson, always a sentimentalist, was still baffled and even hurt by Florence's seeming allegiance to "the competition," especially when she would share meals with them rather than with The Supremes.

Diana and most others on the tour were more realistic about the so-called "bonds" they all shared. They had common, self-centered goals, all having to do with fame and stardom. Though they were friends, they were not blood relations to each other. Only a few idealists, like Mary, thought that what was being shared on these tours was genuine sister- and brotherhood. In the light of nostalgia, that's a pretty picture, but it's not true.

Perhaps it was at this time that the real differences in the girls' backgrounds began to have an impact on their lives. Diana's was certainly very different from that of her singing partners.

Florence Ballard's father was a hobo who slept in graveyards and picked the blues on guitar. He married her mother when they were barely teen-agers. Flo was from a big family—the eighth of thirteen children—and so fighting for attention and recognition was a way of life for her. Most of the time, Florence acted sassy, independent, quick witted and impetuous, but after the rape she often plunged into deep depressions that only her mother could help her overcome.

Though Mary and Florence bonded together, Mary's background was much different. She had been "loaned" to her mother's younger sister since she was three. For the next six years, Mary grew up in a comfortable middle-class environment, believing the lie that I.V. and John Pippin were her natural parents. I.V., a perfectionist, was long on discipline and short on praise, which affected Mary well into her adult years. She blended in, rarely spoke out against what she perceived as injustices, and always did whatever she felt necessary to insure that all of the other youngsters would like her. As a result, no one disliked her. But no one knew where they really stood with her, either.

Her life changed dramatically when Johnnie Mae Wilson came to claim her when she was nine. Not only did she discover that the woman she thought was her aunt was really her mother, but also that two unruly "cousins" were actually siblings. After a series of run-down apartments, Johnnie Mae, who was illiterate, found a home in the Brewster Projects in 1956. Mary's natural father, Sam Wilson, was a drifter and compulsive gambler who had spent time in jail on charges that were never clear.

Mary's and Florence's parents, unable to overcome financial and racial obstacles, always put traditional Southern values of family loyalty and cooperation above everything else. This certainly wasn't the case in the Ross household.

Diana's parents managed to overcome many of the obstacles Flo's and Mary's couldn't. As a result, or maybe even because of it, the Ross family stressed Northern ideals of competition and achievement. Like her father, Diana became more remote, stubborn, suspicious and—as much as she disliked the quality in him—practical. She was mystified by the bond her singing partners had developed between them. While Mary and Florence had become fast friends, Diana remained the outsider and seemed to like it that way. Music and the sense of purpose it afforded was really the only element of compatibility she shared with these girls.

The tour began on November 2, 1962, in Boston and then proceeded to 19 cities in 23 days. Fifteen of the gigs were in the deep, dangerous South, beginning with a night in North Carolina on November 5. Georgia, Alabama, Mississippi, North and South Carolina and Florida were all on the itinerary. After Thanksgiving, the revue would pick up in Memphis on December 1 and then proceed to New York's Apollo Theatre for a week.

Esther Edwards, Berry Gordy's sister, booked most of the engagements herself. The Supremes were paid $290 a week. All but $10 a week for each girl was sent back to Detroit. The Supremes thought they would get the balance of their money when they returned home, but they learned that the funds were deposited into a Motown bank account to pay for what Gordy saw as the company's expenses on their behalf.

Three days after they left Detroit, their fourth Motown single, "Let Me Go the Right Way," which Berry had produced for them, was issued to the public. It would go on to become another flop.

As the tour chugged along, some of the acts were pulled off and sent on their own separate tours. With the exception of Singing Sammy Ward—who never amounted to much with six single releases but no successes—The Supremes and Martha and The Vandellas were the only groups on the revue who didn't have a hit record to sing. As Supremes' legend has it, they were soon dubbed "the no-hit Supremes" by their label mates, and they were none too pleased about that. But Martha and The Vandellas (Martha Reeves, Rosalind Ashford and Annette Sterling, all from Detroit and a couple of years older than The Supremes) wouldn't even have their first record release for two years.

Every couple of days the entourage would stop at a cheap motel to take much-needed baths and wash their clothing. "But it was the smelliest tour of all time," Diana once recalled. "It was good that the audiences were so far from the stage—they didn't have to smell the stink!"

None of the inconveniences mattered much to these youngsters, however, because they were too excited about their lives and burgeoning careers. They didn't realize they were paying their proverbial dues, but even if they had, they would've gladly paid the bill.

As the tour continued, the young Motown artists were confronted by extreme cases of racism that must have made indelible impressions on all of them. By 1962, the boycotts, sit-ins and Freedom Marches that had started in 1955 with the Montgomery bus boycott were rocking the South. Freedom fighters—black and white college students from the North—had traveled southward by bus and, in an effort to enforce integration, were unknowingly paving a path of anger and hatred for the Motown tour. Somehow, Diana Ross never expected to be confronted with racism.

This wasn't the first time Diana visited the South. In late 1950, Diana's mother, Ernestine, gravely ill with tuberculosis, was sent to the Howell Sanatorium in Howell, Michigan, for therapy. One of Ernestine's sisters agreed to watch the Ross children in Bessemer, Alabama, if Fred would pay her $30 a week to cover expenses. Fred drove them South and left them there for a year.

Diana, who was seven years old at the time, recalls little of 1951, her year in the South.

"I remember going in back doors and drinking from certain fountains, and only being allowed to go to certain places," she once said. "I didn't understand why I had these restrictions. I just thought that was the way life was, and put it out of my head. Children, they don't understand racism. They're too busy being children. What I remember most from that year is that my sisters and I all got majorette boots for Christmas."

When Diana's mother recovered in 1952 and returned home to live, so did her children.

"My first school was all-black and so I thought the world was like that," Diana said. "And then I had a racial mix in high school, and that didn't register because I just thought all people were the same. I can't remember when I first realized there was a racial thing, and that being black somehow made you different. It may have been when I spent time in Alabama as a youngster, but I think it really was when I started traveling as a singer."

Once, in Macon, Georgia, the bus broke down and local service station attendants refused to service it because the bus carried blacks. An understanding peace officer convinced the workers to fix the bus, but they did it while muttering obscenities about "those damn niggers." Most of the more well-traveled musicians carried guns with them in case of trouble.

At another stop, in South Carolina, the rickety bus collapsed in front of a jail house.

"All we could see were black hands clutching at the iron window bars, and before long they all started pleading with us to help them," Mary Wilson wrote in her book, *Dreamgirl*. "We girls hung back, afraid to get close, but the Tempts [Temptations] and Miracles went up and shook hands with the prisoners through the bars. 'Isn't there something we can do for these fellows?' I asked one of the musicians. 'Are you kidding?' he replied. 'We'd better get this bus fixed and get out of here before they throw us in there, too. They don't care about no innocence or guilt down here. That's how they treat niggers in the South.' "

"In practically every city, we couldn't find a restaurant that would let us come in the front door," Diana once recalled. "And we were determined *not* to have to use the back door."

At one stop, one of The Miracles became embroiled in a shouting match with a restaurant owner who refused to let the Motown artists use the front entrance. It almost ended in tragedy. The proprietor reached for his pistol just as Miracle Bobby Rodgers scrambled onto the bus and it screeched off.

"Diana was wide-eyed and scared shitless," Rodgers recalled. "She was quiet, all The Supremes were when these things went down, and just waiting to see who was gonna get killed first. These are the kinds of life-changing experiences I don't think any of us ever really got over. Most of the restaurants had little take-out windows in the back for blacks who weren't allowed in the front door, or allowed to sit down with whites."

Winehead Willie, a relative of Mary's who was on the tour as a comedian, walked into a restaurant one day and asked for a ham and egg sandwich. "I'm sorry," the waitress said, "but we don't serve black people."

"That's good," said Willie, " 'cause I don't eat 'em."

As difficult as it was to find safe restaurants, it was even more impossible to find gas stations that would allow the artists to use the bathroom facilities.

Florence, who had never been to the South before—and who said later that she never wanted to go back—once remembered:

"We all needed to go, *bad*, and so we stopped at a gas station. The Miracles got out of their car and come over to the bus and said, 'Don't worry, we'll handle it!' They went in and asked if we could use the bathrooms and came runnin' back followed by a white man with a shotgun. I grew up with white people living right next door, and I never saw anything like this before. These damn whites in the South were *crazy*. Diane would say, 'What makes them think they're better than us?' She really had no idea."

Florence continued, "Eventually, we made a deal with the guy. He said we could use his water hose and he handed us a bucket. So we had no choice. Everyone cleared the bus and whoever had to would go into the bus and do his business in the bucket, come back out, empty it behind the gas station in the woods and clean out the bucket for the next person, using the gas station's hose. Made me wonder if I wanted to be a star after all. But the most vivid memory for me was the day we all got shot at in Birmingham."

After the show in Birmingham, the troupe was boarding the bus headed for the next stop when gun shots rang out in the night. Mary Wells, who always tended to be dramatic, fell to her knees on the steps of the bus. "Oh, Lord, help me, *Jesus*! I'm hit!" she screamed. "I've been shot!"

"Girl, you ain't been shot," Diana said. "Those are firecrackers or somethin'."

"Like hell they are, we're bein' shot at," one of The Van-dellas exclaimed.

"Them's bullets!" Choker Campbell agreed.

By now, everyone was in a mad scramble to get back onto the bus and out of shooting range. But Mary Wells—who hadn't really been shot but was in shock—refused to get out of the way to let the panic-stricken musicians back on the bus. "And Mary was a big girl," Mary Wilson recalled. "No way could we move her."

Finally, when some of the fellows moved Wells, the bus filled up in 30 seconds and then went barreling down the street. The next morning, the driver found bullet holes in the front of the bus.

"You don't forget those kinds of things," Bobby Rodgers, of The Miracles, observed. "You don't *want* to."

In South Carolina, Beans Bowles found the troupe a motel so that they could wash and spend the night on some comfortable beds. Once they had checked in, some of the singers, including Diana, put on their swimsuits, planning to take a dip to cool off after the long, hot trip. Diana Ross was a superior swimmer, and she couldn't wait to take a running dive into the pool, fol-lowed by everyone else. For each black in the pool, one white would get out. Before they knew it, the Motown artists had the pool to themselves. All the whites had left.

"To hell with 'em," one of The Marvelettes decided. "We don't need them in *our* pool, anyway."

According to Mickey Stevenson, Motown's artist and reper-toire director, Diana was intensely competitive on the tour. "This kid would rehearse with an energy that was simply uncanny for an 18-year-old performer back then. Diane would be extremely upset when it didn't go well, and cry a lot after the shows. She'd go off on her own somewhere and rehearse whatever bothered her. The next night, she'd have it right."

By now, Mary and Florence were well aware of Diana's de-termination and aggressiveness. However, the other artists on the show were not at all happy with Diana's quest for attention, especially since her record sales didn't warrant much acclama-tion. What really made the others mad was when Diana would take bits and pieces from their acts. She would watch all of their performances from the wings or from the audience and then incorporate into her own presentation their very same manner-isms.

"Just a little bit softer now, just a little bit softer now," she would start singing after she saw one of the other singers do the same thing the night before. Then, after her voice had dropped to a whisper, she would begin raising it again while singing: "A little bit *louder* now. A little bit *louder* now!"

Because The Supremes were a minor act, they went on early in the show. Soon it began to appear that the other singers who came on later were imitating *them*.

Recalled Berry Gordy, "She [Diana] stole everybody's act. When the other artists came on, they looked ridiculous. They had to change their show every day, so they all hated her guts."

Soon, the artists were on the phone complaining to Gordy, and he had to extinguish Diana's burning enthusiasm by chastising her. "Find your own style," he told her. "You don't have to steal from them. Make *them* want to steal from *you*!"

Diana and Gladys Horton of The Marvelettes always amused the Motown gang over their silly arguments concerning issues like who in the troupe wore dirty underwear. Diana and Mary Wells argued about Wells' accusation that Diana should wear a girdle, " 'cause you jiggle so much." Diana accused someone else of stealing her shoes. They were still teen-agers, and they acted like it.

Sometimes, though, the rowdiness got dangerous. At one point, Gladys and Diana were feuding over some criticism Gladys had about The Supremes' dresses. Before she went on stage that night, Gladys was handed a note by one of the theater employees: "Diana is gonna kick your butt after the show."

After the performance, Horton was accompanying Lee Garrett, a blind youngster, across a parking lot when Diana made her move. She was sitting behind the wheel of a station wagon waiting for Mary and Florence. When she saw Gladys, she stepped on the gas pedal and headed straight for her and the boy. The two of them stood frozen in the parking lot. Diana hit the brakes and the car came to a screeching halt just a few feet away from Gladys and Lee. Gladys was understandably infuriated. She stood in front of the car and began screaming at Diana, "Go on ahead, hit me! Hit me! You crazy bitch!"

Diana rolled down the window, gave Gladys the finger, rolled it back up and sped off, laughing.

The next day, word of this incident got back to Berry and he was furious with Diana. He forced her to apologize to Gladys.

Gladys recalled she never knew what to expect from Diana in those days. "Once we were riding along in the bus and she said to me, 'Gladys, you are so damn lucky. You came out with "Please Mr. Postman" and it was an immediate hit,' " remembered Horton. " 'I'm awful sure that we could have a hit,' she told me, 'but the lady [Billie Jean Bullock] who helps Berry pick the songs for release, she hates me. So she won't release my best stuff.' ''

Horton continued, ''Diana started crying, and next thing I knew I was comforting her and crying with her. 'Don't worry,' I told her. 'You'll have your hit, too. Just you wait.' And there were we, boo-hooing because she didn't have a hit and I did. Diane was really complicated. She'd be runnin' your ass down with a car one day, and then have you cryin' your eyes out feelin' sorry for her the next.''

The tour took a tragic note when Beans Bowles and Eddie McFarland were in an automobile crash enroute from North Carolina to Florida. The two always acted as scouts for the revue, leaving earlier than the busload of artists so they could make plans and accommodations at the next stop. McFarland, the driver, seemed as if he'd had too much to drink the night before at a company party. Still, the two drove off in the direction of Florida early in the morning. Beans took Choker Campbell's gun since they were traveling with the proceeds from the previous night's show.

Hours later, the Motor Town Revue bus came upon their twisted and mangled automobile. Both passengers were missing, money was scattered about the scene. The bus screeched to a halt and everyone rushed out gasping at the horrible, bloody scene.

''Jesus Christ! What happened to 'em?'' Choker Campbell wondered. There was nothing to do but continue on to Florida. When they arrived, there was a message from Esther Edwards telling them to expect her by plane in a couple of hours. When she arrived, she informed the stunned artists and musicians that Eddie had apparently fallen asleep at the wheel and the van had crashed head-on into a truck.

Beans had been practicing his flute in the back of the van, and on impact the instrument plunged through his armpit and came out the back of his neck. He was alive, though both of his legs were broken and doctors predicted he would never walk again.

Eddie was dead. His head had been sheared off when the car was crushed under the semi trailer. It was shocking news and everyone began to cry. This senseless death almost made it impossible for them to continue with the revue.

Most of the theaters in which the artists performed were segregated with blacks in the balconies and whites seated on the floor level, or with whites on one side of the theater and blacks on the other. In Macon, the theater hosted a ''Colored Folks

Night," which meant that, for one evening only, blacks were allowed to sit on the first level while whites were relegated to the balcony. This was a rare occurrence. Segregation was the norm.

If there was no balcony, a rope would be put in place from the center stage straight down the aisle to the back of the theater: blacks on one side of the rope, whites on the other. Some of the lead singers complained of not knowing which side of the rope to sing to. They were afraid of giving too much attention to one side and, thus, angering the other. During these shows, Diana Ross would stand right smack in the center of the stage with her feet planted at the point where the rope began. As she sang, she would look straight ahead, trying to ignore the segregation and, no doubt, hoping everyone would stay on the "proper" side of the rope so that a race riot would not break out.

It's not difficult to imagine the kind of impact these early tour experiences had on the Motown performers. Racism was certainly nothing new to any of the young adults on the revue, but to be confronted with it so blatantly—and to have it intrude on their show biz fantasy world—made the ugliness of it all even more revolting.*

Fred and Ernestine Ross were certainly well aware of the racial problems in the South. They could only hope that their daughter was being protected, as Esther Edwards had promised she would be. Though Diana would telephone home regularly, she was always careful to sugarcoat her experiences. The last thing she wanted to do was worry her parents and then have them demand that she return home, contract or no contract.

Diana's brothers and sisters, all in school, were very impressed that she toured with the revue. For instance, whenever anyone would ask Margretia where her older sister Diana was, she would feign nonchalance and respond: "Oh, she's out with the Motown Revue, entertaining and bein' a star."

*In interviews that some of the singers gave to the media after this tour, the subject of racial discrimination was never brought up. Berry must have told his artists that there was no reason to ruffle any important feathers by making statements regarding their experiences in the South. So, instead, they all talked gleefully about being on the road for the first time, and about how grateful they were to be with Motown. Many years later, however, the singers would share sad, and sometimes bitter, memories with reporters and in autobiographies; apparently none of them was left unaffected by what they saw in the South in 1962.

(After the passing of Federal Civil Rights legislation in 1964, many of these acts would go back to these same theaters and find that the ropes were gone. The audiences were now integrated.)

Barbara Jean, meanwhile, had just entered college where began her long road to achievement in the medical profession. "It seemed like she studied from the very first moment I knew her," Diana would recall. "I know now that she was always as determined as I was to see that her dreams came true."

The tour finally ended with a ten-day engagement at the Apollo Theatre beginning December 7, 1962. A drab, gray three-story pile of bricks on 125th Street in Harlem, the Apollo was one of the most famous presentation houses in the world. Working the Apollo was usually the dream of most young black entertainers at the time. In his book, *Showtime at the Apollo*, writer Ted Fox observed, "[The Apollo was] not just the greatest black theater but a special place to come of age emotionally, professionally, socially and politically."

"The Apollo was the top," said bandleader Andy Kirk. "It was *the* thing. You had to play the Apollo, and once you did play it, you had made it."

Early soul stars such as James Brown, Ray Charles, Sam Cooke and Jackie Wilson had made the Apollo their home. Audiences were known to be brutally frank. If they liked you, you knew it. And if they didn't, you knew that, too, by the sound of their boos and hisses. All of the Motown artists were as nervous as they were excited about the opportunity to play the Apollo, and the competition among them to be the best of the group was stronger than it had ever been.

For The Supremes, a big disappointment came when they ran out to look at their names on the marquee and discovered that they weren't listed with the other acts on the show. Florence got on the phone to Berry and demanded to know why they were omitted from the billing. He told her to be quiet about it. "You're lucky to be there at all," he said.

Diana remembers her first date at the Apollo as being a career highlight. She has been quoted as saying, "I was so happy, I just couldn't stop laughing."

But Mickey Stevenson remembers just the opposite. "The Apollo audiences didn't really like Diane and The Supremes because they were a lot more sophisticated than what those audiences were accustomed to. Opening night was a heavy moment for Diane because the audience was very cool. She was upset because she had worked so hard, and for what? I distinctly remember Berry saying to her on the phone, 'Look, don't worry about it,' and Diane coming back with, 'But they didn't like us. They didn't like *me*!' "

Berry reassured Diana by explaining to her once again the

theory in action behind his Motown movement. "We have to *teach* them to accept our brand of sophistication." Berry was referring to the "cross-over" strategy he'd always had in mind for most of his artists.

"She listened and maybe even agreed," Stevenson concluded, "but she was still very upset."

It wasn't surprising that the Apollo audiences found The Supremes unusual because they were nothing like their colleagues on the revue. The Contours' acrobatic choreography accompanied their gruff, soulful harmonies. The Marvelettes high-stepped their way through medleys of songs that were well-known to the audiences.

But The Supremes were sweet, talented and low-key. Their leader sang through her nose, made funny faces and popped her eyes. They didn't dance about the stage, rather they swayed in unison. There was only one word for them: *elegant*.

In 1981, Diana recalled that a recording studio technician told her he had seen her perform at the Apollo and that one of the stage managers had pointed her out and said, "If Berry Gordy spends time with that girl, she's going to be a big star."

During this engagement, a local disc jockey was responsible for bringing The Supremes off the stage and then introducing the next attraction, comedian Stu Gilliam. The jock wasn't in place one night to do his job, so Gilliam went out to encourage the audience's applause and make the group's bows worthwhile. "Let's hear it for The Supremes," he'd say, trying to incite some enthusiasm from the crowd. Then Gilliam would do his comedy set.

The same thing happened at the next show. No disc jockey was present and Gilliam encouraged The Supremes' bows and prompted the audience's applause. The third time the disc jockey didn't appear, Gilliam decided to let the trio fend for itself, "just to keep a bad habit from starting," he said. The group walked off on their own to a mediocre response.

After his set, Gilliam was summoned to The Supremes' dressing room by one of the roadies. Mary and Florence let him in. Diane whirled around from her make-up mirror to face him.

"So, where were you?" she demanded to know.

"Beg pardon?" he asked.

"I'd like to know why weren't you there to take us off?" Diana responded.

Gilliam explained to her that he wasn't the master of ceremonies, but rather a comic who, for two shows, had done them a favor. "Comic, master of ceremonies, what the heck difference does it make?'' she asked. ''You shoulda' been there to take us off!''

''Hey, you listen here, little girl,'' Gilliam began. ''Rather than spend your time fussing with me, why don't you go out and try to get yourself a hit record?'' He turned around and walked out the door.

''Well,'' Diana huffed. ''The *nerve*.''

''Yeah,'' Mary and Florence agreed. ''The *nerve*.''

Chapter
6

By January 1963, Berry Gordy had decided The Supremes were to be a company priority. Berry's interest in the group was heightened when he saw how adept Diana had become as a performer. He was already excited about her voice, but the fact that she seemed to be such a natural, charismatic performer made Berry even more interested in her potential. Even if Diana hadn't been The Supremes' lead singer, it would have been difficult not to pay almost exclusive attention to her, she was that energetic and electric when she was in front of an audience. But Diana was a part of a group and so all three girls would benefit by Berry's enthusiasm for her.

Every writer and producer at Hitsville wanted to satisfy Berry Gordy and ingratiate themselves with him. He was a father-figure to most of them, also the man who doled out the dollars, so it's not surprising that everyone vied for his attention. If he had a fixation about The Supremes, then so be it. That was his prerogative. Or as one producer put it, "If Berry wanted me to shine his car, I'd be waxing it before he could get the words out." Suddenly, everyone on staff clamored for the opportunity to work with The Supremes.

One producer, Clarence Paul, had the girls in the studio in February 1963 recording a country-western album which, though it boasted probably the best harmonizing the girls recorded, was considered by people around Hitsville as the oddest music the company had ever churned out.

"Gordy had said that he wanted Diane in the studio separately from the other two," Clarence Paul remembered. "But I told him that I wouldn't go for that because I felt I was recording a group and so I wanted a group sound. Diane was such a little

74

egotistical kid, anyway, who knew she could do it all, whatever I asked. Most of the album was recorded in the early morning hours [because the group had a local club appearance at the time]. I remember personally having to pick up Mary and Florence at four in the morning and Diane would already be waiting there for us, wondering where we were.''

Florence once recalled another moment during the recording session. She, Mary and Diana were in the sound booth each singing a lead vocal to a song when Diana suddenly walked away from her microphone, out of the booth and to the control panel where Clarence Paul was seated.

"You know *I* am the lead singer. So why are *they* singing leads, too?'' she wanted to know.

Paul patiently explained that he wanted to have one number on the album on which each girl sang a verse.

Diana looked at him petulantly. "Well,'' she said, "we'll just see what *Mr. Gordy* has to say about this.'' Then she returned to the recording booth.

As Mary and Florence glared at her, she smiled innocently. What she didn't know was that her partners had heard the entire conversation between her and Paul through the intercom system of their headphones.*

In March 1963, around Diana's nineteenth birthday, Gordy decided to release *Meet The Supremes*, a compilation of all the group's flops and flip sides up until that time. Needless to say, it wasn't a big seller. In June, Berry issued a song they had recorded with Smokey Robinson producing: "A Breathtaking Guy,'' one of the group's better songs but not a hit.

There was one writing-producing team at Hitsville that seemed to be having terrific success with the other Motown girl groups: Eddie Holland and Lamont Dozier were lyricists; Lamont would collaborate with Brian Holland on composition. These three young fellows would go on to create the music that would be considered the very pulse of what's come to be known as "The Motown Sound.''

Many have actually said that they *were* the sound but that's not really true. The "Sound'' belonged to all of the writers and producers, but H-D-H originated many of the original elements: a muscular rhythm section, immediately involving hook lines and choruses, clever lyrics. Their music was so impassioned and creative, it's very easy, in retrospect, to forget just how young

*The album they were recording at this time, *The Supremes Sing Country Western and Pop*, would go unreleased for two years, until March 1965.

these guys were: in 1963, Brian and Lamont were 22 and Eddie
was 24.

Their work with The Marvelettes ("Locking Up My Heart")
was just a harbinger of what they planned to do for Martha
Reeves and The Vandellas. The Supremes couldn't help but feel
envious when The Vandellas—who up until this point were nothing but background singers and had only had one unsuccessful
single release—suddenly became *instant* stars thanks to Holland-
Dozier and Holland's 1963 output for them: "Come and Get
These Memories," "Love Is Like a Heatwave" and "Quick-
sand." The couple of songs H-D-H had written for The Supremes were mediocre and had yet to be released.

Martha and The Vandellas were an excellent vocal group. In
fact, almost all Motown historians agree that Martha Reeves was
one of the real major musical talents the company ever turned
out. A genuine artist and arguably the most creative singer at
Hitsville, Reeves had extensive training and experience in jazz,
gospel and even opera.

It was well known among the artists, writers and producers at
Motown that Diana was jealous of Martha, and that Martha
wasn't very fond of Diana either. Diana would complain that
Martha was unfriendly, while Martha would accuse Diana of
snubbing her in the hallways of Hitsville. There were rumors of
"cat fights" between the two—both of whom were once secretaries at Motown—but Martha has denied them.

"I never touched her," she said. "But we did have—*debates*."

The problem between these two was that Martha was considered by practically all of Motown's writers and producers to be
a better singer than Diana. Now and then, Diana would overhear
some of the staff comparing the two voices, and hers would
usually come out on the losing end. The comparisons were unfair since both women had qualities that were special and extremely commercial.

This rivalry would continue for years. Martha would accuse
Diana of coming to her concerts in the Detroit area, sitting ring-
side just to make her nervous—and, to make matters worse, have
Berry Gordy in tow. Ross and Gordy, Martha has charged, would
whisper to one another, while Berry took frantic notes. "Then
they would get together later and go over the notes, and steal
from my act," she would complain.

Diana told Berry in no uncertain terms that she wanted
Holland-Dozier and Holland to come up with a winning formula
for her, just as they had for Martha Reeves. Berry wasn't sure

this would be a good idea; after all, what would Martha think? Certainly, Diana didn't care what Martha thought about her idea.

As Berry tried to make up his mind, Diana apparently decided to take matters into her own hands. She began to pursue Brian Holland, hoping to convince him he should produce her group with his partners. Brian was interested. Soon he was writing notes to Diana and, trying to be discreet, asking Janie Bradford to deliver them. Before long, Brian's wife Sharon, a small but very tough and determined woman, would show up at Hitsville looking for "the other woman" and threatening to "kick Miss Diane Ross' ass if she don't stop messin' with my Brian." Sharon was no passive, sweet and naïve Claudette Robinson-type; she was jealous and very protective of her relationship with her husband. Nevertheless, Holland-Dozier and Holland were in the studio with The Supremes by May 1963.

Eddie, Brian and Lamont came up with a frenetically arranged song called "Run, Run, Run" and had The Supremes record it. Then there was a rush release in October, "When the Lovelight Starts Shining Through His Eyes." It packed a wallop unlike anything else the girls had recorded. The full range of Motown effects was at work here, including a conga beat and grunting male chorus. Diana's lead was more assertive than ever and her delivery was surprisingly strong and full. It was a solid effort that was a bit more of a success than anything they had previously recorded.

The Supremes seemed to be off to a new start, but their future was threatened when Sharon Holland set out to separate her husband, Brian, from Diana. She accosted Diana in the 20 Grand nightclub, where she was partying with Florence, Mary and a female singing trio who called themselves the Velvelettes. According to witnesses, Sharon Holland shouted obscenities and screamed at Diana, "If you don't stay away from my man, you are a dead woman."

Diana wasn't one to run from a challenge. She was ready to fight Sharon Holland if she had to. In fact, she seemed eager to. But her friends managed to get her out of the nightclub just in time.

"Well, he *likes* me," Diana explained to Mary and Florence on the way home.

"She didn't have to mess with Brian Holland to get H-D-H to produce us," Florence said years later in a 1975 conversation with a journalist. "I ain't sayin' that she *did*, I'm just sayin' that she didn't have to. Not that we were any more innocent, I gotta say, because I don't know what we would have done if we'd had the chance. Brian *was* cute. There were other guys besides Brian that Diane—liked. But I ain't sayin' who 'cause it ain't nobody's business, and, besides, she'd kill me.''

Florence said that Brian and Sharon were not happily married and that Brian was seeing other women besides Diana. That's how it was at Hitsville back then, a hotbed of sexual activity.

"Berry Gordy was leading the way, and he'd be up in his room freaking with whoever was in his life that night," Marvin Gaye remembered. "He was the father figure. So why wouldn't all the 'children' follow suit."

Mary Wilson said that Diana Ross and Brian Holland were seeing each other from late 1962 to late 1963, the period of time when Holland-Dozier and Holland first began working with The Supremes. If Diana was, indeed, having an affair with Brian Holland, it apparently ended shortly after the confrontation with his wife in the nightclub. Luckily, the end of the relationship did not mean the end of Holland-Dozier and Holland's work with The Supremes.

Meanwhile, Martha Reeves and her Vandellas were going on to fame and glory while Diana and her Supremes seemed to be stuck in a rut. The battle lines were drawn. Berry made the mistake of booking both groups on a show together at the Howard Theater in Washington, D.C., with The Supremes an opening act.

As The Supremes walked out onto the stage, radiant and proud in the new stage gear Diana purchased for them with money she begged Berry to wire to her, the Howard Theater audience offered polite applause. In the middle of their second number, "I Am Woman," Mary and Florence realized that two Vandellas were standing in the wings and glaring at them.

Florence would later recall that Diana was fully involved in her performance when out of the corner of her eye she noticed Martha Reeves standing just off stage to her right. Her fists were clenched.

After the third and final tune, The Supremes took the requisite bows. Mary and Florence exited stage left and ran head on into two of The Vandellas. Florence gave them a once-over from head to toe: "Hey. You got our dresses on."

"Like hell we do. You got *our* dresses on," they replied.

"Uh-oh."

Diana was supposed to exit from the right but she was still on stage alone thanking the audience profusely over and over again, obviously stalling for time. As the small band droned on, Choker Campbell, the confused conductor, motioned for Ross to leave the stage. She was afraid to make her exit because waiting there for her was Martha Reeves. Suddenly, Flo remembered, Diana dashed across the stage and made a hasty exit on the opposite side. "Quick, let's get to the dressing room!" she screamed as she raced down the hall.

As Mary and Florence followed, Martha sprinted across the backstage area, weaving in and out of the startled stage technicians who were standing in her way. The Supremes screeched in unison as they scampered up the flight of stairs barely out of Martha's reach. They dashed into the dressing room, slamming the door behind them.

"I'm gonna get you, Diane Ross," Martha warned her. "You just wait!"

"You mean to tell me you found out where they got their dresses and bought three just like them?" Florence asked Diana once inside the dressing room.

"Well, we looked good, didn't we?" Diana answered. "I mean, we don't have any hits, at least we can *look* good."

Florence recalled that she shook so hard with laughter her insides began to ache. *"Girl, Martha is gonna kill you."*

While The Supremes leisurely changed clothes and commiserated about Diana's probable fate at the hands of Martha Reeves, The Vandellas—wearing cheaper, tackier stage wear, because of Diana's stunt—wrapped up their star set. "We shoulda' left early and gone back to the hotel," Florence decided. "Honey, you're in trouble now."

"Looky here, I can handle Miss Martha Reeves," Diana said cockily. "If she messes with me, *she'll* be the sorry one. She ain't nuthin' anyway."

"Yeah, she ain't nuthin' anyway," Mary piped in, caught up in the moment. She grabbed a hairbrush, the only available weapon.

Right on cue, a loud pounding on the locked dressing room door startled all three of them. "Open up!" the voice on the other side demanded.

Diane quickly picked up the telephone and began dialing frantically. Mary, always the chicken, politely opened the door. Then, she and Florence took three panic-stricken steps backwards.

Martha Reeves remembered what happened next. "Quite simply, I told Miss Diane Ross that I felt like scratching her eyes out for what she had done," Reeves recalled, laughing at the memory. "And she said to me, 'But Martha, here, the phone, it's Mr. Gordy. . . .' By now her voice had risen an octave. 'He's got somethin' to say to you!' she insisted.

"Then Diane shoved the receiver at me," Martha said. "And I put it to my ear."

There was a patient voice on the other end. "Now, Martha, Diane didn't mean you no harm."

"But Mr. Gordy, she . . ."

"Now you leave Diane alone," he continued, "and when you get back I'll buy you *all* new dresses." His sing-song tone was that of a tolerant father trying to calm down his cranky child.

"Yes, Mr. Gordy," Martha said obediently. After she hung up, she looked around the room but Diana Ross was long gone. "Where'd she go?" Martha demanded. Mary and Florence answered by shrugging their shoulders.

As soon as Martha stormed out and slammed the broken door behind her, the two young Supremes collapsed in laughter.

"You know what I wonder?" Florence asked, shaking her head, "How many times are we gonna have to save that girl from getting her *ass* kicked?"

The Dells, a popular rhythm and blues group, were also appearing on that same show in Washington. Diana was said to be romancing one of the group members, and everyone involved with the revue was whispering about it.

Ardena Johnston, the girls' chaperone at that time, once remembered, "Berry called me on the phone and let me have it. 'How could you allow this to be happening?' he screamed at me. And I said, 'Look, Mr. Gordy, this girl is very difficult and I'm having a hard time controlling her. She does what she wants to do. The others listen to me, but she won't. And I'm sorry, but I don't know what to do with her.' "

Berry's response: "Don't be ridiculous. That's your problem."

Johnston recalled, "To Berry, the most important thing was keeping these girls—all the girl groups for that matter—in line. He did not want them dating the male groups, and that was always a problem. It made the chaperone look bad if she couldn't abide by his wishes."

After talking to Gordy, Ardena searched for Diana and found her in the basement dressing room of the Howard Theater with her friend from The Dells, eating lunch.

"How *dare* you socialize with this young man," Johnston said. "From now on, you follow *my* rules or I'm sending you home. The group will continue without you."

"I can talk to a fella if I want to," Diana protested. "I know my rights! I can say hello to a guy if I like—and you can't tell me what to do, *Miss Johnston*." Later, Diana would recall, "I really whipped it on her."

"You're doing a lot more down here than just talking," Ardena said suspiciously. "Don't you think I know what's been going on around here? You just wait until I tell Mr. Gordy."

The next day, when they returned to Detroit, Ardena told Berry what had happened, and he called Diana into his office.

"Look, I don't care what nobody says," Diana said in her defense. " 'Cause she was wrong and she embarrassed me and I ain't apologizin' to her. No way."

She recalled later, "Berry said I had to apologize to her but I insisted that I wasn't going to do it. Finally, I said I would but only because he said so. So I wound up saying I was sorry, though I really felt that she'd been wrong."

"It wasn't that I didn't like Diana, I did," Ardena Johnston recalled before she died in 1985. "She was a wonderful girl when she wanted to be. But I had a job to do, and if I couldn't keep her in line, it was a poor reflection on me. Mary, too, was difficult to control. She had a lot of boyfriends but was more discreet and would listen to reason. Diane wouldn't listen to anyone except her mother, I guess."

After that incident, Ardena apparently asked Berry Gordy to reassign her to another group. She never again traveled with The Supremes, and Mary has said that Diana didn't miss her very much. Berry's sister Esther Edwards had often traveled with the girls when Ardena wasn't available, and now that she was out of the picture, Esther was back on the job.

Esther Edwards has remembered this story, told to her by Florence.

Once, Mary was determined to spend the night with a man she'd just met and she plotted with Diana for her freedom.

That night, Diana and Florence, wearing their robes with their hair in curlers, watched as Mary, in an evening gown, bouffant wig and earrings, prepared for her getaway. Taking two pillows from the head of her twin bed, she put them in the middle, covered them with a blanket, and molded them into what she thought looked like the shape of a human being. "There," she said with a satisfied grin. "Now no one will ever know the difference."

"But Berry's gonna be mad at you," Diana warned.

"Now, how's Berry gonna know," Mary said. "Unless someone tells him." She shot Diana a menacing look.

"I'll never tell," Diana promised.

"Me neither," Flo chimed in.

As she squirted perfume on her neck, Mary explained that she really had no choice, she just had to see this fellow. "He's so fine, and, well, you know how it is."

"Vaguely," Florence said with a resigned smile.

With that, Mary was gone, trusting her friends.

Five minutes later, there was a knock on the door. Diana opened it, and it was Esther Edwards.

"What are you girls doing?" Esther remembered asking.

"Well, we're just straightening up the room, fluffing pillows and all," Diana said, signaling for Esther to keep her voice down. "Mary's already asleep."

Florence turned away from filing her nails. "Shhhhhh! You'll wake Mary."

"Time you two got to bed yourselves," Esther said before opening the door to leave. She took one more look at the form in the bed. "Mary sure is lookin' lumpy these days, ain't she?"

Esther said that as she turned to leave, she glanced over her shoulder and winked at the two girls.

The door closed. Diana and Florence looked at each other and burst out laughing.

As 1964 began, The Supremes continued to work in the studio with a variety of writer-producers with all sorts of sounds and techniques. Though they had been at Motown for three years, it still seemed as if the group had no identity at all, especially with each of them doing lead singing. After listening to all of their music—most of which the public would never hear—Berry Gordy made an "executive decision." On that day, the group was in the recording studio when Berry walked in, greeted them warmly and said, "Girls, from now on, I think Diane should do all the leads."

He waited for some comment, but there wasn't one. Diana, who sat in a corner with no expression on her face, gazed up at Berry with big, round, innocent eyes; Mary and Florence looked at each other quizzically but didn't say a word. All three girls knew this was a turning point, but no one knew what the decision would mean.

"I know you all sing lead, but she's the one with the most commercial sound," Berry said, pointing to Diana. Berry walked out of the studio and the girls went back to their work without discussing the boss' bombshell.

"I can't say we minded that Diane was going to be doing all

of the lead singing," Mary said later. "We wanted to be a success, and if that's what it took we were willing to go along with it. Plus, we just *knew* that we'd have our chance eventually."

Mary and Florence didn't really know Berry Gordy well enough to realize that once his mind was locked into a decision, it would be difficult to alter his opinion. They thought that despite what he said, they would be able to sing a song if it was "right" for them, like when Florence sang lead on their second single, "Buttered Popcorn," which sank without a trace. They didn't realize that from this point on, no song would be "right" enough for them.

Berry's fateful decision was based on plain business sense: Diana really did have the best, most so-called "commercial" singing voice. Florence's was bigger and louder, but didn't have the character, discipline or assurance of Diana's. Mary was a pleasant enough vocalist, but hers was an indistinctive singing style with no range and certainly no real personality.

Because of its nasal tonality, Diana's voice seemed to cut right through any orchestration—you paid as much attention to her *sound* as you did to the insistent Motown rhythm. Plus, stylistically she was really quite amazing; she knew how to caress a lyric or turn a phrase in such a way that you had to wonder whether it was the result of careful tutoring in the studio or sheer instinct. And her producers insist her style was instinctive. In listening to unreleased versions of songs made popular by The Supremes in later years, it's easy to see that Ross could record the same song many different ways, and all of the performances would be worthy of release because she would always give a real performance in the studio. Moreover, Diana's enunciation was almost impeccable. Indeed, her critics would say that it was sometimes too precise and affected. That didn't matter. Berry wanted his Motown songs to tell a story and he knew that when Diana sang them the listener could always understand every word. Remember that this is what he most admired about Doris Day.

Berry Gordy simply felt that once his writers and producers could focus on exactly which voice they would be writing for, it would be easier to break the group out.

Lamont Dozier, of Holland-Dozier and Holland, recalled the next step: "One evening after a writing session for The Marvelettes, Eddie, Brian and [writer-producer] Mickey Stevenson were playing a game of cards while I was tinkering on the piano. All of a sudden I came up with this melody and the question 'Where did our love go?' Brian heard it and said, 'Hey! That'd be just great for The Marvelettes. Let's work it out.' So we quickly finished it and, at the time, it seemed like just another song on an upcoming Marvelettes album.''

When the fellows played the song for The Marvelettes, they were unanimous in their disapproval. It's surprising that the girls had any say in this at all—usually the artists didn't—but they did have veto power, and they used it because *they* thought "Where Did Our Love Go" was, as Wanda Rogers of The Marvelettes said, "absolutely ridiculous. The most pitiful tune we'd ever heard. We never dreamed it would amount to anything.''

Gordy suggested the fellows offer the song to The Supremes. It was melodic and easy-going and he thought it more their style anyway. To accept material rejected by the competition was more than The Supremes could bear. Not only that, the girls hated the song more than did The Marvelettes.

It was Eddie's idea to have Mary sing lead on the song, a soft, rocking ballad, right up her alley. But Brian reminded everyone, "Diana's the lead singer. Didn't you hear what Berry said?''

Mary was quite disappointed—she didn't particularly like the song but a lead was a lead, and they were becoming more and more scarce. Fatefully, had this decision gone another way, it could have changed a lot more than just a song arrangement. Diana Ross' entire life and career might have been a very different story, not to mention Mary Wilson's.

Lamont Dozier recalled that the session for "Where Did Our Love Go" in April 1964 was "a pretty trying experience." He said, "After it was over, we played the song for Berry. His verdict: 'It'll go Top 40, maybe Top 20. Not good enough for Number One, though.' ''

Against this backdrop of frustration and disappointment, a small miracle was about to happen. Dozier distinctly remembers the breakthrough: "We were used to cutting Diane in the higher key than we had recorded her in previously. For this one tune, we decided to drop the key. The result was surprising: in a lower key, she sounded, well, *sexy*. We were very impressed with that, but we didn't think too much more about it.''

Meanwhile, Dick Clark's annual "Cavalcade of Stars" was gearing up for a summer tour. Taylor Cox, who was a Motown Management department head, recalled, "At the time, Brenda Holloway [a Gordy discovery from Los Angeles] had a monstrous record called 'Every Little Bit Hurts' and Clark wanted Brenda on his tour. Berry was interested in doing *something* with The Supremes in order to generate a little money in their account to pay for all of their flop recording sessions. I told Dick that he could have Holloway, but he'd have to take Diane and the girls. He balked, didn't want 'em, but then offered us $600 a week for them, which wasn't even enough to cover their traveling costs. We sent them out there anyway.''

Motown hurried the group into a rehearsal session to pull together a new act that would consist of their most recent material, including "Where Did Our Love Go." In June 1964, The Supremes began the Dick Clark tour, billed as "others" on a show starring Gene Pitney, The Shirelles, Brenda Holloway and "others." ("Others" included Bobby Sherman, The Crystals, Brian Hyland and Dee Dee Sharpe.) Berry Gordy gave Ernestine Ross the job of chaperone on this trip, replacing Ardena Johnston and Esther Edwards. Perhaps he felt that Ernestine could better handle her own daughter. The Supremes were 20 years old; Florence would turn 21 on this bus tour.

"When my mother went out with us, she loved it," Diana Ross recalled. "She taught us a lot of things about, for instance, going into a nice, beautiful dressing room and leaving it that way. Or going into a messy one, cleaning it up and leaving it better than we found it so that when someone else came after us they would say we left them a clean room instead of how nasty it is. Before long, everyone started calling her Mama Supreme. She wasn't like some authoritative person over us. She was there mostly as a friend.

"They even played tricks on her. She was afraid of spiders and somebody on the bus had a rubber spider, put it over her and she went running through the bus scared and screaming. Everybody just cracked up. I'll never forget that. She was too much!"

"We had only enough money for two rooms on the road," Ernestine Ross remembered, "so the girls had to take turns rooming with me. They always hated to room with me because I'd make them pick up. Diane and Mary used to go out every night after the show, but Florence hardly ever dated. Florence and I would stay in the room and play cards and wait for the other two to come home."

Ernestine was very fair with the girls, showing no favoritism to her daughter in any of the usual squabbles. However, having her mother around seemed to make Diana nervous; she was more reserved on this tour than she had been on the others; still, there were tensions and arguments, as to be expected. At one point, Diane and one of the members of The Crystals were evicted from the bus by the driver, much to Ernestine's embarrassment, because they had gotten into a screaming match over a pair of shoes.

Dick Clark had a fond memory of The Supremes. ''I was walking through the backstage area of one of the auditoriums we played and as I passed by a dressing room I heard three a capella voices singing 'People.' Someone told me it was The Supremes. 'How odd,' I remember thinking. 'Three black girls from Detroit singing Barbra Streisand songs on a rock 'n' roll tour. There must be something there, something . . . *special*.' ''

During the time The Supremes were on the road, Motown reorganized its national record distribution and finally, after five years in business, solidified its ties with radio station program directors. When ''Where Did Our Love Go'' was released on June 17, 1964, the song benefited greatly from the company's stronger media ties. In the midst of Presley-mania and the first inklings of an upcoming British invasion, this glossily arranged tune seemed to fill a void and was eagerly accepted by record buyers. If the record had been released earlier, though, Motown probably wouldn't have been able to fill all of the orders for it, and it would have been lost. The song bulleted up the charts, and as it did, The Supremes began to receive billing and their position on the revue was moved closer to the end of the show.

''We'd go on stage every night and sing the song and the kids would just start screaming,'' Diana Ross recalled. ''We'd look at each other and look around the stage wondering what the fuss was about. Doing these one-nighters, we never had the time to think about what was happening with the record. When I called home, my sisters told me that it was being played—but that didn't matter to me because they played *all* of our stuff in Detroit. They just never played the records anywhere else.''

The group was about a month into the tour when ''Where Did Our Love Go'' began outselling all of the other pop and rhythm and blues songs released at that time. It was also receiving more radio airplay than any other record. All of this momentum and popularity catapulted the song to the Number One spot on *Billboard*'s charts. By the time the revue was over, The Supremes were headlining over Brenda Holloway, Gene Pitney, The Shirelles and all of ''the others.'' Dick Clark had accidentally secured the Number One act in the country for $600 a week.

The ''Calvacade of Stars'' performed in major cities throughout the East Coast and Midwest and when the tour finished in Oklahoma, Berry called to tell the girls they could take a plane back to Detroit, instead of the bus. That's when they knew they had finally made it.

Some pop music historians have theorized that it was the combination of Diane's sultry lead and Mary and Florence's hypnotic, almost mechanical, background vocals ("baby, baby, ooh baby, baby") that made this song unique. The record begins with what sounds like a foot-clomping army (the sound was actually made by clapping two boards together). Drums, guitars, tambourines, xylophones and handclaps relentlessly keep time.

Diana's voice in its new lower pitch did seem to convey a certain sex appeal, but also an appealing naïveté about love and romance. This seemed to be an *honest* performance from her. Perhaps she really was beginning to question love's many mysteries because certainly her superficial affairs hadn't offered her many answers. It's easy to think of most of the other Motown songs and artists prior to this time as being interchangeable, but it's almost impossible to think that anyone other than Diana Ross could have recorded "Where Did Our Love Go."

These were stressful times. The country's aggressive attitude in Vietnam and elsewhere and the racial crisis on the homefront were scaring many youngsters who wondered if there would be any world left at all by the time they were adults. Self-awareness was a growing movement and, consequently, self-examination. Maybe Diana's plaintive questions about love echoed the same inquisitiveness that was beginning to consume a whole generation of record buyers. Or maybe, as Lamont Dozier says, "The record just was a good one, the voice was a strong one, the timing was the right one—and nothing else really matters."

Whatever the reasons for success, Berry Gordy was convinced that H-D-H had hit paydirt; The Supremes now had a "sound." H-D-H were immediately pulled from their other company projects to devote themselves full time to The Supremes. Quickly, they constructed two more songs directly patterned after the first hit, both written and produced with the newly-discovered, kittenish Diana Ross "sound" in mind: "Baby Love" and "Come See About Me," issued in September and October, respectively, both eventually sailing to Number One on the pop music charts.

"Where Did Our Love Go," "Baby Love" and "Come See About Me" are considered historic touchstones for The Supremes, their writers, producers and record company. Each was a sparsely orchestrated, pop-washed, rhythm and blues song with catchy lyrics, but the simplicity was deceiving; the art at work here was that all of the elements—voices, music, lyrics—seemed heartfelt and genuine . . . *real*. Or as Brian Holland put it, "Berry said that if the kids believed this material, that belief would translate into sales, which it did." These songs would become the generic standard for what would one day be called "The Motown Sound."

The group was rushed into the studio for the *Where Did Our Love Go* album, the next obvious step from Holland-Dozier and Holland. It would become one of the biggest selling albums of 1964. With three Number One records on it, it remained on the charts for well over a year and sold 922,009 copies.

After they finished the album, Berry booked the girls into the 20 Grand nightclub in Detroit with The Temptations for a two-week engagement. It was The Supremes' first major nightclub appearance. During the second week, a friend of Flo's came back to the dressing room before a show, pulled her aside and had a brief talk with her. Diana and Mary watched as Flo's face dropped. The woman walked away.

"What happened?" Diana demanded to know. "Who the hell was that?"

"Keep your voice down, girl. She's a cop," Flo whispered. "I used to know her. She said we can't go on 'cause you and Mary ain't 21 yet."

"What? That's crazy!" Diana exclaimed. Then she went to find Berry.

As the girls waited in the dressing room, Berry and the policewoman had an urgent conversation in the hallway.

"Look, if those two go on, I'll arrest 'em," she said finally before storming off.

Berry walked into the room and told the girls to pack up their things. "We got no choice," he admitted.

"We got a choice. We can go on," Diana said. "I'd like to see her just *try* to arrest me."

Berry grinned at her. "You know what? I'd like to see that myself."

The Temptations finished the engagement without The Supremes, who were replaced by Motown singer Kim Weston.

The rest of 1964 was a whirlwind starting with a two-week tour of England in October. (There they were referred to as "Negresses," a term they had never before heard. "At first," Diana Ross said, "I was insulted!") When they returned, they were sent to Hollywood where they appeared on the TAMI (Teen-Age Musical International) Show with the Rolling Stones, The Beach Boys, Chuck Berry and others, and then to New York for their debut appearance on Ed Sullivan's show.

The Supremes would be the first Motown act to appear on the Sullivan program and receive that all-important prime-time exposure. Immediately after any Sullivan appearance, a recording artist could expect record sales to triple. In those days, most popular vocalists were either nightclub chanteuse types, rock 'n' rollers, or slickly choreographed rhythm and blues singers. The Supremes' wholesome image was more like that of The McGuire Sisters'. (At first, The Supremes presented themselves like The McGuires by using one microphone and placing the lead singer in the middle of the trio. However, in The McGuires' ensemble, Phyllis, the leader, was the only one who seemed to come alive during a performance, but each of The Supremes had animated personalities.)

Mary was beautiful and very collected while Florence was statuesque and endearingly awkward. Diana, though, was obviously the focus of the group, gesticulating, mewing, popping her eyes and demanding attention, much like early Lena Horne in her best MGM movies. For Diana, this was an amazing, even startling, performance and demonstrated the beginning of what can only be called "star charisma."

The girls were dressed simply in blue, tiered dresses. Their make-up was lightly applied and limited to heavy eyeliner and lipstick. (Sullivan's make-up artists seemed to have had no idea what to do with The Supremes because of the color of their skin and when they finished with them the three looked Egyptian. Before going on, they quickly wiped off the excess make-up and re-applied it themselves.)

Though Mary and Florence were excited about this opportunity, as Diana remembers it, the group's first appearance on December 27, 1964, left a lot to be desired: "I was very unhappy. We were supposed to do two songs and we ended up doing one. We didn't have any great stage setting. It was like they pulled a screen down and we stood in front of it. We sang our little song ['Come See About Me'] and then off, which is no different than any other act that does the Sullivan show for the first time. They always told you to prepare two songs, but by the time the actual show rolls around they cut it down to only one. After we did the one song, I just cried because I thought we had done something wrong. Maybe I didn't sing strong enough at rehearsal, I thought. Maybe I hadn't given my all and maybe that's why they cut one of the songs. After that we started doing interviews and someone asked me about the Sullivan show, and I really put Sullivan down because I was hurt."

Back in Detroit, the Ross family was enjoying local recognition thanks to daughter Diane's great achievements. Ernestine couldn't even go to the supermarket without being stopped constantly by well-wishers complimenting her on her daughter's success. Fred's co-workers slapped him on the back and offered hearty congratulations. He had to admit that his daughter's "overnight" popularity had made him proud but, still, he was cautious and warned her to "save your money because you never know." Diana's brothers and sisters found themselves on the guest list of practically all of Detroit's house parties and, T-Boy once remembered, "Everyone in Detroit wanted to be friends with us just to be closer to one of The Supremes."

The success of The Supremes spelled out immediate acceptance for the rest of Motown's roster, most of whom had been experiencing only marginal and occasionally major hits. Junior Walker and the All Stars, The Miracles, Marvin Gaye, The Temptations, Mary Wells, The Four Tops—now it seemed that everybody was having hit records with titles like: "Shotgun," "Ooo Baby Baby," "I'll Be Doggone," "My Girl," "My Guy" and "I Can't Help Myself." The so-called "Motown Sound" was the only sound that rivaled The Beatles' success in America. Gordy and his Detroit kids were on a magical roll.

Motown has often been touted as the only record company in history to have a distinctive "sound" that was identified more with the Gordy empire than to the artists themselves. But musical movements in contemporary sound link and develop from—and because of—each other. Patterns, styles, successes and failures of what would be Gordy's "Motown Sound" all hinged on certain approaches characteristic to '50s rhythm and blues, which itself emerged from the scars of what was called race music. Like most phenomena of the late '50s and early '60s, the key word was simplicity. Berry's sound reached for the youth of America with basic rhythms and simple harmonies and, most important, an emphasis on co-mingling the pop style of a white-bread group like The McGuire Sisters with the rhythm and blues approach of soul-shouters like the Isley Brothers. It seemed like an impossible marriage, but history has shown that it worked.

Often, Berry was accused of "selling out," of stealing from white culture so his groups could appeal to whites. But fusing different styles together is a hallmark of popular music, and certainly where rock 'n' roll "thievery" is concerned, the black culture had been more victimized than that of any other race.

Chuck Berry and Bo Diddley, both black artists, are clearly responsible for the birth of rock 'n' roll—though neither is ever really credited. Both introduced rhythm and blues in the 1950s, a style in which beat took precedence over melody and lyrics. Disc jockey Alan Freed gave the music another name when he introduced Diddley as the man who was going to "rock 'n' roll you out of your seats." Once it was renamed, new artists—white artists—like Buddy Holly took over. Soon, indigenous American black music was being revealed to whites in a new form when the songs and styles were co-opted by white artists, for example when Pat Boone took Fats Domino's gritty "Ain't That a Shame" or Little Richard's raucous "Tutti Frutti" and turned them into sanitized pop hits.*

For many years, white musicians tried to emulate black music, and often did a good job of it. Certainly Duke Ellington's swing jazz of the late '20s and '30s was copied with flair and ingenuity by such white bandleaders as Benny Goodman, Artie Shaw and Tommy Dorsey. Blacks were never surprised when whites were credited for their work. For instance, in 1940 when the state of Virginia decided to make "Carry Me Back to Ole Virginny" its official song, most people assumed that it was written by Foster. The author was James Bland, who was black.

In decades to come, if the songs themselves weren't stolen, often the styles were. Elvis Presley's technique, for instance, was directly influenced by rhythm and blues singer Arthur "Big Boy" Crudup, whom most people have never heard of even though he recorded dozens of songs for RCA Victor on its "race label" in the late '40s and early '50s. When Elvis got hold of Big Mama Thornton's hit, "Hound Dog," most people soon forgot the original. This co-opting of artistic expression was grossly unfair to black artists who created so much indigenous American music, many of whom were never able to reap the full rewards of their work. How whites appropriated black art would be one of the subjects touched on during a Diana Ross TV special in 1987 called "Red Hot Rhythm and Blues."**

After the first string of successful Motown records, a disc

---

*But this kind of musical thievery happened all the time and goes back to the days of slavery. Although whites considered black music inferior, they did not ignore it altogether. Mammies sang it to white children, and plantation owners used their slaves to provide singing and dancing entertainment for their visitors. Soon the whites were entertaining themselves with music they had picked up from black slaves and calling it their own.

**The Beatles made it possible for white teen-agers to identify with a kind of rhythm and blues. That the "Fab Four" was influenced by American Negro music is a matter of history. Two of the tunes in their first album were Motown songs; they have often credited Gordy and his sound as being an influence on theirs. The group helped wipe out racial distinctions when they became popular, which no doubt helped give Berry Gordy's music mainstream acceptance. When The Beatles crossed the Atlantic, they brought with them a score of other artists, most of whom also credited black American blues makers as their inspiration.

jockey interviewed Berry Gordy and asked "What do you do when people say you are stealing from white music?"

Berry answered, "I laugh my head off."

When Berry Gordy founded Motown he knew the only way he could succeed was to present the vitality of black music in a way that was non-threatening to whites. He wasn't "stealing" anything, rather he was creating something new, a "Motown Sound."

There's always been a nostalgia for a mythical "Motown Sound" but the fact is that there were, and are, many different "sounds." Besides simplicity, the overriding quality of all of them is elegance: the elegance of a gospel choir soaring on the wings of rich female voices. Of swirling strings and chugging horns. Of handclaps, bells, tambourines. And underlying it all, an insistent, persistent, four-four drumbeat moving forward like a train hurtling down the track.

It's often been said that Motown approached its music assembly-line style, and that's very true. Everything was done in-house—songwriting, producing, publishing, booking and management. Gordy's in-house staff of producers would be told when an artist would be off the road and available to record. A producer then would eagerly begin work on tracks for the singer while writers went to work on lyrics. Often several artists would record the same song with the same tracks. Then Gordy and his quality control staff (consisting of almost everyone who worked for him) would select the best material in Friday morning meetings in his office. Berry locked out anyone who wasn't there by nine o'clock sharp. His criterion for releasing a record was basic, and very human: "Would you buy this record for a dollar?" he'd ask. "Or would you buy a sandwich?"

"The answer to that question could mean the difference between a major hit and a waste of time, considering the financial status of a large part of his market," observed Lamont Dozier.

If someone on staff became too technical in his or her assessment of a song, Gordy cut him off quickly.

"Do you like it, or not? Does it move you, or doesn't it?"

Those were the key questions he wanted answered. "Rhythm is basic. If you get that, that's what people want," he'd insist.

At one Friday morning session, 87 songs were presented to Berry, and only one was released: "Jimmy Mack" by Martha and The Vandellas, which had been in the can for years before Gordy allowed it to be presented to the outside world. Hundreds of songs would be shelved, never to be heard by the public.

Berry Gordy usually knew a smash when he heard one, and

he was also able to pinpoint a problem in a song and then strengthen the record by making the necessary changes. Sometimes it was a complicated matter of changing lyrics or rhythms, which Berry tackled easily; he rearranged countless Motown songs, like The Miracles' "Shop Around" and Marvin Gaye's "Can I Get a Witness?" Often the problem fell in a gray area: "It just don't sound right." So some finishing touches would be added: heavy chains shaking in an echo chamber for The Vandellas' "Dancing in the Street"; other sounds were made by beating cardboard boxes and blowing into bottles filled with water.

"To Berry, either a song was a hit, or it was garbage," said Gil Askey, a musician who would become The Supremes' musical conductor. "He wasn't the most tactful person in the world. He'd call your music junk in a minute, and if you got offended he took that as a sign of weakness. 'Garbage! Garbage! Garbage!' he'd yell at the songwriters. They'd get real pissed, but Berry got the desired results."

Berry was a tough taskmaster, often very much a dictator. He encouraged intense competition among his artists and staff writers and producers, all the while maintaining a single premise: "Do your job, do it well and you'll be rewarded." There were rules, and plenty of them. Despite the advice of his legal staff, Berry instituted fines against writers and producers who broke his rules: no playing cards in the offices before sunset ($50); no losing tapes of recorded music ($40); no loafing ($100). If Berry observed too much "goofing off," he would run throughout the offices shouting, "Hey! Money's not on strike, is it? Get to work!"

By using the same musicians on practically every session, Berry and his producers were able to create a standard sound. He refused to allow these valuable session musicians to be credited on the Motown albums because he did not want them to be stolen from the company. Any musician discovered playing on a session for another company would be fired immediately.*

Throughout the years, many of Motown's writers and producers have complained bitterly of being taken financial advantage of by Gordy. This is ironic considering that in part Berry started

*The foundation of the music was always provided by James Jamerson on bass, Benny Benjamin on drums, with Robert White, Eddie Willis and Joe Messina on guitars, Earl Van Dyke on keyboards and Johnny Griffith on piano. James Gittens and Mike Terry were responsible for the baritone-sax solos found on so many Supremes singles.

Motown because he felt that he, as an independent songwriter/producer, was being treated unfairly by the record companies with whom he did business in the late '50s.

"Just about everyone got ripped off at Motown," Clarence Paul said in an interview with British journalist Sharon Davis. "The royalty rates were substandard. Motown had their own songwriting contracts which were way below the rest of the industry. Tunes were stolen all the time, and often credit wasn't properly assigned."

Gordy had Smokey Robinson write a company anthem, the lyrics of which included: "We are a very swinging company/working hard from day to day/Nowhere will you find more unity/than at Hitsville U.S.A." Gordy required that members of his staff sing it at the beginning of most company meetings. Sometimes he would choose one staff member and force that unfortunate person to sing it in front of his or her co-workers.

There was no time for manners, in Berry's view. Once he called a staff meeting to criticize one of his departments and called the whole group "a dumb bunch of niggers." One of his white executives raised his hand timidly and said, "I'm not a nigger, Mr. Gordy."

"You bet your ass you are," Gordy shot back.

Berry's contracts were ironclad in Motown's favor. If any artist wanted his own lawyer to look over the agreement, Berry took that as a sign of disloyalty and a strike against everyone involved. The first time an artist was allowed to take a contract home with him, Berry told his lawyer, "I guarantee you will not get that contract signed." And he didn't.

Berry found that if potential signers had too much time to go over the offered deal, the percentage of those who signed on the dotted line dipped dramatically. Thus was born Motown's unorthodox and unpopular way of negotiating a new contract: Berry's legal adviser was told not to allow the contracts out of his sight. He would sit with the outside lawyer in an agreed-upon location; the lawyer would be permitted to peruse the paperwork under the supervision of the Motown attorney, but at no time would the outsider or his client be able to take the contract home until it was signed.

Once they signed, the artists could expect their very existences to be taken over by Berry Gordy. Most welcomed his domination over their lives though it may not always have been in their best interests.

"Berry is such a mentor and strong personality that you find yourself relying on that," Diana Ross has said. "You don't grow.

You put yourself in the hands of someone to take care of you and tell you what you have to do next. Berry gave everybody as much as he knew how. But he wouldn't let anyone have the freedom to grow on their own. It was a stultifying existence.''

And whatever it took to get airtime on the radio, that's what Berry would do. Once, while Motown was still in its struggling stage, a popular white disc jockey in Detroit was moving into a new home and asked—demanded—help from Berry. "I need some big black bucks," he told Gordy, "to help with the move."

Gordy sent The Supremes' songwriters and producers Holland-Dozier and Holland, along with a moving van.

Nineteen sixty-five was to become The Supremes' year; Diana and Mary would turn 21 in March, and Florence would become 22 in June. The year started off on the best possible note when, on January 5, the girls went into the studio to record "Stop! In the Name of Love."

"Stop! In the Name of Love" was inspired by an argument between its composer Lamont Dozier and his girlfriend. Just as his woman was about to walk out on him, Lamont shouted out, "Please, baby, stop in the name of love!"

"It was so corny and silly that we burst out laughing," he recalled, "and it ended the fight."

"Stop! In the Name of Love" deposed The Beatles' "Eight Days a Week" when it went to the Number One spot on the charts (in March 1965). *Rolling Stone*, 23 years later, would name the song tenth of the 100 most important singles of the rock era.

A check of The Supremes' discography reveals that there were 17 commercial releases by the group between 1965 and 1966—nine singles and eight albums. After the terrific "Stop! In the Name of Love," all of The Supremes' singles were memorable: "Back in My Arms Again," "Nothing But Heartaches," "I Hear a Symphony," "My World Is Empty Without You," "Love Is Like an Itching in My Heart," "You Can't Hurry Love" and "You Keep Me Hangin' On." All but three of these would become Number One records. (A holiday-themed single, "Children's Christmas Song," was issued as well.)

For their fans, much of The Supremes' music of this time became the more positive side of the '60s experiences. Unlike the folk/rock of the era which reminded us of war, pollution and social injustice, and painted vivid pictures of the sorrows, failures and atrocities of our times, The Supremes spoke to more universal natures: love, disappointment, the vibrance of youth.

Still today, it's difficult not to feel young again whenever "I Hear a Symphony" is heard on the radio. And how can anyone resist the heavy bass introduction of "You Can't Hurry Love"? Today, music by The Supremes is constantly utilized for atmospheric purposes in television programs and in motion pictures. We return to this music over and over to recapture the age—and what's more, the music in its exuberant simplicity still holds up.

Diana Ross may have sung lead on all of these songs, but Mary Wilson and Florence Ballard's work in the background should not be overlooked. The importance of their contribution to The Supremes' records hearkens back to the origins of black music.

Unlike most people who emigrated to the United States for personal freedom or economic opportunity, blacks came in chains. While others, no matter how poor, were able to carry their personal belongings on their backs, the slaves were only able to carry what they had in their heads. Ship captains and later plantation owners mixed members of various tribes together because they felt there was less chance of revolt if the slaves lacked a common language. Music became that common language, at first for solace, and later for communication. Work music made the rough life style go a little smoother. Black work music took the form of call and response songs; one person would sing a verse and others would answer in a chorus. The call and response songs would later find their place in the church as gospel singing, and then even later as important parts of rhythm and blues, and contemporary black music. This is why Mary Wilson insists that she never felt slighted in her *responding* role behind Diana Ross's *call*.

"In the days of early black music, the call was as important as the response," she's said. "It was all part of the whole. I had no problem at all with that. I was purely satisfied." Certainly there is almost as much "response" in Supremes songs like "Nothing but Heartaches" and "I Hear a Symphony" as there is "call." It should be noted though that among African tribes it was never the same person who did the calling; tribal members alternated callers and respondents.

The Supremes were very aware of the roots of their music; it was part of their education not only in the schools but in the streets when they performed call and response songs on street corners in the form of rhythm and blues. While it's true that because of Diana's sense of individualism she was happier when she got to sing lead, the girls understood that each job in the group was a vital one. The problems would begin later when status and recognition became more important issues between the girls than the history and roots of their music.

During this banner year, 1965, The Supremes appeared on over 15 national television programs. They were seen tap dancing with Sammy Davis and swapping jokes with Bob Newhart, Steve Allen, Dean Martin and Joey Bishop, all the while squeezing performances of their current hit records somewhere in the midst of all of the schtick. When they recorded commercials for Coca-Cola, it said that The Supremes were becoming just as much a part of the American tradition as Coke itself. The ultimate endorsement irony came about when they endorsed Supremes White Bread, and their smiling faces were emblazoned across the cellophane wrapping.

This was also the year The Supremes met their pop music peers, The Beatles. The Beatles were scheduled to perform at Shea Stadium while The Supremes were in town for promotional interviews. Both groups were staying at the Warwick Hotel in New York. The "historic" meeting, set up by Beatles manager Brian Epstein and Don Foster, Berry's assistant, did not go well. When The Supremes—all dressed in smart outfits with furs and gloves—arrived in The Beatles' suite, they found the "Fab Four" slovenly dressed in dirty jeans and T-shirts, stoned on drugs and almost incoherent. John Lennon just stared blankly at them, not even rising to shake their hands; he wound up a toy car and sent it speeding across the floor in their direction.

When Paul McCartney, George Harrison or Ringo Starr asked The Supremes about the musical mechanics of the Motown sound, their answers were so superficial ("I think it's got something to do with the knobs on the control board") that the fellows were nonplussed.

As George Harrison put it later, "These broads don't even *understand* how they make this music we fellows love so much!" The Beatles were profoundly disappointed. They were expecting esoteric insights into the production values of soul music, something they would never get from The Supremes. Plus, the boys from Liverpool were amazed that three black women from Motown were so utterly square. Perhaps they expected the three of them to strip to black lace underwear and party into the night.

Diana, Mary and Florence were equally disenchanted by The Beatles, whose image was as clean-cut as their own yet even more of a put-on. The girls had not experimented with drugs, and when they smelled the pungent scent of marijuana in that hotel room, their instincts told them to turn around and walk the other way. Which, after about 20 minutes, they did.

Later in the year, The Supremes would share the bill with Judy Garland at the Houston Astrodome. All of the girls, and even Berry, were starstruck by the very idea of having the opportunity to meet Garland. Diana told Berry, "Maybe if I talk to her I'll find out why she's a legend."

But Judy was in the decline of her life and career; she had more pressing matters on her mind than sharing show business secrets with Diana Ross. Garland recalled, "At five o'clock, the phone rang in the hotel room and they [The Supremes] asked the gentleman who was with me might they come up and meet me? And he explained no, he was sorry, but Miss Garland was taking a nap. And Diana Ross said, 'Well, can we just come up and watch her *sleep*?' "

Finally, right before showtime, Judy Garland stuck her head out of the dressing room as the girls walked down the hall backstage. The three of them spun around. "It's her!"

"Hello," she said. "It's nice to be on the show with you." And then before they had a chance to respond, she shut the dressing room door abruptly. The girls looked at one another for a second and then burst out laughing.

They had really made it.

While The Beatles ushered in the British musical invasion of the United States, Berry and his Motown machinery strategically began planning their own invasion of Europe in 1965. London, Paris and Hamburg—and all with first class accommodations. Stevie Wonder, Martha and The Vandellas, The Miracles and The Temptations joined The Supremes on a show billed as a Motor Town Revue.

"We girls weren't even talking to each other by the time we got to Europe," Diana Ross recalled. "Berry was on that tour with us. That's when I decided that we would sit down and have a meeting. I said, 'It's time for us to talk like adults and regroup.' I felt that everybody was spreading apart and doing individual things and having arguments. I felt we should be grown up enough to talk about them. So we got our whole organizational thing together where I handled the gowns, Mary handled the music and Florence collected the money."*

The European Motor Town Revue Tour was a financial disas-

---

*Diana's memory notwithstanding, no member of a Motown group "collected the money." Payment for concert appearances was always handed over to one of Gordy's representatives and then sent back to Detroit. Some of it would be deposited into bank accounts for the singers, and most of it would be used to offset other company expenses. Never did The Supremes or any of the other Motown groups know exactly how much they were paid for their performances.

ter with half-filled houses everywhere the troupe went, mostly because The Supremes were really the only act to score abroad with hit records—and the Brits weren't even sure what to make of them. There was dissension among the artists because of the caste system that Berry had created: The Supremes, Berry and his entourage were in the "A" group and traveled by stretch limousine. Berry's sister, Esther, lawyer George Shiffer, his children and parents were in the "B" group. Everyone else on the tour—artists, roadies and musicians—were in the "C" group and resenting it. The "B" and "C" contingents traveled by bus.

Dusty Springfield convinced the BBC to do a Motown special broadcast, which she would host. Right before the taping of the program, The Temptations were in the men's room with Berry Gordy "paying the water bill," as Otis Williams put it, when Diana suddenly burst in. "We need some choreography quick for 'Stop! In the Name of Love,' " she said, as everyone quickly zipped up. After a few moments of deliberation, one of The Temptations came up with the traffic officer "palm-out" hand gesture that would quickly become the hallmark of The Supremes.

According to most people's memories, Diana and Berry first began dating during their European tour, even though Mary has insisted that the romance started a year before, in 1964. It had been a long time coming; the attraction between them was there almost from the beginning, but until Europe was platonic. Said one Gordy friend, "No one was ever able to figure out who initiated it. Berry told me that Diane needed 'fathering,' as he put it. He was always gentle and patient with her, but warned her not to mention what was happening between them to anyone because he was still married, though his wife Margaret had given up hope of having Berry to herself. It was their little secret."

But there are other points of view that aren't quite as romantic.

By now, Berry Gordy was a man intoxicated by great power. His record company was a financial success, and he was doing it *his* way. As Marvin Gaye once said, "Berry could make you think what he wanted was what you wanted, when actually what he wanted was what he wanted and not even in your best interest."

Berry controlled the lives and income of everyone who worked for him, and because he was so volatile, he was feared by most of his staff. It always filled Berry with pride whenever he was able to get someone to do what he wanted done. Sometimes he got cooperation as a result of his great charisma; other times he got it because no one wanted to be on the receiving end of his bad temper. To Berry, it didn't matter how he got it, as long as he did.

He had already seen in Diana the possibilities of great stardom. Not only did she have a unique, "commercial" voice, she was a striking performer as well. Audiences may have had trouble figuring out which one was Mary and which was Flo, but everybody always knew Diana. All three would make the same moves, but hers were more graceful. All three would smile, but hers was the widest. All three wore the same clothes, but somehow Diana looked the most glamorous. She had a radiance which captivated the audience—and Berry Gordy. The possibilities for her future in show business seemed limitless. Berry wanted to harness that potential—and own it. Moreover, he saw her not only as the person who could bring fame to Motown, but also as an exciting woman.

After they consummated their relationship, Berry Gordy might have been thinking to himself: "I got her. She's mine."

Ironically, Florence Ballard has said that this is precisely what Diana told her about Berry.

"I got him," Florence remembered Diana announcing.

"Who?" Flo asked.

"Berry. I got him."

"So?" Flo asked nonchalantly, acting as if Diana's accomplishment didn't really matter, or change anything.

"So I just wanted you to know . . . *I got him.*"

And then Diana turned and walked away, smiling to herself.

Chapter
7

IN MID-1965, GORDY found $30,000 homes for each of The Supremes on Buena Vista Street in Detroit; Mary and Florence were on the same side of the street, and Diana was across Buena Vista and down the road a bit. At first Gordy wanted the girls to pay cash for the homes, but his advisers told him that they should secure as large a mortgage as possible for the houses since they might not be content living in this middle-class racially mixed neighborhood as their stature as celebrities grew. Though the area was far from palatial, it was well kept, clean and respectable. One of Berry's chief attorneys remembered that Diana was satisfied with her new home, but still hoped for a more glamorous environment one day.

The Motown lawyer took each girl to the bank individually to sign the mortgage papers. Mary and Florence signed quickly, no questions asked. But when he brought Diana in, it was a different story. Bank employees and customers kept interrupting the meeting by asking for photographs and autographs. The attorney explained to the loan officer that "Diane really wants to close this deal, wants to understand what's being done and concentrate on it. However, we can't do that under these circumstances."

Then Diana had an idea. "Just let me buy this damn house," she told the loan officer, "and after we close the deal I'll take a half hour to chat with everyone and sign autographs." The loan officer agreed. The meeting was very thorough; Diane was quite meticulous in her questioning.

"She proved to me that she's no dummy," said the attorney. "She wanted to know about mortgage insurance policies, interest rates, fixed mortgages, everything. It took an hour to close the deal.

"Later she told Berry that she thought the meeting was just fantastic—and then she spent equal time signing autographs for the employees."

While Florence purchased one home, Mary bought two on the street, one for herself and the other for her mother and family. Diana didn't spend much time in hers; mostly she was with Berry in his, so Ernestine lived in the house with some of her other children.

"The upstairs was for me, but I traveled so much I didn't really use it," Diana recalled. "When my brothers, who had been away at college, came home for vacation, I gave it to them for a bachelor apartment. They were going through a long-hair, slightly rebellious stage—nothing serious but it made my mother unhappy, and it was better if the boys had their own place."

After a particularly good performance at the Michigan State Fair, Berry and Diana offered a limo ride home to one of Gordy's chief attorneys who happened to be white. Knowing Diana was in the car, fans swarmed all over the stretch limo, pounding on the windows and peering in to see. Finally able to pull out of the crowded fair grounds, the chauffeur drove his charges through the inner city before arriving at the exclusive, white, upper-class suburb where the attorney lived. Diana may have been the toast of the inner city, but what would it take before she would be allowed in *this* neighborhood? With wide-eyed wonder, she surveyed the scene all the while commenting on its opulence. Turning to the attorney, she asked, "Gee, do you think one day they'll allow Negroes to live in this kind of area? I mean, I would love to live in this kind of place one day."

"You will," the attorney told her. "You just wait."

As she pondered the possibilities, Gordy and his attorney smiled and nodded at one another knowingly.

Berry Gordy was now controlling every aspect of The Supremes' finances; none of the girls ever even saw a tax return. When they needed something, Berry would buy it for them; on holidays and birthdays, he purchased minks, chinchillas and sables. Sometimes he charged these gifts against their royalty accounts, sometimes he didn't. In one of her many lawsuits against Gordy and Motown (this one filed in Los Angeles in September 1977), Mary Wilson said that in 1965, The Supremes were on a salary of "$200–300 a week"; that they could not purchase personal property, including their automobiles, without Gordy's consent; that Gordy's signature was needed before any withdrawals could be authorized from their personal savings account, and that this was still necessary as late as 1974.

Gordy said that he invested heavily for the girls in TWA and railroad stock. Though Mary and Florence have complained over the years of not having any money left from these early days, The Supremes were anything but frugal. For instance, Mary, the biggest spender of them all, says that she shelled out $20,000 on a 4½-karat heart-shaped diamond ring. Even if she was exaggerating for the sake of glamour, and doubled the amount she really paid, it is still not sensible considering the money she was earning. To put that purchase into context, remember that The Supremes were making about $2,500 a week in the biggest clubs they played, and not only did that have to be split three ways, it had to cover all of Motown's expenses as well, over which the girls had no control.

Along the way, Diana, Mary and Florence picked up furs, pieces of art, and expensive furnishings. They would fly off to New York just to shop; a chauffeured limousine would take them from one expensive Fifth Avenue store to the next. It was a wonderful way of life, but it never occurred to any of them to save their money, and though they were earning more than they ever had, they weren't making as much as they thought they were.

For that matter, they never really knew how much money they were generating. If they had, they would have been surprised. In fact, "Where Did Our Love Go" and "You Can't Hurry Love" were the only instant million-sellers The Supremes had between 1962 and 1968, this being contrary to what Motown claimed—that there were at least eight.*

Berry Gordy did not allow access to the company's books to the Recording Industry Association of America (R.I.A.A.) which officially certifies million-sellers, and with good reasons. He didn't want to pay the escalating charge the R.I.A.A. demanded, a fee that was based on the amount of records sold. He also didn't want the R.I.A.A., or anyone else for that matter, to know how many records he was selling. He was trying to boost the company's image as well as all of his artists' morale by claiming

*Though Motown's sales figures from the 1960s are said to be incomplete, it still seems unlikely that The Supremes had more than the two million-sellers these statistics show, based on the surprisingly meager sales accounted for by the other Motown artists. In years to come, other Supremes songs of this time would become million-sellers as the records continued to sell. When the songs originally entered the marketplace, the artists were paid for sales they were generating, certainly not for projected sales.

that Motown's records were selling much more than they really were, and it worked. When Motown presented an artist with a "gold record," it was often just an ordinary Motown release spray-painted gold and framed. Once, Marvin Gaye actually took one of his "gold records" out of the glass frame and played it on his stereo. It was a Supremes record.

When the Motown lawyer handed out royalty statements and checks to all of the producers, writers and artists, most of them never questioned a single deduction, charge or earning. They were just glad to get what they got. Berry Gordy personally dealt with the royalties of only two of his acts: The Supremes and The Miracles. Both groups had their taxes computed by Gordy's accountants; they may have had many kinds of money problems along the way but none of the singers of those two groups ever had disagreements with Uncle Sam in those days. Gordy's accountants were very conservative in their tax preparations and never underpaid the government (more likely, they always overpaid).

Motown's royalty structure for its artists was astonishingly low, but many recording artists have said that it was the norm for rock 'n' roll stars of the era.

In the beginning of their careers, prior to 1965, The Supremes were each making one percent of 90 percent of the suggested retail price of each 45 RPM and album sold, less all taxes and packaging costs—that is .00675, not even 3/4 of a cent per record. After 1965, each girl made eight percent of 90 percent of the wholesale price, less taxes and costs, or .0091—nearly a penny for each record. Motown practiced cross-collateralization, which meant that any profit the girls made from a successful record had to pay the costs of the preceding failures and any other outstanding expenses before they saw a dime. Also, the girls had to pay for the expenses of their recording sessions: musicians, lead sheets and other arrangements, studio time, etc. In putting these figures to work, it's easy to see why The Supremes never became rich.

"Where Did Our Love Go" sold 1,072,290 copies.* According to their contracts, each girl's immediate royalty would be $7,237.96. First, though, they paid whatever they may have owed on the eight singles released before that song that didn't do as well, and for the costs of the 50 or so songs they recorded by

---

*This figure could be low because Motown never was known for keeping very accurate sales data in the '60s. But since it probably included sales that were registered after the song's initial release, it could also be high.

this time that were never released (they were always charged for unreleased songs, and practically half of the songs they recorded over a 10-year period went unreleased), and for whatever other expenses that were charged against their accounts (none of which they had any control over). It is doubtful that they had much money to show for their "million-seller," especially after taxes. And "Where Did Our Love Go" was the biggest selling record the girls had between June 1964 and July 1966 when "You Can't Hurry Love" was issued and sold 1,104,012 copies.

It was difficult for the Supremes and all of the other Motown acts who had the same recording contract to fully comprehend how little money they were making, particularly because they thought they were selling millions of records, when they really weren't.

For instance, "Nothing but Heartaches" sold 368,267 copies in 1965. If the girls believed Motown's press release that year that "the song is a solid gold, million-selling, smash hit—another in a long string of million sellers," imagine their surprise when they each received a royalty check for $2,982.96, minus studio time, other expenses and taxes. The Supremes and their Motown recording colleagues never had a problem with their expenses or the royalties; rather they believed they were being lied to about their sales, which was not the case. They simply were believing their own publicity. Ironically, Gordy was trying to bolster their public images by inflating their sales—but he failed to let them in on his secret.*

There were always other unpredictable charges. For instance, if two or more artists recorded lead vocals over the same pre-recorded instrumental track (which happened all the time) and the best vocal would be released as a single for one of the acts, the other two acts would also be charged for the cost of the instrumental track even though their versions of the song would go unreleased.

Curiously, after 1965, each Supreme also made a "whopping" $12.50 for each master the group recorded. Whereas they may have thought they were earning almost 13 bucks every time they recorded a song that was never released, Motown defined a master as a two-sided single record, which meant, of course, that it

*These figures are based on the conservative assumption that a single 45 RPM in the '60s sold for 75 cents each. Also, these are based on American sales. Motown's sales in other countries in the '60s were low and would probably not add much to the girls' royalty considering the charges for international shipping and other taxes and packaging costs that would eventually be charged to them.

had to be released. They were still never paid for songs that weren't issued: rather they were charged for them.

Motown was organized under the Internal Revenue Code as a Subchapter S Company, which meant that Motown's money was solely Gordy's, and vice versa. It is said that he made many millions of dollars in the '60s. He was reluctant to share any of his stock, though eventually he did—with Smokey Robinson and his sister Esther.

In many ways, it seemed that Berry Gordy was controlling everything having to do with the private lives and professional careers of all the young people signed to his company. Where Diana Ross was concerned, the relationship was even more complex.

Diana had always felt a need to please her father, which she never seemed able to do, and now she had re-channeled her energies into pleasing another older "father figure"—Berry Gordy. She knew that it pleased Berry when she did what she was told, and beyond that she would allow herself to be controlled because she was smart enough to know it was in her best interest in terms of career growth.

It should be remembered, however, that Diana Ross had always had an independent streak. After all, she may have craved approval from Fred when she was a youngster, but not so much that she would abide by his wishes that she give up entertaining and go to college. She was driven and ambitious and, as she became a successful young adult, she would often demand to have her own way. Berry would usually let her.

If Diana had a problem on the road, she could telephone Berry personally and have the matter rectified in her favor, something the other Motown artists could only dream of doing. Many of her peers thought it was she who was controlling Berry—not the other way around. But Berry knew the score. He let his protégée prevail over the smaller matters—an uncooperative chaperone, a choreographed move that displeased her, a song she didn't want to sing, a dress she wanted to wear—because he knew that these compromises would keep her in line. After all, Gordy had a bigger picture to think about that involved Motown's future corporate interests in Diana Ross' career. He also had the vision to know that as long as his star was content and satisfied, she would be cooperative and agreeable.

When Diana Ross stood before her public, *that's* when she was in absolute control. Mary and Florence couldn't hope to compete with her for attention. They simply didn't have the stage presence of a Diana Ross. No one at Motown did. She was the consummate performer at a very early age, able to thrill critical audiences into giving her standing ovations, able to be just as convincing with her delivery of a show tune as she was with a Motown hit. For instance, when Smokey Robinson sang a Broadway standard, you knew he didn't believe a word of it and was just anxious to get back to Motown where he could better relate to. But when Diana Ross sang one of her favorite Streisand songs, like "I Am Woman," you not only believed her, you actually felt she *lived* the experience, that's how much she personalized her performance. Moreover, you somehow seemed to sense that if she never sang another Motown hit, she would still enjoy a long, fulfilling career as a musical comedy star.

The biggest points of contention between Diana Ross and Berry Gordy were always the result of his trying to tell her how to hone her stage persona, when he tried to take control of her one true freedom. "I would hate it when he would come backstage after a show with his note pad and all his criticisms," she recalled. " 'Leave me alone!' I'd tell him. 'I *know* what I'm doing.' "

And she was right. Diana Ross knew what she was doing. Soon, Berry Gordy would see that.

Although The Beatles-led British invasion dominated the American music scene, parents of middle-class American youth did not share their children's enthusiasm for this Liverpool sound. Many felt threatened by what it represented, especially when the more defiant, sloppier-looking groups like The Rolling Stones and The Animals started invading American shores. The Supremes remained a pleasant alternative and were one of the three American groups able to compete with the British invasion (the others being The Four Seasons and Beach Boys).

Berry Gordy was determined to see The Supremes' run of popularity continue, but not just with the youth generation. Looking to their future, he had the amazing foresight to build a catalogue of albums that could appeal to adults, in order to ensure record sales to another generation. Berry dipped back into the group's canned material to compile a number of special-project albums, including that country collection, an album of their versions of British hits, and also a compilation of Sam Cooke songs. No hit singles were ever culled from these albums; that was not their purpose. Rather, they were part of his master plan that The Supremes be perceived as more than just another rock group, that they would cross racial, cultural and age barriers. Berry wanted The Supremes to solidify an "image" and break out into what Berry used to call "the white world."*

Berry had been negotiating with the owners of New York's Copacabana nightclub to have his girls headline there. This was no place for a rock 'n' roll group but, again, Berry was making certain no one thought of The Supremes in those terms. The Copa was a haven for white stars like Frank Sinatra and a small, elite group of blacks—Sammy Davis, Jr., Billy Eckstine and Sam Cooke. "Diane has the potential to be another Sammy Davis, Jr.," he once said. "And where Diana Ross goes, so goes Motown."

Berry had vision enough to realize that if he could break Diana and The Supremes into Sammy's world, performing for the parents of the youngsters who purchased the girls' cutie-pie hits, she would be guaranteed success in other major white-owned establishments across the country, "and that's where the bucks are," he said. If they succeeded, then each of the other Motown artists would get a shot at this kind of success and money as well. "There's more to this ball game than black clubs and the chittlin' circuits," he told Mickey Stevenson, the man who headed up Motown's A & R department. "And Diana Ross is going to take us there."

In April 1965, a booking at the Copacabana was secured; The Supremes would headline in July. But first there was work to do.

The Supremes already had a sophistication seldom found in rhythm and blues or rock 'n' roll acts in the '60s. They had an aura of "class" and this was something that eluded all of the other girls at Motown, who were earthy and "soulful" rather than sophisticated and worldly. Still, Berry decided that a little extra honing and polishing were in order.

In March 1965, Berry had Harvey Fuqua, former singer with The Moonglows, recruit a staff of professionals who would train The Supremes in the art of showmanship. Gordy had purchased a building next to Hitsville specifically to be utilized as a studio for these new "artist development" classes. He couldn't charge the girls for these lessons because he knew that if he did, only Diana would pay. So the classes would be free—and if they

---

*Sales of these albums were usually very low. *The Supremes—A Bit of Liverpool* didn't even sell 175,000 copies. This compared to over 922,000 copies of the *Where Did Our Love Go* album which preceded it. *The Supremes Sing Country, Western & Pop* did even worse—38,081 copies. *We Remember Sam Cooke* collection sold barely 85,000.

worked, if The Supremes were glossed to perfection—all of the other Motown stars would be automatically enrolled at no charge.

Diana, now 21 years old, was thrilled with Berry's idea and couldn't wait to begin. She remembered how helpful her Hudson modeling classes—and the cosmetology classes Smokey Robinson had paid for her to take—had been and was eager for more advanced training. Diana realized that Berry's concept promised to dress her up with the kind of worldly sophistication and, more importantly, technical prowess that would have otherwise taken years of experience to develop.

Diana Ross had always been very concerned about being so thin. Friends note that she seemed self-conscious about her sticklike figure, especially when standing next to the busty Florence or curvy Mary. In the late '50s and early '60s, the prevailing attitude in most black neighborhoods was that, in order to be considered truly sexy and appealing, a black girl had to have "tits and ass."

For Diana, and only for Diana, Berry decided to augment the Motown training by sending her to the John Robert Powers School for Social Grace in Detroit. While attending modeling and then make-up classes there—independent of the other two girls—Diana discovered that the major criteria for beauty and sex appeal in a '60s pop white culture was simply a matter of skin and bones. Though this was at first difficult to comprehend because it was such a new concept, it didn't take long before she realized that her size five was not only acceptable, it was actually *"in."*

But, still, a little help with the hips couldn't hurt, she decided, so she began wearing hip pads. Sometimes she padded her behind with foam rubber to insure her "shapely" figure, which the John Robert Powers teachers encouraged. The teachers there also discouraged Diana's wearing too much perfume. She loved a scent called Jungle Gardenia and used to wear it so heavily you could still smell her five minutes after she was out of the room. She stopped wearing it after a few months at John Robert Powers.

In 1965, there weren't many black models in the pages of *Vogue*—a magazine Diana read voraciously—but, with Berry's encouragement, she felt that she could rise above and beyond a restrictive black look. During her training in Motown's artist development classes and at John Robert Powers, she began to experiment with different handmade wigs made of human hair. A black girl vying in the white world for the so-called "ideal" of beauty had to deal with the competition, after all, and none of the major starlets sported "naturals" in 1965. She was particularly fascinated by Twiggy, the trendy fashion model of the era, and the technique with which she applied her makeup—dark and dramatic eye shadow and heavy, *heavy* lashes.

Some of her Motown enemies accused Diane of "selling out" when she would show up at the studio looking like an ebony cross between Annette Funicello and Mia Farrow. They obviously didn't understand her and Berry's strategy, the subject of hours of discussion between the two of them. Diana certainly knew that on a philosophical level she was equal to any woman of any race, but she realized that, to the public, she was first a black woman bound by social restrictions. Diana Ross despised social restrictions.

Back in 1965, most of the other female Motown stars eagerly followed Diana's example with heavy, sometimes startling eye makeup and flamboyant wigs. Not that Diana Ross invented cosmetics and fake hair, but at Hitsville she was certainly the one responsible for defining standards of glamour for the other female artists—whether they wanted to admit it or not. "I didn't know what to do with a wig when I first put it on," Martha Reeves admitted. "Diane Ross, she knew right away."

Maxine Powell was a professional model who, since 1951, had operated the Maxine Powell Finishing and Modeling School prior to being hired by Motown at the urging of Berry's sister Gwen. She had been friendly with the Gordy family since the mid-'50s when she hired the family print shop to prepare programs for one of her fashion shows. A black woman who always began practically every sentence by saying something like, "To be a proper young lady, you must always . . . ," Powell was largely responsible for much of The Supremes' offstage poise and onstage presence. She constantly reminded them that they were being trained to play "everywhere from Buckingham Palace to the White House."

Maxine Powell said, "They were taught how to handle an audience. And Diane, specifically, was taught not to 'soul,' as they used to call it. In other words, she would not bend all over and act like she was going to swallow the mike while making ugly faces. I told her that in a first-class place like the Copa, no one's gonna pay good money to watch someone make faces. I wanted her to get rid of the eye-popping routine, and she did."

Powell would criticize the girls constantly, even when they weren't in class. Everything from their posture to their nail polish to the way they got into an automobile or sat on a stool was subject for serious, sometimes heated discussion. And if any of the fellows at Hitsville ever addressed her three students in a flirtatious, or unflattering, manner, Mrs. Powell quickly, and very sternly, admonished them. "These are *ladies*," she would say. *"Not pick-ups."*

Gil Askey, The Supremes' musical conductor, was one of Gordy's employees given the job of designing a slick nightclub act for the Copacabana engagement. He remembered the novel way he presented his ideas to Berry: "We were sitting in his office and I had all of my notes compiled after days of kicking this around in my head. I was explaining my concept, but Berry wasn't getting any of it. Finally, I decided to act it out."

As Berry watched, Gil went into his routine:

"First the three of 'em come out and sing somethin' like 'Put on a Happy Face' [he sings a chorus and dances around the room] then they'll do 'I Am Woman' [he sings four bars] and after that I'll write some bit that'll introduce a couple of their hit records. Then, I figured, something like 'Make Someone Happy' would be great."

Berry was smiling broadly by now, nodding his head and encouraging Gil to continue:

"See, the whole thing is we gotta keep the action movin', with not a moment for these white folks to get bored. Diane will introduce the girls by assuming that no one knows who they are—see, she'll be humble as hell. Then they'll sing 'Somewhere' from *West Side Story*—he sings the chorus—and maybe we'll throw in a hit after that. Maybe not. No one cares about the hits anyway; so we'll re-arrange them to sound like show tunes.

"After that we'll try 'From This Moment On' and 'The Boy From Ipanema,' and then . . ." Gil continued at a clipped pace until finally Berry said: "Enough! Enough! I am sold! Write it up. Supremes at the Copa!"

Cholly Atkins was responsible for the girls' stylized choreography. Atkins had worked with stars such as Ethel Waters and Lena Horne over the years and, with tap dance partner Honi Coles, he had been a top Broadway song-and-dance attraction. Atkins, considered by many a bit of a snob, seldom socialized with any of the Motown people. Still, he did his job well. Immediately prior to being recruited by Harvey Fuqua to join Motown, he was working with Gladys Knight and The Pips.

"It's important to remember that these kids were from ghetto-like environments and had never even done anything like tap dancing with hats and canes," he observed. "With Diane, I had a lot of cramming to do because Gordy wanted her to be ready [for the Copa] and he wanted no excuses. One of the major production numbers was a straw hat and cane rendition of 'Rock-a-Bye Your Baby With a Dixie Melody,' which ended with a difficult hat trick that Diane had a helluva time with. She went out and got herself a practice hat at Hudson's department store, and every time I'd turn around, she was in a corner somewhere practicing this trick. Finally, she learned the trick so well she could do it in her sleep.

"There was plenty of dancing, plenty of complaining, too, mostly from Florence," he continued. "Florence hated the choreography and felt it was unnatural. There was also an order—and it came from Berry—to keep Diane off to the right side as much as possible, separated from the other two. I didn't ask questions about it, I just did what I was told. To me, it was obvious what he was planning—to single out Diane as the star."

Maurice King had conducted shows at the Flame Show Bar for years before Gordy brought him into the fold to help teach Diana how to relate to an audience and also, as musical director, to re-arrange those hit records into a big band, Broadway style. Arrangers Gene Kee and Johnny Allen assisted King with the music, but where Diana's patter was concerned, Maurice worked with her personally. "Diane and I spent hours and hours practicing little speeches and elocution," he said. "I worked with her on stage patter and on how to appear to be improvising when actually every single word was scripted. She wasn't very articulate so she had a lot of memorizing to do."

There was more than the usual tension among the three girls during the learning period, this time because most of their teachers simply felt that Mary and Florence weren't working as hard as they should have been. Of course, both girls were certain that Diana was trying to make them look bad by being so utterly conscientious. Some of the artist development teachers have claimed that Diana didn't really care about how the other two looked; her main concern, of course, was how *she* looked. "If you think she learned all of that stuff in artist development for the benefit of The Supremes, forget it," A & R head Mickey Stevenson concluded. "She learned it for herself." However, in later years, with 20-20 hindsight, Mary and Florence may have realized they would have been well served to work a little harder to keep up with her.

At the end of their three-month Motown training program (and two extra months for Diana at John Robert Powers), the three Supremes were polished, poised and groomed within an inch of their lives. Each had become a girl/woman, still youthful but now disciplined beyond her years. Diana and Mary were excited about everything they had learned, but Florence wasn't. "Why are they trying to make us so phony?" she kept asking. "I think we look silly with hats and canes."

"We're stars now, Blondie," Diane would remind her, "And Berry says it's time to *act* like stars."

"Well, *I'm* no star. I'm just Flo," she would say. All of this was fine with Diana; if Florence wanted to be normal and earthy that was her prerogative. Diana, on the other hand, had different aspirations.

In many ways, everything The Supremes accomplished after the Copacabana was due primarily to the extensive training they received for that date. Diana's experiences of the last five months only served to reinforce her perspective on show business: she was committed to her life as an entertainer, to Berry Gordy who had made so much available to her, to Motown, and—for the time being, anyway—to her role with The Supremes.

Gordy said of Diana at this time, "She wants to be somebody and she wants that for her audiences as well as for herself. And she's going to *be* somebody because she works at it. I know she's going to be a great, *great* star because there is nobody who works as hard at it as Diana does . . . and there's nobody better than her at it."

In *Cosmopolitan* magazine, Rona Jaffe best summed up the Diana Ross mystique—honed and polished by Berry's artist development courses: "She is a delicately boned, gentle, intelligent, trembling, electric wire of a girl—part guts, part geisha, *all* radar. She can sit perfectly still in a corner and seem to jump out at you. It's what makes her a star. Chic, witty, high-fashion taste in clothes, with a style of her own. The curviest skinny girl I've ever seen—5 feet, 5½ inches, 103 pounds—she's not a skinny girl but a mini-girl."

By now, Diana and Berry were making love, music and money together, and he was constantly prompting and coaxing her into expanding her horizons almost to the point of exhaustion. But he was tender with her, as well. One former Motown publicist remembered the stories about Berry purchasing a full-length fur coat for Diana, and then making luxurious love with her on the fur.

There are others at Motown who remember how concerned Gordy was about her welfare. "Berry made me talk to all of the dietitians of every hotel we stayed in to make sure a special menu was prepared for Diana," recalled Joe Shaffner, The Supremes' road manager. "He was very specific: bacon and eggs and hotcakes for breakfast every morning. She had a terrible time maintaining her weight while rehearsing for the Copa because she was being pushed constantly and there was no time for eating. Plus she was a bundle of nerves and had no appetite."

Many of Berry's co-workers have raised questions about Berry's motives for being concerned about Diana's health. Was he really worried about her? Or was he worried that if she was in poor health, the group would suffer?

Diana herself complained privately, "All Berry and I ever talk about is my work and The Supremes. I don't feel like I really know him like I want to. Is he interested in me? Or just my career?" But because of her busy schedule and turbulent lifestyle, Diana never really had the chance to pursue the answers to her questions.

In truth, even though Berry was quite the womanizer, he remained absolutely devoted to Diana Ross and always wanted what he perceived as the best for her. Gordy was certainly mercenary where some of his other artists were concerned—Florence Ballard would have attested to this—but his bond with Diana was too strong and personal for him to disregard her health or welfare. True, he pushed her to the limit, but not because he didn't care but rather because he cared so much. Indeed, Berry Gordy was controlling and manipulative. Those were facets of his personality he himself couldn't deny, and Diana often felt the brunt of his machinations. But he did love her in his own way.

As a lover, Diana told one of Berry's former girlfriends, "Berry is like nothing I have ever experienced. He's as demanding in our private lives as he is in business."

She was never any more specific, but this former girlfriend elaborated in an interview, "He's a terrific lover, but also a mean-minded one because he uses sex more as a tool to keep a woman in line than as an expression of true love. He's the greatest manipulator of all time, and he had Diane eating out of his hands for years. He became everything to her very quickly: confidante, father, lover, best friend. He didn't always treat her well—was often cruel to her—but when he did good by her it was so good that he kept her wanting more, more and *more*. She was in a trap, only she didn't know it at the time."

Mary and Florence have said they never once discussed with Diana her sexual relationship with Berry. These three girls were in their early twenties, an age when love and romance are surely on the minds of most people. One would think that the subject would have been broached somewhere along the way, considering all of the time they had to spend in each other's company, and the impact the relationship between Diana and Berry was having on the group. But, apparently, it never was. Just as Florence's rape was overlooked and never dealt with again, Diana's affair with Berry was another taboo subject among the girls.

Obviously the three Supremes really were not the best of friends. Rather, they were just girls from the same neighborhood who sang together and, as a result, became inextricably tied to one another because of their fame.

Mary Wilson still cannot come to terms with the reality of her relationship with her two partners. "Flo and I had been parts of Diane's life—and she of ours—for so long now, we weren't just dealing with a friend but a family member," Mary wrote of this period in her 1986 memoirs *Dreamgirl*. "The Supremes became partners in a kind of marriage; each partner sees the others' flaws but tolerates them, because divorce is out of the question and fond memories of the courtship and romance refuse to die."

Diana Ross is much more realistic about her relationship with Mary and Flo. Mostly, she doesn't discuss it publicly and, often, when she does, it's in a superficial, disingenuous way. But every now and then, a little reality slips out, like in a 1985 interview when she recalled, "I wish I'd had [a close] relationship with Mary and Florence. We would go onstage and sing together, but we never really got deep down inside of how we were feeling. You know, 'Are you *mad* at me because I'm the lead singer?' 'Does it make you *mad* that I sing in front of you?' "

She concluded sadly, "We never talked about the *heart*."

In Manhattan on July 29, 1965, temperature and humidity were both in the seventies with evening thundershowers predicted—the kind of weather to frazzle the nerves. July 29 was the night The Supremes would open at the Copacabana after four long months of rehearsals. Every song, every gesture and every word—including Diana's ad-libbed comments—were practiced over and over again. As the date grew closer, Berry Gordy ordered his staff to attend rehearsals and carry notebooks to write down their comments. No other Motown act had received such scrutiny before an opening, but the Copacabana was not an ordinary gig.

Around since the early 1940s, the Copa, as it was usually called, was (and still is) located at 10 East 60th Street—a small nightclub, decorated with pseudo-coconut palms, its minuscule round tables packed so close together that private conversations were impossible, and its postage stamp-sized stage doubled as a dance floor. New acts were booked during the summer when its regular clientele escaped the city heat, but management never had to worry about patrons. Summer, winter, spring and fall, the Copacabana was a mecca for New York visitors.

Even tourists had heard the stories about organized crime controlling the entertainment industry. Mafia involvement in the record business was commonplace in the late '50s and '60s as rock 'n' roll became a burgeoning million-dollar affair. Racketeer Benjamin "Bugsy" Siegel—indicted for murder in 1940—was known to have started the Las Vegas boom with underworld money, beginning with the Flamingo Hotel where in the '60s The Supremes would appear for two engagements. In the '50s, the Copacabana was owned by syndicate boss Frank Costello. By the time Gordy brought in his Motown Sound, Costello was long gone but rumors persisted that the Copa was still run by criminal elements.

It was a formidable undertaking on Berry Gordy's part to book his "girls" at an exclusive and prestigious nightclub like the Copacabana, and in the other clubs in which they would play in the next few years, because the majority of these spots rarely featured black entertainers below the stature of a Nat Cole, Lena Horne or Sammy Davis, Jr. As Berry probably learned when he started dealing with the Copa's management, many of these clubs were run by shady underworld figures who, if they weren't the real thing, were as frighteningly close to anything resembling the Mafia as he had ever encountered. As Gordy became exposed to such people, Motown and The Supremes would continue making millions of dollars, and there were grumblings that some outside "businessmen" wanted a piece of Berry's action. There were also stories that Berry had gone to "investors" for capital, and now they wanted to control his company. No one ever had any proof.

The Mafia had also long been rumored to have involvement in the record industry. Record distributors, those who transport records from the manufacturing plant into different cities, and rack jobbers, who take the records into the stores, were said to be heavily influenced by the underworld element. All record companies had to deal with these distributors and jobbers, so it was difficult to avoid problems.

Most nightclub devotees and music fans didn't care who was behind the scenes as long as nothing interfered with their entertainment. And there was always plenty of entertainment to choose from in New York City. On the night The Supremes opened, Xavier Cugat's band was at the Latin Quarter, home of the longest legged, most glamorous showgirls in town. Walter Matthau and Art Carney were playing on Broadway in *The Odd Couple*, Zero Mostel in *Fiddler on the Roof*, and Barbra Streisand in *Funny Girl* (where the top price for orchestra tickets, including Saturday night, was $9.60). Many theater goers would drop in at their favorite nightclubs afterwards for drinks and to watch the second show.

Considering the importance of this engagement and all of the pressure on Diana, it was surprising that one of her biggest concerns seemed to be to make certain that Gladys Horton, the lead singer of The Marvelettes, and Martha Reeves, of Martha and The Vandellas, fully understood the fact that she had finally made it big. Throughout the years, Diana had been in competition with both women—and many others at Motown as well—and now that she was becoming a star she wanted them to know it. It appeared that she was so insecure, and so fiercely competitive, that headlining at the Copa wouldn't mean as much to her if the people she considered "foes" weren't present to watch her hit the big time.

"The rumors were that she wanted Gladys and Martha sitting up front," recalled a Gordy intimate. "Diana wanted to look out and see the expression on their faces as everyone applauded her. She kept insisting, 'I want Gladys and Martha to know. I want them to *know*.' It was sad, really."

Whatever it took to relax Diana during this important engagement, that's what Berry would do. Martha Reeves was working in another part of the country, so she could not be present, but Gladys was opening the following night with The Marvelettes at the Apollo Theater in Harlem. Berry promised Diana that Gladys—who sang lead on "Please Mr. Postman" and most of The Marvelettes' big hits up until this point—would be at the Copa to cheer her on. He had his sister Gwen call Gladys at her New York hotel to tell her that Berry and Diana wanted her present for the "big night."

Gladys tried to beg off, explaining that she wanted to rest up for her own opening, so finally, Berry called and insisted she be there. When she explained that she had nothing to wear "to a fancy place like that," Berry told her that Gwen would take care of the details. Before she knew what was happening, Gladys Horton was in Gwen Gordy's hotel room deciding what she would wear to the Copa.

"She had bought all of these beaded dresses for me to choose

from, and matching beaded purses and shoes," Horton recalled.
"She dressed me up in a wonderful gold outfit, really did me
up. Then, to make sure I didn't change my mind, Berry insisted
that I drive to the club with him in his limousine. I didn't understand at all why they wanted me there so badly."

At the first show, comedian Bobby Ramsen was putting the
audience in a good mood. It was important to Berry that the
media people and celebrities he had invited—people like Ed Sullivan, Earl Wilson, Joey Bishop, Jack Cassidy, Joe Louis and
Sammy Davis, Jr.—be happy. He did his best by making certain
they had enough to eat and drink. His *opening night* liquor tab
came to $4,000. The Supremes' salary *for the week* was $2,750.
If Berry had known what was going on in the girls' dressing
room, he might have been even more generous with the liquor.

Still dressed only in their slips and biting their false fingernails, The Supremes were waiting for Maxine Powell to help
them get ready. All of their new gowns, selected by Berry's sister
Gwen, were still in the closet, hanging in plastic wrappers. As
the time for their entrance grew closer, Cholly Atkins' wife,
Mae, tried to help the girls decide which outfits to wear, when
Powell came in.

"You have no business selecting their gowns," Powell huffed
at Atkins. "You just leave them alone. This is *my* business."

"I was just trying to help. You were so late and . . ."

"I don't care *who* helps us." It was Diana. "Just get us into
one of those dresses fast, or I am really going to get mad."

There was a knock on the door. It was Berry.

"Diane, look who's here," he said with a wide grin.

He stood aside, and Gladys Horton walked in.

Diana jumped up. "Berry, you brought her. I just knew you
would." She sized up Gladys from head to toe. "Oh my goodness, she looks like a princess," Diana cooed. Then she turned
her back on The Marvelette and resumed the business at hand.
She never said a word to the visitor.

Berry quickly ushered Gladys out of the dressing room.

Diana continued her argument with Atkins and Powell. "When
do I get dressed? *When do I get dressed?* Who decides on the
gowns?"

"Now, Diane, young ladies do *not* raise their voices," Mrs.
Powell said.

Diana glared at her. "I'll decide then," she said, heading for
the closet.

"The blue ones, you'll wear the blue ones," Mrs. Powell
interjected, once more in control.

"If these don't look stupid, I don't know what does," Flo muttered loud enough for Mrs. Powell to hear. "I bet these things flap up in your faces, too," she said, indicating the over-size blue and pink flowers Gwen had hastily attached to the collars after declaring the blue chiffon dresses too plain.

"Never mind, we can fix them later," Diana said. "It's time. Now!"

"Ladies and gentlemen," came the announcement. "Mr. Jules Podell is proud to present—The Supremes!"

The applause was loud and full while the three girls from Detroit walked through the cheering crowd. As they made their way up onto the small stage, they nodded confidently and appreciatively at members of the audience whom they would pass. The girls took their places behind three microphones, their smiles brilliant and their manner calm; one would never guess at the pandemonium that had just transpired in the dressing room. Once on stage, Diana, Mary and Florence were just an arm's length away from the ringsiders, that's how packed the club was.

The show was an exercise in precision, but it was quickly obvious to the audience that Diana did not consider herself a group member from the way she took the microphone, separated herself from the line-up, and began walking about the stage while performing. Now and then, she would melt into the group's choreography for just a moment. But then Diana would extract herself from the gentle swing of group unison, leaving Mary and Florence to the practiced routines so that she could go off on her own.

Earlier in the day, Berry and his family had buried his sister Louyce who had died following a brief illness. After the funeral, he had flown to New York for the opening. As the girls performed "Make Someone Happy," Berry leaned over to Mickey Stevenson and whispered, "She's incredible, isn't she?"

"Diana?"

"Yeah, Diane," Berry said. "Isn't she amazing? Just look at her. Look at her eyes. They're *hungry*, man. She ain't gonna be in this group too long, no way. She don't need those girls, Mickey. She's got it, whatever it is. *She's got it*." Then, softly he added, "It's a shame that Louyce . . ." He left the sentence unfinished. The Gordy family was a close one, and Louyce had been involved with Motown from the very beginning. But this was not a night for sorrow. He turned his attention to the stage once more.

Diana was making the introductions. "I know if there were teen-agers in the house they'd know our names." (The Supremes, after all, had just enjoyed five consecutive Number One singles.)

"But if you don't know us," Diane continued, "on the end is Florence Ballard. She's the quiet one. In the middle is Mary Wilson. And she's the sexy one. My name is Diane Ross." (She was not yet referring to herself as "Diana.") Then after a long pause, and peering shyly out from long eyelashes, "I'm the intelligent one."

Into the next song, "Somewhere," from *West Side Story*. "Yes, there's a place for each of us, a place of peace and quiet, and we must try to pursue this place where love is like a passion that burns like a fire and also the fulfillment of two hearts' desire," Diana said in the middle of the number. "Let our efforts be as determined as that of a little stream that saunters down the hillside seeking its level only to become a huge river destined to the sea."

She enunciated each syllable as clear as a bell, while Mary and Florence harmonized in the background.

The girls closed with "You're Nobody Till Somebody Loves You." Diana directed the first few bars of the song as a ballad to a member of the audience before the song picked up to a jazz/swing rhythm. When she sang "But gold won't bring you happiness," Florence suddenly interjected, "Now wait a minute, honey. I don't know 'bout all that!"

Flo's delivery was droll, impeccable and very reminiscent of what Pearl Bailey would have done with the line. The remark was also spontaneous; the only unplanned moment of the night. Everyone at Berry's table immediately turned to him to get his reaction. Observers said you could see the blood drain from his face.

But then Sammy Davis, Jr., stood up and shouted, "All right, girl! You tell it like it is!" The place broke out in applause. Flo had her moment, and the expression on her face indicated that she had never expected such an enthusiastic response.

"She's always been like that," Diana said with a wide grin before continuing the number.

Just as their opening song's title, "From This Moment On" was prophetic, so was their closing. "You're Nobody Till Somebody Loves You" drew applause and shouts of "More! More!" Clearly, The Supremes had triumphed. They were nobodies no more.

After the first show, the Motown entourage—except for Berry—crowded into the dressing room, hugging and kissing. Florence and Mary were in tears. Wrapped in a white terry cloth robe, but still wearing her wig and stage make-up, Diane stood in the corner by herself. Berry walked in.

"What did they say?"

"How'd they like it?"

"What'd you write down?"

Ignoring everyone, Berry walked straight to Diane and whispered something in her ear. Her face lit up. Everyone in the room tried to mask his or her curiosity about what Berry had said to her by acting profoundly disinterested, but all eyes were on the two of them just the same. He kissed her gently on the cheek and they embraced.

"Okay, everyone, listen up," Berry said, pulling out his notebook as he and Diane parted.

The room quieted. Pencils, pens and notebooks quickly replaced glasses of champagne in everyone's hands.

"What's up, chief?"

Berry Gordy grinned from ear to ear. "We got things to do."

Chapter
8

THE MORNING AFTER the Copacabana triumph, The Supremes were scheduled to pose for publicity photos in the club's lobby. They stood in front of a poster with their picture on it and accompanying words: "The Copa Rains Supremes!" After the session, Berry pulled Florence aside. "Not bad, Blondie, that little line you dropped into the last song," he told her. "Real funny stuff."

Flo recalled that she wasn't sure if he was complimenting her or being sarcastic.

"Diane loved it," he continued.

"Oh, she did, did she?" Florence said.

"Yeah, we're gonna keep it in the act. Maybe give Mary a line, too. But listen, next time, I want you to say . . ."

"Now you just hold it right there, Berry," Florence interrupted him. "*My* way worked. I'll do it *my* way. Or *I'll* come up with a new way."

"Fine. Suit yourself," Berry said. Then he walked away shaking his head.

That night, Diana made the group introductions, as she always did. When she said, "On the end is Florence Ballard. She's the quiet one." Flo interjected, "Honey, that's what *you* think." Again, her delivery and timing couldn't have been better.

The place erupted in shouts and applause.

"All right, Flo! You tell her! That's what *she* thinks!"

Diana looked out at Berry in the audience.

He wasn't smiling.

Neither was she.

After the Copacabana success, artist development went into full swing for all of the Motown artists, most of whom didn't take too kindly to the concept. "I have *never* offended anyone with my eating habits before, so what's the problem?" Martha Reeves wondered when Maxine Powell tried to teach her table etiquette.

Marvin Gaye refused to attend most of the classes. "I won't be Berry's idea of a white singer," he said.

Smokey Robinson wasn't thrilled with the idea, either, and said he felt awkward singing show tunes when he finally made it to the Copa. Indeed, thanks to artist development at Motown, practically all of the major company names followed The Supremes into the Copa and other clubs of that class, and just about all of the artists complained about everything having to do with Berry's concept—everything that is, but the money they made playing those places.

Most of Gordy's artists simply didn't understand the significance of what he was trying to do, indeed of what he had done. Starting with The Supremes at the Copa, Berry Gordy made loving black artists a point of pride to much of the white population. Of course, Motown's artists had a black following; that was to be expected. But the company's white fans were also very proud to be Motown fans and they loved these black artists for what they were. They didn't want them to be white.

Historically, whites had always thought of blacks as exotic singers who sang raucous music that didn't mean anything to the white culture. Wrong though they were, many did not think of blacks as intelligent human beings, equals to them. What Berry had done with The Supremes, and was hoping to do with the others, was to relate them to whites in an artistic way. But he never compromised the artists' integrity, which is important to note. He simply gave to black entertainment a new dimension. It wasn't a better one because black art in itself was perfectly fine, but rather it was a dimension that not only blacks could enjoy but also whites.*

After Berry's artist development team would finish with a new show for one of the acts, Gordy would have the department meet and sit with him as he watched a run-through of the complete act. Then he would give every song a rating from one (worst) to

*The irony is that, as adults, Mary Wilson and Diana Ross insisted that what was done for them in artist development when they were young is all a matter of what Mary calls, "The Motown Myth." She says, "Berry never signed anyone to the label who had to be remade. I hate that this lie has been propagated over and over. If you weren't already polished you couldn't get in the door. We were *not* molded . . ."

Diana agrees. "It's just not true. We were all already polished."

10 (best). After they finished this task, the group would go back and try to bring every song up to a 10 rating.

"Don't you think we could have a little more time to do this?" Maurice King asked after all of The Vandellas' routines scored below a five.

"No, I don't," Gordy said. "I like to see you work under pressure. You do better when you're being pressured."

Most of the artists chosen by Berry to go through the company's artist development classes benefited. Now and then, there were failures. Former Motown employees still laugh among themselves when anyone mentions the one and only Oda Barr, a fat girl from Las Vegas whom Berry was crazy about because of her voice. He brought her to Detroit and showed her off to the artist development personnel. Despite her 240 pounds of girth, she was signed to a contract. The team went to work on her; a careful diet program was outlined. Then one day, someone was sent to the hotel room to get her and caught Oda eating a whole box of Hershey bars. When Berry found out about it, he canceled her contract.

The distance from the Brewster Projects to the Copacabana is measured in more than miles. "From This Moment On," the title of the opening number in The Supremes' nightclub act, said it all.* From this moment on, The Supremes were more than "a nationally advertised all-girl product of the rock 'n' roll age," as *The New Yorker* magazine announced their Copa opening in a one-line blurb. The Supremes were *somebodies*, playing before an integrated audience from all over America.

The Supremes were now head and shoulders above the rest of the Motown stars; in October of 1965, they played Philharmonic Hall in New York to a standing-room-only crowd and grossed $15,000 ($6.80 top ticket price). Diana has remembered this evening as "one of the highest peaks" of the group's career.

For The Supremes, 1966 continued to be a heady time. The year started out with their return to Detroit, the first major nightclub engagement there since becoming world famous. All of the success on the road and abroad thrilled them, but it didn't mean quite as much as acceptance in their hometown. Not that there was any doubt that Detroiters would warmly welcome The Supremes' return. Certainly this group was something to be proud

---

*"From This Moment On" was the original opening number at the Copa. Later it was changed to "Put on a Happy Face," which appears as the first song on the Motown album *The Supremes at the Copa*.

of. These three black girls from the Motor City who dubbed themselves The Supremes and sold millions of records were more than just a coup for black music. They were a social phenomenon.

It was January 17, 1966, when The Supremes opened at the Roostertail nightclub in the heart of Detroit—only four and a half miles away from the Brewster Projects but a million miles away in experience. When the girls, wearing yellow chiffon, walked out onto the stage for their new opening number, "Tonight" from *West Side Story*, they peered out into the packed house to a sea of recognizable faces—close family members, distant relatives, former schoolmates and teachers, record wholesalers, disc jockeys and Motown employees. It was one of the most exciting nights they'd ever experienced, and neither jealousy nor bitterness could dampen the joy of coming back home. At about 22 years of age, each girl was a hometown champ.

"When I used to live in the Brewster Projects, I always thought it would be fantastic to have a phone," Florence Ballard said at this time. "I would dream about a phone, dream about getting out of the projects. We had nothing much before, me, Diana and Mary. Now—well, now we're The Supremes!"

During this engagement, an interview was scheduled with a reporter from *The Detroit News* in the Motown offices. The angle: "Hometown Girls Make Big." It was just another of the many interviews the group had been doing of late. In the middle of the conversation, Diana suddenly announced, "I'd like to say that, from now on, I'm going to call myself 'Diana,' not 'Diane.'"

Even though Florence and Mary have claimed that this was the first time they heard of the name change, she was already called Diana on the liner notes of *Meet the Supremes* (March 1963) and on other albums released after that. Moreover, Berry often referred to her as Diana. Perhaps she decided that she would now *officially* do so as well; to her it may have sounded more glamorous. Even if Florence and Mary had known about it, the way Diana broke the news to the press probably made them feel it was just one more facet of her master plan to separate herself from her singing partners.

But this was not Diana's intention. More than likely, she didn't think the name change would matter to her partners. Flo and Mary made much more of it, but, as was always the nature of the girls' relationship, they never discussed it with Diana.

In the winter of 1966, The Supremes were booked into the El

San Juan Hotel in Puerto Rico. By this time, Diana and Berry were sharing a suite and didn't seem to worry what anyone thought of their romance; no one dared question it anyway. Diana's days were all spent with Berry, walking on the beach or gambling. She was mesmerized by him, and by practically everything he had to say about anything. "How did he ever get so smart?" she asked a fellow artist. "When I'm with him, I just hope some of his smarts will rub off on me."

That Motown colleague has remembered arguing with Diana over Berry's lack of loyalty to her. "I pulled her aside one day and, because I thought we were friends, decided to level with her. Berry Gordy was the freakiest man I'd ever known. He could make love to five different women a night and if Diana was one of them, that was okay. But if she wasn't, that was okay, too. So I told her this and tried to make her see that Gordy was not serious about her as a woman, only about her as a star. But she was like a teen-ager in love. She was blind to Berry's philandering. He was two-timing her right under her nose with women he'd have fly into San Juan from all over the country. How Diana Ross could be so smart, yet so stupid, was beyond me."

A person like Berry Gordy had to deal with all sorts of shady characters in order to make any kind of impression on the white music world. Many people who worked for Motown felt that this Puerto Rico engagement signaled Gordy's and Motown's downfall.

Starting with Ping-Pong games in the studio, Berry was the consummate gambler. He always enjoyed playing games with his writers and producers, games that started out friendly and ended up heated. Whether at Hitsville or on the road, most of his employees would lose their shirts to Berry. But when his luck turned, Berry could lose thousands of dollars without thinking twice about it. "He was a reckless gambler," Ralph Seltzer, Gordy's chief attorney, confirmed to Marvin Gaye's biographer David Ritz. "On any given day, he could lose $50- to $100,000."

At one point, Gordy bet a house producer the right to work with Chris Clark, a newly-signed white artist he found attractive. Berry won the game and before long he was in the studio writing and producing songs for Clark's *Soul Sounds* album. He could have worked with her anyway if he really wanted to, he was the boss after all, but there was something about *winning* the right that made it all the more sweet to Berry Gordy. Or as Marvin Gaye once said, "Berry's such a hardcore bettor that if you were in his office and it was raining, he'd pick out two raindrops that hit the window at the same time. He'd take one, you'd take the other, and he'd bet you 10 bucks that his raindrop would slide down and hit the bottom of the window before yours.''

According to popular belief among Gordy intimates, Berry hit it big at the gaming tables in San Juan and won tens of thousands of dollars over the course of the first few nights. But then, later in the week, Gordy began to lose heavily. The theory was that a well-known racketeer had hired a cardsharp to swindle Berry, first by letting him win big and thereby luring him to bet even greater sums of money, and then losing his proverbial shirt. Eventually, Gordy was dropping $75,000 a night, and was in the hole for many hundreds of thousands of dollars by the end of The Supremes' engagement. If this is true, exactly to *whom* Berry was indebted is a mystery, and whether the party really did have underworld connections is an open question.

Diana was totally oblivious to any of Berry's "business problems" since Gordy's policy was always "ignorance is bliss," where she was concerned. "Berry likes to gamble," she told a friend. "I think it's good that he has something to take his mind off business. Everyone needs to relax, sometimes."

A former booking agent for General Artist Corporation (the Madison Avenue agency that organized The Supremes' nightclub appearances and, with Motown officials, planned the group's itinerary) would only speak about this subject anonymously. "The one thing I recall of Puerto Rico was all the thugs in dark suits sitting in the audience. These menacing-looking creeps seemed to be following The Supremes from one stop to the next—it had started just before the Copa gig—and in Puerto Rico their number had multiplied."

Some of the more sophisticated members of the Motown entourage had strong suspicions about Berry's dealings with several rather ominous-looking characters. This particular booking agent recalled approaching Berry on the third night of the San Juan engagement and asking him very directly, "Hey, man, what's with all these thugs in the house? It's bad for business, and for image, too."

Berry snapped, "Those aren't thugs, man, those are my gambling buddies."

When the agent responded: "Man, those fellows are not your buddies," Berry shot him a mind-your-own-business look and walked away.

The next night, The Supremes had three curtain calls and left the stage to a strong ovation. Backstage, the scene was loud, noisy and disorganized as well-wishers descended upon the girls before they even had a chance to change from their stage costumes into street clothes. While all of the attention was focused on The Supremes, three of Gordy's white "gambling buddies" had cornered him next to one of the equipment rooms.

"Hey, man, how'd you like the show?" Gordy asked one of the men. The visitor mumbled something and Gordy, his brow sweating, began looking nervous and uncertain about what to do next. A few more words were spoken and then suddenly the four men adjourned into the equipment room and shut the door behind them. They were in there for about 15 minutes when people began asking for Berry. By now, Florence had changed into her street clothes and was watching the whole scene with great curiosity because, apparently, she had seen Berry and his friends slip away into the back room.

An aide knocked on the door, went into the small room, probably told Berry that someone was looking for him, and quickly came out. Instead of closing the door behind him, he left it ajar. By now, most people had cleared out of the backstage area and had begun congregating in the girls' dressing rooms where chilled champagne was being served and press photos were being taken.

Gordy, his two bodyguards and three "gambling buddies" continued their discussion for about another 20 minutes. Recalled the booking agent, "I came back looking for Berry, and then I remembered he was in this meeting. So I walked down the hall and standing there next to the partly open door was none other than Florence Ballard. So I walked behind her, tapped her on the shoulder and she just about jumped out of her skin. *'What the fuck is wrong with you?'* she shouted at me."

Just then, one of the men suddenly came bounding out of the room. He looked at Florence suspiciously. When asked what she was doing standing there, Florence said she was simply waiting to ask Berry a question. She swore that she hadn't been eavesdropping, even though that is certainly how it appeared.

No one other than those present knows what was being discussed in that meeting. And no one knows what, if anything, Florence Ballard overheard or even if she understood what she was hearing. But from that night on, Florence Ballard would claim that she had "something" on Berry Gordy—and that was a threat that he didn't like hearing from anyone.

The next night, Berry's sister Esther told him that a singer, Barbara Randolph, was appearing in the lounge. Randolph was an exciting vocalist, California-born and quite attractive. Esther suggested that her brother catch her act, and when he did he was very impressed.

"She'd work in The Supremes, wouldn't she?" he asked one of his staffers. "Look good next to Diane, huh?"

The staff member was confused. "Well, who's leaving?"

Berry ignored the question.

After Puerto Rico, the boss had bodyguards with him at all times. Some people speculated he needed protection because the Mafia wanted to infiltrate Motown, and Gordy wouldn't let them. Others suspected they were already in, and Gordy was protecting himself from them anyway. These are questions which, to this day, are unanswered.

Nelson George addressed the subject in his history of Motown, *Where Did Our Love Go?* "It has become a record industry truism that Motown is controlled by underworld figures," he wrote, "that they grabbed power at Motown by lending money to Berry when he was caught in a perilous cash-flow bind." But George also allowed that no proof of any Mafia tie to Motown has ever been found.

Whatever the case, one fact remains: where Berry was once a very accessible person, by early 1966, he was usually accompanied by 1,000 pounds of beef—four hefty bodyguards weighing in at 250 pounds each. Sometimes they would be right at his side, but often they would just be in the area, watching. Gordy certainly gave the impression that he was afraid. Of what or whom only he really knew.

It was reported in the *Rock* magazine issue of July 6, 1970, that after the Puerto Rico engagement Berry Gordy was "beaten and left unconscious, supposedly by a squad of Mafia toughs. He suffered a broken arm and cracked ribs. Gordy won't discuss the beating or its purpose." *Rock*'s allegations were reprinted by the *International Times* in London, giving them worldwide exposure and credibility. The *Times* reported the rumors that Berry had received a million-dollar loan from the Teamsters Union pension fund, possibly to pay off his gambling debts—and if this is true, one wonders what Gordy arranged to use as collateral. It has never been proven, however, that such a transaction ever took place.

Of the Mafia stories, Berry has said, "That was one of the biggest stumbling blocks in our way. I lost some potential executives because of those stories, and some of our competitors have helped to keep those stories alive. But there's never been any of that stuff. Of course, when I first heard about it, I wanted to sue everybody. [But] I've been in legal battles where I've had to give depositions of ownership. So it's a matter of record that there's absolutely no tie with any kind of underworld thing.''

Smokey Robinson concurred with Gordy in a separate interview: ''Those kinds of charges have always been with us—that we're owned by the mob. They were lies when the rumors first started and they're still lies.''

Marvin Gaye agreed: ''Bullshit. Utter bullshit.''

A friend once asked Diana Ross to comment on the stories about her man and the mob. Her reaction: ''That's absurd! Don't you think *I* would know about it if it were true?''

After Puerto Rico, there was a marked difference in Berry's attitude toward Florence. Florence would say years later that she never knew what to expect from Berry: either he would be extremely friendly to her, buying gifts for her that he had not purchased for the other two, or he would go out of his way to embarrass her.

When The Supremes were booked into the Copacabana again from March 17 to 23 at double their original salary—$5,000 a week—Florence began complaining of a nagging flu. A tour of West Germany and Scandinavia was planned, and Florence's doctor recommended that Berry cancel it. Reluctantly, he did.

After a week, Gordy scheduled a recording session. An album of spiritual songs was being planned as a tribute to his recently deceased sister, and The Supremes were scheduled to record ''He.'' Diana, Mary and Berry waited for Flo for over an hour, and when she didn't show up Berry became disgusted.

''But she's sick,'' Mary said, trying to defend Florence.

''I talked to her doctor. She ain't sick no more. She's lazy, *that's* her problem,'' Berry shot back.

''And not only that,'' Diana added, impatiently, ''but it's costing us money and I'm tired of it.'' (The Supremes were required to pay for their own recording sessions. The cost of recording time was automatically deducted from the group's royalties.)

This was not the first time Florence missed a recording date. In October 1965, she didn't show up for the session of ''My World Is Empty Without You'' and Holland-Dozier and Holland hired Marlene Barrow, one of the Andantes (a Motown female singing group who specialized in backing vocals) to sing with Mary on the song. When Berry heard the single, he couldn't tell that Ballard wasn't singing in the background. ''No shit,'' he said, amazed. ''That really sounds like Florence to me.'' The public was none the wiser when "My World Is Empty Without You" was finally released as a single.

For the "He" session, Berry sent Mary home and had Diana record the song alone. She finished it in about 30 minutes. "Now, *that's* what I call cost-efficient," Berry told Holland-Dozier and Holland later. "No more sitting around waiting for those two girls to get it together anymore," he told H-D-H in a meeting. "If one doesn't show up, send the other one on her way and record Diane alone. It's quicker," he said, "and it's cheaper. No aggravation. Diane's a pro."

That week, Florence continued to miss rehearsals for the upcoming Copa date. If Ballard had been so easily replaced in the studio, was it just as possible to replace her on the stage? Berry and Diana discussed the option, and they agreed that they had no choice but to try.

One of Berry's aides remembered a Motown staff meeting that took place in February 1966: "Berry called together a bunch of his closer confidants—Gil Askey, Maurice King, Harvey Fuqua and a few others—and raised the simple question, 'What would happen if we replaced Florence at the Copa?' We all looked at him as if he were crazy. He started chewing on his tongue, like he does whenever he's in thought, and he asked, 'Is Diane good enough to carry the show regardless of who she is singing with?' Everyone had to agree that, yes, Diane could be put with any two girls and people would still be impressed. Berry seemed relieved. He said that he was pulling Flo out temporarily, that she would return after The Copa. He was hoping to teach her a lesson."

After the meeting, Berry told Diana that he would find a new third girl for the group. "Don't worry about it," he said. "All you have to do is sing."

"But Diane wasn't that much of a pushover," said the Gordy aide. " 'Look, I want to know who the hell I'm singing with,' she told him. 'Whoever this girl is, she has to meet with *my* approval if she's going to be sharing my stage.' "

Harvey Fuqua, the producer of the tribute album to Berry's sister, suggested that Marlene Barrow should join the act since she had already worked with Mary in the recording studio. Diana and Berry agreed that the attractive and talented Marlene would be a suitable replacement for Florence—and that Mary would be the one to teach her the routines. Mary obediently went along with the plan, venturing no opinion one way or the other.

"The next thing I knew, I was working night and day at

Mary's house trying to learn The Supremes' stage act," Marlene Barrow recalled. "I was also given a budget to go to Saks Fifth Avenue to buy expensive clothes, because I ordinarily didn't dress like they dressed. Then I had to be fitted into the stage costumes. I was basically Florence's size though I wasn't as tall. When I was finally ready, Diana, Mary and I appeared at a debutante party at the Grosse Point Country Club in Detroit. Then the next day, a white limousine pulled up in front of my parents' home. My mom and dad were everyday folks so all of my neighbors came out onto their porches to see what was going on. It was Berry's car coming to pick me up to take me to the airport. This, to me, was like a dream. We went to Philadelphia, Ohio and, finally, into Boston where we played a small club as a dress rehearsal for the Copa.

"Basically, I never saw much of Diana," Barrow said. "I don't remember ever rehearsing with her, only Mary. All of my dealings with Diana were on stage."

Berry flew in to Boston to see how the show was faring. "He was impressed with it," Barrow said. "I was nervous, wondering if the audience would question who I was. I was told to say Florence had the flu, and that was that. The audience was appreciative and Diana, of course, was wonderful, working harder than ever. There was a standing ovation. It was the most beautiful experience for me."

Now that one of the girls had been replaced successfully, Berry became more confident than ever that Diana Ross was the focus of The Supremes and that tolerating any aggravation from Florence, or even Mary, was not very necessary. But then Berry's plans for The Supremes' Copa lineup were thrown into turmoil by Jules Podell, the owner of the club. When Podell discovered that Florence would not be on stage, he became angry. He enjoyed Florence tremendously, remembered that she was a crowd pleaser during the last engagement, and made it clear that he wanted the three original Supremes. If Berry could not guarantee the presence of all three, the commitment would be canceled.

Both Berry and Diana were quite amazed by this turn of events.

Berry had no choice but to call on Flo. With Diana, Mary and Florence on stage, The Copa engagement turned out to be a great success. But Flo never knew how popular she was with Jules Podell. No one ever told her.

Following the Copa, there was a week of one-nighters before another engagement in Boston, this one at Blinstrub's. Because the schedule was so grueling, Gordy didn't accompany the ladies on one-nighters. Each stop along the way was typical of all the others.

First on the itinerary was The Aire Crown Theater in Chicago.

The plane carrying The Supremes and their entourage was two hours late landing at busy O'Hare Airport. The first lesson of life on the road the girls had learned long ago was that nothing ever happened on time. As soon as they touched down, a troupe of solicitous booking agents and secretaries ran to greet them as they were dragged down the concourse. "No water, no coffee, no explanation," Diana snapped at one of them.

A reporter for the *Chicago Tribune* magazine covering their arrival recalled that Ross was wearing "giant celebrity glasses" with artificial flowers woven into her curly wig, a black suede fox-trimmed coat and matching suede boots. Gordy had allowed her to buy the $400 coat on the installment plan from the same Hudson's department store in which she had worked five years earlier.

As the troupe quickly walked down the concourse in one big cluster, Diana stalked behind them, alone and miserable. She knew that the day would be spent indulging disc jockeys at popular radio stations by acting as if she were genuinely interested in meeting them and then by agreeing to participate in taped interview broadcasts. It was the same routine everywhere the group went. The first stop of this trip was at WLS radio. As soon as The Supremes appeared in the lobby, the jocks who had helped make them famous by playing their records swarmed all over them. How could the girls not be nice? Diana, Mary and Florence stood in front of a white wall with the jockeys, and when someone said "Smile, girls," they did.

After gobbling down sweet rolls, the three were seated in the studio for a hastily taped interview. "Hi! We're The Supremes. I'm Mary. I'm Florence. And I'm Diana," they each recited like little robots programmed to be congenial. Then they launched into their "routine": innocuous anecdotes about the Brewster Projects, The Primettes, Berry telling them to "finish school" and how "we never dreamed we'd be so successful." After finishing, they were herded into another booth for an on-the-air interview. They posed for more photos before everyone retreated into a meeting room for chicken club sandwiches.

Lunch lasted four minutes. Then The Supremes and their entourage were hustled out of the building and back into the waiting limousine, late for their next appointment. *"Now we don't have enough time and I am really getting mad!''* Diana screamed at the promoter.

Now nervous and upset, Diana began to talk incessantly to herself, remembering questions and answers from the last interview. Florence and Mary just gazed out the windows and watched wearily as Chicago passed by them. ''What do The Supremes dream about?'' was an interesting question posed earlier. Diana's thoughtful on-the-air answer: ''Oh, we dream about getting married, having children and settling down.''

But in the back seat shadows of their limousine and away from the glare of publicity, Diana now had a very different, more honest answer: ''What do The Supremes dream about?'' she asked no one in particular. ''One night I dreamed of a cat leaping on me, digging his claws into my skin.

''Just what do The Supremes dream about?'' she repeated. ''All frightening, terrifying things like that because we're *always* being harried and rushed.'' She sighed loudly. ''You know what? Sometimes I feel like a machine.''

Still looking out the window, Florence muttered, ''Yeah, but even a machine stops sometime.''

Chapter
9

As 1966 CONTINUED, Diana and Berry's fascination with one another grew. "I am a student of Berry's," she said. "He is constantly teaching me about the business. I am constantly sitting in on his meetings. It really is fascinating to watch that little genius at work. He's an amazing man when it comes to dealing with people. You know the saying, 'Walk with kings, but have a common touch'? He can do just that. There's no one like Berry Gordy to me in this world."

"She has a very intelligent mind, but she's lazy," Gordy said of his star student. He was always very critical of her. "She's been trying to improve her vocabulary because she knows it will help her, but lately she hasn't been working at it. She's a very emotional, sensitive person. If there's a little smell in the room, she's the only one who notices it. If the food doesn't taste just right, she can't eat it."

By this time, all of the other artists at the company felt that Berry's interest in Diana had hindered their own careers. "I was sick of hearing about Diana all the time from Berry," Marvin Gaye said. "I always thought of myself as the Company Prince, because Berry was the King. But Diana was the Queen. I couldn't compete with her, no matter how hard I tried, for the King's attention."

Motown executive Mickey Stevenson explained Gordy's position on the matter of favoritism. "Motown had a lot of people to support," he said, "and if Berry told me that he was going to take all of the money The Supremes were generating and disperse it among all of the other artists so that we could all go out of business together, I'd say he was crazy. I'd tell him to put the money on Diane because she's the winner and I want to be paid on Friday. The thing for the other artists to do would have been to take Diane's example and get their own acts together so that they, too, could be winners. And if that was too much to ask, Berry felt they should just get their hats and find themselves another record company.''

In March, the girls opened at Blinstrub's in Boston, a good engagement because it meant two weeks in the same place. By this time, Diana was down to 93 pounds and exhausted because of the hectic schedule and severe insomnia; she was fortunate to get two hours of sleep a night. Berry was in Detroit and unable to accompany The Supremes because he was co-producing some tracks for The Temptations. When he talked to Diana on the telephone she was very restless but amiable. Certain that something was seriously wrong, he asked Mary and Florence if she had confided in them about her health, but of course she hadn't. ''They said she seemed like she was blacking out on stage, but kept herself going by sheer will,'' Berry would recall years later.

On the third night, the group went out on stage for the show and midway into the act, as they performed ''I Hear a Symphony,'' Diana suddenly stopped singing and began slowly backing away from her microphone. Mary and Florence sang their background parts loudly and executed their choreography more broadly in the hopes of filling in the gaping hole left by Diana's silence. The confused audience watched as Diana put both hands up to her ears as if she was trying to block out the droning music. Florence, standing to her left, remembered Diana swooning and moaning, ''What's happening to me? I feel so small. I'm getting smaller, smaller and smaller.''

''What's wrong with her? What's happening?'' the backstage staff asked each other. ''What do we do?''

Road manager Sye MacArthur calmly walked out onto the stage, put his arm around Diana and escorted her off as she muttered and complained incoherently. Mary and Florence, by now very concerned about Diana, finished the song and followed. An announcement was made to the alarmed audience that the show had to be canceled, ''due to the illness of Miss Diana Ross.''

Backstage, the scene turned frantic. Diana lay on the dressing room couch, her head in Florence's lap. As Florence massaged her temples and tried to reassure her, Diana wept. ''I have this pain in my head,'' Flo remembered her crying. ''I can't go on, not another show. I just can't go on, it's too much.''

''Be quiet, baby,'' Florence comforted her. ''You don't have to go on any more. You'll be all right, we're all here for you.''

She turned to MacArthur. "Get me the phone," she said, taking charge. "I need to call Berry."

"You understand, Flo," Diana continued to ramble. "You're the only one. I just can't continue . . ."

Mary, her eyes spilling over with tears, stood in the background, too upset to do anything. "Is she gonna be . . . all right?" she stammered.

Gordy was at home and, instinctively, he picked up the phone on the first ring: "What's wrong? What's happening?"

"Diane's sick, that's what's happening," Florence snapped. "I told you we've been working too much and now look what's happened. She's sick, Berry, and we can't continue." She handed the receiver to MacArthur. "Now look, you tell this man we gotta cancel. This is all his fault, goddammit!"

Sye MacArthur got on the phone and apprised Berry of the situation, but Berry told him that he didn't think it would be necessary to cancel. Florence, now infuriated, got back on the line. "Look, I know a whole lot more about what's goin' on than you think I do." It sounded like a threat, but no one knew exactly what Flo was talking about—there's a chance that she didn't either.

Gordy shouted something at her, and she hung up on him.

"*Sonofabitch!*" Flo said, as she cradled Diana's head in her arms.

Berry was on the next plane to Boston. When he saw Diana, he immediately canceled the rest of the engagement, took her back to Detroit and checked her into the Henry Ford Hospital.

Berry and Diana never discussed the reasons for the hospitalization with anyone in the entourage; she stayed for a week, and while she was there, Berry gave her a scrapbook filled with Supremes' memorabilia, which must have lifted her spirits. Berry promised her that he wouldn't work her so hard in the future, but that vow was quickly forgotten.

From this time on, Florence would measure time in terms of "before Diane's breakdown" and "after Diane's breakdown."

In a 1975 interview, Ballard recalled a touching moment she and Diana shared on the day she went to visit her in the hospital. "I wasn't sure I should go," Florence remembered. "I didn't want to start nothing with her being so sick and all."

According to Florence, when she arrived, Diana was alone, wearing a bathrobe, sitting on her bed and looking very frail. Flo remembered that Diana was listening to the instrumental track of a song Berry had brought over for her to learn, an arrangement that when completed would go on to become "Love

Is Here and Now You're Gone." She sat on the bed next to Diana.

"Maybe you should sing some more leads, now and then," Diana said to Florence as they listened.

"Oh yeah?" Flo responded.

"Yeah. You know what? You should Flo. I'll tell Berry you should."

"Oh, I can't do that," Florence said. "Berry, he'd never let me."

"But you can," Diana urged. Flo remembered that Diana reached over and clasped her hand tightly. "Blondie, you know you can do anything you want to do. Don't you know that? I mean, haven't we proved that? Look at us, just look how famous we are. You can do anything, Flo!"

"I don't think so, Diane," she said sadly. "You, you're the one who can do anything she wants to do." Florence began to cry.

The two girls were silent for a minute before Flo turned to Diana and asked her a very direct question: "Diane, are you gonna leave us? You leavin' The Supremes?"

"I don't know, Flo," Diana said with genuine uncertainty. "What do you think? Berry probably thinks I should."

"Who cares what Berry thinks? Who's gonna take care of you if you leave us?" Flo remembered asking her. "Who's gonna help you when you're sick? Not Berry, no way! He don't care about you, Diane, all he cares about is money."

Florence recalled that as soon as she mentioned Berry Gordy's name, Diana's eyes filled with tears. Soon, they were streaming down her face.

"Thanks for helping me, Blondie," Diana said finally, not addressing the questions at hand about Berry or her future with the group. "Thanks for what you did in Boston."

"You don't have to thank me, Diane," Flo said, also crying by now.

The two girls sat on the hospital bed, and as they held hands and sobbed, "Love Is Here and Now You're Gone" played over and over again on the tape recorder.

At this time, *Look* magazine profiled The Supremes in an article entitled "From Real Rags to Real Riches" (May 1966). It was a strong piece, but caused anxiety for Berry because the girls were so candid and not concerned about the image of innocence Gordy propagated on their behalf.

Diana used the feature as a platform for her own ambitions.

"I'm a hardworking ham," she boasted. "I can be anything I want. I'm ready to do all the extra things—acting roles in movies, be the star of a big Broadway show. But where are the offers? We've had six Number One hits in a row, but we're still treated like some ordinary rock 'n' roll group.

"On TV shows like Ed Sullivan's, we're pushed on and off the stage fast as if we're nothin', and there are The Supremes, cryin' behind the wings. On 'Hullabaloo,' they give me a cue card with a stupid speech to say. How dare they do that! I could be the mistress of ceremonies, but they never ask me. I see all these phonies who never even had a Number One hit runnin' around actin' like big stars. But I've got something they don't have, and the kids know it. I'm for real, and every time I sing a song, it's part of my body."

Of course, what Diana said was true enough, but her comments infuriated Gordy. "What are you *crazy*? Talkin' 'bout Sullivan like that? Do you know how tough it is to get you on his show?"

"But . . . but . . ."

Mary used the magazine to make known her feelings about Diana's constant lead-singing. "We've got to take the load off Diana," she observed. "It's endangering her voice. We must even things out."

Berry called the three of them into a meeting and scolded them for being so candid. Florence and Mary were contrite, but Diana couldn't understand why Berry was so angry.

The article also created a problem between Diana and her mother when she told the reporter that Mrs. Ross once had had tuberculosis, and it was printed. There was still a stigma attached to TB at that time, and when Ernestine Ross read Diana's words, she was at first shocked and then angry. It's extremely unlikely that Diana meant to hurt her mother; probably she became impulsive and said the first thing that came to mind.

On September 2, 1966, Berry and the group embarked on a tour of the Far East. While the group performed in Tokyo, Mary and Florence began to see what Berry really had in store for them.

At press conferences in the past, the girls usually arrived together but, beginning in Tokyo, Berry engineered it so that he and Diana would walk in first, followed just a little later by Mary and Florence. The waiting reporters had already been told who was the leader of the group. Sometimes, Berry would have his aides tell Mary and Florence that a press function was to begin 30 minutes later than it was actually scheduled, and then have

Diana arrive punctually. By the time the other two got there, nobody cared. Diana told an aide, "Mary and Florence understand their position in the group. I'm the leader and the spokeswoman. There's nothing wrong with that, is there?"

While in Okinawa, the group visited army hospitals and talked to wounded soldiers. Diana has recalled feeling "dizzy" when she walked into the room of a double amputee who had been shipped in from Vietnam; he smiled at her and asked for an autograph and all she could do was swoon as her eyes filled with tears. His eagerness for her signature in the wake of his personal tragedy was almost more than she could bear. One of the Motown aides had brought a portable record player along, and the girls sang along with their records to the bedridden patients. The results of the Vietnam carnage were so heartbreaking, though, it was almost impossible for them to smile and act "Supreme."

When in Japan, the girls loved to shop and would spend thousands of dollars on fabrics they hoped to have made into stage wear. In one store, they were suddenly ambushed and surrounded by a troupe of gawking, curious Japanese women touching their hands and trying to feel the skin on their faces. One tried to explain to the girls that many Japanese were familiar with black American men but had never been so close to black women, and they were surprised at how beautiful they were.

While in Tokyo, Florence started dating Tommy Chapman, Berry Gordy's chauffeur, and soon they were sleeping together. Berry was incensed when he learned of the relationship; after all, she was one of his prized "girls" and Chapman was only a "lowly" chauffeur. But Diana, who had Berry, of course, and Mary, who was having an affair with Duke Fakir of The Four Tops, were happy to see that Florence was romantically involved with someone.

It seemed that after she was raped, Florence was never very interested in romance, and when she did get involved, it was with the wrong men. An affair with Obie Benson of The Four Tops ended sadly when he wasn't able to commit to her; one with Bobby Rodgers of The Miracles also broke her heart when he went back to his wife, one of The Marvelettes. When Florence fell in love with Otis Williams, a tall, dark and very good-looking member of The Temptations whom she called "Big Daddy," it seemed that it would last.

"It was Flo who taught me the expression 'shoot the habit to the rabbit,' which means make love," Otis Williams recalled. But The Temptations had become almost as popular as The Supremes, and the two schedules prevented the lovers from spending time together.

When she was with Chapman, she seemed more self-assured and confident, and he was also able to take her mind off her obsession about Diana's growing fame. Flo had become interested in Tommy shortly before they left for the Orient. The two of them were alone together in a limousine in Detroit and he was driving her home after a press function where Diana had been the center of attention. Florence was upset by the way Diana seemed to encourage the writers to ignore her and Mary.

Tommy once remembered that his first in-depth conversation with her was while they were driving along; he looking at her through the rearview mirror, she with her head tilted back staring at the ceiling of the limo.

"If you don't mind me saying so, you're really messin' things up," he told her. "The way you're handling Diane, or Diana, or whatever she calls herself . . ."

Florence was at first surprised that the chauffeur would be so direct with her.

"I'm not listenin' to you. You just drive. You got some nerve."

He told her that if she had problems with Diana, she should talk to Berry about them.

"I been knowin' Berry a lot longer than you, whatever your name is. And I can't talk to him."

"Well, what about Diana?" Tommy asked, still driving. "You should be close by now. Like sisters."

"Yeah. I know. It's a shame, ain't it?"

"Ain't what?"

"That we ain't like sisters."

"No, that's even better," Tommy remembered offering. "Makes it easier to handle her."

"So how do *you* think I should handle *Diana*?" Flo wanted to know.

"Ignore her," Tommy said simply. "If you ain't sisters, what the hell's the difference." He smiled at her through the rearview mirror. "Ignore the bitch and before you know it, *poof*!, she'll be gone."

Flo did a double take. Then she smiled.

"You know what? I think I like you," Tommy remembered her saying. "Let's go dancing. You and me."

After that night, Flo and Tommy began seeing each other regularly. The big problem would arise, though, when Tommy wasn't on the road with the group, and Florence had an excuse to drink because "I miss him so." Although Florence always drank more than Mary or Diana, she never drank alone until now; and now, she was drinking more than ever.

At photo opportunities in the Orient, Gordy had the girls dress in geisha outfits and wigs, with Diana always getting the most attention. His tactics to promote Diana to the media were upsetting to Mary, but absolutely infuriating to Florence. She understood Gordy's motives—she had grown to despise him and so nothing he did surprised her—but she was mystified as to why Diana seemed to want to hurt her and Mary. Out of frustration, Florence continued to drink on the tour and, as a result, her appearance seemed to grow increasingly sloppy. When she wasn't at peak performance, Diana would be angry at her. Rather than admit to what was ailing Ballard, she only harped on the symptoms.

When they got back to the States, the group was scheduled to perform at a benefit in Boston when Florence came down with what was diagnosed as walking pneumonia. It was ironic that this should happen in the same city where Diana became sick and had been cared for by Flo.

Florence had missed a rehearsal for the Boston engagement, and Berry considered sending the two girls on their own when she showed up, even though she was ill.

"What are *you* doing here?" Diana snapped at her when Florence walked in.

"I told her to come," Cholly Atkins, the choreographer, jumped in. "She's too sick to sing but she can sit and watch the routines and maybe learn that way."

"Nobody can learn that way," Diana argued. "If she's too sick then she's too sick, and I don't want to catch whatever it is she thinks she has. Blondie, turn around and go back to the hotel. I think you got rheumatic fever, or something."

Now Florence was angry. "Listen, Missy, don't nobody tell me where I should be or where I shouldn't be," she blustered. "Why are you so mean, anyway? Why are you such a nasty bitch?"

Finally, Atkins realized his mistake and ushered Ballard out of the rehearsal. Tommy drove her back to the hotel.

Ultimately, the group had to cancel their performance when Florence complained that her throat was too sore to allow her to sing that night. Backstage as they were packing to go back to Detroit, the scene was very methodical and quiet. Everybody just doing what they could to implement a quick departure after the sudden cancellation. Diana, a garment bag over one shoulder and make-up kit over the other, eased over to Florence who was sitting on a couch sipping hot tea. "You know you're not sick," she told her.

"Why don't you just go to hell," Florence shot back without thinking.

"Lead the way," Diana countered. Then, true to form, she ran back to Gordy and said, "Berry, Florence told me to go to hell. She can't say that to me. Can she?"

"Now, Diane, just be nice to Florence," Berry said patiently. "She thinks she's sick."

Berry was more than willing to put up with these outbursts because he felt that much of Motown's survival depended on The Supremes. However, he must have wondered how long he could allow this dangerous dissension in the group to continue.

A week later, The Supremes were scheduled to tape a television appearance at Belle Island, a park area in Detroit. Gordy called Ballard's doctor to see whether she would be able to make the appearance. The doctor said she was still sick and probably shouldn't perform outdoors, but if she would only be on stage for an hour, he would give his permission. Gordy promised. Florence was on stage taping from nine in the morning to six at night until finally she went over to Berry and complained.

"Look, Blondie, there's a lot of money to be made and we're very busy tryin' to make it," he told her. "If you're too sick to be in this damn group, then you should take time off. I don't know what else to say to you."

"Why are you trying to force me out of the group?" Florence asked, her feelings genuinely hurt. She began to cry and ran off the set.

For Flo, the most mystifying person in this drama was Mary Wilson, who wouldn't say one word to defend her, or to discourage Berry and Diana. No one knew where she stood. It seemed as though she was waiting to see whose side it would be safest to take.

Before an appearance on "The Ed Sullivan Show," Mary had a private talk with Florence and suggested that she "wise up. Don't you know that every time Berry and Diana come at you, they're trying to antagonize you so that you'll say something and they can fire you."

"Well, what am I supposed to do?" Florence asked.

"Just do what I do. Nothin'. Don't say nothin' back."

"Fuck that!" Florence said. "I'm not kissing Diana Ross' ass, or Berry's either. I'm fightin' both of them, and I'll win."

"You won't win, Flo," Mary said, shaking her head sadly. "No one ever wins."

On September 25, 1966, the group appeared on "The Ed Sullivan Show" to promote a medley of hits and then sang "My Favorite Things" from their current Christmas album. For the performance, the girls wore pink chiffon dresses and ornate earrings. During the dress rehearsal, one of Florence's earrings fell off. Diana stepped on it with her high heel and crushed it. To witnesses, Diana's actions appeared to be purely accidental.

After the performance, once the dressing room door was closed, Florence lunged at Diana and ripped off both of her earrings and started pulling her hair.

"Help. *Help me.*" Diana screeched as Mary cowered in a corner, watching in horror. Two of Berry's bodyguards pulled Florence off Diana, who by now had tears streaming down her face and was crying. *"What'd I do? What'd I do?"*

In retrospect, it's ironic to find two "innocents" singing about "doorbells and sleighbells and schnitzels and noodles" one second and then grappling on the floor in a screaming cat-fight the next. It was obvious that the pressure was building to an explosion point.

After the Sullivan show, Florence's drinking became more serious, especially when she went on a two-day binge after the group recorded a live album at the Roostertail, which was never released. Either she wasn't allowed to sing her solo "People" in the show, or she didn't want to. According to Gil Askey, "she was complaining that her voice was hoarse and she couldn't do the tune. Diana heard this and said, 'Okay, why don't we do the Symphony medley,' comprising five standards from their *I Hear a Symphony* album, on all of which Diane sang lead. When Flo realized that we had replaced her one song with five Diana songs, I think she got depressed."

But Flo said in an interview that when they were rehearsing "People," Gordy taunted her by telling her that her voice was weak and she looked overweight on stage. Finally, he took the number out of the act. She never did it again. Florence drowned her despair in drink.

"Do you see how bad she's making us look?" Diana asked Mary.

"Yeah. Pretty bad," Mary agreed half-heartedly.

"Well, I'm gonna do somethin' about it," Diana said.

Florence was beginning to lose hope that the group would ever be the same ol' gang again, or least as she had perceived it. She realized that Diana was not only becoming a major star but also had Berry under her thumb. "Why couldn't *I* have been born skinny, ugly and big-eyed?" she once jealously asked another Motown artist when she was in a drunken stupor.

The more Florence drank, the more weight she gained and the more uncomfortable her tight, form-fitting stage wardrobe looked on her. Berry could be cruel when he wanted to be. "You know somethin', Flo," he told her one day. "For a fat girl, you don't sweat much."

Diana was an emaciated size three, Mary a reasonable size seven, and by this time, Florence was a 12 and growing fast. One night, while out with Diana and his sister Gwen, Berry noticed Flo in the 20 Grand nightclub nursing a martini. He sidled over to her and told her that he and Diana had discussed the matter and had come to a conclusion. "We think you're fat, Flo."

"Oh, you think so, huh?" she said calmly. Then she threw her drink in his face, spun around on uneasy footing and walked away laughing loudly.

As Florence drank and Mary brooded and both complained, Diana made plans: she wrote down her goals very specifically in lists and determined when she would achieve each one. Still suffering from insomnia, she slept very little. During the evening hours, she and Berry would often be in the studio as she recorded and then studied the techniques of engineers and technicians who mixed and mastered her vocals. Diana was interested in everything that had to do with show business. She would shop for hours trying to find just the right outfit that would make her distinctive and then model it for Berry. If he liked it, she would wear it the next day and "surprise the girls." She was obsessed with entertainment and how to be the best at it, so bringing a temporary new girl into The Supremes didn't affect her. As long as she was still singing lead, what difference did it make?

At the end of 1966, Berry asked Diana what she wanted to do with her future. She was uncertain, and only knew that she was unhappy with the way things were working out in the group.

Florence's discontent had obviously become a problem, and she seemed close either to getting fired or to quitting. When Ballard visited her friend Gladys Horton of The Marvelettes backstage at the Fox Theatre in Detroit, she complained about how miserable she was. " 'I am an alcoholic behind all of this,' she told me," Horton recalled. "She said she was afraid of flying. 'I got to get stoned to get on those planes,' she said.

Then she told me she was ready to quit. I was shocked. I thought she had it so good.''

When Diana heard about Florence's backstage confession, she turned livid. She didn't like the idea of Florence being so frank about her problems—and about The Supremes' private business—with a member of one of the competing Motown groups.

Berry told Diana that she could quit The Supremes if she wanted to, and that if this was her decision, he would support her in a solo career. However, he recommended that she continue with the group, but with Barbara Randolph—the girl he had seen perform at the El San Juan Hotel in Puerto Rico in January 1966—taking Florence's place. (Marlene Barrow had decided that she did not want to be a full-time Supreme.)

Diana felt ambivalent. A solo career was certainly what she had in mind, but leaving the act was a gamble she wasn't sure she was ready to take. Replacing Florence certainly seemed logical, but she feared she would be blamed for the move by a gossiping public and press. Also, say Ross intimates, she was suspicious of Barbara Randolph, simply because Randolph was so beautiful and Gordy was obviously interested in her if he kept her in mind all of this time.

"She wanted to know who this Randolph woman really was to Berry," said one of Diana's former associates, "and Berry assured her that he was not having an affair with the singer. He really wasn't. He just thought she would be perfect to replace Flo. She was extremely talented. The more he talked about her, the more suspicious Diana became."

"Berry said there were problems and dissension in the group and that I would be replacing Flo," Randolph recalled. "But he said the final decision was Diana's. All final decisions were Diana's. And he wanted me to discuss it with her. I had mixed emotions because I knew that she was the Queen of Motown. I wasn't sure I wanted to get involved. I felt that she used her position to keep anyone that might outshine her, or have the potential to do that, in her place."

The Supremes—now with Florence back—were appearing in the same New Jersey city with Barbara Randolph when Berry decided to arrange a meeting between Barbara and Diana. "He took me backstage and I was very excited and nervous," Barbara recalled.

Berry knocked on the dressing room door and opened it.

"Diane, I got Barbara Randolph here," he said very pleasantly. "Remember her from San Juan? Now would be the time to talk."

"I *don't* want to talk to her! I *told* you that!" Diana screamed at him.

Berry, embarrassed, quickly closed the door. He turned and looked at Barbara sheepishly, and shrugged his shoulders.

"She was not willing to even speak to me," Barbara said. "I knew then that I wasn't going to be a Supreme. It never was mentioned again."*

It seemed that Diana had made her decision: she would strike out on her own. The last couple of records had not really done very well: "My World Is Empty Without You" sold barely 500,000 copies; "Love Is Like an Itching in My Heart" had done worse, a little over 368,000. But then they rebounded with "You Can't Hurry Love," a huge hit that sold over a million, and the album *The Supremes A Go Go*, which became the girls' first Number One album replacing The Beatles' *Revolver* on the charts. The time was right to break up the act while it was hot. Gordy had someone in his publicity department feed an item to columnist Earl Wilson about all of the "movie offers" Diana had been getting, perhaps hoping she would get a few. She didn't. Still, the group's schedule for 1966 was set with only tentative dates.

An album titled *The Supremes Sing Holland, Dozier and Holland* was completed, conceived as a tribute to the guys who had written and produced all of the group's major records. A single, "You Keep Me Hangin' On," was planned as the last Supremes record. Mary and Florence had no idea that the group was about to break up. Their futures were not a consideration at this point. The announcement of Diana's departure would be made after The Supremes' next engagement, at the Flamingo Hotel in Las Vegas where they would open on September 29, 1966.

But then, Diana changed her mind. The group would continue, and with Florence, for the time being.

The Vegas gig was an important, high-stakes engagement for which Florence had decided to clean up her act. Berry Gordy loved Las Vegas because his biggest weakness, besides women, was gambling. Some of his employees speculated that the main reason he wanted his acts to play Vegas—and The Supremes were the first—was so that he would have a legitimate reason to be close to the gaming tables.

Diana shared Berry's enthusiasm for gambling. Road manager Joe Shaffner recalled an incident that happened later during the

---

*Barbara Randolph was signed as a solo act by Motown, and had a hit single in September 1967, "I Got a Feeling."

course of this engagement: "She was ahead maybe $20,000, but Diane never quit when she was ahead. The more excited she got, the more she gambled. In a casino, Diane was like a kid in a toy store with a pocket full of change. She was playing five blackjack hands at $500 a hand, and she got busted on each hand and lost. 'Oh no, not all my money!' I heard her shriek. After that happened, I had the unenviable task of having to tell her it was time for her to get ready to perform. I walked up to her, tapped her on the shoulder and she whipped right around and threw a drink in my face."

The afternoon they arrived in Vegas, Gordy took some heavy losses at the tables, and, since she was trying to keep up with him, Diana found herself losing heavily as well. Before they knew what was happening, Berry and Diana were $25,000 in the hole. Afterwards in Gordy's suite, the atmosphere was morbid, as if there had been a death in the family. No one liked to see the King and Queen lose; it was bad for company morale.

There was a knock at the door. Diana answered and it was Don Foster, one of their road managers, carrying a briefcase under his arm. Berry, who acted as if he didn't know what the contents were, suggested to Diana that she open the package. She did. "Money! Just look at all of this money," she squealed as everyone gathered around. Berry, a man who certainly knew how to infuse a little life into a party, grinned broadly. Apparently, he hadn't felt very lucky that morning when he woke up, and so he called back to Detroit to arrange for $100,000 cash to be delivered to his suite in big notes. It arrived at the best possible moment.

"Let's go back and gamble," Diana begged Berry, which is precisely what they did.

Florence and Mary felt uncomfortable with this display of wealth and by Berry and Diana's frivolous attitude. They still remembered what it had been like when there was no money being made, when they were the "no hit Supremes." Even though Berry would tell them to "stop living in the past," it wasn't easy for them to shake the memory of being poor, especially since Florence had brothers and sisters back in Detroit who were always on the phone with her begging for money, which she always sent to them. Florence doled out $10,000 on Christmas presents for her family that year, but she felt that that was money well spent.

The girls had been rehearsing daily for the Vegas engagement. On the day of the opening, rehearsal was in the showroom. Berry, Maurice King and road manager Sye MacArthur were sitting in the middle of the empty theater. The Supremes and the orchestra were running through the show. When they finished "Queen of the House," Maurice King stood up, "Okay, here there will be applause, applause, applause. Now, Diane," he said, pointing at her. "It's your intro."

"Thank you," she began. "Ladies and gentlemen, before we go into the next number, I'd like to introduce the girls. On the end is . . ."

Berry stood up.

"You know what, Diane? I can't understand one goddamn word you are saying. Sye, can you understand her? Can you understand one goddamn word she's saying?"

"Not really," Sye said with uncertainty.

Diana looked hurt.

"Thank you. Ladies and gentlemen," she began again, very deliberately. "Now, before we go into the next . . ."

"Slow down," Berry commanded her.

"*Enunciate,*" Maurice King suggested.

"Yeah, *e-nun-ci-ate!*" Gordy repeated.

"Thank you," Diana began again. "Ladies and gentlemen, before we begin the—our—number . . ."

"Goddammit, Diane," Berry shouted at her, approaching the stage. "It's '*before we go into the next number.*' Get it right! What is the matter with you, anyway?" He turned to face Sye MacArthur. "Sye, what is the matter with her, anyway?"

Sye shrugged his shoulders. "Tired, I guess . . ."

Mary and Florence just stood on the stage silent, their eyes focused on Diana who was, by now, close to tears. "Berry, please. I'm trying," she pleaded.

"Well, try harder."

She took a deep breath, trying to choke back the tears. "Thank you. Before we go into the *next* number, I'd like to introduce the girls. On the end is Florence Ballard . . ."

Diana finished the speech perfectly and then left the stage in tears as Berry, Maurice and Sye watched silently. The orchestra began playing "Somewhere" and Mary and Florence dutifully continued rehearsing their background parts.

"You're too rough on her,' Sye said to Berry. "She's just a baby, you know."

"I know it," Berry said. "But I got to be, Sye."

"Why?"

" 'Cause she's gonna be a star. She's got to get used to pressure. And anyway," he said with a conspiratorial grin, "Wanna know a secret?"

Sye nodded his head.

"I understood every goddamn word she said from the start." Berry winked at Sye and then went after Diana.

Later that day, a newspaper reporter from the Las Vegas News Bureau interviewed The Supremes in Diana's room. Berry was present with the three girls, and so was musical conductor Gil Askey and road manager Sye MacArthur. The reporter first asked Mary and Florence questions. Both gave charming answers. He then turned to the lead singer and asked, "What do you think, Diana?"

She was about to answer when Berry suddenly blurted out, "Miss Ross."

Diana, thinking she was being addressed, gave Berry a quizzical glance. Berry jabbed his finger at the reporter. "Miss Ross. Call her Miss Ross."

Florence shot Mary a pained and exasperated expression. No one in the room said a word.

After an uncomfortable silence, the reporter carefully rephrased his query: "And what do you think—*Miss Ross*?"

Berry smiled with satisfaction, obviously remembering the heady mixture of respect and power when, in 1965, he made the transition from being "Berry"—everybody's buddy—to "Mr. Gordy"—everybody's boss. Gordy was discussing business with an influential concert promoter backstage at the Apollo Theatre when one of his artists slapped him on the back, called him "Berry, baby," and asked him for a loan. Berry felt humiliated by this blatant display of disrespect. Prior to this incident, he had complained to his sister Esther about not being given the "proper respect" from associates who had known him before he became wealthy and successful and still fancied that underneath the gold chains and bravado he was the same guy. He wasn't. Now he had power.

After the incident at the Apollo, the word was handed down that he was to be called Mr. Gordy, and that if any artist was in need of money he or she had to go through proper accounting channels. No one argued with him.

So now that Diana was acclaimed as the star of The Supremes, Berry felt that she deserved similar respect and the distinction of being known as Miss Ross. It would be good for her ego. It would also keep her happy. When she was happy, she worked harder, was less argumentative, and caused less of a problem for Berry and everyone else.

But the two girls who sang with Diana—and were still mistakenly operating under the notion that they were, in Berry's eyes, somehow on the same level as she was just because they sang in the same group—didn't quite agree with Berry's decision.

"Miss Ross, *my ass!*" Florence huffed after the interview was over and she and Mary were going back to their rooms. "I'll be damned if *I'll* call her Miss Ross! I think *Miss Ross* is gonna have such a big head now that we're not gonna be able to stand her."

"I gotta agree with you, Flo," Mary said, sadly.

Florence stopped in her tracks and, with a very serious expression on her face, looked at Mary for two beats. "Listen, you, from now on you call me *Miss* Flo," she scolded, mocking Gordy's dictate. "After all, I am *quite* a *big* star!"

"*Miss* Mary, that's what you call *me* from now on," Mary insisted. "And don't you ever, *ever* forget it! *Honey!*"

The two girls became hysterical with laughter.

"It was hard for them, I think, to admit that Diana was 85 percent of the group, and they were 15 percent," observed Taylor Cox, who negotiated the Motown contract for the Flamingo engagement with GAC. Cox was division head of Motown's Multi-Media Management division from 1964 to 1972, and his observations strongly reflect those of others in power positions at Motown at that time.

He noted, "Without Diana Ross, The Supremes were basically nothing. I don't really think the story of The Supremes would have been much different had it been Diana with any other two girls. Mary and Florence were not wise enough, though, to realize that Diana was making their money for them, making them famous, taking *them* with *her*. What they should've done was everything they could to keep her happy."

More revelations were forthcoming for Mary and Florence. That night, the girls descended to the showroom to prepare for the concert and were escorted to their dressing rooms—Mary and Florence in one, and Miss Ross in another. It was the first time Gordy had decided to separate the girls' dressing quarters, and it wasn't a good omen. It obviously did nothing for group spirit. Opening night, and the rest of the engagement, was tense, especially when Gordy ordered fresh roses for Diana's dressing room every night, and nothing for the girls. Also, all of the congratulatory telegrams were sent to Miss Ross' dressing room.

Though Diana didn't have much to say about any of this special treatment, it was obvious that she enjoyed the attention. Berry was forcing Mary, Florence and everyone else in the entourage to recognize her power and importance. How could Diana Ross help but allow herself to be spoiled by the man she loved?

Chapter
10

NINETEEN SIXTY-SIX ENDED with The Supremes recording a double album of Rodgers and Hart standards. After a guest appearance on an ABC television special saluting their music, the girls and Gil Askey went into the Detroit studios to record the new collection. It turned out to be some of their finest, most revealing work. On tunes like "With a Song in My Heart," "It Never Entered My Mind" and "The Lady Is a Tramp," Diana proved herself to be a vocalist who was much more stylistically mature than even Berry had imagined.

Mary and Florence were also coming into their own with this work, and it seemed that, as a group, The Supremes were never more cohesive—amazing, considering all of the turmoil behind the scenes.*

The new year began with the group in the recording studio again, this time cutting sides for an odd collection of songs associated with Walt Disney films. The album, *The Supremes Sing and Perform Disney Classics*, would be completed but never released. Their latest single, "Love Is Here and Now You're Gone," was Number One in the country, and the group had recently performed it on Andy Williams' NBC series. The Supremes were scheduled for an appearance at the Elmwood Casino in Ontario, Canada, at the end of January, and then off to

---

*Only half of the songs they recorded during these sessions were immediately released as *The Supremes Sing Rodgers and Hart*; the rest were issued by Motown almost 20 years later in a special collection. The group's public probably wouldn't have tolerated all of the songs in one release anyway in 1966 because, as it was, the initial album was a commercial failure, selling barely 135,000 copies.

a few more dates in the area before returning home to the Roostertail in Detroit.

One of the biggest problems between Florence and Berry was that whenever they would have a disagreement—which was happening more frequently as weeks passed—she would inevitably threaten him by implying that she knew information about his business that could prove to be somehow damaging. By now, he must have known that Florence's threats were empty. Perhaps she did have information that could prove to be harmful to his empire. But she really wasn't shrewd enough to know what to do with it. And who would believe her, anyway, if she simply went to the media? Whatever she thought she knew would just be more fodder for gossip mills, and Berry was so accustomed to gossip about Motown and its alleged underworld ties that it no longer bothered him.

Certainly, now, Berry was probably bored with Florence Ballard and with her ambiguous threats. "And if I can't control her I don't want her around," she remembered him as having said.

There was more at stake here than just strife within The Supremes and bitter animosity between Berry and Florence. Berry had to look at the bigger picture. Florence Ballard was dangerous, not because of anything she thought she knew but because she was making Berry look weak. Word had begun to filter down to the other artists that she was a troublemaker, that she pushed Gordy to the limit, calling him and his girlfriend names, and actually got away with it. He had to show that she was expendable, and if *she* was—one of the high and mighty Supremes— then so was everyone else at the company who might challenge him and his authority.

His task would be easier if the other two girls just insisted she be ousted. Often Berry would try to pit them against one another. For instance, once, when they were exhausted by a series of recording dates and concerts, he had a meeting with them and said, "I was going to give you girls 10 days off, but I've decided not to do that."

When they protested, he explained, "You could've had the time off, but Florence *thinks* too much." Then he walked out of the room leaving the three of them to argue over an issue they couldn't even pinpoint.

Berry had been in business long enough to know that often an enemy will come along whose cunning and even common sense are impaired by some kind of weakness. When he found these kinds of weak opponents, he knew they would always do themselves in eventually. Perhaps Berry believed that if he waited long enough, Florence would probably destroy herself because she was weak, unhappy, and had a need for alcohol. But he didn't have time to wait. The Supremes were more marketable and profitable than ever. Diana's star continued to ascend and Berry believed in capturing the moment.

At the end of March, Berry posed the question to Diana: "What do you think we should do about Florence?"

"She's got to go, Berry. She's ruining everything."

Berry was glad to hear her say it. They were in agreement.

Later in the week, he called Diana and Mary to a meeting at his home in Detroit.

"I think we have to replace Florence," Berry said to the two girls. He was trying to make this matter appear to be a group decision, even though his mind was already made up. Bringing Mary into this discussion was a formality, a courtesy. But then Berry found that he had an unexpected ally when Mary actually agreed that Florence had to go. Years later, Mary would always take Florence's side in every disagreement that pitted her against Berry and Diana, but the truth is that Mary was aligned with the "enemy" in the decision to get rid of "the troublemaker." Not only did she fail to tell Florence about the meeting, she also kept secret the fact that she, Diana and Berry had conspired to find a quick replacement.

Florence once said of her relationship with Diana and Mary, "I would rather deal with Diane than I would with Mary because Diane is honest even though she's mean. At least you know how she feels and you can deal with it. But Mary, she can say one thing and do another. She's not always honest with you."

"Mary has been the most marvelous person in the world," Diana said in an interview. "When we had problems, I didn't ever have to worry about Mary because she was always there with me. I started off making decisions for the group out of necessity because Mary was the type of person who wasn't the decision-making sort. She wasn't the kind of person who would say, 'I think we should do so and so.' Whatever the majority decided, she would go along with.

"At this time, Mary and I sat down and had a talk," Diana continued. "We decided that if Florence leaves the group we'd either try to find another girl to sing with us—and maybe the public wouldn't accept her—or, Mary said, maybe I'd get married. Then I said I had no real ideas about getting married. So I thought maybe if this did come about, perhaps I'd go out as a single."

If Diana left the group, Berry knew that a logical direction

for her would be to film. She wanted to be an actress, too, if
that would mean expanding her appeal, making her a bigger star.
She welcomed the challenge. Berry realized that Diana would
have to prepare herself for her new ambition, but how should
she go about that? Who could advise her? Who better than one
of Berry's biggest influences, Doris Day. Day had, by this time,
appeared in 37 motion pictures.

No one seems to remember how he got the assignment, but
Hollywood columnist Jim Bacon was to take Diana to meet Doris
on the set of her latest movie, *The Ballad of Josie*. With this
film, Doris was experiencing one of the bitter aspects of her
bittersweet life as an actress. "It was nothing more than a
second-rate western that required me to get up at 4:30 every
morning," she wrote of *Josie* in her memoirs, *Doris Day—Her
Own Story* (written with A.E. Hotchner).

However, before taking Diana to meet Doris, Jim Bacon
brought her to The Actors Studio, an acting workshop in Los
Angeles. Jack Garfein, who was then a director, suggested that
Diana consider private lessons. He told her that the best teacher
in Hollywood was an actress who wasn't working much, Lee
Grant. Diana listened attentively.

Though Doris Day may have been having her problems on
Josie, she welcomed Diana Ross onto the set with the kind of
cheeriness for which she's always been noted.

"Tell me, please, what do I have to do to be an actress?"
Diana asked.

"You just do one thing," Doris remembered telling her. "You
be yourself."

"But what about acting lessons?"

"Maybe you're a natural," Doris suggested. "And maybe
lessons would destroy that naturalness. I'd check into that, if I
were you."

Diana and Doris then posed for pictures. It was a quick meeting, but one the two women have never forgotten.

While she mulled over the possibilities of single stardom, Diana suggested that Cindy Birdsong, a member of Patti LaBelle
and the Bluebelles, a popular rhythm and blues group originat-
ing out of New Jersey, be considered as a temporary replacement
for Florence in The Supremes. Gordy had one of his aides, Larry
Maxwell, find her. Diana had liked Cindy ever since she first
met her when The Supremes shared a bill with the Bluebelles at
the Uptown Theatre in Philadelphia.

"In those days there was a lot of rivalry among girl singing
groups," Birdsong recalled. "So it wasn't a good idea to so-

cialize with the competition. Our girls, the Bluebelles, definitely hated The Supremes because they seemed like they were stuck up, so classy and all. We also had feuds with The Shirelles, but that's the way it was back then. I sort of liked The Supremes, though. They seemed different, as if they really had nice personalities under all of the sequins and glitter.

"So one night between shows I decided to sneak over to their dressing room and meet them. I wanted to know what made them tick. I loved the way the girls did their make-up. We Bluebelles hardly wore any at all—just a little eye pencil and lipstick—because our manager insisted that we not. When I knocked on their dressing room door, Diana opened up and immediately welcomed me in. Mary and Florence were quite aloof, and I suppose it's because they thought I was spying on them. But Diane, she was open and warm. So I asked her for make-up tips."

Diana pushed Cindy down in a chair and eagerly began to divulge her make-up secrets. She opened her cosmetic kit and proudly lifted out a tray of false eyelashes—dozens of them, each pair in its own special plastic case. After choosing just the right ones, she carefully applied the heavy lashes and thick liner to Cindy's eyes. Cindy stared unbelieving at her magically changing image in the dressing room mirror. Heavy lipstick and blush were added as finishing touches.

"Well, just look at you, Miss Cindy Birdsong," Diana said happily. "Just look at how *glamorous* you are. Do you like it?"

"Do I like it? I *love* it!" Cindy enthused. "But my girls, they are gonna *hate* it!"

"Oh, no they won't," Diana insisted. "How *could* they? Here put this on." Diana reached over to a white Styrofoam mannequin head and handed Cindy a fluffy wig. "Try this. I know this will make all the difference."

"Oh, no, I couldn't possibly . . ." Cindy hesitated. She looked around to find Mary and Florence and realized that both girls were standing in a corner looking disapprovingly with their arms folded over their chests.

"Sure you can," Diana urged, ignoring her singing partners. Before she realized it, Diana had pulled Cindy's hair back and began to secure a net around it. Then she put the wig on and started brushing the curls into place. Suddenly Cindy looked like one of The Supremes. In fact, she looked almost like Florence, which probably didn't sit well with Flo.

"Now you go over there to *your* girls and you tell them that if they need any help at all, they should come over here and see me and _my_ girls," Diana said proudly. Cindy thanked her profusely and left.

"You know what?" Florence offered. "That girl is gonna be dead in about two minutes."

Birdsong walked down the hall, into her dressing room and as soon as Patti LaBelle saw her, she nearly fainted. "What have you done to yourself?" she asked suspiciously. When Cindy explained Diana's handiwork, her singing partners were not at all happy with the transformation. "Well, I think you look ridiculous," Nona Hendryx said as she grabbed the wig from Cindy's head. "And you can tell Miss Diana Ross what to do with her fake white-girl's hair."

The door opened and, as the three Supremes stood watching in the doorway of their dressing room, a wig came sailing down the hallway. Diana caught it in mid-air. The girls couldn't help but laugh.

Now, it seemed that Diana Ross had more plans for Cindy Birdsong, and this time Gordy was involved. Larry Maxwell located Birdsong's mother, Annie, and telephoned her in Camden, hoping to track down her daughter. When he finally found Cindy and explained why he was calling, she promptly hung up on him, thinking the call was a prank. When he called back, Birdsong agreed to see him. Maxwell was on the next plane to Camden and spent hours with Cindy explaining the situation. "When I got the whole story, I wasn't sure I wanted to do it," she said. She went back to Detroit with Maxwell to meet with Gordy, Ross and Wilson. As far as everyone was concerned, Cindy was in. Now it was just a matter of getting Florence out.

Diana, Mary and Berry must have all agreed not to mention Cindy Birdsong to Florence, because no one ever did.

March 1967 started off as an exceptionally productive month but ended up a nightmare. On the second day of the month, the girls were scheduled for studio time with Holland-Dozier and Holland, and they cut, in a single day, three songs that would go on to become major hits for them when finally released: "The Happening," "Reflections" and "In and Out of Love." Not a bad day, at all. Afterwards, it was off to the Deauville Hotel in Miami, Florida, and then a series of one-nighters in the South. After the Deauville, Berry decided to return to Detroit and tend to company affairs.

On the way to Memphis, Florence got drunk on the airplane, and by the time the group arrived at the hotel, she could hardly walk up to her room. Diana was so upset she called Berry from the lobby, complaining, "How's she gonna do a show? She can't even walk."

They got through that concert, and the next morning everyone congregated in the hotel lobby ready to take cars to the airport for the plane ride to the next stop, New Orleans. Everyone but Florence. The last anyone had seen of her, she was on the phone talking to her family and sobbing. She would stay on the telephone, her lifeline to the "real world," and spend hours having conversations with family members she grew to miss more every day. Diana and Mary rushed to Florence's room and found her asleep on the bed, a half empty bottle of liquor at her side.

"Oh no," Diana shrieked. "Not again."

"It's all right, it's okay," Mary said, trying to smooth things over. "I'll help her. She'll be all right. Just don't call . . ."

"Berry," Diana finished Mary's sentence. "Well, I *am* calling Berry," she decided and with that, she ran down the hall. Diana couldn't reach Berry at that moment. Meanwhile, one of the group's road managers helped Florence get dressed for the trip to New Orleans. In the plane, she refused to speak to anyone. As soon as they were checked into the next hotel, Diana contacted Berry and told him what was going on.

"Diana could see that this Supremes machine was breaking down, and since she was the driving force she felt it reflected poorly on her," Joe Shaffner, the group's road manager at the time, observed. "There's a coach on every team and if the coach says you ain't able to play you don't play. Diana was the coach. Flo wasn't allowed to play."

Shaffner remembered what happened next. "Berry told me very calmly to put Florence on the next plane back to Detroit. He wasn't angry, he was just disgusted. I put her coat on for her, grabbed her suitcases and drove her back to the airport. Before we left, she went up to Diana and just smiled in her face, as if to say 'You ain't got to me, lady. I was leavin' anyway.' It was the most heartbreaking sight. On the way to the airport, she just cried and cried, she was so miserable, so unhappy. It was then that I knew that success was the worst possible thing that could have happened to The Supremes where Flo was concerned. I used to date her when they were three nobodies, and she was much happier then than she was in the car that night on the way to the airport. I hated what was happening to these three innocent girls—I hated every goddamn minute of it."

Diana and Mary went on that evening as a duet. Marlene Barrow was flown in to finish the tour.

When Diana and Mary returned to Detroit, Berry Gordy arranged for them to be featured in a commercial endorsement for the United Foundation, a Detroit-area charity group. Along with Flo, the two of them would be shown singing, and then discussing the charity work done by the U.F. The Brewster Projects were to be used as a backdrop for the commercial.

"Hello," the girls said in unison, standing in front of one of the homes in the housing development. Then Mary began. "The Brewster Projects in Detroit hold . . ."

"Uh, Berry, can we stop for a minute?" Diana interrupted.

"Cut!" Berry said.

The two conferred.

In an interview later, Florence recalled that Berry and Diana began whispering angrily to each other. "If you wanted to do it, you should have said something before now," Berry told her, his voice rising. "Now, what am I supposed to do?"

Diana just looked at him innocently.

Gordy turned to John Fisher, public relations director for U.F., and whispered in his ear. Fisher shrugged his shoulders helplessly. At this point, Flo recalled, Berry began chewing on his tongue as he always did when he was trying to handle a problem. Finally he said to Mary, "I know we've gone over all of this but now I think Diana should do the whole speech. Don't you?"

Mary glared at him but didn't say a word.

"Well, *I* don't agree." It was Florence. "And I ain't playin' second fiddle to *Miss Ross*. Especially here in the projects where we used to be equals. I'm just trying to be fair. And this isn't fair. Is it, Mary?" She looked to Mary for support. Mary just stared at her.

"Jesus Christ!" Florence said to her. "Thanks for nothing. I'm just trying to protect you."

Suddenly, Diana whirled around to face Florence. "Well, who the hell *asked* you to?" she snapped. "Why don't you just be quiet? This is *Berry's* decision."

"I was so sick of her by that time, I just kept my mouth shut," Florence recalled later. She said that people who lived in the projects were gathering around to watch the argument, and the scene became embarrassing.

After Berry calmed everyone down, Diana stood in front of the two girls and read the cue card marked "Mary": "Hello. The Brewster Projects here in Detroit hold a lot of early memories for us. We grew up here . . ."

As Diana gave the speech, Mary stared straight ahead.

Then Diana read the card marked "Florence": "Detroit is our home. Our families are here . . ."

Florence's face was expressionless.

Finally, Diana read her own card and finished the commercial.

Later, George Walker, a reporter for *Detroit* magazine, asked Diana how she felt about being back at the projects. "I don't feel like a stranger at all. After all, I left only a couple of years ago. There's a lot of love here. So many children, and a lot of love. We had good times here."

"Yeah," Flo said sadly. "*Those* were the good old days."

Diana was asked to account for the fact that the three of them made it from the Projects to the big time.

"We were just lucky," she said simply.

He turned to Flo for a reaction.

"Just like she said." Then a pause. "Luck."

After the taping, Berry's assistant, Janie Bradford, called the girls to inform them of a scheduled meeting at his house on April 23.

On that day, Florence brought her mother Lurlee for emotional support. Mrs. Ballard always seemed rather eccentric with brown hair that was almost waist-length. She had never before openly involved herself in Florence's career. The last time she had anything to do with Supremes' business was the day the girls signed their first Motown contracts. Because they were minors, their mothers had to be present. With the exception of Diana's mother, who was well educated, the mothers were pretty useless in terms of offering advice and guidance. Lurlee didn't understand what her daughter was getting herself into, and Johnnie Mae, Mary's mother, was of little help because she could neither read nor write.

Florence and her mother took their places in the den on the gold velvet couch. Mary sat next to them on a bar stool. Besides a few quiet pleasantries, there was no conversation. After about 20 minutes, two tall double doors opened and Berry and Diana made their entrance together, followed by one of Berry's bodyguards, Nate McAlpern.

"I think I have good news for you girls," Gordy began. Mary and Florence perked up. It had not occurred to them that good news would be imparted at this meeting.

"Starting at the end of the year, the group will be known as Diana Ross and The Supremes."

"That's good news?" Florence asked under her breath.

Ignoring her, Gordy then went on to explain that with Diana's name added to the billing, the group would be able to command a larger concert fee, "because it'll be two separate entities, two star attractions," his voice rising with excitement. "It's gonna be great! I think we'll start it with the next single. 'Reflections,' is it?'' he asked McAlpern.

"Yeah, boss. 'Reflections.' ''

Mary has remembered that Diana said nothing, but listened with great interest as if this was the first time she was hearing about his decision.

Then Berry changed the mood. "Now, about Blondie,'' he began. With all eyes turned to her, Flo sunk deeper into the gold velvet. Pacing back and forth, Gordy very calmly reprised the points of contention, counting the grievances on the fingers of one hand: Florence was drinking too much and looking sloppy on stage because of her weight. She was missing shows and "what happened in New Orleans can never happen again.'' He said that he felt that she was unhappy being a part of the group. Therefore, he decided, she was to be out of the group.

Nobody said a word. Finally, Florence's mother suggested that Mary, at least, wanted her daughter to continue with the act. All eyes turned to Mary who was now fidgeting nervously in her seat and looking over at Florence hoping for some indication as to how she would like her to respond. Florence turned away.

"Mrs. Ballard, Flo doesn't want to be in the group anymore,'' Mary has remembered saying. "Yes, I want her in the group but what can I do? *She* no longer wants *us*.'' Diana didn't say a word.

"Well, if that's the way you want it . . .'' Lurlee Ballard said, tears welling up in her eyes. Florence just sat slumped beside her, looking defeated. Finally, Berry went over to Florence, took her arm and helped her out of her seat. He then assisted her with her coat.

"Are you going to be all right?'' he asked. She nodded listlessly. Then she turned to leave, walking by Diana and Mary without looking at them.

When Florence suddenly opened the French doors of the den and walked out into the living room, she discovered a startled Cindy Birdsong sitting there. Birdsong had been met at the airport by Motown staffers, driven directly to Berry's home and told to wait in the living room. She knew a meeting was taking place in the den, but she had no idea who was in there.

"Oh my goodness. Flo!'' Cindy said, flustered. "What's going on? What's happening?''

Florence, now in tears, rushed by her.

Cindy sat down again and waited. "I wondered what I had gotten myself into,'' she recalled years later.

As Nate McAlpern said good-bye to the Ballards at the front

door, Diana and Mary came into the living room. Diana looked at Cindy and smiled. She hugged her warmly. Mary, ignoring them both, pulled open the gold drapes and watched silently as Florence and her mother walked out onto the driveway with their heads bowed. The two women stopped in front of the car and suddenly embraced, holding each other tightly and sobbing.

After a few moments, both got into Flo's Cadillac and drove away.

Cindy's was a soft second soprano voice which was nothing at all like Florence's first soprano, but she and Mary were able to approximate a harmonic blend in time for a concert appearance at the Hollywood Bowl on April 29, 1967, a benefit for the United Negro College Fund.

"Diana was really gung-ho about the idea of me in the group," Cindy recalled. "Berry and I liked each other instantly. Mary didn't have much to say to me other than rehearsal suggestions. She was antagonistic, in a way, because I was replacing her friend and she, after all, was the one who had to teach me Florence's parts."

Diana's version of what had been happening at this time came out in an interview several years later: "We had a talk with Flo and her mother and wanted to find out if leaving the group was really her final decision. And that was really what she wanted to do. She had made up her mind. She felt it just wasn't the right thing for her. Plus she wanted to get married and have her own family. She was dating very strongly with this one guy. So that's the way it happened when Florence left the group. It was a case of getting off our buns and doing something about a problem. Instead of sitting back and brooding about the situation."

There were no problems with the show at the Bowl. No one seemed to notice that Florence was even missing, probably because of the distance between the audience and the Bowl's stage, and Diana decided not to mention it.

Diana recalled, "We told Cindy that if she had any problems, just keep moving fast and smile like mad and don't get nervous. During the show, we had to run down a ramp onto the stage and sing 'From This Moment On' at the same time. So I sang my heart out and got to moving around the stage because I didn't want anything to appear missing. I didn't want the audience to miss Florence, but Cindy stood in there strong and did very well."

Afterwards, a party was given for the girls in Beverly Hills and the guest list included Shirley MacLaine, Natalie Wood,

Robert Wagner, Henry and Jane Fonda. No one would ever have guessed that there was any problem in The Supremes' camp. The girls were gracious and congenial, never once mentioning Florence's name. The next morning, an exclusive store on Rodeo Drive in Beverly Hills opened its doors early for The Supremes as a favor to Gordy.

"Diana and Mary went tearing through the store buying everything in sight," Cindy remembered. "I just stood there with my mouth wide open wondering how these girls had learned to spend so much money so quickly."

Cindy didn't realize that her contract with the Bluebelles would not be easy to break. (To this day, Bluebelles' member Nona Hendryx will not speak to Cindy Birdsong, whom she apparently considers a traitor.)

These details couldn't be worked out in time for The Supremes' next engagement at the Copa in May. It was just as well. Berry remembered what happened the last time he tried to give Copa owner Jules Podell a Ballard replacement, and he didn't want a repeat of that. Florence agreed to come back to the group on what she thought was a trial basis. She was distant, now, and didn't seem to care about group politics anymore. Her boyfriend Tommy Chapman was with her, and the two of them spent most of their free time together. Gordy had Birdsong with the entourage in New York, and she had been given tapes of The Supremes' show to learn. As they performed, she watched from the audience. Her presence only served to unnerve Florence even more, especially when she was invited to share the group's limousine while Florence traveled with Tommy in a Lincoln.

Tommy Chapman remembered a conversation he and Florence had during the Copa engagement as they drove back to the hotel.

"Did you see that Cindy girl in the audience watching every move I made?" Florence asked. "Studying me? Stealin' all my best stuff, stuff I worked years on? How can Diane and Berry do that to me?"

"Diane and Berry ain't doin' *nothin'* to you. You're doin' it to yourself," Tommy said sharply.

"Bullshit!"

"Look, Flo, I don't blame Diane and Berry," Tommy recalled telling her. "You're the one messin' up. And I don't blame Mary, that Cindy girl, nobody but you. You got the best spot in the best group and you're throwing it away 'cause you're jealous of Diane."

"Thanks," Flo responded with tears in her eyes. "Thanks a lot."

"Anytime," Tommy said angrily.

"Nobody can take my place in The Supremes. Nobody!"

Tommy pulled up to the hotel. "Wake up, Flo," he told her. "Somebody already has."

When The Supremes appeared on Johnny Carson's show during the Copa run, Carson asked if it were true that the group was breaking up. Diana jumped in with, "We're breaking up over you, Johnny."

Florence, who was making her last television appearance with The Supremes, and probably knew it, added, "If all of the rumors were true, we'd have six children and would've all been married six times." Diana then went on to talk about what she called the group's "understudies."

"We have, just like in a Broadway show, a stand-in," she said. "The show must go on. Except for me. They can't have a stand-in for me. But for Florence and Mary, we have two young ladies that will stand in their place." Diana was speaking of Barrow and Birdsong, but Wilson and Ballard, who certainly knew about these "two young ladies" standing in the wings, didn't need to be reminded of their expendability.

There was a five-day engagement at the Cocoanut Grove in Los Angeles beginning June 13 before the group was booked for its annual visit to the Flamingo Hotel in Las Vegas. Once in Vegas, Cindy Birdsong was staying across the street at Caesars Palace "just in case we need her, which I think we will," Berry said. Then on opening night, June 28, the Flamingo Hotel's luminous pink and white marquee read: *Diana Ross and The Supremes*. Nobody could miss it.

Before the show that night, Florence confronted Berry in a hallway backstage. Members of The Supremes entourage tried to act busy but couldn't help but hear.

"So, I see you've finished the dirty job," Florence once remembered saying to Berry. "I'll bet Diane just loves that marquee, don't she?"

"Now, Blondie, don't you start with me . . ."

"Don't you Blondie me," she said, her voice rising. "After I finish tellin' the world what I know about you, Mr. Berry Gordy, you'll be sorry you started this war with me. And you know what I'm talkin' 'bout so don't act like you don't."

"Florence," Berry began, shaking his head in disbelief. "What did I *ever* do to you to make you hate me? I'm the guy who made you a star, remember? We—" he was almost too upset to continue, "—*loved* you! We're *family*!"

With that, witnesses recall that Gordy turned and walked away muttering, "I just can't figure her out . . ."

"Don't you walk away from me, Mr. Berry Gordy," Florence shouted down the hallway.

By now all of The Supremes' musicians were congregated in a corner listening to the exchange. "And the hell with you, anyway," she continued even though he was long gone. "*Diana Ross* and The Supremes, *my ass.*"

With those words, she leaned against a wall for support and started to sob.

"I'm finished," she said to herself, her voice choked and her mascara running down her cheeks. "I'm finished with all of 'em. They can have their goddamn group. I can't take it no more."

Florence went back to the dressing room she shared with Mary and poured herself a stiff drink, and then another. When she dressed for the show, her wig was askew and her make-up took on the look of a clown. She had been wearing heavy layers of black shadow and mascara since her return to the group, and the effect was startling. Her costume, a silver two-piece bare-midriffed job, didn't fit. Her stomach stuck out, and the outfit looked tasteless as the group made its way through their opening number, ironically called, "Put on a Happy Face," from *Bye Bye Birdie*.

Throughout the show, Flo was off her mark and singing flat. Diana and Mary did what they could to cover for her, but it was difficult. In the act, before their closing number there was stage patter where Diana said, "I'll have you know thin is in," to which Florence, à la Pearl Bailey, always responded, "Thin may be in, but, honey, fat is where it's at." This night, when she delivered that line she stuck her stomach out to underscore the word "fat." It was an unattractive thing to do, especially considering her appearance. When Gordy saw her do this, he bolted up from his chair and headed backstage.

When the girls got off the stage, Florence went straight to her dressing room. "I need a drink," she said. Berry was standing there waiting for her.

"You are *finished*," he told Florence. "I want you to pack your things and get the hell out of this town."

"Berry, you get the fuck out of my face," Florence snapped as she pushed him out of her way and slammed the door.

Infuriated, Berry stormed out of the backstage area and into the casino, where Diana joined him. The two spent the night at the tables commiserating over what had happened. The next morning, he called Florence's room. When she picked up the phone, he realized that she was hung over. "I'm calling to tell you that you're finished," he told her.

"I'm what?"

"You're *fired*, Florence. Finished! I want you to go back to Detroit. I want you out of my life, goddamn it."

"Like hell, I will. I'm goin' on stage tonight," she said.

"If you go on stage tonight, I will have you thrown off," Berry threatened. And he hung up on her. Ten minutes later, his sister Gwen called Florence and convinced her to leave town.

Joe Shaffner recalled, "Florence quickly packed her bags and, again, it was my job to drive her to the airport and arrange for her return trip to Detroit. This time, I don't recall any tears, just hostility and anger."

As Shaffner drove Florence past Caesars Palace, Cindy Birdsong crossed the street and headed toward the Flamingo Hotel on her way to a rehearsal in Diana's suite. When she got there, Diana hugged her warmly and told her that she had never before been so happy to see anyone. Berry, smiling broadly, reached out to Cindy and also embraced her.

But Mary sat in a corner with tears in her eyes. She nodded at her new partner half-heartedly as Berry set up a reel-to-reel tape recorder on the dresser. He flicked a switch and a tape began playing the upbeat orchestral track to "Put on a Happy Face."

The three girls lined up in front of a full-length mirror and took a collective deep breath.

"Gray skies are gonna clear up . . ."

Chapter

11

IN JULY 1967, the worst riots in Detroit's history left 43 people dead. More than 7,000 others were arrested; 1,200 homes and businesses were destroyed. The riots were more than 40 years in the making as a volatile mix of poor whites and blacks began moving northward in the '20s. It was said that most of the rioters were "hard-core unemployed." Many black neighborhoods were ruined, including the area where the Hitsville offices were located.

While this was happening, Diana Ross was in Las Vegas, hobnobbing with Johnny and Joanna Carson at one party, and then with Milton Berle and his friends at another. Berry also was in Las Vegas with Diana and couldn't return home because the airport in Detroit was closed. Martha Reeves was on stage in Detroit singing "Dancing in the Streets." She was asked to stop the song in mid-performance and urge everyone in the audience to go home because Detroit was on fire, and their families were in danger. Marvin Gaye's duet partner, Tammi Terrell, reported that the home across the street from hers was burned to the ground.

Perhaps out of respect for the Gordy empire, now worth $30 million, the rioters left his buildings unharmed. Gordy had sent all of his employees home and had hired security guards to watch the premises, but there were no problems.

However, a few weeks later, his office received an anonymous phone call with the message: "Motown will burn by Halloween," and Gordy became worried. Detroit was no longer "the place to be" but where else could he go? Berry decided to move Motown out of its bungalow premises to a 10-story office building on Woodward Avenue in the heart of the city. This new building was much easier to keep safe because access to the offices was impossible without going past security guards stationed in the lobby, and up elevators. In the next year, Gordy's security measures would be beefed up considerably.

Tension continued to build within the group. A Ross confidante remembered, "Diana was feeling that Mary hated her guts and she was right. Mary did. Especially when Melvin Franklin (of The Temptations) sent her [Mary] a telegram at the St. Moritz Hotel in New York saying 'Stick by Florence. It may happen to you. Think about it.' The more Mary thought about it, the angrier she got. Diana used to tell her, 'You'd better let it all out, Mary, because if you don't, it'll hurt you.' As it turned out, all of this anger was hurting not only Mary, but the whole group. Diana wanted out. The Supremes had served their purpose."

When the media asked Diana why her name was being featured in the billing, she replied with a poker face. "Now all of that was done through the offices at Motown. They met with Mary and Florence because contractually it's easier and for money reasons and purposes you can sell and get a bigger price for a lead singer and a group. Like Smokey and The Miracles and many other groups in the country. But I was really not aware of this change until Florence left the group. They had talked about it before with Mary and Florence, but it had never come to my attention because I was working hard and doing a lot of sessions alone. I even took *my* vacation to do a whole Christmas album while the other girls went on vacation."

Rumors of Mafia intervention in Motown business were running rampant. Recalled a former Motown executive, who was still nervous about discussing this question and therefore asked for anonymity, "The word was that Berry had merged with outside businessmen and had received a huge amount of money from them. Most people at the company believed that Berry was being maintained as a front man in the organization so that it would still be respectable. This way, outside influences could pull money from Motown's profits without drawing attention to the matter. Money made through illegal gambling operations could also be filtered through Motown. There were many new white executives at the label and everyone was intimidated by them. None of the artists knew these guys, and all of these men were in decision-making positions."

If any of this is true, it surely must have been a problematic situation because Berry was used to running his company his way, and, supposedly, now there were others he had to answer to. As the story went, the chief man responsible for Motown was Michael Roshkind, a hard-nosed but brilliant New Yorker in his late thirties who had the title of Corporate Vice President. Roshkind was said to have worked for John F. Kennedy and Adlai Stevenson in public relations. One reporter described Roshkind this way: "Heavy-set with thick hands and the kind of tired, jowly face that makes you want to splash cold water on it, Roshkind gives the impression of a man who has learned the ropes in a cutthroat business."

"I know this for a fact about Roshkind," said a former publicist for Motown, "I saw him give orders to Berry Gordy. He didn't ask, he told. Mike Roshkind would tell him what to do, saying, 'This is what *I* want *you* to do.'"

"I've been called everything from the real boss at Motown to the Mafia's representative," Roshkind once said in an interview, "but this is Berry's company. Motown is an extension of Berry Gordy, not the other way around."

After the Vegas engagement, Florence Ballard met with Mike Roshkind—not Berry Gordy—on July 26, 1967, to negotiate the terms of her future. Her friends say that she had heard the stories about Roshkind and was intimidated by him. "I'm scared of this white man," she had said. "Who is he, anyway? Why can't I talk to Berry about this?"

She later recalled the meeting with Roshkind in a conference room at the Northland Inn in Detroit: "I was told I had no right to the name Supremes, ever. He promised me $2,500 a year for the next six years [a total of only $15,000]. I thought, 'Is that *all* I'm worth?' Then he said I had no right to say that I was ever a Supreme. And he said that if I didn't sign this paper, Berry wouldn't have anything more to do with me. I told him I didn't care if I ever saw Berry again."

Though she had no attorney accompanying her, she signed the agreement without even reading it all the way through. It stated that she would not receive any future royalty earnings from Supremes recordings. She must have felt helpless in the face of all of this intimidation and legalese. Roshkind apparently also offered her an extension of her recording and management contract with Motown, which she turned down. In claiming that she had "no right to say that [she] was ever a Supreme," Roshkind meant that Ballard would not be permitted to bill herself as "a former member of The Supremes" if she decided to go solo.

As the 24-year-old ex-Supreme, ex-Brewster Project girl signed the document, her whole body shook inside. Memories of all she had achieved, and all she was now losing, must have flooded her senses. Choked with resentment, she took a deep breath and stood up proudly. With her eyes spilling over in tears, she studied the stranger on the other side of the table. To her, he seemed contemptible; she smiled bitterly at him.

"You can take this paper," she told him, "and you can shove it right up your ass."

In the beginning of the Diana-Mary-Cindy union, Berry tried to reestablish a group unity among the girls because he realized that the tension among them shouldn't continue. "We had a good rapport with Berry," Cindy recalled. "It wasn't like he was the king and we had to ask to be in his presence, or if we did something wrong he'd say, 'Get rid of that one and get me a new girl in 24 hours.' Berry wanted to be sure that what happened with Florence didn't happen again. So at the rap sessions, we would all be able to say whatever we wanted, but he did most of the talking. He would tell us how important it was not to let the money and fame and fortune go to our heads. I thought he was an uncanny person, and so honest. He told me that when he first got money he got tied up in the flesh thing—girls, girls, girls. And he didn't want me to get involved with a lot of men now that I was becoming rather wealthy. There were things that he didn't like concerning Mary and some guys. But she was usually discreet. He would make a snide remark in passing or in a rap session to let her know she was out of hand."

This sense of unity didn't last very long. Diana began doing little things to hurt Mary's and Cindy's feelings. For instance, at the end of performances on television, she would often throw her arms dramatically into the air with her head ecstatically tilted back. Actually, she was positioning her head so that she could see the television monitors that were suspended above her in the studio. By looking at the monitor, she could see where Mary and Cindy were standing behind her and then maneuver her arms so that her hands would be directly in front of their faces.

"It took me a long time to catch on to this," Cindy admitted, "because I was like a little girl off the farm, so naïve. It was done very subtly. At first, I couldn't believe it was intentional. So I started maneuvering around, thinking, 'Well, she must not know that her hand is in front of my face.' But as I moved to the left, her hand moved to the left. As I moved to the right, her hand moved to the right. She knew all the time."

In concert, after one of the bigger numbers, Mary and Cindy would take short curtsies while Diana took long, swooping bows at Berry's direction.

The new name seemed to warrant an entirely new look for the

group. Chiffons were replaced by more sequins and beads. Hairstyles became even more flamboyant. Diana Ross and The Supremes' look was fashioned in a Broadway musical show style: pure glitz.

Diana's look, in particular, had also changed dramatically in just a year. She had taken what she had learned in artist development courses to a new level of sophistication—on and off stage. Where many of her critics once felt that she looked like a youngster wearing grown-up wigs and make-up, now there was no doubt that she was a mature, sophisticated woman.

Moreover, there was also a marked difference in Diana's stage attitude. In the beginning, she was anxious—almost desperate—to please her audiences; she performed with a bubbly, energetic enthusiasm that shouted "Love me! Love me!" Indeed, she was always in control, yet she still acted as if she had something to prove every time she walked out onto a stage. But those days of proving herself were behind her. Now she was much more experienced and self-confident. It no longer surprised her when she got a standing ovation. If she had any butterflies, there was certainly no sign of them.

At about this time, Holland-Dozier and Holland began expressing great dissatisfaction with the Motown machinery, especially when Berry promised to give them stock in the company in appreciation for their contributions. Instead, he gave the shares which were valued at over $1 million to his sister Esther. He offered H-D-H $100,000 a year each in advance against their royalties, but they decided that wasn't nearly enough.

Eddie Holland fancied himself an entrepreneur and convinced his brother and Lamont that the three of them should leave the Gordy empire and strike out on their own. Gordy spent so much time on the road with The Supremes that he had no idea that the fellows had begun to work on independent projects. When he found out, he became upset, especially considering that he had paid H-D-H nearly $2.5 million in royalties from 1965 to 1967. After an acrimonious discussion, H-D-H walked out of Berry's office, never to return. Soon after, Gordy hit them with a $4 million lawsuit. The three men countersued for $22 million and would be miserable for years—living far above their means without making any money to justify their expenses—before settling out of court with Gordy.

Finally, they started their own label in Detroit and enjoyed limited success for a short time, but nothing like the chart-topping success they had become accustomed to as part of the Gordy empire.

   As a result of the defection of Holland-Dozier and Holland,
The Supremes and many other Motown artists were left without
their valuable writing-producing team. This loss, combined
with the Florence fiasco, spelled the end of The Supremes' con-
sistency on the record-selling charts.

   By the beginning of 1968, Diana, at 24 years of age, and
Berry, 39, had almost totally distanced themselves from Wilson,
Birdsong and the rest of the entourage. Even though Berry played
around behind Diana's back and suspected she occasionally did
the same, they felt a strong, undeniable passion for each other.
Perhaps these complex feelings might have been interpreted as
love. Berry simply felt that Diana was the most sensual, en-
chanting woman he knew. The more powerful and confident she
became—in other words, the more she began to assert herself
within The Supremes' structure—the more attractive she seemed
to him.
   Also, Berry enjoyed a good challenge and Diana never failed
to deliver just that. Whereas once she would always abide by his
wishes, now she often did so only after putting up a fight. "Their
arguments were as exciting and as passionate to them as their
lovemaking," said a Berry Gordy confidante. "Berry knew that
Diana was strong-willed and uncontrollable, but that when he
got her in the sack, all of her defenses melted away and she was
his and did what he said."
   According to most people who knew Diana and Berry at this
time, Diana fully realized Berry thought he was totally controlling her. But she was still smart enough to use his inflated ego
to her advantage. Many important career decisions regarding her
upcoming solo ventures were supposedly made over pillow talk
when she knew she could sway whatever corporate power he had
to her advantage. Berry Gordy and Diana Ross were totally enveloped in each other as 1968 began, and, to most observers, it
was difficult to know just who was dominating whom.
   The year began with an exhausting European tour for The
Supremes—Paris, Amsterdam, Madrid and Stockholm—which
included the group's socializing with the Duke and Duchess of
Bedford: a luncheon was arranged at the beginning of January
and then a party hosted by royalty at the end of the month. The
party was held at the Club Dell-Aretusa, a Chelsea nightclub,
and attended by some of Britain's biggest celebrities, including
Mick Jagger, Vanessa Redgrave, John Paul Getty and Tom Jones
(Jones was having an extra-marital affair with Mary Wilson at
this time). The girls were impressed when Gordy arranged an

invitation for them to visit the Duke's 3,000-acre estate, Woburn Abbey, where they sipped tea and viewed the lovely woodlands for a day. Much to their delight, they also discovered that the royal couple had a copy of every Supremes album.

While in England, Diana Ross and The Supremes recorded a live album at the popular Talk of the Town nightclub and garnered rave reviews for their performances. But the real focus of attention during the overseas tour was on Miss Ross, who by now had become a much bigger pop sensation than Twiggy, Mia Farrow or any other doe-eyed "innocent" of that era.

"The great goddess of pop music is, without a doubt, Diana Ross," wrote a reporter for the music publication, *Disc and Music Echo*. "Mention her name and a thousand breathless men will fall at your feet." Diana reveled in the media's perception of her as an unaffected, benevolent and good-natured superstar. "She has managed to remain untainted by the effects of power and success. If anything she is even nicer than before," reported British writer Penny Valentine.

But Cindy Birdsong remembers a very different picture of Ross during the tour. The group held a press conference at London's Mayfair Hotel in January. The scene was typically chaotic. Birdsong recalled, "We were practically crushed by the reporters, all of whom were yelling at us at one time. Flashcubes were going off from a hundred different angles. But we ate this stuff up. We loved the attention, every minute of it."

To the enthusiastic press corps, Diana proudly gushed, "Today we know where we are going and what we want from life. At one time we might have given up and got married and had families. But now it's our career before anything or anyone. This is the life we want to lead—a life in the glamour of show business."

However, when a reporter inquired as to the status of Diana's relationship with Berry Gordy, she seemed truly annoyed. "Look, that's all people want to know about," she said. " 'Mr. Gordy this and Mr. Gordy that.' As far as I'm concerned, my relationship with Berry Gordy is just nice and cool and going along well. And that's all I have to say on the subject."

A big, warm smile melted the edge from her answer.

"Is that your own hair?" a reporter then asked Diana.

"Sure it is," she said with a twinkle in her eye. "I bought it myself." Everyone laughed.

Diana then mentioned the possibility of recording albums saluting the music of Walt Disney and the score of the film *Doctor*

Dolittle (never recorded). Someone then asked Cindy how she was adjusting to the group's hectic schedule.

Birdsong opened her mouth to answer and just as the words were about to tumble out, Diana quickly cut in, "Cindy thinks that a lot of sleep and regular meals are very important. It's no good skipping food when you're working until 2:00 A.M. every morning and traveling hundreds of miles a day."

The red-faced Birdsong was left with her mouth wide open. Casually, she leaned over to Diana and whispered in her ear, "Diane, I'd like to answer the questions that are directed at me, if that's all right with you."

Diana fixed her with an imperious look and then, turning to the reporters, forced a thin smile and said, "But of course, Cindy has an answer to that question."

Later, Cindy would recall, "Diana didn't like that at all. Usually at these press conferences, Mary was very quiet, not saying anything. But I was the new girl and very excited about these things. I wanted to talk as much as possible. I really didn't think it was fair that Diana did all of the talking. But I didn't have the sense to realize that I would be cutting my own throat by speaking out."

Immediately after the press conference, Gordy asked Wilson and Birdsong to meet him in the lobby of the hotel. There he laid down the new law. "We were instructed that from that moment on, Diane would answer all questions at press conferences," Cindy recalled. "I guess I really hit a nerve," she added, laughing. As he spoke to the two girls, Diana slipped into the hotel's drug store where she waited. After the meeting was finished and the obedient little Supremes went on their chagrined way, Diana popped out of the store with new pink sunglasses.

"Did you tell her?" she was overheard to have asked Gordy as they walked hand in hand out of the hotel. A busy and determined entourage of Motown employees led the way, clearing their path of fans and gawkers, and listening in on Diana and Berry's conversation.

"Who?"

"Cindy," she responded.

"I told them both. You speak, they don't," he said. "You're the leader, Diane. These press guys only care about what you have to say anyway," he added as they approached the black stretch limousine parked at the curb. The very British chauffeur got out of the driver's seat and walked around to the passenger's door to open it for them, but before he could get there, Berry held out the palm of his hand. "No, let me," Gordy insisted as he opened the door for Diana. Diana gazed at him for a moment, a confused look on her face.

"After you," he told her with a big grin.

Berry must have known how much Diana would love this grand gesture. He stood with the door open and his arm extended toward the seat.

But instead of getting into the car she reached over to Berry and hugged him. As the limousine driver and entourage stood and watched, Diana and Berry embraced and kissed very tenderly. It was a rare public display of affection between two people who, for just a few minutes, didn't care about anything else in the world.

Shortly after Florence Ballard was fired from The Supremes, her boyfriend Tommy Chapman quit his job at Motown after announcing to Berry that he planned to marry Flo. Later, Tommy said, "Berry told me that if I changed my mind about quitting, I always had a job with him."

When Tommy told Florence what Berry said, she was furious. "Why is he being so nice all of a sudden?" she wanted to know. "Sure, now that I'm out of the group, he's a real fuckin' nice guy." Tommy said later that Flo decided to call a newspaper reporter from the *Michigan Chronicle* in Detroit and tell him everything she knew about Berry Gordy and Diana Ross.

"I'm gonna expose them both," she told Tommy.

"Girl, what are you talkin' 'bout?"

"They been sleepin' together for years!" Flo said.

"So?"

"So I'm tellin' *everyone*. And a lot of other stuff, too. I know stuff about Berry that would surprise people. I know a whole lot of shit."

Tommy said that he grabbed her by the shoulders.

"Look. You got enough problems," he remembered telling her. "Whatever you know, you keep to your own goddamn self. You hear me?"

Flo thought it over for a minute.

"I can't do it anyway."

"Why not?" Tommy wanted to know.

Tears began to well in her eyes. she didn't answer.

"Why not?" Tommy repeated.

" 'Cause I think I care about them," Flo finally answered. "I never really knew it, but I think I care about them both. And I don't—want—to—hurt—them." She began to cry. Tommy held her. "Ain't that crazy?" she said, sobbing. "Ain't that the craziest goddamn thing?"

"It is," Tommy said, now also crying. "It's the craziest goddamn thing."

Florence hired independent legal counsel and was able to get $160,000 from Berry: $20,195.06 from The Supremes' account; $5,000 from the Diana Ross and The Supremes' account (paying Ballard for stage wardrobe she had been charged for, but had been unable to take with her); and $134,809.40 from Motown Record Corporation. There was still no offer of future royalties.

Florence, her attorney Leonard Baun and Mike Roshkind finalized the agreement at the Motown offices.

"I wish you'd reconsider this, Florence," Flo remembered Mike Roshkind as having said. He was genuinely concerned. "You should have payments spread out over a few years. Otherwise, the government is going to kill you."

"Well, maybe . . ." Florence began.

"Look, a clean break is the best way to handle this," Leonard cut in.

"Yeah, it's the best way for *you*," Mike said.

Baun was unruffled. "Look, I have tax shelters lined up for her. So don't act so worried."

Mike Roshkind handed the nine-page signed agreement to Florence. When she reached for it, Leonard Baun intercepted it and quickly put it in his briefcase. That was the last Florence ever saw of it.

"Take care of yourself, Flo," Mike Roshkind said as she was leaving. He hugged her. "I mean it. If you need us, you call. Me. Or Berry." As he embraced her, she was stiff in his arms.

"Don't hold your breath," she said as she walked out.

A couple of days after that settlement, Florence married Tommy on February 29, 1968, in Hawaii.

When they returned, Florence tried to get some of the $160,000 from Leonard Baun but wasn't able to. It was verified that the three checks were sent from Motown's accounting department to Baun's office, but Flo said later that she never saw a penny of it. Baun, who is now deceased, was later disbarred on an unrelated matter.

Florence signed a solo recording agreement with ABC Records for a $15,000 advance; Chapman, with no experience at all as an entertainment manager, decided to take on that job for his wife. Of the dozen songs she recorded, only two were issued as singles and both were commercial failures.

Then the record company dropped her.

* * *

In the middle of The Supremes' successful tour, Gordy and
the girls returned to the United States for a couple of days to
attend the reaffirmation of Mr. and Mrs. Berry Gordy, Sr.'s wedding vows. Berry's parents had now been married 50 years and
the ceremony was organized by Berry's sisters Esther, Anna and
Gwen. After the touching ceremony at Bethel A.M.E. Church,
2,000 of the Gordys' "closest friends" attended a reception at
the Detroit Veteran's Memorial.

What most guests remember about the affair is the air of sus-
pense that hung over it. Berry had at least two armed bodyguards
at his side at all times, and two more were always in the vicinity.
Many observers expected there to be some sort of violence at
any moment—especially at a champagne breakfast for the family
at the Pontchartrain Hotel where he spent a lot of time looking
over his shoulder. What he was looking for, no one seems to
know, but there was never any trouble. Diana, who was wearing
a white-jeweled mini-skirt, seemed more concerned about it riding up when she sat down than by any undercurrent of danger.

Berry Gordy was now spending much less time in Detroit. He
had begun to implement plans for offices and a home on the
West Coast. When he was in Detroit, however, he always seemed
to be nervous and uneasy. His skittish public appearances gave
even more credence to the rumors that underworld figures had
infiltrated his Motown operation. The *Rock* magazine July 1967
report on Motown's underworld connections said that one of
Gordy's former bodyguards was masterminding a Motown take-
over by the Mafia, and that the FBI had begun to compile a
dossier. No such dossier has ever been found.

Of the Mafia rumors, Gordy told the *Detroit Free Press* at
about this time, "There's no truth to them at all. I have never
been approached by anyone whom I would consider Mafia in
any way and I know a lot of people in and out of the record
business. There's absolutely no truth to the rumors. We have
had a policy of ignoring rumors generally because our business
is really one that creates them."

Berry also admitted that an outsider offered Smokey Robinson
$1 million in cash to leave the label. He refused the offer. "We
all came up in the same area in Detroit, the lower east side, what
is now called the ghetto, and it would be extremely hard for
anybody to pressure us into doing anything."

The belief among Motown personnel was that Berry Gordy
was losing his grip on his own record company. Maybe none of
his employees was connected to the underworld, but Gordy cer-

tainly didn't act as if everything was normal. It was as if he were playing a role in the science fiction thriller *Invasion of the Body Snatchers*—not knowing whom to trust anymore. Gordy tried to discover what was happening within his organization in some rather primitive ways.

Said one former Motown publicist, "Berry Gordy used to encourage people to spy on each other. He used to put tape recorders in people's offices, and then play them back later for shock value. He would go to the office of the PBX operators, pick up the headphones and listen in on people's conversations. That's the kind of man he was, and the kind of paranoia from which he was operating."

Diana Ross and The Supremes were headlining at the Copacabana in New York on April 4, 1968, when Martin Luther King, Jr., was shot on the balcony of his second-floor room in the Lorraine Hotel in Memphis. That night, 80 riots broke out. Federal troops were sent to Baltimore, Chicago, Washington and Wilmington. Forty-six people were killed, 3,500 injured, 20,000 arrested. Chicago's Mayor Richard J. Daley—who had criticized Dr. King and his work when King went to Chicago in 1966 to organize for open housing—ordered police to shoot to kill arsonists and to maim looters.

Everyone at Motown was deeply saddened by the tragedy. King had once visited the Hitsville building and was impressed. "What you are doing here is important," he told Berry Gordy. "History will show just how important."

Even though The Supremes were not involved in the Civil Rights movement—life on the road made it hard for them to be involved in anything beyond their careers—they still had empathy for King's work and admired him very much. If not for the Civil Rights movement which culminated in the 1965 Voting Rights Act (the triumph of Dr. King's Selma campaign), the story of Motown and all of its artists might have been a very different one. The movement demanded that blacks deserved equality, a concept that most certainly helped Berry Gordy's cause.

Most of the other Motown acts had to perform the evening of Martin Luther King's death. The Temptations faced a hostile crowd in Charleston, South Carolina, in no mood to have a good time. But Gordy canceled The Supremes' show at the Copa.

The next day, he received a call from the producer of "The Tonight Show" asking that the group appear with Johnny Carson to honor King. Where Gordy was concerned, good exposure was good exposure, no matter what the reason. Still, he knew that this could be an important television appearance and he wanted it to be a significant one.

He confirmed the booking and decided that the group would perform "Somewhere," a number from their nightclub act.

Usually, in the middle of that song, Diana delivered a spoken interlude about romance which was always a crowd pleaser. "Let our efforts be as determined as that of a little stream which saunters down a hillside . . ." Diana would say very seriously, and with the most perfect diction this side of Helen Hayes.

Right before the Carson show, Gordy and Shelly Berger decided to rewrite the speech in an effort to pay tribute to Dr. King. Now Diana would say, "Let our efforts be as determined as that of Dr. Martin Luther King, who had a dream . . ." She would then go into a recitation about "all God's children, black men, white men, Jews, Gentiles, Protestants and Catholics"— and then finally close with the line "Free at last, free at last, great God almighty, free at last!" The text was culled almost directly from the historic "I Have a Dream" speech delivered by Martin Luther King on August 28, 1963, on the steps of the Lincoln Memorial. To have Diana Ross echo King's heart-wrenching words was risky. This was too important to do haphazardly; she would be speaking not only for herself and The Supremes, but also for Motown. It would be the company's only public statement about the tragedy.

Gordy didn't give Diana much time to rehearse the speech and she was insecure about it. After hearing her practice it a couple of times, he was worried.

"Do it again," he ordered.

She did.

"And again."

She did.

"And again."

"I know the words, Berry," Diana finally said, exasperated and with tears in her eyes. "Leave me alone, please."

When she went on the air, Diana was extremely nervous and became tongue-tied, saying "gentles" instead of "Gentiles," forgetting how to pronounce the word "Protestant" and blowing the "great God almighty" line. She was under too much pressure to deliver a speech for which she was not fully prepared.

Johnny Carson's show was the first talk show appearance on which Diana sat at the panel alone, without the girls, and she was apprehensive about the idea. As always, she craved Berry's approval and wanted to make a good impression, but the subject at hand—the King assassination—was an emotional one and she didn't know if she would be able to express herself properly in front of a nationwide audience. She did have great respect for the slain Civil Rights leader and wanted to make an important public statement. But she had already tripped her way through that speech and didn't want to say anything to make matters worse.

"Just say what you feel," Berry had told her earlier. "Be honest. You're best when you're honest."

"I didn't sleep very much last night, Johnny," she began thoughtfully and very softly. "I'm very sad. And I'm angry, too, but I don't think it's good to be angry. I really don't know what to say . . . all I can say is what's inside."

Carson watched silently as Diana's eyes began to moisten. She could barely continue. "I'm Negro and I respected and loved Dr. Martin Luther King very much. And I know he lived and died for one reason—and I want all of us to be together. Not just the black man but the white man and everybody. I think we should walk together . . . It's very important because, uh, well, just *because* . . ."

By the end of the program, Diana was so nervous she had trouble concentrating. After Carson thanked her "and the gals" for appearing, she said, "Well, I think the cause is more important than the reason we're here."

When the show was over, Berry told an aide, "Man, she was somethin'. So real. So honest. We oughta have her say more shit like that."

"Yeah, boss. We oughta do that," the Motown employee said, carefully.

Once offstage, Diana began walking down a long hallway to her dressing room. Mary and Cindy had already changed from their black-beaded, long-sleeved and high-collared gowns and into their funky street clothes. They were standing near the stage door sharing a laugh, waiting for Diana and also for the limousine.

"You have to get changed, Miss Ross. Time to go," one of the road managers told her. "We got a lot of stuff to do and Mr. Gordy wants you to . . ."

"In a minute," she said in an exhausted, emotionally spent tone.

"But Mr. Gordy wants you to . . ."

Before she could get to the dressing room, Diana collapsed into a folding chair next to a water cooler. "I said, in a minute!"

Burying her face in her hands, she began to cry.

"Why can't I please—just—have—a—minute?" she asked, sobbing.

Without question, 1968 was the most violent year of the decade, with the assassinations of Martin Luther King, Jr., and then Robert Kennedy. The war in Vietnam had taken a turn for the worse. Campus riots, antiwar demonstrations and racial turmoil all pointed to the fear that America was about to explode. It was difficult for Gordy or his Motown artists to remain aloof from taking some stand on black issues. Considering the way the country was being rocked, public figures who were black were almost obligated to be involved, or to at least act as if they were.

Gordy began experimenting with various concepts to contemporize the group's—and particularly Diana's—persona. Most of the time, these plans didn't work. As much as Gordy and everyone else at Motown hated to admit it, though Diana Ross and The Supremes were a big concert draw, they were not appropriate spokespeople for any political causes because they were simply not that articulate.

The Gordy family was politically active in Detroit, and Gordy had often sent The Supremes to perform at fund-raising functions for the Democratic Party. This was usually done as a favor to someone with whom Gordy wanted to ingratiate himself. Most of the time, the girls didn't even know why they were raising funds, or what politicians they were even entertaining—to them, the date was merely another engagement on an exhausting tour.

In June 1968, Coretta King, Martin Luther King's widow, telephoned Berry to ask if he could arrange a concert benefit in Atlanta in honor of the Poor People's Campaign. With only two days' notice, Berry canceled the previously scheduled dates of The Temptations, Stevie Wonder and Gladys Knight and The Pips so that they could perform at the benefit. He decided to make Diana Ross and The Supremes the headliners.

Among the over-capacity audience in Atlanta's Civic Center were 1,600 poor persons enroute to Washington from Mississippi, Alabama and south Georgia, on what was called a Poor People's March. Before The Supremes' show, Mrs. King presented Gordy with a bound collection of her late husband's books, which she had personally inscribed. Berry was also given a citation by The Rev. Ralph Abernathy, president of the Southern Christian Leadership Conference and sponsor of the Poor People's Campaign. Then Diana Ross and The Supremes finally came out to perform, but not to say anything political.

When the benefit was over, Berry and Diana met with Rev. Abernathy backstage and posed for pictures.

Three weeks after the assassination of King, Hubert Humphrey announced his presidential campaign. After the benefit in Atlanta, Humphrey's headquarters contacted Motown and asked for a black act to support his presidential campaign. Diana, Mary, Florence and Berry first met Hubert Humphrey in June 1966. The Supremes performed at a dedication ceremony for a swimming pool that had been built by the city in a Detroit housing development. So Gordy decided to let Humphrey borrow The Supremes for the endorsement.

Of Hubert Humphrey, Mary Wilson has said that the entire group had met with him and was convinced that his policies were sound. After carefully considering the matter, they decided they'd be glad to endorse his campaign. While it's true that The Supremes would be more inclined to endorse Humphrey, because of his support of the Civil Rights movement, than they would Richard Nixon, his opponent, it's difficult to believe they really had the time to do much research on Humphrey's total platform. Considering the fact that Humphrey's office was just looking for any black group, and Gordy sent him The Supremes because he probably felt it would be good exposure for them, it certainly seems that this endorsement was mostly motivated by purposes of publicity.

The press conference to announce their endorsement was set for July 23 in New York at the Waldorf-Astoria. The day before, Diana apparently began to realize what she was getting herself into when she read an analysis of the endorsement in the press and started to have misgivings about it. She told Gordy she didn't want to make the endorsement because she didn't feel prepared.

Berry usually paid attention to Diana's sharp instincts when it came to any kind of performance—which is really what this endorsement was about—because he knew that she was almost always right. But now it was too late to turn back. He calmed her by telling her that all she had to do was "read this statement, smile, look pretty and act conservative." So she wore her cerise felt hat and raspberry mini-skirted silk suit and hoped for the best.

Diana, Mary and Cindy met briefly with Humphrey and, apparently, the conversation centered mostly on how much he enjoyed their music and liked their clothes. Then it was time to face the media.

The first surprise to everyone was that while Diana, Mary and

Cindy would be photographed with Hubert Humphrey, only Diana would be at the press conference.

As Humphrey stood at the podium in front of the noisy contingent of reporters and photographers, he said, "I would be less than honest if I did not tell you that I am deeply moved today." Then in a choking voice and with tears at the ready, he promised not to let The Supremes down and "to do my very best to merit your trust. And now, Miss Diana Ross has a few words to say."

Diana, sitting on a chair at his right, her legs crossed demurely, said, "Thank you. Thank you so very much."

Then she stepped up to the podium and read from a prepared statement that she had reached her decision to endorse Humphrey's campaign "only after thoroughly researching his record and talking to him for hours and hours. Thank you. Thank you all so very much." Just as she was getting ready to step down, someone from the press corps shouted out, "Miss Ross, we have some questions."

A Motown representative shot out of his seat and ran up to the Humphrey campaign publicist who had organized this press conference. "Questions? Hey, man, nobody told me nuthin' 'bout no questions. She can't answer no questions."

Witnesses recalled that Diana took a deep breath and reluctantly stepped back up to the podium. "Miss Ross, can you give us an idea of the kinds of changes the Vice President will make once he is in office?"

"I . . . uh," she stammered. "I mean, he, uh . . ."

Humphrey cut in quickly, "Look, let me handle this press conference," he told Diana. "And just don't be impatient," he scolded the inquiring reporter. "Now just cool it!"

Suddenly, the place exploded with a barrage of questions directed at Diana.

Humphrey made it clear that the press shouldn't attack her and severely reminded the media that "Miss Ross is not a one-issue person. This is a very well-rounded citizen here. We've discussed a greater emphasis on urban problems and Miss Ross is *very* interested in the quality of life in the United States."

"Yes. Yes I am," she said.

"We have not yet discussed the war in Vietnam in depth . . ." Humphrey added.

"No, no we have not," Diana added, interrupting him so she could appear involved.

". . . but a position paper on Vietnam will be forthcoming to all of you in the next ten days."

"Yes, yes, it will," she agreed.

"Well, exactly what *did* you talk about with Mr. Humphrey, Miss Ross?"

She was back in the hot seat. "Oh . . . *a lot* of things," she said uncomfortably.

"Like?"

"Well, like he said he wants to stop the shootin' and talk later," she said, making a reference to Vietnam.

"But I thought he said you two didn't discuss Vietnam."

"Well," she squirmed. "We didn't . . . not exactly . . . I mean . . ."

Usually when Diana was on stage, she generated such warmth that the audience was quick to respond. Although her stage patter was carefully rehearsed, she could make it appear spontaneous. No one had to teach her how to smile, to make eye contact, to let each person in the audience feel she was singing to no one else. It was a kind of magic. When she was performing, she was in control. This time she was not performing.

Afterwards, Hubert Humphrey caught up with Diana in the lobby of the hotel. "When I'm elected, you'll be invited to the inauguration," he told her. "You will also be invited to the Inaugural Ball, and when we're settled in the White House, you'll be among the first honored guests we will invite to dinner."

Diana forced a smile. "What are you gonna serve?" she asked. "Soul food?"

Diana was heartbroken about the way the press conference went and later wondered why Berry didn't protect her from looking so foolish. She was used to holding court for reporters and photographers who grabbed onto every word she said. She was not used to being badgered by a group of unruly journalists. Gordy apologized profusely. As far as he was concerned, it was simply a matter of everyone involved being in over their heads.

After the Humphrey endorsement, The Supremes were rehearsing a new routine in Detroit with Cholly Atkins when Florence's name came up. During a break, Cholly mentioned that he was working with her on her new nightclub act. Mary remembered that she asked enthusiastic questions about Florence and the show, and Cholly told her that Flo was well and that the act was coming along nicely. Diana didn't say anything.

When Mary asked Atkins if Flo had any bookings, he told her that she didn't and explained that Flo's husband-manager couldn't secure any club dates for her unless she had a hit record. Suddenly, Diana perked up.

"Well, then, Berry should help her," Diana said.

Mary recalled that she and Cholly turned to face her, surprised.

When Diana realized the attention her words had garnered, she became self-conscious. "I just mean—well, Berry has connections, you know? Maybe he can help her. I think he should, don't you?" she turned to Mary, who was too stunned to answer.

"Well, don't you?" Diana asked again, slightly miffed.

"Sure I do," Mary finally answered. "I'm just surprised to hear . . ."

Diana was hurt. She said that all she ever wanted for Florence was the best, "and why doesn't anyone believe that?"

"Doesn't matter anyway," Cholly cut in, shrugging his shoulders.

Diana and Mary waited for an explanation.

"She's pregnant."

By the summer of 1968, Diana had become fascinated by Barbra Streisand. In the beginning, it was Berry who recognized that Streisand enjoyed the kind of pop appeal and worldwide popularity he wanted for Diana. He suggested "I Am Woman" from *Funny Girl* in one of The Supremes' first acts. He knew that Diana excelled in this kind of material.

Later, he told friends that he realized he was falling in love with her the first time he saw her perform the song at the Apollo. He wanted her to think of herself as being special—so much so that he encouraged her not to tell Mary or Cindy where she bought her personal wardrobe, or what kind of lipstick she used. (If she found out one of them was wearing her perfume, she would switch.) There could only be one black Streisand at Motown.

Of course, Berry's vision for Diana was what she wanted for herself as well. Diana certainly wanted Barbra's fame. But she wanted more than that: Barbra controlled her own career—from records to live shows to movies. Barbra did not have a Berry Gordy pulling her strings. Barbra had power. And respect. And that's what Diana wanted, too. What better way to start than by doing Streisand-style music?

There was no other Motown artist who could handle the dramatic theatrics of Broadway show tunes the way Diana could. Most seemed uncomfortable with any music other than rock and roll, but Diana settled in comfortably to all musical challenges. She proved herself in Berry's eyes with the Rodgers and Hart sessions. "And now I want her to do a whole Streisand album," Berry told Gil Askey. "We need a Streisand concept."

"Diana's always measured herself against Barbra Streisand," Marvin Gaye once said. "She's worked hard for everything she's achieved. If she had been white, like Barbra Streisand, it would have been a hundred times easier for her. Her older sister's name is Barbara. She's also very pretty and smart and Diana had to compete against that."

It just so happened that in August, Streisand's much-heralded $12-million film *Funny Girl* was set to be released. Gordy had the shrewd idea of beating the original soundtrack recording into the stores with a *Funny Girl* album by Diana Ross and The Supremes. "It was what you would call a rush job," recalled Gil Askey, who produced the album with Gordy. "We did the whole album in two days in New York. Diane was in her absolute glory every step of the way."

Jule Styne, who wrote the music for *Funny Girl* and produced the Broadway show, assisted Gordy and Askey in the studio with Diana's lead vocals and also consented to writing liner notes for the album. "I'm proud that they chose *Funny Girl* for their first full-scale show and movie album," he wrote. "My life is now complete. From Frank Sinatra to Barbra Streisand to Diana Ross—what a parlay!"

"I just don't like the idea of her singing my songs," Barbra Streisand reportedly said of Diana, "and with my musical arranger. Who the hell does she think she is? The world doesn't need another Streisand!" She was particularly upset that Gordy had timed the album's release to coincide with the upcoming movie.

Diana Ross and The Supremes Sing and Perform "Funny Girl" was regarded by most pop music critics as some kind of a practical joke—not because the performances were bad but because no one took them seriously. Few seemed interested in hearing Diana Ross sing anything other than Motown songs, which was a shame because the *Funny Girl* album contains some of Ross' best vocal performances. She is in full-bodied and spirited voice on songs like "The Music That Makes Me Dance" and "People," all of which were carefully and lavishly arranged. Ross' pleasure in the album comes through; she's never sounded more alive on vinyl.*

***

*The *Funny Girl* album was a huge flop for Motown, the poorest charting album released by The Supremes since the very early days of their career. It sold only 76,508 copies, about 2,000 more than the first Supremes album, which was

"I think we should have the girls do a big concert in Central Park, like Barbra did," Berry told Gil Askey. "One day, that'll happen." When this idea was mentioned to Diana, she thought it was terrific. But the event never materialized for The Supremes. It would take almost 20 years before Diana would fulfill Berry Gordy's Central Park prophecy.

By the summer of 1968, The Supremes' recording career was in a slump, for a number of reasons. First of all, with the exit of Holland-Dozier and Holland, Gordy wasn't sure how the company should rebound. Music had become much more aggressive and less cute than it had been in the early and mid-'60s, influenced by hard rock, heavy metal and the social climate in the country. Also, Gordy really was preoccupied with Diana's Streisand fixation and simply not as interested in The Supremes making hit records. The group hadn't had a major hit record since "Reflections" more than a year before; the most recent release, "Some Things You Never Get Used to," sold only 202,963 copies.

"But one thing that was always inevitable was that when Diana Ross had a hit record, the whole company benefited," said Deke Richards, a Motown writer/producer. "It was good for company morale: if the Queen had a hit, so did the rest of the court. Berry decided she should have one, and it should be something contemporary and exciting. He put together some very strong forces—Frank Wilson, R. Dean Taylor, Pam Sawyer, Hank Cosby and myself—and locked us up in the Pontchartrain Hotel in Detroit until we came up with a hit song. He would check in on us now and then asking 'Did you get it? Did you get it?' Eventually we got it. It was called 'Love Child.'"

Gordy's instincts told him that the song was going to be a big commercial success—even though some of his associates disagreed with him. So he scheduled a recording session in September. But Mary, exhausted by the group's schedule and by the emotional turmoil that had surrounded Florence's dismissal, demanded that she have some time off. "This is not a good time for that, Mary," Berry told her sternly. "We're getting ready to cut this new record and it's hot. Don't you want to be in on it?"

"I need a vacation," Mary insisted. "I'm serious about this."

"Okay with me," Gordy told her. "But one day you'll be

released before anyone really knew who they were. Still, Gordy remained undaunted. "Jerks don't know great performances when they hear it," he said of the record buyers and critics who thumbed their noses at Ross' Streisand opus.

sorry you didn't work every day you could. You'll look back on this and regret it.''

"Yeah, right," Mary said.

Wilson flew off to Los Angeles to buy a new home in the Hollywood Hills. When she wouldn't tell Berry about the next leg of her vacation, he became suspicious. He liked to know where the girls were at all times, partly out of habit but mostly because he never wanted them to forget who was boss. Apparently, Gordy coaxed a member of The Four Tops into snooping on Mary and finding out where she was going.

When Gordy found out that Mary was booked into the Las Brisas Hotel in Acapulco, he apparently asked The Four Tops singer to go along with her and try to find out what she was up to. He promised that he would give a little extra push to the next Four Tops record if he kept him posted. Of course, he wouldn't commit himself on any important details. Either Mary never knew why she had an escort, or she just didn't care, because the two had a grand time in Acapulco together while Diana slaved away in a Detroit recording studio.

Cindy was also in Detroit while the "Love Child" single and album were recorded, but Gordy decided there was no point in using her if he wasn't using Mary.

"Well, who do we use in the background?" one of the producers naively asked Gordy.

"What the hell difference does it make?" he stormed. "That's *your* problem. Don't be ridiculous."

Anonymous studio background singers were added to the track of "Love Child" after Diana finished with it and most of the accompanying album. Diana's solo recording career was now in full swing, and she wasn't even out of the group.

The lyrics to "Love Child" were timely and explicit: an illegitimate child's plea to her boyfriend that they not sleep together and take the chance of her becoming pregnant. The song spoke to a prevailing problem among the youth of America who were submerged in the sexual revolution of the '60s. Ross' performance is strong and heartfelt. "Love Child" is the perfect pop record and easily soared to Number One on the charts, replacing The Beatles' "Hey Jude." It would become one of the four instant million-selling songs The Supremes had with Diana at Motown.

The group lip-synched the record when they debuted it on Ed Sullivan's program. Wilson and Birdsong learned the background vocals to their own hit simply by listening to it repeatedly and trying to figure out the "oohs" from the "aahs." Their fans around the world were duped, and no one was the wiser. In fact, after Ballard was fired, Wilson and Birdsong never appeared on another Supremes single.

As far as Diana was concerned, she was doing all of the hard work—spending many hours in the studio recording practically all of The Supremes' output alone, not to mention the many dozens of songs that she would give her all to but which would go unreleased. Yet she was being compensated exactly the same amount of money as Mary and Cindy were in royalties, and not a penny more. Even though they weren't on the singles and albums, the other two Supremes were still paid for their sales.*

The fact that Diana was making the same money as Mary and Cindy for concert appearances also seemed unfair to her when she considered her position in the group and importance to the show. But Berry didn't do anything to rectify these problems because he felt that there was already enough dissension in the group at this point. To realign the royalty and concert payment structure now would only make matters worse. The main reason Mary and Cindy weren't recording on singles wasn't because they were unavailable or unwilling but rather because they weren't asked. So why should they be penalized?

In the fall of 1968, Diana Ross and The Supremes continued to tour, promoting their "Love Child" release. Their lives on the road were, for the most part, isolated, privileged and sheltered. To outsiders, it probably seemed that it was easy for The Supremes to forget that the country was in such chaos, that racial tensions were still running hot. Indeed, for these fortunate three, it was always the finest hotels, the best restaurants, people fawning over them.

But Diana reminded a reporter, "I'd like to have my own television show, but it is very hard for a Negro. I think we have to work twice as hard to get that. I mean, if there were three *white* girls who had as many hit records as we do, they probably would have their own show by now."

Though Diana, Mary and Cindy may have been naïve in many respects, when it came to racial restrictions they were not. Diana

*Mary Wilson still receives about $85,000 a year in royalties today for titles like "Love Child" and "Someday We'll Be Together," hit songs she didn't record but which are still popular and always in release. Unfortunately, Birdsong relinquished her royalties in a 1972 agreement with Motown—just like Ballard—when she left The Supremes on maternity leave.

In 1968 and 1969, Mary Wilson did appear on three singles that teamed The Supremes with The Temptations.

and Mary's early adventures on the road in the South during their first Motown tour were full of life-changing experiences. Both would never forget being refused service in restaurants simply because of the color of their skin, or the sight of all those white people jumping out of the pool when they jumped in, or being shot at. How could they forget the sight of those black men with no hope begging them for food and money from behind bars? "They don't care about no innocence or guilt down here," one of the musicians had said. "That's how they treat niggers in the South." Cindy had also had similar experiences during her early road tours with The Bluebelles.

By 1968, some things had changed, but not everything. During another tour of the South that year, Diana was reminded that no matter how successful she might be on the stage, she still was not immune to racism. One night after a sold-out concert date, she and road manager Shelly Berger dropped by a pizza parlor after the show. While he ordered, she went over to the juke box to see if any of The Supremes' records were there. As she was looking, she heard a voice growl, "Hey, nigger!"

At first it didn't register. She looked straight ahead at a menu on the wall, stunned.

Then, again, "Nigger!"

Louder, "Hey, nigger!"

Diana whirled around. The men at the table were smirking. She couldn't tell which one had spoken. Her first reaction, fear, was quickly replaced by the kind of blind anger which makes people do foolish things. She started to approach their table. Shelly Berger grabbed her arm.

"Let's get the hell out of here, quick!"

"Wait a minute, let me . . ." she began to protest.

"No. It's not a good idea. Let's just go."

"One of these days—you just wait!" she muttered under her breath.

Before walking out of the door, Diana Ross took one more long look at them. When she turned her back to leave, she heard the angry voice again.

"Over here, nigger!"

In retrospect, it may have been foolish in the deep South of 1968 for a black woman to walk into a public restaurant with a white man. But Diana had just finished a successful show before a mixed audience where she had been cheered by blacks and whites alike. Ironically, had she still been dressed in her stage outfit she probably would have been recognized and the men who were shouting racial slurs would instead be respectfully requesting her autograph.

A few weeks later, in November, Diana Ross and The Supremes embarked on another European tour—London, Stockholm, Copenhagen, Malmö and Brussels. Because of his work schedule in the States, Berry could only accompany the group for part of the tour. Shelly Berger, road manager, and Suzanne dePasse, Berry's trusted "creative assistant," were sent to head up the Motown entourage of 13 people. But no matter what titles Berger and dePasse might have held, it seemed to many that it was Diana who was really in charge. "I'll have to ask Miss Ross," became a constant refrain.

She may not have made more money than Mary and Cindy but she certainly had more perks. The entire Motown contingent soon realized that Diana Ross had to be fully accommodated, especially in Berry Gordy's absence. She was always called "Miss Ross." The other Supremes were "Mary" and "Cindy." Diana had her own personal assistant, Roger Campbell, to keep track of her outfits, wigs, perfumes. Mary and Cindy took care of their own belongings. Diana made important decisions and conferred with dePasse and Berger. Mary and Cindy played Scrabble with the roadies.

Except for carefully orchestrated events, Diana avoided the press. Mary and Cindy were usually good for a quote whenever newspeople could get to them. Mary, especially, loved to be provocative. She confided to one reporter, "I would love to get married. And I think that Diana and Mr. Gordy are thinking about doing that very seriously. They have been going out now for at least three years."

On every tour, there were always a myriad of details to be coordinated, but on this tour some of the tasks grew to epic proportions because of Diana's demands. For example, she insisted that The Supremes' limousine at the backstage exit be parked facing the proper direction so that after the performance she could be whisked off without interruption—especially from the media. First the crew had to determine Diana's or the group's postshow destination and then locate it on a map. The placement of the limousine became even more challenging in London because people there drive on the left side of the street, not the right as they do in the United States.

The Motown tour arrived in London the morning of November 11, 1968, in time for the rehearsal of their Royal Command Performance at the London Palladium that evening. One of the acts to share the bill was a British group, The Black and White Minstrels. As Diana waited, she watched them rehearse.

Established in 1962, The Black and White Minstrels immediately became popular through their stage and television appearances. Dressed in black and white blazers and white trousers and carrying straw boater hats and canes, they wore traditional minstrel black face make-up. Their hands were covered with white gloves. Thus disguised, the 30 male performers could have been white or black. The audience would never know.*

The more Diana Ross watched The Black and White Minstrels with their Black Sambo make-up, the angrier she became.

"I think this is despicable," she told one of the crew. "How can they do this? They're making fun of Negroes, aren't they? I think it's very disrespectful."

Finally, she announced that she would not perform unless The Black and White Minstrels were removed from the show. The news people covering the rehearsal started scribbling away furiously. The Motown entourage were understandably upset. But Diana reasoned that if The Supremes appeared with an act which seemed to ridicule black people, it would look as though they approved. It took an hour's worth of talking until Diana was finally convinced that canceling their act when the Queen Mother, Princess Margaret, Lord Snowdon, Prince Charles and Princess Anne were all to be in attendance was not the proper thing to do. Such behavior would be interpreted as an insult to the British Royal Family, not as a plea for racial equality.

Diana continued with the rehearsal, but when it was time for the spoken part in "Somewhere," she turned her back to the press corps and kept silent as Mary and Cindy sang their oohs and aahs and looked at each other in confusion. Diana had apparently noticed the reporters taking notes during her protest about the Minstrels. There was no need to let them know her thoughts about Martin Luther King—at least not yet.

Most of the major London theaters have a royal box reserved for the monarch and her guests. Outwardly it resembles the other boxes, but its interior and furnishings are more elaborate. It

---

*Minstrel groups from the United States had performed in Great Britain as early as the 1840s. In America, minstrel shows effectively died out with the advent of vaudeville, although black face remained. Al Jolson and Eddie Cantor performed in it regularly. Judy Garland and Lucille Ball appeared in it as well. One of the last on-going public black-faced performances had been the Mummers Parade, a New Year's Day tradition in Philadelphia, with origins traced back to the 17th century. In 1964, the Mummers were prohibited from appearing in black face after Civil Rights leaders complained.

displays no bunting when the royals are in attendance but people always glance to see if anyone is there. Whenever the box is occupied, as it was that night, there is a special excitement in the audience and backstage.

When the show began, Diana, carrying a microphone, walked down a center aisle graciously shaking hands and singing the opening number, "With a Song in My Heart." When she ascended the stairs onto the stage, she was joined by Mary and Cindy. All three girls managed to project an image both demure and sexy. Their elaborate pearl-encrusted gowns were such a pale pink that they almost looked white until the spotlights turned them into an iridescent glimmer. Though high-necked and long-sleeved, the dresses hugged their bodies, showing every curve. Their hairstyles were upswept and elegant. Their earrings, though large, were not gaudy. The Supremes looked regal, as princesses are supposed to look but seldom do. If they were a bit nervous at first, they managed to overcome it, buoyed by the audience's approval after each song in their opening medley. The show went along smoothly.

In the middle of their last number, "Somewhere," the music softened and the lights went to blue. Diana stepped forward, stage left, and faced the royal box. She began to speak, softly and deliberately.

"Yes, there's a place for each of us, and we must try to pursue that place where love is like a passion that burns like a fire. Let our efforts be as determined as that of Martin Luther King who had a dream that *all* God's children—black men, white men, Jews, Gentiles, Protestants and Catholics—could join hands and sing that great spiritual of old.

"Free at last!" she exclaimed, her voice thick with emotion. Still looking up at the royal box, she repeated, "Free at last!"

Diana extended her arms to the Queen Mother as though in supplication. By now tears were streaming down her face. "Great God, almighty!" She couldn't keep her voice from cracking. *"Free at last!"*

As she segued back into the song, Diana never took her eyes off the royal box. She took the microphone from the stand, put it to her mouth, and sang the last few notes while bent over backwards as far as her spine would take her. When the music stopped, she raised both arms into the air and bowed her head. Then the spotlight snapped off—the perfect dramatic gesture.

The applause was immediate. Mary and Cindy bowed and smiled their thanks as they went into the reprise. But Diana stepped back, almost staggering. Her head still bowed and her hair swinging in her face, she began to sing again. By now she was singing so intensely that when she tilted her head back to gaze up at the royal box again, the veins in her neck were clearly visible. Tears streamed down her face.

"Somehow! Someday! Somewhe-e-e-e-re!"

Arms raised. Heads bowed. Stage black. The perfect dramatic gesture—in triplicate.

Traditionally, all members of the royal family are polite but reserved at public performances. However, on this occasion the Queen Mother was not only applauding heartily, she was also the first to her feet. Her diamond tiara sparkled as she nodded her head when the other royals joined the two-minute standing ovation. Those who consider the British unemotional would have had to revise their opinions that night.

At a reception following, the Queen Mother had a few words of small talk and handshakes for all the cast. When it was Diana's turn, the Queen Mother paused longer than usual. As the 68-year-old matriarch and the 24-year-old performer shook hands, their eyes met. Both smiled. No words seemed necessary.

The next day, much of the British press chose to focus their reviews on the Martin Luther King statement. Don Short of *The Daily Mirror* wrote, "The colored Supremes had obviously planned it as a moment of high drama. But the impact was lost. They got the coolest reception of the evening." Perhaps Short had been visiting the loo during the two-minute standing ovation.

Derek Malcolm from *The Guardian* wrote, "It was a rather mawkish tribute that seemed inappropriate for the occasion."

To counter any bad feelings, Motown arranged a press conference. As Mary and Cindy watched, Diana explained, "It wasn't meant to shock people. And it isn't really that revolutionary or militant, if you'll just think about it."

"But, Miss Ross, in front of the royal family?" one reporter asked.

"Why *not* in front of the royal family?"

As the photographers snapped pictures and reporters furiously jotted down her words, she repeated, "Why shouldn't I have said this in front of the royal family? They're human and they must know what's going on in this world as much as anybody else. I didn't say anything bitter. This is more like a prayer. It's something we should all believe, something we should strive for."

A journalist asked about her feelings in regard to The Black and White Minstrels.

"I think it's old-fashioned," she answered quickly. "I'm sure that today's young people don't want minstrel shows. Those shows bring back memories of sadness for colored people."

"Do you agree with the black movement?"

"It's not a black movement," Diana insisted. "It's a *people's* movement. And we should pay attention to activists like Stokely Carmichael. He has a good philosophy. If it wasn't for people like him, things wouldn't be happening for Negroes today. Why should I feel different because of my skin color or why should my brothers and sisters feel different because they have kinky hair and their noses aren't pointed?"

Mary and Cindy nodded their heads. They must have had a few thoughts of their own on the subject, but they had been told not to speak so they didn't.

After a few more questions and answers, Diana stood up, signaling the end of the press conference.

Mary and Cindy also rose, on cue.

Members of the Motown entourage engulfed Diana and attempted to lead her away from the podium, but she pulled away from them.

"I'd just like to add one thing," she said as she approached the microphone again. "James Brown says something and I agree with it. 'I'm black, and I am *proud* of it!' "

The press corps applauded; Diana turned and walked away, smiling.

Just six months ago, she had been nervous and insecure about making a Civil Rights statement on "The Tonight Show." But the previous night she had carried a plea for racial equality to the British royal family. Today, she took on the formidable British press corps and won. In public or in private, nobody would ever call her "nigger" and get away with it again. Nobody was going to make her feel ashamed about being black.

Chapter
🌿12🌿

In late 1968, Berry Gordy came to an agreement with NBC to star Diana Ross and The Supremes in their first network television special, called "T.C.B.—Taking Care of Business." The group would co-star with The Temptations, with whom they recorded a major hit that year, "I'm Gonna Make You Love Me."

A year prior to "T.C.B.," The Supremes and The Temptations had made a joint appearance on "The Ed Sullivan Show." During the Sullivan rehearsals, David Ruffin, The Temptations' lead singer, was excelling in a medley in which the two groups sang each others' hit records. Ruffin was one of the most powerful singers Gordy had ever signed to the label and, with this performance, he was definitely outsinging the label star, Diana Ross. "That's because the key is too low," Diana complained to musical arranger Maurice King.

When she overheard King tell one of The Temptations, "Don't worry about her. She's just pissed because David's embarrassing her," she went to the dressing room and called Gordy in Detroit and complained about "this horrible medley." Five minutes later, King had his orders from Berry: "Raise the key half an octave." When he did so, the entire arrangement was squarely out of Ruffin's range and into Ross'.

"It's sounds a lot better now, don't you think?" Diana asked David.

During rehearsal breaks, Diana always retreated to her dressing room. She never socialized with any of her former peers. Later, she would complain to Berry Gordy, "Those people hate my guts and I don't know why." She was lonely, but she did not seem to know how to rectify her own unhappy situation.

During one lunch break, everyone gathered about a piano on

the stage and, as someone played, Mary and Cindy and the five Temptations sang old doo-wop standards to each other, having a fun time together. In a dark corner Diana sat alone, her legs crossed and her arms folded. Whenever anyone would look her way, she would avert her eyes and act uninterested. But when she didn't think anyone was watching, her mouth would move along to the songs' lyrics and her head would bop up and down to the rhythm. Even the most casual observer could sense her loneliness and isolation. She obviously wanted to join in and be a part of the fun, but she had distanced herself so far from her old friends that now there seemed to be no turning back. So she just sank deeper into her solitude.

Later that day, Martha Reeves and The Vandellas stopped by CBS studios to pick up new musical arrangements from Maurice King. Clustered in the tight hallway together, The Vandellas, The Temptations and two Supremes were enjoying a warm, and also rather noisy, reunion of the old Detroit gang when suddenly Diana's dressing room door swung open.

"Will you all please shut the hell up. I am trying to rest in here!" she exclaimed, and then she slammed the door shut.

"What's *her* problem?" one of The Temptations asked.

"Who the hell cares," one of The Vandellas cracked. Then the loud reunion continued.

For the most part, The Temptations thought that all of the attention Diana received, and the way she handled her burgeoning stardom, was some sort of bad joke. They had to agree that she was a dedicated performer, but since most of them knew her when she was just an emaciated-looking kid in the Brewster Projects, it was difficult for them to think of her as "Miss Ross."

"What's with all of this 'Miss Ross' bullshit?" one of the fellows asked. "And how come I can't get no one to call me Mr. Franklin?"

Still, some of the guys couldn't help but be impressed by Diana, despite any problems they may have had with her. She was an extremely attractive, sexy woman. Beyond that, any performer serious about his craft had to marvel at her talent and versatility even if she was difficult. Diana slapped Eddie Kendricks of The Temptations in front of everyone during one rehearsal—and Kendricks has never said what happened between the two of them to anger her so—but years later he would still be awed by her. When one of the other Temptations said something derogatory about Diana, Eddie jumped to her defense. "She's the *queen*," he said, quite seriously. "And you don't say that kind of stuff about the queen!"

At this time, The Temptations were having their own internal ego problems. David Ruffin decided the time had come for his group to follow The Supremes' lead and rename themselves David Ruffin and The Temptations. Ruffin, preoccupied by his romance with Dean Martin's daughter Jeannie, had grown more independent of his fellow Temptations. He now rode in his own limousine rather than share one with the rest of the group; his singing partners were on the verge of dropping him from the act. Ruffin was certainly a tremendous talent; no one who ever heard the man sing "My Girl" or "Beauty's Only Skin Deep" could disagree. As a solo, he just might have found success. Unfortunately, he was miserably out of step in his bid for fame, especially in trying to parallel his ambition to Diana's. Ruffin's game-plan was missing the crucial elements that made Diana's work so well for her: her versatile, superstar talent and Berry Gordy's support.

When Gordy had a conference with The Temptations to inform them that they would be co-starring in a television special with The Supremes, David had the poor sense to question the show's billing. "Why should it be Diana Ross and The Supremes with The Temptations?" he argued. "How in the hell can that happen? I think it should be David Ruffin and The Temptations with Diana Ross and The Supremes."

A month later, David Ruffin was fired.

Dennis Edwards, a former member of The Contours singing group, was brought into The Temptations' fold; his appearance on "T.C.B." was one of his first with the act. The rehearsals for the show were tense, partly because they were working with a new lead singer, mostly because The Temptations had to face the fact that nothing really mattered except the answers to questions like "Where does Miss Ross stand?" and "What does Miss Ross think?"

Paul Williams of The Temptations told one of the producers, "If it wasn't for me, *Miss Ross* would still be in the Detroit ghetto, and now I can't even have a conversation with her unless I clear it with half a dozen people."

Donald McKayle, who choreographed the program, remembered, "Though I don't think I saw Diana say two words to any of The Temptations, I do recall that she spoke to one of The Supremes . . . once."

McKayle echoed Berry's thoughts about Diana when he said, "The others at Motown were pretty much who they were, but Diane had the actress in her and could create personas at will, and she delighted in doing this. The pressure on her at this time was tremendous. But to my way of thinking, she was mature beyond her years, always there on time—which I couldn't say about the other Supremes or about The Temptations. Not only was she willing to work, she was capable of almost anything—which I also couldn't say about any of the others. She was special, they weren't."

The NBC special aired on December 9, 1968—a treat for the eyes as well as the ears. Gordy and producers George Schlatter and Ed Friendly invested an enormous amount of money in the program for futuristic state-of-the-art Plexiglas staging and dazzling costumes. In the opening, The Supremes sparkled in form-fitting gowns beaded in pink and green. When Diana Ross, with her big, hungry-looking eyes, sang "The Impossible Dream" together with The Supremes and The Temptations, one had to marvel at the fact that these Brewster Projects kids were living an honest-to-goodness, American rags-to-riches dream.

Berry usually encouraged Diana's alienation from her friends by telling her that she was "too good to hang around those clowns, anyway." His control over her in this area was absolute. Perhaps she had days when she resented him for encouraging the bitterness and estrangement that was now a hallmark of her life-style but, except for an occasional weak or vulnerable moment, Diana usually went along with Berry Gordy's suggestions.

Berry had always been attracted to blondes, and when Diana wasn't around, he and his cronies enjoyed talking about "those beautiful blond white girls." He became interested in Chris Clark, an extremely attractive, white California-born singer. He was so smitten with Chris that he signed her to the label. He did so despite the fact that some members of his staff felt her to be just a marginally talented singer. Mostly, the ambivalence about Clark's talent stemmed from the fact that she was white and Gordy's staff was never certain that signing white artists was such a good idea.

"She may be white, but she's got the sound," Berry would say in her defense. Clark had a great commercial style similar to Dusty Springfield's, and Berry was intrigued by her.*

Diana felt she had every reason to dislike this tall, *zaftik* platinum-blonde, especially when she discovered that Gordy was producing some of her music himself. When Rona Jaffe, on as-

---

*Diana needn't have felt threatened where Chris Clark's music was concerned; the total sales of the latter's two Motown singles, "Head to Toe" and "Whisper You Love Me, Boy," would amount to a mere 17,171 copies.

signment for *Cosmopolitan*, covered one of The Supremes' engagements in Puerto Rico, she was warned by a dutiful Motown publicist not to mention Chris Clark's name in Diana's presence. Jaffe had never even heard of Chris Clark, and so she certainly had no reason to bring her up.

Later that day at a meeting Jaffe attended, Berry began praising Clark's latest recordings, her fair-haired beauty, and the company's big-budget plans for her career. "She's gonna be Motown's next major artist," he enthused. As he talked, Diana sat directly behind him watching with disapproval and making faces to demonstrate her distaste. Apparently, one of Berry's bodyguards told him about Diana's reaction. Later, when Berry reprimanded her, she argued that if he had any real respect for her he wouldn't bring up Clark's name, especially in front of a reporter who was there doing a story on *her*.

The next day, Diana made a point of mentioning to Rona Jaffe how much she enjoyed Chris Clark's records and what a wonderful, lovable person she found Clark to be. She rattled on about Clark's attributes for another ten minutes. Jaffe said that she wasn't sure if Diana had done this of her own volition, or whether she was following orders.

"I know one thing," Jaffe reported at the time. "This poor kid won't even allow herself to express the normal emotions, like jealousy; no wonder she hums with tension like an electric wire."

What Diana did not know—luckily for Berry—was that Chris Clark was probably safely tucked away back at the hotel. According to Mary Wilson, at Berry's instructions Chris began following the group's itinerary and popping up wherever they were booked. Berry would have the road managers arrange to reserve Chris' room to his left and Diana's to his right.

Chris, of course, knew of Diana's presence but Diana never knew of hers. Often Berry's guys would pay hotel guests to find other accommodations so that they could make the necessary arrangements. Berry loved Diana but, as he told one of his assistants, "Those blonde chicks, man . . . what can I say? I can't resist 'em."

Diana was always cordial to people who were friends of the Gordy family, and she always scored extra points with Berry when she impressed those who he cared about deeply.

Blues singer Mabel John, the first female Gordy signed to Motown, was still extremely close to Gordy and his mother, Bertha. Diana, of course, had known John for years (since Ross and The Primettes recorded background vocals on her early records) but always regarded her with envy and suspicion, as she did any woman close to Berry Gordy, Jr. Though she had checked with mutual friends, she wasn't sure whether John and Gordy ever had an affair, but she probably suspected that they had.

When Mabel John was first signed to Gordy's company in 1960, the label featured gospel and blues. But by 1964, Gordy's sights were firmly set on the pop charts and, in particular, Diana's cross-over fame. "I had a talk with Berry and he told me that Diana was going to be Motown's major star, not me," John remembered with a note of sadness in her voice. "I'm a realist. I loved Berry very much—I wanted him to be number one—and so I accepted his interest in Diana. In her company, once, Berry told me, 'You are two of the smartest women I know. But there's one difference between you and Diana. Diana knows how smart she is and how to utilize it. You don't.'

"I told him I would always be his friend, but that I wanted out. We both cried. Berry is very sentimental, though he rarely shows that side of him. He told me that he loved me, sent me a bouquet of roses and $1,000 to go shopping. Then he gave me my contract release."

In 1968, Mabel John's brother, the popular blues singer Little Willie John, died in the Washington State Penitentiary of pneumonia. Willie was hailed as one of the best soul singers of the late '50s. James Brown used to serve as his opening act. "I loved that man's voice to death," says Brown. But Willie's life took a violent turn when he was arrested for fatally stabbing a man in a Seattle café brawl. He was sentenced to a long prison term.

Because of his relationship with Mabel, Gordy also felt close to her brother. When Willie died, Gordy apparently told Diana, "I want you to be nice to these people. I love these people— they're family—and I want them to love you, too."

Mabel John recalled the day her brother died: "The first person to call me at my mother's house was Diana Ross. 'I heard you lost your brother,' she told me, 'and I want to know what you want me to do for you.' 'All I want is my brother back,' I cried. 'Well, I can't do that for you, but if there's anything else, call me and it's yours,' she said. Diana and Berry organized the funeral arrangements together, including a 50-car procession, most from the Motown family. The morning of the funeral, I was in my robe and curlers, the house was filled with people, and Diana Ross came swooping in, taking charge. Everyone had to do a double-take, they couldn't believe it was really her."

Mabel was dazed with grief when Diana took her upstairs to the bedroom. She watched helplessly as Diana went through her clothes closet, coordinated an outfit for her and helped her dress. "She assisted me with my make-up and hair," John said. After the services, Diana and Berry took Mabel back to Gordy Manor where they unwound in the pool. "Diana did everything she could to take my mind off my tragedy and were it not for her I would never have gotten through that day."

During this time, Berry brought a new young lady into the fold, an aggressive, very attractive 21-year-old black woman named Suzanne Celeste dePasse, a Syracuse University dropout who had worked as a talent coordinator for Cheetah, New York's "in" spot of the day. Suzanne, of the long flowing dark hair and impeccable taste in clothes, was a friend of Cindy Birdsong. Birdsong had introduced her to Gordy while The Supremes were working the Copa; at first he thought she was a go-go dancer. DePasse's family was said to have been a part of Harlem's black elite; the theater, ballet, museums and circus were all part of her early life. As a young adult, she traveled by limousine wherever she went at night, rented at $8.00 an hour on her $125-a-week salary, "because New York cabbies were reluctant to pick up blacks after dark."

Gordy was fascinated by this gorgeous woman, partly because she reminded him of his aggressive, bright sisters. Suzanne was educated in the best schools (her grandfather was a physician, her father a Seagram's executive, her mother a teacher) and she somehow knew which buttons to push to impress Berry. In about a year, dePasse and her trusty steno pad had infiltrated his organization. At first, Gordy had her secreted away in his New York office with little to do.

One day, she called to ask exactly what her job was.

"What do you think I am, stupid?" Gordy stormed. "When I have something for you to do, I'll let you know."

After that call, before anyone knew what was happening—or why—Suzanne dePasse had started making important decisions on Gordy's behalf. However, it was not easy for her. She remembered "crying all the time" while trying to fit into the clannish Gordy structure: "He would say to me: 'This will either make you or break you,' and sometimes I was convinced it would break me."

At first, Diana didn't know whether or not to be jealous. "And what's her job supposed to be?" she asked Gordy one day.

"Never mind that, you just do yours," he told her.

During rehearsal for "T.C.B." Diana discussed a wardrobe

problem with designer Michael Travis one afternoon when Suzanne dePasse burst into her dressing room and asked her a question.

"Hey. You wait just a moment," Diana snapped at her. "Can't you see that I'm busy? I will talk to you later."

"Oh, I'm so sorry, Miss Ross," dePasse said, bowing out of the room. "Please forgive me."

"Ay yi yi," Suzanne remembered, "I couldn't get that girl to talk to me."

(Today, over two decades later, Suzanne dePasse is the president of Motown Productions and one of the most powerful women in Hollywood.)

Friends of Diana say that she was sure Gordy and dePasse were somehow romantically involved, but that she could never prove it. Diana could not be certain of their relationship, especially since everyone thought it odd that Gordy would elevate a female so quickly to Motown's upper echelons. Diana's insecurity about Suzanne was compounded by the fact that she was so utterly intimidated by this woman's self-confidence and business savvy. Whenever Suzanne and Berry would discuss company business, Diana would stand on the sidelines and watch suspiciously.

Eventually, she decided to befriend Suzanne dePasse. Perhaps she thought that if she and dePasse were friendly she would be able to keep her eye on what was happening with Berry. So befriend dePasse she did, with a vengeance, by monopolizing her time and ignoring the fact that Suzanne was also Cindy's friend. Suddenly, anyone who worked for the group heard "Me and Suzanne this" and "Me and Suzanne that."

For dePasse, befriending the boss' girlfriend could only solidify her standing at Motown. But she insists today that there was no sexual relationship between herself and Gordy. "Berry Gordy and I were not lovers," she stated emphatically. "Everyone in Detroit thought I was his girlfriend. But I would never have had to work so hard if I had been his old lady."

Cindy must have known that she'd lost Suzanne dePasse's loyalty on the day that Suzanne betrayed a confidence. "I told her that I hated Diane," Cindy said, "and as soon as I said it I was sorry I had uttered the words. Diane had just driven me to the edge, and I was speaking out of emotion. I felt that she didn't care about me, that her world was centered around herself." When Suzanne shared that bit of information with Diana, it only served to drive a wedge further between Diana and Cindy. (It is one of life's small ironies that, 15 years later, Cindy Birdsong would find herself working a nine-to-five job as an assistant to Suzanne dePasse at Motown Productions.)

Diana Ross and The Supremes embarked on a month-long European concert tour in the winter of 1969, and when they returned, Berry Gordy's plans for Diana's solo career began to solidify. He booked her to make solo television appearances, first on a Dinah Shore television special called "Like Hep" and then on "Rowan and Martin's Laugh-In." Diana had become accustomed to working on television with show business stalwarts like Sammy Davis, Jr., Ethel Merman and Bob Hope. "What I'm most sad about today is that I didn't keep any photographs or scrapbooks," she said in 1985. "Now I wish I had."

Gordy used to encourage her to watch Sammy Davis and Bobby Darin perform so that she could see how to work an audience and overcome stage fright. "He wanted me to see how natural they were and learn from that. I used to get so nervous when I'd be on stage, I'd turn into a big knot," she said.

But some of show biz's old guard were not very gracious in welcoming Diana to the ranks. Bing Crosby, who had recorded some of his best songs with The Andrews Sisters, was particularly chilly when The Supremes appeared on his 1969 television special. One set insider on "Like Hep," said "Lucy [Ball] and Dinah gave Diana hell. They treated her like a real novice, took advantage of her inexperience at comedy and tried to make her feel inadequate."

The Supremes also hosted the popular "Hollywood Palace" television show for ABC—actually Diana did the hosting and the girls, whom she referred to in a sketch as "the other two McGuire Sisters," joined her now and then for a number. Ethel Waters, a memorable guest on the program, sang a duet with Diana on the old blues song "Bread and Gravy." Whenever the group appeared on Ed Sullivan's program, they continued to introduce new Motown music. At the same time, Diana became more versatile. She was called upon to learn songs by such diverse composers as Fats Waller, Cole Porter and Irving Berlin for television appearances. It wasn't all easy work, but she certainly made it appear that way.

Diana Ross and The Supremes opened a two-week sold-out engagement at the Latin Casino in Cherry Hill, New Jersey, on June 2, 1969. Berry decided to visit the group, supposedly because of rumors that Diana was secretly dating Tim Brown, a football star with the Philadelphia Eagles. In truth, it wasn't a serious relationship. Brown, now an actor, has said, "I can hardly remember anything at all about Diana Ross. It's all a dim memory to me.''

Even taking into account that Brown might be chivalrously defending a lady's honor, Diana, had she been serious, certainly would not have used the local promotion men in Philadelphia to act as intermediaries for her "rendezvous" with him. It seems more likely she wanted word to get back to Berry and make him jealous.

She succeeded.

On the morning of July 6, Berry exploded in her hotel room at the Rickshaw Inn where The Supremes were staying. "He was furious with Diana and had a huge fight with her," said a friend of Gordy's. "He shouted at her, 'How dare you make a fool of me?' Anyone on the same floor could hear this going on.

" 'What kind of relationship is this, anyway?' I heard Diana shout back. 'You date other people. Well, so can I!'

" 'The hell you can see other men. It's over between you and the football player, as of now. You'll be sorry you did this. Just wait and see!' ''

Although the tension between them was apparent, Berry was backstage for both shows that evening.

Years before, Mary and Florence had decided to buy Yorkshire terrier puppies to keep them company while on tour. When Cindy joined the group, too, she got a terrier. Diana never cared about animals before, but when she saw how popular their dogs had become on the road, she decided that she simply had to have not one, but two animals—a Maltese named Tiffany and a Yorkie called Little Bit. Mary and Cindy kept their dogs leashed or locked in their hotel or dressing rooms. Diana let hers run free.

The first show at the Latin Casino went off without a hitch. So did the midnight show, until it came time for the encore. After their performance of "You're Nobody Till Somebody Loves You," The Supremes were to make a "fake exit" and then return to ovations and their encore finale. As always, Wilson and Birdsong exited stage left, Diana stage right. As soon as Diana was offstage, she let out an ear-piercing scream. The audience, of course, heard her and immediately thought one of the girls had been injured, especially when they heard an announcement asking for a doctor in the house.

It was not one of The Supremes. Diana had found Tiffany and Little Bit staggering in the wings, shaking and vomiting.

"What's wrong with them? What's wrong? This is *your fault*, Joe Shaffner," Diana shouted at the group's road manager. "You should have kept an eye on these damn animals!"

Sobbing, she picked up Tiffany, who died in her arms. "Call an ambulance. Call an ambulance."

One of the Motown entourage suggested that the dogs might have ingested rat poison left on the floor in her dressing room.

"Rat poison," Diana shrieked. "There are innocent animals around here. Where are the warnings? There should be signs. I'm suing this place."

By now the scene turned chaotic. Diana was screaming and the Motown entourage and fans were milling about, trying to discover what was happening and to help, if they could.

Berry tried to reason with her. "Now Diane . . ." he began.

"Don't you now-Diane me," her voice rose. "I want to leave. I'm not performing here again, Berry. Ever! Pack my stuff. I'm leaving!"

"I'll help you," one of her fans offered, following her into the dressing room.

"Not that way, this way!" She pushed him aside, grabbed the garment he was folding, and threw it on the chair.

By now, Dave Dushoff, owner of the Latin Casino, appeared. "Miss Ross, I don't see why you can't continue," he said, obviously trying to calm her down. "Listen, we had a very famous singer here recently whose mother died." And he continued, "These are only dogs."

"Only dogs." Her voice rose an octave. "*Only dogs.* Berry, get my coat."

Berry scurried about trying to find her fur wrap. As Mary, Cindy, road manager Sye MacArthur, assistant manager Joe Shaffner, and the rest watched, Berry and Diana left. When someone suggested that perhaps the other two girls could finish the engagement without her, a Motown aide said, "No way in the world. Forget it." Cindy and Mary just looked at each other and shrugged.

The next morning, Berry called a group meeting in Diana's room. "Berry told us that we weren't going to complete the engagement because Diane didn't want to," Cindy Birdsong recalled. "We talked about the possibility of being sued. We agreed that we weren't going to say anything at all to the press about the incident, and then that was it. We just packed up and left very abruptly."

"You guys go wherever you want," Berry told Mary and Cindy. "I'm taking Diane back to L.A. with me."

Dave Dushoff held a press conference. "She left without calling the management, without saying good-bye, without our knowledge. She tore her contract to shreds, did everything to it in the whole world. There was nothing for us to do but close down."

The Supremes were going to be paid $55,000 for the two-week engagement. (Twenty years later, Diana would make at least twice that for a single performance.) Even though Motown would lose money, the Latin Casino would lose a lot more. The supper club had a capacity of 4,000 people and was sold out with reservations for two shows every night for the remaining 10 nights. It was the final engagement of the season before closing for the summer; food worth many thousands of dollars spoiled. The Latin Casino sued and eventually settled with Motown years later. Diana Ross never appeared there again.

Her actions might have had as much to do with exhaustion as with grief. "Sometimes I find myself working so hard I get tired from the outside in," she once complained. Still, she was a professional, and for a professional the show must go on.

"That was very poor behavior," recalled Taylor Cox, who contracted the engagement for Motown. "There have been artists who carried on and performed with problems much worse than dying dogs. And, yet, if you knew Diane it would not surprise you that this is what she'd do. It was completely within her character—unthinking, unfeeling and showing a complete disregard of the problems her actions created for others. We had a hell of a time cleaning up that mess."

The week after the dogs' deaths, Joe Shaffner bought Diana another white Maltese which she wouldn't let out of her sight and would smuggle onto airplanes, usually in her fox stole.

Touring for The Supremes continued half-heartedly throughout 1969 as they fulfilled contractual commitments. By now, Mary and Cindy were fully prepared for Diana's leaving, even though she never once discussed it with them. The girls read about her and Gordy's plans in newspaper accounts just like everyone else. Without actually explaining to her that Diana was leaving, Berry informed Mary one day in June that he had found a replacement. He and Shelly Berger had found Jean Terrell performing in a group at the Fontainebleau Hotel in Miami Beach, Florida, and signed her to the label as a solo artist before deciding to drop her into The Supremes. Mary and Cindy accepted this decision and just waited to see what would happen next.

Gordy hoped to make it appear that everyone involved was happy and that the separation was an amicable one. His press agents immediately released the information that Terrell would be joining The Supremes, along with the untrue story that Diana was helping Jean "learn the complicated and effervescent style of The Supremes."

In September 1969, Diana Ross and The Supremes taped another television special with The Temptations, "G.I.T. on Broadway," which would air two months later. Produced by George Schlatter, the special was a rather dreary affair heightened only by a wonderful medley of "Leading Lady" songs that Diana performed with typical vivacity—songs made famous by the likes of Ethel Merman ("Everything's Coming Up Roses") and, of course, Barbra Streisand ("People"). The medley was masterfully coordinated by Billy Barnes and Earl Brown, both "special material" writers who obviously knew of some of Diana's secret aspirations. Costumes were designed by Bob Mackie.

Mackie, who still designs for Diana, recalled, "With every costume I designed for her in that medley, Berry Gordy told me to try to create the impression that she originated the role on Broadway. I got the impression that he and she both wish she had." There was no doubt left in anyone's mind that Diana had long outgrown The Supremes and any possibilities the group could afford her.

By that fall, Berry Gordy had moved to the Hollywood Hills into the former home of comedian Tommy Smothers. Motown still had its offices in Detroit—and Gordy maintained the three-story, million-dollar mansion he owned at Boston and Hamilton in Detroit—but now he was living thousands of miles away. "I've had it with Detroit," he told one friend. "There's too much going on here."

Earlier in the year, Berry had invited a group of visitors to Gordy Manor in Detroit, including a member of one of his female singing groups. They found the place in complete disarray. It had obviously been ransacked. The Persian rugs were muddled and some of the expensive paintings that decorated the walls had been slashed (but not the one Berry's sister Esther commissioned of Berry as Napoleon Bonaparte). Most alarming, the marbled fireplace and frescoed ceiling had been splattered with what appeared to be blood.

"I don't know for sure that it was real blood, or even human blood," recalled the singer who witnessed this scene. "Berry immediately rushed us all out of the room, and then out of the house. No one I know had the rest of the story, or a full understanding of what that episode was all about. The next day I saw

Berry and he acted as if nothing had happened. I didn't ask any questions.''

Later, it was rumored that one of Berry's house pets was killed by the intruders, which might account for the blood on the walls. But what happened at Gordy Manor—and more importantly, *why*—is an unsolved mystery.

At this time, most Detroiters familiar with show business whispered among themselves about "Motown's dark secrets," and anytime anything unusual happened at Hitsville, it became the talk of the town. In February 1969, the *Sunday Free Press* reported that there had been a shooting at Motown that terrorized an entire department and that one of Gordy's female employees had quit as a result. Stories of murder and mayhem at Motown spread like wildfire and Berry was angry. He felt that Motown was already suffering from poor public relations because of some of the other stories that had been circulating and that, as a result of this latest one, even business associates would be afraid to go to the company for meetings.

"Agents will not want to sign their people to Motown," he reasoned. "They'll say, 'If I go up there for a meeting, I might get shot.' "

Gordy's version of the shooting was that a sharp crack was heard in a room where ten women were doing secretarial work. The women shrieked and scattered about, believing they were being shot at. Berry said that the Detroit police were called. An investigation revealed a hole in a window, big enough, Gordy said, to be made by a BB, but too small to be the result of a bullet. The police were unable to find the object that made the hole, and nobody quit as a result of the incident.

"It's rough in Detroit," Berry reasoned. "It's really rough."

But life 2,000 miles away in Los Angeles was also not without its problems. On the night of December 2, 1969, Cindy Birdsong returned home to her Hollywood apartment after rehearsing with Mary and Diana's replacement, Jean. She was greeted by her boyfriend Charles Hewlett, who had keys to the apartment, and one of his buddies. When Cindy went into the bedroom to change her clothes, she found an intruder waiting for her. A desperate white man in his late twenties, with a crazed look in his eyes and, wielding two butcher knives from her kitchen, pushed her back into the living room. Apparently he had been hiding while Cindy's boyfriend was waiting for her in the apartment. Holding a knife at Birdsong's throat, the man forced her to bind her guests' hands behind their backs with their ties and then dragged

Cindy, kicking and screaming, out of the building and into her car.

With Cindy in the passenger seat, her kidnapper began to drive along the Long Beach Freeway for what Cindy described as "30 minutes of terror." Traveling at high speed, the two struggled in the car, his knife slicing all of her fingers on both hands. He threatened her with what was going to happen after he met up with two of his friends. In a moment of desperation, Cindy opened the car door and leaped into the cold, dark night. She hit the hard concrete of the freeway and rolled down a dirt embankment.

Though panic-stricken, Cindy Birdsong kept her wits about her and realized that if she ran in the direction of oncoming traffic, her assailant wouldn't be able to follow her unless he exited the freeway first. Hoping to buy some time before he pursued her again, she tried to flag down passing motorists but cars just whizzed by; no one would stop to help. Fortunately, two California highway patrolmen noticed the bleeding woman crying hysterically and running down the side of the road. She was taken to Long Beach Hospital where she required stitches and other treatment for her cuts and bruises.

When Berry Gordy was awakened in the middle of the night with the news that "one of the girls has been kidnapped," his first thought was probably "Thank God it's not Diane!" She certainly would have been the more obvious victim. Gordy intimates say that he was certain the attack was somehow directed toward him, that someone was trying to either get to him through one of The Supremes, or teach him a lesson by grabbing one of his "girls." Gordy was especially tense because the Sharon Tate murder by the Manson "family" had happened only three months earlier, and just miles from where he was living. Immediately, security was beefed up at his home until the next day when Charles Collier, Cindy's kidnapper, was apprehended.

"When Berry realized that the attack probably wasn't directed at him, he was relieved, but shaken up just the same," recalled a former associate. "Berry always had this intense paranoia that someone was after him. No one really knew why he was so scared, but all of us in the inner circle knew something was very wrong in his life."

Collier eventually surrendered to authorities in Las Vegas the next day. He was an ex-convict on an alcohol and drug binge. When asked why he kidnapped Birdsong, he responded, "for the money." Though Gordy seemed certain there was more to the story than what Collier had explained, it appeared from all available evidence that the kidnapper had been working alone. He was apparently just a loser who was going to hold Cindy captive for ransom.

Cindy would be released from the hospital in time for Diana Ross and The Supremes' final appearance together on "The Ed Sullivan Show" later in the month. On the day of her release, there was a small party in her room. Diana had a drink in one hand and a cigarette in the other. She walked over to Cindy, who was obviously still shaken, and asked her, "Well, did he try to rape you?"

"No," Cindy said, "he didn't."

"He didn't?" Diana pushed.

"Well, I asked him if he was gong to rape me," Cindy recalled, "and he laughed at me. 'Hell no, I'm not gonna rape you,' he said. 'Don't flatter yourself.' "

Diana's eyes widened and her mouth dropped open. "He told you *that*?" she asked incredulously. "The nerve of him! *I* would have slapped his face!"

After the first reports in the press about the kidnapping, nothing more was ever published about the matter. "It was all quieted down by Berry," Cindy said. "He had the power to do that, I suppose. There was nothing about the court case in the papers. To my knowledge, not a single word. Motown wanted to forget it happened. I was afraid to face the kidnapper in court, but decided that I must. When I finally saw him again—after having months of nightmares about the guy—I must say I felt sorry for him. He was just so pitiful. He was convicted [of kidnapping, armed robbery and felonious joy riding] and thrown into jail, but nobody outside of the immediate 'family' ever knew what happened to the guy."

Berry was in Los Angeles when Bobby Taylor brought to Motown a group of youngsters calling themselves Jackson 5. Taylor was a Motown artist whose biggest claim to fame should have been his discovery of 10-year-old Michael Jackson but it was a distinction of which he would be robbed. The group's father, Joe Jackson, drove his youngsters from Gary, Indiana, to Detroit in a bus for the audition. Since Berry wasn't available, their audition was videotaped at the Greystone Ballroom nightclub.

The tape was sent back to Gordy, who was extremely enthusiastic about the boys and decided to sign them to the label.

Berry hadn't been this excited about an act since the day The Supremes hit Number One on the charts. For their age, Michael Jackson and Jackson 5, which is how Berry Gordy originally intended to bill them until father Joe drew the line, were truly an explosive little band of entertainers. Gordy flew them out to Los Angeles and lifted their spirits by telling them they were going to be "the biggest recording group in history." He predicted then that they would have three Number One records in a row. They ended up having four.

Gordy felt that he needed some sort of promotional hook to introduce Jackson 5 to the public, and his strategy was to associate them with Diana Ross. At first, she didn't understand why he wanted to lie to the world and claim that she had personally discovered the boys in Gary, Indiana. Certainly Bobby Taylor also had questions along those lines. When Diana met the boys, however, she thought they were so adorable and talented, and was so taken with them that she decided not to question Berry's judgment.

Diana then hosted a party in honor of Jackson 5 at the Daisy Club in Hollywood. She told the 300 guests, including press members, that she discovered the group while touring with The Supremes. Wearing a British bowler over his Afro-style hair, 10-year-old Michael Jackson explained, "I had just about given up hope. I thought I was going to be an old man before being discovered, but along came Miss Diana Ross to save my career." Young Michael was learning about show biz hype at a very early age.

Diana later introduced Jackson 5 as a supporting act on The Supremes' show at the Forum in Los Angeles on August 16. That appearance was followed by the boys' first national audience when she and The Supremes hosted "Hollywood Palace" in October 1969.

Gordy decided to use Diana's name to promote Jackson 5's first album, which he allowed Bobby Taylor to produce. Diana also wrote the liner notes to the album, *Diana Ross Presents Jackson 5*. "Honesty has always been a very special word for me . . ." she began. Then she wrote that Mayor Richard Hatch of Gary, Indiana, brought the boys to her attention.

Diana thought that would be the end of her involvement with Jackson 5. But a year later, she would discover that Gordy arranged for little Michael Jackson to move into her house.

By then, Diana had already relocated to the West Coast. Mary, Cindy and Berry all had homes in Los Angeles at the end of 1969. Flo was still living in Detroit. Berry arranged for Diana to lease a house in the Hollywood Hills as he searched for a permanent home for her. The first order of business, however, was to pull Diana out of The Supremes. The official announcement was made by Motown's press department in October:

"Diana will strike out on her own as a single star."

"You know, to be honest, Mary and I never really thought Diane would leave," Cindy Birdsong recalled. "We really didn't believe it. Or maybe we didn't *want* to believe it because who knew what it meant for us, really. I don't even think we were told. I'm almost sure we read about it in the papers."

During those last few months, Diana was annoyed when Mary Wilson and Cindy Birdsong distanced themselves from her while they planned for their own futures. It was one matter for Diana and Berry to separate themselves from everyone—as they had done for over two years now. But Diana became nonplussed when her singing partners started making it clear by their indifference toward her that they couldn't wait for her to become "a single star."

"To say we were anxious is an understatement," Mary Wilson said. "By this time, Cindy and I had been rehearsing with Jean and were excited about the prospects of the new Supremes. Anything we had to do with Diana—farewell appearances or whatever—was just a matter of formality none of us wanted to bother with. But Berry insisted we go out with a bang, even though we already felt we'd gone out with a whimper."

The "whimper" Mary Wilson referred to was the sound made by the group's recordings of the last year. More than anything, Berry wanted Diana Ross and The Supremes to have a Number One single as their farewell effort, which was easier said than done.*

Diana had been complaining to Berry that she wanted to make some final decisions about her future career. The fact that Mary and Cindy now seemed to despise her was finally beginning to bother her, and she was pressuring Berry to do something about it. Berry called a staff meeting of writers and producers, slammed his fist on his desk, and said, "Goddammit! I want Diane out of this group and we got to have a hit or she ain't goin' nowhere."

---

*By this time, The Supremes were considered passé by most radio station music programmers, partly because the material Gordy had ordered released by them after "Love Child" was just not up to par. Two singles recorded with The Temptations in 1969, and another produced by Smokey Robinson—which sold barely 200,000 copies—didn't amount to much. Berry even produced a number for the girls—rather, *girl*, since Mary and Cindy were not on the release—called "No Matter What Sign You Are." That, too, was a disappointment, #31 on the pop charts, and not even 300,000 sales.

Someone suggested releasing "Someday We'll Be Together" written by Johnny Bristol, a tune Diana had recorded earlier. Berry had planned it as one of her first solo records, not as a Supremes song. On "Someday," Diana was backed by a choir of voices that only the most naïve fan would have ever taken for Wilson and Birdsong. Still, this was a superior record—a gospel-flavored mid-tempo arrangement with a composed, easy-going delivery from Diana—and it began climbing the charts as soon as it was released in October. Eventually, it would become a Number One record, the biggest song of their career (over two million copies eventually sold) and the fourth instant million-seller recorded by Diana as a member of The Supremes, including "Where Did Our Love Go" and "You Can't Hurry Love" and "Love Child." ("I'm Gonna Make You Love Me" [with The Temptations] also sold a million.)*

A final appearance on Ed Sullivan's show was scheduled for December 21, 1969. Wearing gold lamé and chiffon gowns with dolman sleeves, the girls sang a fast-paced, exciting medley of their hits and then "Someday We'll Be Together." Sullivan had certainly been good to The Supremes over the years—12 appearances in all—and this was an appropriate forum for their last TV appearance together. As they performed, the girls seemed tired and not as enthusiastic as they'd been on past Sullivan efforts. Still, there were a few sad glances among them during the last number. Sullivan announced that "Diana Ross will continue her career as a solo star." No mention was made of Mary or Cindy's future.

As Diana finished the song, she began walking toward the television camera and, because of an odd shooting angle, it seemed that Mary and Cindy literally shrunk away behind her.

The group opened in early January 1970 in Las Vegas at the Frontier Hotel. A live album was then recorded over three nights

*Other Supremes singles that sold a million copies or more during the time of their original release were "Where Did Our Love Go?" "You Can't Hurry Love" and "Love Child." "I'm Gonna Make You Love Me," which they recorded with The Temptations, also sold a million. Though Motown's sales figures are said to be incomplete, it seems that "Baby Love," "Come See About Me," "Stop! in the Name of Love" and "You Keep Me Hanging On" probably all eventually sold a million copies as years of sales were tallied, but they were not million-sellers during the time of their original releases. Press hype to the contrary, other famous Supremes singles—like "Back in My Arms Again," "Nothing But Heartaches," "Love Is Here and Now You're Gone" and "Reflections"—did not even come close to selling a million; most sold roughly half that much.

of performances with Diana at the Frontier Hotel. Produced by Deke Richards, it would be issued with the title *Farewell*.

"The nights we were recording the *Farewell* album were extremely tense," Cindy Birdsong recalled. "Mary and I knew that this was going to be the end of something, but we didn't know exactly of what. In those last days, we never saw Diane, but Mary and I knew that she was elated about leaving. It made it rough to perform with her. None of us was happy, yet we had to project happiness to our audiences. The last show with Diane was particularly difficult to get through."

Diana Ross and The Supremes' final performance took place on January 14, 1970.

Onstage in the Music Hall of the Frontier Hotel at 11:30 P.M., ventriloquist Willie Tyler scolded his dummy Lester and ripples of laughter spread through the room. In the wings, witnesses recall, Diana Ross waited, nervously toying with a cigarette. She took a heavy drag, exhaled and then waved the cigarette from her mouth with a theatrical gesture. The glare of the spot made it impossible for her to see beyond the stage into the audience, but she must have known there was a full house. She dropped the cigarette to the floor and ground the butt with her high-heeled shoe.

Her face was pensive in the semi-darkness. Seen up close and without the smile, wearing heavy stage make-up, she looked tired and older than her 25 years. The last few years, in particular, had not been easy ones. She sighed and gave a half-hearted wave to band leader Gil Askey when he held up 10 fingers to indicate that it was 10 minutes till showtime.

Meanwhile, in their dressing room, Mary Wilson and Cindy Birdsong were sharing a bottle of champagne. Before leaving, they took a quick look in the mirror to check their make-up. Long red fingernails fluffed out, then smoothed down elaborate wigs. A glance over the shoulder made sure the back view was right.

"Well, this is it," Cindy has remembered saying. "I don't know about you, but I feel sad and happy all at the same time."

"Me, too."

"It must be harder for you. You've been in it from the very beginning."

Mary shrugged. "Hey, don't talk like this is a wake. Just because *she's* leaving doesn't mean we're dying. This is a happy night. The Supremes aren't dead." She poured the remaining champagne into their two glasses. "Come on, we can finish this while we wait."

As they left their dressing room, they saw that Diana had been joined by Berry Gordy and that the two were engaged in deep conversation. Berry's back was toward them. Diana's arms were around his neck. He was holding her waist. Diana glanced up, saw Mary and Cindy, but gave no sign of recognition.

"You're a star, baby. This is your night. Forget about the girls," Berry said to Diana just as Mary and Cindy walked by.

Cindy looked at Mary. Mary said nothing, but by the way she straightened her shoulders, it was obvious that she had heard.

Willie Tyler was offstage by now. Houselights dimmed. Spots flashed on. Cue music played.

Diana Ross entered from stage right.

Out of darkness. Into light. Into applause.

She flashed her megawatt smile.

Mary Wilson and Cindy Birdsong entered from stage left.

Their smiles, too, were brilliant.

Diana, Mary and Cindy, all together now, looked for all the world like best friends forever as they started right out by taking care of business with the song "T.C.B." that segued into "Stop! In the Name of Love." The audience cheered as The Supremes outstretched their arms like traffic cops. Only no cops ever looked like this: pearls and gold braid punctuated the low-cut vees of black velvet dresses, trumpet-shaped skirts flared out at the knees to liquefy every step, and sleeves embellished with gold-sequin paisley bedazzled. This was glamour with a capital G, and the audience loved it.

Bathed in three soft beams of blue light, the women sponged up energy from the crowd and performed a medley of their best-selling songs. The music was arranged in a big band Las Vegas style—there were horns and strings where they shouldn't have been any—and had little in common with the recorded versions that became popular. But the songs—"Come See About Me," "My World Is Empty Without You" and "Baby Love"—were charged with memories just the same and the die-hard fans in the house applauded the beginning of each one.

By the time the group finished "The Lady Is a Tramp," this audience of over a thousand people—celebrities, special invited guests of Motown, friends and family—clapped, really clapped, none of that pitty-pat-ten-fingers-barely-touching kind of noise.

"Thank you, thank you, thank you," Diana cooed.

And then it was time for Mary's solo number, "Can't Take

My Eyes Off of You." Mary bit into the song as though it was her last meal.

"You're awful nice. Now get back to your microphone," Diana said when Mary was done. Everyone laughed.

By half-past midnight the show was strictly high voltage. "My Man" put on the brakes, giving some in the audience a chance to exchange knowing looks and snide remarks, a reference to the sepia Streisand was probably the least offensive. Some viewed it as the first of several songs—love songs except for "Hey, Big Spender"—meant exclusively for Berry Gordy. Diana walked off the stage and down the center aisle where she delivered "My Man" with passion and longing to Berry at his table. "For whatever my man is, I am his," she sang to him unashamedly.

As the show proceeded, cigarette smoke drifted in front of the spots and gave them a hazy, blue look. Drinks were refilled before the ice even had a chance to melt. And with a fine sense of irony as the applause for "Love Child" died down, Diana chose *that* moment to introduce "the people who go way, way back for us, our mothers."

The spot found Mary and Cindy's mothers with no trouble at all. Diana's was nowhere to be found.

"Mama, where are you?" Diana cried out in a little girl's voice. "You're not there?" The spotlight crisscrossed the room.

She had always been able to count on Ernestine. "Mama, where are you?"

The crowd's embarrassment was almost palatable. Diana's smile grew even brighter. Someone from the Motown table shouted, "She's probably trying to make it the hard way." That gambling reference broke the tension. "The devil made her do it," Mary volunteered as people laughed.

"I'm so sad," Diana said, still smiling, smiling, smiling, tossing her head back so they'd know she wasn't really sad, not tonight. "Anyway, my brother's here."

Later, Diana told the crowd, "We're going to groove together" as she glided off the stage and into the audience. Despite the fact that some of the spectators she was about to face had long memories, smiles masked personal hurts and animosities. You are all my brothers and sisters, the incredible Ross smile seemed to say. Disarm with charm. No one would dare argue tonight, not in public, not to her face. Tonight they would sing "Let the Sunshine In" whenever she asked.

On stage, Mary and Cindy were on about the 25th chorus repeat by the time Diana strutted over to where Smokey Robinson and his wife Claudette were sitting.

"Join in, Claudette." Diana stood over her. Claudette's grip tightened on her glass. Her frozen smile was almost as bright as Diana's. "You gotta sing," Diana insisted, holding the mike out to her.

Claudette stood up next to her. "Let the sunshine, let the sunshine in," she sang in a sweet, clear voice before Diana chimed in.

"You could have been the lead singer of The Supremes, Claudette," Diana said after she and Smokey's wife finished their brief duet.

"I tried."

Diana smiled.

"Come on, Smokey, you sing now." He stood up and obliged without hesitation.

Diana turned away with one more parting shot to Claudette. "Show him how much I love him."

Claudette said nothing.

"Let the sunshine in."

Diana announced, "Marvin Gaye! Before I go to this cat, I have to go to his wife because she accepted me as one of her family. I am now a part of the Gordy family. I am a sister. And I want all of my sisters to sing with me."

Berry's sister Esther went first. The others hesitated. Sister Anna looked at her husband Marvin's stony face.

Diana insisted, "Come on, Anna. Let the sunshine in! Come on, Gwen," she said to Berry's third sister. "You know you could have been one of The Supremes, too. Okay, Mr. Gaye. You stand up."

As soon as Marvin Gaye let loose with his improvised chorus, hands started clapping. Diana laughed, a silvery peal.

"I'm your biggest fan, you know that," she said. Then she whipped the mike out of his hand. "Is that Dick Clark over there? Let's make *him* sing."

"Let the sunshine in."

"And there's Steve Allen."

"Let the sunshine in."

By now, they had all become a part of it. The whole room was madly involved, people jumping up and starting to sing without even being asked. Diana wound her way back to the stage, all the while moving, singing, clapping.

"One more time," she shouted.

And they kept on singing, stomping. The Music Hall of the Frontier Hotel reverberated with the fervor of an old-fashioned gospel meeting. This was a magic fusion of star and audience, again with Diana Ross in command. No matter what some of the people in the crowd felt about her, they couldn't help but want more, and the explosion of "Let the Sunshine In" was so intense it made everything that followed anticlimactic—"The Impossible Dream," "Someday We'll Be Together," a telegram from Ed Sullivan and a rambling address by the senator from Nevada. (In his speech, he noted that the success The Supremes have enjoyed is an example of what can happen when people don't rely on backstabbing and hypocrisy.)

When Diana Ross brought Berry Gordy up to the stage, the audience gave him a thunderous standing ovation. He embraced Diana and kissed her passionately. Cindy approached him. He grabbed her by the waist and kissed her gently on the cheek. Then he went over to Mary and hugged her. Tears were streaming down her face as she and Berry held one another for what seemed like an unusually long time. When he went to kiss her on the cheek, she turned abruptly and startled him by kissing him squarely on the lips. He broke free of her embrace, just as Diana walked over to stand next to him. Flustered, he hurried back to his seat.

Jean Terrell, the woman who had been selected to replace Diana Ross in the group, was then brought onto the stage. "I think she should be here right now," Diana said. Jean was dressed in black polyester crepe with gold brocade sleeves, a poor imitation of the exquisite gowns the others were wearing. With the four women posing together, never losing their smiles and holding bouquets of roses, the photographers at the edge of the stage could not contain their enthusiasm. Their shutters sounded like live crabs clicking, clicking, clicking.

As the audience craned their necks to catch one final glimpse of the glowing Supremes, the curtain dropped and the glow vanished.

"It was all acting," Cindy Birdsong would confess later, "the smiles, the tears, all of it. Just acting. Afterwards, there was a big scene backstage—an argument over something I don't remember."

No one would have suspected any sort of problem as the Motown entourage entered the Cabaret Room for a farewell party, complete with a cake that looked like a record of "Someday We'll Be Together." A journalist from United Press International poked a tape recorder in front of Diana's face, and she said, "What a meaningful evening this is for us all. Really it is," before Berry pushed it away. Another reporter, from *Soul* magazine, later wrote, "Diana, Mary, Cindy and Jean moved into a booth and toasted each other with champagne, displaying much love all around.''

Mary left almost immediately. Cindy recalled: "I went along for protocol, but Mary's attitude was 'If that's the end then let's end it.' Jean [Terrell] was there for a while and then it was just me and Diane and the photographers. I remember watching Diane and wondering how she was feeling. Was she relieved? Was she happy? Was she sad? I really had no idea. To work with someone for so long and then really not know what was going through her mind on this important night, well, I guess it said a lot more than I care to remember.''

As the party broke up, a group of agents and managers followed Diana to the tables. Berry, who usually loved to gamble, did not join them. "You go ahead," he told them. "I gotta think.''

Berry seemed to be mulling over the events of the evening and one of his aides remembered that Jean Terrell was on his mind.

Berry headed for the house phone. It was 3:00 A.M. After trying her luck at the tables, Mary had gone to her room with a bottle of champagne. She was sound asleep when the phone rang.

"Mary? I want to replace Jean [Terrell].''

No answer.

"Mary? You hear me? I want her *out*.''

"I don't know what you're talking about, Berry. I'm still asleep.''

"Then wake up, dammit. This is important. I'm gonna replace her with Syreeta." (Syreeta Wright was another Motown artist.)

"You can't do that. We just made the announcement about Jean. What happened?''

"Never mind what happened," he said. "Syreeta's a better singer anyway. Sounds more like Diane. We'll just say we changed our minds.''

"No way," Mary shot back. "We want Jean in the group, so you can just forget it!''

For Mary, this was no supreme act of will as much as it was the foolishness of a person making an important decision half asleep.

"And that's final," she concluded.

Berry held the phone receiver out at arm's length, as though he couldn't believe what he was hearing. There was a frown on his face. "Fine then," he said. His voice rose. "You're on your own. I wash my hands of the whole goddamn group."

He slammed the phone down.

Turning to one of the ever-present aides, he snapped, "When's that new Supremes single coming out?"

"Next month, boss."

Berry scowled. Then he picked up a pencil and snapped it in his fingers. "Damn!" he muttered. "How'd these women get to be so ungrateful?"

Gordy turned and walked into the casino where Diana was surrounded by people. All eyes were on her as she bought a stack of $25 chips. Berry watched as she drew blackjack on a $200 bet.

"All right," she squealed.

She bet another $200. Again, blackjack. "Hey! Fantastic!" In about a minute, she won $1,000.

"How about that?" she shouted to Berry. *"I'm a winner!"*

"Great," he said with no enthusiasm.

Diana was too excited to notice.

He broke through the crowd and walked over to her.

"Hey. Wait," she protested, as he grabbed her by the arm. "I'm not done *winning* yet . . ."

"C'mon, Diane," he said.

"But . . ."

"Let's go," he insisted, pulling her along. "You're done here. We got some things to do."

Chapter

13

IN A GREEK myth, Pygmalion carved a statue from ivory, fell in love with his creation, and she became a mortal. Years later, Henry Higgins would create a lady from a flower girl in George Bernard Shaw's play *Pygmalion*, which in turn became *My Fair Lady*, the musical.

There were many who saw a parallel in the Gordy-Ross legend when a powerful older man refashioned a young unknown girl into a star. As she rose, he became full of pride and wonder at her energy and ambition, and she fell in love with him.

However, unlike Galatea who was created from ivory and Eliza Doolittle who probably would not have risen above her station in life without Higgins, Diana Ross was fiercely ambitious from the beginning. She could just as likely have become a top fashion designer if music—and Berry Gordy—had not come into her life. But he *was* there, and a lot of people wondered about their future together.

As soon as Berry Gordy finally separated Diana Ross from The Supremes, most people assumed that this would be the ideal time for the two of them to wed. Diana seemed to think so herself after the group's final show, and shared this belief with more than a few of those inside the Motown circle.

If Berry had married Diana while she was still a member of the group, it would have caused even more complications. There would have been no way she could have continued a working relationship with Mary, Cindy and especially with Florence. One of the important facets of her romance with Berry was secrecy. During the whole time Diana was singing with the other girls, she never discussed her affair with Berry with any of her musical partners, and none of them would dare broach the subject with her either. But if she and Berry were legally man and wife, how could they all have avoided the issue?

After she left the group, it seemed that marriage was still out of the question. Publicly, Berry Gordy addressed the question of marriage to his star singer in an *Ebony* magazine story in 1970. "I tried to marry her a couple of times," Berry confessed. "Why should she marry me when she's got me anyway? She's free and rich and talented. Get married for what?"

In this same candid interview, Diana admitted her feelings for Berry in a manner so direct that it surprised the Motown staff. "I love Berry Gordy very much," she said, "and I think most people know that. I think he feels the same way about me."

Despite what Berry told the reporter, it's doubtful that he really did try to marry her "a couple of times." Not only did he already have three failed marriages and was not eager to add another to the list, he also found Diana's egocentricity increasingly difficult to take.

"Black is sort of bitchy, isn't she?" he asked one close friend. (Berry and Diana called each other "Black," a nickname of endearment whose origin only they know.)

"Well, I think that's putting it a bit mildly," was the careful reaction.

"How the hell did that happen?" Berry wondered. "That's not what I expected."

Like Henry Higgins, Berry Gordy was genuinely baffled by his creation. She had always been temperamental but lately she was becoming more and more obstreperous. He shouldn't have been surprised by this development because for the last six years he had spoiled her, giving her everything she seemed to desire: money, power and sex. She had become just as single-minded about her career as he had always been, but she was no longer willing to defer to his judgment without question. Berry had to confess to friends that Black had become one of the most self-centered women he had ever known and he didn't find this part of her personality at all attractive. It was one matter to work with and spend most of his time with her; actually living with Diana Ross—and having to put up with her as his wife—was not an idea that appealed to Berry Gordy.

On the other hand, Berry didn't live up to Diana's expectations either. She was no longer the naïve girl who would not listen to friends trying to convince her that Berry was a womanizer. Her eyes were now wide open to his philandering ways. She probably thought that after all their years together he would have settled down, that he would find that she was enough woman for him.

But that wasn't the case. Berry was a single man and still thought of himself as a lady-killer. Diana could hardly keep tabs on the women in his love life.

"I want to have a family and be able to grow up with my kids, but I have to come right out and tell you that the whole marriage thing is going right out the window," she despaired in a 1970 interview. "I know that I can't have children without getting married even though it's getting to be very popular. It's just not the kind of thing for me and it wouldn't make my mother happy."

"Diana definitely wanted to get married and she wanted a baby," said Cindy Birdsong, who married in May 1970. "This, I think, was the one frustration in her life. We sometimes talked about how many children we'd have, how wonderful it would be to have a family. That part of her was important, and it was missing. She had everything she wanted—power, fame, money—but not a child, and I do think she was determined to have one."

In early 1970, Diana and Berry continued to argue constantly about the terms of what had become a tug-of-war relationship. At one point, she was said to have given him an ultimatum: "Marry me, or we're finished." But it was an empty threat because she knew their lives were firmly interwoven. Too much money was now riding on their working together. Before, she needed Berry to make it to the top. Now he needed her just as much to keep *him* Number One. How could they end it all now?

After the Motown contingent returned home from the Las Vegas "farewell," Berry still had the problem of dealing with Mary Wilson and Cindy Birdsong. Wilson and Birdsong really had already served Gordy's purpose as background scenery for Diana. Although it may appear as though he had exploited them, they nonetheless had made a good living and achieved a fair amount of fame in the process. Now they were irritations to him, a man not much interested in sentiment. If the two of them had simply accepted his choice of Syreeta as Diana's replacement, there probably wouldn't have been any further discussion among them.

But instead, Wilson and Birdsong challenged Gordy's authority and in doing so they dragged him into a bitter battle over something he really didn't even care about. To Berry, Diana's replacement had now become a matter of principle—"These women are supposed to do whatever the hell I say!"—much more than genuine concern over the future of the group that had helped put Motown on the map.

In retrospect, it would seem that the main reason Birdsong

and Wilson were so intent on having Terrell as the New Supreme was that they were trying to defy the boss. They may also have suspected that Berry's sudden lack of interest in Jean had more to do with a personal problem between the two of them than it did with a question of her talent or image. After all, she had been his first choice.

"There was a big clash over this when we got back to Los Angeles, and Berry was very angry with us," Cindy recalled. "He had never been that angry with the two of us before, to the point of threatening that we must do what he said, or else. But he made his choice in singling out Diana. He got what *he* wanted. So we demanded Jean Terrell."

All the more reason for Berry to, as he put it, "wash my hands of the whole goddamn group."

Surprisingly, "Up the Ladder to the Roof," The Supremes' first recording with Terrell in the lead, was a hit even without Berry's support. He hadn't counted on the public's overwhelming curiosity about the "new" group. Also, their appearance on "The Ed Sullivan Show" helped record sales. It sold a little over 800,000 copies.

Audience reaction to the Ross-less Supremes was strong, proving not only that the new grouping was an exciting one but also that people are attracted to underdogs. Most of the press was a bit more jaded. Of the "new" Supremes, a reporter for *Time* magazine wrote, "Without Diana, audiences have to memorize their wigs to remember which is which."

Many observers at Motown predicted that Berry Gordy would never allow the "new" Supremes to be successful for too long. How would it look, after all, if a young girl from Belzoni, Mississippi, named Jean Terrell, could come out of nowhere to fill Diana Ross' high-heels and then take The Supremes on to even bigger success? Diana was supposed to be a major star and, as such, indispensable.

Diana was oblivious to all of this conflict over her successor. In her mind, she had no reason to be concerned. She was in her own exciting world now. "Oh, I'm sure they'll be just fine," she nonchalantly observed of Wilson and Birdsong. "After all, Berry won't let them down."

Diana Ross' initial starting price as a solo attraction was to be between $30,000 and $70,000 a week—and now she didn't have to split the profits with two other girls. At the time, Berry said, "She's not really taking a big chance because people are buying her like mad. Vegas is buying her, Miami is buying her, the Waldorf in New York. Like the stock market, she's up now because everything she's done has been a total success. If Diane is going to do it, she's going to be the best out there. She will be sensational if she does nothing but stand up there and sing.''

In the spring of 1970, Diana purchased a home in Beverly Hills at 701 North Maple Avenue for about $350,000 from film producer Donald L. Factor, grandson of the late cosmetics manufacturer Max Factor, and his wife Lynn Paula. The house was sold as part of a divorce arrangement between the Factors. The property is located in what is known as the Beverly Hills flatlands, a very exclusive, very rich and very white area of Los Angeles. Diana loved this house, despite its angular, foreboding appearance, no windows in the front, only skylights above. The front door was an imposing block of solid wood, and beyond that was an uninviting steel gate.

Eventually, Diana would design an additional wing and a two-car garage. Part of the new structure was a recording studio, but because she didn't know what she was doing when she ordered the renovations, the studio was practically worthless because of inferior acoustics. In between the studio and a brightly decorated guest bedroom was a sauna which she never used because she couldn't figure out how it worked.

Still the house became her glittering pride and joy, especially after she put her own design imprint on it: a glass and silver-plated grand piano; a silver, mirrored fireplace; a sunken living room splashed with hot pink pillows; an Andy Warhol tapestry of Marilyn Monroe; and a life-size poster advertising The Supremes' 1965 Lincoln Center engagement plastered on a gleaming white wall beneath a ceiling skylight. Soon, her mother and brother Chico would come to live with her and keep watch over the place while she was on tour. Berry bought Diana a new Rolls-Royce, his way of welcoming her to Los Angeles.

The first order of business for Ross' new career was the selection of that all-important debut solo single. When she recorded "Reach Out and Touch (Somebody's Hand)," written and produced by Nickolas Ashford and Valerie Simpson, she decided it should be her first release. But Berry was certain that this song, with its waltz-like rhythm, would not be the Number One record he wanted to inaugurate her solo career. "Kids don't like waltzes," he told her. "This won't sell!"

Diana claimed that the song spoke to a prevailing drug problem among America's youth. Berry had recently taken her back to the Brewster Projects during a trip to Detroit to remember the old days and, possibly, to put her present good fortune and success into some kind of perspective. At first, Diana didn't want to go, but once she was there, she was struck by how rundown the area now seemed, and how prevalent the drug problem had become among the Brewster Projects' youth. Some of Diana's former neighbors who were having problems with their children on drugs report that she gave them her Beverly Hills phone number and urged them to call if there was anything she could do to help.

There is a generous, benevolent side of Diana Ross that many people do not know about because it is in such contrast to that "other" side of her for which she's better known. Perhaps one of the reasons Diana Ross is so suspicious of people today is that she has often been taken advantage of when she's extended herself.

For instance, a month before she left The Supremes, she met a female fan who said she was depressed and suicidal. After talking to her, Diana became alarmed. She wanted to help and gave the girl her private home phone number. A while later, the girl called Diana in the middle of the night and unloaded all sorts of psychological problems on her. Diana listened and offered patient, loving advice. What Diana didn't know is that the girl was tape-recording the whole encounter.

That conversation revealed quite a bit about Diana Ross and the way she was thinking at this time. "You have to make yourself stronger, I told you that," Diana urged. She suggested the fan improve her life one day at a time. "At least *try* because no one else can do it for you but you. It really is worth it."

"You really think so?" the girl asked, baiting Diana perhaps to keep her on the line, and then moaning that her life had no purpose.

"You have to make your own purpose," Diana offered. "Nobody has any purpose when they start off. You'll find something you enjoy and like and it'll be your purpose in life. Some people were put here to be very religious and some were put here to follow Dr. King and nothing else. Some people were put here to *be* a Dr. King. You'll find yourself as time goes on. You're very young, and you've got time. We're all still searching. You don't always know what your life is going to mean to other people. As long as it means something to you, that's what's important. And I want you to call me each and every time you feel depressed," Diana said. "And we'll talk about it and see what we can do about it."

Later in the conversation, she urged the girl to "write down all your ideas about how you feel when you're depressed or when you're happy, so that when you read them back you'll know how you felt. You can remember those feelings and learn from them. Life is hard,'' Diana continued earnestly. "Things *have* to be hard. Otherwise they're not worth any time. Anything you want to do in life is going to be hard, it's not going to come easy.''

Finally the caller threatened to turn to drugs. "You don't want to get involved,'' Diana said, raising her voice. "You don't really believe what you're saying. You've got to mix with other people. If you don't even try, they won't try to be friends with you.

"Just continue to call and I'll talk to you. And when things get rough just try to be a little bit stronger.''

It was an emotional conversation, and Diana appeared genuinely concerned about the caller. However, anyone listening to the tape could sense that the caller was trying to prolong the conversation by bringing in irrelevant issues. Then, to make matters worse, she copied the tape and distributed it among her friends. Imagine how manipulated Diana Ross might have felt if she ever learned of this betrayal. The tape still circulates among Diana's fans. "Don't make yourself too available to them,'' Berry always warned her about her following. "It'll backfire on you in the end.''

Diane, inspired by her Detroit trip, may have wanted "Reach Out and Touch (Somebody's Hand)'' released because, as she said, "I think it's a very important message—it's time to stop being selfish.'' Or she may have been trying to defy Berry because he didn't want it issued. The more Berry rejected the song, the more adamant Diana became. Finally, he allowed the record's release. "Reach Out and Touch,'' a really uninteresting sing-along kind of song, made a dismal debut. It didn't make it into the Top Ten. To make matters even more embarrassing, it sold barely 500,000 copies, which means that the new Supremes' first record, "Up the Ladder to the Roof,'' did much better.

Today, almost 20 years later, when Diana uses "Reach Out and Touch'' as an audience participation number, it becomes peace, love, brotherhood and hope, all rolled into one. It's always wonderful to watch the way she can entice an audience of strangers to hold hands with each other and sway back and forth to the rhythm of this song. As long as Diana's in control, polyester-clad grandmothers and snakeskin-shoed con men, wide-eyed innocents and jaded gamblers, people who have sat next to one another for the whole performance and not even made eye contact, audience members who knew it was coming and swore they wouldn't be drawn into it—there they all are, holding hands, humming, singing, swaying, whatever she tells them to do, loving this feeling, loving each other, loving Diana. Her use of this song and the brilliant way she's related it to her audiences have become one of the hallmarks of her career.

Walter Burrell conducted the first major interview with Diana after she left The Supremes, for *Soul Illustrated* magazine. He recalled, "When we did this interview, natural hairstyles were in vogue, and Diana was toying with the idea of wearing a big bushy natural wig for the photographs. So while she was trying on these wigs, Mike Roshkind, who was running the show that day, told her, 'No! You're not wearing any such thing. Your public knows you with the flowing white girl hair, and that's the way I want you to be.' Well, she was infuriated by this, and with good reason I thought. After all, wasn't she [at 26] old enough to make these decisions? She had a big fight with Roshkind, and after that she was in a terrible mood.

"Every time I asked her a question, I would get a curt and disgusted 'yes' or 'no' answer. Finally, I pulled her out of Roshkind's earshot to talk to her privately. I said, 'Look, Diana, you use toilet paper just like everybody else. Now we both have a job to do so let's get this damn interview out of the way. Then you can go and deal with your wigs and with this white man and I can get the hell out of your ugly house with no windows.' After that we had a wonderful interview. And she never did wear that wig.''

In her interview with Burrell, Diana updated him on her family, having recently attended a July 4th family reunion, on her father's birthday: Sister Barbara was now married. She had dropped out of college to have two children—and during that time taught school—but was now re-enrolled and looking forward to becoming a doctor. Margretia (Rita) was also married; she and her husband—"who is somewhat of a genius"—had one child and lived in Raleigh, North Carolina. "She is basically being a housewife," Diana reported.

(Rita and Tommy Gardner divorced after a few years. In an interview, Gardner indicated that Diana apparently wasn't particularly warm to her in-laws. "I never even had a conversation with her," said her former brother-in-law. "I'm sure she's a very nice lady, but I never talked to her. I'd see her at family reunions but I don't think she ever said two words to me.")

Fred Earl was in the Air Force and stationed in Texas. Diana's younger brother Arthur, "T-Boy," "is very involved in black problems of today." Wilbert Alex, "Chico," the youngest Ross family member, was now living with Diana in Beverly Hills, and attending Beverly Hills High School. "He is my protector and friend, and we are very, very close," she said. Though Diana didn't mention it, Fred and Ernestine were separated though not yet divorced. Ernestine and Aunt Bee were living together in Detroit. Fred continued to work for American Richfield there.

"And I've finally gotten a chance to meet his family," Diana explained. "I had never known my dad's relatives, except for his sisters and aunts who live in Detroit, but none of the others. When I went down to Rogersville, Tennessee, to visit his Uncle George [for the reunion], it was really wild because when I got there at least 500 kids were outside the house. I signed autographs for hours. Then I went in to eat and the kids were standing around the table looking at me. I said, 'Hey look, I don't eat any different than anybody else.' It was like I was in a fish bowl."

Diana reiterated that Fred "never wanted me to go into show business," and mentioned that she had offered to buy him a new car as a birthday present "because I've never really done anything for him."

Fred declined the offer. "Save your money," he told her sternly. "Put it away. One day you might need it."

"He's like that," Diana said, sadly.

Diana's first solo dates were difficult experiences. The $100,000 nightclub act Gordy ordered overwhelmed her, and the audience response was very cool. There were costume changes galore—eight in all, from sequined sarongs to bugle beaded mini-skirts. Besides a band, she had three female background singers and two male dancers. "Welcome to the Let's-See-If-Diana-Ross-Can-Make-It-On-Her-Own Show," she told her audience.

"But the people were coming to see her with a bad attitude," her opening act, ventriloquist Willie Tyler, remembered. "It was as if she had gotten a bad reputation just by leaving The Supremes—her partners—behind. Also, she was trying too hard. Now she had to prove herself, prove that her ability warranted a solo career, and so she was singing, dancing, changing clothes, doing everything she could think of to razzle-dazzle 'em. At first, I recall her being very disappointed by the reception she was receiving. But Berry told her to take her time and wait it out. Soon, he said, the audiences will come to her side."

When Diana brought her new show to the Frontier Hotel in Las Vegas for the first time, the advance reservations were very few for opening night. "This place has got to be full," Berry said, "or else it just won't look right." He then went out onto the street with his pockets full of $20 bills, tore each one down the middle and handed one-half to people walking down the Vegas strip. He promised that they would get the other if they came to Diana's show. Berry's idea worked. The place was filled to capacity.

It didn't take long before Diana found her solo niche as a performer. "The only time I miss Mary and Cindy," she said with a mischievous grin, "is after a show when I have no one to argue with."

Upon the release of her second single, an exciting new arrangement of the Marvin Gaye-Tammi Terrell pop classic, "Ain't No Mountain High Enough," Diana's solo career seemed to be guaranteed success. Complete with spoken verses and gospel-influenced climax of soaring male and female voices, this really is a classic pop record. It's also a heartbreaking song, especially considering the status of Diana's lovelife at this time, because of its message of unconditional love and the solemn, emotional way Diana delivers it. The song went to Number One on the charts and would eventually be nominated for a Grammy Award.

Harry Langdon was responsible for taking all of the photographs for all of Diana's early solo album covers, as well as for press purposes. Langdon recalled how constantly involved Berry Gordy was in the work:

"Berry used to come to her sessions and insisted on standing next to me and prompt her on. I thought he was abusing her to a certain extent by forcing her to get up to a performance peak for action shots—which we took a lot of. He wanted it to appear that she was in full performance swing and so he badgered her unmercifully to sing at the top of her lungs and dance about. But then when I saw the pictures blown up on a Sunset Strip billboard, it really did look like they were lifted from one of her shows and I understood what Berry was going for.

"He really is quite a creative person," Langdon said. "I never allowed a manager to sit in on a photo session, let alone direct it. But with Berry, I really had no choice. He was surrounded by bodyguards and I wasn't about to keep him out. It is also an unwritten law that a photographer does not allow anyone to grab his camera and start taking pictures. Again, I could never stop Berry. The first time he tried to take my camera, I protested and one of his fellows glared at me menacingly. So I let him have the camera, and you know what, he was terrific. He knew how to generate energy in Diana, and also how to bring out the essence of her glamor. He taught me quite a bit. We got along famously.''

Rather than have Diana appear on the cover of her first solo album, *Diana Ross*, in standard Ross regalia of sequins, beads and swooping wig, the photo selected showed Diana in cut off jeans and a T-shirt, eating an apple, barefoot and with hardly any makeup on at all. Langdon shot it with a wide-angle lens, which distorted Diana's image and made her appear even thinner and more angular than she really was. She looked about 15 years old.

Harry Langdon recalled that the photo was taken as an afterthought when they finished one of his grueling 12-hour glamour sessions. He developed the print ''just for the fun of it'' and had a mock billboard made using it with type that announced ''Over 400 Million Records Sold!'' He then sent the billboard up to Berry Gordy's house as a joke, '' 'cause I thought he would get a kick out of it. But when Berry received the photograph, he didn't know what to make of it.'' Certainly this wasn't the image he had ordered and paid thousands of dollars for, yet he was captivated by it just the same. A week later, Harry Langdon was summoned to Gordy's mansion for ''a corporate meeting.''

Langdon recalled, ''I drove up to his huge estate which was protected by massive electrical gates and surrounded by intimidating security guards. After I arrived, Suzanne dePasse, whom I found to be totally charming, escorted me into a large conference room where all of the officers of the Motown corporation were seated around a giant oval table. I had never before encountered any of them, all rather stuffy types in suits and jackets. Without saying anything at all, they stared up at me and then back down at the table, in the middle of which was my mock-billboard of Diana. I began to get nervous and sat down quickly. Then Suzanne asked me very nicely to please get up and find another chair. I was sitting in Berry's.''

After a few uncomfortable moments, the doors swung open and Berry Gordy made his entrance, wearing a jogging suit and holding a golf club. It wasn't what Langdon expected. He asked Langdon to stand up in front of everyone and explain just why he had sent him this odd photo of Diana Ross.

Langdon knew he had to come up with a more impressive reason than it had been a practical joke. He stood in front of the Motown hierarchy and took a deep breath. ''Gee, you know, Diana's been so successful with the world's rich movers-and-shakers, maybe it's time you guys used a picture of her that relates back to her own people in the projects and appeals to those who can't afford to buy her records and see her performances."

Everyone around the table looked at him with confused expressions, as he continued. "I call this Diana's Biafran refugee picture because she looks hungry, don't you think?"

Mike Roshkind glanced at Berry and cleared his throat loudly. Berry ignored him as Harry continued, "If you want to break Diana out as a solo star, you shouldn't lose your black base. Get back to basics and she'll continue being a winner.

"And then," Harry Langdon said, "I sat back down and waited."

After a few beats of silence, Berry stood up and applauded. "Bravo!" he exclaimed with a broad smile. "Now this man has a good idea. We'll take Diana back to her roots for this album jacket. How come none of you people came up with this idea?"

His manner suddenly became accusatory as he pointed to the executives before him. "All the money I pay you people and we have to get such a terrific idea from an *outsider*." By now, everyone at the conference table was squirming.

"At that moment, I realized I was in big trouble," Langdon said. "I had scored points with Berry, but the rest of the organization was obviously not pleased with what I had done, and by the way Berry was berating them. After that meeting I had a very, very difficult time with everyone at Motown. I'm sure the only reason I continued working with Diana was because Berry insisted upon it."

As Diana's solo career was getting underway, Motown's promotional efforts made sure she was the topic of public discussion. Since she was single and beautiful, there was always a lot of media speculation as to whether or not she would marry and have children.

Diana had said that she desperately wanted a child and Berry Gordy certainly seemed to outsiders the most logical candidate as the father. But Berry was not interested in marrying Diana. In his mind, he would say later, there was no question about that. He loved her, no one doubted that. Loving Diana was easy, but living with her would not be. Though Berry might not have been interested in formally committing himself to her, he was still vitally concerned about her career. A child out of wedlock could ruin her.

Many of Diana's peers would go on to have children without marrying—including Berry Gordy himself—but she said that she would never do so because her mother would not approve. An unstated, but equally compelling reason was that her fans would never understand. Nothing would ruin her image more than Diana Ross in a maternity dress without a gold band on the third finger of her left hand. At one point, she considered becoming a single mother by adopting a child.

In 1966, a 22-year-old Diana had said, "I want the biggest wedding of all. I want what every young girl wants—to have a big fabulous wedding, to wear a lovely white wedding gown with a long, endlessly long, train, to see my mother and father all dressed up, and my husband waiting for me down the aisle in a tuxedo. That's my dream. And then a romantic honeymoon afterwards far, far away."

But five years later there was no Prince Charming in sight.

Names of prospective husbands for Diana, including Berry, continued to grind in the rumor mill, but that's all they were—rumors. No one was prepared when *Soul*, a Los Angeles-based bi-weekly newspaper with strong ties to Motown, ran a cover story with Diana's picture next to a handsome white man's, and the headline: "What You See Is What She Got!"

Diana Ross, 26, had married Robert Silberstein in Las Vegas on January 20, 1971. As soon as the news services picked up the story, the Motown phones wouldn't stop ringing. The New York office refused to confirm that a wedding had taken place at all, and the Los Angeles office referred all calls to New York. "The runaround," as one former Motown employee explained it. Everybody wanted to know. "Who is Robert Silberstein?"

Silberstein, from Elberon, New Jersey, is the son of a wealthy garment manufacturer. A year younger than Diana, he graduated from West Virginia University with a Bachelor of Arts in Theater. Supposedly, he tried teaching but quit after a dispute with the school board. He moved to Los Angeles in 1970 and, taking the less ethnic surname Ellis, he began working for a public relations firm in Hollywood. His clients included some Motown artists. Berry Gordy liked him. He was aggressive, had a winning personality and was perceived by everyone who knew him as a PR *wunderkind*.

"Bobby was somewhat of a celebrity in Hollywood just by virtue of the fact that he was so charming and handsome," remembered one woman who used to date him. "And he also knew how to be a good friend. I have nothing but wonderful things to say about him because, still to this day, he's a prince of a guy. But he was the type of personality that could be taken advantage of in Hollywood because he was a bit naïve, too generous and giving.''

Diana Ross legend has it that they first met in a Beverly Hills men's clothing store where Diana was shopping for a gift for Berry and asked for Bob's advice. She discovered a "rare thing," she said later, "a gentleman who is young, alive and very handsome—all of the fantasy things you think of in a husband.''

Many people greeted this story with skepticism. Said a Motown publicist, "It's what everybody in Hollywood was talking about: 'How'd she meet this white man?' But Berry Gordy was a fearsome person in those times. He was powerful as all hell, and the press didn't ask a lot of questions of anyone close to him.''

(After a few years of telling the shopping spree story, Diana finally decided to tell curious reporters, "How we met is just something we don't discuss with other people.'')

Diana apparently went on a couple of casual dates with Bob Silberstein in February 1970, first in Las Vegas and then again in Los Angeles. According to photographer Harry Langdon, "They were very secretive about being together. I remember they would drive around totally incognito, dark glasses and all, in Bob's charming MG roadster. I didn't know what their relationship was. I didn't think it was serious, though.''

That was understandable. Dating Diana Ross was not without its problems. "You see, when I first met her," Bob has recalled, "I didn't know exactly what she was doing because I was just out of college and I only knew from football players. Those were stars to me—football players and tennis players. So my friends used to tease me. On the radio, when one of her songs would come on, everyone would wait for me to move my foot or at least perhaps react. But I'd just sit there like an ass.''

Later, presumably to cure his discomfort, Diana gave Bob a present: 27 of her albums. The perfect gift for the man who has everything.

Cindy Birdsong recalled, "When she first started seeing Bob, she asked me and Charles to go with them on the first date. I think she wanted to double-date so that she could break the ice with Bob. [Birdsong's then-husband, Vietnam veteran Charles Hewlett, is white.] We went to a restaurant in the Sands Hotel in Las Vegas and I remember Diane being a little nervous and unsure of herself. This was really the first time she had ever been serious about a white guy. She had never even dated a white man before. I'm sure she never, ever thought she would marry one.

"I found Bob to be very personable and outgoing, a great personality. And what a sense of humor. He was also extremely intelligent and articulate. But, still, I was as surprised as everyone else when she ran off and married this guy."

Why Diana Ross decided to marry Bob Silberstein remains a mystery today. If the two of them were in love, it was the best kept secret in Hollywood. One of Diana's friends has this theory: "She was tired of waiting for Berry to come through for her, and she wanted a child. Bob was there. So she married him."

The wedding was a far cry from the lavish affair of Diana's dreams. It was suddenly decided that they would marry, and impulsively they flew from Los Angeles to Las Vegas. The ceremony took place at one o'clock in the morning at the Silver Bells Chapel. Suzanne dePasse was Diana's "witness." She appeared to represent Motown's corporate interests rather than Diana's. None of her other friends were there.

Ernestine and Fred Ross were not present. Ernestine was staying in Diana's Beverly Hills home at the time and so it seems odd that Diana would not have invited her. Fred was in Detroit.

Berry Gordy was also not present. (When asked to comment on the wedding, he refused to do so. Then he went into what one of his aides called "hibernation" for a few weeks. But, according to the source, "He wasn't particularly upset. I felt he was just putting on the show he felt was expected of him.")

Diana, wearing a simple paisley pantsuit and dark sunglasses, was barely recognizable. "I didn't even know who she was," said Reverend Frank Hutchinson, who performed the ceremony. "The cab driver had to tell me." Silberstein wore a sports jacket and slacks.

The newlyweds didn't have much of a honeymoon, either. The day after the wedding, Diana telephoned Ernestine to tell her what she'd done ("She was shocked," Diana recalled) and then she and Bob returned to Los Angeles so she could complete work on her first ABC television special.

"I'm proud to be her husband," Bob said. "I don't want anything from her. I know she didn't get where she is today because someone up there said, 'Okay, Diana Ross, let's make you a star. Let's make you a singer.' She drives herself, man."

Bob Silberstein was both white and Jewish. Diana's appearance and singing style were meant to appeal to Caucasians, so a white husband would certainly not hurt her image—in fact, it would enhance it—and Jewish men were perceived to be shrewd and intelligent. (People in entertainment circles believe that Jewish men who are drawn to black women respect their independence and the strength they've needed to survive.)

If Diana's friends questioned her motives for marrying Bob, his friends were equally curious. One of his former girlfriends in Los Angeles has said that Bob telephoned her one day to say that he could no longer see her. When she asked why, he told her that he was marrying Diana Ross. She remembered by his tone that he didn't seem to be very much in love. In fact, he had never even mentioned Diana prior to this. Before hanging up, he apologized to the girlfiend. "I just didn't want you to read it first in the newspapers," he said.

Within two weeks of the wedding, Diana announced that she was pregnant. And then, a month and four days after the ceremony, she decided to separate from Bob. She said later that "a friend" changed her mind.

Obviously, this was not the happy beginning to a long life together for the Silbersteins. But in an interview with writer Rennie Walters, Diana insisted that Bob was the first man she ever loved. "When Bob and I met it was kind of love at first sight," she said. "People were surprised at our marriage because we didn't do a lot of talking about how serious we were. I'd never dated a white man before so I couldn't believe this thing we had would last. Frankly, I expected there would be a problem marrying someone white. But if there is a problem it's in other people's minds, not ours. I'd had very little experience dating. I could count the steady boyfriends I've had on one hand. Bob and I are very happy."

However, despite Diana's romantic sentiment, when the newlyweds were seen in public there was an odd indifference between them. Indeed, that smiling mask of inscrutability that has always been part of the Diana Ross mystique was evident. After all, she was in show business. She knew how to hide her feelings. Although Diana could put on a cheerful face when the couple appeared in public, Silberstein was not so convincing. He always seemed in a dark mood. His friends said they didn't know what his life was like with Diana Ross but sensed that he had gotten himself into something he wished he hadn't.

Berry made it clear that his connection to Diana was now strictly business. "My concern is with her career development," he announced at the time. "If the home life is a happy one, then the career will be, too."

It seemed to most observers that there were quite a few secrets being kept by Diana Ross, and maybe even by Berry Gordy and Bob Silberstein. "Bye baby, see you 'round," were the haunting first words of Diana's current single release, "Remember Me" (produced by Ashford and Simpson). Her performance seems charged with painful memories; through the lyrics she is dejected and helpless in the face of a cruel twist of fate. "I gave you my *best*," she sings passionately. Diana Ross never sounded more convincing.

As a newlywed with a child on the way, she seemed more forlorn than happy; the famous Ross zest for love and career was depleted. "We had a tough first year," Diana confirmed later of her marriage. "And I don't like to think about it."

She doesn't like to talk about it either. Whatever was happening in 1971 is a secret that Diana Ross, Berry Gordy and Bob Silberstein still keep today.

Back in 1969, movie producer Jay Weston had approached Berry Gordy with the idea of starring Diana Ross in a movie based on the life of Billie Holiday. Weston, a former publicist, met Holiday in 1957 when she performed at the Newport Jazz Festival and was so enchanted by her that two years later he optioned her autobiography *Lady Sings the Blues*, which was cowritten with William Dufty. In the mid-'60s, with a script by Terence McCloy, Weston cut a deal with CBS Features to mount the film. His first choice to star as Holiday was Abbey Lincoln, whom he had cast opposite Sidney Poitier in *For the Love of Ivy*. His second choice was Diahann Carroll.

Billie Holiday was born Eleanora Fagin to 13-year-old Sadie Fagin on April 7, 1915. She died at the age of 44 in 1959, just about the time Berry Gordy began seeking seed-money for his empire. Holiday was one of the greatest jazz singers of all time, successor to Bessie Smith and precursor of Ella Fitzgerald. But her life was a very difficult one and her addiction to drugs eventually led to her downfall. Prostitution, rape, narcotics, bisexuality, prison life and bigotry were all parts of the Billie Holiday story.

In May 1969, Weston and CBS Features President Gordon Stulberg saw Diana Ross and The Supremes perform in the Empire Room of the Waldorf-Astoria. During the show, Weston nudged Stulberg, pointed directly at the lead singer on the right and announced, "There she is! That's my Billie Holiday."

Stulberg frowned and then huffed, "That's crazy. She's no Billie Holiday." The next day, Weston continued to try to convince Stulberg that Ross would be right for the role, but he was unsuccessful.

"She's just a Supreme," Stulberg said. "If you change your

mind, come back to me. CBS will do the movie with Diahann Carroll, but never with that Diana Ross girl.''

In June, Weston proposed his concept of Ross as Billie Holiday to Berry Gordy. Gordy was hoping to establish himself in Los Angeles and seemed depressed by whatever troubles he was having back East. He was glad to be out of Detroit and eager for new opportunities.

Berry didn't really know whether Jay Weston's idea was a good one. But rather than try to determine that on the spot, he decided to play hard ball with Weston.

"Hey guy, there is no way I'm going to give you my girl to do a movie about a black junkie singer," Gordy told Weston. "It just ain't gonna happen, so you might as well forget it."

"He turned me down flat," Weston recalled. "He was suspicious and acted superior. But it didn't sour me on the idea because I knew she was right for the role."

Though Weston was a movie producer, he didn't realize he was facing a terrific actor. Gordy feigned lack of interest and tried to appear smug, but secretly he was thrilled with the idea that this big-time film producer actually came to him with this great idea. He didn't particularly care what the movie was about. The fact that it was a film, and that his creation, Diana Ross, could star in it, excited Berry. This was the kind of opportunity he had hoped to find in Los Angeles and now this project was falling right into his lap.

"If he wants her bad enough, he'll be back," Berry said of Jay Weston.

As soon as Weston left that meeting at Motown, Gordy summoned his receptionist. "Get me Diane on the line."

"She's in Washington performing at the Carter Barron," came the answer.

"I don't care where she is, just get her!"

Propitiously enough, *Look* magazine had recently called Motown to arrange a cover story on The Supremes. Gordy's staff convinced the editors that the focus of the story should be on the possibility of Diana leaving The Supremes, and the cover photograph should be of just her, alone. When he finally reached Diana, Gordy asked her, "What do you know about Billie Holiday?"

"Who?"

"Billie Holiday. Billie Holiday. Find out what you can about her," Gordy instructed. "And then talk about her to the guy from *Look*. Sound interested, like you really know what the hell you're talkin' about. Talk about the blues and stuff like that."

"The blues? But why?" she asked.

"Just do it." And he hung up.

A few months later, *Look* published the cover story.

"Just listening to Lady Day brings a sadness to me," Diana told writer Jack Hamilton, "and I'm trying to find out everything about her. I want to sing about blues and sadness, a natural part of life. I'm trying to find out the real psychological reasons Billie Holiday gave up and took to drink and drugs."

Gordy, ever the shrewd operator, was using the media to find out just what options might be open to him. His feeling was that if one movie producer was interested in Diana starring as a most unlikely Billie Holiday, maybe there would be even more interest in Hollywood to feature her in other kinds of biographical films.

"What was that Billie Holiday stuff for," Diana would ask Berry later.

"Oh, never mind about that. I'm workin' on something," he would answer.

As soon as the article appeared, Jay Weston went back to Gordy, just as Berry knew he would. But Gordy turned him down again. Weston's mere interest in Diana wasn't good enough. Gordy wanted this man to *hunger* for her. After a disappointed Weston left a second time, Gordy said confidently, "Don't worry. He'll be back."

Chapter

14

ALTHOUGH BERRY WAS waiting for the movies to come to him, he did not neglect television. It wasn't difficult for Berry Gordy and Mike Roshkind to strike a deal with ABC-TV for Diana Ross' first solo special. The time was right. People wanted to see how she was faring as a solo act. They planned a one-hour *tour de force* to prove that Berry's protégée could make it on her own and that a corporate mistake had not been made in lifting her from The Supremes. The show's centerpiece was made of three silent film sequences in which Diana portrayed—in full make-up and costume—Charlie Chaplin, Harpo Marx and W.C. Fields. Rubber-faced and animated, Diana mugged her way through the three sequences, displaying an amazing flair for comedy and timing. It was the happy surprise of the hour.

Meanwhile, Jay Weston hired Sidney J. Furie to direct *Lady Sings the Blues* and began negotiating with Diahann Carroll to play the lead. He had no intention of ever meeting with Berry Gordy, Jr., again.

Sidney J. Furie, a Toronto-born director, had become internationally known because of *The Ipcress File*, starring Michael Caine. He had also directed Marlon Brando in *The Appaloosa* and Frank Sinatra in *The Naked Runner*. When he asked who Weston had in mind for the starring role in the film, and was told Diahann Carroll, he said to Weston, "You got the wrong Diane. It should be Diana Ross."

Furie added, "Jay told me he had tried to get Ross and couldn't, that he was finished with Berry Gordy and that was the end of that." But Furie had seen the *Diana!* television special and, like much of the viewing audience, was taken by surprise by the silent-movie spoof. "It was obvious to me. If you can play comedy, you can play drama," said Sidney Furie.

"That girl Ross, she's an actress. I'm convinced of that," he insisted to Jay Weston.

"Well, then, dammit, let's go get her once and for all," Weston decided.

Furie's agent at the William Morris Agency, Joe Schoenfeld, also represented Motown. In May 1971, a meeting was set between Sidney Furie, Jay Weston, Schoenfeld and Gordy in the Motown offices at 6464 Sunset Boulevard in Hollywood. Gordy showed his three guests to plush fabric chairs in front of his desk, on top of which sat a tape recorder. Gordy told them that he records all his meetings "for posterity."

After a few pleasantries, Weston and Furie reiterated their interest in Diana Ross as Billie Holiday. Berry listened intently, all the while sizing up his white visitors and trying to figure out the best way to play the game this time.

"You fellas wanna play a little pool?" he asked.

They retreated to the conference room which contained a pool table, Gordy with tape recorder in hand.

Once there, Gordy selected an expensive cue stick, but didn't offer one to his guests. Chalking the tip of his cue, he began thoughtfully, "The only problem is that Diane can't act." His guests looked at one another quizzically, wondering whether it would be a good idea to agree or disagree. As Gordy set up the "T" on the table—the balls in a perfect triangle formation—he asked, "Why her? Why a girl who can't act?"

Furie decided to challenge him. "What're you talking about?" he asked. "What about that special? I know she has the ability from seeing her work on that special. The Chaplin thing, W. C. Fields and Harpo. Hey, she can act."

"That was acting?" Berry asked incredulously. "No shit?" He bent over, took his best shot and busted the "T." The balls went sailing across the felt table.

Furie said he thought comedy is more demanding than drama, and since Diana Ross had a natural comedic flair, she could probably fare well as a dramatic actress. "I know she can be nominated for an *Oscar* in this kind of role, a classic Hollywood role."

"No shit?" Berry asked. He took another shot.

"No shit!" piped in Jay Weston.

"Yeah, no shit," repeated agent Schoenfeld.

Berry then recounted the story of Diana's "acting debut" as the benevolent Sister Therese on Ron Ely's *Tarzan* TV series in

January 1968. The plot involved three nuns, Therese from the African village of "Muganda," Sister Martha (Mary) from Chicago and Sister Ann (Cindy) from Pittsburgh who return to Therese's village in hopes of building a hospital there. The episode was taped on location under a scorching sun in Cuernavaca, Mexico, and was intended as a dramatic vehicle for Diana Ross. Birdsong and Wilson's few lines were added to the script as afterthoughts so that there would be some reason for their presence.

"See, the opening had the girls in this canoe paddling down a river, three beautiful nuns coming back to the village," Gordy explained to Furie and Weston, all the while continuing his solo pool game. "They're singin' this song, 'Michael Rowed the Boat Ashore' and Diane's squeezin' a box accordion for accompaniment. Funniest damn thing I ever saw in my life. The script called for the canoe to be knocked over by a hippo. The two girls were to swim to shore but Diane, of course, would be rescued by Tarzan. So on the day of the shooting, I said, 'No way am I gonna let Diane get knocked into that freezin' water. We need a stand-in.' "

Berry angled up another shot and continued his game and his story.

"So anyway, there were all these poor Mexicans all over the place. We lined up a bunch of 'em. I picked out three that were kind of shaped like the Supremes. 'You! You! And you!' I said."

He used his pool stick to pick out three imaginary Mexican Supremes.

" 'Wanna make some money? *Dinero? Dinero?*' 'Sí! Sí! Sí!' they said. So we put them in these heavy-as-shit nun's habits, sat them in the canoe, set the thing to sailin' and then tipped that baby over. Splash! The Mexicans fell into the water. So we're waitin' and waitin' and waitin' and, Jesus Christ!, the three of 'em never came back up. Everyone started panicking. 'What the hell's going on?' the director was asking. I turned to him and said, 'Holy shit! Did anyone ask them if they could swim?' "

Berry started laughing and slapping his thighs. His guests joined him. "Man, they were drowning. You dig what I'm saying. Drowning! So Diane is on the sidelines screaming, 'Save 'em. Save 'em. Oh, Lord. Save 'em.' And the director is yelling, 'No. No. Keep filming, this is great stuff.' And the next thing I know, Tarzan jumps in and actually *rescues* them. It was terrific. We kept a lot of it in the show.

"Anyway," Berry concluded. "Diane was horrible in that

role. The worst. Couldn't have been any worse. When we saw how bad she was we were glad she wanted to be a singer and not a nun.''

"Yeah, but that was then and this is now," Sidney Furie insisted.

"As he played pool," Furie later recalled, "Berry then made a long involved speech about how he'd reached a pivotal point in Diana's career, how leaving The Supremes was a risk and how he wasn't about to take any chances with her future. He talked about how Motown was interested in getting into films, and how he wanted to be a movie mogul. This was what he wanted most of all, I sensed, to prove himself by making it in Hollywood, and by making Diana a star. Well, we thought he was the most charming, friendly, candid and charismatic guy in town.''

Gordy sized up the last play of his game, as well as everything that was said at the meeting. Then he took an angle shot, banked the white cue ball off several sides and sank the black eight ball into the corner pocket, an almost impossible shot. "You fellas got yourself a deal," he said with a wide grin.

Two months after Gordy decided to bankroll the script for the Billie Holiday story, he received the preliminary screenplay from Furie and Weston. He called Diana into his office, and recorded the meeting on tape so that he could later send it to the producer and director. There was some question in her mind as to whether she wanted to make this movie. But Berry knew how to take care of that. He appealed to her fascination with Barbra Streisand by telling her that Streisand would do it if she were a black woman. Suddenly, Diana became very interested.

"But why are there so many scenes in this movie?" she asked. "I mean, this is so long. How am I gonna remember all of this? Why can't there just be four or five scenes?''

Berry replied, "Cause this is a movie, Diane. A movie has fifty, a hundred scenes. Two hundred. And you're gonna be in every one of 'em. But listen, don't worry about it. They want you. They want you bad. Jesus Christ, they came to me three times with this thing!''

Berry realized this role would be a challenge. He had known and admired Billie Holiday; a photograph of the two of them with Mabel John hung in his living room in Detroit. Diana had once commented about how young they all looked. Holiday had performed at the Flame Show Bar in Detroit where Maurice King conducted the house orchestra, and where Berry's sisters ran the photograph concession. He felt an emotional link with Billie. He also believed her life would make a good movie and strong Diana Ross debut vehicle, but then he had second thoughts when he began remembering the lurid realities of her biography.

"He called me and was nervous about the fact that this might be too heavy-handed for Motown and Diana," Furie said. "But I told him I didn't want to make a serious, deep, important movie. I wanted to make a piece of entertainment that would make big money for all of us. He agreed. Anyone who knows Berry knows that there is no color in his eyes but green, the color of money."

Originally, *Lady Sings the Blues* was to be episodic, dealing with each of Billie's relationships with three husbands. But Berry decided that the three romances were too confusing. At his insistence, Furie and Weston agreed to combine all three into one—the one she had with Louis McKay—for dramatic unity.

"But that's not truthful," Diana argued. "It's not the way it happened."

Berry, who has always subscribed to Henry Ford's theory that "history is bunk," said, "The hell with being truthful. White people certainly don't worry about changing the facts to make good movies. Why should we be saddled with it just because we're black?" Diana had to agree.

Berry financed the writing of a revised screenplay, which was then submitted to every movie studio and source of financing in Hollywood. No one wanted it. It quickly became apparent that the rest of Hollywood wasn't quite as enthusiastic about Ross and Gordy's entrée into the filmmaking community as were Weston and Furie. With the exception of an occasional Sidney Poitier film, black movies and black screen stars were not considered money-makers then and, except for Eddie Murphy, they still aren't today. Or as one white movie studio head put it, "White people just don't go to see black people in the movies."

Until the early '70s, the black woman's image on the screen had been largely confined to broad Hattie McDaniel and Butterfly McQueen-like portrayals. Lena Horne had really been Hollywood's only black screen legend. And even her screen image as a mulatto temptress never really elevated her to the kind of celebrity that the white glamour girls of her era enjoyed. Often her scenes were shot in such a way that they could be edited from the movie when they were shown in the South.

But at about the time *Lady Sings the Blues* was being hawked around town, Hollywood was about to realize a huge and untapped box office market in the black community. A genre of films referred to as "blaxploitation" emerged in the early '70s —movies such as *Superfly* with Ron O'Neal and *Shaft* starring Richard Roundtree. Though these films were, for the most part, dreadful in every possible way—propagating stereotypical images of black life with each frame—black moviegoers would still bring Hollywood studios big-buck profits just the same.

Frank Yablans received his copy of the script of *Lady Sings the Blues* on the first day of his new job as president of Paramount Pictures. He immediately called Weston and offered him a deal. By six o'clock that evening, he had agreed that Paramount would finance the film to the tune of $2 million. Today, it would cost at least 15 times that to do the same film.

It was time for Berry to let Diana meet the men in charge. "I remember very well the first time I met her," Sidney J. Furie recalled. "It was at Le St. Germaine restaurant just down the street from Paramount Studios. She and I had lunch alone, and as we drank expensive French white wine, I fell in love with her. I thought she was the most incredible thing I had ever met. So charming and magical. I told her I wanted to make *Funny Girl* and the people in it would happen to have black skin. And I told her that by the time we were finished with this film, she would fall in love with me, too."

Film critics, jazz purists and Holiday fans lashed out against what they saw as outrageous casting. Diana certainly bore no resemblance to the buxom Holiday and she had nothing in common with her musically. It also seemed that she simply hadn't had enough life experiences to draw upon to bring Billie Holiday's tortured existence to the screen. To a certain extent, that was true. She and Holiday were very different in terms of their upbringing and lifestyles.

On some levels, though, Diana could certainly relate to the prejudice Billie faced. She and Gordy may have perceived her public persona as a white one—and by extension the public did as well—but, obviously, she was still a black woman. Privately, she had to deal with the kinds of problems inherent to the black experience. She may have been protected in her career, and in most of her private affairs, by Berry Gordy but her family was just as vulnerable as the rest of black America to the racial climate of the '60s and early '70s. It so happened that at the time *Lady Sings the Blues* was being mounted, the Ross family was facing difficult times.

Earlier in the year, Diana received an alarming phone call informing her that her 20-year-old brother Arthur, "T-Boy," was in jail in Bessemer, Alabama. T-Boy had never been in any serious trouble with the law, so this incident came as quite a surprise to the family. Apparently. Arthur Ross went into a corner store, picked up a bag of potato chips and a pack of cigarettes and put a $20 bill on the counter to pay for the items. The owner of the store claimed that he didn't have change for a twenty; Ross said he didn't have anything smaller. "Okay, then I'll just keep the twenty," the white man said. When Ross protested, the man pulled a knife on him. T-Boy yelled and just at that moment a white police officer happened by. He immediately assumed the problem was caused by T-Boy. He slapped him, kicked him and threw him out into the street.

Ross' aunt (daughter of Diana's grandfather, the Reverend William Moten, pastor of the Alabama Bessemer Baptist Church) heard the scuffle and came running down the street screaming at the officer to leave her nephew alone. The police officer took a swing at the old woman, knocking her to the ground.

"Man, are you *crazy*?" T-Boy protested as he approached the cop. Before anyone knew what was happening, the officer pulled his revolver from his holster and fired off a shot directly at T-Boy's head.

Luckily, the bullet just grazed the side of Ross' skull, shattering the store window behind him. As T-Boy lay on the ground bleeding—and his aunt lay next to him in a half-conscious state— the officer handcuffed him, dragged him into the police car and took him to jail.

That is the Ross family's version of the story. Most likely it is very close to the truth considering the racial climate in Alabama at the time. Diana was horrified when she heard this news. "What if that cop had killed Arthur?" she asked later. "We would never have known the truth!" She sent a high-powered lawyer to Alabama, and he managed to get the charges dropped and clear her brother's name. But Diana still had to pay for the store window that was shattered by the police officer's bullet.

Of course, there were serious problems in Detroit, too, at that time. Before Diana's brother Fred went into the Air Force in 1969, he worked part-time at Motown as a recording engineer. One day, while driving down a Detroit street in Diana's expensive white Jaguar he noticed a police car following him. He pulled over.

"What'cha doing in this car, boy?" the cop asked suspiciously.

"It's my sister's," he responded just a bit defensively.

"I don't like the tone of your voice," the officer said, pulling

Fred out of the automobile. After a scuffle, Fred found himself stretched out in the middle of the street, his hands cuffed behind his back, and being kicked by a white policeman. He was taken to jail and, Diana said later, "He got beat up real bad. He wears his hair in the natural way. And right off, I suppose, Detroit cops assume he's a militant because of all the riots."

When the Detroit police department decided to press charges against Fred, Diana paid for his defense. If her brother had a police record he would never be able to join the Air Force, which was his goal at that time. There was a court case. Fred Ross' name was cleared.

"There are times now when I'm just as angry and bitter as the black militants who are asking 'Why should it be this way?' " she said to a reporter at this time. "I'm asking too, but the next question has to be 'What do you do about it?' Dr. King had his way and Rap Brown had his and the Panthers have theirs—and I have mine. I follow my instincts. I've followed them all of my life, about everything, and they have never let me down, especially when it comes to people. All I can do as a black woman is follow my instincts and live my life as best I can."

In another interview, Diana said, "I saw a picture once of a black grandmother sitting on the steps of a tenement. Sitting next to her was her daughter, and her daughter's daughter. Generation after generation, they stay in the same place, the same building. If I could only convince one black person from that kind of background that there are a lot of nice things in this world they can have if only they try for them. Obviously, you have to work hard and not everybody can make it clear to the top. But it's worth it, no matter what. It's worth it if only to accomplish the smallest thing. If only to be free."

Diana Ross certainly understood and could relate to white prejudice against black people. Still, Paramount's publicity departments would face a huge challenge in attempting to overcome the hostility surrounding her casting in *Lady Sings the Blues*, especially when Louis McKay, Billie's real husband, shot off a warning through his lawyer to Weston and Motown that "you guys better not make a movie about my wife using that singer girlfriend of Berry Gordy's." The producers ended up having to bring McKay into the project and pay him handsomely as a consultant.

At first, Diana was hurt by the negative reaction to her upcoming film debut. "My God, what had I done to deserve this total resentment? And from my own race and people?" she said.

"There was such a total 'No, you can not do it' that it frightened the hell out of me."

She called Berry late one night and said simply, "Get me out of this." But he told her it was too late—it really wasn't—and that she should toughen up, take the flak and turn it around and make it work for her own benefit.

Diana did just that. First she got angry—"How dare they question my ability?"—and then she got to work to prove her critics wrong. She studied the situation, asked lots of questions, and then took action. On the cover of her copy of the script, Diana wrote: "The most important thing in my life is to have my baby. The second most important thing is this movie."

Months before shooting began, Diana immersed herself in the Billie Holiday legend in preparation for recording the soundtrack album. The thought of singing blues and jazz was intimidating to her at first. So much so that someone suggested she simply lip-synch in the film to Holiday's recordings. Diana quickly rejected that idea as "an insult to me as an artist" and decided that her goal would not be to sound like Billie Holiday but rather to capture the strong moods, hues and interpretive genius that Holiday brought to her records.

Diana had already been exposed to Billie Holiday's music when Gordy decided to have her sing "My Man" on a Bob Hope TV special in 1969. She agreed to sing the song because she wanted to emulate Streisand's *Funny Girl* performance. "But that version sucks!" Gordy told her. "You gotta sing it like Billie Holiday."

"But I've never even heard Billie Holiday sing that song," Diana argued. "I don't think I've ever heard Billie Holiday sing *any* song!"

Gordy sent his aides to scour record stores in Los Angeles in hopes of finding Holiday's version, but with no luck. Finally musical conductor Gil Askey came into the office with the Holiday recording. Berry summoned Diana and played it for her in front of Askey. "Now you listen to this and you sing it exactly the same way on the Bob Hope special," he told her.

Which is precisely what she did, though she didn't think Billie's performance was very good ("I listened to that first record and thought, 'What's so great about Billie Holiday?' " she would later admit). Perhaps to pacify her Streisand obsession, Gordy allowed Diana and The Supremes to perform two more Barbra Streisand songs on that same program: "Sam, You Made the Pants Too Long" and "Cornet Man."

Gil Askey had been working with the "new" Supremes at the

Frontier Hotel in Las Vegas when Berry decided to pull him out that engagement to work on the soundtrack of *Lady Sings the Blue* With years of experience as The Supremes' musical conductor, h contributed a lot to the Ross-less Supremes' success.

"But who cares about them?" Gordy decreed. "Now Diane needs him again."

Gordy instructed Askey to choose 18 Holiday songs he believed Ross could handle, and then give her tapes of all of them to study. "Every night, Diana would lie in bed with her earphones on and listen to that music," Askey recalled. "For weeks, she would fall asleep with Billie Holiday's music in her head. She got into Billie by osmosis, a brilliant way to go about it."

Gordy and Askey recruited many of the musicians who had actually worked on Billie Holiday sessions—including trumpeter Harry "Sweets" Edison, bassist Red Holloway and guitarist John Collins—for the recording dates at Mowest Studios, Motown's West Coast recording studio.

The double-album soundtrack to *Lady Sings the Blues* contains some of Diana Ross' best work by far. Many women have attempted to cover Billie Holiday's music—Peggy Lee, Judy Garland and dozens of others have recorded songs like "I Cried For You" and "God Bless the Child" with their own style and approach, but, though technically proficient, their performances never seemed to fully capture the humanity that was Billie Holiday's. Billie's truly was a voice of experience. Perhaps only Carmen McRae approximated the range of emotion unique to Billie in her interpretations of Holiday's music and, noted one observer, "That's because Carmen didn't imitate, she loved."

There are those who claim that Diana Ross was successful with her Holiday recordings because she had grown to love Billie Holiday as much as Carmen McRae. At the time she recorded the album, nothing could have been further from the truth. When Diana first went into the studio with these songs, she hadn't filmed the movie yet and knew only a small part of the Billie Holiday story. By way of mimicry or maybe, as Gil Askey believes, osmosis, or even genuine empathy for what little she had learned about Holiday up until this time, the final result is convincing. Diana didn't attempt an imitation of Holiday's timbre, but she did emulate her nuances and phrasing with great accuracy. In "You've Changed," the resemblance is amazing.

Most critics were absolutely dumbfounded by the excellence of these recordings—as if the only material Diana Ross ever waxed were the Holland-Dozier-and-Holland-produced commer-

…hese same critics never paid any attention at all to …orded Rodgers and Hart performances, or to her tele-…ditions of the Irving Berlin and Fats Waller catalogues, …anything else she ever recorded that didn't soar into the …fen. It shouldn't have been surprising to anyone who was …ly familiar with her diverse body of work that Diana Ross was …ole to tackle the music of Billie Holiday. Don't forget, this is the same woman who was determined to out-Streisand Barbra just a couple of years earlier on the Jule Styne score of *Funny Girl*. Not that Holiday has anything in common with Streisand but, to Diana Ross, a challenge is a challenge. She is astonishingly versatile in the recording studio.

"I have never felt I was a great talent," she once said. "I have to work hard on everything. I really do. When I record, I stay in the studio a long time. I know I'm the total of all the intense work, and of all my experiences. Nothing I've learned from my life is wasted."

After the sessions, she told Gil Askey, "You'll never go back out on the road with Mary [Wilson] and the girls. You're too valuable. I want you to stay with me."

Once she felt satisfied with the recording sessions, Diana became consumed by the *Lady Sings the Blues* project. She continued her research into Holiday's life by studying photographs to associate facial expressions and posture and the fact that "she probably had bad feet." She even noticed the combs, brushes and peanut brittle wrappers in photos of her dressing room. She began asking questions about drug abuse of people she knew to be addicted, or who had quit. She read up on Lenny Bruce's life. She interviewed people who had known Billie personally.

"I found that if I talked to three or four people about her, they all knew a different Billie Holiday," she said. "Which is just like if you talked to people about Diana Ross. Some remember her as a bitchy so-and-so—Billie," she hastened to add. "Not me."

While Diana studied for her role, Jay Weston discovered that dealing with Gordy and the Motown structure was not easy. "An unhappy moment for me came when I found I had to share production credit with some Motown lawyer [James S. White, formerly of the William Morris Agency]," he said. "Motown is not an easy partner to be in business with. I found dealing with Berry and his people extremely difficult. Motown originally did not have production credit, but through various influences the movie became a Weston-Furie-Motown Production."

By now, Berry Gordy was also brimming with enthusiasm

about the project, especially when he realized Diana's devotion and saw how good she was in screen tests filmed with five potential leading men in a Paramount Studios office. Berry agreed to invest from his personal savings an amount that would surpass the studio budget of $2 million. Eventually Billy Dee Williams, who had just finished work on the television film *Brian's Song*, was selected to be her co-star after he showed up for the audition in a white suit and white hat and swept Diana off her feet. When she saw the film of their scene together, Diana sank down in her seat and told Jay Weston, "I just got chills, I'm in love."

Berry, who made it clear that his major interest was in Diana Ross' future, now began to ignore the rest of the Motown "family" by delegating more responsibility and power to others at the company. Most of these people were white, like attorney Ralph Seltzer and "collections man" Barney Ales, both of whom had been with the company since the early '60s. In fact, by 1970, four of Motown's eight vice presidents were white. Seven years later, whites would hold four out of every five power positions at Motown.

The Motown offices were officially located in Los Angeles. While the move to the West Coast proved great for Gordy's kingdom, it was devastating to Detroit's blacks. Motown had stood as a symbol of what a black man could accomplish with business acumen and organization. So when Gordy and Motown moved from Detroit, it left a void in the community that had given the company its start.

Around this time, Martha Reeves returned to Detroit from Europe and called the Motown offices to see if any recording dates were scheduled for her. "Oh, they moved," she was told by the answering service.

"They *what*?"

"They all moved to California, girl."

"But nobody told *me* nothing about that," Martha said.

"Well, they're *gone*," the operator on the other end said impatiently before hanging up on her.

Other Motowners weren't so anxious to follow Gordy westward.

"I knew I'd lost B.G. a long time ago," Marvin Gaye told writer David Ritz in Gaye's biography, *Divided Soul*. "Diana dazzled him, just like she would dazzle the world. She meant everything to him—Vegas, Broadway shows, movies. In my heart, I knew I could do the same. But Berry was off on his Diana trip. His head was in Hollywood, and we were all supposed to follow after him like little puppy dogs. Let the others go. Let them chase after the bright lights. No me. I was cool in Detroit. I stayed out and wasn't about to move until I got damn well ready.''

Marvin had bitterly resented Diana for years, feeling his own career suffered because the boss lavished time on Diana at his expense. Berry dismissed these claims as the "gripes of wrath."

The Supremes were still doing fairly well having made the charts with a couple more hit records ("Stoned Love" and "Nathan Jones"). But as it turned out, Berry Gordy wouldn't have to work very hard at destroying the new Supremes. They would self-destruct.

"Without Berry being around, there was a lot of pressure off of us," Mary Wilson once recalled, "and I guess it was easy to slip up. Also, I found that working with Jean was difficult. She had no real loyalty to The Supremes or to Motown, so that made it tough.''

New to Motown, Jean Terrell was unfamiliar with the way the company traditionally handled artists' finances. She once complained, "Gladys Knight never got the money that she made, neither did The Supremes, nor Diana Ross, nor any of the other artists who ever worked at Motown. Somebody just put it in his pocket. So don't tell me you can give me two pennies just because I was only making one at first, and that I'm supposed to be happy with it."

First Cindy Birdsong would leave the group to have a baby in 1972, and in doing so, she would sign away all of her future royalties to Supremes' recordings, the same big mistake Florence also made. She would be replaced by Lynda Tucker Lawrence. Then, Jean left. Like Florence and Cindy, she also signed away her royalties. She was replaced by Scherrie Payne, a remarkable singer. By this time, without Gordy's interest in the records, royalties were no longer a matter of consideration because the songs—though they all had great potential to be hits—were commercial failures.

The end was in sight when Mary married Pedro Ferrer, a dashing, unemployed Latin. She then decided to make him The Supremes' manager, even though he had no experience.

Mary felt she had no choice. Somebody had to do it if Berry wasn't going to. Ferrer certainly wasn't shrewd enough to know how to deal with Berry Gordy and the politics of the Motown structure. Ultimately, he would kill off The Supremes. Indeed, just as Berry Gordy predicted, the group that had been used as a launching pad for Diana Ross' ascension to superstar glory simply fizzled out after its purpose had been served.

It seemed that, for the most part, Berry Gordy's life became calmer when he moved from Detroit to Los Angeles. However, his bodyguards went with him, strong and seemingly invulnerable, but not always as invincible as Berry may have believed. At a surprise 17th birthday party for Hazel Joy Gordy, Berry's daughter, at his home, the guest list included Diana and her brother Chico, Sugar Ray Robinson, Jim Brown, Dionne Warwick and many other celebrities.

"Security was so tight that many of the handsome men you might want to chat with over coffee could easily be carrying a gun," reported one party guest, writer Judy Spiegelman.

After Berry's daughter blew out her birthday candles, her father presented her with a small ring box, which contained a key that belonged to a new Pontiac Firebird. The automobile, with a big red ribbon on top of it, was parked in the driveway. When Hazel saw the car, she let out a shriek and jumped into it for a test run down the hill. As the confused guests watched, three muscular fellows packing guns bolted for another car and went screeching down the driveway after her. For many of the guests, this was the first time they were aware of the tight security precautions. When Hazel returned a few moments later, the security men were right behind her, barely a foot remained between their automobile and hers.

Berry Gordy always had security guards at his side, even when he entertained guests at his home. At one party, one of these bodyguards was shot to death under what are still mysterious circumstances. One former Motown executive who attended the party and asked for anonymity recalled, "All I know is that this man was killed at the party, and I remember being scared to death about it. The rumor was that the perpetrators were some of Berry's 'buddies' from Detroit who were trying to prove to him that they could still get to him if they wanted to."

No Los Angeles Police Department file could be found relating to this incident. According to one informed source, the security man was killed by another of Berry's guards. The surviving guard claimed that both men had been drinking and his gun went off accidentally. Apparently, there were no witnesses to the shooting, and no one was prosecuted in connection with the incident.

Photographer Harry Langdon recalled of the victim, "Whenever I did photo sessions with Diana, he would always be in the room with her if Berry wasn't. This was the security guard Berry trusted most, a very large, husky man. I never refused him anything he ever asked for. After the meeting at Berry's house with his staff members in which he berated them in front of me, I had a very difficult time getting other ideas about Diana channeled to him. The only way I could do it was to sneak them to this particular bodyguard, with whom I had a terrific rapport. But then he got into that shootout at the house. Next thing I knew, he was off to that big Motown studio in the sky.''

Early in the morning on August 14, 1971, Diana Ross gave birth by Caesarian to her first daughter, Rhonda Suzanne, at Cedars of Lebanon Hospital in Los Angeles. Berry Gordy, Michael Roshkind and Diana's husband Bob were all at the hospital awaiting the birth. Bob explained that they named the child with an "R" for himself and Suzanne after Suzanne dePasse. Mike Roshkind said later there were so many nervous men in the waiting room, "you couldn't tell which one was the father."

The next day, Florence Ballard read in the newspaper that Diana had given birth to a baby girl. She said that she wanted to telephone her, but that she felt awkward about it. So, instead, she put together a lovely package of infant baby clothes and matching booties. She carefully wrapped the box with bright pink wrapping paper and a large pink bow.

"But why, Flo?" her husband Tommy wanted to know. "Why are you doing this for Diane?"

" 'Cause I feel like maybe I messed up in the past," Flo said. "I think it's gonna be up to me now to reach out to Diane. And this is a happy time for her. I want to do this."

Flo signed a card and taped it to the box. Then she wrapped the whole thing with brown paper and addressed it. She took it to the post office.

Two weeks later it was returned to her, marked "Undeliverable."

She didn't have Diana's correct Beverly Hills address.

Chapter

15

PRINCIPAL PHOTOGRAPHY FOR *Lady Sings the Blues* was to begin in mid-October 1971, but three weeks before the starting date, Berry called Sidney Furie into his office and announced to him that the script was "all wrong."

"What the hell are you talking about?" Furie said.

"Just look at this," Gordy replied, opening the script to a confrontation scene between Diana Ross and Billy Dee Williams. "Louis McKay can't take that abuse from Billie lying down. He's gotta walk out on her, or he'll be a pussy. And this guy cannot be a pussy, not in a Diana Ross movie, anyway."

"But it's about conflict," Furie argued. "If he walks out, that's the end of the scene. Where's the conflict?"

"The hell with that," Gordy shot back. "This is life. In real life, no real man takes abuse from any woman. Listen, I'm gonna rewrite this whole goddamn script on the plane on my way back to Detroit this weekend."

Furie marveled at Berry Gordy's naïveté. "You cannot rewrite a whole movie screenplay on a plane to Detroit," he said, his voice rising.

Gordy dismissed Furie's apprehension with a wave of his hand. "Leave it to me," he said, showing him to the door.

When Gordy returned on Monday, he had only rewritten that one confrontation. He announced to Weston and Furie that filming would have to be delayed until Suzanne dePasse and Chris Clark—neither of whom had any prior scriptwriting experience—could rewrite the rest of it. "I reminded him that this would cost us more money," Sidney Furie said. "And I'll never forget his words: 'We'll pay everyone. Forget about the bucks, Furie. We're makin' a classic here.' "

Production was delayed six weeks while dePasse and Clark revised the Terence McCloy script. "Ninety-five percent of McCloy's script was rewritten," Jay Weston said. "I don't know that there were more than a couple lines left on the original. I knew then more than ever what I was up against with Gordy."

Finally with a 100-page shooting script and 168 different scenes, principal photography for *Lady Sings the Blues* began on Monday, December 6, 1971.

From that point on until the movie was completed in early February 1972, changes in dialogue were made virtually every day. "Most of Diana Ross' great moments were improvised as the camera rolled," Sidney Furie said. "For instance, I'd know what I needed and I would explain it to her: 'Here's what's happening, you feel this way, he feels that way, and you say something like . . .' and then I'd turn the camera on and film whatever she did. That would be take one. Then we'd do it again and again. In each of those takes we'd get a little of something that when we went back in and edited a piece here and piece there we had a scene. Actually, I don't know that Diana was acting as much as she was reacting. But whatever it was, it worked,"*

Gordy and his staff made script changes every day, and these revisions would be sent out late at night to the actors at home. The new lines had to be learned by early the next morning. Once, Billy Dee Williams had gotten his new lines in the middle of one night, and had to be awakened out of a sound sleep in order to memorize them and be ready the next morning to report to work. When he got to the studio, Berry told him, "Forget about the lines we sent over, we're just gonna make it up as we go along. Diane's better at that." Billy was upset, but could do nothing.

Williams' attempts at improvisation in *Lady Sings the Blues* proved awkward and uncomfortable to watch. Later he would admit that he had never worked like that before, and hoped he would never have to again.

Two days into the film, Diana detonated what set-insiders called "the gown explosion." She finally had a chance to take a look at the wardrobe she was expected to wear and decided it was unacceptable. Diana got on the phone with Berry and began to cry about the wardrobe. He explained to her that the gowns

---

*When the film was finally released, respected *Los Angeles Times* critic Charles Champlin noted that the improvisational tone of some of Diana's more moving scenes "explains their harrowing immediacy and the fact that they play as drama rather than melodrama."

were authentic in that they were designed from period photographs taken in the 1940s. "But they look crappy," she argued. "I don't want these. I want the best."

"So all of the gowns were dumped," Sidney Furie recalled. "Berry just came in one day and said, 'These clothes are no good, throw 'em out.' By now I was used to these sudden turnabouts and last minute Motown decisions. 'Diana needs better than this,' he said. He got the money together to hire Bob Mackie and Ray Aghayan to do the wardrobe.

The new costumes were certainly much more suited to a glitzy Diana Ross persona than they were to an earthy Billie Holiday's, and Berry realized this as soon as he saw all of those chiffon and sequin gowns hanging in the wardrobe room.

"The producers felt she was a temperamental bitch," he said later. "So did I. But because of what I felt were emotional ties between Diane and Billie Holiday, I completely gave in to her wishes."

Certainly Berry realized that any "emotional ties" between Diana and Billie had nothing to do with the 43 expensive gowns Ross ordered to be made for the film. She wanted to look good in her first movie, which was certainly her prerogative.

"Diane is very shrewd," Berry said later. "She'll make you think she's not. I know that she's the world's worst when she doesn't like something."

Motown insiders say that Gordy offered Diana control over the wardrobe but only after striking a private deal with her. "No more tirades on the set," he reportedly told her. *"Ever."* Gordy realized that the Hollywood community is small and clannish, and that if word leaked out in the film industry that Diana Ross was, as he put it, "a temperamental bitch," studio heads would run the other way when approached with future projects that involved her. "I want your reputation in this damn town to be flawless," he told her.

Diana kept her part of the bargain. Most people who worked on the set of *Lady Sings the Blues* insist that she was always willing, giving and eager to please.

"She is as much a pro as I have ever worked with in over 20 years of filmmaking," director Sidney Furie recalled.

"She's the most incredible actress I have ever worked with," said producer Jay Weston. "She was the most disciplined, the most professional. I never had one moment of problem with her. She exceeded all of my expectations, and everyone else's."

Berry had to admit that he was surprised at Diana's ability as an actress, but then in thinking it over he realized that he should have expected as much from her. "There are winners and there are losers," he observed to writer Michael Thomas, "and there are heavyweights, middleweights and lightweights. Diana has always been a heavyweight. And my thing is, people should have the opportunity to do any fucking thing they want."

Lady Sings the Blues was very loosely based on Billie Holiday's autobiography which she wrote with William Dufty. The film told the story of how Holiday, a child rape victim and former Manhattan prostitute, eventually became the toast of the town with a triumphant engagement at Carnegie Hall. Along the way, she has a stormy relationship with Louis McKay (Billy Dee Williams), faces segregation in the South, witnesses a lynching in an open field, suffers the anguish of an attack by Ku Klux Klan members while on the road with a band of white musicians, and the murder of her friend Piano Man (played by Richard Pryor) by two drug dealers.

It was an extremely physical movie: Ross had to grapple with Williams (with switchblade in hand, she actually cut him), bang about a padded cell and scream through a drug withdrawal scene. But musical arranger Gil Askey says that it wasn't the physical or wildly emotional scenes that were difficult for Diana.

"The ones that dealt with anything sexual were tough," he recalled. "Like when she's sitting on the toilet wearing her bra and shooting up. She was more concerned about the bra thing than she was about the drug depiction. In another scene she had to act like she was picking up money with her thighs while the audience leered and cheered her on. Diana was a wreck about this. She is very, very modest about her body. She didn't even like to change clothes in front of anyone, not the other Supremes, not even her mother. Only time you ever saw her body was in a swimming suit. Not that she was gonna be showing any skin in the scene, but the idea of all that attention on her you-know-what freaked her out. After she told me she was nervous, I went out and got her a bottle of Courvoisier, told B.G. I was gonna do it.

"'C'mon girl,' I said, 'Drink this, it'll make you relax.' She gulped a couple of shots, took a deep breath and went in and did the scene."

When the movie was nearly finished, it was four hours long and there were still scenes to be shot. Paramount brass insisted that the film would have to be edited to 90 minutes before it could ever be released. "They want to butcher it," Gordy complained.

Berry said that he fully intended to edit the movie before

releasing it, but that he had to continue shooting excess film in order to get what he wanted. To Berry, this whole process was comparable to cutting ten different versions of a Motown song, combining the best parts of each one to make a single version, and then trashing the rest.

"That might be a good way to make records, but it's a shitty way to make movies," Paramount president Frank Yablans told him. Yablans said that he would close down production as long as Gordy continued to spend Paramount's money filming scenes that would end up on the cutting room floor. Ultimately, Berry negotiated to buy out Paramount and, as he put it, "protect Diana Ross and the Billie Holiday legend." Not only did Gordy pay back the $2 million Paramount put up in the first place, he would eventually take another $2 million from his personal savings account before the film was finished. As Marvin Gaye put it, "Berry was betting the bank on Diana."

Berry Gordy—a man used to owning the names of singing groups, all of their music and their contracts—now owned *Lady Sings the Blues*, which was the way he liked it, but certainly not the way Jay Weston or anyone else involved expected things to turn out.

For the rest of the filming, Gordy watched over the set like an eagle protecting his nest. Berry's influence on the project escalated to such an extent that Sidney Furie would not start shooting—even though they were rehearsed and set up—until Berry arrived to confirm everything.

Producer Jay Weston said, "Berry did interfere with the directing to the point where he was behind the camera, in front of the camera, telling Diana what to do. But when Berry gets the bit in his teeth, there's no holding him back. He started editing the movie himself, with no experience whatsoever, taking cassettes up to his house every night. Sidney Furie just threw up his hands and tried to work with him as best he could under the circumstances. Motown, Gordy, just completely took over."

Berry's behavior was that of "a self-made, talented, creative person, and that's not easy to come up against," Suzanne de-Passe remembered years later in an interview with the *Los Angeles Times*. "He was kind of like a bear coming through the woods. Crash, crash, crash."

Gordy tried not to make an issue of the fact that Billy Dee Williams had a habit of arriving 15 to 20 minutes late practically every day. One day, Gordy pulled him aside. "Man, are you crazy?" he told him. "The cameras are rolling and my money's going down the drain because you're late." When Williams explained that he was used to taking his time on the set, Gordy exploded. "That's good with somebody else's money, but this is costing me $29,000 a day. Diane has the starring role, and she's always here 20 minutes early, if not earlier. You don't see *her* making a grand entrance." Billy Dee Williams was on time for the rest of the shoot.

Williams today says that he enjoyed working with Diana, even though she was often distant and removed. "Sometimes, you feel an aloofness from her, as if she is not available. Even on a film set, Diana is nice to people but again not often available. She keeps a distance. She is a secretive person, self-protective."

Also, he said, "That woman has a fantastic mouth. We had to do one of the kissing scenes over ten times, and each time, there was Berry Gordy, moving around in the background, trying to get a closer look at what we were doing to make sure we weren't enjoying it too much. Things were fine when I didn't have to contend with Berry."

"Billy Dee tried to kiss too much," Berry said. "I'd let them rehearse the scene until they got to the kissing part and then I'd yell, 'Okay. Cut! Cut! You got the scene down. You two certainly don't need to rehearse the kiss!' "

Her co-stars were always baffled about Berry's hold over Diana. "Why do you rely on that guy so much?" one asked her on the set.

At first, she was surprised by the question. Most people never asked her about Berry, they just accepted the relationship. Her answer, however, was quick: "Because he's the only man in the entire world who can handle anything for me the way I like it done. There's nobody else I can trust totally. There's not one person like Berry Gordy, Jr."

"Even your husband?"

Diana's face froze. She turned and walked away.

"She's in love with the guy, still," said her co-star. "Face facts."

Richard Pryor's role as Piano Man began as a very small one, one line in fact, at the start of the film. "It was Berry's idea to use him," recalled Sidney Furie. "Pryor was so brilliant, and he improvised so well with Diana, that his part just kept getting expanded. He had his problems. He drank, but he was always very, very funny."

On Christmas Eve, the cast was shooting a radio station scene in a Los Angeles theater. According to the script, Billie has been hired to sing on a Manhattan broadcast sponsored by Sunray Soap, but because she's black—"and, after all, this is a soap product"—she doesn't get to perform as promised. She is humiliated and disappointed when other vocalists, all white, perform with her band. It was a tense day. Everyone involved was anxious to finish the shoot and get home in order to celebrate the holiday with families. Some of the cast members, including Pryor, sat on the sidelines to lend Diana moral support, and then to commiserate with her afterwards.

The filming proved slow-going, and after each take, Richard Pryor would reach beneath his seat and pull out a fifth of brandy, take two swigs, and then quickly hide the bottle again. As the brandy went down, Richard would close his eyes, inhale deeply and then exhale with a shudder.

When Diana, who was on stage with the orchestra, figured out what was going on, she began shooting dirty looks at Richard. He pretended not to notice. Then the very second she would turn her back, Richard would reach for the bottle and take two surreptitious swigs before hiding the whiskey again. When she turned around to face him, he would wink up at her, flashing what Berry called "that big shit-kickin' grin of his."

After about an hour of this game, Richard was feeling pretty good, and Diana was pretty angry.

"Stop. Cut. Or whatever you call it!" she announced. "Black, I wanna talk to you."

"What's the problem?" Gordy asked as he pulled her aside.

Pryor sank down into his seat with a guilty "Oh-boy-I'm-in-trouble-now" look on his face.

"Do you see what Richard is doing?" Diana said. "Why does he have to bring booze on the set? Why? It is so distracting and he's gettin' drunk right here in front of us."

Gordy told her to leave Pryor alone. "At least he ain't doin' drugs," he said. "And besides he's really funny, he's a genius. Whatever road he takes to get there is his business, not yours."

Diana protested a bit more, but finally she relented, rolled her eyes at Berry, and then went back up onto the stage. Once in place, she looked down at Richard indignantly. This time he averted his eyes like a schoolboy caught cheating on a test by the teacher.

The scene continued with "a commercial actress" who was playing both voice roles of mother and daughter for the radio broadcast. Daughter had been complaining to mother that she didn't understand why none of her friends would play with her. Mother realized it was because her girl's complexion was dull and listless, and suggested that she wash her face with Sunray soap. Later that day the girl came home from school and enthused, "Mommy, Mommy, what am I going to do? I have so many friends I don't know who to play with first . . ."

"Why don't you play with yourself?" Richard ad-libbed from the sidelines.

Everyone on the set broke up laughing. Diana looked over to Berry, shaking her head and flashing a broad grin. Berry shrugged his shoulders as if to say, "What'd I tell you?" Then Diana looked down at Richard. He winked at her.

She winked back.

The line stayed.

On the day the movie was finished, Berry discovered he owned only domestic rights. He went to Paramount that very same day and bought the foreign rights. He was fairly certain he had a blockbuster on his hands, even if Paramount was sure he didn't. At Gordy's direction, the Motown hype-machine revved up immediately and did everything it could to disassociate the film's white producer and white director from the "black project." First, Gordy didn't want Weston and Furie to attend the film's opening in Manhattan. He wanted all of the glory for himself.

"But finally Paramount agreed to spring for a ticket and hotel for Sidney and me," recalled Jay Weston. "Motown was doing its best to freeze us out so that Berry could claim the movie for his own."

Diana became pregnant again the evening of the last day of filming. When she discovered the pregnancy a couple of months later, she was utterly dismayed; she didn't plan on having another child so soon. But, she admitted to close friends, her doctor wouldn't allow her to use birth control pills "and Bob is very frisky." She lamented, "I really don't have enough time to spend with myself. I don't even have time to get my nails or hair done anymore. I'm just not used to this."

Most of her friends feel that had she not become pregnant, she would have sought to dissolve her marriage. Bob was only living at the house with her occasionally by this time. At one point he rented his own apartment in the Hollywood Hills and threw a housewarming party. Diana was hostess.

"I don't know anything about their personal life," Berry claimed. "I stay out of it. They fight, they're happy, they're sad, whatever . . ."

This did not seem to be a "normal" marriage by even the most bizarre Hollywood standards. Both insisted, however, that their problems had nothing to do with race.

"Bob's being white has never been a problem," Diana said.

"Not for me. It has been a problem with other people, I'm sure. I am so tired of people like Barbara Walters asking me what it's like being married to a white Jewish man. Talking about the differences in race or religion becomes a kind of discrimination when it's made a point of all the time. It bugs the hell out of me."

Admitted one of Bob's close friends, "I don't even know they were still seeing each other, let alone sleeping together. When I heard she was pregnant, my first reaction was total disbelief. She and Bob didn't seem to get along, I thought."

Eddie Carroll, Diana's Hollywood hairdresser at the time, said of the couple, "She used to come into the shop on Sundays to have her hair done, with her husband and kid. All they did was fight constantly. He was a very nice guy but, to me, it looked like he only paid for the gardener, and she paid for everything else. He was mellow and soft-spoken, while she was tense and a real screamer. He never argued back. He would just stand there holding Rhonda and taking a lot of verbal abuse from his wife. You could say he was 'henpecked.' She didn't seem to care who heard these arguments, which really surprised me about her. Why would she want everyone in a beauty shop to know her private business? I couldn't figure her.

"The only other thing that stands out in my mind about Diana Ross is that whenever anyone asked her for an autograph while she was having her hair done, she would refuse. I remember the young daughter of one of my best customers happened by one day and asked me if it would be okay to ask Diana to sign a photo. I didn't think it was a good idea, but the kid was so cute I was sure Diana wouldn't be able to resist her. I sent the girl into the back room where Diana was, and about a minute later she came back out crying, sobbing like crazy. She said Diana told her off, but since I wasn't in the room with them I don't know what really happened. I do know that she didn't get her picture signed. But that was Diana—very moody, very unpredictable, a very strange lady."

Sometimes, the strain between Diana and Bob became apparent even in press interviews. When Joseph Bell went to the Silberstein household to interview Diana for *Good Housekeeping*, he asked Bob, "Exactly what is it you do?"

Bob fumbled, trying to come up with an answer, and Diana cut in, "You're just what you are. A total nothing."

As Diana prepared for the birth of her second child, Gordy and his crew prepared for the birth of Motown Productions' first motion picture.

Diana had to face a solid schedule of concert and recording dates with an uneasy stomach and strained emotions. The fact that she was ordered to stop smoking served to make her even more tense. "It was hard for her to turn herself off, or even to slow down," said Cindy Birdsong.

Even when she was off the road, Diana didn't want to wind down. Instead, she became one of the most beloved Beverly Hills party hostesses. One of the gala parties she and Bob threw at the Maple Avenue fortress was for Mick and Bianca Jagger; at this time, Bob was managing Billy Preston who was on tour with the Stones. There were 16 Beverly Hills policemen and 20 hired security guards (courtesy of Berry Gordy) holding back groupies and fans wanting to get a peek at the celebrities, including Bette Midler, Ringo Starr, Liza Minnelli and Hugh Hefner, who attended the party. There were no gate-crashers because each guest had to have four security checks to get inside the house.

Said guest Warren Beatty, "One thing you can say about Diana Ross, she really knows how to be a Beverly Hills hostess. The trick isn't who comes to the party, it's who you manage to keep out. She had tighter security there than what they have at the White House!"

Chapter

16

IN THE SUMMER of 1972, Berry Gordy took another look at an unedited cut of *Lady Sings the Blues* and began having doubts. Was this movie going to be a success? He honestly didn't know. He was too closely connected to the film and its star to be objective. Sidney Furie was so unhappy with the last third of the film that he asked that his name be taken off the screenplay credits. This request only served to make Berry even more apprehensive. Diana had spent so much time on the film that her recording career had slipped considerably. The current material proved to be mediocre and resulted in low chart ratings. Berry wanted a hit for Diana. So once again the call went out to the Motown troops.

Ron Miller had worked with The Supremes in the '60s as a writer/producer, but made his biggest impact late in the decade with his classic song "For Once in My Life." Written in honor of his daughter on the day she was born, and recorded by Stevie Wonder in 1968, the song became an instant standard. Most people do not even realize it's a Motown song because so many versions have been recorded by traditional artists like Perry Como and Andy Williams. Miller, who is white and looked like a rumpled college student at the time, was known at Motown as being the resident curmudgeon; he was critical of everything. If he actually liked a product, Berry would say, "It must be good 'cause Ron don't like shit." Berry asked Ron to take a look at the film and render an opinion.

"I had heard that Motown was the laughingstock of the film industry with this movie," Ron Miller said, "so I was really prepared to hate it. I sat in a little screening room alone and saw a four-hour unedited version of it. To tell you the truth, I cried because she was so good.''

When he told Berry that he was deeply touched by Diana's sympathetic portrayal, Berry's reaction was, ''Well, I don't know. Some people say it's gonna be great and some say it's gonna ruin her. She's on my back, man. If the movie flops, I'm in deep shit with her. I have to follow it with a natural hit, something so magical no one will question that it's a Number One song.''

Meanwhile, Suzanne dePasse had met a young composer, Michael Masser, at a cocktail party. ''Would you like to start at the top?'' she asked him. ''If so, we need a song for Diana Ross.''

Masser went into the studio with Ross immediately and cut a couple of songs that were of no consequence. Then he composed some music that Gordy felt was strong but could use Ron Miller's compositional and lyrical finesse.

Miller had already dreamed up the title ''Touch Me in the Morning,'' but, as he recalled, ''I didn't have the vaguest idea what it meant. So I analyzed Diane as a person and realized that she was a contemporary woman who was probably liberal about expressing her sexual values, like most *Cosmo* women in a '70s society. Once, it was the man who might give a woman the brush off after a one-nighter telling her 'nothing good's gonna last forever'; now it could be the other way around. So I started writing. I wanted something more adult than 'Baby Love' but pop and r&b enough to cover all markets. It was a cold, calculated, precise job of crafting.''

Miller worked with Masser on a demo Berry loved but Diana did not, saying, ''It's okay for an album but it'll never be a hit.''

''At this point she had a tendency to look down upon her record career as something subservient to the ultimate goal: movies,'' Miller said. ''Her message to me right from the start was: 'I'm only doing this shit 'cause Berry said I have to, but I'm really a movie star. When my movie comes out, don't expect me to keep recording these silly songs.'

''And she's got this big Barbra Streisand complex. I'd heard about it, but didn't really know it until I started conversing with her. Man, she would rather be Barbra Streisand than anyone else in the world. And I don't think she will ever achieve that goal because part of talent like Streisand's has to do with comprehension and artistic vision, which Diane doesn't have much of.''

''Like it or not, record the song,'' Berry ordered Diana. ''It's a hit.''

That week, Ron Miller had to arrange a meeting with Diana in order to rehearse the number with her. She asked him to arrive at the windowless fortress at seven in the morning, and when he protested the hour, she insisted, "I can't help it, Ron. I have to go to New York to buy hats."

When Miller showed up for work, Diana greeted him at the door in a white satin dressing gown trimmed with maribou feathers, the kind of outfit stars wore in the movies of the '30s. Her make-up and hairdo were more suitable for 7:00 P.M. than 7:00 A.M., but if that's what it took to get her in the mood to work, Ron had no objections.

He followed her to the living room, sat down at the glass-plated baby grand, and ran through "Touch Me in the Morning." Diana leaned against the piano while he played, her arms crossed, a frown on her face.

"Play it again," she said when he finished.

After he played it a second time, she shook her head. Her "I don't know" wasn't encouraging.

"Why don't you try it?" he remembered asking her.

Diana came around and stood behind him. After humming three bars, she stopped. "It's too early. My throat hasn't opened up yet."

"But you said seven."

"I know what I said. I can't help it if I can't sing."

"Why don't you try a glass of water or something?"

"You know, you may be right. I haven't had my breakfast. Wait right here."

After what seemed like an interminable wait, Diana returned holding a silver tray with a glass of orange juice, three miniature Danish, a pot of coffee and one cup. She sank down into the couch and began to eat leisurely, looking up from her reading only once to ask Ron, "You have eaten, haven't you? I thought you must have, getting here so early and all."

After her second cup of coffee, Diana pronounced herself ready to proceed. As Ron played, she strained her way through the arrangement.

"It's not right. You've done it differently this time," he remembered her saying.

"It's B-flat, your usual."

"It doesn't sound right," Diana insisted.

"Look, why don't you just run through it again?"

"I don't want to. I know it's wrong. Take it down to A-flat and don't fight me on this, Ron."

After lowering it, he told her, "Now it sounds like shit, Diane."

"But that's my key," she insisted, "and that's where I want it."

"You wouldn't know your musical keys from your car keys," Miller said under his breath. Diana may often be a brilliant vocalist but has never been a technical one. When he called Gordy for support, he got Berry's catch-all reaction: "That's your problem. Don't be ridiculous."

While Diana was in Manhattan, she began practicing the song in her head in A-flat, but meanwhile Ron Miller and Michael Masser decided to use their better judgment and orchestrate the song in the more pleasant sounding B-flat. After returning to Los Angeles, Diana was quickly booked into the Motown recording studio with Miller and Masser for what they both knew was to be a moment of reckoning.

"She was due in the studio at eight in the evening and arrived at 11," Miller said, "with her babysitter, her kid, her so-called husband, her entourage, her white wine and her grapes. And then she got on the phone for hours and fooled around until four in the morning. I knew she wasn't interested in recording at all."

Finally, she was stationed in the sound booth behind a recording microphone, and with the track playing into her ears through headphones, she began singing A-flat melody to a B-flat track. It was all out of tune. A couple of technicians snickered at her. She stopped abruptly.

"Hey. What key is that?" she asked through the intercom system connecting the recording booth to the mixing console.

"It's your key, Diane," Miller said from the other side of the glass window.

"The hell it is," she retorted. "You guys screwed this track up, and are wasting my time."

Now, recalled Ron Miller, he was upset, too. "Well, what key do you think it is, Diane? You tell me."

"How the hell do I know what key it's in," she shouted back. "I just know it's not right. It's supposed to be in, uh, A-flat."

"It is A-flat," Miller lied. He got up out of his chair and began to lumber menacingly toward the sound booth. Michael Masser cringed. He was the new boy on the block and not yet used to this kind of Motown musical melodrama.

"I'll prove it to you. We'll go to the piano right now," Ron said. "And when I finish with you, Diane, you'll know it's A-flat." As he walked toward her, all the while wondering if she would call his bluff, Michael Masser sank deeper into his chair.

"Oh, never mind, goddamn it," Diane said. "I believe you. Let's just cut this goddamn thing so I can go home."

The rest of the session was slow and laborious. Because of the hour, Diana wasn't up to her vocal potential. Miller and Masser had her record the song 12 times and then edited a final product together. "Phrase by phrase," Masser remembered. "There aren't three syllables from a single performance together on the final product." A week later, Ron brought the finished patchwork product to Diana so that she could hear his and Masser's handiwork. He played her the tape. "Gee, that's great, Ron. What take was that? Two or three?"

"Uh . . . two."

"See that. I knew it. I just knew I was hot that night," Diana exclaimed. "So why'd you make me do all those other takes? Just to waste more of my time?"

The next step in Berry Gordy's plan to refortify Diana Ross' recording career was to team her with his brother-in-law, Marvin Gaye, for an album. Marvin had enjoyed great success with his self-written and produced *What's Going On*, despite the fact that Berry thought the record was self-indulgent and didn't want to release it. Marvin had continued to be jealous of the attention Berry lavished on Diana, insisting to friends that he could be every bit the star she was if he only received half the care. So when Berry asked him to record an album with her, Marvin laughed in his face and told him, "*No way!* I wouldn't go in the studio with that crazy woman for a million bucks."

But Berry knew how to get to Marvin. He sweet-talked him into the project by telling him that Diana needed his help now that her record sales were slipping and that, as Gaye put it later, "the prince is in a little stronger position than the princess." Gordy also told Gaye that—who knows—perhaps if there was magic between the two of them in the studio, "I just might be able to work you into her next movie." Marvin became interested.

Marvin attempted to negotiate a deal by which he would get top billing over Diana, the way he'd always had it when he recorded duets with Mary Wells, Kim Weston and Tammi Terrell. He probably should have known better than to ask for star billing. He didn't get it.

"The chemistry was all wrong," recalled Art Stewart of the Ross-Gaye recording sessions. Stewart was a Motown staff engineer and his comments were made to writer David Ritz. "It was extremely tense. Marv would wander in, sipping wine and smoking a joint, ready to sing, while Diana was much more formal. Then, adding insult to injury, he sang circles around her. She just couldn't keep up with him.''

Most people at Motown knew that Marvin Gaye rarely recorded without a marijuana cigarette in his hand. Diana tried to reason with him in the sound booth before the first session that she was pregnant and didn't want to inhale the smoke. With Marvin standing at her side in front of a microphone, and Diana sitting in a rocking chair in front of another mike, she asked him very nicely to put out his joint.

Marvin remembered telling her, "I'm sorry, baby, but I gotta have my dope or I can't sing."

"What kind of crap is this?" Diana exclaimed as she got out of her rocking chair and walked out of the recording booth. Going over to Berry Gordy, who was sitting at the control console on the other side of the glass, she announced, "I am not going back in there unless he stops smoking that stuff."

By now, Marvin was behind the glass panel taking deep dramatic puffs and then blowing smoke into the air as if each cloud somehow punctuated his independence. Berry got on the intercom and addressed Marvin, who had, by now, fogged himself in behind the glass.

"You know, Diane's pregnant," Berry said, choosing his words carefully. "Can't you put the drugs aside just this once?"

Marvin didn't want to record this duet album in the first place, and he probably felt if he was going to do it it would be on his terms, marijuana and all. "Sorry, B.G., gotta have my stuff," Marvin said casually with a grin.

Berry turned to Diana and shrugged helplessly.

Marvin recalled that Diana reached over a bowl of fruit on the console, grabbed a bunch of grapes, and threw them at Berry's face. Then she turned on her heels and stormed out of the studio.

"Must've been something you said, chief," Marvin joked as everyone collapsed in laughter.

After that, Diana Ross and Marvin Gaye recorded their parts of the album separately, though listening to the warm, loving sound no one would ever guess it. Perhaps the jacket provides a clue: a smiling Ross and Gaye each in profile—back to back and looking away from each other.

"But I was dealing with two very emotional people," producer Hal Davis said. "I had to check myself into a hospital after we finished. I had these tremendous breakouts."

Marvin Gaye's assessment of the situation: "During this album [Diana] was on pins and needles. She was pregnant and her marriage seemed shaky. Professionally, she and B.G. were still together for the same reasons that Anna [Gordy] and I were hanging on. Fear and money. I could have been a little more understanding. But I'm afraid I went the other way. It's hard for me to deal with prima donnas. We were like two spoiled kids screaming for the same cookie. It was definitely not a duet made in heaven."

Diana and Marvin was finally released a year after they recorded it. Diana's succinct words about the album: "Marvin was great to work with. He made it very easy for me."

The ads trumpeted "Diana Ross *is* Billie Holiday." But Diana could not attend the premiere of *Lady Sings the Blues* on October 12, 1972. Because she was so close to giving birth to her second child, her doctor forbade her to fly.

"There's only one first for anybody, whatever his profession," Diana said later. "I hated missing that premiere. It would have been the biggest day of my life."

Instead of going to New York with Berry and the Motown staffers, she had to remain in Los Angeles. Berry's basket of two dozen long-stemmed red roses with the note, "Tonight everyone will know what Diana Ross is," were little consolation.

"Why doesn't he call?" Diana once remembered asking herself at 8:00 P.M. the night of the premiere. She'd been pacing back and forth in her bedroom for the last hour.

"It's too early. It's three hours' difference from New York," her husband Bob said.

"Why didn't they have the premiere in Los Angeles? Why didn't that damn doctor let me go? Why'd I have to be pregnant now?"

For Diana, the circumstances seemed too cruel to be true. She was 30 pounds overweight, suffering from shooting back pains and stuck in Los Angeles when she wanted to be in New York.

Later, Diana would recall that she started throwing away maternity clothes that night, vowing never to get pregnant again.

At midnight the phone rang.

"We're a hit, Diane! The movie's gonna be a smash."

"Oh, thank God. Just thank God."

After hearing all the details, Diana and Gordy said their goodbyes. Just before he hung up, Diana said, "You really didn't have to call to tell me all this, Black. I could've just read about it in the paper tomorrow.''

Three days later, Diana gave birth to another girl, again by Caesarian section; this child would be named Tracee Joy. Sidney Furie's wife, who also became pregnant on the last day of shooting, had her baby on the same day as Diana. Ernestine Ross came to California to stay with Diana when the new baby was born ''because I really needed her,'' Diana said. ''But I did have to remind her that all through my life I've been capable of doing most anything.''

The relationship between Diana, Berry and Bob continued to baffle all observers. The three of them took skiing vacations together, and the two men competed on the tennis courts—26-year-old Silberstein would always defeat 43-year-old Gordy. Gordy and Silberstein thoroughly enjoyed pacing each other in competition: on 200-yard foot races on the beach at Malibu, Berry always beat Bob.

In interviews promoting *Lady Sings the Blues*, Diana would often be joined by both of the men in her life. In discussing the Silbersteins' private life, one writer asked Diana if she thought she was a good wife. As she pondered the question, Berry jumped in.

''I think she's a great wife.''

''And I think he's an excellent husband,'' Berry concluded of Bob.

The two men grinned at each other.

''Actually, I'm a fantastic husband,'' Bob corrected.

''Who asked you?'' Diana said under her breath. Then she smiled to show she had been jesting.

The reporter continued to question Diana's domestic ''bliss'' by asking what kind of father Bob was.

''That's something we don't get into too much,'' Berry snapped, as Mr. and Mrs. Silberstein sat silently.

Bob and Berry then retreated to the next room and the backgammon table. The reporter, feeling he was getting a terrific story, asked Diana about her future plans. When she responded that a trip to Europe was in the offing, she was asked whether Bob would be joining her.

''No, I don't think so,'' she said.

''I'll be in Europe ahead of you,'' Bob shouted from the other room.

''Me, too,'' Berry piped in.

''You'll both be in Europe ahead of me?'' Diana asked, suddenly sitting bolt upright. She appeared to be very exasperated. "You're just doing that so you can *both* be there when I'm there."

"I'll be skiing with Berry," Bob said, ignoring her comment. "While you're doing one country a day, we'll be in Gstaad, me and Berry. It's just fantastic this time of the year."

Diana groaned and sank down into her leather couch. The look in her eyes made it clear to the reporter that this interview was over.

Diana's former lover and present husband actually seemed to like each other quite a lot, especially when Diana wasn't around. She often appeared more uncomfortable with the two of them than they were with each other, probably because she was the focal point of both of them.

But despite those moments of uneasiness, Diana would never consider breaking free of Berry entirely. And Berry wasn't about to let her go, either. Bob seemed to be in love with Diana, now, and willing to put up with almost anything just to be with her.

Just as Berry Gordy had expected, most reviewers and friends of Billie Holiday's criticized the many biographical inaccuracies in *Lady Sings the Blues*. The film is approximately 90 percent imagination and 10 percent fact. Or, as Berry puts it, "The picture is honest but it's not necessarily true."

Billie Holiday didn't have a full orchestra at Carnegie Hall as Diana did in the movie—she had only piano, bass and drums. Holiday didn't wear lovely designer clothes, hers were usually cheap, store bought items. Billie certainly never dreamed of as much continuity in her life as the Motown script allowed.

But Gordy and company didn't intend to make a documentary about the life of Billie Holiday. Rather they hoped to capture Lady Day's essence poetically on film, and maybe bring into focus the hopelessness of ghetto life and how only the strong survive.

"It's a love story," Berry observed. "Love is love. It's universal. Billie Holiday was a human being, a beautiful and lovely human being who had a tragic life. It didn't matter about color. Everybody's the same when it comes to love. Black people have joy like everyone else, as well as tragedy. When someone in the ghetto falls in love, she hears bells, the same bells someone uptown hears when she falls in love."

Through her amazing screen performance, Diana Ross elevated the *myth* of Billie Holiday. Leonard Feather, a close friend of Billie Holiday's, doubted that Diana could ever be convincing in this role. "To my amazement, I confess it, this newcomer destroyed almost all of my reservations," he said. "Miss Ross brought to her portrayal a sense of total immersion in the character. Dramatically, this is a *tour de force*."

As a result of all of the improvisations, it seemed that Diana Ross created a series of impressive scenes, rather than a real character who grew and coherently changed through the film. But, still, she appeared believable. She tackled the tragic legend of Billie Holiday with power and pathos and, in spite of acknowledged inaccuracies in the plot, came out a winner.

Billie's friend, the late music critic Ralph Gleason, wrote for *Rolling Stone*, "I never thought someone so young could have loved Billie so much. How glad I am now to have been so wrong."

Most of the promotion Diana Ross did for the movie was via press interviews at her home (later, after the baby, she would begin making appearances on "Tonight" and other shows). She appeared on the cover of *Life* magazine's December 8, 1972, issue, a real coup for Motown's press department. Often she would talk intelligently about Billie Holiday and her life.

"There are parts of Billie I could relate to," she told a reporter for the *Philadelphia Inquirer*. "The insecurities, the courage, the ups and downs, her spirit—the way she just wanted to live and be good at it. I get angry when all I see are pictures of her with tears in her eyes because I'm sure, I'm just sure, there weren't always tears."

In another interview, Diana talked about growing older (she was 28) and the effect it seemed to be having on her: "A woman starts worrying about her age after she has two children, and they begin to take up all of her time. You look at yourself and you don't see that teen-ager you used to see. You see a woman. I guess the film did that to me, too. When I looked up at that movie screen and saw how I was magnified, it frightened me."

Diana had expressed to many reporters that she somehow felt different, almost alienated from herself after making the movie and having her two children. Her life had changed so dramatically, and in such a short time. "She can't quite shake off this queasy feeling that it's not her anymore," one writer reported. "She hasn't quite caught up with herself yet."

Probably Diana Ross was suffering from a touch of postpartum depression, but with a show biz twist. She wondered how she could continue her regular career as a pop vocalist, performer and recording actress, as if nothing had happened, after this movie experience. How could she just move on to another

Vegas engagement, another record album? "It's a long way from 'Baby Love' to 'Good Morning Heartache'," she observed.

Diana felt let down. She had given pleasure to millions of people through her work, but what about herself? For instance, she couldn't even remember how many times she had been to Europe. Despite at least four visits, Europe was to her a stage door in Milan, a hotel room in London, a fight with Florence in Paris. She never saw any of the sights. Now, she was beginning to equate her life with her European experiences. She was missing out. At 28 years of age, she suddenly felt empty inside.

Was she really an actress like everyone was saying? Or just a lucky singer? Her husband would say that the way Diana coped with this life crisis was "to cry a lot." One magazine reporter called her "The Princess of Plastic Pop." Is that who she really was? She hoped not. The writer signed himself J.C. She said that she almost wrote back to him: "Dear Jesus Christ, Since you know so much, you tell me how you know what I am."

She didn't have the answers and, unfortunately, no one around appeared particularly interested in the questions.

"I feel lost," Diana complained to Berry. "I don't know where I'm going, what I should be doing." The two were lunching at Le St. Germaine restaurant; she was wearing a green and white dyed foxtail coat and large, matching "celebrity sunglasses." Everyone in the restaurant seemed to be staring at her, the nouveau movie star.

Berry Gordy, natty in a well-trimmed beard and expensive pinstriped suit, just shook his head and smiled at her.

"Jesus Christ, Diane," he said, as he poured her another glass of French white wine. "What a bunch of crap!"

Chapter

🌼 17 🌼

AT THE END of January 1973, the Academy Award nominations were announced; no one was really surprised when Diana Ross was named in the Best Actress category. Certainly she deserved this recognition for such an impressive cinematic debut. The film was also nominated in four other categories, including a nod to Gil Askey for his work on the musical score. Other nominees in the Best Actress category included Liv Ullmann (*The Immigrants*), Maggie Smith (*Travels With My Aunt*), Liza Minnelli (*Cabaret*) and Cicely Tyson (*Sounder*).

The Golden Globe and all sorts of other awards had come Diana's way, and she was thrilled by most of them. Some of her other awards did not prove as thrilling. For instance, when she was awarded a Golden Apple as "Most Promising Newcomer" from the Hollywood Press Association, she was offended. "Newcomer? How dare they," she exclaimed to reporter Joseph Bell.

"I don't think she even wanted to go to the luncheon," a Motown publicist recalled. But Berry forced her to play this political game. You *are* a newcomer—in films, he told her.

Diana posed and smiled with other winners, Peter Falk and Burt Reynolds, and then afterwards said, "They were all so full of that Hollywood crap, it made me sick."

Now Diana had to socialize with Hollywood's so-called "movers and shakers" and be interviewed by the same Tinseltown columnists who, before, hadn't shown the least bit of interest in her. Depending on her mood, she enjoyed the attention but certainly not the control Motown maintained over all proceedings. If Berry wasn't pulling the strings, someone else from the company always was.

"Diana will probably do a live concert tour to coincide with all the openings of *Lady Sings the Blues* in Europe," Mike Roshkind told Joyce Haber during her February interview with Diana Ross.

"I will?" asked Diana, obviously surprised.

"She hates my guts," Roshkind told Haber.

To impress her Hollywood interrogator, Diana wore a sable coat, silk blouse, green velvet skirt and silver jewelry from Gucci. She looked stunning and seemed very much in control, but Roshkind still insisted on finishing Diana's sentences, much the way Diana used to finish Cindy Birdsong's and Mary Wilson's.

"I'd really be thrilled if I won the Oscar," Diana began. "But then if I didn't . . ."

"You'll cry," Roshkind jumped in.

Most people felt that Diana really had a chance. Even Liza Minnelli said, "I've got two words to say about the Oscars: Diana Ross."

Only Diana's husband Bob and Berry Gordy really knew how much she wanted the Academy Award, the ultimate confirmation of her ability as an actress. Berry wanted it for himself as much as for Diana because it would secure him a place in the movie business. One of Berry's new Hollywood cronies told him that it was customary for motion picture studios and production companies to purchase advertisements in trade publications—primarily *The Hollywood Reporter* and *Daily Variety*, that specifically publish for those in the industry—touting their films and stars. First, the advertisements are placed to encourage members of the Academy of Motion Picture Arts and Sciences to consider Oscar nominations. Once nominated, more ads are purchased to encourage voting. Some people feel this is just a method of swaying votes, as well as financing the production of these trade journals. When Berry heard about how influential these advertisements can be, he was thrilled with the idea because he was under the wrong impression that the Academy Award was up for sale. "You mean you *buy* the award?" he asked one of his staffers. "Hey, I can handle that."

Berry then spent many thousands of dollars touting *Lady Sings the Blues* and Diana Ross in one of the most ambitious advertising campaigns in recent Hollywood history. Day after day, there were full-page ads of Diana, as Billie, looking her very worst: being photographed for her mug shot, her lips chapped and wig askew; going through cold turkey withdrawal in a padded cell; sitting on a toilet wearing just a bra, shooting up; snarling at Billy Dee Williams with a switchblade in her hand; screaming and smearing lipstick all over a dressing room mirror in a fit of hysteria. There was never any accompanying type.

Gordy wanted to prove that Diana was an actress and had selected the most melodramatic moments to illustrate that point. He also started to plant stories in the trades about upcoming film ventures that were not true. (The front page headline in one publication reported that Diana was "tapped" for two new films "and negotiations are under way with a leading European co-star.") When the columnist of one entertainment magazine supported Cicely Tyson's Oscar bid, Berry tried to get the journalist fired, offering the publisher a new columnist "who will see things the right way" and a fat Motown-sponsored advertising budget as well.

Walter Burrell, a black entertainment journalist, said, "I'm a member of the Academy and I was personally offended. I was insulted not only by the ads but by the expensive gifts Berry bought for the voters and by the lavish dinners he hosted for them. His white advisers must have encouraged him in this because Berry liked to put all of his trust in white people; he believed that if white people were involved, it had to be right."

On March 26, the night before the Academy Award ceremonies, Diana hosted a 29th birthday party for herself at the Silberstein home. Many celebrities, the Motown coalition and the key players in the _Lady Sings the Blues_ project attended. As a gift, Berry gave Diana an enormous scrapbook of photographs of herself.

Bob's gift to his wife was a toy poodle. Everyone was in a partying spirit when Diana kneeled down in front of the dog. Bowing before the animal, she implored, "Oh, creative one, name my dog. Name my dog."

Berry shouted out, 'I dub thee Oscar" as everyone cheered.

Diana had invited her mother and father to attend the award ceremonies with her. At first, Fred was reluctant to go because, as he put it, "I'm not too crazy about that Hollywood stuff." But Ernestine convinced him to attend. The next evening, Diana, Berry, and Bob and Fred and Ernestine Ross attended the 45th Academy awards presentation at the Dorothy Chandler Pavillion in Los Angeles.

Diana decided to keep her hairstyle simple for this occasion: short and extremely conservative looking. She wore a silver satin pantsuit with matching sequined vest, white blouse and black ascot. A red corsage on her lapel perfectly matched her lipstick. Later, she would change into a slinky black evening gown.

When Liza Minnelli's name was announced as the winner of

The original Supremes in December 1966. Diana Ross, standing, Florence Ballard in the middle and Mary Wilson, kneeling. (*Murray Laden/Groove Tube Photos*)

The Brewster Projects home, where Diana Ross was raised in Detroit, Michigan (*courtesy: Reginald Wilson*)

Tenth-grade homeroom class at Cass Technical High School (Diana, age 15, is farthest to the right in the middle row) (*J. Randy Taraborrelli Collection*)

The Primettes in 1961: 17-year-old Diana (top, center) and (bottom, left to right) Barbara Martin, Mary Wilson and Florence Ballard. (*Groove Tube Photos*).

Florence, Mary and Diana perform in Philadelphia in 1964. By this time, Barbara Martin had dropped out of the act and The Supremes were having their first string of hit records for Motown. (*J. Randy Taraborrelli*)

The Supremes appearing on the popular television program "What's My Line?" in New York. (*Groove Tube Photos*)

After months of coaching and grooming, The Supremes made their debut at the Copacabana in New York on July 29, 1965. Opening night at the Copa, July 14, 1965. (*J. Randy Taraborrelli Collection*)

Diana Ross in Japan, 1966. (© 1966, *Soul Magazine. All Rights Reserved.*)

Berry Gordy always had his eye out for a new female conquest. Here he is posed with Diana and a friend, and clearly has his mind on the friend. (*Eric Fowler/*)

Florence Ballard was kicked out of the group in 1967. Here is a rare publicity photo of Flo taken by her new record label, ABC. She was not legally permitted to promote herself as ever having sung with the Supremes. (*J. Randy Taraborrelli Collection*)

Mary Wilson was always considered "the sexy one." By this time, however, she was also "the confused one," not knowing to whom she should be loyal—Diana, or Florence.

Diana Ross and the Supremes. A new name, a new look and a new member (Cindy Birdsong on the left). By early 1968, the group was a glitzy showcase for "Miss Ross." Mary and Cindy were miserable, though one would never know it by looking at this picture! (*Groove Tube Photos*)

A star-studded line up . . . with Sir Lawrence Olivier on September 14, 1967. (© *1968, Soul Magazine. All Rights Reserved.*)

. . . and Paul McCartney (*Groove Tube Photos*)

. . . and Ethel Merman, Ed Sullivan and Cole Porter (*Groove Tube Photos*)

Diana Ross appeared as a nun on an episode of the "Tarzan" television program in 1967. This was Diana's first acting experience; here she is on a break. (*J. Randy Taraborrelli Collection*)

Cindy, Diana and Mary were not always pleased with Berry Gordy's advice. Here, they look less than enchanted by Gordy during a rehearsal for "The Ed Sullivan Show" in 1968. (*Groove Tube Photos*)

By 1969, Diana Ross was poised for solo stardom. Her singing partners were more than anxious to see her leave the group. (*J. Randy Taraborrelli Collection*)

Cindy Birdsong was kidnaped in 1969. Many observers believed that the kidnaper was trying to intimidate Berry Gordy by snatching one of his "girls." (*Groove Tube Photos*)

A pensive moment during a photo session at Motown. (*Groove Tube Photos*)

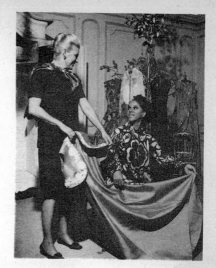

While Florence Ballard selected wardrobe for a solo career that never got off the ground . . .

. . . Diana Ross and the Supremes continued flying high. Here they are seen with Bing Crosby, performing on one of his television specials. (*Groove Tube Photos*)

The final show for Diana Ross and The Supremes, January 14, 1970, at the Frontier Hotel in Las Vegas. "It was all acting, the smiles and everything," recalled Cindy Birdsong, far left. Next to Birdsong are Mary Wilson, Jean Terrell (Diana's replacement in the group) and Diana Ross. (© 1969 *Soul Magazine. All Rights Reserved.*)

Diana, Berry and Jean Terrell cut the "Farewell" cake at a party after the concert . . . (*J. Randy Taraborrelli*)

. . . then Diana, Berry and Cindy take a stab at the cake. Mary Wilson refused to attend the post-show party. She was too upset about Ross's departure and Berry's lack of interest in the group's future to celebrate. (*J. Randy Taraborrelli*)

Diana Ross, now a solo star, in 1970. (*Groove Tube Photos*)

An early solo photo session. (*Seawell/Groove Tube Photos*)

Diana married Robert Silberstein in January 1971. Twenty years later, Berry Gordy's ex-wife, Raynoma Singleton, would claim that Diana was pregnant with Berry's child when she married Silberstein.

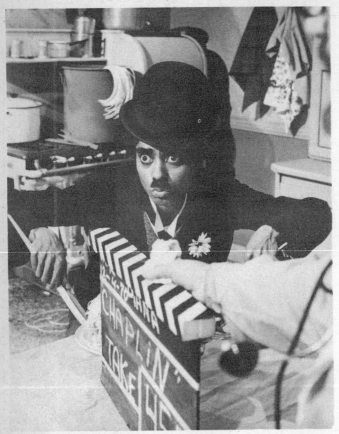

Diana as Charlie Chaplin in her 1971 "Diana!" television special. (*Groove Tube Photos*)

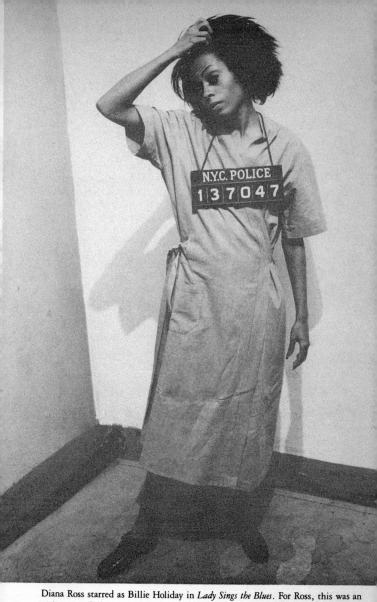

Diana Ross starred as Billie Holiday in *Lady Sings the Blues*. For Ross, this was an acting tour de force. Here she is pictured during a break in filming. (© *1972 Soul Magazine. All Rights Reserved.*)

Robert Silberstein, Diana, Fred Ross (Diana's father) and Berry Gordy arriving at the Academy Awards ceremony in March 1973. Diana was nominated as Best Actress for her portrayal of Billie Holiday in *Lady Sings the Blues*. She lost the Oscar to Liza Minnelli. (*Soul Publications*)

Diana and husband, Robert Silberstein, with Henry Kissinger. (*Groove Tube Photos*)

During a break in the filming of *Mahogany* (*Groove Tube Photos*)

Diana's daughters, Rhonda Suzanne (l) and Tracee Joy (r) welcome their new sister, Chudney. November 1975.

Diana Ross at Florence Ballard's funeral, February 1976. Some observers say she stole the show.

Berry Gordy, Diana Ross and Diana's daughter Tracee share some lighthearted moments backstage in Las Vegas (© 1977 *Soul Magazine, All Rights Reserved.*)

Diana has always wanted to portray Josephine Baker in a film about that entertainer's life. Here, she dresses in Baker-esque garb for her concert act. (*J. Randy Taraborrelli*)

During a break in filming *The Wiz*. (*Groove Tube Photos*)

Diana with her protégé, Michael Jackson. (*Danny Romo Collection*)

Diana told friends she wanted to marry Ryan O'Neal. But after their brief romance in 1979, he said of her, "Diana Ross doesn't want to show her body, doesn't want to do sex scenes on the screen, and doesn't want to be black." (*Groove Tube Photos*)

Mary Wilson continued her love-hate relationship with Diana Ross into the '80s. (*Photo by Mark Vieria/© 1980 Soul Magazine. All Rights Reserved.*)

For Diana, after Ryan O'Neal came rock star Gene Simmons, Cher's former boyfriend. "I know that my fans want to know who I'm sleeping with, but it's really none of their business." (*Groove Tube Photos*)

On July 21, 1983, Diana Ross braved the elements during her much-publicized rain-out concert at Central Park (*N.Y. Daily News Photo*)

Diana performed at Radio City Music Hall in September 1984, a difficult time for her because her mother was suffering from cancer. At the opening night party, ex-husband Bob Silberstein posed with daughters, Tracee Joy and Chudney Lane and Diana and Rhonda Suzanne (*N.Y. Daily News*)

Ross in repose. (© 1977. *Soul Magazine. All Rights Reserved.*)

The Supremes reunion-gone-bad at "Motown 25." "Did you see what that bitch did to me?" Mary Wilson fumed after Diana Ross shoved her during the performance. (left to right): Cindy Birdsong, Diana Ross and Mary Wilson (*Groove Tube Photos*)

Diana Ross, hard at work. (*J. Randy Taraborrelli*)

Diana Ross and Arne Naess were married for the second time on February 2, 1986. Here they are in December 1988, after her fifth child was born (*Albert Ferreira/DMI*)

Diana, on stage in Las Vegas at Caesars Palace. (*Photo by R.W.T.*)

Still a glamorous star at the age of 46. (*Photo by R.W.T.*)

the Best Actress award, Diana applauded immediately then took a deep breath and tilted her head back. Trying to maintain her composure, she closed her eyes and exhaled deeply. Then she reached over to Bob and held his hand tightly. "When we left the ceremonies, there were tears streaming down her face," her father said. "I gave her a handkerchief."

"I cried," Diana admitted. "I opened my eyes real wide, but still the tears came. I was looking forward to being up there and getting it, looking gorgeous and saying all the right things."

Berry was characteristically optimistic that evening in front of the press. "We'll be back. We'll definitely be back," he said firmly.

Most observers were certain that Berry Gordy's aggressive advertising campaign cost Diana the Oscar. "Obviously, Berry was literally trying to buy the award," said Walter Burrell. "He's from Detroit, from the school that believed and practiced the concept: 'If I can't scare you then I can buy you. One of the two will work.' Well, those kinds of tactics don't work in Hollywood; they're a bit more subtle here. The saddest part about it is that Diana might have won if Berry hadn't been so greedy and obvious. As it was, the vote between Ross and Cicely Tyson was split, so Liza Minnelli won. And both of those black actresses were better than Liza Minnelli."

"I tried to tell Berry and Suzanne just that," Jay Weston complained. "But they wouldn't listen. Motown money at work, that's what it was. They didn't understand that the Academy voters are older, conservative and, for the most part, white and easily insulted."

(It should be noted that while Berry's advertising campaign was unsettling, it was not nearly as offensive as those of producers and studios in Hollywood today.)

Walter Burrell was more to the point: "White Hollywood is only going to let a few blacks in, the ones they choose to. This is a racist town, let's face it. And when these white big shots found this out-of-town black man telling them to vote for his black protégée every damn day of the week, they were outraged enough to vote against her."

"So how much did I lose by?" Diana was said to have asked. She wanted to know how the voting went, how many voters were for her. Of course, she never found out. The Academy doesn't divulge that information.

The day after losing that award, Diana didn't even want to get out of bed. She was emotionally spent. It was good, she told Suzanne dePasse, that she was scheduled to embark on a European tour later in the week to promote the movie abroad. She was happy to leave the country and didn't want to have to explain to anyone in America how she felt about losing.

Lady Sings the Blues did wonders to broaden Diana's international appeal and for the next couple of years she would be treated like royalty everywhere she traveled overseas. But, on this first trip, the big question to her was, "How did you feel that night?"

"I just felt I had the strongest performance," she told Barry Newman of the *London Times*. "I really felt I had a chance. We had a beautiful [advertising] campaign and I probably never will forget the moment they announced Liza's name."

On the day Motown held its London press conference, she appeared even more pampered than she had been the last time she was in England with The Supremes in 1969. The reporters were asked to give her a standing ovation when she entered the room. "There are always people swirling about," wrote Lisa Robinson in *Disc* magazine. "'Could we have a drink for Miss Ross?' 'Are there any Kleenex for Miss Ross?' 'Have you something to stir Miss Ross' drink?' "

The overseas Motown brass became irritated with Diana because she had insisted on wearing a see-through blouse for the occasion. "I can wear it if I want to," she told the European company representative.

"But Miss Ross . . ."

"Miss Ross nothin'," she said. "I'll put a jacket on over it, don't worry."

During the press conference she coyly took off the jacket to reveal the cream-colored blouse and the fact that she had no bra on underneath.

Upon Diana's return, her recording career was quickly reactivated. "Touch Me in the Morning" had been put on the back burner while Gordy concentrated on *Lady Sings the Blues* propaganda. He released "Good Morning Heartache" as a single. It was Diana's only single release in 1972 and did not become a hit. After he heard the finished version of "Touch Me in the Morning" again, he decided it was too long and that Diana should go back into the studio and record a double-track fade-out. After losing the Oscar, she wasn't interested.

"She went into hiding when she got back from Europe," Ron Miller, the song's writer and co-producer remembered. "She was sure that she would go into the supermarket and everyone would point at her and say in sing-song fashion, 'Na-na, na-na, you didn't get it!' ''

"This is bullshit," Berry told Diana. "You call Ron Miller and arrange studio time for this song."

She did. "I promise to be on time, Ron," she said very timidly. Obviously she realized that Miller wouldn't be very eager to work with her again, not after their last studio fiasco. He remembered Diana as being almost despondent when she called. The two of them discussed the birthday party she hosted the night before the awards, and how she had papered an entire wall so all of the guests could write congratulatory sentiments. As they were doing this, she asked Ron if he thought she would win the Oscar. He told her he doubted it; that the Academy would probably give it to Liza Minnelli to appease its guilt over the fact that Judy Garland never won one. He urged her, however, not to change the name of the dog Bob had given her, the one Berry named Oscar.

"Call it Oscar, anyway, if you lose," he told her.

And that's what she called the dog after she lost: "Oscar Anyway."

A new recording date was scheduled. "Berry Gordy came with Diane and with half of his family for support," Miller said. "It was the first time she had come out of hiding, and the tension was unreal. Berry had warned everyone not to dare say a word about the Oscar. 'Don't mention it, or she'll blow up and leave.' ''

Diana tried to record the new ending to the song. But after a dozen takes, her performance still remained inadequate. Finally, Berry turned to Ron and said, "Man, this song ain't shit."

"The session was going down the drain and so was the enthusiasm for my song," Miller recalled. He then did what he called "the unthinkable." He stopped the session and asked everyone in the studio, "Does anybody in this room remember who won the Best Actress Oscar last year?" At the question, somebody groaned loudly. Ron believed it was Berry.

The winner had been Jane Fonda for her performance in *Klute*, but no one knew the answer. Miller then walked out of the studio and came back in a few moments later with a security guard. He asked him the same question. The man shook his head; he didn't know the answer either.

"There. Now can we finally get on with our work?"

There was dead silence. Then Diana smiled and went back into the recording booth where she finished the song.

When "Touch Me in the Morning" was finally released (in

May 1973), it was off to a slow start but began to catch on after about a month. Eventually, it went to Number One, stayed on the pop charts for over five months and was nominated for a Grammy Award.

A *Touch Me in the Morning* album followed, on which Diana seemed to be defining a new, more mature image. She dug into the material and performed it all as if she'd suddenly remembered her station in life as a recording artist. Her performances on songs like Rodgers and Hart's "Little Girl Blue" are sensitive and almost dreamy.

In 1973, *Lady Sings the Blues* was the final spotlighted film at the prestigious Cannes Film Festival. This was a gala affair attended by Berry and Diana, but not by the movie's producer or director, Jay Weston or Sidney Furie.

"To my horror, I found that we were not invited," Weston said. "Berry Gordy wanted the honor all to himself. The Motown machinery went into action and, as far as they were concerned, this was a Berry Gordy Production. Bob Evans [who came into power at Paramount after Frank Yablans] was a personal friend of Berry's. They did everything they could to shut us out and I'm still sore about it."

For Diana Ross, this was a night to remember: the night Motown's queen was treated like royalty.

Miss Ross was met at the airport by festival dignitaries who arranged for her to be chauffeured in a classic 1923 Rolls-Royce to the posh Carlton Hotel. She was escorted there by a motorcade of French police officers. That evening, she performed a concert at the Palais des Festivals. The prestigious Garde Républicain, imported from Paris, assembled along the Promenade de la Croisette from the Carlton Hotel to the concert site, wearing their medals, capes and white holsters and standing along the bright red carpet.

"Miss Ross is ready," someone announced.

A door opened and Diana made her entrance wearing a white sequined Bob Mackie gown, a matching cape and a Billie Holiday gardenia in her hair. Then she slowly walked down the red carpet, her head held high, as the human corridor of soldiers stood at attention. The red carpet seemed to stretch on forever to the main concert hall. When Diana got to the end of it, 2,000 people stood and cheered as she walked onto the stage and took deep, graceful bows as the Nice and Paris Symphony orchestras heralded her arrival.

After her concert, *Lady Sings the Blues* was screened and then Diana, now wearing a ruffled, polka-dotted gown, was brought back onto the stage for a five-minute standing ovation. Berry Gordy, resplendent in a bronze velvet tuxedo, was himself caught up in the ovation.

Afterwards, on a grand staircase, Diana Ross was greeted by Josephine Baker, the black entertainer who left rural America for France in the 1920s and went on to become the darling of Paris. The French people never lost their affection for Baker, even after she retired from the stage. Baker, who never forgot her own early struggles, was generous to Diana. "Honey, you sure showed them what acting—what show business—is all about," she told Diana when the two were introduced. Then Josephine Baker and Diana Ross embraced warmly.

Chapter
18

LADY SINGS THE BLUES changed the way people perceived Diana Ross' abilities; she had surprised her critics as well as herself. Many of her friends felt that when Diana Ross began acting, this was a turning point, professionally and personally. It provided her with a sense of self-fulfillment that she said she had never experienced as a recording artist. Perhaps she felt what she performed in front of the cameras proved even more creative than what she did in the recording studio. There she would sing as she was told, and then record the song a dozen times or more until it was deemed satisfactory. In films, even if she was forced to play a scene a certain way, she felt she had more freedom to use her own judgment. She had a little more control.

As an actress, Diana Ross was forced to crack her fragile, well-crafted façade and explore a wide range of human emotions and feelings. Perhaps the heartbreak, anger and sense of intangibility associated with Billie Holiday forced her to take a much deeper look at herself; she was always complaining of feeling "lost" at this time. Her work as an actress was probably also stretching her as a human being.

Many critics said that *Lady* would be Diana Ross' springboard for a long and fruitful acting career. Given the success of her first film and her proven box office appeal, Diana was certain that many juicy roles would come her way. Unfortunately, Diana's possibilities were being limited by Berry Gordy.

"She was over-managed, and the great material that was being submitted for Diana was not actively being considered," said Jay Weston, producer of *Lady Sings the Blues*. "Berry didn't want to work with outside producers anymore. After *Lady*, I wanted to remake *Sabrina*, a Paramount property, as a musical for Diana. I wanted to do it with an interracial twist, and have her star with Jack Lemmon. Lemmon was excited about it, but Berry said, 'Forget it.' Diana was never even consulted, I'm sure. It would have been a great property for her, but by this time I was shut out, and so were all of the other Hollywood producers interested in her. She didn't even know it.''

During this time, Berry brought Rob Cohen, a young, white 23-year-old whiz-kid, into the firm to head up Motown's film division. Cohen, who had worked previously for 20th Century-Fox, recalled, ''Like a lot of white people, I came to think of powerful men to be cut out of the Kennedy mold,'' he recalled. ''I always thought the real leaders and visionaries went to Harvard, which is why I went to Harvard. I patterned my ideas of leadership and manliness after the Kennedy brothers and, in turn, expected the leaders of the entertainment world to be just like them. So when I met this black man in tennis clothes who had this kind of crazy energy about him and surrounded himself with wacko henchmen, I was shocked. He was one of the real moguls of show business, but what was he? Later, I would learn he was a genius of the first order.

''When he heard what I wanted in return for working for him— an ironclad contract, big money and the kind of respect where I would not be some kind of glorified white boy script-reader— he howled with laughter. He thought I was very ballsy and he liked that. 'I'm a very very rich man,' he said, 'and if that's what it takes to get you here, you got it.'

''From age 24 to 29, the major male figure in my life was Berry Gordy,'' Cohen said in another interview. ''In some ways we were chalk and cheese—I was a white, middle-class, Jewish, Harvard graduate, and he was a black, Golden Gloves champ, high school dropout. He inspired me to want to kill myself to do the best for him.''

Berry introduced the man he had entrusted with Diana Ross' film career to her one evening at a cocktail party at Gordy's home.

Diana felt Suzanne dePasse should have been awarded this important job, not some young white *wunderkind*. She told Berry as much but he didn't listen. DePasse was also very upset by Berry's decision. ''The work you did and the credit you got, for a long time, were not commensurate, in my opinion,'' she said of her position at Motown at that time. ''I really wanted to play a part in the movie business, and there were other people running it . . . white men from the outside who did not have a sense of who we were and what we ought to be doing.''

"At my first meeting with Diana Ross, we did not become bosom buddies,'' Rob Cohen said. "She was not charming. Rather, she was aloof. This was a time when Diana was obviously feeling constrained by Berry's will and desires, and here I was—one of Berry's boys—watching over her. She would rather have dealt with Suzanne, with whom she had already developed a rapport and, in a sense, could control.''

One day, Rob Cohen got a call from the William Morris Agency, which represented Diana Ross. They wanted him to come to their Beverly Hills office for a meeting to discuss what they all perceived as being the perfect vehicle for her, a remake of the Judy Holliday classic *Born Yesterday*.

"You mean you want her to play the Judy Holliday role?'' Cohen remembered asking. The answer was affirmative.

"And who's gonna play the Bill Holden character?'' Cohen asked. "Who's gonna teach this black chick the ropes of life? Billy Dee Williams?''

"Oh no,'' one of the agents answered. "We'll get some white guy.''

"Yeah, a white man who will whip that black girl into shape,'' offered another agent.

"You mean you're gonna have an ignorant black woman being educated by a smart white man?'' Cohen asked.

"Yeah, that's it,'' another agent responded enthusiastically. "It's the perfect Diana Ross movie.''

"I don't think so,'' Rob Cohen said as he got up to leave. "Listen, Diana Ross is a very smart woman. She's not Judy Holliday, that's not her essence. Her essence is being shrewd and self-determined. No way am I going to present this lame idea to her.''

Cohen recalled, "They looked at me like I was a psycho and then someone said, 'Listen, you chicken-shit idiot, we're telling you what we have planned for Diana Ross and that's the way it's going to be.' ''

Cohen slammed the door behind him.

As soon as he returned to the office, Berry quizzed him about what happened at William Morris.

"What do you think of their idea?'' Gordy asked.

"Personally, I think it stinks,'' Cohen remembered having told him. "I look at Diana Ross, this artist you created, and I know she's brilliant and I've only met her once. I don't think you want to build a movie around her being stupid. She's not stupid, is she?''

"Hell, no, she's not," Gordy shot back. "Fuck those idiots at William Morris. This is the kind of shit I've had to put up with ever since I got to Hollywood.''

Now Berry was fuming. "Just because she's black, they think she's stupid. It's racism, that's what it is. Diane doesn't know it but this is what the real world is like. I wonder what she'd think if she did know.

"If she has to make movies like that, then forget it. She'll make records and be happy doing it. At least, she'll be respected. I didn't work all of these years to have her be some kind of fool on the screen.''

Cohen told Gordy he felt Diana should play the same kind of ambitious woman she was in real life, a woman who was a role model for many young blacks. "I want Diana Ross to do a film that's inspirational," Cohen said.

Since they were both so obviously on the same wavelength, Gordy and Cohen agreed that Cohen should come up with his own Diana Ross vehicle. He had recently read a script by Bob Merrill—the lyricist of *Funny Girl*—about a New York model who meets a politician who stutters. This girl assists him in getting over his speech impediment and, in the meantime, goes on to become a famous fashion model. Richard Harris was Merrill's choice for the male lead. And his choice for the female: Barbra Streisand. Streisand, however, thought the idea was too wacky. Eventually the concept ended up on Rob Cohen's desk.

"Just don't tell anyone that Barbra turned it down," Merrill was warned, "because if Diana finds out you can forget it. She'll never touch anything Barbra wouldn't.''

When Cohen and Merrill met, they decided to make some changes in the concept. "I want to do a Joan Crawford movie, a tear-jerker, with Diana Ross as the star," Cohen told Merrill.

Berry was paying Diana $1 million a year to tie her to Motown as an actress and Billy Dee Williams $250,000 for the same purpose. So they would have to be teamed together again. Cohen and Merrill began theorizing about what Diana Ross possessed that wasn't musical, but yet was a strong part of her persona. The answer was obviously her glamour. There probably were few black women as glamorous as Diana Ross. Cohen and Merrill decided to develop a story around Ross' glamour and not have her sing one note in the entire film.

Cohen remembered, "Bob and I thought, 'Hey, we should do a film about a black woman who wants to be a fashion designer and who has to have this shitty job just to pay the bills. And she'll have a black boyfriend who's a politician, and he wants her to devote herself to his cause. But all she wants is to get up, out, and away from the misery and poverty of her background. Eventually, she meets a fashion photographer who wants to turn her into a model, but he's off his rocker. When she goes to Europe and becomes a big-shot model, she misses her boyfriend and feels empty inside. She realizes that she has no roots. So, she goes back to her man and they live happily ever after.' And in that one conversation we had the whole premise of a film Bob Merrill wanted to call *Mahogany*—and the concept never changed one iota.''

How to present the idea to Berry? Cohen knew that Berry Gordy did not like to read scripts, and that he would simply pass any treatment on to Suzanne dePasse or one of his flunkies who would probably just veto it for political reasons. Rather than try to force Berry to read the treatment, Cohen thought the best way to present the story would be as an audio-visual experience.

He hired an artist to draw pictures of Diana and Billy Dee Williams on story boards, in different scenes from the movie. Then Bob wrote a love theme (not the one that was eventually used in the film) and hired a pianist to play it at the exact dramatic moments. Someone else was hired to flip the boards as the story progressed. Bob Merrill offered to read the script aloud. It was an unorthodox way of presenting a film, but Cohen realized he was dealing with unorthodox people.

At Berry's mansion one evening, Berry, Suzanne, Diana and a host of other Motown people sat in front of the easel and Bob Merrill began.

''Fade in,'' he read. ''Tracy Chambers is a young girl living in the inner city who has a big dream . . .'' and on he went.

(Rob Cohen explained, ''The lead character's name would be Tracy Chambers, I decided, because my nanny's name was Ophelia Chambers, and she was one of the brightest women I'd ever known.'')

The love theme was played, the story boards were flipped, the little saga went on and on and then ended on a melodramatic note.

''Well, what do you think?'' Berry asked Diana.

''I don't know. What do you think?''

''Edna, get me Robert Evans'' was Berry's response as he turned to his assistant, Edna Anderson. She dialed the number of the president of Paramount.

"Bob, it's Berry. I got the movie we're gonna do next. It's brilliant."

Diana was cautious about the idea. "Miss Ross never jumped, because when Berry made a decision that was it. He owned her," Rob Cohen said. "At least, this was something happening. She had been eager for the last year and a half to do something and I had the feeling she had been led down the garden path by Berry a few times and was disappointed. She told me immediately after the presentation that, coincidentally, she had been interested in fashion designing as a youngster in Detroit."

"Is that so?" Rob Cohen said to her. "You know what? You do have a unique flair for fashion. No one dresses like you, Miss Ross."

She smiled demurely.

"Why don't you design the costumes for this movie?"

"Oh, my, do I dare?" Diana asked.

"Yeah, why not?" Rob replied. "You'll be brilliant at this."

She smiled, then turned to Berry. "Guess what? You'll never guess what Rob said I could do."

As Diana excitedly relayed Bob's suggestion to Berry, Berry turned and smiled at his new genius producer.

Rob Cohen had scored another point.

Rob Cohen gave Berry Gordy two choices for director of *Mahogany*: John Avildsen and Tony Richardson. Berry Gordy chose British director Richardson feeling that he would give the movie the sort of sophisticated finesse required during the location-filming in Europe. Richardson had directed *Look Back in Anger* and *A Taste of Honey* and had won Academy Awards for producing and directing *Tom Jones*, so Berry was impressed by his credentials. Diana also relished the idea of working with an Oscar-winning director.

Diana and Berry didn't know it at the time, but Tony found *Lady Sings the Blues* "pretty dreadful." Said an associate of Berry's, "From the outset, Tony looked at Berry and Diana like monkeys in a cage, these weird animals he couldn't make heads or tails of."

Tony Richardson remembered the first meeting with Berry Gordy. "He asked me to his house in Bel Air. There were a couple of cars waiting for us at the bottom of the hill with security men in them. We had to drive up the hill with one car in front of us and one behind.

"When I was in his home, I noticed that there were cameras on me the whole time. It was quite fascinating, the Gordy empire

and all. There were animals all about [among his wildlife men-
agerie, Berry had a doe named Diana] and it was like a wild
jungle on one hand and a prison on the other. Berry was really
nice, charming and absolutely adorable. But I could see immediately that there was this very dangerous side to him.

"The first thing to deal with was the Berry Mafia. He always
had these goons about, and I had heard that he was perfectly
capable of acting in very violent ways. Later, I learned that when
he walked down the street there would be four gunmen with
him, two in front and two behind. But I enjoyed this. I actually
enjoyed the dangerous side of Berry Gordy, Jr."

John Byrum, who had been hired to write the final screenplay
of *Mahogany*, was also at this meeting and he remembered,
"Berry and Tony were alike in many ways, but also different in
frightening ways. For instance, the first time we were at the
house, he had peacocks all over the place, these wild, colorful
tropical birds. Well, Tony has peacocks roaming about his home
in St. Tropez. Both guys loved the way these wild birds looked
scampering around the estates, so they had that in common."

Byrum recalled that during the meeting, Tony turned to Berry
and said in his very proper British way, "My good fellow, I
must say that you have the quietest peacocks I have ever encountered in all of my days."

Berry laughed. "Oh, them?" he asked, motioning to one of
the birds as it waddled by.

"Yes, they're so silent."

"That's 'cause I had their fuckin' voice boxes cut out," Berry
explained very matter-of-factly. "I hate the way those little fuck-
ers squawk."

John Byrum remembered the first time he met Diana Ross, at
a chic Hollywood restaurant, The Cock 'n' Bull on Sunset Boulevard. "She was alone, and it was very strange because I got
the impression that she hardly ever went out alone. She was like
a kid with a charge card and the power to run it up as high as
she wanted. She pulled out this thick notebook and every page
was filled with lists and lists of ideas. Then she showed me a
page of questions and answers: 'Who is Tracy Chambers?' 'I
am Tracy Chambers.' 'What do I do?' 'I am a fashion designer.'
'What are my goals?' 'To be successful and happy.' It was as if
she was a high school student preparing for the lead in the school
play. But as basic as she was approaching it, she was right on
the mark. After all, you can't play a role unless you know what
it's about, can you?

"I wondered if she had a similar list as a member of The

Supremes: 'Who am I?' 'I am Diana Ross of The Supremes.' 'What are my goals?' 'To leave those other girls in the dust and make movies.'

"I was very surprised at how straight she was," he continued. "I expected this real rock 'n' roll mama, you know, this wild-eyed Supreme who sang "The Happening' on 'The Ed Sullivan Show.' But she was so calm, reasonable and polite. When I walked her out to her yellow Rolls-Royce and she got in it and drove off toward Beverly Hills, it struck me that she was really a Beverly Hills housewife with a great job. I liked her quite a lot."

The matter of casting *Mahogany* was at hand; so far, only Billy Dee Williams was definite. Rob Cohen, John Byrum, Diana Ross and Berry Gordy met one afternoon in Gordy's office to decide about the rest of the cast. Berry handed Diana a copy of *The Academy Players Directory*, a catalogue of practically every actor and actress in Hollywood, pictured in alphabetical order, along with the addresses and telephone numbers of their agents or representatives. "Okay, Diana, you pick who you want to work with," he told her.

"How 'bout him?" Diana said, pointing to an actor.

Berry would lean over and look at the picture. Then he would scratch his head and turn to Rob Cohen.

"How much for that one?"

"Too much," Rob would say, and then he'd whisper a figure in Berry's ear.

Berry winced and said, "Uh, gee, that's a whole lot, Diane. Who else would you like?"

Diana continued flipping through the pages. Finally, she made another choice. Jack Nicholson. "Oh, I *love* Jack Nicholson," she said brightly. "I want him. Can we have him?"

Berry scratched his head again and squirmed in his chair.

"Nicholson," he said. "How much for Nicholson?"

Rob Cohen gave him a figure.

"Jesus Christ. *That much for Jack Nicholson?*"

"Hey, he's a big star," Rob responded with a wide grin.

"You can't have him, Diane," Berry said. "Costs too much." She frowned.

"Well, look, I'm sorry," he told her, shaking his head apologetically. "Just keep looking."

Finally, they settled on Anthony Perkins.

Even though Berry and Diana may have been naïve, what they were doing that day is exactly what the Hollywood casting system is all about—it's a meat market. Every actor has a price.

Berry Gordy was used to dealing with street people and with the bottom line. People in the movie business think they're more elegant than that. They have shinier veneers, but the bottom line is still the same. How much? Berry's approach may have been unconventional but, to him, the results were always what mattered, not the method.

"The only point of contention I remember is that Diana didn't want Billy Dee Williams in the movie," John Byrum recalled. "She kept saying, 'Do we *have* to have Billy Dee? But *why*?' One of the reasons I wanted to write the screenplay was because I wanted to duplicate the Lombard-Gable quality the two of them shared in *Lady Sings the Blues*. But we found out quickly during rehearsals for *Mahogany* that Billy Dee had spent too much time sitting in his home in the Hollywood Hills getting rusty. By the time he got to *Mahogany*, he was weak. Diana just didn't feel comfortable with him anymore. I also didn't get the impression that they liked each other much."

For the next few months, Diana began designing costumes for the film. She designed 50 outfits in all, from casual sportswear to elegant evening gowns. Diana supervised every phase of the operation from purchasing the fabrics to beading and color and fabric coordination. Some of the fabrics cost as much as $1,000 a yard. She always did have a sense of style, color and texture, and for her *Mahogany* wardrobe, she was influenced by Grand Kabuki Theater, a form of classical Japanese entertainment, and the French designer Erté.

Diana was given her own space at the Goldwyn Studios. Soon drawings of beaded dragons covered all the walls, and seamstresses were everywhere. In the middle of it all, there was Diana giving them hell. It was a scene which would be duplicated for the movie.

The outfits for *Mahogany* were all a reflection of Diana's personality—pure glitz and fantasy—and Diana was very proud of them. She had a showing of her costumes in a small boutique on the Sunset Strip.

"The whole point, I thought, was to impress her mother," recalled John Byrum. "So she flew the woman in, a very nice, pleasant lady. Berry was there and I remember him frowning at a model as she paraded around in this shiny, dragon-sequined, yellow-satin Chinese thing that Diana would wear in a fashion show in the film. 'What the hell is that supposed to be?' he asked. Long-legged models came out wearing Diana's other designs, and we all 'oohed' and 'aahed' at them while Diana just sort of basked in all of it."

Before principal photography began, it was decided Diana would record the theme for the movie, "Do You Know Where You're Going To?" The song had been floating around Motown for years and singer Thelma Houston had a version of it that was being readied for release as a single. When Rob Cohen heard it, he was struck by the lovely melody and used his influence with Berry to have Thelma's version killed. Berry agreed with Rob that this was the perfect Diana Ross love theme. Michael Masser, who composed the melody, played it for her on her piano one day at her Beverly Hills home.

"She looked over to a picture of her children on the wall and had tears in her eyes," he said. "That's how we knew we were close." Gerry Goffin rewrote some of the lyrics, and the recording session was, said Masser, "quick and very painless."

By this time, trouble began brewing between Tony Richardson and Rob Cohen. Richardson felt that Cohen was too inexperienced to handle this monolithic project and was unhappy with many of Cohen's decisions. "I was young and naïve," Cohen said. "But it was my picture and I would be damned if I was going to let him try to rule the roost."

Just before they left for Chicago, where the first third of the film was to be shot, Cohen received a phone call from Berry Gordy.

"We got a problem with Tony," he said. "He's trying to poison Diana against you by telling her you're just a kid, still wet behind the ears."

"Well, what did you say to Diana?" Rob wanted to know.

"I told her that you and me and she are family," Berry said. "We are the team. We're Motown. He's the outsider. And that she should remember that family's what's important."

Cohen was grateful for Berry's support. Later, he found out that Diana went to Tony Richardson the next day and asked him point-blank: "If Rob is so goddamn stupid, then why'd he pick you?" Tony Richardson was careful about what he said to Diana Ross from that point on.

"She'd obviously been trained by Berry to do exactly what he said. There were some deep insecurities there," Richardson said of Diana Ross. "Berry always said of her, 'Oh, Diana isn't a personality, she's a product.' That was his favorite line about her and though it was unkind, there was probably an element of truth to it."

The script of *Mahogany* went through many changes along the way, but ultimately it was about a girl named Tracy Chambers who climbed from a secretarial position at the Marshall Field store in Chicago to become an international fashion model and then tops her career with equal recognition as a designer. Anthony Perkins portrayed the psychotic photographer who dubs Tracy "Mahogany" because, in his eyes, she is a "rich, dark, beautiful and rare" but also inanimate object, or as Berry Gordy would put it, "just a creation, a product but not a personality." That aspect of the film certainly may have been close to the real Diana Ross.

Soon after, Tracy's boyfriend tells her that "success is nothing without someone you love to share it with." She gives up her lucrative career and returns to Chicago to spend the rest of her life helping her boyfriend's cause.

On November 12, 1974, shooting for *Mahogany* began in Chicago in a tough neighborhood at 51st Street and Ellis Avenue. A few months earlier, Gordy and Cohen had selected a rundown tenement apartment there to be Tracy Chambers' home, but when the Motown coalition arrived, they discovered that the owner of the complex had been so excited about having a Diana Ross movie filmed there that he made drastic renovations.

"It looked like a goddamn Beverly Hills mansion in the middle of the ghetto," John Byrum said. "The art director had to go back and mess it all up, sandblasting the paint off the front of it, smashing the windows and trying to make it look like a ghetto again. We laughed a lot over that. It was one of the only light moments we had in Chicago."

"The atmosphere on the set of *Mahogany* was tense, I thought. There was quite a lot of drugs there," Tony Richardson recalled. "Berry was still in Los Angeles at first—he came in during the second week—and he refused to believe that this was going on. One of Diana's co-stars was certainly on the stuff at the time and, as a result, his timing was off. Naturally, he would throw off the people who were not on drugs. Diana, who was never on anything, didn't realize how strongly this co-star was on the stuff.

"After she discovered this, she really didn't want to work with him. He was throwing her off and this made Berry bully her. He was always saying how terrible she was, how awful she was as an actress, always berating her, putting her down. I tried to tell him that it was all because of this actor that she wasn't up to par, but, no, he wouldn't admit that. Finally, when he was convinced of the drug abuse, he got his goons to immediately put an end to it. But he never apologized to Diana."

There were also problems with gangs in the neighborhood. One night there were four murders reported in the area in which

Diana was filming. Diana was very aware of her surroundings. She recalled, "You could almost see the faces of those who are going to stay where they are and the ones that are going to grow out of that and want something better. It hurt me to see people begging. I kept asking myself, 'Don't they want anything better than this?' It made me proud that all the black people that I know want better. They're fighting for better, to make it better, knowing there's a much better way of life and going for it."

Making image matters worse, Tony Richardson would show up on the set in expensive fur coats and, to many of the poor people in the area, this proper, white, British gentleman seemed extremely out of place. Often he was jeered, which must not have been very pleasant for him. As far as Berry was concerned, Tony's presence was becoming an embarrassment to the Motown image.

To many it seemed that Tony Richardson could not relate to black people. In a story conference with Billy Dee Williams, Tony discussed a scene in which Williams was trying to drum up votes from women and older people. Tony said, "Get very passionate and excited, and say a few swear words. You know how you people swear."

Billy Dee became incensed by the racist implication of Tony's statement. "What do you mean 'You people'?" he snapped. "I wouldn't swear in front of a woman, and especially in front of old people. I don't know any black people who would. And you can forget about that Sambo line in the script." (There was a toast scene in the original script where he and Diana were supposed to lift their glasses and say, "To all the Sambos in the world.")

Berry observed this confrontation, but didn't say anything. "He was eyeballing the whole thing and taking mental notes," said Rob Cohen. "Tony Richardson thought black people were these charming little imps. He was looking at blacks with what I personally perceived as a racist perspective: that Diana, Billy, Berry and the rest were charming little children. Diana didn't see this, though. I think she was just glad to be taking direction from someone who wasn't Berry Gordy."

Gordy and Richardson clashed practically every day of the shooting, much to Diana's dismay. "I can't act with all of this tension," she complained. "Berry, why don't you go back to Los Angeles, *please*!"

It was obvious to everyone on the set that Berry really wanted to direct this film, but didn't quite know how to go about getting rid of Richardson. Instead, he insisted on rehearsing Diana and

Billy in their scenes as Tony—who had never before encountered such insolence from an executive producer—fumed at the interference.

As time went on, Berry started to feel that the storyline was weak. He was beginning to sense that perhaps *Mahogany* hadn't been such a good idea and that Diana wasn't actress enough to pull it off.

"His whole thing had become, 'Write to the lowest emotion, the simplest dialogue,' " said screenplay writer John Byrum. "I wanted to write long eloquent speeches for Diana, and he kept saying 'No, it's wrong. She can't handle it. Make it simple. So I thought he was dumb, and his ideas were dumb. But in the end I found that he was right. He knows how to reach the people on a basic, human level. The only thing I thought he was wrong about was that Diana couldn't handle the speeches. She could have. She was very good."

Berry and Diana telephoned John Byrum one night and asked him to underline the words in the script that Diana should emphasize. "That's up to you," Byrum told her, "not me."

"Don't leave it up to me," Diana said. *"I have enough problems."*

One evening after a hectic day of shooting, Berry, Tony Richardson and a few other members of the crew watched the "dailies" (that day's filmed footage) in a small Chicago movie theater. Afterwards, they were standing in the parking lot having a conversation about the day's work, when suddenly a car went into reverse and began screeching toward them forcing Berry to jump out of its path. The young man behind the wheel rolled down his window and shouted at Berry, "Get out of the way, asshole!" One of Berry's bodyguards took down the license plate number.

"He did a slow burn, and eventually became absolutely furious," Tony Richardson remembered. "The next day, he found out that the guy in the car turned out to be the projectionist who ran the dailies. Then he actually wanted his goons to go and break this projectionist's legs for insulting him. Luckily for him, the guy went on vacation the next day and never returned."

Berry Gordy apparently blamed Richardson for the projectionist's sudden disappearance. "Gordy literally thought that I had protected him from his goons by warning him about what was to happen," Richardson recalled, "which I had not."

Associate producer Neil Hartley explained a possible reason why Berry's reaction to this incident was so volatile. "There were stories among the crew that Berry had been run out of

Detroit a few years back by the underworld. Now he was in Chicago—maybe just a little too close to Detroit and to his enemies. Mind you, I don't know that this was the case, but I do know that this is what everyone in his camp was saying, that security around him was tight and that when anything out of the ordinary happened, he reacted strongly.''

"I only remember one bodyguard in particular, a big, tough guy," recalled Hartley. "He would make trouble on the set and was often threatening, but I didn't make an issue of that. Berry was certainly allowed security if he felt he needed it. I wasn't intimidated by this, but rather fascinated by it.''

The final disagreement between Berry Gordy and Tony Richardson came over a simple matter of casting a bit player. In the disputed scene, Diana was to be pursued by a rapist. To show her character's spunk, Berry wanted her to confront the hood and offer him "a piece of ass," in order to intimidate him and scare him off.

Richardson was appalled by the whole idea of Diana offering herself to this thug, no matter what the reasoning. Berry found an actor to play the rapist and had been coaching him on the scene. Meanwhile, Tony found another actor. Finally, the two of them disagreed on who should do the scene and, according to Tony, "He blew up and I refused to give in. It was as if he was saying, 'Hey, look, I know black rapists a lot better than you do.' I knew he was using this as an excuse for an altercation. Finally I said, 'Berry, you should just fire me. You really want to direct this movie. You've got the money, so do it.' The only person I felt sorry for was Diana who I knew was very sad that I was going and that Berry wasn't.''

No one is certain where Berry Gordy got the idea of directing the film, but friends say that his then-fiancée, a beautiful blond woman named Nancy Leiviska, encouraged him. Berry was a bit tentative about the idea, since he'd never officially directed a film, but Leiviska, who was working at Motown in different creative capacities, apparently convinced him by asking him, "You direct everything else, and you're great at it. Why not this?''

So Berry Gordy was in and Tony Richardson was out—he reportedly received a cushy termination settlement of over $200,000 and now says that he's never even seen the completed version of *Mahogany*.

"Diana wasn't happy about this change at all," Rob Cohen said. "She enjoyed Tony Richardson. He's brilliant, well-traveled, well-read, articulate, extremely witty. They really liked each other. She loved having this Academy Award-winning director to work with, and now she was faced with having Berry on her back again, telling her what to do, criticizing her. Theirs was an odd relationship by this time. Every time he would criticize her, it became a whole psychodrama. He would push her way beyond her limit.''

Neil Hartley indicated that Diana telephoned him to discuss her anxiety over the transition. ''She had some legitimate concerns. She was worried about how she was going to come across in this movie. How could this man who had never directed a film bring out the performance in her? To her way of thinking, he couldn't. She knew that Tony could bring qualities out of her that Berry, as a non-director, would not understand. But, of course, she wasn't consulted about any of this.''

Rob Cohen had been at his father's funeral at the time of the final confrontation. Berry had promised that he wouldn't make any decisions until Rob returned to Chicago. But Rob had heard about what had happened and telephoned Berry from New York.

Cohen recalled, ''When I reached him, he was flying, just as happy and giddy as can be. That's when he told me he was going to direct. It was a shock, but I understood it. If anyone could get a performance out of Diana Ross, it was Berry Gordy. 'I'm sorry, Rob. I'm sorry, I'm sorry, *I'm sorry*,' he told me. "But I had to do it. I did it for Diane. I can't let this guy ruin Diane's movie.''

Richardson's British crew stayed on with Berry. They all called Berry ''Gov'nor.'' On the first day of shooting with Berry Gordy as director, exterior scenes were to be filmed. It was snowing and freezing cold. Diana, wearing a Maximilian sable coat, watched Berry suspiciously as he prepared Billy Dee for the scene.

''Okay, let's get started,'' Berry ordered the cast and crew.

No one budged.

''I said, 'C'mon, let's do it,''' Berry shouted.

Again, everyone ignored him. Finally the assistant director leaned over to Berry and said, ''Gov'nor, you gotta say 'Action!' '' Berry nodded his head and smiled.

''*Ac—shun!*'' he said, drawing out the word with a wide grin. Then everyone fell into place.

After the scene was played successfully (Berry *did* know how to get the performance out of Diana Ross and Billy Dee Williams), there was plenty of applause and lots of enthusiasm for the new director's work. Everyone milled about, laughing and slapping each other on the back, and no one seemed to realize that the cameras were still rolling. The assistant director leaned over to Berry again. "You gotta say 'Cut!' " he told him.

Berry's mouth fell open. "You mean they're still rollin'?" he asked.

"*Cut! Cut!*" Berry shouted as everyone cheered. It was quickly apparent that with Berry Gordy as director, the atmosphere on the set had become much more comfortable. He may not have had experience, but he did have a winning personality, charisma and instinct, which is how he'd gotten that far in the first place.

To explain what had happened with Tony Richardson, Berry's press people told the media that Richardson didn't "understand the black experience."

"Utter bullshit," Tony Richardson claimed.

"*Mahogany* was certainly not of a black perspective, it wasn't a black subject," he observed. "It was obviously an attempt to make a commercial white movie. There was nothing black about it. Diana Ross was never about being black. She was about proving herself in a white world, and that was what the character was about."

Said Berry, "I could better relate to the black brothers and sisters who were being used as extras and for atmosphere purposes in Chicago because they talk and act like I talked and acted when I was coming up in the Detroit ghetto. I'm doing this to protect Diana Ross' interest."

Diana didn't quite see it that way. She thought that Berry once again found a way to control her. He invaded the one creative area of her life she thought was her own. Her last bit of freedom was gone.

"I don't like it at all," she told one friend as she hurled a $20,000 powder-blue lynx coat across the room. "What's gonna happen to me now? I am sick and goddamn tired of having to do what Berry Gordy tells me to do, and I'm not gonna do it anymore!" Unfortunately, her declaration of independence was a bit premature. After finishing in Chicago, the *Mahogany* coalition would begin shooting in Rome on January 13.

Once there, Diana Ross would give Berry Gordy hell.

Chapter

🌿19🌿

In January 1975, sad news about Florence Ballard made headlines across the country: "Ex-Supreme Broke and Living on Welfare!"

Accompanying the news reports were photographs of a dejected-looking Florence posing in front of a picture of the original Supremes in shimmering red sequined gowns. Now Florence was 31 years old with three children supported on A.D.C. (Aid to Dependent Children).

For the last eight years, ever since that night in Las Vegas when Berry Gordy ordered her off the stage, Florence's life had been slowly slipping downhill. Her standard comment, published in *Ebony* magazine in February 1969, as to why she left The Supremes:

"Oh, I was just tired of traveling so much and wanted to settle down. I don't know why people are still interested in all that past history. I get so tired of answering questions about whether Diana and I had hair-pulling fights. I've told people over and over again that we didn't have any fights. I'll be back. I'm like Richard Nixon. Remember how everybody thought he was washed up? Now look at where *he* is today!"

Of Berry Gordy, she would only allow, "We are very cordial to each other. He's a very nice man."

A troubled history always seemed to embrace Florence Ballard's solo career. One former Motown publicist who went on to work for Florence now insists that she was intimidated about continuing as a solo performer, especially after she went to play in Atlantic City and received a threatening phone call that she should not go on stage. One of the writers who worked on Florence's ABC Records material claims that he received a telephone call from somebody who threatened that if he wrote any more songs for her, his fingers would be broken.

Meanwhile, in her official ABC Records biography, Florence was not allowed to mention the fact that she was a former member of The Supremes because of her release agreement with Motown. How ironic, considering that it was Florence who chose the name in the first place from the list provided by Motown. ''For the past several years, Florence was a member of the world's most famous entertainment trio,'' was the only allusion to The Supremes in Ballard's press material.

In 1970, she filed a lawsuit against Motown, Berry Gordy, Diana Ross and The Supremes charging that she had been ''maliciously ousted'' from the group and asking for $8.7 million.

''You can't buck the boss no matter how wrong he may seem,'' she said privately at the time. ''And to get in the way of an aggressor bent on being a superstar is to get trampled for sure.''

Her suit was dismissed by the courts, saying that her release from The Supremes was legally binding unless she could return to Gordy the $160,000 she received as a settlement, which she couldn't do.

The Chapmans' marriage had been unstable for years and the couple finally separated in 1973 after a now-paranoid and often inebriated Florence accused her husband of secretly working with unknown enemies she felt were bent on ruining her life.

''And you probably still workin' for Berry Gordy, too!'' she accused her husband.

''But, Flo . . .''

''You been plotting with Berry Gordy. I just know it!''

For the most part, Diana and Mary had nothing to do with Flo after she was fired. When it became obvious that she was going to lose her home, Diana did try to save the house by paying off the mortgage. She and Tommy Chapman were unable to come to terms on how the transaction should take place. Though Mary knew that Diana tried to help save Florence's house, she decided not to mention this in her *Dreamgirl* memoirs. In her book, she also didn't address the question of why she never tried to help her friend financially.

After Florence was forced to move her family out of the home—by this time she had a third daughter, Lisa Marie—*Jet* magazine contacted Flo to do a story about her problems. She posed in front of the boarded-up home looking miserably anxious and seeming to be overcome by loneliness, and maybe even fear. She was wearing a fur coat, one of her only treasures from the good old days. The photograph was so sad that Supremes fans around the world were shocked by it. Certainly Motown and The Supremes had never represented *this* kind of pain and sorrow.

"I keep saying to myself, well, at least couldn't I have kept my house for the sake of my children," Flo said. "Couldn't that have been paid for, somehow? And it tears me up inside."

Flo, who now weighed about 190 pounds, moved into a $150-per-month apartment on Detroit's west side with her mother and sister. Most of her days were spent watching television game shows and wishing she could compete for the big money prizes.

"If I had all your talent, girl, I sure wouldn't be sittin' 'round all day watchin' game shows," Lurlee Ballard would scold her daughter. "Why are you wasting your time?"

"Just leave me alone," Florence would say sadly.

"But you should do commercials," Lurlee suggested.

"Sure, if I lost 40 pounds," Florence responded.

On Aid to Dependent Children, she received $135 every two weeks. "I put off going on welfare for as long as I could," she had said. "I had been suffering a lot of mental anguish and had to see a psychiatrist. During one period, I stayed in the house for over a year. I felt I couldn't take it any more. I lost faith in everything. How could this have happened to me? How could I have it all—and then nothing?"

At this time, she was offered a job at an inner-city nursery school paying $80 a week. She turned it down.

"No matter what happens now," she said, "I'm determined to keep on. I don't want my kids remembering a mother on welfare. I want to give them something better."

Some of Florence's fans would send her money in the mail. She would send them thank you cards.

During a party at the home of one of her brothers, Flo drank more vodka than she could handle. As she walked home, a car pulled over to the curb. A man rolled down the window.

"Hey, bitch, ain't you that broke Supreme?"

Florence kept on walking.

"I said, hey, bitch! Ain't you that broke Supreme?" the voice shouted at her again.

Florence, now with fire in her eyes, turned to face him. As she approached the car, her fists clenched, the door swung open and before she knew it she was being pulled in, kicking and screaming. She was pushed into the front seat. The car sped off. Soon, she and her two kidnappers were parked in a vacant lot.

Flo once said that she could barely remember what happened

next. "All I knew is that I was going to be killed," she recalled. "I started praying for my life. I started praying for my girls."

One can only imagine the terror she must have felt, especially considering what had happened to her when she was a teen-ager.

Once the car was parked, the two men got out and began talking, apparently trying to figure out what to do with Florence now.

"It's time to make our move," she remembered hearing one of them say through the cracked window.

"But, hey man, she was one of The Supremes," said the other voice.

"Who the fuck cares!"

As they stood next to the automobile, talking and laughing, Florence reached over and locked the door on the driver's side.

"Hey, bitch, whatcha doing?"

Then Flo quickly locked the other door.

She looked down at the ignition. The keys were in it.

"I remember thinking, 'Thank you, Jesus,' " she said later.

She started the car and drove away. As one of her assailants ran in front of the car to try to stop her, Florence stepped on the gas and tried to run him down. He jumped out of the way just in time to save his life. When she got home, Flo called the police. Then she went to bed and cried herself to sleep.

Diana Ross, wearing an elegant, full-length, mauve one-shoulder gown and holding a matching marabou feather muff, was posed on the edge of a baroque fountain atop the Gianicolo, one of Rome's most spectacular attractions.

"Ac-shun!" Berry Gordy shouted through his bullhorn.

On cue, Anthony Perkins put his hand on Diana's waist, and gently pushed. She fell backwards into the freezing pool and proceeded to thrash about in the chilly water, while screaming at Perkins at the top of her lungs.

"Cut!" Berry commanded. "One more time, Diane."

"What?" she asked unbelievingly.

"I said one more time," Berry repeated.

"Enough is enough!" she screamed. Diana climbed out of the pool. This was the sixth take. She had been dunked, dried off, changed and dunked for the last time. Her once-wavy wig now looked like a drowned rodent, her make-up was streaming down her face, and her soaking wet gown clung to her body.

One of her effeminate assistants approached the shivering actress with a fluffy white towel.

"Oh, my, my, *my,* Miss Ross! Just look at you now! You poor darling *dear*! Let me help you. Please!''

"You just get away from me," Diana snapped. "Goddamn it!''

"You think we got a good take in there somewhere?" Berry asked one of his aides. He was totally oblivious to his star's fury.

"Certainly hope so, Gov'nor, because she isn't doing another.''

"Oh, she'll do another—if I tell her to," Berry said confidently.

From the beginning, when the Motown crew arrived in Spoleto, Italy, it was obvious that Diana Ross was miserable. By now, Berry had seen all of the footage he directed in Chicago and was thrilled with it. Every scene Diana shot involved dozens of takes, with Berry Gordy working as he liked to do in the recording studio: repeating an effort over and over and then editing a portion of each attempt into the final product. By the end of the first week in Italy, Diana was totally disgusted with Berry and with *Mahogany.*

At the end of January 1975, Berry's mother Bertha suffered a cerebral hemorrhage while preparing to go to church. As soon as the family contacted Berry, he left Rome for Los Angeles. He was at his mother's side in the hospital when she died. Many of the Motowners attended the funeral, including Billy Dee Williams. When Berry returned to Italy, he brought along his grieving father who had had a leg amputated recently because of an illness.

In Rome, before they got back to work, Berry was presented with a special American Music Award given to him by Diana Ross and transmitted via satellite during the Awards ceremony in America by Dick Clark Productions. A couple of days later, in the second week of February, work resumed. Matters between Diana and Berry were worse than before.

Everyone seemed on edge, especially with the knowledge that Diana Ross—Berry's former girlfriend—was a few months pregnant with her third child (not showing yet), and Nancy Leiviska—Berry's fiancée—was also some months pregnant with her first. The whole crew knew of the double pregnancies, but no one really wanted to discuss the irony of it all, because of the obvious tension.

"I'm not sure I like the idea of *her* being here in Rome with us," Diana told a friend. "But what can I do about it? Berry seems to love her.''

"Diana stayed clear of Nancy," said that friend. "Mostly, she liked her. Nancy was very giving and friendly to Diana. She was the most generous, understanding girlfriend Berry had ever had. But the fact that she was Berry's girl made Diana extremely nervous. 'Who knows how much she knows about me?' was her main concern. 'How much did Berry tell her?' Nancy had a calming effect on Berry Gordy that Diana never had, and I think Diana must have known that. She had to be a bit jealous. I'm sure it added to the tension. Bob was in and out of Rome a lot. When he was in, he and Diana never spent time with Berry and Nancy.''

It was costing $35,000 a day to film *Mahogany*—a pittance considering what it now costs to make a movie, but a sizable amount 15 years ago. Each extra day Berry spent making Diana re-film scenes put the production further into the red. To emphasize the cost overrun, Rob Cohen made his point dramatically. He withdrew $35,000 in cash from the Motown Productions' bank account and began to throw the money into a trash can in front of Berry every time he would go above eight takes. With each extra take, a few thousand more dollars went into the garbage. It was his way of illustrating to a man only concerned with ''the bottom line'' how much his behavior was actually costing him.

''Berry's a crapshooter and he didn't understand the significance of $35,000 on paper, but cash, that's another story,'' Cohen said with a smile. ''Seeing cash go into the trash, *that* Berry understood.''

Bob Silberstein stayed with Diana for most of the filming in Europe, and was well-liked by the crew. ''He was a very attractive and nice fellow,'' associate producer Neil Hartley said. ''I liked him enormously. But she had to be the boss, and I got the feeling that she was driving him away. She was very charming, very classy, but a bit on the bossy side.''

Near the end of the schedule, Diana was working with a queasy stomach because of her pregnancy and a hot temper because of dealing with Berry. One particular day, the script called for her to run up and down a long flight of outdoor stairs, all the while shooing away pigeons. After about two dozen takes, she was tired and irritable.

''Goddamn, Berry, isn't that enough?''

''No, Diane, I gotta . . .''

''You got to do nothin', I'm finished!'' she blustered as the startled crew looked on.

''Like hell you are,'' Berry said angrily, getting down from his director's chair. ''Now, listen, you get back up on those stairs and . . .''

Diana looked like she had finally reached her boiling point. Before Berry could finish his sentence, she took a swing at him with the palm of her hand and made stinging contact with the side of his face. There was a loud smacking sound and Berry's sunglasses flew a yard into the air.

"Hey! What the hell are you doin', woman? What's goin' on?"

"I hate you! I hate you!" Diana screamed. "That's what the hell is goin' on!"

Then she spun around and ran away. Four assistants trailed behind her, nervously asking "Miss Ross" what they could do to help. She threw her pearl-and-gold button earrings at them.

"You can just leave me alone, that's what you can do. Goddamn it." Diana shouted at them as she stepped into her trailer and slammed the door behind her. "And you pack my make-up," she screamed at someone inside the trailer. "I'm getting out of here."

The rest of the crew and other actors squirmed in embarrassment.

"Does this mean we're done?" someone asked.

"I think so," was the answer.

"I got this call in my office that Diana had hit Berry and stormed off the location," recalled Rob Cohen, who was away planning the next day's shoot. "By this time I was fairly seasoned to the ups and downs of that relationship, so I can't say I was surprised that she hauled off and slapped the guy. She was always half-seductive but angry, and he was always tolerant but mad. Their relationship was so complicated—everything a man and woman can possibly be to one another: father, daughter, mother, son, lovers. Damned if I could figure it all out.

"I don't think Diana ever went back to the villa in which she was staying. She went right to the airport. I remember having to ship all of her clothes back later. When I saw Berry that day, he had a cut on his nose but was fairly philosophical about the whole thing. He kept saying, 'Gosh, Rob, hell if I understand her anymore. She never used to do shit like that.' "

Later, Gordy's press people released this statement to the media: "I thought we might be too close for an effective director-star relationship. As director, I was naturally compelled to put on pressure to draw from her every emotion the script calls for. And this can be hard going between friends. She's nonetheless responded with resounding success."

After Diana left, Berry's secretary, Edna Anderson, filled in for her by doing "insert shots": a woman's hand holding a candle that drips wax during a party scene, a woman's figure in a red Iso-Rivolta sportscar speeding down a bridge headed for disaster, and so forth. A montage sequence with Diana would be filmed in Los Angeles later after her temper had cooled. By this time, Berry had plenty of completed film ready to edit.

In September 1975, "Theme to *'Mahogany'* (Do You Know Where You're Going To?)" was released.

Prior to its release, Gordy and Michael Masser, who also composed the soundtrack to the film, argued over the music mix; Gordy wanted one version released and Masser another. As a last resort, Masser snuck into the recording studio and erased the version Gordy liked. At first Berry was furious, but then he began to laugh. "That little blond shit-head," he said with a grin. "Okay. Release his version."

Michael Masser's version went to Number One on the charts and is one of Diana Ross's most popular songs. Her performance was dreamy and compelling and set the stage beautifully for the release of the movie, which almost never happened.

The advance trade reviews for *Mahogany* were dreadful and when *Time* magazine accused Berry of "squandering one of America's most natural resources: Diana Ross," all hell broke loose.

"See, what'd I tell you? Berry's ruining me," one friend of Diana's remembered her saying. "I'm one of America's most *natural* resources and he's *squandering* me," she cried.

"I got a call from Berry and he said he was going to pull the picture," Rob Cohen remembered. "I said, 'Berry, *please* listen to me. This is not a picture for the critics or for Hollywood. This picture touches a human nerve and it's gonna work. You listen to me.' "

"No, Rob, Diane's screamin', and I made a mistake and . . ." Berry fumbled, his vulnerability showing.

"Did'ja see what *Time* magazine said about me? Jeez, I really worked hard on this goddamn thing. What the hell am I gonna do now, Rob?"

"You release that film," Rob recalled having insisted. He realized that if Berry Gordy pulled the movie from release now, it would probably never come out. "Think about all the great things in that movie," Rob urged. "Think about all your hard work, all those long, endless nights editing, how the people in the crew loved you. Forget Diana, man. Think about you for a change. You did a fucking incredible job, Berry. You deserve this."

Berry did not answer immediately.

"Okay," Berry said. "Good advice. You always have the best advice, you know that?"

The two men laughed.

"We'll see what happens," Berry added. "Forget Diana."

In its first two weeks, *Mahogany* grossed nearly $7 million and the demand for it was so strong that the Loews State in New York was forced to stay open around the clock in order to accommodate the crowds. (It broke the opening day record at the Manhattan movie house which *The Godfather* had previously held for three years.) Suddenly, it became stylish to sit in a movie theater at 3:00 A.M. and watch Diana Ross in all of her splendor. People in ticket lines were controlled by mounted police.

Despite the film's less-than-critical acclaim—"the worst reviews in the history of the world," Berry said later—some of Diana's notices were very good. Wrote Charles Champlin in the *Los Angeles Times*: "She is out of the [Louis B.] Mayer '30s— a genuine movie queen who wears her heart and soul close to the surface . . . she is the absolute essence of the star as symbol of enviable escape from the humdrum ordinary ball."

Other critics weren't so generous. Rex Reed, who praised Diana Ross for her work in *Lady Sings the Blues*, observed: "*Mahogany* exists as a hymn to the celebration of how glorious it is to be Diana Ross." He also criticized Diana's designs, writing that they looked like "Halloween costumes at a Harlem relief ball."

Michael Roshkind, by now Berry's right-hand man, was so outraged by the reviews that he shot off a letter to *The Hollywood Reporter* and suggested a new method of critiquing movies. He proposed that each new film should be viewed at special public previews across the country. Ratings would then be released to the press and television as official "authorized" reviews. He wrote, "This would be much more accurate as to the public taste than that of a single professional whose tastes are probably jaded and prejudiced," he wrote.

According to Roshkind's logic, which certainly underscores the Motown system of total control, these screenings would be beneficial because "[they would] be held by the producer or releasing company and controlled by them for their benefit." Needless to say, the Motion Picture Association of America (MPAA) never considered adopting Motown's proposal, but it did raise a few eyebrows.

Berry Gordy brought *Mahogany* in at almost double its $2-

million budget allotted by Paramount (which means that the additional money came out of his pocket), but in the end it was a profitable film. *Mahogany* was not a blockbuster; it had a large black audience but never the white acceptance Gordy thought it would enjoy. Still, though it isn't a brilliant movie, it is a touching one. People do remember it.

"I'll admit that if I had been the producer or director, I might have made some different choices," Diana said about the movie. "All in all, I have no regrets. The whole experience was good for me."

Soon "Do You Know Where You're Going To?" became a catch phrase with Diana Ross' employees. Shelly Berger, one of her managers under Gordy, would say that the question was asked about 15 times a day as sort of a practical joke, until at last Diana had had enough.

"Do you know where you're going to?" Berger asked Diana good-naturedly during an interview.

"No! Goddammit, no," she snapped at him. "And I don't care either!"

Chapter
20

"DO YOU KNOW where you're going to?"

It was a question to which Florence Ballard never had an answer. Life had never gotten any better for Blondie. During one Christmas season, in the early '70s, a despondent Florence took her three children to the boarded-up house on Buena Vista Avenue. She was almost incoherent as she stood in front of it with her daughters at her side and talked about how wonderful it once was when they all lived in this home. She complained that "now Mommy can't afford no Christmas presents for her babies." Then she and her girls sat on the snow-covered front steps and pretended that they still lived there.

In August 1975, Mary Wilson arranged for Florence to visit her in Los Angeles. She brought her on stage during one of The Supremes' shows, and the sight of Florence was heartbreaking. She had never stopped drinking and the effect of years of alcohol showed. The warmth and softness in her face were gone. But the audience cheered loudly anyway. With tears in her eyes, Florence stood in a soft blue spotlight before 2,000 people, all of whom were standing and applauding.

The next night, she was backstage before the show. "Got a cigarette?" she asked one fan.

The fan stared at her, barely able to believe his eyes. "Aren't you . . . ?" he began. "Oh my goodness . . ."

"Yes, it's me," Florence acknowledged, her voice deep, raspy and hard-sounding. "Got a cigarette?"

The fan reached into his coat pocket and pulled out a pack of Marlboros. With her eyes fixed on the pack of cigarettes, Florence took one out and shoved it into her mouth. With shaking hands, she struck a match and lit it, barely able to align the match with the cigarette. She took a heavy drag and exhaled loudly. The fan shuddered. Florence, realizing she was under heavy scrutiny, shifted from foot to foot.

Suddenly, Mary Wilson swept grandly by wearing a low-cut white sequined gown, matching turban, black and white feather stole. She held a flute of champagne in her hand. Grinning, she said something to someone about how fabulous she thought she looked. "It took me three hours to get my make-up to look like this," she gushed. "Three hours! Can you believe it?"

Florence tried to ignore her. "Goddamn, I need a drink," she said, twitching. "A double shot, that's what I need right now."

The fan wished he could reach out and let her unburden her heart. Instead, he turned and walked away. It was too painful to see her like this. One of his friends caught up to him and, pointing to the woman in the floral-print dress leaning against a wall, asked, "Isn't that . . . ?"

"No, it's not," the fan said as he shook his head and continued walking.

After Florence left Los Angeles that summer of 1975, she and Mary Wilson didn't speak to each other until the following November when Mary hosted a family reunion in Detroit. Mary decided not to invite Flo to the party. She showed up anyway. It was the last time Mary would see her alive.

"I talked to Diane just the other day," Florence had told a friend after she returned to Detroit in 1975. "I just felt like I wanted to talk to her. So I called 'round and got her number in Beverly Hills and I just called her."

Florence remembered that the phone rang three times before a male voice on the other end answered very formally, "Miss Ross' residence."

"May I speak to Miss Ross, please?" Florence asked politely.

"Whom shall I say is calling?" he intoned.

"Florence . . . Florence Ballard."

"Who is this, really?" the person on the other end demanded impatiently. "Miss Ross is extremely busy and certainly has *no* time to . . ."

"Just tell her it's Florence."

Suddenly, Diana picked up an extension.

"Blondie? My God. Is it really you?"

Florence recalled that, for the next hour, the two of them enjoyed the nicest conversation they'd had in many years. Mostly, they discussed motherhood, their children and Diana's career.

"I saw that new movie, *Mahogany*," Florence remembered telling her.

"Well, did you like it?" Diana asked.

"Not really," Florence said. "You looked great, girl, but that ending. To go back to the ghetto after seeing the world and bein' the toast of the town. That would *never* happen."

"It was a very strange call," Diana would say years later. "She said she was ready to go back to singing. The next thing I knew, she was dead."

After her conversation with Diana, Florence received an "unexplained cash settlement." Now that Florence had $50,000 in her bank account, her husband was back in the picture. They reconciled. She considered going back into show business but confided to one friend that she still didn't know the difference between a recording contract and a management contract. She purchased a new home, paid cash for a Cadillac and gave her children the nicest Christmas they'd ever had with a huge tree and many presents. Some said that she had won the lawsuit against the lawyer who had absconded with her Motown settlement. Others insisted that the money came from Diana Ross.

"Maybe it did come from Diana Ross," was all Tommy Chapman had to say. "What the hell difference does it make?"

Two months later, on February 22, 1976, Florence Ballard was dead. Records filed with the Wayne County medical examiner's office listed the cause of death as "cardiac arrest." Florence weighed nearly 200 pounds. An autopsy revealed a blood clot in a major artery. A doctor confirmed that it was "unusual but possible" for a 32-year-old woman to suffer a heart attack, especially considering Florence's history of high blood pressure and the medication she was taking for weight-loss.

"But I think she died of a broken heart," Lurlee Ballard said of her daughter.

"It didn't last too long," Florence had said of The Supremes' success. "We were bound, someday, to go our separate ways."

Diana Ross set up a trust fund for Florence Ballard's three daughters. The amount each girl will be entitled to when she turns 21 has not been revealed, but it is said to be in the six figures. Certainly, this was a generous gesture on Diana's part.

But then a month after Florence Ballard's death, Diana Ross told *People* magazine, "Did I cry? Yes, I cried." She said, "People tried to help Florence. I tried to help her. She had it all and she threw it away.

"She quit The Supremes, we didn't quit her. Don't make too big a thing of this," she cautioned the reporter. "Florence was very important in my life, but I'm not dead. She did this to herself."

* * *

Rhonda Suzanne came bounding into her mother's bedroom after school one afternoon. "Why is my skin brown when my girlfriend has white skin and blond hair?" the five-year-old asked. Diana kneeled down to her level and smoothed down the little girl's dress.

"That's the breaks, kid," she said. "That's the way it is. My skin is brown, too. Don't you think I'm beautiful?"

The girl nodded her head and grinned broadly. Then she ran out of the room to play.

Diana Ross started 1976 as the mother of three. Another daughter, Chudney Lane, had been born to her and Robert Silberstein in November of the previous year. Bob was in the delivery room with Diana. "He thought he'd never make it through," Diana recalled. "But he was fine." The couple was expecting a boy and planned to name him Robert Silberstein, Jr. When a girl arrived, they were at a loss for a name. Diana couldn't think of one, and she remembered, "The lady kept comin' back and saying 'We need a name on the birth certificate!'

"Look, this name has got to be with this child for the rest of her life," Diana said to the nurse. "Will you please give me a break?"

She decided to name the child after the spicy fruit relish, chutney. She misspelled the word on the birth certificate which is how her daughter ended up with the odd name Chudney.

Diana seems to be an excellent mother. "I like to spend as much time with them as I can," she had said. "I don't mind if I spoil them by giving them a lot of love. If loving them means spoiling them, that's just too bad."

Diana has talked of bathing with her three daughters in their old-fashioned bathtub with legs in the mirrored bathroom. "You guys are so beautiful," Diana would say of the images of her three tots reflected on the mirrors. "You look just like me."

Once, five-year-old Rhonda asked, "Mommy, who are The Supremes? They say we [she and her sisters] look like The Supremes."

"That was a long time ago, Rhonda," Diana said patiently. "A lifetime ago."

Another time, Rhonda was watching television when a commercial came on announcing the sale of a new collection of Diana Ross and The Supremes hit records. The girl sat in front of the tube with her legs crossed and a confused expression on her face as photos of the three Supremes flashed across the screen—with the skinny doe-eyed singer front and center. "Diana Ross?" Rhonda asked. "Who _is_ Diana Ross?"

"I don't know," Diana said. "I really don't know _who_ she is."

Diana would bring her children with her on tour and often they would drop in on her press interviews. During one session backstage with a reporter, four-year-old Tracee came waltzing in with a small ring box and handed it to her mother. "Open it," she said. "It's a surprise."

Diana got up from her chair and kneeled down in front of her daughter. "You didn't get this from Mommy's dresser, did you?" she asked very patiently.

"No, Mommy," the little girl said, shifting from one foot to the other.

"Well, what is it?" Diana asked.

"A surprise."

Diana opened the box. It was empty.

"Surprise," Tracee exclaimed, giggling.

Diana scooped up her daughter in her arms and hugged her.

During another interview, this one with _Rolling Stone_, Diana complained to manager Shelly Berger, "What a day. Six o'clock this morning I wake up and find out that one of my girls has peed all over me."

"She what?" Shelly asked.

"She peed on me. She crawled up in bed with me in the middle of the night, and at some point . . ."

"Jesus, you oughta do something about that!"

"Yeah, I should do something," Diana agreed, "But I don't know what it is I should do. I can't get angry with her when something like this happens because it's not her fault. This happened once before and I did that. I got angry. I woke up to this terrible smell, and before I knew what was happening, I was shouting. And my daughter, you know, she wouldn't even look at me for the rest of the day. I felt just terrible."

Diana said she was reading a book that explained what to do with your child after she wets the bed, but that now she'd decided to buy another book—"what to do so that your child won't wet the bed in the first place."

Of her marriage, Diana Ross said at this time, "We never thought it would last this long [five years], but here we are."

Shortly before Chudney was born, Diana got up in the middle of a sleepless night and wandered into her bathroom where she began to cry uncontrollably. "Emotionally, everything seemed out of whack," she said. "I finally told Bob I wasn't happy with my career or my life or my marriage—that nothing seemed to be working the way I want it to. And yet I was feeling all of this guilt because I had everything: beautiful children, a warm home, a good job, love.''

Disgusted with Diana's continuing dependency on Berry Gordy—even though he and Berry got along famously—Bob introduced her to the est (Erhard Seminars Training) philosophy. Bob wanted her to realize she was successful because of her talent, not only because of her connections with Berry Gordy. The older she became, the more she began to analyze what had brought her success in the past and what she should do in the future. Bob was tired of hearing about it. Who was responsible for her fame? Was she? Or was Berry Gordy? Or the teachers in artist development? The songwriters? Producers?

The principles behind est are simple—a person is responsible for himself and his own decisions. Erhard had told her that there are some people who have success, and others who are had by success. She had to stop and think about that.

''It was the most wonderful experience I've had up to this date,'' Diana said of est. ''Afterward, I just felt good about everything, you know? It's just like I seemed to understand other people more, their fears. I was interested in other people more, not just in myself.''

Diana may have thought she was more caring, but it can be argued that to live the est way, one must be selfish, considering one's own life, wants and needs before those of others. Many people think it's not the best way to continue a partnership in marriage.

Later, she told *McCall's* magazine, ''Even today I'm not sure what I was crying out for that night [when she was pregnant with Chudney] except that up to that point I had simply been doing what I was told and letting other people think for me. I'd never really looked inside myself for answers—or even questions. I was ready to start.'' Diana could not reconcile wanting to become more independent while being married.

After Chudney was born, it was reported that Bob walked out on Diana. ''He'd had it with her obsession with Berry,'' said a friend. ''There was a big blow-up over something Berry had said to Diana, or perhaps it was the other way around. Who really knows? Berry was always involved in that marriage and it was impossible to keep him out of it.''

Diana even invited Werner Erhard to her home to meet Berry Gordy and explain the theory behind his training. Berry wasn't impressed. His own philosophy wasn't much different from Erhard's. He certainly didn't want someone telling him what to do with his life. "Sounds like a pretty good racket, though," Berry had to admit.

Despite the problems in their marriage, Diana and Bob posed for a loving *People* magazine cover in January 1976. The photo spread featured the couple at home with their three children. The reporter made note of the Silbersteins' "cook, English secretary, a yardman, a housekeeper, a nanny" to look after Diana, Bob, their three children, her brother Chico and her sister Margretia's son, Tommy, who was living with them because his parents were separated and Margretia's job with the airlines kept her away from home. Fans couldn't help but notice that Tracee and Chudney looked very much like Bob, while Rhonda, the oldest, looked nothing at all like him.

When the reporter wrote that Bob never considered himself "Mr. Ross," Diana reacted. "I'd certainly not considered him that, nor had he thought of himself that way before," she said after the story was published. "Of course, this may have had deep roots and we never admitted it. I suppose the story made us both stop and take a look around and ask if people are really thinking that way."

Of her relationship with Berry, Diana admitted in the article, "At first he was a dictator, and I really hated him. Then I loved him more than anything. Then I started to hate him again, and now I really like him."

Later that year, Diana said of Gordy, "He's in charge of my career, always has been and always will be. But he's not the director of my life."

Despite whatever was going on in her personal life, the career, as always, continued. During the 1960s, the most popular dance music originated with Motown. Motown's artists and its unique sound were dominant in pop music, but then Woodstock and psychedelia swept in. Janis Joplin, Jimi Hendrix and others changed the face of popular music. The Motown Sound had entered a period of stagnation; the fervor and magic it once had was dissipating. But black music was still preserved in the Philadelphia Sound and the Chicago Sound. By the early '70s, the popular black music field was flooded with artists, songwriters and producers creating a sound of their own, all of it very much influenced by the early Motown era.

One of the music trends surfacing at this time was called "disco music"—usually 132 beats-per-minute of rhythmic, pounding percussion. Motown got into the disco forum with some of Eddie Kendricks' and The Jackson Five's work ("Girl You Need a Change of Mind" and "Dancing Machine"), but for the most part stayed away from it until Diana Ross teamed up with producer Hal Davis for "Love Hangover." The record became another hit when it was included on her February 1976 album, *Diana Ross*. "Love Hangover," an exciting dance record perfectly suited to the times, went to Number One on the charts and was nominated for a Grammy Award. It also exposed Diana to a new generation of young record buyers totally unfamiliar with her earlier work.

Now, more than ever, Diana seemed determined to extricate herself from Berry Gordy's hold. One of her first moves in that direction was putting together her own nightclub act in 1976. It would be her best, most creative show to date. To assist her, she hired Joe Layton, known for his work with other pop music queens of the day such as Bette Midler and Cher.

"We went through all kinds of emotional drama together," Layton recalled. "She was upset about her marriage and always in tears. I was upset because my wife had recently died, and also always crying my eyes out. Out of all of these sobbing bouts, somehow came creativity. Even though she was still recording for Motown, she wanted to split from Berry, and that was very clear. His image of her was something she wanted no part of, so he wasn't consulted about the show. I'm sure it must have made him crazy, but she was cutting the cord that was around her neck."

In this new 90-minute nightclub act, Diana Ross became the ultimate glitz-queen; she really knew how to give her fans—who were now paying to see a movie star as well as a recording artist—what they craved most. It was *Mahogany* come to life. For her opening numbers, "Here I Am" and "I Wouldn't Change a Thing," she stood center stage in a white dress with her arms extended to each side. As mimes unfurled the yards of material on her arms, projected images of Diana Ross in all of her splendor graced the sleeves. Diana Ross always knows how to make an entrance.*

---

*During this time, Diana began talking of making a film based on the life of Josephine Baker, "an absolutely incredible, multi-faceted woman." She had been approached with the idea by a couple of Hollywood producers, and said that she was very interested. For the next 15 years, the Baker project would grow to obsessive proportions for Diana, and would prove to be difficult—if not impossible—for her to mount. Interestingly, before she died in 1975, Josephine Baker reportedly had offered to sell her life story to Berry for Diana to do—for $1 million. Berry was stunned: "A million bucks? Forget it."

"It's like a stylish stage adaptation of 'This Is Your Life' with Miss Ross playing both host and honored subject," said Robert Hilburn of the *Los Angeles Times*. That didn't matter, though. Eight spectacular Bob Mackie costume changes and that effervescent Diana Ross personality, spirit and voice made the show more than memorable. Another critic noted that "the enthusiasm from her audience was so fervent at times that it suggested the beginnings of a Judy Garland-ish cult around her."

At the Palace Theatre in New York, "An Evening With Diana Ross" broke the Broadway showplace's 63-year-old box office record. Diana would win a special Tony Award for the concert. During that engagement, Maxine Powell attended a performance. Powell is the very charming etiquette teacher who helped to prepare Diana for her important Copacabana opening in 1965. Diana graciously introduced her from the audience as "the woman who taught me everything I know." Afterwards, she and Maxine spent time together backstage. Diana was genuinely moved to see the lady who, just ten years earlier, promised to groom her so that she could play "everywhere from Buckingham Palace to the White House."

Diana, with tears in her eyes, hugged Maxine warmly. "I just want you to know," she told her, "that whenever I walk out onto a stage you are with me."

"When I perform, I'm not as afraid as I once was," Diana said later. "It's not that I'm that much surer about what I'm doing, but I'm not scared anymore. I've faced my fears about what I was afraid of onstage. Mostly I was afraid I wasn't going to sound good. I'm skinny. I'm not pretty. I used to walk out and I was competing. I was afraid that I wouldn't be up to what was expected of me."

After the show at the Ahmanson Theatre in Los Angeles, press and record promoters congregated backstage—25 people in all—and just as in every city, Diana held court. The room was filled with invited guests, all breathless with anticipation. Everyone held glasses filled with champagne. Three men cleared a path through the crowd between the door and the middle of the room. Conversations turned into whispers; there was a hush of expectancy. Mike Roshkind, wearing a three-piece suit, walked in, his hands clasped in front of him. The hush deepened. "Ladies and gentlemen," he announced, "Miss Diana Ross."

There was enthusiastic applause as Roshkind opened a door. Diana swooped in wearing a white silk evening gown and a matching sequined jacket. The dress was cut low to reveal the curve of her breasts. She was in full make-up, her hair pulled back severely and accented by two gardenias on one side. Diamond earrings provided the perfect finishing touch.

"Oh, thank you," she cooed, absolutely beaming. "Thank you so much."

The applause continued.

"Yes, thank you. Thank you. Thank you!"

"A *fabulous* show," someone shouted as the applause rang out.

Diana raised her hands to her head and ran her palms over her slicked back hair. When her ten fingers touched at the nape of her neck, she tilted her head back ever so slightly. As she held that pose, the clapping persisted.

"A wonderful performance," someone else yelled. "Just marvelous in every way!"

"Oh, thank you. Thank you," she said, now blowing kisses.

Finally, the applause died down and there was stunned silence. Everyone took her in as she walked about, shaking a hand here, kissing a cheek there.

Later, five-year-old Rhonda was brought in by her nanny. She looked up at her mother with wondering eyes and said, "Mommy, people love you because you're a *star*. Right?"

Mommy just smiled.

Diana was riding the crest of a very successful "Greatest Hits" album during the summer of 1976 and seemed happy with her career. "My audience—I need their love in a way I can't describe," she said after the Ahmanson engagement. "Maybe that's because I didn't get enough love when I was little. Perhaps it's because I was a second child and I needed more attention. I was always striving to make an impression."

Wrote Liz Smith for the New York *Daily News*, "I have never seen an audience so genuinely, healthily in love. Hers is the warmest and best live performance I've ever seen."

In the summer of 1976, Diana worked at Caesars Palace in Las Vegas. Just before going on, she wrote on her dressing room mirror with soap: "You can have it any way you want it." Her mind was apparently made up.

Following that engagement, in June while appearing at Radio City Music Hall in New York, she filed for divorce from Bob Silberstein after saying simply that "I don't want to be married anymore." The est philosophy postulates that the decision to end a relationship should be done quickly and painlessly. Unfortunately, Bob wasn't ready to end the marriage and told friends that he was bitter about the way Diana just seemed to discard him. He felt that he had somehow served his purpose in her life, and now that was the end of his usefulness to her. He also discouraged a good friend from going into show business, "because it's more awful than you can imagine."

In September, Liz Smith reported in her column that they had reconciled and gone to Hawaii to try to put the marriage back together "for the sake of their three little girls. Now they are back in L.A. and I understand that divorce proceedings are under way."

In an interview a few years later, Diana mentioned that it seemed to her that Bob had a problem when someone accidentally called him Mr. Ross. "I don't think he admitted it, but I think finally it did get to him. It's just something that . . . it's not fun." When asked if that's what broke up the marriage, she said, "I think, yes."

"Of course that wasn't it," Bob insisted. "She just didn't want to be married anymore. It was as simple as that."

Bob's comments at that time seem to indicate that he was frustrated with his wife's continued obsession with her Svengali. "My wife *belongs* to that company," he complained shortly before the divorce. "She is totally dominated by a man who has never read a book in his life. I just can't stand it anymore to hear them calling Stevie Wonder a genius. Whatever happened to Freud?"

People who knew them had their own opinions about what had happened, but an actress friend of Diana's who asked for anonymity probably best explained it when she said, "Partly it was a career thing. Remember, Diana's an incredible celebrity, as in 'legend,' and she needs that huge audience of hers. To Diana, the audience is number one, so she began to think, 'How dare these men manipulate me?' Berry Gordy. Her husband. She wanted her freedom to make her own choices, at whatever the cost."

Chapter

21

In March 1977, after Diana's divorce became final, she starred in a one-woman 90-minute television special for NBC using her nightclub act as a focal point for the show. The highlight of the special was a sequence in which she portrayed Billie Holiday, Bessie Smith and Josephine Baker, complete with look alike make-up jobs by Stan Winston. According to the script, Diana "imagined" that these three legendary performers suddenly materialized before her in an empty theater and reflected about their experiences as entertainers. Certainly, from a historical perspective, Diana Ross had a lot in common with these great singers. But this sketch was clearly an attempt to include herself among the greats rather than an effort to pay tribute to her predecessors.

In June, Diana recorded an excellent album produced by Richard Perry, *Baby It's Me*. Then, later that summer, one of Diana's friends convinced her that if she enjoyed est, she should take matters a step further and visit the guru, Swami Muktananda, who had taught Werner Erhard many of his principles. It was faddish at this time in Hollywood to turn to the teachings of Muktananda: John Denver, Olivia Hussey, Marsha Mason and many other celebrities swore by him and he was considered a saint among his vast international following. (He died in 1982.)

Shortly thereafter, Diana was off to Ganeshpuri, India, to visit the guru. In trying to find herself, she became surrounded by people who had a transcendent devotion to God. She had never been exposed to anything like this. She meditated in the special room that the guru himself meditated in for 12 years. Most observers felt that this trip was somehow connected to a publicity gimmick. The photos of a beaming Diana sitting atop an elephant and posing with the guru that appeared in magazines and newspapers around the world did little to dispel that notion.

By mid-1977, Motown had acquired the hit Broadway musical *The Wiz* as a film property through a production deal with Universal. *The Wiz,* an all-black fantasy conceived by Ken Harper and Charlie Smalls, is based on L. Frank Baum's classic *The Wizard of Oz*, which had already been adapted to a variety of stage and film versions, the most notable, of course, being the Judy Garland classic of 1939.

In the Broadway show, the role of Dorothy went to Stephanie Mills, barely a teen-ager at the time. Suzanne dePasse was so impressed with her that she signed her to the label. Mills had no success at Motown, however.

Motown's *Wiz* project began to take shape in 1975 when Rob Cohen and director John Badham enjoyed the play in New York while casting Badham's Motown film, *Bingo Long and the Traveling All Stars*, starring Billy Dee Williams and Richard Pryor. Cohen felt that *The Wiz* could be successfully adapted to the screen, and in May 1976, he and Universal negotiated with Ken Harper for the screen rights. The Motown/Universal production was announced to the film industry in July.

The concept was to surround an unknown Dorothy with big-name stars playing the other characters. Stephanie Mills was campaigning for the role. Cohen and Badham wrote a script, which Universal rejected, then a fallow period transpired when nothing was happening with the project. During this time, Cohen and Badham met with a number of black stars whose connection they felt could cause Universal to become more interested in the project—including Sidney Poitier and Bill Cosby. There was no interest from these celebrities. Cosby was particularly outspoken and wanted to know why both the producers and director of this Motown production were white.

Diana first heard of Motown's plans over dinner with Suzanne dePasse. When actor Ted Ross joined them briefly at their table, he and dePasse enthusiastically discussed the upcoming venture in which he had already been cast to repeat his stage role as the Lion. Diana was immediately interested. Here was a Motown film and she hadn't been asked to be a part of it. She had seen *The Wiz* twice on Broadway. "Darn, I would love to be Dorothy," Diana said to Suzanne. DePasse told her that it probably wasn't possible—it was such a small-budgeted film—and quickly changed the subject.

According to Diana, that night she lay awake thinking about both *The Wiz* and *The Wizard of Oz*, "maybe even dreaming,

I'm not sure." At two in the morning, she said, she got up, watched a videotape of the Garland original and then telephoned Berry.

"I want to play Dorothy," she said.

"Who is this?"

"It's Diane. I want to play Dorothy in *The Wiz*," she repeated.

"Have you been drinking?"

"Of course not. I've been watching *The Wizard of Oz* and I had this dream or something about being Dorothy and . . ."

"Forget it. What are you, nuts? You're too old to be any damn Dorothy. Now go to sleep."

With that, he hung up on her.

Diana may have thought that Berry completely dismissed her idea, but he had too much confidence in her instincts to disregard the phone call. He called Rob Cohen. It was four in the morning.

"The phone rang and I jumped awake, my heart beating wildly," Cohen recalled, "because I knew it was Berry, and I knew something was up. It was his secretary Edna telling me to please hold. So I held for 15 minutes laying in the dark while Berry did business with someone else on another line. I swear to God, the man never slept."

Suddenly, Berry got on the line. No hellos, just straight to business.

"Man, I was on the phone with Diane a second ago," Rob recalled Berry as having said. "And she had a dream or something that she played Dorothy in *The Wiz*. So what do you think about that?"

The thought of casting Diana in this film had never occurred to Rob, but he didn't have to think too long to make a decision about it. "There are a lot of reasons why it's wrong," he said carefully. "There's only one reason that it's right."

"What's that?"

"Universal will pay her $1 million to do it," Rob replied. "And it'll mean getting this movie made."

"And what's wrong about it?"

"She's too old. She's in her 30s. This character is one of America's beloved icons and to put Diana Ross in the center of it may, in fact, be condemning it to being hated even if it's a great movie."

"That's the same goddamn thing I told her," Berry said. "But she's insistent about doing it. And you know how she is once she's made her mind up about something."

"She's too old, I think," Rob continued, "and also . . ."

Berry cut him off. "Hey. Wait a minute. Did I hear you right? Did you say a million bucks?"

Rob remembered that he was suddenly on the spot. The million-dollar figure was one he had offered, impulsively.

"Yeah, that's what I said. One mil."

"You mean to tell me you can get Diane a million bucks to do this thing?" Berry asked incredulously.

"Well, I, uh . . ."

"Look, you get her a million, and I'll tell her she can do it."

"But . . ."

Berry hung up.

Rob said that he spent the rest of the night pacing. At 6:00 A.M., he started making phone calls and, after not very much negotiation, Tom Mount, one of the executives in charge of *The Wiz* at Universal, told Rob that the powers-that-be at the company would be interested in having Diana do the film—and that Universal would, in fact, pay her $1 million to do it. Rob then called John Badham and asked how he would feel about directing Diana Ross in this film. Badham said he thought it was a terrible idea, and he wouldn't have anything to do with it.

"You can have her, but I don't want her," he said. "She's all wrong. If Diana Ross is in, I'm out." John Badham quit the project and went on to direct *Saturday Night Fever*.

Cohen called Gordy to tell him about the Universal deal, and about John Badham. Before Berry had a chance to call Diana back, she was on the phone calling him.

Diana recalled, "I told him that I absolutely believed in Dorothy and in her search to find who she is and that it seemed so very parallel to who I am. I thought that identity would carry over to anybody who watched the picture, whatever their age, sex or color. And that it was something I really wanted to do."

Berry still felt that this would be a mistake. He saw nothing in this role for Diana. The more he denied her, the more she hungered for it. At this point, Diana didn't want to abide by any of Berry's decisions, and *The Wiz* very quickly, in a matter of hours, became another point of contention in their relationship.

"But you are just too old," he told her. He did not yet tell her about the million-dollar offer.

"I am not too old for that role," she insisted. She became more determined than ever. "It's ageless. It's right for my career."

He told her that the role was hers, and so was a million bucks—the deal was set and no one even had to leave their homes.

Berry then apparently washed his hands of the whole matter. It would be the breaking point in his and Diana's professional relationship—the first major project in which she would be involved without him. He knew she was cutting her ties with him, and that there was no holding her back.

The Wiz was budgeted as a small film, no big problem for anyone. Once turned into a star vehicle for Diana Ross, it became a big problem for everyone. Where this project was concerned, when Berry repeated to Rob Cohen those three words he'd been using for years, he meant them: "That's your problem."

"The actual truth is that there was a lot of magic involved. And you can't explain magic," Diana told a reporter who asked how she got the role.

Finding a new director was not easy. Cohen talked to Herb Ross and then Bob Fosse, but they showed no interest. He paid for a plane ticket to fly in Britisher Alan Parker (who had directed *Bugsy Malone*) from London to see the Broadway show, *The Wiz*. After the performance, Parker went back to the Plaza Hotel, where Motown Productions was putting him up, and made a deal with Peter Guber to direct *Midnight Express*.

Finally, Sidney Lumet, who had just finished working with Richard Burton on *Equus*, was hired as director. Lumet decided that the best way to make the film work would be to turn it into a modern-day Manhattan fantasy, so New York locations would be utilized. The budget was now up to $30 million, three times the total production costs of *Lady Sings the Blues* and *Mahogany* combined.

Screenwriter Joel Schumaker's script had Diana playing a 24-year-old schoolteacher living in Harlem who gets caught up in the vortex of a blizzard and ends up in Oz, a souped-up New York City, with her dog Toto. Once there, she somehow convinces the Scarecrow (19-year-old Michael Jackson), Lion (Ted Ross) and Tin Man (Nipsey Russell) that the qualities of knowledge, courage and compassion they're hoping the Wiz will give them are qualities they already possess. Richard Pryor played the Wiz and Lena Horne (at the time, director Sidney Lumet's mother-in-law) the Good Witch.

Producer Rob Cohen remembered, "Joel Schumaker, Sidney Lumet and Diana Ross had an interpretation of Dorothy that was neurotic. Dorothy was a scared adult, a peculiarly introverted woman. It was nothing like what John Badham and I had first envisioned. But Joel and Diana were involved in est and Diana was very enamored of Werner Erhard and before I knew it the movie was becoming an est-ian fable full of est buzz words about knowing who you are and sharing and all that. I hated the script a lot. But it was hard to argue with Diana because she was recognizing in this script all of this stuff she had worked out in est seminars.''

When Judy Garland filmed *The Wizard of Oz* in 1938, she was 16; Diana now was 32. When news of the casting was announced, most critics felt that Berry was giving his princess something else she wanted without any consideration to realism or artistic control. Berry didn't have much choice.

At about this time, Diana considered selling her home on Maple Drive in Beverly Hills where her fans felt no compunction about walking up and ringing her doorbell. There was a constant parade of strangers. Recalled John Mackey, a former employee of Loeb and Loeb, the law firm that represents Diana Ross, "Even though she could be a real witch to the people working for her, if the doorbell rang and it was a complete stranger oohing and aahing at her, she would turn on the charm. I have seen her in the foulest of moods, swearing, and then turn around and do an about-face to show some gawking fan a courteous person.''

Finally, Diana decided to move into a home in Bel Air but at the last moment she decided to become bi-coastal and live in New York. She leased a house on Long Island with her three children (Rhonda, then six; Tracee, five; and Chudney, two). While rehearsing for *The Wiz*, she lived at the Pierre Hotel as a temporary apartment was being refurbished at the Sherry Netherland by Angelo Donghia.

"She was away from Berry at long last," Rob Cohen said. "It was not Berry's money. It was all MCA's money. And Diana had said, 'Look, if you want me to stay at the company then let me go and do my own thing and stay the hell out of it.' It was liberation to her. I remember having very deep discussions with her about freedom and est. Half the time I didn't know what she was talking about, nor did I care. But she was very determined to break free, to do the movie, to have a life.''

"For the first time, I feel grown up," she said at the time. "I am responsible for more aspects of my life than I ever was when I lived in Los Angeles. I still depend on Berry for many things, but slowly I am also finding that I can handle just about anything that comes my way. It's like Dorothy in *The Wiz*—I believed that I could be independent and, though it scared me to death, I found that I could—that I had it in me all the time.''

She added, "What was happening to me in California was

that I was becoming a recluse. And I'm too young [32] not to have any fun. I decided that I was going to deal with my life, be public, and know that everything happening to me would be positive not negative. I decided to stop being afraid that someone would interrupt my meal in a restaurant and ask for an autograph.''

Diana enjoyed New York's pace and rhythm, though it took her awhile to get used to the taxicab drivers. She would take a 30-minute cab ride from the Pierre in Manhattan where she was staying during the week to the St. George in Brooklyn where rehearsals were conducted. On the first day of rehearsal, true to Manhattan tradition, the cabby drove recklessly, weaving in and out of traffic. Diana, appalled at his frantic driving, pounded with her fist on the shield separating her from the driver.

''What the hell are you doing?'' she demanded. ''You in some kind of hurry I don't know about?''

The driver turned to face her, without even slowing down.

''You're turning around? Are you *crazy*?''

''Say, ain't you Diana Ross?'' he asked.

''No, I ain't Diana Ross!'' she shot back. ''I'm a whole lot tougher than Diana Ross, and if you don't slow this goddamn car down you're gonna see what I'm talking about!''

He slowed down.

Rehearsals started in July 1977, but filming at the Astoria Studios in Queens wouldn't begin until Monday, October 3, 1977, for a 13-week schedule. Diana was uneasy the first day of shooting and, as she was putting on her make-up in her dressing room (which was once the original suite of offices used by Paramount founder Adolph Zukor), an aide said to her, ''You have nothing to fear but fear itself.''

Diana stopped and spun around in her chair. ''What was that?''

''You have nothing to fear but fear itself,'' he repeated.

Diana asked where that saying had come from, and when she was told that it was from Franklin Delano Roosevelt, she honestly did not know who Roosevelt was. ''I never even heard of him,'' she said. ''But what a powerful saying, and what a brilliant man he must have been to come up with it.''

She took her eyebrow pencil and wrote it on her dressing room mirror: *You have nothing to fear but fear itself.*

''That's just marvelous,'' she repeated as she continued putting on her make-up. Later, she decided the reason she'd never heard of Franklin Roosevelt was because he died the year after she was born. "My feeling was that she was two sandwiches short of a picnic," said the backstage aide.

Sidney Lumet disagreed: "I've never met a woman anywhere to compare with Diana. Anywhere. She is a person going through a most extraordinary metamorphosis right now. She's absorbing everything, experiencing everything with unquenchable energy."

People magazine reported some immediate problems on the set: "Diana Ross made like the Wicked Witch of the West [when] told that she'd have to share apartment sitting rooms with Lena Horne. [She] tempestuously vetoed any such notion."

A dangerous moment occurred in filming when Diana was playing a scene with a huge steel head with spotlights for eyes. She stared at the lights for too long and was almost blinded. "I remember that she had gotten herself so stoked up into thinking she was actually seeing some kind of Wiz that she wouldn't blink for a second, staring and staring all day into these lights," Rob Cohen remembered. "The next morning she woke up and she was having trouble seeing. Slowly, she was losing her vision. She was terrified. 'What's happening to me?' she was crying. And I thought to myself, 'Oh, Christ! No! This can't be true.' "

Diana was immediately flown to Jules Stein Eye Clinic in Maryland. "We had some real emotional moments there," Cohen recalled. "For a few terrifying hours, we didn't know if she would ever see again. The doctors said that she had suffered retinal burns. It was very scary."

Diana spent the next two uncertain days in the hospital with her eyes completely bandaged. Doctors told her that if the retinas were burned badly enough, they would not heal. The one in her left eye was particularly damaged. Slowly, full vision returned and everyone was relieved.

The next week, Diana returned to the film, but her eyes have been extremely sensitive to light ever since that time; they flood with tears and ache when exposed to sudden bursts of light. She has often requested that paparazzi not use flash bulbs when photographing her. Soon after this *Wiz* incident, she went to The Red Parrot nightclub in Manhattan to see Nona Hendryx (formerly of Patti Labelle and the Bluebelles) perform. Despite her pleas that he not do it, a photographer continually snapped pictures of her with his flash. Finally she just hauled off and punched the guy on the arm, neck and shoulder.

After the accident, Diana's sister Rita Ross became her stand-in during the filming of *The Wiz*. Her job was to stand in Diana's dress while the camera crew planned shots. This freed her superstar sister to do more important things.

Sidney Lumet originally wanted to cast Jimmie Walker as the Scarecrow. Walker played J.J. Evans (and popularized the phrase "dyn-o-mite!") on the '70s sitcom "Good Times." Cohen hated that idea. He thought that Walker was a caricature of a comic. He wanted to cast Michael Jackson.

"I had always been impressed by Michael because there was something very pure about him," he said. "I felt that the scarecrow needed youth and purity, not a jaded stand-up comic approach. Plus, Michael could sing and this was a musical, after all."

It was Diana who encouraged Michael to audition for the role of the Scarecrow and assured him that she would make certain that his family's leaving the Gordy empire to sign with CBS would not influence anyone's decision as to whether he would get the role. But once he got the part, she became upset with him because he was so adept at the complicated choreography that he made her, the star, look like an amateur. She pulled him aside one day during rehearsal and told him that he was embarrassing her. Michael lightened up on the virtuosity.

Diana Ross and her *Wiz* co-star Michael Jackson became so linked in the public's mind that most people never thought of one without the other. Diana and Michael had enjoyed a friendship since Berry "foisted" the young Jackson on her when he and his family moved from Gary, Indiana, to Los Angeles in 1970. Michael later claimed that Diana, an art fan, encouraged him in that field and that the two would go out practically every day and buy art supplies or go to museums where, he has said, Diana introduced him to the works of Michelangelo and Degas. That seems unlikely considering Diana's schedule in the early 1970s; she was rarely at home, and when she was, she seemed too self-consumed in her own problems—her solo career, her unusual marriage—to spend her days teaching a ten-year-old how to paint.

"She was Motown's superstar and she was at the level that Michael strove to attain," observed long-time friend Joyce MacCrae in an interview. "Diana was certainly his first impression of a celebrity. He liked the way she carried herself, her style, and tried to emulate her."

"There was an identification between Michael and me," Diana told writer Gerri Hirshey. "I was older. He kind of idolized me, and he wanted to sing like me."

Michael revealed that, during the filming of *The Wiz*, he shared with Diana Ross "his deepest, darkest secrets." That's not likely. It's more likely that Michael wished he could. But not only is he unable to share these hidden parts of his personality with anyone, it's doubtful that Diana Ross would have even particularly cared to hear them—unless she's as curious as his fans about the secrets Michael is hiding. It's more likely that the "deep, dark secret" Michael shared with her was that he had a blotchy complexion then and was glad to have the opportunity to wear the Scarecrow's make-up to hide that fact.

They did have some funny moments on the set. In one scene, Diana was supposed to faint and be picked up by Michael. Try though he might, Jackson couldn't budge her. She was too heavy for him. He kept puffing away, until he finally lifted her, but by that time Diana had broken up in convulsive laughter and the scene had to be reshot.

In hiring Michael Jackson to be the Scarecrow, and arranger/composer Quincy Jones to score the film, Rob Cohen had inadvertently put two forces together that, in the '80s, would go on to make music history with *Thriller*, the biggest-selling album of all time.

One day during a dance rehearsal, choreographer Louis Johnson tried to organize a couple of hundred dancers all with skateboards and hula hoops. The scene turned into absolute pandemonium by the time Diana arrived. She stood and watched as Johnson tried to figure out how best to use all of these dancers and paraphernalia. Diana started laughing hysterically.

Johnson walked over to her. "What's wrong?"

"Man, when I dream," she said, pointing at the chaos and still laughing, "I dream big!"

Filming on *The Wiz* wrapped on Friday, December 30, 1977, just short of three months after it began.

During 1978, Diana started her tour at the Universal Amphitheatre with a spectacular new show. At one outdoor theater engagement, an airplane hovered, blinking out the message: "Thanks for being a part of my life. Have a good time. Love, Diana Ross." Fans were treated to close-ups of nearly every part of Diana's carefully garbed anatomy on stage-screens as lasers danced above their heads. Suddenly, Diana's face appeared on the giant screen, center stage. A closeup revealed Diana, fully made up, a jeweled turban cocked on her head, mouthing the words to "Ain't No Mountain High Enough": "If you need me, *call* me . . ." In a full-length shot, the projected image showed Diana descending a staircase that seemed to stretch into infinity.

At just the right dramatic moment, when the filmed Diana reached the bottom step, the real Diana stepped out of the screen in person, wearing the same silver lamé gown, turban and full-length fox-lined coat.

It was a memorable beginning. Long hours of planning paid off. No doubt about it—she had that audience with her and she stayed in control all the way. At the end of the show, her six dancers—one of them her brother Chico—carried her back into the screen, and from there the projected image had them carrying Diana Ross into the heavens.

Unlike Ross' current concert appearances, which were getting raves, *The Wiz* was released in October 1978 to generally mediocre reviews. If anything, the film proved that lots of money, publicity and promotion couldn't *guarantee* a blockbuster Diana Ross movie.

Wrote one critic, "In *The Wiz*, the first thing Dorothy does when she lands in Oz is to inadvertently kill the Wicked Witch of the East. She should have aimed for the Wicked Witch of *est*. [The film] is injected with every self-help jargon of the last fifteen years."

The Wiz had a short life and Motown lost a bundle. Berry was truly disappointed by this blot on his company's record. So eager is he to forget *The Wiz* even happened, he cut all mention of it from Motown's 25th anniversary network television special in 1983.

"It was a big, big dream that got away," Cohen said in retrospect of *The Wiz*. "A brilliant idea gone very wrong. The knowledge that two years of my life, $23 million of Universal's money, thousands of man-hours of labor, and all the love, hopes and dreams of everyone involved had gone into this movie that didn't stand a chance absolutely made me sick."

Diana was believable in her first two film roles, but certainly not in this one, and it wasn't because of the age factor. The differences between Diana and the Dorothy personality transcended the obvious question of age to become a question of character. Perhaps the American public could not accept Diana Ross, one of the most sexy, ambitious, self-confident black women to emerge in the last decade, in the role of an insecure, scaredy-cat plain-Jane. Plus, Diana played the role with a firm seriousness, never considering that perhaps a sense of humor was needed.

What mattered most to Diana, though, was that she had broken her tie with Berry and did what she wanted to do her way. "It was just so important for me to get out there and do something on my own," she said. "I don't care that it didn't make money. It wasn't about the movie as much as it was about me."

But Rob Cohen said that Diana's feelings about the film's failure went deeper than that. "She loved success very much and Diana was very burned by *The Wiz*. She really believed it would have been a good idea and was totally traumatized by the critical reaction to it."

After *The Wiz*, Rob Cohen left Motown Productions. He said that there was no connection between the movie's flop and his leaving the Gordy empire.

"When I went in to tell Berry I was going to leave, he was very hurt and upset," Cohen recalled. "He told me, 'I knew you wouldn't stay at Motown forever, but I didn't think you'd leave so soon.' It had been five years. But to him, Motown was a lifetime thing. I loved Berry, but I wanted to move on and get away from the Motown pressures, which included dealing with Diana's movie career. It was getting harder and harder to come up with properties for her.

"We had tried to cast her in *Tough Customers*, a film where she would have played Stephanie St. Clair, the girlfriend of gangster Dutch Schultz, a very fine script. But no way could we find a white co-star who would take second billing to her, or even co-star with her. No way could we find a studio to back it. *The Wiz* had hurt her bank-ability. It was extremely frustrating.''*

In November 1978, Barbara Walters planned to interview Diana for one of her prime-time television specials. Diana had met Walters before and, like many other stars, was tremendously intimidated by her. "I think she knows me too well," Diana had said at the time. "I'm afraid of her."

Walters is known for the manner in which she cracks the carefully constructed celebrity façade, and Diana had worked too hard on hers to have it shattered on national television. Naturally, she was reluctant to do the interview. Perhaps one of the reasons she consented was to face her fear of Walters; it was her decision to do it. No one else's.

"But she was frantic," said one of Diana's employees at that time. "Just absolutely desperate to make a good impression on this woman, to win her over. She considered it a real challenge. She took the time to read everything that she could get her hands on having to do with Barbara Walters. 'God, what if she asks

---

*After Motown, Rob Cohen went on to become a top movie producer with, among other films, *The Running Man* and *The Witches of Eastwick*.

me *that* question?' she kept saying. She was referring to the obvious one about Florence Ballard."

Diana Ross has always appeared disingenuous when asked about what happened to Florence Ballard; therefore people usually assume that she alone was responsible for Florence's downfall. That, of course, is not true. Diana has never once been open about what really happened to Florence and why she had to leave the group. Instead, she's only made veiled excuses like "Oh, she was just tired and wanted to get married," which she told Rona Barrett in 1973. Perhaps Diana would be treated more fairly by her public if she would only be more forthcoming about what happened.

Now and then—not often—she would try to make the relationship seem like much more than it ever was. "It was like losing a sister, really," Diana told *Ebony* of Florence's death. "My relationship with her had become so close over the years." Mary Wilson makes the same kinds of public statements about her relationship with Florence and no one seems to mind because they're believable even though they're apparently not true. But when Diana Ross does it, the public is jolted because the sentiment seems so implausible.

The day before the Walters interview, Barbara and her crew visited Diana's home to see what colors she had in the living room in which they were going to tape. They wanted to be certain to bring the proper equipment, and of course Barbara wanted to make sure her clothes matched the color scheme in the room.

That night, Diana appeared at the Universal Amphitheatre in Los Angeles. Barbara Walters came backstage to visit after the show.

She told Walters, "I'm scared of what you're going to ask."

"Don't be afraid of me," Barbara said, winking at her.

The next day, Barbara and crew arrived and discovered that Diana had had the room completely refurnished and repainted a totally different color—all in 24 hours. "I just wanted it to look pretty for you," Diana explained.

During the interview, Barbara did not waste a moment. "People say you are cold and difficult and testy." Diana visibly squirmed in her seat. "Where does that stuff come from?"

"Gee, uh . . ." Diana began, almost at a loss for words. "I *have* been cold and testy. That is one of the things that . . ." Her voice trailed off. She had to stop to choose her words carefully. "Well, when you're wanting everything to be right a lot of times you make a lot of mistakes and you are quite rough on people and you forget . . . Lately, in the last couple of years,

I've gotten better in my relationships with people. I'm not . . . I don't know. I've gotten better. I'm not half as frightened. I'm not half as afraid.''

"Diana, when Florence died and she died penniless . . .''

Anticipating the dreaded question, Diana cut Barbara off. "Yes, it's so funny,'' she said as she nervously ran her fingers through her hair. "I knew exactly what you were going to ask.'' She sounded irritated.

"You can't help but ask that,'' Barbara continued, ignoring Diana's agitation. "Why did she leave The Supremes?''

Diana took a deep breath, then sighed. "I think it was, you know, the point of 'I'm tired and I wanna quit.' You know?'' Suddenly she seemed very defensive. Her words were all running together. "We were working very hard. We were like, exhausted, you know? We looked older than we probably look now.''

Later in the Barbara Walters interview, Diana talked about her life as an entertainer. "What else would I be doing that's better than this? You have to remember where I'm from and what we had offered to us. My sister being a doctor was incredible in our lives. She fought hard. My sister studied from the time I knew her. She was always studying to be a doctor. It's an important thing to do. And my dad . . .

"My dad . . . well, my singing, you know? He said I should do something important,'' Diana continued. "He didn't think my singing would amount . . .'' She stopped and shook her head.

And then, "I'm going to be singing for the President next week, you know?''

Barbara then asked her what she was most proud of in her life.

Diana's quick response: "I'm proud of myself.''

At the end of November 1978, Berry Gordy's father died at the age of 90 after a long illness. Berry was deeply saddened by the loss, as were many of the Motown artists. "Pops'' had been the patriarch of the Motown family and, without him, many of the artists felt that things would never be the same. "It's not that he was involved,'' Diana said at the time, "but you just knew he was there and part of the family.''

At about this time, toward the end of 1978, director John Boorman submitted a movie treatment to John Calley, head of Warner Brothers. The film, entitled *The Bodyguard*, was intended as a vehicle for Diana Ross and Ryan O'Neal. Calley forwarded the eight-page treatment to Ryan, who thought it was excellent. He wanted to do the movie. What about Diana? When the treatment was sent to her, she was immediately intrigued. She had known Ryan for four years, since she and Bob once owned a $500,000 Malibu Colony beachfront home close to one Ryan owned. Ryan, who had been married twice, used to jog on the beach in the nude; he wasn't easy to ignore.

Diana had someone in her office read the treatment and this person told her that the idea was clever and that she might want to consider doing the film. Diana then called Ryan to discuss the movie and to reacquaint herself with him.

The Bodyguard was envisioned as an exciting, tense, mysterious, sexy drama with a musical backdrop. It was about a black female singer who was making a career change and, in the process, distancing herself from her mentor/manager, a man very jealous of her and resistant of the idea. When the singer begins receiving death threats, she becomes frightened and decides to hire a bodyguard. She interviews dozens of men—most of whom are black and solidly built—until she chooses Ryan O'Neal, not because of his muscles but because of his sharp instincts.

In the next scene of the treatment, the singer is rehearsing for her act and out of nowhere in the darkened theater a shot rings out. She clutches her chest, which begins spurting blood. She drops to the floor, dead. Then, out of the wings but still hidden by the shadows, steps a horrified Diana Ross. It was all a plan she and her bodyguard, Ryan, had concocted. They had hired a "double" to see just how far whoever was after Diana would go to get her. Unfortunately for the phony-Ross, the hired killers were quite serious about their work. Ryan convinces Diana to leave town with him for her own protection. While on the lam, they are overcome by a strong magnetism between them and fall in love.

Berry had reservations about *The Bodyguard*, not because of the obvious sensitivity of the subject matter but because he didn't see it as a suitable vehicle for Diana Ross. But foremost in Diana's mind by this time was the opportunity to work with Ryan O'Neal.

Besides his sandy-haired, blue-eyed good looks, there were many reasons why Diana found Ryan O'Neal, who was three years her senior, so appealing. One of the biggest reasons had to be his association with Barbra Streisand. At this time, Ryan was completing *The Main Event*, his second film with Barbra. Diana knew that he and Barbra had been lovers. Her friends say she was thrilled beyond words to have the opportunity to get close to someone who had been one of Barbra's paramours.

Besides his affair with Streisand, Ryan O'Neal had also enjoyed tempestuous romances with a wide array of Hollywood notables, including Joan Collins, Barbara Parkins, Ursula Andress and Bianca Jagger. But he had never before been linked to a black woman. Diana would be the first.

Berry used to tell her, "You're not too beautiful, but you have character in your face." Now, she *was* beautiful and able to attract handsome movie stars.

"He is an incredible lover, totally devoted to giving a woman pleasure," his ex-wife Joanna Moore said.

"What? Are you kidding me?" Ryan told Diana when she inquired about his playboy image. "How can I be a playboy when I've got my kid sleeping with me in my bed? It's just not true, Diana."

It is not clear if Diana Ross was aware that *The Main Event* had actually been developed with her in mind. Howard Rosenman, the executive producer of the project, said that the script was sent to high-powered Hollywood agent Sue Mengers, who was working with Diana at this time. Rosenman asked Mengers if she could somehow secure Ryan O'Neal, whom she also represented, to star with Diana in the movie. But then Mengers, who had packaged *What's Up, Doc?* for O'Neal and Streisand, decided instead to bring those two together again. So Barbra Streisand ended up working with Ryan O'Neal in *The Main Event*, a successful film that was intended for Diana Ross. Surely, if Diana knew anything about what had actually happened she would have been upset. While she was waiting for a movie property to come her way, a vehicle intended for her that would have been perfect was offered to Barbra Streisand, her obvious competition in the movie business.

Because Diana was searching for business direction and simultaneously trying to seize control of her career, she wanted to be in the company of someone who was shrewd and could advise her. She had heard how Ryan O'Neal had masterminded his daughter Tatum's career as her manager, and she was impressed by his business acumen.

"People want so much out of me, you know?" she said at this time. "Making the right choices can be so hard. There's always some new obstacle to get through. When I left The Supremes, I had to establish my own sound, my own identity. For *Lady Sings the Blues*, I had to learn a whole new style of singing. Then when I had to take charge: the expression is show *business*. That last word, I finally found out, is no accident. I am a *business* woman.''

When Diana discussed her problems concerning Berry Gordy and Motown with Ryan, he would listen carefully, and try to offer sound advice. ''If I had what you make, I'd be rich forever,'' Ryan told Diana one day over a Beverly Hills lunch as he advised her on investments.

But, for the most part, Ryan O'Neal avoided serious discussions with Diana Ross. He wasn't particularly interested in her life—The Supremes, *Lady Sings the Blues* or show *business*. He had a movie to make. Without Berry Gordy running interference for her, Diana would have to decide for herself who were Hollywood's prince charmings, and which ones had ulterior motives.

Chapter

22

In January 1979, Diana Ross, who was about to turn 35, opened her own offices in the same building as Motown on Sunset Boulevard and Vine Street in Hollywood. "Why the hell does she need her own offices?" Berry Gordy asked Suzanne dePasse. At this time, Diana sent a letter to all of her business associates, on gold-embossed stationery with her picture on the left hand corner (one eye, half a nose and half a mouth in a box).

Dear Sir or Madam:
All future invoices and/or statements should be directed to *my* office:
   Diana Ross Enterprises, Inc.
   6255 Sunset Blvd.
   18th Floor
   Hollywood, Ca. 90028
   I wish to express my sincere appreciation for your patience and cooperation in this matter.
   If you need any assistance and/or information, please call my office collect.
   Sincerely,
   Diana Ross

Usually, a chief assistant would lay down the law. "Call her Miss Ross," she would tell new employees. "Never, *ever* call her Diana. And never *Ms*. Ross. She hates that."
   "I want respect," Diana had said. "Like Berry had respect. Even I call him Mr. Gordy in public. There's nothing wrong with respect, is there?"

Finally, behind her back, her staff began to call her "Miss-Ross-To-You," a tradition that's been handed down to her employees over the years.

"Did Miss-Ross-To-You call yet this morning?"

"Better not leave for lunch because Miss-Ross-To-You is on her way up."

Often, employees were hired to live with Diana in the Maple Avenue home and oversee the day-to-day operations there. Diana didn't particularly enjoy having strangers live with her and the home wasn't big enough to insure total privacy for either her or her employees. It was difficult for her to maintain the aloofness she feels is important in order for her to be the boss. Diana Ross constantly struggled to keep the upper-hand with staff members, always trying to distance herself from these interlopers in her home whom she felt were getting too familiar with her.

One assistant who worked for and lived with Diana for about six months remembered that she and the boss had a fight over what the employee called "the Miss Ross thing." It happened innocently enough. The phone rang and the assistant answered it. "Diane, it's Mr. Gordy," she said. After conversing and hanging up, Diana glared at the employee and said, "You call me Miss Ross, or you're out of here." The disagreement ensued when the assistant said that she could understand calling her boss Miss Ross in public, but why in the privacy of home when it was just the two of them? "Because I said so," was Diana's explanation. It was a short argument.

Despite all that she had achieved in her life and career and the way in which she was revered by her public, Diana still obviously felt very insecure, and often even easily intimidated. Certainly this part of her personality became apparent the night Natalie Cole visited her backstage and began to impulsively sing at a piano during a small gathering. As Nat King Cole's daughter sang, backstage visitors cheered. Diana, who watched silently, looked disappointed and hurt. After all, she had graciously welcomed Natalie into her private domain, and now it seemed that Cole was showing off in front of her (Diana's) friends. After listening to Natalie for a few minutes, Miss Ross pulled an employee into a corner and told her that she did not want "that woman" singing in her dressing room. The employee had to tactfully get Natalie away from the piano.

(Perhaps Diana was still smarting from Natalie Cole's comments to *Rolling Stone* in the early '70s that she can "out-sing Diana Ross any day of the week," even though Cole has since said that she was misquoted.)

Though it may be understandable that Diana Ross would feel a need to be competitive with a beautiful, black, female entertainer like Natalie Cole, why she would feel any insecurity around her was baffling, considering her own superstar status. That Diana was also in steady competition with members of her female staff members also seemed perplexing.

Just as she wouldn't tell her Supremes partners which perfumes and lipsticks she used, she was still just as determined that her "look" remain unique. Some women who have worked with her have said that they were not allowed to use the same cosmetics the boss used, nor could they have their hair styled by whichever Beverly Hills coiffeur was responsible for Diana's hair at that time.

One assistant said that she was reminded by Miss Ross that any telephone calls that came in from men, "are just because they're trying to get to me. Not you. And don't you forget it." The assistant said that she was later reminded that the desk she used in Miss Ross' home, "is my desk, and don't you forget it." Most of Diana's employees could never determine whether she was being serious, terribly insecure, or merely testing them to see how much pressure they could take. Diana, like Berry Gordy, subscribes to the theory that the more stress a person endures, the better he or she will be for it. "Anyone who works for me is going to be successful in this life," she proudly told an employee.

Diana requested that anyone who was to work closely with her take _est_ classes. She felt that Erhard's courses had done her so much good that she did not want to associate with anyone who didn't share the same philosophies. But after employees graduated from Erhard's classes, enlightened and newly-independent staffers were usually not willing to take unlimited pressure from Miss Ross. They often ended up getting fired for talking back or asking soul-searching, _est_-like questions of her that she often asked herself but didn't appreciate hearing from "the help."

"Why are you always so angry?" one _est_-trained staffer asked Diana shortly before she was dismissed. "You're the star. You have nothing to be angry about."

Often, Diana was at her wit's end as to how to handle someone who, in her viewpoint, simply would not take direction. She often appeared mystified by the fact that there were people working for her who often did not agree with her. Firing a person often led to another problem—replacing that employee with someone unfamiliar with the Ross program. When Diana was at a complete loss—which was often—Suzanne dePasse acted as intermediary between boss and disgruntled staff member. A typical day found Diana and an employee sitting in Suzanne's Motown office—an angry Miss Ross steadfastly refusing to talk directly to the indignant assistant.

"You tell her she is not doing her job properly," Diana commanded Suzanne.

"And you tell her I am not a baby-sitter," the employee told dePasse. "And I am not a dishwasher, either."

"And you tell her that she better not use that tone with me," Diana told dePasse.

DePasse threw her hands up in the air and exclaimed, "Ay yi yi!" Then she refereed dutifully. It was all in a day's work for a woman known to be one of the slickest, most articulate officials in the Berry Gordy camp. After Suzanne finished her arbitration, Diana and the employee would leave, smiling. They would appear to be friendly—until the next time.

In the Diana Ross Enterprises office, Diana's employees had the responsibility of coordinating her tour schedules, solving her personal problems, dealing with Motown on promotion for her records, and assisting her with anything else she needed. However, as soon as she hired her own staff, she found that Motown no longer promoted her music with the same verve as it once had. This was customary behavior at Motown and even Diana wasn't exempt. "If you bring outsiders in, the members of the family resent it and stop giving you their all," Berry had warned her.

Those on Diana's first staff remember her as learning how to be a tough taskmaster, even though she lived and worked in New York most of the time. She always phoned her office fifteen minutes before her five employees had to report to work at eight o'clock to learn who arrived early. Everyone had to stay until six, and she would call a few minutes before that hour to make certain everybody was still there. When she was in town and on her way up to the 18th floor, one of the parking attendants would phone from the garage to warn her staff, "Miss Ross is headed up there. Better watch out!"

"Miss-Ross-To-You didn't want you smiling or talking to anybody in the hallway, either," remembered one former employee. "She was always gracious to any visitors in the office, but as soon as that person would leave, she would snap at the rest of us. I liked her—*idolized* her—until I worked for her. Then I saw her in a whole different light. Her average fan would have been mortified by the experience of working for the real Miss Ross."

Two cardinal rules at Miss Ross' new office: No one was to

play old Motown music, and there was to be no mention of The Supremes. Once, one of her employees looked in the cupboard underneath the sink in her private bathroom and discovered all of her Supremes gold records.

In January 1979, Diana Ross was scheduled to meet with writer Tom Burke for a *Cosmopolitan* feature. She agreed to have lunch with him at a Beverly Hills restaurant. The maitre d' prepared a private dining room for Diana and her guest. He obtained a large arrangement of fresh camellias from the same posh Beverly Hills florist who did arrangements for her home, then placed the flowers on her table as well as on surrounding tables that wouldn't be occupied.

"I know *all* the stars," the maitre d' enthused to Tom Burke, who had arrived a few minutes early. "They all come here. But Diana, she is special among all of the ladies up there on the screen. Forever she will be special."

His loyalty and devotion to Diana was a perfect example of Ross' fans' feelings for her. "Diana's got sophistication, finesse. She is the definition of cool. And look what she's *been* through . . ."

The force of her personality always draws people to her when she's in public. They find excuses just to be near her. There are some performers who are admired for their brilliant work, but they are not adored. They may get top billing, but when they appear in public they are rarely besieged by fans. On the other hand, talent does not always guarantee superstardom. Looks help. So does charm, and other assets.

Marilyn Monroe, for instance, combined sophistication and a sexual body with an underlying little-girl-lost quality. That worked for her. When she was in public, she was hard to resist.

But Diana Ross' charisma is a combination of beauty, a sexy singing voice and worldliness. There used to be a childish quality to her persona but, as a result of years of experiences, that part of her was replaced by a new cosmopolitanism. So strong is the total package, it is difficult not to be dazzled when she walks into a room. Diana knows that she possesses a magnetic persona. She thinks of it as a hit record and always sings it for all it's worth.

Tom Burke recalled that, dressed in earth tone silks, she "materialized at the door of our private dining room, smiling," exactly on time. "A white orchid at her clear brow . . . her presence filled the room more seductively than the flowers." As soon as they sat down, "a maniacal young waiter burst in on us with *more* fresh flowers." Diana was startled by the waiter and spilled a few drops of water on the tablecloth. A team of nervous busboys cleared the table and they laid a new brocade covering cloth in a moment.

A few minutes later, another waiter burst in with another flower for her. "Miss Ross," he said reverentially. "This is a tiger lily. And I removed all of the pollen so that it wouldn't soil your clothes. Oh, please, Miss Ross," he begged, his hand trembling, "let me cut the stem. Let me pin it on."

"Oh, my, yes. Please do."

By now Diana had also learned to be much less pliable in the hands of reporters. In the '60s, she and The Supremes were taught to say anything for the sake of a good story. Now Diana didn't have to care as much. When Elin Schoen from *Ladies Home Journal* needed more interview time with her, Diana said bluntly, "Really, you got enough, my dear. I mean, that's enough. I think maybe if you put yourself in my shoes, you would see why it's difficult."

Diana's public and much of the media loved her celebrity status. For those who had to work with Miss-Ross-To-You, it was a different story. One of Ryan O'Neal's former business associates recalled that Ryan thought Diana was "extremely spoiled. I think the main thing on his mind was *The Bodyguard*. He was determined to do this film with her because his movie career was very inconsistent at this time. He would do anything to get her to do this movie. I doubt that Ryan was interested in her as a woman. Ryan likes to control women. Diana was working against being controlled at this time."

But Ryan had told other friends that even though the film was what brought the two of them together, he soon found Diana to be a fascinating, exciting woman. He admired her determination and ambition, both traits that reminded him of Barbra. Also, Ryan never liked shrinking violets, and Diana certainly did not fall into that category. Her insistence that all of her employees call her "Miss Ross" fascinated him; he thought he had seen it all when he was in Barbra Streisand's company. Ryan had said that even Barbra didn't insist upon being called "Miss Streisand," which absolutely amazed Diana.

Regardless of how he really felt about her, it is true that Ryan's film career had been inconsistent and he apparently could not get a commitment from Warner to release *The Bodyguard* unless he and John Boorman could get Diana to agree to star in it. The studio heads perceived the film as an interracial love story, the co-star would have to be black, and Diana was the biggest black female box office draw at the time.

Diana wanted to take the relationship at a slow pace. After

all, it was based on business. She would have one of her female assistants accompany her and Ryan on dates. "If anyone asks, you say he's your boyfriend," she would instruct the employee. Perhaps an indication of how she at first felt about Ryan O'Neal came on the day he called her "Diane" in public, and she corrected him. "Diana," she said with a gracious smile. "You can call me Diana." They were getting close—he was certainly closer to her than anyone who was supposed to call her "Miss Ross"— but Ryan O'Neal was not yet privileged enough to call her "Diane."

Diana finally read the treatment more carefully and discovered, much to her horror, that the film would include a nude scene. Diana decided then that she could not appear in it, but Ryan urged her to reconsider. He wined and dined her for the next few weeks showering her with affection and giving her expensive gifts. She was, quite simply, swept off her feet; Diana Ross was falling in love. She thought that they were the most perfect couple the world had ever seen, and, indeed, they did look striking: he, muscular, blond and dashing; she, thin, dark and glamorous. Diana was said to be put off by Ryan's conceit but, she said in his defense, "nobody's perfect."

Diana's road manager Michael Browne told writer Diane Albright, "The man that she had picked to be her husband was Ryan O'Neal. She thought he was the man of her dreams, even though he really wasn't. He didn't have the kind of money she wanted in a man. But he was so damn good-looking, she couldn't resist him."

On March 26, 1979, Diana hosted her own 35th birthday party at her Beverly Hills home with guests including Tony Perkins, Gregory Peck and Tony Curtis. Diana's brother and sister, Chico and Rita, were also present. She greeted 50 guests in a James Galanos bare-shouldered black silk crepe gown, which she wore with a white jacket beaded with textured flowers and leaves. Her hair was slicked back into a bun. "She looked every inch the heiress to a throne," someone observed.

The dinner party was lavish. She decorated the house with calla lilies and lit it with candles. As party favors, Diana handed guests small wands and bottles of detergent for bubble blowing. She invited her guests to visit the bathroom in the children's wing where Michael Jackson had painted graffiti on the walls. "God bless Diana," said the late actress Joan Hackett, who came to the party holding a huge potted ficus tree as a gift. "She's revived fun in Hollywood."

For her birthday gift, Berry presented Diana with a new sable jacket.

"Not baaad," Diana said.

Mary Wilson, seven months pregnant with her third child, also attended the party, telling everyone she was now embarking on a solo career. "And I asked Diane to go to my opening night in New York in August, and she said she would!!!"

"Oh, please call me Mary, honey," she told a friend. "Never Miss Wilson!"

In the middle of the party, Ryan took off his jacket and, in a tuxedo shirt and slacks, strutted onto the dance floor and broke into wild gyrations to the Sister Sledge song "The Greatest Dancer." As everyone gathered around and applauded, Diana stood starry-eyed on the sidelines.

"Isn't he wonderful!" she said happily. "Don't you just love him?"

This was the first time some of her friends met Ryan O'Neal and he certainly made a positive impression on them. He was gorgeous and very physical with her, hugging and kissing her tenderly on the cheek, but never on the mouth. He had given Diana an amethyst ring with inset diamonds as a birthday present. He was very fatherly toward Diana's three children. They sat on his lap. He told them stories and tried to keep them busy as mother flitted about being the gracious star hostess. Even Berry Gordy found him to be charming and witty. "Man's got the whitest damn teeth I ever seen in my life," Gordy said of O'Neal.

At this time, Diana and her children spent a couple of weeks with Ryan and his youngsters at the O'Neal family home in Malibu. The two of them would share picnics with their offspring on the beach in back of Ryan's house, and then a governess would herd Rhonda, Tracee, Chudney, and Ryan's children, Tatum and Griffin, back into the house and prepare them for bed. Meanwhile their parents shared white wine and intimate moments on the sand. During this stay at the O'Neal home, Diana and Ryan attended a private party at Alice's Restaurant on the Malibu pier, and another partygoer claimed that "they were sitting very close together and gazing into each other's eyes . . . like they were hungering for each other." He said that later while they were having Ryan's car filled with gas, the two of them embraced and kissed "like lovesick teenagers right there at the gas station."

The only sour note in this duet came from Ryan's 15-year-old daughter Tatum who, it was said by friends of Ryan's, didn't like

Diana Ross or anyone else her father ever dated. Diana must have noticed that Tatum was spoiled. She got away with much more than her daughters ever did.

When one of Diana's friends at Motown told her the following story, she must have wondered about Ryan as a father. After Tatum won the Oscar for her role in *Paper Moon*, Ryan took her out of the private Beverly Hills school she was attending to have her tutored at home. When Tatum announced to her friends that she was leaving, they stood up and applauded. She was mortified and complained to Ryan. "But, Tatum, that's what actors live for," he said, very seriously. "Applause."

"Oh my God! I can't believe that story is true," Diana said.

"That's Ryan," the friend concluded.

"Well, I'm sorry. Ryan is just too sweet to have said that. It's not true."

On April 5, 1979, Diana embarked on a six-week, 28-city concert tour of the United States.

On April 9, she took a break to fly into Los Angeles from Baltimore and be a presenter at the Academy Awards. Since she had to be at the Dorothy Chandler Music Center for rehearsals during the day and return there well before the 7:00 P.M. ceremonies began, Diana booked an expensive suite at the Bonaventure Hotel, not far from the Music Center. This way she could dress in leisure, and also, she told her staff, "You can watch the show from my suite and then I can get in touch with you people if I have a terrible emergency."

By 5:00 P.M., three members of Diana's staff milled about eating from the lavish buffet she had set up in the suite. She was pacing back and forth in her white silk James Galanos gown, upset because *"someone"* had forgotten to bring the matching wrap. One of her employees, Jeffrey Wilson, was supposed to pick up the tulle accessory from Galanos' offices in West Los Angeles and bring it to her so that the outfit would be complete.

When Wilson failed to show up at the appointed time, Diana called her office.

"He left a long time ago, Miss Ross. He should be there any minute."

Other employees in the suite remember that Diana slammed down the phone. She lit a cigarette, stubbed it out, and lit another one almost immediately. She looked at the clock and swore under her breath. There was a knock at the door. One of her staff members answered it.

"It's Mr. O'Neal."

"Ryan," he corrected.

"Oh, it's you," Diana said.

"That's a hell of a hearty greeting. You certainly don't seem happy to see me."

"Oh, Ryan, don't talk that way." Diana put her arms around his neck and gave him a kiss on the cheek—there were employees watching so she had to be discreet. "I was expecting my wrap. He hasn't gotten here yet."

Ryan O'Neal consulted his watch. "It's still early."

"But I'm so worried."

Ryan told her to do whatever it was she had to do, and offered to answer the door when her employee arrived.

"Let me make a phone call first." She dialed a number. It rang and rang. Her lips tightened. She slammed the receiver down. Ryan relaxed in his chair, watching her with amused eyes. She never ceased to make him smile. "She's just so silly sometimes," he would say.

The others in the room acted as if they were glued to the television, when actually they were all hoping she wouldn't take her anger out on them.

Diana retreated into the bedroom and slammed the door, leaving Ryan with her staff.

There was a knock. "Will someone answer that?" Diana shouted from the bedroom.

"Well, look who's here!" Ryan's voice was jovial. "Come in, come in. Diana, it's Tatum! Just joking," he said, almost choking in a burst of laughter. "It's your wrap."

"Is it all right?" she called.

"Looks great to me. I'll bring it in."

"I better go," Jeffrey Wilson said, handing the wrap to Ryan.

"No, no. You wait here," Ryan insisted. After bringing the wrap into the bedroom, he returned to the employee. "You look like you could use a drink."

"Yeah, I probably could. But I better not. She'll kill me. I bet I'm in real trouble, anyway. When I saw how late it was getting, I took a chance and drove on the shoulder. I didn't know what was worse, getting a ticket or . . . or . . ."

"Or facing the wrath of Ross?" Ryan laughed. Wilson looked uncomfortable, but Diana's entrance saved him from having to answer.

"How do I look?" she asked. Wilson recalled that Ross posed in the bedroom door, wearing her white Galanos sheath with draped bodice and spaghetti straps. Her necklace and earrings were simple so as not to detract from the elaborate white-on-white embroidered straight skirt. The white tulle wrap was the perfect accessory against her bronze shoulders. Her hair was pulled straight back from her face.

"Ravishing! Sensational! Gorgeous!" Ryan pronounced. He knew all the words she needed to hear. "Almost too good to be true."

"And you?" she asked the employee. "Do *you* think I look pretty?" She batted her eyelashes at him.

"Yes—Miss Ross," he said nervously. "You certainly do."

"Fine. You ride in the elevator with us then. Why were you late?"

"The traffic was . . ."

"But, you see, you must *plan* for those things."

"Yes, Miss Ross."

Ryan clapped the employee on the shoulder. "You got here with the wrap. That's the important thing. Now, doesn't Diana look great. Tell her how good she looks."

Diana smiled and slicked back her hair with her hands. She took a small bottle of perfume from her purse and squirted it on her wrists.

"You look great, Miss Ross."

She ignored him.

"No, call her Diana," urged Ryan. "Diana. Di-an-ah."

"I . . . I can't."

"Sure you can. She won't mind, will you, Diana?"

Diana turned around and faced Ryan. Her lips curved in that overpowering smile. Her eyes were hard as granite. She didn't say a word. The elevator door opened. She hurried through the lobby, O'Neal at her heels, to her waiting limousine.

Recalled Jeffrey Wilson, "It was the longest elevator ride in my life."

As Ryan and the employee watched, the chauffeur opened the door and Diana got in. Ryan had decided he wasn't going to go with her to the ceremonies, probably because he didn't want to encourage the gossip about them. Berry and Suzanne were waiting for her inside the limousine. They would accompany her to the awards. The door closed and the car sped off.

Back in the suite, Ryan watched the television ceremony with Diana's staff. When Diana walked out onto the stage, he burst out laughing. "Jesus! Look at that."

Jeffrey Wilson sank deep into the couch.

Diana didn't have the wrap on.

On April 19, when Diana Ross appeared at the Omni Theatre, Ryan showed up in Atlanta to see her, as well as Tatum, who was filming *Little Darlings* there. While there, Ryan and Diana attended a B.B. King concert.

"They were very close during the concert," said Alun Vonyillius, general manager of the hall at which King was appearing. "They joined King on stage for his encore. Diana did a lot of prancing around with Ryan, who was playing the tambourine."

In May 1979, to coincide with her current tour, Motown released what many consider to be one of Diana Ross' finer albums, *The Boss*, produced by Nickolas Ashford and Valerie Simpson. *The Boss* not only gave Diana another hit on the dance floor, but also reflected her new independence—it was the first album release that Berry Gordy had nothing to do with.

When they cut the album, Ross, Ashford and Simpson resided in New York City, miles away from Gordy's influence. Gordy must have realized that his former protégée was determined to keep him out of her life and career by now. Still, Berry was persistent. A few months before the album's release, he gave Diana a $175,000 diamond bracelet. This puzzled Berry's friends, who thought he was trying to win her back. If that was Berry's intention, it didn't work.

Said her producer, Valerie Simpson, of the album, "Diana had some things she wanted to say in a particular way. Listen to 'It's My House.' The song is about a modern woman who tells her lover, 'I'm independent and may fit you into my space . . . but on my terms.' Those are Diana's ideas."

The album's cover boasted a new look for Diana: long mane of hair and scant clothing that revealed plenty of leg and chest. The apparent message: I'm the boss of my own image now.

As she worked to promote *The Boss*, Diana discovered that her independence from Motown had a price. While she was out on the road, Motown was doing little for her in terms of record promotion.

"As soon as she would leave town, the wheels of promotion would always come to a grinding halt," recalled a former employee of Ross'. "She came back in town for a day or so and I remember that she and Michael Roshkind were having a fight about the way Motown was treating her since she'd become so independent. The door was closed and the secretary told me not to go in there. I could hear them arguing outside the door. Later, I learned she was screaming at Roshkind and pulling him by the tie. Berry was out of the picture and all hell was breaking loose."

Diana also discovered that she was losing money on the tour. It was an expensive show—to date, the last big-budgeted spectacle she would do—and she was under the impression that Motown was helping to defray the exorbitant costs. However, Gordy's company did not do so. "Diana Ross Enterprises, Inc." was on its own. Berry probably took the position that if his protégée yearned for independence, she had to pay the price. Between the poor promotion of *The Boss* and what was happening out on the road, she felt betrayed by Mike Roshkind, Shelly Berger and Suzanne dePasse—who were responsible for her day-to-day career—but mostly by Berry in whom she had long ago entrusted practically her entire life. On a professional level, she felt that he had a responsibility to her as Motown's biggest artist to make certain that she made money, not lost it. On a personal level, she was surprised to learn that Berry wasn't watching out for her.

After the fight with Roshkind, she sat at one of the desks in a Motown office and began to compose a handwritten letter to Gordy. As she wrote, she began to sob. Finally, she became so upset, she went to the ladies' room, and then left the building, leaving the letter behind. One of her employees found it, read it, and saved it.

"The letter detailed a lot of love for Berry that she could not express verbally because she was in such pain over what she felt was being done to her," said the employee. "She was hurt because, to her, it was obvious that he was trying to teach her a lesson. She felt that he was making sure she would lose money on the road so that she would come crawling back to him. She was torn, I think, between Ryan and Berry, and maybe trying to make Berry jealous. And she was hurt because that didn't seem to be working. Ultimately, perhaps she thought that if Ryan would marry her, that would have sent Berry over the edge. But that didn't seem to be in the picture, either. This confusion and vulnerability was a side of Diana Ross I rarely got to see. I saw the magic of the star at night and I saw the bitch by day, but not much in between. I realized then that she was carrying a heavy load, that she was hurting and, of course, taking it out on all of us who had to work for her."

By this time, *The National Enquirer* had learned of the romance between Ryan and Diana and featured the two of them on the cover of its May 29, 1979, issue. The story indicated that they were desperately trying to keep the "hot and heavy" romance a secret "for fear that their interracial love affair will hurt their careers." That didn't seem likely considering the fact that Diana's former husband was white. If Ryan O'Neal did not want to be seen in public with her, she probably would have dropped him.

After another month with her, Ryan O'Neal realized that Diana Ross is as temperamental as she is determined. He admired her ambition but disliked her emotional outbursts. As he watched the way she handled her life and business—the constant chaos that swirled around her, not to mention the stormy mood swings that have become so much a part of the Ross mystique—Ryan was becoming less enchanted with her. This is ironic, since O'Neal is not known in Hollywood as being a particularly easygoing person himself.

It was becoming apparent to anyone who cared to watch that Ryan O'Neal considered himself a free man. During this time, he had a one-week affair with Margaret Trudeau, who said later that she found him shallow. "I had enough of Ryan's conceit, his self-obsession," she said.

Finally, the moment of reckoning had arrived. Ryan had to have an answer from Diana about the movie. John Boorman flew to New York to meet with her to get her final decision. The meeting did not go well. Diana, understandably, did not want to make the wrong decision now that she had seized so much control. *The Wiz*, her idea, was a mistake in many ways and she didn't want to follow it with another one. She wasn't certain that she liked the treatment to *The Bodyguard* and told Boorman that she didn't understand the need for all of the violence and bad language. She also would not do the nude scene, didn't want to sing in the film, and wasn't happy with the title because it emphasized Ryan's character and not her own. In other words, she was going to pass on *The Bodyguard*.

Boorman realized that the movie would never be made and reported as much to John Calley of Warner. Calley begged Boorman to fly to Los Angeles and discuss a plan to convince Diana to do the movie. As much as they tried, that's how much she was determined that her mind was made up. Two years later, she would tell writer Roderick Mann, "I never actually saw the script, just a treatment, and I didn't want to commit on that. So it collapsed as a project, which was a pity. Of course, I'm lucky. I don't have to do films for a living."

"You want to do a black/white love story?" Berry, ever the competitor, asked her. "Fine, we'll get you one." Then he and Chris Clark wrote an interracial romance called *All Is Fair*.

Diana did not do that movie either.

Ryan was not able to change her mind about the film, "but

he must have talked her into something because they are still *steammmmmmeeee*," reported gossip columnist Suzy.

Suzy apparently misread the smoke signals. Ryan was upset— maybe only because Diana took months to decide and then said no. He was tired of Diana Ross now. He wanted out. But Diana has never accepted rejection of any kind, at least not without a fight. She had six months invested in this relationship and decided to pursue Ryan when she returned to Los Angeles. She wanted to convince him that there was more to their romance than just a film. Or perhaps there's a simpler explanation: Hell hath no fury like a woman scorned.

"She would call him and pester him from my shop while she was having her hair done," said her hairdresser Eddie Carroll. "Apparently, he would instruct his secretary to tell Diana that he wasn't at home. She would hang up the phone so hard I was afraid she'd break the receiver. One day, she went to the beach house in Malibu, barged in and started screaming at Ryan. 'You sonofabitch, you! I'm calling you and you're ignoring *me*? How dare you!' Her feelings were hurt. She was pursuing him, and didn't care who knew it. Certainly everyone working in my shop knew it. But the guy had cut her loose and that was the end of it."

Diana was never able to understand why Ryan O'Neal ended the romance. "She thought she had him tied down," observed assistant road manager Michael Browne, "and when she found that not to be true, she was absolutely miffed. She wore the amethyst ring for years after Ryan O'Neal was out of her life. But because of what happened with O'Neal, she decided the hell with beauty. Next time, she'll go for money."

Ryan O'Neal—who started romancing Lee Majors' ex-wife, Farrah Fawcett, after ending his affair with Diana (and is still with Farrah today)—put the romance with Diana in perspective when he said, "All of a sudden she didn't want to play a woman guarded by a white bodyguard because Diana Ross doesn't want to show her body, doesn't want to do sex scenes on the screen, doesn't want to sing, and doesn't want to be black," he concluded bitterly. "As you can see, we are obviously no longer an item."

Diana Ross has never had many female friends. She's said that she's never felt a need to have girlfriends in show business. This attitude may be a holdover from the days when Berry Gordy used to discourage her from having such relationships. Once, when asked about her idol, Barbra Streisand, she had to admit that she had only admired her from afar because Barbra gives the impression of "being untouchable." The two of them have been at the same cocktail parties, but have only made eye contact and have never had a full conversation.

Diana and Suzanne dePasse have remained friends over the years, but it's a relationship that seems mostly based on what Diana needs, what Diana wants, and how Diana feels. One day, Diana was depressed about a business problem and complained to Suzanne about all of the things she felt she couldn't achieve because she hadn't gone to college. This was certainly ironic, considering what her father had wanted for her.

"Bullshit," Suzanne said. "You're one of the smartest women I know. It has nothing to do with going to college. That's your cop-out."

Diana must have been surprised when Suzanne continued: "That's how you run away from things you don't want to deal with."

Ross had to admit that dePasse was right. "I never had a girlfriend as close as her," she said later. "I cherish the relationship and hope it will always be there. I wish I'd had it with Mary and Florence."

Diana also claimed to have a close relationship with Cher. "I can be close with her and talk with her and it's straight. There's no shit. She calls you dirty names . . . a terrific lady," Diana had said in 1976. Cher is always honest and frank and seems completely unaffected by her success. Cher was also fun and fearless, which Diana liked about her. She and Diana were complete opposites.

Diana became friendly with Cher during a lull in Cher's career after her initial television series and before her movie success—a time when Diana's career was thriving.

There were some good times during their five-year friendship. Once, Diana and Bob and Cher and Cher's then-boyfriend David Geffen were joined by Bette Midler and Elton John in New York where they all went to see a performance of *Grease* together. (This was unusual because, according to Cher, Diana and Bette did not get along, "so I go out with one or the other of them, but never both of them together.") When they left for some fresh air during intermission, half the patrons followed to gawk at them.

"The people were pouring down from the balconies," David Geffen recalled. "The second act was 30 minutes late because of the madness."

After the show, they went dancing in gay discos, drawing a

lot of attention. "All of these divas in silver sequins and span-gles," one fan said. "The guys were throwing themselves at their feet, touching and feeling them to make certain the whole thing wasn't an apparition."

"Guess who got the biggest attention?" Diana asked. "My husband." She remembered the men on the dance floor reaching between Bob's legs and grabbing him. "Now you cut that out," Diana said, pushing one overzealous admirer away. "That's mine."

When Diana and Cher would drag Bob and David on shopping sprees for shoes, it was always a major production. The four of them would pile out of a limousine, dash into an expensive shoe store and then as the fellows watched, the ladies proceeded to try on every shoe in the shop. Soon, the chauffeur would be sent for sandwiches. When he returned, everyone ate, right there in the store. After lunch, the couples would argue about who should pay for the shoes and how they can best be deducted from their taxes as business expenses.

Diana and Cher would swap secrets about baby nurses and the problems they had raising children and maintaining their ca-reers. When Cher's daughter Chastity was sick in the hospital with a 105° temperature, and Diana was on the road, Bob sat up all night with her in the hospital. "I don't know what to do, where to go," Cher would complain to Diana, because she con-sidered her to be an excellent mother.

"She's always complaining, that Cher," Diana would say. "She's a tragedy queen for sure."

"Diana needs her kids," Cher has said. "They're her rock, her anchor. Only her kids can cure that special loneliness. And don't let all that noise about her fool you, she's got the 'lonelies,' too. You can't be that big and escape them."

Some of the problems in Diana's relationship with Cher may seem slight in retrospect, but would cause dissension just the same. In one of her nightclub acts, Cher decided to have three female impersonators portray herself, Diana and Bette.

When Diana saw the act in Las Vegas, she wasn't so much concerned with the impersonation as she was horrified to find that the performer was wearing an almost exact replica of one of her most treasured Bob Mackie gowns. "You'd think she'd have enough taste to not rip off my clothes," Diana said after the show. "I paid a lot of money for that goddamn dress and now how am I gonna be able to wear it?"

Back in August 1979, Cher hosted a surprise birthday party for her latest boyfriend, rock star Gene Simmons. "I'm just crazy about Cher," Gene said at the time, "just nuts about her. She's my first love." At the party, Cher introduced Diana to Gene. Diana found him fascinating. He was intelligent and, to her way of thinking, extremely sexy.

In May 1980, Cher celebrated her 34th birthday. As Cher tells it, Gene was undecided about what kind of birthday gift he should buy for her, and she suggested he take Diana along.

"She knows what I like," Cher said.

Soon Diana and Gene were romantically involved. With commendable restraint, Cher made no public comments.

Diana insisted that Cher and Gene had already ended their relationship when she became involved with him, and that her friendship with Cher didn't suffer as a result of what had happened. "I can call her up and complain to her when I think Gene is being ridiculous," she said. Apparently, Cher didn't hold any grudge. She paid Gene special thanks on an album she released at that time, crediting him with helping switch her over from disco to rock 'n' roll. It didn't take her any time at all to find a new boyfriend, Les Dudak, another rock musician.

"What's wrong with swapping boyfriends?" Cher asked writer George Haddad-Garcia. "After I've found out what a man is like . . . why not let another girl have him."

Diana's romance with Cher's hand-me-down, who is five years her junior, proved tumultuous. It lasted off and on for about three years. Simmons is a member of the shock/rock group Kiss, which, at the time, was known for its bizarre stage make-up. On stage, he dressed like a fire-breathing, vampire-costumed ghoul and was known for the way he would lap his snake-like tongue at his audiences. ("My tongue is long enough to make your girlfriend leave you and come with me," he once told a reporter.) He wore 12-inch-high platform boots, each shaped like a demon's mouth complete with bladed teeth. Part of the gimmick meant the group was never seen in public without its make-up, so whenever the guys would venture out into the world it would be with handkerchiefs covering the lower halves of their faces.

Simmons, a former sixth-grade schoolteacher, is six-foot-two with a ruddy face, deep dark eyes and thick black hair. Despite his image, he did not smoke, drink or take drugs. He claimed that he has never once been high or drunk and that the only time he ever sipped wine is during Passover services. Gene Simmons was born in Haifa, Israel.

"What a nice Jewish boy he is," observed Diana, who says that she takes a strong position against drugs.

Simmons is also a brilliant and confident businessman and rock 'n' roll merchandiser. Diana said she admired the way he was able to pinpoint any problem and deal with it. She would confide in Gene regarding her problems at Motown, and he would always offer the same advice: "Get the hell away from there. What are you nuts?" He acted as though he didn't think she was particularly bright, or strong-minded.

"If this business hasn't made you tough, especially workin' for Motown, then forget it," she would counter. "All the est in the world won't help you."

Even though Simmons didn't have as much money as she had, and she had sworn that after Ryan O'Neal she would not get involved with men who had less money than she, Diana was hopelessly attracted to him. Dating Simmons could not have helped Diana's image. He is extremely sexist, considers women to be nothing more than objects, and is known for his scrapbooks containing pictures of over 3,000 women with whom he says he's had sex. He enjoys taking pictures of them in the act with his SX70 camera; it's become part of the lovemaking ritual. "If one goes hunting and never takes a picture of the trophy, what good is it?" he's asked.

By now, Berry Gordy must have realized that Diana was dating some of these men partly to defy him. "I don't even care anymore," he had said. "I don't care who she makes a fool of herself over. I've just had it with her."

Most people at Motown felt that Gene Simmons—a man who once said he wanted his epitaph to read "What are you doing tonight?"—was not the right fellow for Diana Ross. "But he is completely different in private life," she insisted. "He is so gentle. Not at all like the monster he looks like on stage." The more she heard of the company's outrage, the deeper she threw herself into the relationship.

Diana was determined to keep her affair with Simmons out of the public eye. One wonders how Simmons felt about this because when he was dating Cher, he got a lot of mileage out of it, and even a *People* magazine cover. But there was nary a word in the press about the blossoming Ross/Simmons affair, and certainly no cover stories.

Diana was friendly with Victoria Principal at that time and was never able to understand how Victoria could accept so much press coverage about her relationship with singer Andy Gibb, who was quite a few years younger. One day, Diana sat in her office with a secretary, reading a magazine feature about Principal and Gibb. "Hmmm, oh, that Vicky, she just loves those little boys!'' she said, laughing. ''But why must she let everyone know it?''

Later she insisted, ''I know that my fans want to know who I'm sleeping with, but it's none of their business. It's really not!''

Soon, though, Gene was said to have convinced Diana that his affair with Cher did nothing to hurt her (Cher's) career, so why the big secret? Eventually, Diana became more open about the romance—but still there would be no features.

''Gene Simmons was the great love of her life,'' insisted John Mackey, who had worked as a paralegal at Loeb and Loeb, the law firm that represents Diana Ross. ''He was staying at her Beverly Hills home while Diana was in New York. It was said around the office that it was hot passionate sex between them. But they would have fights all of the time, and I recall that when Diana would come into town she would stay at the Beverly Hills Hotel rather than at the house with Gene. So, in effect, he was living in her house while she was staying at a hotel. It was an odd love affair.''

By the summer of 1980, Diana and Gene were in full throes of passionate romance. He was following her around like an obedient puppy as Kiss tried to work out its tour schedules to suit Diana. She was busy promoting what would turn out to be her biggest solo album at Motown, *diana*, produced by Bernard Edwards and Nile Rodgers of the group Chic.

Between 1976 and 1978, Edwards and Rodgers had revolutionized the sound of disco music with their unique sound: striking guitar riffs and vigorous female voices all hued with multiple keyboards and strong string orchestration. The duo had produced a number of hits for Chic, ''Dance, Dance, Dance (Yowsah, Yowsah, Yowsah)'' and ''Everybody Dance,'' and then went on to work with Sister Sledge (''We Are Family'' and ''He's the Greatest Dancer''). As producers, they had developed their own personal and very identifiable sound. But when work on the *diana* album was completed, Diana decided that the material sounded too much like Edwards and Rodgers and not enough like Ross.

After reviewing the final mixes, she sent the masters back to the producers with ''suggestions'' on how she would like to have the music remixed. They probably thought she was just being temperamental—after all, what did she know about *mixing*. They placated her with a slightly altered version of the album. She still wasn't satisfied. When they suggested she go into the studio and do whatever she wanted to the record, she actually did it. Motown recording engineer Russ Terrana remixed the entire album.

"I was shocked," Nile Rodgers said. "I was furious and got on the phone right away and called Motown." There wasn't much Rodgers could do, however. Diana's mind was made up that Terrana's mixes were better.

"I proceeded to make the record more Diana Ross and far less Chicish," she said. "Besides, they've only been in the business, what, two years? I believed my 20 years experience in show business would be of great value to the project."

Rodgers and Edwards demanded that a disclaimer be added to all trade advertisements purchased by Motown, crediting Ross and Terrana with the new mixes. After it was completed, Diana began to have second thoughts about the album, and Motown's promotional staffs thought it was certainly going to be a failure. But, as is often the case in the record business, the first single appealed to the buying public. Despite the fact that "Upside Down" seems like a nursery rhyme set to disco music (she told Rodgers and Edwards that she wanted songs her children could sing, and that's precisely what she got), it was a huge hit—Number One for over a month and nominated for a Grammy. The follow-up, "I'm Coming Out," a much better, more challenging record, went to Number Five. Gay discos promoted it as a dance theme of self-expression and acceptance.

"I'm Coming Out" also seemed to convey another more obvious personal message from Diana Ross, who was definitely coming out from under Berry Gordy's thumb, and having great success with it as well if this album was any indication. *diana* was certified platinum and is considered one of the biggest-selling albums in her career. The album's success seems ironic because it's one of her least exciting ones. Most of her performances were weak, uninspired and mechanical, but the music sounded hot and driving which, apparently, was enough for her many fans. The album peaked at Number Two on the national sales chart. Number One was held by, of all people, Barbra Streisand (and her *Guilty* album).

The Gene Simmons romance continued through the summer. "I have a wonderful relationship," she said in an interview with *Women's World*. "It's really a most unusual scene for me. We met as people, not as performers. We find it difficult to find time to spend together since we both work hard most of the year, and when I go out to events like award ceremonies and I want Gene to come along, he can't because it's a big deal about his face."

When she appeared at Caesars in Vegas that June, Gene came with her. The women in Ross' entourage probably didn't feel safe when he was there, but the guys got along famously with Gene because, as one musician put it, "He was a helluva nice guy. A real man's man."

Diana's ex-husband, Bob Silberstein, and his new wife, Suzin, were also in Las Vegas as her guests. Bob wanted to spend time with the children. He and Gene seemed friendly to one another. "It's so wonderful that we're all so wrapped up together," Diana said.

People who know her, though, say that the more Diana thought about her divorce from Bob, the more she regretted it. She had even told Bob's wife that she still loved him, "and I just hope you don't mind." Diana now felt that, perhaps, she and Bob should have worked their way through the bad times in their marriage. "We only had one bad year, you know," she was saying (no one was certain if she was referring to their first one together or their fifth and last).

In her nightclub act, Diana introduced "Remember Me" with the line, "I wouldn't change a thing . . . well, maybe *one* thing." She confided to one long-time associate that that "one thing" was her divorce from Bob. "I really do regret it," she said. "I think that, perhaps, I made a mistake letting him go."

Diana didn't think that Bob would remarry so quickly. It was barely a year and a half after their divorce that he took a new wife. "She wasn't used to being quite so dispensable in anyone's life, least of all Bob Silberstein's but she's the one who ended the marriage," noted one of Bob's friends. "I think she took comfort in the fact that the children would still tie her to Bob."

In the middle of the Vegas engagement, Diana and Gene traveled together to Colorado Springs for a day—accompanied by 15 members of her entourage, all aboard three private jets—where she taped a Bob Hope special at the Air Force Academy. They arrived at five in the morning, checked into the Sheraton Motor Inn, and left instructions not to be disturbed. Diana had two guards stationed in front of the door to insure their privacy. Six hours later, Diana and Gene emerged for her rehearsal in matching his and her outfits: black leather pants, boots and white silk shirts.

For her performance of "Reach Out and Touch," Diana was to wear a low-cut, backless, orange, sequined gown, which was in Los Angeles. It had to be shipped to Colorado Springs and to insure that it would be handled with care, Diana purchased a seat for it on a Western Airlines flight. Many of the airline employees seemed to be anticipating the arrival of "Miss Ross' dress" as if being near the gown was as momentous as being near the star herself. When someone from her office checked the outfit in at the ticket counter, the agent could barely fill out the boarding pass, she was so taken by the moment. "Oh, my! Is this it?" she gushed. "Is this really Diana Ross' dress?"

During the taping, Diana, with hair pulled back and cascading down her back, performed her numbers to the enraptured servicemen and women. Gene sat in the performers' tent transfixed by her image on the television monitor. No one knew who he was, and when someone asked why he was so interested in her performance, he pointed at Diana and said, " 'Cause that's my lady!"

"We have an agreement, Gene and I," Diana insisted at the time. "He's not fooling around and I'm not fooling around."

It doesn't seem like Gene Simmons kept his end of the agreement; he's never been known to be monogamous. "I am aware that the whole time he was sleeping with Diana, he was dating other women," said a woman who worked for Diana Ross. "I'm also aware that she didn't know it."

Maybe what they say in Hollywood is true: nothing succeeds in the world like a little deception.

Once, when Diana and Gene were dining in a Manhattan restaurant, Gene saw a shapely blond woman he apparently knew sitting by herself. When Diana went to the ladies' room, Gene went to the other lady and struck up a conversation. Suddenly, he kissed her fully on the lips in front of everyone in the bistro, and then, using an eye-liner pencil she'd pulled from her purse, he jotted something on a matchbook. He kissed her again, got up and went to his own table just as Diana returned. She apparently had no idea about what had happened. She beamed as he rose to help her with her chair.

Diana may have tried to be oblivious to Gene's indiscretions at first, but it didn't take her long to figure out what was going on.

"Soon, she wanted him by her side every single minute," Michael Browne said in an interview. "And that's not Gene's style. Diana started getting very jealous and at one point went out and hunted him down in the middle of the night. He was out romping with the boys. He got pissed, stuck her in a cab and sent her home. But, as always in her relationships with men, Diana was determined to make this guy her own."

It is ironic that such powerful and successful women like Diana Ross and Cher would want to associate with a man who would go to bed with almost any woman. "A man can have a girlfriend and be devoted to her, and still have a hundred lovers on the side,'' Gene Simmons reasoned. ''That's perfectly acceptable behavior, I think.'' With such a harem, Diana and Gene would often encounter one of his many girlfriends, usually aspiring actresses working as sales clerks. Gene would be very friendly—and Diana would storm off in a huff. Many of these women attest to the fact that Simmons is, as one of them put it, ''the consummate lover.'' She added, ''No way could Diana resist being under his influence. He could make any woman happy. Knowing Gene, that romance had to be based on great sex.''

In September, Diana Ross followed Gene Simmons and Kiss to England. She had never seen him perform and wanted to see what his stage persona was like. Now she was a glorified groupie. While there, she held a press conference at the Inn on the Park Hotel in London, ''. . . in order to discuss,'' observed British writer Danny Baker, ''. . . uh . . . well nobody was actually sure of that.'' Diana was described by Fleet Street journalists as ''the famed girlfriend of Gene Simmons.'' During the press reception, she was presented with a platinum record for *diana*.

''So what do you think of Kiss' music?'' one reporter asked.

''I like all forms of music, so I'm not stuck for having to give an opinion about Gene,'' Diana said.

''Well, what did you think of their show at Wembley?''

''I was mostly backstage. So I don't know . . .''

''Do you think we can discuss Miss Ross' exciting new movie projects?'' piped in a Tamla-Motown representative, trying to move the questions away from Kiss. Diana was still trying to mount the Josephine Baker project at Paramount, but had reached an impasse. She wanted to produce it herself, and the studio felt she didn't have enough experience to be able to handle that responsibility.

If she was going to England to be with Gene Simmons, Diana would have been better served by keeping a low profile. As it was, she had no theatrical business there except to tape an episode of ''The Muppet Show.'' After the press conference, *New Musical Express* ran a photograph of Diana with the caption: ''Unveiling of the Kiss Army mascot.''

''Why is she here?'' one of Gene Simmons' fellow bandmembers asked.

'' 'Cause I love her,'' Gene replied.

As passionate as the romance may have been in private, publicly Miss Ross demanded respect. In the past, Gene used to grab his girlfriends' asses or tweak their breasts. There would be none of that with Diana Ross. She may have been a groupie, but she drew the line at public humiliation.

Gene told one of his fellow bandmembers. "Can't grab her ass whenever I feel like it. She'd kill me. She's a real lady."

"Well, then," said the musician, "what the hell is she doing with you?"

Chapter

23

It HAD BEEN 22 years at the close of 1980 since Berry Gordy founded Motown Records. But it was the company's first decade—the '60s—that stood unchallenged in terms of Motown's impact and influence on popular music. These were certainly the label's most innovative and prolific years.

Back then, Motown, a communal hotbed of artistic spirit and imagination, stood at the vanguard of the pop music revolution. Gordy's artists were promoted to the world as a "family" and none of their fans would have believed that eventually those fraternal bonds would be broken. When the "kids" started to leave home, never to return, it was a shock to everyone who loved the music they made. The refrain from The Supremes' first hit record, "Where Did Our Love Go," began to seem poignantly apropos.

The exodus began with Mary Wells in 1964 when she turned 21, the age of consent, and decided that she should not have to renew a contract she signed when she was a teen-ager. One by one, over the next 15 years, most of the Motown stars who traveled the South by bus, who found fame and fortune in prestigious supper clubs and theaters in the country, who entertained for kings and queens abroad, indeed, who popularized Gordy's Motown Sound to an international audience, left the label, many of them disgusted and angry.

Martha Reeves, The Temptations, The Four Tops, The Isley Brothers, The Spinners, The Miracles, Mabel John, Gladys Knight and the Pips, Kim Weston, Chris Clark, Barbara Randolph, David Ruffin, Eddie Kendricks, The Marvelettes, Edwin Starr, Brenda Holloway, Ashford and Simpson, Jr. Walker and the All Stars, Michael Jackson, Jackson 5, Florence Ballard,

Cindy Birdsong and even Mary Wilson. Sadly, the list went on and on and would continue into the next few years and include Marvin Gaye.

There would be many reasons why the singers would defect, but often the problems had to do with disagreements regarding Berry Gordy's domination over their lives and careers. Gordy also did not agree with the ambition of some of the artists—like Jackson 5—to write and produce their own music, thereby seizing more control of their careers both financially and artistically. A common complaint, though, had to do with Berry's single-minded attentiveness to Diana Ross. When Motown moved from Detroit to Hollywood, many artists felt that they and their careers were being neglected, that Berry only cared about pleasing Diana and fulfilling his aspirations for her to be a movie star.

Fans and much of the record-buying public remained loyal to the artists after they defected. They followed with great curiosity the new lives of the former Motown greats, sometimes with excitement and often with disappointment and sadness for those—like Martha Reeves—whose careers faltered after leaving Motown. They also still believed in and supported Berry Gordy and Motown and, in retrospect, it seems that Diana Ross had much to do with this devotion. In the '70s, she embodied the spirit of Motown in that she was a testament to the success of the past and a symbol of hope that the future would still be exciting. It seemed that no matter how many ways Motown's royal family disintegrated, Diana Ross would remain the reigning queen of whatever kingdom was left.

Toward the end of 1980, Michael Masser produced what most critics still consider to be Diana's most passionate ballad performance, "It's My Turn," the title theme to the motion picture starring Jill Clayburgh, Michael Douglas and Charles Grodin.

"It's My Turn" seemed to reflect Diana's own life at the time, an evocative statement of self-affirmation delivered in a truly compelling style. She sings of having once seen her entire life "through someone else's eyes." But not anymore. Now, "It's my turn."

"The first time Diana heard 'It's My Turn' was when I played it for her on the piano in Berry's office," Michael Masser recalled. "She immediately felt it captured something that she was experiencing at that particular time. The story was significant to her, and when she sang it, I got goosebumps."

Considering her life at this time—the way she, too, was trying to break her ties with Berry Gordy—it was obvious to many company insiders that Diana Ross now could relate to her material in a very personal way. Her fans who knew nothing about her problems were fascinated, though a bit confused, by the way she seemed to be revealing herself. The possibility that the song actually had personal meaning for her—that the lyrics might be somehow prophetic—seemed remote, yet intriguing.

On the record, her voice is clear, strong and emotional. She had never sounded more appealing. "I never wanted to overkill or bury her voice on my productions," Masser explained. "I kept her sound up front because no one sounds better than Diana Ross when she's giving her all to a performance."

Following right behind "Upside Down" and "I'm Coming Out," "It's My Turn" was a natural for the Top 10 and rounded out 1980 as a stellar year for Diana as a recording star, three Top 10 singles. She was on a magical roll. Because of her success, Diana was justifiably filled with self-confidence about her future. When rumors began to surface that she might be leaving Motown in order to facilitate a final break with Berry, many observers were not as surprised by the possibility as they might have been just two years earlier.

She had been under contract to Motown since January 1961. For almost 20 years she was obligated to defer to someone else's judgment. And when she refused, a battle would ensue. It had apparently finally occurred to her that Berry Gordy was not—as she and her label mates had been led to believe all of these years—"The Boss." Diana's recording contract with Motown was not a work-for-hire pact, but rather an artist's agreement whereby a record label produces, manufactures, distributes and promotes the results of an artist's talents. She received royalties, not a salary. The additional agreement that made Berry her personal manager primarily called for his obligations to her. In other words, *she* was *his* boss; he had the *privilege* of recording and managing her.

When Diana and her Motown peers first started out, many still in their teens, they were hungry and naïve, and if Berry fostered the image that he was the boss, fine. Many who came from broken homes—like Florence Ballard and Mary Wilson—were probably looking for father figures, anyway.

Now Diana had become an adult. Her eyes were wide open. She wanted to negotiate a new contract with Berry in which she would have total control over her career. And she also wanted to exclude him from decisions regarding her personal life. If she couldn't have those guarantees, she threatened to make arrangements with another recording company.

In November 1980, after "It's My Turn" was released, Diana's contract with Motown expired. For the first time, she did not rush to renew it.

Berry felt she was bluffing. She already had more freedom than he felt she needed and deserved, and some of her solo decisions, like starring in *The Wiz*, had proved to be bad career moves. He didn't mind her moving to New York, he tolerated her romances with Ryan O'Neal and Gene Simmons, and he accepted the fact that she was purposely excluding him from creative involvement in her albums because, as he told friends, he felt all of this was just a phase. "She'll come around," he said.

Berry was always one to look at what he called "the bigger picture." No matter how free this woman thought she was, she was still under contract to him and to Motown. Diana may have felt that she was acting like an adult—moving away from Berry's domination, having affairs, making some of her own decisions— but actually, where Berry was concerned, she was just "playing grown-up."

Backstage at one of Diana's Caesars Palace shows, she and Berry had a loud disagreement about the terms of her re-signing with his company. When she told Berry, "Listen, we need to hammer out a new contract if I'm going to stay here," he was indifferent to her.

"If you can get a better deal somewhere else, go on and get it," Berry said.

"I just don't understand him," Diana told a former girlfriend of Berry's backstage in Vegas. "Does he really want me to leave? Because if he does, I will. I can get a lot more money somewhere else."

She was right, of course. Thanks to her recent string of hits, she seemed more valuable to the record industry than she had been in years. But Berry held the position that Diana had consistently high recording and promotion costs and that her sales were spotty. In terms of prestige, certainly it was a coup to have Diana Ross on the label even if financially it often was not so. In many instances she would follow up a major hit with a series of monumental flops.

For instance, "Ain't No Mountain High Enough" sold 1,243,738 copies in July 1970. The next release, "Remember Me," sold 540,940 records just five months later. And then "Reach Out (I'll Be There)" sold only 254,307 copies four months after that.

"Touch Me in the Morning" sold 1,504,909 copies in May 1973. The next release, "Last Time I saw Him," sold 643,740 records seven months later. Then, "Sleepin' " sold 46,162 copies four months after that.

As Berry pointed out to Diana, her studio costs—the amount of money it took to record one of her albums—were very high. The cost of promotion also proved exorbitant. Because of her erratic sales, Motown could never break even. Berry held the position that since Motown always covered her expenses when the company lost money on her, when she was making money and her sales were up, she should remain loyal because, as he always put it, "we're a family."

But Diana had become much more concerned with personal freedom than with Berry's check and balance system. She said, "All of a sudden I felt like, here I was, 37 years old, with three children, but not yet able to take full responsibility for my own decisions. I don't want to have to pick up the phone and call Berry, Motown or anybody else if I want to buy a car. I want to know where my bank accounts are."

As has often been the case where Gordy's other artists were concerned, Motown could not provide an acceptable accounting of royalties when Diana demanded one for recent releases. Ironically, the figures they gave her were probably accurate. Like the other singers who made similar complaints, she was fooled when Motown touted her record sales into believing the figures to be higher than they really were. This hype always worked for Motown in terms of public relations and image, but never failed to backfire on the company when it was time to come up with the money those figures would justify.

Just as The Supremes' sales had been exaggerated by Motown, so had Diana's. "Ain't No Mountain High Enough," "Touch Me in the Morning," "Love Hangover," and "Upside Down" were the only four million-sellers of her solo career up to this point. Motown contended in publicity releases she had had at least a dozen, including songs like "Theme From Mahogany" (888,272 copies sold) and "The Boss" (barely 250,000 copies).

According to close associates, the breaking point came when Diana thought Gordy was lying to her about the sales of "It's My Turn." After all, the record had reached the Top 10, and it certainly seemed like it should have sold more than the confidential tally of 434,794 copies she was given at royalty statement time. Perhaps Motown used some influence with the trade publications to keep the record in the Top 10 while the company was negotiating Diana's contract—this kind of chicanery certainly is not unheard of in the record industry, though Motown has never been accused of doing it—but Gordy was not lying about the record's sales. As strong as the song happened to be, it simply was not a big seller. Diana was not savvy enough to understand what Motown was doing for her—and to her.

Diana has alluded to having had serious money problems at this time. "I got ripped off," she said later. "I was gettin' ripped off left and right. People were taking my money. And that's when I realized I'd better figure out what the hell was going on."

"Diana said that Berry kept telling her that she wasn't selling records," said John Whyman, a friend who discussed the problem with her in Las Vegas. "She believed she was. She confided that, by 1980, she was practically bankrupt. I think she may have been exaggerating, but she was definitely having financial problems."

Other associates do not seem to think Diana exaggerated at all, and some contend her public would have been surprised to learn how little money she really had at this point, Ironically, Diana ended up like Florence when she began investigating the question of just how much money she had to her name. Not much, she discovered.

She told one employee, "I have a few hundred thousand dollars that I can actually put my hands on. And that's it. After all that work, that's it. I have three kids, I have responsibilities, and damn it, I can't believe how Berry has run my money so that it's mostly his money. How could he do that to me after all of these years? What have I done to deserve this?"

Apparently, it was time to economize. One day, she was shopping in a chic Beverly Hills boutique and examined a pair of slacks that cost $180. She held up the pants in front of her and carefully deliberated whether to purchase them.

"I like these, but it's silly for me to pay this much money," she said. "I can have these *made* for less than that!"

"I know what you mean," the employee agreed.

"In fact, I could have five pairs made for this."

Later, Diana told a reporter, "Little silk pants like that—well, I'll just sketch what I want, then call one or two of the three good seamstresses I'm always in touch with. They'll bring over some silk samples. I'll choose, then they'll sew for me, at a total cost of about $60 per pair of pants, what they ought to be in the store."

Columnist Janet Charlton said that, in the late '70s, Diana would stand in front of shop windows in Beverly Hills with a sketch pad. Pencil in hand, she would copy designs, and then take the sketches back to her seamstresses to have "knock-offs" (cheaper versions) made for herself.

"She had a woman who did nothing but copy designer clothes for her," Charlton said. "Worse, she would buy expensive gowns on consignment in the most exclusive stores, only to have her seamstresses stay up all night making duplicates. The next morning, she would return the dresses saying she had changed her mind. Of course, she would always get a full refund."

Despite Diana's financial situation, Berry Gordy could not entertain the thought that Diana would actually leave the label. She embodied the spirit of Motown. Arm in arm, Gordy and Ross had made a most significant contribution to entertainment by breaking the racial and class barriers that had kept black music from commercial acceptance. They had also conquered the worlds of film and television. Of course, there had been others who made major breakthroughs—Billie Holiday, Lena Horne, Louis Armstrong, Harry Belafonte, Sammy Davis, Jr., to name a few—but in terms of contemporary popular music and the acceptance of blacks in that field, the impact Berry Gordy and Diana Ross made is of major importance.

Indeed, timing certainly played an important part in Diana Ross' success. Had she come along at any other time or place in the evolution of American entertainment, she might not have been able to enjoy such a multi-faceted and commercially successful career. Early black pioneers like Bill Robinson, Ethel Waters and Bessie Smith gave American culture some of its best entertainment. Yet no matter how extraordinary their achievement, these performers' opportunities were limited by the color of their skin. Unable to perform in certain clubs and sections of town, many great black artists of the '20s and '30s were forced into oblivion with no claim to their creations. If, after reaching the pinnacle of her career, Josephine Baker hadn't lived another four decades, all the while showcasing the risqué entertainment style that elevated her to the fast-paced life reserved for the very rich, we may not have understood what the Baker mystique was all about.

But Diana Ross was just coming into her own as a star just as Berry Gordy was about to realize his fate as a pop music mogul. Because of the Civil Rights movement, the two joined forces when society truly began to accept blacks as equals, thus allowing Gordy and Diana to participate in and enjoy to the fullest the rewards of show business.

"In the scenario of their lives, I would say they did it all," observed Diana's producer Michael Masser. "Nothing could erase from their hearts the time and place in which they created all of that wonderful magic.''

"Wonderful magic'' aside, Diana Ross had a decision to make, and it would be based on economics. She knew that Berry Gordy had never been much for sentiment before. As far as she was concerned, now was no time for him to become sentimental about the past.

In February 1981, Diana produced her own television special for CBS in association with television producer Steve Binder and without Berry and Motown's official involvement. Entitled *diana* (again with the lowercase "d''), the 60-minute show combined taped footage of her concert before 18,000 hysterical fans at the Los Angeles Forum with studio footage that teamed Ross with Larry Hagman and Michael Jackson.

The live footage captured on tape the maniacal enthusiasm of Diana Ross's loving cult. She performed "in the round,'' a simple, no-frills staging for which she had become known in recent years. There was no Vegas slickness—no leaping dancers and elaborate settings—just a one-woman presentation with a small orchestra and a group of background singers.

The taping of this show provided the first of the many Diana Ross/Mary Wilson confrontations of the '80s. Hearing that Diana was interested in bringing the life of Josephine Baker to the screen, Mary decided that *she* should play the role instead. Mary went so far as to pose in Baker-esque costumes for publicity photos and postcards, but unfortunately no one really cared except her fan club members, and least of all Diana Ross, who must have thought that if *she* was having trouble launching the Baker project, what hope did Mary Wilson have?

When Diana was scheduled to play the Forum in Los Angeles, Mary wanted to attend the concert with John Whyman, a longtime friend of Diana, Mary and Cindy's. Diana Ross' office, though, refused to make tickets available. Undaunted, Whyman secured tickets from a temporary office worker in producer Steve Binder's office.

The night of the show, Whyman and Wilson pulled up to the Forum without the required VIP parking pass.

"Hey, I got one of The Supremes here,'' Whyman said, hoping to gain entry.

"Who cares? Go park at the Holiday Inn,'' was the guard's annoyed response.

Mary, embarrassed, sank down in the car seat.

Once they parked at the Holiday Inn, several thousand feet away, Mary, wearing a gorgeous white foxtail coat, used a short-cut but had to traipse through weeds and bushes in order to get to the Forum. When she arrived, she wanted to attend a private Diana Ross party at The Forum Club, but didn't have a "backstage pass" and so wasn't permitted to enter. Four other people were with Wilson and Whyman, but the couple had only four tickets so the Mary Wilson party of six squeezed into the four folding chairs as best they could. For Wilson, it was one indignity heaped upon another, and all to see a woman she doesn't even like very much perform in concert.

But when Mary strolled into the concert hall, the Forum erupted in wild applause at the sight of this svelte, beautiful black woman walking proudly to her seat. She may have had to park at the Holiday Inn next door, but she was still Mary Wilson, former member of The Supremes, looking, at age 37, like a million bucks, and all of Diana Ross' fans knew it. She received a standing ovation just for being there. Perhaps it was worth the trouble of picking a few weeds out of the crushed glitter of her hot pink jumpsuit.

Then minutes later, the lights were lowered and out came Diana making her entrance through the audience, in practically the same coat Mary was wearing.

Diana's was full length, but since most of the audience had already seen Mary in a similar outfit, Diana lost much of the impact of her grand entrance. She managed to cover her feelings long enough to allow Mary to join her for a few bars of "Reach Out and Touch (Somebody's Hand)," much to the crowd's delight. But after the show, Diana vented her anger, backstage witnesses say. When her aides told her that the footage of Diana and Mary singing together would be an exciting addition to the program when broadcast, Diana vetoed the notion. She felt that Mary had tried to upstage her, and she wasn't going to do her former singing partner the favor of giving her national TV exposure.

Though footage of Diana singing with other celebrities—Muhammad Ali, Larry Hagman, Michael Jackson—was included in the program when it aired, the duet with Mary Wilson had been excised.

In the spring of 1981, Diana teamed with Lionel Richie for what is considered the biggest hit record of her career, "Endless Love." Richie was still a member of The Commodores, a Motown group Suzanne dePasse brought to the company. However, he was beginning to make a solo impression much the way Diana had done when she was with The Supremes. His contribution to his group far overshadowed the appearance of other members. Thanks to artfully commercial ballads he had penned for his group ("Still," "Easy" and "Three Times a Lady") and for Kenny Rogers ("Lady"), Lionel was considered Motown's "golden boy" by 1981.

Franco Zeffirelli contacted Lionel Richie to write the theme song to his film, *Endless Love*, starring Brooke Shields. The title tune was planned as an instrumental and after it was finished, Zeffirelli suggested that Richie write some lyrics and that perhaps Diana Ross could record them. Eventually, the performance became a duet.

"At first it wasn't a Motown single," Diana recalled of the song. "I didn't come into the picture until later. Lionel's agreement was with PolyGram (Records and Pictures). When I got into the picture, Lionel and I agreed that it was only fair that Motown get the single. [Note: Actually, Berry Gordy insisted on it.] I was really pleased with it because it was one of the most beautiful songs I've ever recorded."

It was difficult to coordinate Lionel's schedule with Diana's for the recording date. Lionel, producing Kenny Rogers in Los Angeles, locked in recording studio time in Reno for the Ross session. Diana, working in Vegas, finished her club date and took a limousine to Reno to meet Lionel, who had flown in from Los Angeles. Lionel recalled that "Endless Love" was recorded from three to nine in the morning.

Though the film proved dreadful, the song was a hit, one of the biggest records of 1981. "Endless Love" claimed the Number One spot on the charts and, amazingly, remained there for nine weeks. Lionel's group, The Commodores, had turned this song down when he submitted it for one of their albums. It was nominated for an Academy Award, and Ross and Richie performed the song at the Oscar presentations in 1982. The song was also nominated for several Grammy Awards, including Record of the Year. Though it lost both the Oscar and the Grammy, "Endless Love" is one of those timeless, classic Motown songs.

Diana apparently became angry with Lionel after the record's release. The Commodores were appearing in Las Vegas, and she had attended their show. Backstage, Lionel invited her to his group's upcoming concert at Radio City Music Hall, and she agreed to go. Shortly after that, she came storming into her Manhattan office with a rolled up copy of the New York *Daily News* in her hand. She slapped it down on an aide's desk. "Look at this. Look at this!" Underneath her picture was the announcement, "the special guest on opening night of The Commodores' show will be none other than Diana Ross."

"I'd never seen her in a rage before. This was the first time," the employee recalled. "And she said, 'Call Ticketron and find out if The Commodores are saying I'm going to be on that show.' I did, and they were. I thought, 'Oh mother of God, this is the end. How do I tell her this?'

"I told her and, of course, she started swearing and screaming, saying that she felt exploited, and how could Lionel do this terrible thing. I'm sure she was more hurt than angry—because she likes Richie a lot—but Miss Ross often lets her emotions run away with her. Eventually, there was some quick legal work done and Miss Ross' name was taken off the billing. Radio City Music Hall had to do a retraction."

Diana had enjoyed the biggest record of her entire career, and she was no longer signed to Motown as a recording artist. Now she found herself in a very powerful position. With Diana Ross as a free agent, show business was a-buzz with the possibilities. Many music industry moguls considered they had a golden opportunity to sign her to their own labels.

The late Neil Bogart, who launched Donna Summer's career for Casablanca Records, offered Diana $15 million to sign with his newly formed Boardwalk Records. David Geffen, Cher's former boyfriend who had signed John Lennon and Yoko Ono to his new Geffen Records, matched Bogart's offer. PolyGram also came up with a substantial proposal. Diana had always believed she was worth much more than Gordy was willing to pay her. Now that she was certain, she was flattered and filled with new confidence. "A lot of people have offered me incredible amounts of money," she boasted.

"Listen, Diana Ross will never leave Motown," Mary Wilson said. "Not in a million years. She and Berry are together for life."

Cindy Birdsong agreed. "I just can't believe that can happen. Not after all they have been through together."

Both of Diana's former singing partners were wrong. Once Diana had received these outside offers, she decided she would not re-sign with Berry Gordy. Despite her contention that this was a difficult decision, some close associates say it really was not. For her, the issue now transcended a matter of control over her career, which she wanted desperately. She finally realized how much she was worth, and she wanted at least that much money. Berry claimed that he could not afford to match any of the offers. He told her that if she felt any gratitude for what he had done for her over the last 20 years, she would stay with Motown. That kind of sentiment infuriated Diana.

"What he did for me?" she would exclaim. "What about what *I* did for *him*? What about what I did for Motown?" She certainly had a point.

Deciding to leave Motown was easy for Diana. Doing it was not. She was ending a professional relationship with Berry, but she didn't want to lose him as a friend, even though their friendship had certainly become strained during the last few years. She also knew that Berry was not a sentimental man, and that if she left him he would consider it a betrayal and probably not want to have much to do with her again.

To whom could she turn? She didn't know anyone who could give her objective advice, so she called Smokey Robinson who, as a vice-president of Motown, was hardly unbiased. He urged her to stay with the company that had made her a star, "with the people who understand you and have taken care of you." She asked if she could fly to Los Angeles and discuss the situation with him. When they got together, he again encouraged her to stay.

"But what about the money?" she asked.

"If that's your main concern, then what can I say, Diane? We can't compete with the money."

"After the meeting with Smokey, she flew back to New York. She told me she cried on the plane the whole way," said a former associate. "Her decision was made. It was heartbreaking for her, but she said that she vowed that she wouldn't cry one more tear over it. 'What's done is done,' she said. 'I'm a businesswoman, and Berry's the one who always told me that it's not good to do business with friends. If the tables were turned, he would do the exact same thing.' "

In March 1981 it was official. Diana signed a seven-year contract with RCA for a reported $20 million, said to be the most lucrative recording contract up until that time. She was obligated to deliver one album a year. Her deal was with RCA for record distribution in the United States and Canada, and with EMI for distribution throughout the rest of the world.

Ebony magazine asked her: "Was it the money you were offered that made you leave Motown?"

Her answer: "I don't think I should comment on that."

Thus ended the golden years. Now, she said, "I want a company that will pay you exactly the amount of money for each album that they say they're going to pay you. My deal with RCA is one in which they have to check everything with me. Everything."

"It was the most important decision I've made in my life and

I have made a lot of important decisions," she said at the time. "My relationship with Motown over the past 20 years was the greatest, and I know the inference of my leaving is that there was something wrong. But that's not entirely true."

If Diana learned anything at Motown, she discovered that public relations and her image could be very important. She decided that she wanted her decision to be perceived as part of a growing experience, not a choice based on finances.

"I don't think that children leave home because there's something wrong, exactly," she said. "There are just other areas of who they are that somehow need to be expressed. Berry has been the most influential person in my life, yet at a certain point all of the things he taught me I had to be able to experience myself in order to know what they're really about. Many of the things I've done in my career I've never been able to take credit for because they've been done for me. It was not an easy decision. It was a decision I never thought I'd have to make."

Diana's actions certainly put an end to the rumors that she and Berry would one day marry. "That sure would have been the answer, wouldn't it?" she said sadly to the *Ebony* reporter. "But that's a fairytale story where relationships seem like they're just wonderful. That's not real.

"We'll always have communication," she continued. "I don't think there's any reason not to. When you love somebody, you don't stop loving that person because you no longer have a working relationship with him. If our love is as strong as it was said to be, then I'm sure we'll always have a relationship. We're too close. It's family. Our children. My children. His family."

Berry Gordy has never been perceived as a loser, so losing Diana Ross was as much a blow to his professional ego as it was to his personal pride. He simply could not understand how she could be so cold, so calculating. Certainly, her need for independence baffled him. He told his friends that she was one of the most independent women he had ever known. To his way of thinking, he had never been able to control her. "So what the hell is she talking about?"

"It was a tragedy the way she left the label," observed Suzanne dePasse. "She didn't get her necessary blessing from Berry."

For the next few months, Berry ruminated over what Diana had done. Where he was concerned, after all he had done for her—20 years spent devoting himself to her every need, to all of the important facets of her career development, not to mention the romantic entanglements—it all boiled down to the fact she could get more money somewhere else, from a white man named Robert Summers, president of RCA. Indeed, as mercenary as even Gordy is, Diana's decision was a bitter pill to swallow. "Jesus Christ! I even spent my goddamn savings to make *Lady Sings the Blues*," he exclaimed.

"I felt personally insulted and very hurt," he said. "And to leave as she did, strictly for money. I would think that if any person leaves for that reason, they should *not* be with Motown. If they don't understand what we did for them—understand about the care and love and all the other stuff they had—and rate everything in dollars, well, that, to me, is not very bright.

"But with Diane, I felt even worse. I felt like a failure. I will always love her, but I will always be disappointed in her, too."

"I know Berry loves me," Diana countered very confidently. "He can't stop loving me in one day."

After that comment was published in *Soul* magazine in the winter of 1981, Berry Gordy cancelled a plan to issue an album of previously unreleased Diana Ross material. He sent a memo to his department heads referring to Diana's statement about him, saying that he didn't want to do anything to interfere with her upcoming RCA material. He was being a good sport. But, still, a cold war would ensue between Diana and Berry for the next two years. That's how long it would be before they would see each other. She would telephone him occasionally, and often he would not take her call. When they would speak, Diana would usually be effusive about "the incredible sense of freedom that I didn't know was possible before"—something she told him one morning after waking him up. Her observation did little to brighten Berry Gordy's day.

"I was like a kid leaving home," Diana explained in an interview. "It felt like walking out in the blue sky, but I just had to trust myself and do it. To my amazement, every time I took a step alone in the unknown, there was something there to support me."

Berry Gordy, at 52, was a changed man after Diana Ross left Motown. His love-hate relationship with her had consumed his life for two decades. When it was over, there was nothing to replace it. He told one former girlfriend that he would spend hours mulling over details of the past. He wondered where he had gone wrong, just as a lonely, anxious parent frets when a child leaves home unexpectedly. "Whatever was going on, whether we loved each other or hated each other, at least we were there for each other," he said sadly. "Now she's alone. And I'm alone."

As far as many of Motown's fans were concerned, Diana's leaving Motown closed the final chapter in Berry Gordy's book of dreams-come-true. Stevie Wonder was still with the label, so were Smokey Robinson and a few of the other stalwarts. But without Diana Ross as Queen, the kingdom just didn't matter much anymore. Motown would never again be the same.

Berry Gordy was nothing if not brilliant at the art of saving face. He soon began telling his friends that it was actually *he* who masterminded Diana's multi-million dollar RCA contract. "Yeah, she wanted out," he said. "So I got her this big deal. What the hell. I thought it was the least I could do."

But as for her future at RCA, Berry held little hope. He realized that her success at Motown was the result of teamwork, of careful planning on a corporate level, and also on his insisting that she make career moves she either didn't believe in or was uncertain about. She was a magnificent entertainer and vocalist, but Diana Ross was not an entertainment manager. Gordy predicted that now that she was on her own and master of her own fate, no one would ever be able to tell her what to do again.

Her ego would all but ruin her.

Berry was more prophetic in his analysis than anyone would have ever guessed at the time: "I feel that Diana, big as she is—and she's certainly the biggest artist we ever had—if she doesn't have the right team behind her, she will have trouble. And she does *not* have that team."

One of Diana's road managers has said that her greatest fear had always been of "ending up old and poor." There was certainly not much she could do to prevent herself from aging, but where her finances were concerned she no longer had reason to fret. After banking the RCA money, she bought a five-acre baronial estate in Greenwich, Connecticut. The manor was purchased from tobacco heiress Nancy Reynolds—the only surviving child of the original R.J. Reynolds—for a little over $1 million.

To insure that she would have no neighbors, she also bought six acres of adjoining land.

Now, more than ever, she was alone.

RCA was a brand new world for Miss Diana Ross. She was completely surrounded by "yes" people. No one to disagree with her. No one to tell her what to do.

These next few years would not be easy ones. Diana had become more lonely—since Gene Simmons was proving to be an undependable lover—and more confused than ever. She was determined to forge her own way and prove wrong anyone who felt she had made a mistake by leaving the security of Gordy and Motown. In trying to run her own career, she would make many blunders, some of them serious, some of them foolish. In her quest to achieve what she would call "perfection in my life and career," she would make enemies along the way. Of course, it's often unfairly difficult for women to be taken seriously in business. This probably can be compounded if the lady is also emotional, volatile and self-centered.

"I'm just doing the best I can," Diana would say in her defense. "And it's not easy." But without Berry Gordy, Mike Roshkind, Suzanne dePasse or any of the other shrewd and capable Motown executives to anchor her, it often seemed as if Diana was some sort of madwoman running amok—causing one scene after another and hurting feelings along the way—all the while firming up her reputation as a difficult, unpredictable pop diva.

By this time, Diana was being managed by Howard Marks of Glickman-Marks Management in New York. Since Berry no longer guided her, she needed someone to handle the tedious details of her career. It had to be someone who would do it her way, and apparently company partner Howard Marks fit the bill. Gene Simmons had suggested Glickman-Marks because his group, Kiss, had been managed by them for some time. Glickman-Marks employed staffers who specialized in tour management and other services that could make Diana's transition from Motown to RCA an easier one.

"My relationship with RCA has been great so far," she said at the beginning of her love affair with the new label. "There has been nothing I've wanted that they haven't done. They trust my instincts and decisions 100 percent. When I say something, they do it. There are no hassles. Nothing goes out without my approval, and that's the kind of thing I've always wanted."

RCA was a structured organization and very impersonal, which was fine for Diana Ross. After Motown, she no longer wanted personal ties with anyone in business. The executives at her new label made her feel that no one would touch her or ask her to do anything, because, unlike Motown, they just didn't know her that well and were all clearly intimidated by the Ross legend. At RCA, she believed everyone would respect her, the same way Columbia respected Barbra Streisand. However, Diana Ross would find that personal friendships did come in handy on occasion. When problems arose, no one at RCA would care about her. In time, she would learn to complain incessantly about the lack of a personal interest in her career from her record label.

Diana said that she had tried to get Bernard Edwards and Nile Rodgers, the duo from Chic who produced her biggest Motown album, *diana*, to produce her first RCA album, "but they wanted creative control and I cannot give up creative control." Finally, she decided to produce it herself. She didn't seem to have a clue about how to do this, but RCA indulged her just the same. She surrounded herself with studio technicians who did know what they were doing and the album, *Why Do Fools Fall in Love?*, was finally released in September 1981, six months after its due date.

The album included as a cover jacket a poster of Diana Ross in a provocative zebra-skin outfit which she designed. After the revealing cover, Diana said, "Actually, I think my body is the best it's ever been in my entire life. All of a sudden, I feel more womanly. I feel like I've got a figure. I was always straight up and down, the skinny one in the middle. I was just like a bean pole and now I'm getting a few curves and I like it. It took me 15 years to do it."

Apparently, it took a half dozen photo shoots, with as many different photographers, to capture Diana's newly acquired womanliness on film. Douglas Kirkland finally came up with a photograph she would approve. Endless hours were spent making her up, then touching up the photos. According to a witness, "Diana would go into Howard Marks' office and she would say, 'We need to brush down the skin here, put more pink in the cheeks, take a line out here.' Every single week it was the same thing until eventually that poster looked like a picture of a white woman. She'd airbrushed herself into Doris Day oblivion. She continued making changes on the shot until it got to the point where we just started bringing the photo back to her with nothing done to it, and she wouldn't know the difference."

When she wanted to re-record the Frankie Lymon and The Teenagers hit "Why Do Fools Fall in Love?" for RCA, most people working with her thought it was foolish. If she was really trying to go forward with her career, why was she doing oldies? But the single would be a Top 10 hit, and so would its follow-up, "Mirror Mirror." The album would be certified platinum, but it was successful mostly because there was still some of the Motown magic dust about. People were curious about her, and she was coming off a long string of Motown hit records.

No one could fault Diana Ross' close relationship with her children. When Rhonda turned 10, she was going through a phase in which she loved horses, so Diana ordered her a chocolate birthday cake in the shape of a horse with a mane and tail of candy. The night before Rhonda's birthday party, Diana had to remain late at the office. She called her daughter and said, "Are you excited?"

Apparently Rhonda said yes.

"Wow! You're not a little girl anymore. Now you've got two numbers to your age." She was a tender and very caring mother.

"Tomorrow's a special day for all of us," she told Rhonda. "And Mommy loves you very much."

At this time, Diana decided to involve her ex-husband Bob—who lived with his new wife, Suzin, 30 minutes away in nearby Connecticut—in some of her business affairs as president of her management company. In that capacity, Silberstein attended most of Diana's meetings, sitting directly behind her and looking over her shoulder. At business conferences at Glickman-Marks, everyone would introduce themselves and then Howard Marks would introduce Diana. She, in turn, would introduce Bob, but rather than portray him as an adviser, Diana would say, "This is Bob Silberstein, the father of my children." It seemed that she wanted to be certain that none of the office employees would mistakenly discuss with Bob her romance with Gene Simmons.

"I was determined that Bob's and my relationship would always be a good one," she had said to *Ebony*'s managing editor Hans J. Massaquoi. "I like him too much. He's too good a man. I've met a lot of strong human beings in my lifetime and he's one. If I didn't admire him in the first place, I would never have married him."

She insisted in another interview that she and Bob were closer now than "we were at any time in the marriage." She also told *Esquire* magazine that she'd been in love "twice, including my husband. The other was a man I knew before I was married." She declined to identify him as Berry Gordy.

Said a former Glickman-Marks employee, "What we didn't know then but learned later was that Bob was preparing to manage her career himself through a company they were starting, RTC Management. Bob had rhythm and blues singer Chaka Khan under his managerial wing at this time, and Diana enjoyed dabbling in the management of Chaka's career. Diana, apparently, was not willing to give Bob up just yet. In fact, I had the feeling that if there was anybody she really trusted at this time, it was Bob. He was extremely sweet, 180 degrees opposite of Diana's boyfriend, Gene Simmons. I did get the feeling that he would have liked not being around so much, that there was tension being in the same office as Gene Simmons.''

Most of the female employees of Glickman-Marks felt hostile towards Simmons and his chauvinistic ways. One secretary recalled the day Gene had nothing better to do than wad pieces of paper together and lob them across the room into her cleavage as she tried to work. But no one would dare say anything to criticize Gene because of his relationship with Diana.

In some ways, it's understandable that Diana tolerated Gene Simmons and didn't recognize characteristics of his personality that made him so unappealing to her female employees. Perhaps the reason she didn't see Gene as being the sexist he was is because she was so accustomed to being around Berry Gordy, a man considered by many of his female employees to be quite the chauvinist. During her years at Motown at Berry's side, Diana witnessed extreme cases of what could certainly be called male chauvinism. Since she herself had never been targeted in a blatant manner by Berry (though, some would argue, she was often victimized in more subtle ways), she was indifferent to the way Berry and some of the other men treated many of the women at Motown.

For instance, once Berry conducted a meeting with Diana Ross and some Motown executives. He was tape-recording the confab, as he always did, when the recorder malfunctioned. Berry contacted one of Diana's female assistants on an intercom and asked that she bring in a new cord for the machine. With cord in hand, she appeared instantly and proceeded to walk across the room in the direction of the faulty equipment.

''What do you think you're doing?'' Berry demanded to know. ''Don't you know there's a meeting going on here?''

''I'm going to fix the tape recorder,'' the assistant explained. ''Isn't that what you want?''

''Well, what we *don't* want is to *see* you,'' was Berry's response.

''Then how do I fix the equipment?''

''On your knees,'' Berry said. ''You get on your knees and walk across the room that way.''

The perplexed assistant looked over to her boss, Miss Ross, for help. But Diana just stared at her with an impatient countenance. Then she watched, along with everyone else in the room—including three other women, all in power positions—as the female assistant got down on her knees. She made it half way across the room before finally scrambling to her feet, exclaiming, ''I'll be damned if I'm going to do this.'' With that, she ran out of the room in tears and slammed the door behind her.

Berry seemed genuinely baffled by the woman's behavior. To his way of thinking, his request wasn't chauvinistic or cruel as much as it was just his way of having an employee appear inconspicuous during a meeting.

To the assistant, Berry's request was demoralizing, not to mention a great indignity. But quite a few women—and men as well—have privately admitted that they were elevated into key positions at Motown only after having their dignity stripped away, and then replaced by something perceived by the powers-that-be as "loyalty."

This is the school from which Miss Ross graduated. The reason she acts the way she does and often treats people in a manner that might be considered thoughtless is because she was so influenced by Motown's—Gordy's—corporate philosophy that the personal liberties and even feelings of employees are simply not as important as absolute devotion to the boss. And, also there is apparently no time for courtesy. Anyone who has ever worked at Motown will attest to the fact that words such as "please" and "thank you" are rarely heard in the offices, especially in those of Motown Productions, the television/film division headed by Suzanne dePasse. This breach of common courtesy is excused by the belief that show business is so demanding, taxing and urgent that there's no time to worry about people's silly sensitivities. Or, as one self-important Motown Productions official put it during a television taping, "We're all under such pressure here. The very least an employee can do is take abuse and not ask questions about it."

In 1981, Diana became involved in a publicity campaign during which she would pose for pictures at an exclusive health club in Manhattan. She was photographed working out on Nautilus equipment and also lounging in the jacuzzi. After the shoot, Diana decided to relax in the steam room. According to a former employee of Glickman-Marks, Diana turned to one of two women who were in the steam room with her and said, "Hey, you. Get me a glass of water."

Perhaps she thought she was directing her command to someone who worked for Glickman-Marks. But these women were not employees. Rather they were highly insulted spa patrons.

"What? Get it yourself, you black bitch," one of the women snapped.

Certainly, Diana realized her mistake quickly. Humiliated, she stormed out of the steam room. The Glickman-Marks staffers said that they heard Miss Ross vent her anger about this instance of mistaken identity for many weeks to come. Giving her the benefit of doubt, perhaps she thought that the club—which only caters to wealthy clientele—would have been completely cleared on this day for her promotional plans. Hopefully, Diana never would have asked that woman to bring her a glass of water if she knew that the woman was a patron and not an employee.

Indeed, Diana Ross has been a privileged person for a long time. It appears that like many, though not all, celebrities, she has grown so accustomed to people abiding by her wishes—servants and staffers who nervously scurry about while making certain that her every whim is satisfied—that she does not always find it easy to relate to the reality of how "normal" people live, feel and act. She seems, as Holland-Dozier and Holland so aptly put it when they wrote her hit record, "Reflections," "lost in a world of distorted reality."

From what can be construed from some of her interviews, Diana Ross does sincerely believe that she is a fair-minded, logical, rational person. Just as she can not relate to the everyday human condition, "normal" people—like that incensed spa patron—cannot understand her. They are just as confounded by her when she acts in an imperious fashion as she herself is taken aback when they won't do what she says.

In the summer of 1981, Diana Ross interviewed prospective candidates to distribute a cosmetics line for one of her new business ventures, JFF Enterprises, Ltd. She envisioned a cosmetics line called *Diana*—*Diana* makeup base, *Diana* blusher, etc. Howard Marks had discussed the concept with Revlon and set up a meeting with executives from that firm in Glickman-Marks offices. This was not to be a line of black cosmetics. Diana Ross, who resents being pigeonholed as a "black star," made that very clear.

The Revlon representatives showed up with graphs and charts, ready to sell Miss Ross on the idea of how much they could do for her in this venture. Everyone was seated around an oblong conference table, with Diana holding court at one end. Four men from Revlon were seated at one side of her, and three representatives from Glickman-Marks, including Howard Marks, on the other side. After a few pleasantries, it was time to get down to business.

"Miss Ross," one of the Revlon spokesman eagerly began, "we are certain that you could do quite a bit for the black women's market of cosmetics. Now on this graph you will see . . ."

According to one of the Glickman-Marks representatives pres-

ent at the meeting, Miss Ross shot Howard Marks an exasper-
ated look. Her fingers tightened on the edge of the table. The
Revlon executive continued talking as Diana rose. He stopped.
Everyone around the table politely stood up in unison and
watched as Miss Ross very elegantly walked out of the room.
Without saying a word, she closed the door behind her.

"Is she going to the bathroom?" one person asked.

"What's happening?"

Five minutes passed. Ten more.

Glickman-Marks employees offered refreshments as everyone
waited. Finally, Howard Marks got up and walked out. "I'll see
what's keeping her."

A few moments later, he returned red-faced.

"Gentlemen, I'm very sorry, this meeting is concluded," he
said before leaving.

One of the Glickman-Marks people told the Revlon representatives as they walked to the elevator, "Miss Diana Ross is *not*
black. Not in her mind and not in the mind of anyone who works
for her. She crosses *all* color barriers."

"But that's foolish when it comes to cosmetics," a Revlon
executive tried to argue. "Makeup and moisturizers vary for
different skin colors, and if you're black . . ."

"Too goddamn bad," Diana's representative said, cutting him
off. "You guys just lost yourself a sweet deal."

Glickman-Marks was said to receive approximately 300 requests a year from black organizations asking for Diana Ross'
involvement.

"Could Miss Ross lend her name to the United Negro College
Fund?"

"Could Miss Ross endorse the Black Women of America
Foundation?"

"Could Miss Ross appear on the Black Gold awards?"

The office staff usually did not bother to ask her about these
requests because Diana Ross rarely involves herself publicly in
any black causes or with any black organizations.

When asked how she feels about being criticized by blacks
for allegedly "abandoning the cause," she gets defensive.
"That's not true. I don't believe they have done that to me,"
she says, turning the tables. "I can't abandon anything. Anyone
who looks at me can tell I'm black. I can't pass."

Diana had many millions of dollars now that she was signed
to RCA, and there was a great deal of discussion as to what she
should do with the money in order to avoid a big tax bite. "My

main concern is that I don't want to end up again like I was when I left Berry,'' she said. "If people think I'm cheap, too goddamn bad. I have my reasons. If people knew what happened to me at Motown, they'd understand.''

Howard Marks suggested a number of sensible real estate investments with the RCA money and, according to someone who claims to have seen Diana Ross' financial records, she would now be making many millions a year in those investments alone. This income had nothing to do with her performance fees. She was enjoying all of the star trappings of limousines, first-class accommodations, furs, jewels, but none of those made a dent in her total worth by 1982. Diana Ross was finally a wealthy woman. "If I shine at what I do, then I'm an example, to kids and blacks who'll realize they can do the same thing,'' she said.

She did spend money on security. It had been a year since John Lennon was murdered by a crazed fan in front of The Dakota apartment building in New York, yet most celebrities still felt a deep need to beef up security measures. Diana Ross was no different.

The Sherry Netherland hotel, where she lived in Manhattan, was exactly two short blocks in a straight line from the Glickman-Marks office. But Diana Ross would not walk that distance, even with bodyguards. Instead, everyday she would descend in the hotel's freight elevator so as not to meet any other guests and then be ushered into a waiting limousine, which was parked in front of the back exit with one door already opened, as per her specific instructions. Because of the surrounding one-way Manhattan streets, the chauffeur had to drive her five blocks out of the way before he could pull up to the back entrance of the Glickman-Marks office, where their service elevator would wait for her. Diana would go up with the elevator operator at her side, never saying a single word to him.

The John Lennon murder became the impetus behind one of Diana Ross' more intriguing rules: "Don't speak to me unless I speak to you first.'' Some former associates say that this edict, which, apparently, exists to this day, started because she did not want to be approached by anyone for any reason simply because she was afraid.

In New York, she was not as protected as she had been in Los Angeles. Much of the travel about the city involved chauffeurs. In Los Angeles she would drive herself in her yellow Rolls. (The part of L.A. where Diana Ross drives is full of yellow Rolls-Royces, so she can be as inconspicuous as she wants.) Also, New Yorkers were less intimidated by her than Los Angelenos.

They would approach her without thinking twice about it. Her East Coast fans were aggressive, and they scared her.

But there are never any absolutes when it comes to Diana Ross and her moods. Some fans have reported approaching her in the streets and being greeted warmly with hugs and kisses. It all must depend on how she feels, the kind of day she's having.

Certainly, though, when Diana would be conducting business in lawyers' or agents' offices, all of the employees were told very specifically that they should not approach her under any circumstances, or talk to her unless she talked to them first. And, of course, she was to be addressed only as "Miss Ross" if, by some chance, she did need a response to a question. Most people would probably call her Miss Ross anyway, just out of respect. But when this courtesy became *mandatory*, it inspired wonderment and gossip about the proportions of Miss Ross' ego.

Despite the fact that she wanted to be protected from her public, Diana continued going out into her audience every night during engagements to sing "Reach Out and Touch (Somebody's Hand)." Once someone asked her how she could still leave the stage considering her concerns for her safety. She said that she was protected by her image when she was on stage. "Those people wouldn't dare hurt me," she said. "I'm a *goddess* to them. But when I'm out in public, I'm at their mercy and, damn it, some of these people scare the hell out of me."

After she made that statement, Diana had a scare during a performance in San Carlos, California. A fan tried to jump up onto the stage. When security guards rushed him, he whipped out a knife and began stabbing at them, before managing to face the startled star on the stage.

He whispered something in her ear. Without showing panic, she kissed him on the cheek, and he fainted dead away. Later, he was booked for assault with a deadly weapon.

At the end of 1981, Diana, now 37, decided it was time to declare total independence. She severed her ties with Glickman-Marks and officially started her own management firm, RTC Management Corporation (RTC are the initials of her three daughters: Rhonda, Tracee and Chudney). At this time, Taylor Cox, who co-managed Diana's career in the '60s through Motown's Multi-Media Management division, observed of Diana: "What she needs more than anything else right now is sane management. Left to her own devices—if she ever tries to plan and guide her own career—she'll kill herself. In Diane's case,

I'm afraid that the old saying about the doctor who prescribes for himself having a fool for a patient will prove all too true."

If Bob Silberstein had intended to be a part of this arrangement, he either changed his mind or Diana changed it for him because from then on he no longer appeared to be involved in her career. Eventually, Silberstein and his second wife, Suzin, opened a dog/cat nutrition store in Manhattan.

RTC was located at 21 East 63rd Street in Manhattan, a brownstone that she now owned near Fifth Avenue. Diana had a member of her staff purchase two portable sign posts that read "No Parking Between Signs." They were placed very conspicuously 18 feet apart from one another in front of the entrance to the building. This way, Diana's limousine could park there and she could dash in and out, even though parking on East 63rd is illegal during weekdays. "Stardom does have its privileges," one of Diana's staffers reasoned. But when word of this particular perk got back to the Traffic Department, the signs came down.

Diana was excited about her new business ventures and instructed RCA to issue a press release entitled "Diana Ross: A Woman in Business," outlining the purposes of the many other new Diana Ross companies:

Diana Ross Productions, "the parent company for all recording activities."

Rosstown Music and Rossville Music were "her own music publishing companies."

Chondee, Inc., handled "tour and concert appearances for Miss Ross."

JFF Enterprises Ltd. directed "the research and development of proposed cosmetics, fashion and merchandising lines." (Diana started this company when she was still with Motown and designing the costumes for *Mahogany*. The initials stand for Just For Fun.)

Anaid Film Productions, Inc., was established to develop and produce "a variety of feature films, television specials and record promotion videos for Miss Ross. Anaid Film's first feature will be *Naked at the Feast*, the biography of Josephine Baker. Miss Ross will star in the production as well as produce it." (Anaid, of course, is Diana spelled backwards.)

Diana Ross Enterprises, Inc., "oversees all business and creative aspects of Miss Ross' entertainment companies."

Loeb and Loeb, the Los Angeles law firm with whom Diana Ross had been doing business, continued to represent her. John Frankenheimer (not to be confused with the film director of that name) was the attorney responsible for guiding Diana Ross' career to her exact specifications. She would no longer have a manager. She would also only hire people to work for her whom she knew had never worked for Motown or Berry Gordy.

"I want to help people," she insisted in an interview with *Soul* magazine. "I mean, I see a lot of the other acts that started out the same time I did, and they can't even get paid now and can't get a record deal. I want to be able to assist them. I mean, I don't even know where Martha Reeves is now. Or The Vandellas, either!"

"Funny you should mention Martha. I just did an interview with her," said the reporter.

"Is she doing fine?"

"Well, she . . ."

"You see, I want to know where these people are!" Diana interrupted. "I care."

"You might like to know that Martha is . . ."

"I saw The Four Tops in Vegas. I just want to know where everyone is, like Holland-Dozier and Holland."

"H-D-H? They're in . . ."

"I'd like to get reconnected to the sources of my career," she continued. "I don't know where they all went, or what happened. Maybe I was too involved in my own career. I don't know . . . I have so many questions. I wish I could find someone who could answer them."

Chapter

24

DIANA TURNED 38 in March 1982 and hosted another party—"my annual 29th birthday celebration"—at the home she still owned in Beverly Hills. A tuxedoed messenger in a chauffeured limousine personally delivered the invitations. As part of Diana's theme, guests were asked to wear either black or white. The party was held on the tennis courts, which had been specially tented for the event. A buffet of bastilla, rice, spinach with mushrooms, and skewers of shrimp, lamb, beef and chicken with watercress and endive salad was served to guests who sat at tables decorated with ceiling-high black and white plumes. Diana greeted all in a stunning black and white sequined Galanos gown, and then as dinner was served she made a costume change into a sexy Vicky Thiel black silk outfit.

Mary Wilson was one of the many celebrity guests. She told George Christy of *The Hollywood Reporter*, "Berry Gordy now says I should have gone solo like Diana, but I told him I didn't have him or Motown behind me." She revealed to someone else that she was considering writing a book, "but whatever you do, don't tell Diane or she'll throw me out."

Diana and Gene Simmons danced the night away. He presented her with a chocolate birthday cake decorated with two long-lashed eyes, framed by 38 candles and bearing the message: "Diana—the two eyes that haunt me—Love, Gene."

"I do know that I want to marry again," Diana said at the time. "I do have Gene—for what it is, nothing more. Gene and I are not even thinking about marriage.

"I guess I'm seeking in a man the same relationship I had with my father," Diana told reporter Colin Dangaard. "He was always strong, sure, sensitive."

Marriage for Diana and Gene was unlikely; the two had been steadily growing apart. It seemed that Diana grew discouraged about the fact that Gene Simmons would not totally commit himself to her.

"They would have fights all the time," John Mackey, a paralegal at Loeb and Loeb, recalled. "And then 24 hours later they were back together again. They never really lived together in Beverly Hills, though. Gene was staying at the house, and when Diana was in town, she would stay at the Beverly Hills Hotel. He might spend the night there, or she might spend it at the house. But living together was, for some reason, not something she wanted to do. She wasn't willing to go that far with him, let him have that much control over her."

Diana asked reporter Arianna Stassinopoulos, author of a biography about Maria Callas, "What is it inside of me that makes me want the commitment of a relationship, that makes me want much, much more than sex from a man? I think it's the nature of every woman that we want to attach ourselves to someone. Sometimes I feel that if we were to look at ourselves under a microscope, we would be a bit like leeches."

Apparently, like Ryan O'Neal before him, Gene Simmons was perplexed and often irritated by Diana's diva mentality. His previous girlfriend, Cher, was much more down to earth and levelheaded. Often, Diana would find one of her male employees sharing a soft drink with Gene, which would unnerve her.

"Don't you have a job to do?" she would chastise the employee.

"Uh, sorry, Miss Ross."

"Don't you Miss Ross me, just do your job."

Gene—or Genie, as she was calling him by this time—would often take Diana aside and suggest that perhaps she was too tough on her staff. However, she wasn't exactly eager for Gene to tell her how to run her organization.

When she insisted that "they are the help," Gene would usually tell her to "shut up." He wasn't one to mince words with her.

Sometimes, though, Diana's eccentricities were amusing. Once, she and Gene walked into Nirvana restaurant in New York and asked for a table by the window so that they could have a view of Central Park. There wasn't one immediately available so they accepted a table elsewhere. When the waiter returned with their drinks, he couldn't find them. They had picked up the table and moved it next to a window.

Finally, Diana decided to break off with Gene. It was quick and quite mysterious. Perhaps Diana's decision was hastened by her apparent jealousy of Cher. One of Cher's children has said that Diana suspected that Gene and Cher spent time together in Simmons' Manhattan penthouse (which Cher had designed in black and marble tile). If Diana believed that Cher and Gene had resumed their affair (which they hadn't), this misunderstanding apparently marked not only the end of Diana's romance with Gene Simmons but also her relationship with Cher.

"Diana was never the same after that," said Cher's child. "She used to be so much fun when she and my mother would be together. But after that, she disappeared. My mother could never understand why she was so upset."

Diana said of Gene, "I've ended a relationship after two and a half years because the commitment, that total sharing that I want, was not there."

Cher, who is known not to have much time for what she calls "life's bullshit," probably thought Diana was being rather silly and melodramatic.

When Ron Delpit, a popular Las Vegas reporter, tried to obtain Diana Ross for a charity concert, she informed him personally that she did not have time. He recalled, "She said she didn't give a shit about the charity because her kids were in Las Vegas for the weekend and she wanted to spend her time with them, which I guess was understandable."

But when he told her that Cher's children were in town for the last concert and she brought them along to the event, he said that Diana Ross' reply was, "Who cares about Cher! She'll go to the opening of a hot dog stand!"

During this time, Diana allowed Michael Jackson to produce a single for her second RCA album, *Silk Electric*, a dreary affair that, with the exception of the Jackson song, she produced herself. This was her most boring, ponderous album, and an indication of things to come from Diana Ross at RCA.

After *The Wiz*, Michael's *Off the Wall* album sold seven million copies in 1979. The more famous he became, the more difficult it must have been for Diana Ross to continue a friendship with him. People who know her well say that she and her career must be the center of attention in any relationship, or she is simply not happy. In 1985 at a taping of Smokey Robinson's television series, "The Motown Revue," someone asked executive producer Suzanne dePasse how Diana felt about *her* work.

Suzanne replied, "What? Us talk about me? That never happens. We only talk about her."

By 1980, Michael Jackson had become so reclusive and eccentric that he had no friends, least of all Diana Ross. He spent most of his time alone except for his animals and a staff that didn't dare disagree with him because they knew how fragile and sensitive he was and they wanted to keep their jobs.

Michael Jackson appropriated Diana Ross' early '70s speaking voice, an uncertain, shy, slightly inarticulate way of communicating. It's been reported over and over again that he had plastic surgery so he could look like her as well.

One chauffeur in Hollywood tells the story of Michael demanding that he be called Miss Ross while being driven around Beverly Hills. "I said, 'Mr. Jackson, would you like . . .' and he cut me off," said the chauffeur. "He said, 'Please, call me Miss Ross.' So I did."

Jackson certainly looks more like Diana Ross now than he did before the surgery—with the almond-shaped eyes, the tweezed, arched eyebrows, the high cheekbones, the nose tapered, tapered and tapered again—actually it's much more pixie-like than Diana's. Now, it seems, Michael Jackson doesn't continue to have cosmetic surgery so he will look like Diana Ross. He has said privately that he has it so he won't look like his father Joseph Jackson.

"I'd do anything so as not to end up looking like him," Michael told one friend. "I couldn't bear to look at myself in the mirror if I had to have my father staring back at me."

As adults, the Jacksons possess a strong resemblance to their father, Joseph, and, for years, Michael dreaded that, with age, he too would look like this man. He and Joe have been estranged since 1981, after the last of their management contracts expired. Joe Jackson blamed Michael for breaking up the family act, The Jacksons, and accused him of betraying and abandoning his brothers. Michael also felt unhappy with the way Joe treated his wife, Michael's mother, Katherine.

After splitting with his father, Michael received an offer from Diana to have his career managed through her RTC Management. "I'm available, Michael. Why don't you let *me* manage you? I don't know if I can handle an artist as major as you, but I'll bet I could. So, what do you think? Huh? Good idea?"

"Uh . . . Thanks anyway, Diana." Michael realized that Diana had her hands full with her own career and he wasn't about to risk his by having her be responsible for it.

(At one point, Diana also wanted to take recording star Prince under her wing. "I wanted him to be my protégé," she said. "I tried to reach his manager to get him a tour with me, but I could never reach him.")

Michael Jackson is childlike and innocent in many ways, but he is also shrewd and manipulative, qualities he and Diana Ross share. Like Diana, he has also worked hard to be accepted by the white world and has professed to being color-blind. The black press views such comments as thinly veiled excuses meant to keep blacks out of their business affairs.

When Joe Jackson said, "I need white help in dealing with the corporate structure at CBS," Michael insisted that he was "sickened to hear him talk like that. It turns my stomach." But after firing his father, Michael worked almost exclusively with Jewish managers and attorneys. After Berry Gordy, Diana Ross has also worked mostly with Jewish managers and attorneys.

Michael enjoys being in the company of women like Diana Ross, Elizabeth Taylor and Katharine Hepburn, all of whom feel they have been unfairly attacked by the media over the years. He feels they can relate to what he's going through in his own life. They enjoy being with him because he flatters them and is awed by them.

Diana's second album for RCA was shaping up to be a disaster, mostly songs that were recorded for the first one but deemed unacceptable at that time. She needed something from a hit writer/producer that would help make it a success. She asked Michael to create a song for her. He agreed and, while returning from London where he'd been working with Paul McCartney on their hit, "Say, Say, Say," wrote a kinky song titled "Muscles." The song's lyrics tell of the joys of a man's muscles "all over your body."

Michael wanted to co-produce this song with Diana, but she was against the idea. Perhaps she felt "A Michael Jackson production" would be better accepted by record-buyers at this time, or she was trying to encourage him to assert his independence. At any rate, Diana insisted that he alone produce the song.

Michael was greatly intimidated by Diana in the studio and couldn't bear to order her around.

"I just can't, Diane," he insisted. "I just can't tell you what to do!"

"You're the man," Diana insisted. "You're the boss on this one."

What a pair these two were. Michael, too awed by her stardom to tell Diana what to do, and Diana, too independent to do anything he commanded anyway, even if he could manage to utter the words.

"But it's really shocking to me," she had to admit later, "that this guy can be so shy. Why does he have to whisper like that?"

Though Diana's voice sounds mushy and indistinguishable on "Muscles," it was a huge hit. She was right in her calculations: *Silk Electric* was a gold album but would have turned into a financial disaster were it not for "Muscles"—which was eventually nominated for a Grammy—since there were no other hits to be found on it.

"He spends a lot of time—too much time—by himself," Diana told writer Gerri Hirshey after "Muscles" was issued. "I try to get him out. I once rented a boat and took my children and Michael on a cruise. Michael has a lot of people around him, but he's very afraid. I don't know why."

Despite the fact that Michael has repeatedly said that Diana is "like a mother-lover-friend" to me, the two have never had a sexual relationship. "It's all been in Michael's head," said a friend of his who would only speak anonymously. "The fantasy of making love to Diana Ross is appealing, but the actual thought of such a thing probably isn't. He is too intimidated by her to ever think of making a pass at her."

Perhaps Diana put her feelings about Michael in perspective when she told one of her audiences during a Los Angeles engagement, that " 'Muscles' was written for me by Michael Jackson. But I don't know whether it's supposed to be *his* fantasy or mine."

Michael, shy and skittish when off stage, has always envied Diana's stage presence and the way she is able to mingle with her fans in the audience during a show. Certainly when he is on stage, Jackson is in his element. But to actually go out among the fans, it's almost too much for him to comprehend. "I'm too scared to do that," he told her. "I don't know how you do it."

Diana could only smile. She knows that she's the happy, bright picture of poise and elegance when she's on stage, as long as everything goes well. Otherwise, the painting darkens somewhat.

During the summer months of 1982, Diana toured Europe to promote "Muscles" and her current album, *Silk Electric*. The tour got off to a rocky start in London at the Wembley Stadium on June 2. Diana was particularly edgy because the sound system was not up to her standards. Critic Moira Petty reported that she "spent far too long spitting and snarling like a rabid kitten."

During the performance before 9,000 people, Diana stopped the show and began shouting at the sound crew. "What's wrong with you people?" she screamed. "What is *wrong* with you! I have just about *had* it with you!" Then she knocked one of the sound monitors off its platform and off stage with a kick the reporter said was "worthy of Pelé."

Needless to say, most members of her audience were stunned. An unexpected intermission was called.

The next day, all the British newspapers panned Diana for her actions. "It was the shoddiest outburst of show business tantrums I have ever seen," wrote Peter Hold for the *London Standard*.

A couple of days later, Diana held a press conference to apologize and explain. "I think I handled it badly. I wanted it to be perfect. I'm not perfect. I'm normal."

Almost 20 years had passed since Diana Ross and Berry Gordy drove through an affluent white neighborhood outside of Detroit and she confessed to him, "I would love to live in this kind of place." In those years, certainly most of her fantasies of wealth and security had been realized, but she was still dreaming about and hungering for more.

Now she wanted to be part of the so-called "Manhattan A-List," people who are immediately recognized by the impeccable clothes, well-coiffed heads and noteworthy jewelry. Maitre d's and salespeople fawn over them. Heads turn when they walk into a room, not only because they look so elegant but because they exude an air of self-confidence. No matter what they feel inside, they give the impression that what they have, they deserve. Though Diana has great flair and can be extremely persuasive when trying to impress a reporter who makes an ordinary wage, or a "hometown" Beverly Hills waiter who's a diehard fan, she doesn't seem at ease in the company of that "A" group she desperately wants to be a part of, as though she fears she'll be unmasked as a fraud.

For instance, true socialites usually don't care when they make mistakes. They feel they don't have to. They're *socialites*, after all. But Diana Ross does not allow herself the luxury of shrugging off a mistake. When she said "vanilla envelope" instead of "manila envelope" on "The Tonight Show," she didn't realize the faux pas. Upon reviewing the tape, she became embarrassed and angry at herself. Berry Gordy had insisted that she improve her vocabulary in the '60s, and she worked at this task constantly because he had told her that mispronouncing a word was a sign of her greatest enemy, ignorance. She once borrowed a reporter's *New York Times Book Review* section in order to make a good impression. "I just *love* to read," she cooed. "I hope you don't mind."

She had spent many hours working on her diction, insisting that she didn't want listeners to have a clue to her race from her voice. "Nobody talked right in Detroit where I grew up," she had said. "I'm going to work on that. I swear it."

She took up tennis because her first husband, Bob Silberstein, once jokingly told her that's what wealthy people did. She delved into classical music so that her rich socialite friends would not think of her as "just" a rock and roll singer. She would attend openings at the Metropolitan Museum of Art, more to mingle with the elite than to admire the art.

Diana's efforts at improving herself were certainly in line with Berry Gordy's artistic development classes, whose purpose was to make his Motown acts more acceptable to white audiences. He considered that good business. Though he was trying to appeal to whites with his entertainment, Gordy was still always involved in black causes. In turn, Diana also had a certain black consciousness in the '60s. But in contrast to her impassioned plea for racial equality 20 years ago, Diana now rarely, if ever, publicly supports black causes or openly identifies with them. It's not that she is ashamed of her background in the Brewster Projects, but she does want to make certain that her public realizes that she has left all of those memories and influences far behind.

In her nightclub act, Diana's humor sometimes betrays her. As she stands dripping in furs and jewels, she has joked: "People ask me, 'Whatever happened to Diana Ross from the Brewster Projects? Whatever happened to that girl?' You know what I say to that?

"I say, 'Who?' "

In one interview, she observed, "I think black people are completely negative about the black situation. Everything bad that happens to them, they blame it on being black."

To help introduce her to East Coast society, she once asked Andy Warhol to escort her to Manhattan's "in" spots. When he suggested the Othello Club where he had once taken Elizabeth Taylor, she loved the idea. She also wanted to go to trendy New York gay leather bars. He told her that even *he* was afraid to go to such places, but she insisted that she would protect him "because I'm not scared of anything." However, when Warhol made plans, Diana would bow out, usually with little advance notice.

One of the people Diana most wanted to meet was Jacqueline Onassis, whom she had admired for years. Former employees remember she wished to learn the identity of the designer of Jackie's clothes and the name of the wine Jackie drank. Friends have remembered she dreamed that she, too, could marry a multi-millionaire and become one of the world's most powerful women. "Jackie has yachts and power," Diana said privately. "I want all of that, and more."

Michael Browne, Ross' former assistant road manager, remembered that Diana had been trying to "pull all kinds of strings among New York society to arrange an introduction." He said that they finally met at a party at the 21 Club in Manhattan in the early '80s. They exchanged telephone numbers and agreed to meet for lunch.

According to Browne, a few weeks later, Jacqueline Onassis telephoned Diana Ross at her RTC office. Diana's employees were quite impressed that the woman considered by many to be the most well-known in the world was holding on the line for "Miss Ross." But, according to Browne, Diana did not hurry to respond. "Tell Jackie I'm busy right now," she told her secretary. "I'll have to call her back."

Browne claims that Diana then sat behind her desk, grinning at the fact that she was keeping the former First Lady waiting. Jackie held on the line for a couple of minutes before Diana had her secretary tell her that she was too busy to talk at that moment. Forty-five minutes later, she returned the call.

Later, when they became friendlier, Jackie confided to Diana that she wanted to have more children, but that she couldn't because of what she called "female problems."

According to writer Diane Albright, who interviewed Michael Browne, "After she learned about Jackie's secret wish to have more children, Diana insisted privately that she wanted to have more children herself. She already had three, and had complained incessantly every time she was pregnant. She never talked about having more children until she and Jackie discussed it. Then she started talking about it constantly, as if there was some kind of competition going on. Now Diana wanted to marry someone like Onassis and give birth to more children, copy Jackie and then go one step further."

When Jackie Onassis became a book editor, she asked Diana Ross if she was interested in writing her memoirs. Naturally,

Diana was flattered that Jackie would deem her life interesting enough. But she turned her down saying, "it's not time yet."

Then, on February 8, 1983, Diana met with Jacqueline, now an editor at Doubleday, at the Doubleday offices in Manhattan. Her mission: to have the publisher stop publication of a Diana Ross photo-biography, which had been under contract since December 1982. Diana was joined by Irving "Swifty" Lazar, a high-powered Hollywood literary agent. Two other Doubleday editors were in attendance.

Jackie wore the kind of conservative suit she prefers when working. Diana had wrapped herself in a full-length white mink coat, which she kept on when she sat for the meeting. The contrast of her mahogany skin and black mane against the starkness of the soft white fur made her appearance striking. She had on diamond earrings and a matching necklace.

She explained to Jackie and the others that she was now interested in writing her own story after all, and that by publishing the other, unauthorized, work Doubleday's chances of acquiring "the official book" would be placed in jeopardy.

"What kind of project do you have in mind?" Jackie wanted to know.

"An inspirational book," Diana said. "A biography, but with no personal details whatsoever."

"No personal details whosoever?" Jackie asked.

"None."

According to one of the principals, Jackie wanted to know what kind of "biography" has "no personal details." Diana responded that she wanted to share with her public sage observations about life and love, but as they relate to other people, certainly not to herself. She was quite serious.

Jackie did not want to insult her by dismissing the proposal as being silly, even though later Jackie would say that she realized that it was.

"That's an idea," she offered sweetly. "Perhaps we can talk about it further."

The other two Doubleday executives looked at each other and tried to suppress a smile.

"Let's have lunch sometime," Jackie said.

Diana beamed. "Oh yes, let's do," she agreed, eagerly.

"But what about that other book?" Lazar wanted to know.

"Yes," Diana piped in. "Will you take care of that?"

"Oh, we'll work something out," Jackie suggested. "Don't you worry about it."

According to others present at the meeting, after Diana and

her agent left, Jackie rolled her eyes, shook her head and declared, "Oh, my, my, *my!*"*

(A few years later, Jackie signed Michael Jackson to write his autobiography which, as it turned out, wasn't much more revealing than the one Diana had planned.)

As much as Ross enjoys publicity, she prefers that it be limited to her public persona. She does not appreciate documentation of her life and career unless it's with her approval. Her life experiences might make for an interesting story, but she prefers that if it can't be told from her viewpoint and with her authorization, it not be told at all. Once, a girl gave her a massage and happened to say, "Gosh, what a great story your life is going to be!"

"This is my *life*. This is *not* a fucking story," Diana snapped at her.

When *Dreamgirls* opened on Broadway in December 1981, she was particularly angry because the show seemed based on her early days with The Supremes. The play told the story of three girls from Chicago who became a popular singing act, The Dreamettes, and then The Dreams. The man who owns the company that records their songs has an affair with the group's lead singer, Deena Jones. After firing an overweight and argumentative member of the group, the boss makes Jones the focus of the act and elevates her to stardom. The group is rechristened Deena Jones and The Dreams. Jones eventually leaves for a solo career. She then stars in a motion picture about the life of a legendary entertainer.

It didn't take much imagination to figure out that *Dreamgirls* was, at least in part, the story of Diana Ross and The Supremes. The late Michael Bennett (*A Chorus Line*), who directed *Dreamgirls*, once admitted that he was a Supremes fan and attended the final performance of Diana Ross and The Supremes in Las Vegas in 1970.

The Deena Jones character was a '60s Diana Ross clone in every visual, clichéd way, flailing arms, thick eye make-up, heavy duty wigs, and a mouthful of sparkling teeth. Sheryl Lee Ralph, who played Deena Jones, did a masterful job of mimicry. She admitted, "I did deny it over and over again whenever anyone asked if it was true that the character I played was Diana.

*The Doubleday photo-biography in question was published in March 1985 under the title *Diana* by J. Randy Taraborrelli and was made a selection of the Literary Guild.

And it was all a big lie because it really was Diana I was playing and trying to look like and sound like.''

"But I wasn't even consulted," Diana Ross complained.

In 1982, Sheryl Lee Ralph finally met Diana Ross at the Russian Tea Room, a fashionable restaurant next to Carnegie Hall in New York. Ralph, who was at a pay phone when Diana came sweeping by, was excited about the opportunity to meet the woman she "portrayed" on Broadway.

"Oh, excuse me, Miss Ross," she said very politely. "I just wanted to introduce myself. My name is Sheryl . . ."

"Ralph," Diana said, cutting her off. "I know you. You're from *that* show."

And then Diana just rushed by her.

Not only did she refuse to see the show ("I don't want to validate it in that way"), but Diana would not allow her daughters to view the musical. From what she had heard, she decided that the show was a gross distortion of the facts surrounding her rise to fame and not one she wanted the girls to relate to their mother. Diana's harsh words against *Dreamgirls* only served to focus even more attention on it.

In contrast, Mary Wilson attended many performances, thoroughly enjoyed the show, and often told the press she thought it was wonderful. Michael Jackson reported to "Entertainment Tonight" that Diana asked him to see the show for her. Afterwards, he said it was the "most fantastic thing I've ever seen in my life."

"I don't want people to walk away thinking it's the truth," Diana told Stephen Holden of *The New York Times*, "because I don't think they know what the truth is."

Diana Ross felt somehow betrayed because Suzanne dePasse was managing the star of *Dreamgirls*, Jennifer Holiday (who played the Florence Ballard character and won a Tony Award for her work), and record industry mogul David Geffen (an ex-boyfriend of Cher's) was its chief financial backer ("We've been almost intimates," Diana claimed). Yet they hadn't consulted her about the play.

"Damn it," Diana said to writer Gerri Hirshey, "this is serious for me. And it hurts me if it's turned to ice cream. There's pain there, and there are wonderful things. It's like in my song 'Mirror Mirror,' where I said, 'You turned my life into a paperback novel.'

"If [only] there [was] some way I can make sure that they [her children] understand from *my* point of view what it's all about. My relationship with Berry, especially.'' In her feature about Diana, Hirshey wrote, ''Real tears began to bead up on her mascaraed lower lashes.''

Chapter

25

In EARLY 1983, Suzanne dePasse began to mount an NBC television special to celebrate Motown's 25th anniversary. Since Gordy started the label in 1959, it had only been 24 years, but dePasse decided not to wait. Naturally, most of the famous Motown alumni were expected to appear. Some of the others, like Mabel John, The Marvelettes, David Ruffin, Eddie Kendricks, The Contours and The Vandellas, were not invited to perform.

Diana Ross wanted nothing to do with "Motown 25—Yesterday, Today, Forever," as the special was called, for two reasons: she felt awkward about the fact that she hadn't seen Berry Gordy since she left Motown for RCA two years before and she was afraid of alienating herself from RCA Records president Robert Summers. She realized that singing the praises of her former record company and boss would not ingratiate herself to Summers.

But the Motown press machinery had already begun planting stories that she was going to be a "special guest star." Her public expected her to show some gratitude to the company and to the man most responsible for her fame and fortune. Now she was backed into an untenable position. If she didn't make an appearance, it might look worse for her.

The night before the taping, Diana was dining in a Los Angeles restaurant when she saw one of Gordy's former attorneys. She greeted him warmly and asked if he would be her guest at the show. He declined. She then said that she was not anxious to see Berry Gordy, and were it only for his benefit, she would never appear on the program, "but I think maybe I owe it to the other artists. I don't know for sure, but I think I do."

After Diana Ross' appearance was confirmed by executive producer Suzanne dePasse, the reunion of the rest of The Supremes had to be organized. Cindy Birdsong's participation would not be a problem, but Mary Wilson's would.

Mary Wilson was suing Berry Gordy and Motown over her right to use the name "Supremes" to promote herself and her nightclub act. In September 1977, she had filed a multi-million dollar lawsuit against Gordy, the first of many such actions over subsequent years, in which she claimed that she was "the sole remaining member of 'The Supremes' and, as such, the sole remaining originator of such name," and demanded that Gordy assign to her "full and complete ownership and control of the name including all right, title and interest therein."

Berry held the position that Janie Bradford, a Gordy employee, was the "originator" of "The Supremes" name, not Mary Wilson. Rather than fight Mary, he settled by offering her a solo contract. When Motown released her first album in 1979, it flopped. After a single titled "Red Hot" sold only 6,120 copies, Gordy unceremoniously dropped Mary from the label. He thought that would be the end of it, but Mary persists to this day in trying to get The Supremes' name for herself.

So Mary Wilson and Berry Gordy had been enemies and wanted nothing to do with one another. Nevertheless, if Gordy and dePasse wanted to capitalize on Wilson's history and exploit her past glory, then they had to have her on the show.

Suzanne dePasse telephoned Mary Wilson personally to convince her to appear. Over the years, dePasse has taken on much of Berry Gordy's mythic stature. She can be intimidating and often will not take "no" for an answer. She worked her way up to president of Motown Productions and was second only to Berry.

"It has been very sweet to see the expressions on people's faces when they realize I'm the boss," she once said. "They understand black women singing and dancing and acting. They understand black women sweeping and ironing. But they don't understand a black woman telling them what to do."

It's a tribute to dePasse's tenacity that she was able to cajole all of the artists into agreeing to participate in this program despite their hostility toward Berry. (She said she had to do so much begging she had "scabs on my knees.") She explained to Mary Wilson that she had not called sooner because she first tried to secure a commitment from Diana Ross, "and it's much harder to get her, you know, because she's such a superstar." Mary Wilson was put off by dePasse's audacity, but consented to appear on the program provided she was given a solo spot singing Barbra Streisand's "How Lucky Can You Get." Mary had apparently not only appropriated Diana's Josephine Baker obsession but her Barbra Streisand fixation as well.

The show would begin taping at 6:00 P.M. at the Pasadena Civic Center on Friday, March 25, 1983, the day before Diana Ross' 39th birthday. At about 5:30, one-half hour before it was time to let the audience into the auditorium, Diana Ross arrived to rehearse with her former singing partners. Diana had a stomach flu. She was wearing a full-length white mink and clutching a bottle of Courvoisier brandy when she arrived, "for my nerves," she explained to one of Suzanne dePasse's assistants. For each former Supreme, Diana granted a quick, obligatory hug and a blown kiss.

"What have you done to your face?" Diana asked Mary Wilson. "You look different. What have you done?"

Before Mary could respond, Diana turned her back and came face to face with Mary's mother, Johnnie Mae. She sized up the older woman from head to toe, and then turned and walked away without saying a word to her. Mary and her mother were left speechless. Diana then went over to Cindy and embraced her warmly.

Suzanne dePasse informed Diana that because of the lateness of the hour, there was practically no time for a worthwhile rehearsal. Diana deliberated and said, "Well, then, we'll simply have to skip The Supremes' medley. The girls will be happy with 'Someday We'll Be Together.' "

She motioned to her former singing partners but didn't look at them. Suddenly it was 1967 all over again; Diana was calling all of the shots. The "girls" whispered to one another angrily.

Suzanne dePasse and producer Don Mischer took pains to explain in great detail to "Miss Ross" exactly what was expected of her. (DePasse may consider herself a close friend of Diana's, but she always calls her "Miss Ross" in public.) Because of Diana's intimidating reputation, most television producers are relieved and grateful she is actually standing before them. They are loathe to give her instructions for fear that she'll storm off the set, even though she never has.

Diana was to introduce all of the acts for the big finale, and then bring Berry Gordy onto the stage from the audience. "We'll prompt you on the TelePrompTer," dePasse offered.

"No, don't do that," Diana said. "Just give me a list of names and I'll memorize them all."

After a five-minute haphazard rehearsal of "Someday We'll Be Together," during which Diana did not acknowledge the presence on the stage of either Mary or Cindy, the three went their separate ways. Diana was then told that, during the taping, she would be entering from the back of the theater and would walk down the center aisle while singing "Ain't No Mountain High Enough." A stand-in had been hired to demonstrate this maneuver. The back door swung open and a young black girl in jeans and sweatshirt came walking down with an elegant gait, her shoulders hunched up to her ears and a big smile plastered on her face. Diana ignored the impersonation, but others tried to stifle their laughter.

Finally it was time to open the doors to the public.

Meanwhile, backstage, Cindy Birdsong found that she had been assigned a small, cluttered dressing room with Mary Wells. Mary Wilson had been given a room with an obscure female Motown artist she did not know. It was obvious that some mis-informed Motown employee had thought that it was Mary *Wells*, not *Wilson*, who had sung with Cindy Birdsong in The Supremes, just another example of Motown's indifference to them.

Soon, Mary and Cindy's escorts arranged it so that the two could share a dressing room, one a great distance from Diana Ross' private and much more lavish quarters where she sipped brandy and con-sumed cherry cough drops. To make matters worse, Mary and Cindy were told that they were not allowed to visit "Miss Ross" or any of the other "bigger stars" like Smokey Robinson, Marvin Gaye and Stevie Wonder in their dressing rooms.

Mary became frustrated and antagonized, especially when she learned that the solo she had been promised had been cancelled. She found solace in champagne. Soon she was telling everyone who would listen that "there's gonna be fireworks tonight. Just wait and see."

Finally, Mary, Cindy and their escorts decided to go to the back of the building, climb through bushes and shrubbery in their long formal wear, and make their way to the front of the Civic Center. They were trying to fake an "entrance," as if they were just arriving by limousine. "Oooh, look at all those tele-vision cameras," Mary gushed as she picked weeds from her black bugle-beaded gown. Cindy, struggling to keep up with her, just smiled graciously.

The fans behind the roped-off area in front of the theater ig-nored both ladies as they sauntered down the red carpet, their heads held high. Finally, one of their escorts hollered out, "Look, it's two of The Supremes!" Immediately, cameras started clicking and fans started screaming.

"Oh, yes, yes, *yes*!" Mary cooed. "We love you *all*! It's *wonderful* to be here tonight! Just *wonderful*!"

Berry and Diana, with a little more finesse, had a limousine pull around to the back of the theater and drive them to the front.

"If we're gonna do this, we should act like we're arriving in style," Berry said.

The program was taped before an audience as a benefit for the National Association for Sickle Cell Anemia. There were many truly memorable moments including reunions of The Miracles and Jackson 5 and medleys by The Temptations, The Four Tops and Stevie Wonder, all pumping Motown magic.

The evening's best moment, however, was Michael Jackson's awe-inspiring, almost surreal performance of "Billie Jean." Jackson refused to appear on the show until Berry personally promised that he would be allowed to perform this, the only non-Motown number of the evening, and also have final say over the edit that would be broadcast. In a black silvery jacket (which he later gave to Sammy Davis, Jr.) and matching baggy, tuxedo pants, he put on an imaginative display of theatrics that brought down the house. When this performance was telecast, it was the first time most of America became aware of Michael Jackson's galvanizing, magnetic stage personality.

Mary and Cindy were slated to deliver a weak speech honoring Motown's songwriters and producers. But Mary was unhappy with the material written for them and took this opportunity to test her resourcefulness. She saluted the writers and producers and with all the panache of a cat-burglar and the poise of a professional newscaster, Mary totally ignored the TelePrompTer and began to ad lib, "I couldn't be here tonight without mentioning some of the people who are not with us . . ." Cindy averted her eyes.

As the producers and writers ran about frantically trying to figure out where she was getting her words from, Mary continued her impromptu but beautifully delivered tribute to "Mom" and "Pops" Gordy, Berry's parents, and Paul Williams, a member of The Temptations who, distraught over finances and failing health, put a gun to his head and killed himself in 1971 at the age of 34. (Williams, who died barely two blocks from Motown's original Hitsville offices, is credited with discovering Diana Ross in the Brewster Projects.)

Gordy, dePasse and producer Don Mischer looked on in utter exasperation as she concluded, "I couldn't be here tonight without mentioning one lady that I love very very much, Flo. Florence Ballard." The Civic Center audience burst into applause. It had been the only mention of Ballard's name all evening. "She's not here with us tonight but I know that wherever she is, she's up there [a finger snap] *Wooo! Doing it!*" It was an emotional, heartfelt speech.

It was also edited from the final broadcast and, hence, never seen by the viewing audience.

Later in the show, British rock star Adam Ant, a non-Motown artist, performed his rendition of The Supremes' "Where Did Our Love Go." Watching from the wings, Diana told Suzanne dePasse, "I'm goin' out there."

"What? No, Diane, please . . ." Suzanne began.

But before dePasse could finish, Diana was on stage doing a solo bump-and-grind routine. The audience may have thought that this was part of the show. One look at Adam Ant's face would have told them it was not. It's to his professional credit that, regaining his composure and without missing a beat, he started dancing toward her. Diana thought that what she had done was spontaneous and fun. Others didn't agree.

Finally it was time for Diana, who entered from a back door, to saunter down the aisle as instructed. She wore a short black satin skirt, low-cut silver-beaded jacket, rhinestone high-heeled shoes, and a white fox stole slung over her shoulder; her hair looked uncombed. The audience began to stand and cheer as she started "Ain't No Mountain High Enough." It was obvious, however, that something was wrong.

She appeared to be disoriented, bewildered and uncomfortable. Instead of the proud air of someone who had come back home triumphantly to family—like everyone else tried to do—she looked like she was trapped in the enemy's war zone. She had never appeared so awkward on television before. Her red lipstick was smeared onto her teeth and her tongue was beet-red from the cough drops she had been eating backstage. It was said that prior to going on, she had tried everything to get the dye off her tongue. But even brushing it with toothpaste didn't help. She even had a run in her stocking.

Once onstage, Diana tossed her fur to the floor as she continued "Ain't No Mountain High Enough."

"When you get out there, step on that fur," Richard Pryor told Mary as she waited in the wings.

"Yeah, kick that goddamn thing off the stage," someone else suggested.

"If *Miss Ross* forgets the words to the songs, you steal the song from her, Mary," another person hollered.

The Motown performers backstage were so caught up in their dislike of Diana Ross that they forgot one thing: she had opened doors for most of them. Without her, many of them might never have had a chance at the Copacabana, at "The Ed Sullivan Show," at crossing over into the lucrative pop music field. Many of her fellow performers had found it hard enough to forgive her competitive ways when she was a newcomer. The passing years had only added fuel to the bonfires of their misery: her apparent abandonment of Florence Ballard, her insistence on being the center of attention, her departure from Motown, her treatment of fellow performers, her self-isolation from people she had known for years.

Tonight, the frustrations of not being as successful as they thought they should be, of not getting as much money as they thought they had earned, of not getting Berry's attention when they thought they needed it, of not getting the right kind of promotion when they did get a release, all came to the fore, and their target was standing on the stage before them. Moreover, if they "got" Diana, they "got" Berry as well. They were looking for a David to attack Goliath, and they chose Mary Wilson for their task. They didn't have to twist her arm. She probably would have volunteered if they hadn't asked. She certainly shared their feelings.

Diana's singing seemed sluggish and off-key. Usually whenever she appeared in front of an audience, the interaction between star and audience turned electric. This time it was polite, but restrained, as though Diana was operating on low voltage and the audience could not become charged up. She seemed to sense it, too. When she started to pay tribute to Berry, she appeared hesitant and unsure of herself.

"It's a strange thing, but Berry has always felt that he's never been really appreciated. Strange thing." She hesitated. "I feel a little emotional." Her eyes filled with tears. Berry watched with a sad, resigned smile.

Diana continued. "But it's not about the people who leave Motown that's important. It's about the people who come back. And tonight everybody came back."

By now, Diana and Berry were looking at each other as though they were the only two people in the auditorium. Seemingly oblivious to the applause, her eyes still locked on Berry's, Diana started to raise a clenched fist. It seemed as though she was making the black power salute, but the movement was so tentative, no one could be sure what she meant by it.

Berry's expression never changed. He raised both fists to chin level, his hands opened wide, his fingers splayed, as if he were freeing a small bird.

The applause grew louder.

Gil Askey conducted the opening chords of "Someday We'll Be Together" and Diana began singing in a weak, thin voice. "Mary? And Cindy?" she called out, motioning to the sides of the stage. Cindy entered from stage left wearing a white silk and sequined gown. She beamed as she walked toward Diana singing and flashing a winning smile. She had never looked happier or more proud to be a Supreme.

"Go on out there, let her have it," someone goaded Mary as she waited for Birdsong to find her mark; Mary would make a grand entrance; she would not walk out at the same time as Cindy.

"Go 'head, Mary, sock it to her!"

Diana motioned to Mary with her index finger, and Mary came strutting out in a red sequined gown with a slit running up the side. Glitter was sprayed into her wig. Tall, dark and provocative looking, she smiled brightly and her presence seemed electric. It was obvious that since the evening Diana Ross left The Supremes, Mary Wilson had developed a keen, confident sense of herself as a performer. Now, 13 years after that night in Vegas when Berry promised her that her career was over, she looked for all the world like the greatest star on earth. The applause was loud and full.

Diana greeted both girls with a wide smile. "That's Mary Wilson," she pointed to her. "And Cindy Birdsong." It seemed that she was happy to be on stage with them. She took a few steps in front of them to her usual position. However, she didn't know Mary had told Cindy that whenever Diana stepped forward, they should do the same. The old days were gone.

Three times, Diana stepped in front of Mary and Cindy, and three times they joined her by her side. Diana also didn't know that Mary had told Cindy to sing very softly during the sound check when the microphone level was being adjusted. By doing that, when it came time for the actual performance, their mikes would be adjusted louder than Diana's.

Soon, Mary took over the lead on "Someday We'll Be Together" and Diana acted lost and disoriented. It wasn't going well. Suzanne dePasse sent Smokey Robinson out to save the moment. With Smokey present, The Supremes reunion was over and so was most of the tension, for the time being.

Diana then began bringing out the other acts as she had been instructed to do: "Richard Pryor, and Billy Dee, and The Temptations." Pryor walked out, kissed Diana on the lips. Finally, with the stage full of performers, Mary Wilson, caught up in the emotion of it all, called out, "Berry, come on down."

Diana grabbed Mary's wrist and pulled the microphone from her lips. "It's been taken care of," she scolded Mary sharply.

An audible gasp came up from the audience. Mary shot Diana a look of disbelief and then froze, stunned at this breach of professional etiquette. Backstage, Motown employees and friends waited for what was coming next.

"Didja' see that? Didja' see that?"

"I told ya' she'd do somethin' like that. Now you owe me a hundred bucks."

One of Berry Gordy's sons turned to a friend and said, "Looks like we might get another hair-pulling fight like the good old days."

Rather than back off, Mary proceeded to sing even louder than before.

"How long will it take for you to come down here, Black?" Diana shouted to Berry, using her nickname for him.

Berry, in a rumpled brown satin tuxedo, came down the center aisle closely followed by three bodyguards.

Once he was up on stage, he and Diana shared a kiss and a long, warm hug. Then Berry and Michael Jackson embraced. "You finally learned how to sing, huh?" he whispered in Mary Wilson's ear when she greeted him.

There were hugs, kisses and handshakes from the other stars and it seemed, if only for a minute or two, that all of these people genuinely loved each other. Artists who had left the company years ago amid acrimonious personal quarrels and contract disputes—The Four Tops, Martha Reeves, Mary Wells, Marvin Gaye, Michael Jackson, even Diana Ross—were together once again, holding hands, crying and saluting the man most responsible for their fame and fortune. It was difficult to hang on to all of the past anger and hostility during this emotional, triumphant moment.

Through it all, Diana struggled to maintain control. "Stand back," she ordered. "Don't shove. Watch out. Move over." No one paid any attention to her. Finally, she retreated to a platform on the orchestra's level above the group of joyous artists and musicians. As everyone sang "Reach Out and Touch," she swayed back and forth above them.

After the show, one of the producers asked that everyone remain on stage for a *Life* magazine photographer. Diana quickly scurried from her perch and worked her way front and center.

After the photo session, as the cast filtered out of the studio, Diana looked at her watch and discovered that it was past midnight. It was officially her birthday.

She exclaimed, "Guess what, everyone? It's my birthday. It's my birthday!"

But only a few people gathered around her to wish her well. Most of the other artists, musicians, writers and producers just turned and walked away.

Chapter

26

"DID YOU SEE what that bitch did to me?" Mary let go in the limousine on the way to the party. "Give me some champagne. Get me a cigarette. How dare she? How *dare* she?"

After the "Motown 25" special, Berry Gordy and everyone else involved, except for Diana Ross, went to a lavish party. "In the '60s, it all happened so fast that we didn't have time to think about it," Gordy said. "But [on stage] I said, 'My God, what have we created here?' I looked around me on stage and, my goodness, the list was endless. I just said, 'Boy, oh boy!' "

It's difficult to know what Diana Ross really felt about the "Motown 25" special, since what really happened and what she apparently thought happened, are two very different things.

Diana Ross' point of view about the show was summed up in a media handout from RTC Management:

"It was amazing. There were some people there I hadn't seen in 13 years. The relationships were all so good. My kids even asked something like, 'Mommy, you know Uncle B.B. [they call Berry Gordy "Uncle B.B."] is like a daddy to everybody that was there.' And it's true. It was just real warm moments there. Michael and Stevie, they were all backstage with me and seeing Billy Dee after I hadn't seen him for a long time. We had a wonderful chat and even seeing Shelly Berger . . . Suzanne dePasse was crying backstage. It was just wonderful. I know that the people in the audience saw a glorious special, but they really didn't see everything . . ."

What had happened between Diana and Mary detracted from the importance of Motown's 25th anniversary and how Gordy and company changed the face of black music and pop culture with such an original, timeless sound. Some of Diana's associates have said that she was mystified as to why Mary Wilson "acted that way." She didn't understand that she was just as responsible for the fracas.

For the next few months, the media concentrated on the altercation between Diana Ross and Mary Wilson during The Supremes' reunion. "Only Ross' prima donna petulance prevented the event from being truly Supreme," wrote a reporter for *Us* magazine. The footage of The Supremes' "reunion" was edited down to just a few minutes for broadcast on NBC on May 16, 1983. The unused tape was locked away and only Berry Gordy and Suzanne dePasse have access to it.

"Motown 25" was the highest rated musical special in the history of television and won an Emmy as Outstanding Variety Program, proving that the public was dazzled by the warmth they saw among the artists and the performances they watched. No one but insiders knew of all of the angst surrounding "Motown 25."

Except for her press release from RTC, Diana said nothing to the media about what had transpired. But Mary, always loquacious with the press, used this event as an opportunity to bask in the spotlight once again. She announced that she would be writing her memoirs and would reveal "the real truth" about her relationship with "Diane." Suzanne dePasse thought that Mary's P.R. campaign was shameless and vowed never again to include her in a Motown television production.*

Since Diana attended "Motown 25," many Motown executives felt "closer" to her and wanted to be back in her life. Suzanne dePasse was suddenly more solicitous than ever, and when Diana appeared at Caesars Palace in Las Vegas three weeks after the special, there was Berry Gordy sitting at his old table, coming backstage, offering advice and criticism. She felt that, somehow, he was trying to control her again and she didn't like it.

Diana put an end to Berry's interference quickly by making it clear that he was welcome to come to her performances but that he would have nothing to do with her life. Though it wasn't a

---

*In the summer of 1985, Suzanne dePasse was planning a Smokey Robinson television program with Lily Tomlin as a guest. Tomlin wanted to do a take-off on The Supremes, using Mary Wilson and Cindy Birdsong. DePasse tried to reason with her, saying that Mary was not available. Tomlin was insistent. She would only do the show if she could have Mary there. "Then if we have to choose between having to put Mary Wilson on network TV again, and losing Lily Tomlin, I say we lose Tomlin," dePasse said. Tomlin did not appear on the show.

big blow-out, that brief confrontation put the relationship in a new perspective. Afterward, Berry and Diana continued to see and talk to each other as friends, and the girls got to see much more of their "Uncle B.B." Berry had said that it was difficult for him to stay angry at Diana for what she had done—leaving Motown—because they had, after all, shared so much over the years.

"Whatever she wants to do with her life," Berry said after "Motown 25," "she'll just have to do it. I can't worry about it anymore. I'm tired of worrying about Diane."

During this engagement in Las Vegas, Diana was still ill with the stomach flu she had during the taping of "Motown 25." Friends say she also seemed emotionally drained, perhaps from the anniversary experience. One night, during her performance of "Mirror, Mirror," she threw the microphone to the stage floor. Turning her back to the audience, she buried her face in her hands and began to sob quietly. Ringsiders heard her mutter to herself, "I can't go on, I just can't." She seemed to be on the edge of a breakdown.

Later during the engagement, she canceled some of her shows and checked into the Desert Springs Hospital in Las Vegas for rest and recuperation from a stomach ailment. Paul Anka filled in for her. She returned to the stage after a couple of nights.

Cindy Birdsong and John Whyman went to Las Vegas to visit Diana during this engagement. Birdsong, a born-again Christian, said that she hoped to "claim" Diana for Jesus Christ.

Though Birdsong and Whyman weren't able to tell Diana they were coming, they decided to go anyway. The night before the show, Berry arranged it so that Cindy, her son David Hewlett, and Whyman could sit at the booth usually reserved by Caesars Palace for him. They thought Diana's performance and their drinks would be complimentary. But since Diana was not aware of their presence in the audience, drinks and cover-charges were not paid for in advance. Neither Birdsong nor Whyman had any money on them at the time.

"Oh, no. What are we going to do when the check comes?" Cindy asked nervously.

"Leave it to me," John replied.

There is a standing regulation at Caesars Palace that whenever a star of Diana Ross' caliber is onstage, waiters and waitresses cannot serve food or drinks or collect money. As soon as she disappears for a costume change, the employees scatter all about the showroom doing their work as quickly as possible. Then, when she walks out again, the help freezes in its tracks and waits.

During one of these breaks, the bill was placed on Birdsong's table. As Diana performed, Whyman charmingly tried to convince the waiter that he and Birdsong were guests of Miss Ross and didn't have to pay for the show. A disagreement ensued with the Caesars' help, and then the showroom management. Diana watched the whole scene from the stage.

The check remained unpaid when John Whyman and Cindy Birdsong went backstage. Looking radiant, Diana Ross came out of her dressing room. Before saying anything to anyone, she turned to Whyman.

"Where's the check?"

He handed it to her.

"Have this taken care of immediately," Diana snapped at a female secretary. "And don't you ever embarrass me like that again. Don't you know who this is? This is Miss Cindy Birdsong, a guest of mine. Her check should never have been put on that table."

Cindy and Diana then went into the dressing room to talk privately.

Cindy Birdsong was the unpretentious, open-hearted woman Diana had selected to replace Florence Ballard in The Supremes. Diana and Cindy worked together for only two and a half years almost two decades ago, nevertheless, Diana has always been generous to Cindy. When Birdsong needs her, she responds.

After her career as a Supreme ended in the mid-'70s, Cindy Birdsong experienced a difficult life that, in some ways, mirrored the existence of her predecessor, Florence Ballard. Cindy's story is so typical of the downside of show business, where glamour and excitement are often just illusory and, unfortunately, sometimes very temporary.

"I had accumulated a lot of money in savings but I hadn't invested it wisely and soon I found myself broke," she said. "Also, at the time, I was going through a divorce. I couldn't handle it all. It was a very hard time for me because I started selling things to live. I had too much pride to go and find myself a job.

"After I lost my apartment, the car, the furs and all that stuff, my child and I went to live with my brother who had a bachelor apartment. I cut off contact with friends. I really felt that nobody cared about me anyway. I found that the friends I had made in show business were really fair-weather friends and I went into a deep state of depression. I thought about taking my life lots of times but I didn't do that. I know now it was because God had his hand on me. I felt that because of my son I had to go on. Most of the time I just stayed in the apartment in a desperate state. The world had loved me—and then it was all gone.''

Cindy Birdsong became a born-again Christian in the early '80s, which, she says, saved her and gave her new determination to live life to the fullest. Unlike Florence Ballard, she found a way to help herself and to feel happy and fulfilled. She obtained a job at the UCLA Medical Center as a lab aide and lived under her married name, her past occupation unknown to co-workers and neighbors.

Diana Ross had no idea that Cindy Birdsong had had such a difficult time, but finding out, she began to lend a helping hand. In the mid-'80s, Motown attempted to negotiate with Diana for the rights to her life story; dePasse was trying to mount a Supremes biography called ''Where Did Our Love Go?'' for television. Most observers felt that dePasse was being naïve if she thought that Ross would ever consider selling her life story to Motown, especially now that she was signed to RCA. Diana probably had no intention of doing so, but she procrastinated long enough for Cindy Birdsong to get $30,000 for her part of The Supremes' story. Then, apparently, Diana pulled out of the deal. The program still has not been produced. Birdsong didn't have to return the advance.

After leaving UCLA, Cindy began working for Suzanne dePasse at Motown Productions. For the most part, dePasse and her staff treated her with indifference and, often, even disrespect. Sadly, many of the upper-level Motown employees were so insecure in their jobs that they took great pleasure in making Birdsong—a former ''star''—feel small and insignificant in the big corporate structure. Ironically, she was once part of the group that helped put Motown on the map and allowed Gordy to hire so many young, ambitious people, many of whom went on to become executives. Finally, Birdsong quit Motown Productions to resume her singing career.

When she embarked on a comeback tour in London as a solo artist, she found herself stranded there with no money. Often, Cindy has borrowed money from Diana Ross and has always found a way to repay Diana's generosity to her. From Europe, Cindy tried to get in touch with Diana to ask for assistance, but Diana's telephone number had been changed and no one who had it wanted to give it to her. Rather than give her Diana's telephone number, Suzanne dePasse simply ignored Birdsong's calls.

Just at this time, ironically, *Us* magazine published a feature about Suzanne dePasse, in which she discussed how she was now in a power position at Motown because Cindy had introduced her to Berry Gordy in 1968. "She was my friend then and she's my friend now," dePasse said. "Let me put it this way: Cindy Birdsong can have anything I've got."

"Yeah, anything but Diane's phone number," Cindy cracked to a friend.

Eventually, John Whyman was able to get in touch with Diana and explain Cindy's dilemma to her. Cindy's story saddened her. "Here is a woman who never once has anything bad to say about anybody," Diana observed. "Anytime I can help her, I want to know about it."

Diana told Whyman to find out how much money Cindy needed and to get back in touch with her at the Sherry Netherland hotel in Manhattan. "Ask for Mrs. Blue," Diana instructed. "That's my code name." (Diana Ross uses aliases when she checks into hotels so that nosy fans won't bother her. On the East Coast, she's usually "Mrs. Blue," and on the West Coast it's "Doris Brewster.")

Birdsong managed to return to the United States without the help of her former singing partner. But she knows that she can call upon Diana Ross whenever she needs her.

Mary and Cindy were not the only people from the past Diana had seen. Janie Bradford, the woman who thought up the name "Supremes" in 1961, had asked Diana for some sort of financial assistance. Rather than loan her money, Diana suggested she write a song for the next Ross album. Bradford composed "I Am Me" with Freddie Gorman, who had written The Supremes' first record, "I Want a Guy."

Diana was not entirely happy with the song but redesigned it to her liking. She then included it on her *Silk Electric* album, and on the flip side of "Muscles," a single that sold over a million copies. Writers of flip sides make as much in royalties as the writers of hit sides, so Bradford and Gorman scored big.

Because her monetary status has far outscaled those of her former peers, Diana is often besieged by requests for financial assistance from people she knew in the early days. This is ironic, considering that most of the artists, writers and producers at Motown were not particularly fond of her. She has never really been able to understand how some people, like Florence Ballard, could allow their lives to get out of control. It's difficult for her to relate to the fact that, often, they have no choice.

Certainly this has never been the case with Diana Ross. Despite what she says happened at Motown toward the end of her career there—that she only had "a couple of hundred thousand dollars" to her name—she obviously has not had a moment of genuine concern about finances in 30 years. As for others who have not been so fortunate, she explained to a friend, "I just have to weed them out. I can't help everybody. I don't want to. Why should I? I think we're all responsible for ourselves."

By the summer of 1983, Diana was still trying to unload the white elephant on Maple Avenue that she had once called home. A Beverly Hills realtor had put the house on the market for $2.9 million, an extravagant price for a home that size. Since Diana purchased the house in 1970 for $300,000, she had added some rooms and made other renovations but it still wasn't worth ten times its original price. But she was certain she could command that amount simply because it was the "Diana Ross house" and, as she herself had asked, "Who wouldn't want to live there?" Although frustrated that she wasn't able to sell it, she still refused to lower the price.

She also wouldn't move back in. Whenever she came to town, she would stay in an expensive, beautifully decorated suite at the posh Beverly Hills Hotel on Sunset Boulevard as "Doris Brewster."

Because the house remained empty, there were always security problems at 701 Maple Avenue. Once, while "Miss Brewster" stayed at the Beverly Hills Hotel, she found herself in need of some clothing that remained at the house. An assistant went to fetch it. When the employee arrived, she was surprised by an intruder in Diana's master bedroom. For a moment, she thought her boss had somehow gotten there before her when she heard a flustered voice saying, "My dear, don't you know to knock before entering a room?"

A figure wearing one of Diana's Bob Mackie gowns whirled around to face the guest. It was a drag queen in full Diana Ross regalia—wig, make-up, gown, the works—even the voice. The assistant somehow managed to maintain her cool and telephone the police. Until the authorities arrived, the ersatz "Miss Ross" and the assistant admired the real Miss Ross' "*faaaaabulous*" gowns in the closet. The intruder was then hauled off and charged with felonious burglary . . . and bad taste!

After many more incidents, Diana decided in March 1983 to have John Mackey, a paralegal from Loeb and Loeb, live at the house. Having it occupied would lower her insurance premiums, which made the idea even more appealing to her.

From June 17 to 19, Diana taped a music video for "Pieces of Ice," her latest single, in Manhattan with director Bob Giraldi, best known for his work with Michael Jackson. Giraldi had directed the taping of the Pepsi commercial during which Michael's hair caught fire because of special effects. The video cost Anaid Film Productions $122,500, even though, said Diana of the concept, "It means nothing but it's interesting."

The song proved a commercial failure because no one, not even Diana, as she would admit later, understood the lyrics with their artsy and confusing imagery, "long entropic nights," "zebra lightning" and "Tunisia."

"Pieces of Ice" was culled from her third RCA album, *Ross*, produced in part by Steely Dan producer Gary Katz. The album's sales proved to be disappointing even though it was not really a bad record, just a dull one. The front jacket photograph seemed startling and unappealing: Diana with her hair looking like a fright wig, her eyes half-closed in a drug-like state, and her face tinted. The cover problem killed the album in the record stores. She was not smiling but, then again, she has not smiled on an album cover since 1971.

Though it seems odd, considering the image of Diana most people have in their minds—that of the broadly smiling diva—she dislikes photographs that show her teeth. Ten years ago, Diana began controlling photos of her that are released to the media. Since that time, the number of recent "authorized" pictures of her in which she is smiling could be counted on one hand.

Diana Ross of the '80s will probably best be remembered for her two Central Park concerts in July 1983. In a way, that's a pity because even though the first concert proved memorable, both performances showed more of her weaknesses than her strengths. Much has been written about these shows, but not about why Diana felt compelled to do a free concert in Central Park in the first place.

No doubt, given her Streisand fascination, she was inspired by Barbra's *A Happening in Central Park* concert-cum-album in July 1967. "There is only one person on the face of this planet that Diana Ross gives a whit about," reaffirmed John Mackey. "Barbra Streisand. And I always believed the real reason she did the concert was because Barbra had done one. I'm sure they still don't know one another, Diana and Barbra. Miss Ross could never handle a social encounter with Streisand. She would be too jumpy, nervous and intimidated."

It's said that the mere mention of Streisand's name unnerves Ross. Once, an employee of hers and one of her lawyers were waiting in Miss Ross' office when the employee mused, "I wonder what Miss Ross thinks of Barbra Streisand's new album." The lawyer threw his hands up. "Don't, *please don't*, ever mention that woman's name in Miss Ross' presence!" Apparently, Diana's staff knows that any discussion with her about Barbra Streisand that might lead to a comparison between careers is not a good idea.

CBS broadcast and recorded Streisand's Central Park special in 1967. A year later, Berry Gordy decided to have Diana Ross record the Motown *Funny Girl* album, and even suggested to Gil Askey that one day Ross do her own concert in Central Park.

By the '80s, many of Diana's show business peers had connected themselves to charitable causes. For instance, Stevie Wonder was a strong supporter of the Dr. Martin Luther King, Jr., Center for Social Change. Sammy Davis was known for his support of the Harlem-Dowling Children's Services, the United Negro College Fund, the NAACP and Operation Push. When *Ebony* magazine, however, asked Diana what charities she had been involved with, she had to answer, "I don't have one. I'm not involved in any project." That didn't bode well for a woman so concerned with public image.

It's not that she is a heartless person. Once, in New York City, Diana rode in a cab along Fifth Avenue when she noticed a drifter asleep on the steps of a church. When she reached her destination, and before getting out of the cab, she handed the driver a $50 bill and asked him to go back to the drifter and try to get him to a shelter. The cabby went back, woke the man up and said, "Here's 50 bucks from Diana Ross."

"Yeah, sure," the drifter mumbled before he rolled over and went back to sleep.

Diana had told the driver to keep the money for himself if the homeless man didn't want it, which is what he did.

Even though she may sometimes be charitable in private, publicly Diana has always been perceived as being self-centered. Diana Ross is much too savvy and shrewd about her image to fail to realize her music often is more popular than she is.

"But now I want people to think of me like they do Stevie [Wonder]," she said to associates. "I want to be an artist who is *appreciated*. Maybe I should do something for cancer research or something."

When Michael Jackson became identified in the media as a humanitarian, Diana must have been spurred on to do something to rectify her selfish public persona. "I really want to make a difference in my life," she insisted in interviews. "I'd like to serve mankind in some way. I want to be a tunnel," she said, though no one was ever certain what she meant by this. "I want to use my life to do good. I want to be exploited." She wasn't very convincing.

Soon, she started The Diana Ross Foundation which, according to the quickly released notices to the press, was "an organization through which Miss Ross will channel her philanthropic activities."

The first "philanthropic activity" would be a free concert in Central Park (Elton John had done one in 1980 and Simon and Garfunkel in 1981), produced by Diana Ross' production company, Anaid. Paramount Pictures would co-produce. Seven-and-a-half percent of the revenue from the sale of promotional items like T-shirts and posters and from the show's cable broadcast and satellite worldwide telecast would be used to reconstruct a children's park to be named after her at 81st Street and Central Park West. In the summer of 1983, she stood by New York Mayor Edward Koch's side at a press conference and made her announcement about the park.

"It's for the children," she said solemnly. "It's my dream."

The concert took place at 6:00 P.M. on July 21, 1983, on the Great Lawn, a 13-acre expanse in the park. The crowd, officially estimated to be between 350,000 and 400,000, began congregating early in the day. By 11:00 A.M., more than 4,000 people were already there, many with blankets, picnic baskets and radios to help while away the time. Alongside the Diana Ross souvenirs, vendors were busy hawking food, beer and marijuana.

For her first number, Diana appeared in the midst of a troupe of African-garbed dancers. She was wearing what can only be described as a multi-colored straw tent which she soon discarded to reveal an orange formfitting bodysuit. Soon that was covered with a sheer orange cape, which blew dramatically in the rising wind. She stood alone on stage because, earlier, she made the decision that the band and background singers should not be seen or even acknowledged. Diana sang for 25 minutes on the open stage until the first raindrops appeared. This rainfall grew into such a wild storm that the downpour knocked out electric power for nearly 40,000 homes.

Far from being daunted, Diana regarded the storm as one more challenge. "I've waited a lifetime to get here," she told the drenched but cheering crowd, "and I'm not going anywhere." With her hair slicked back, make-up dripping and costume clinging to her body, Ross in the rain was an unforgettable sight. Just as awe-inspiring was the sight of her audience, so transfixed and riveted that it too gladly endured the elements for its star. Even the fans ankle deep in mud booed and hissed as park officials pleaded with Ross to stop the show.

Mayor Koch sat huddled under an umbrella for most of the concert. As Diana sang "Endless Love" in the rain, a mysterious male voice from off-stage dueted with her. It was as if the sound of the other voice was somehow connected to the elements because she never introduced the singer. After the performance was officially over, Diana remained on stage to oversee the evacuation of the area. The next day, *The New York Times* would quote City Commissioner of Parks and Recreation Henry J. Stern as calling Miss Ross "magnificent in calming the crowd and gradually emptying the Great Lawn."

Media reaction was swift and favorable. Diana stayed up late into the night watching TV news reports showing her singing in the storm with the audience loving her. What could easily have been a disaster turned into one of the highlights of her career. It had "rained on her parade" and she emerged wet but triumphant. And she'd done it all without Berry Gordy, Jr. Diana was victorious. She should have stopped while she was ahead, while her public had a positive impression of her.

The next morning, Friday, she sat on the floor of her dressing room trailer, surrounded by the local newspapers. She'd made the front pages of all of them, including a page-one picture in *The New York Times*. (Much of the $146,000 set aside to publicize the event would be spent on worldwide promotion of her performance during the storm.) Suddenly, she was receiving more publicity than she had generated in many years. The focus of all of this attention was not on any park "for the children" but rather on Diana Ross and on her magnificence in the face of what had amounted to an almost impossible situation. Diana loves attention. She couldn't let go of "the moment." Not yet.

The concert was tentatively rescheduled for that evening, depending on favorable weather and the Great Lawn not being too muddy; when she learned that the concert would take place, she debated about canceling the dancers, because she apparently felt that her fans did not want dancers, they only wanted Diana. She did, however, change her mind.

Attendance for the rescheduled concert was down by less than half to about 150,000. Thursday, people had been packed shoulder to shoulder. On Friday, some areas were nearly empty.

For the broadcast of the Friday performance, Diana added a

montage of morning-after newspaper accolades to show her bravery and dedication. In greeting her audience, she seemed genuinely moved by their enthusiasm, but it soon turned out to be a different kind of crowd from the day before. Perhaps they were not united by the rigors of weather; perhaps it was Friday and people were getting in a weekend mood. Sensing the unruliness, she told the crowd to calm down. She held her hand to her chin, palm up, and blew air to her audience.

"Can you feel me? Can you feel me?" she called out. It was an odd gesture that seemed somehow egocentric, but most people didn't know what to make of it.

In her nightclub act and concerts, Diana interacts with her audience to the point of going out and touching them at every performance. With the audience in the palm of her hand, she can alternate fast numbers with slow ones, and her fans are always right there with her. But in Central Park, it was impossible for her to leave the stage and go out among the people. By not touching her spectators physically, she lost touch with them emotionally.

"I have a dream come true," she kept repeating. "I want you to listen to me." She seemed edgy. "When I do a quiet song, it's important that you can hear me," she said to the noisy crowd. Her manner was petulant and condescending and there was no humor or warmth to her approach. A telling moment occurred every time a hapless, nervous wardrobe woman, obviously intimidated by "Miss Ross," came out to drape her boss in a sequined cloak or feathered jacket. Diana ignored the assistant every time, never looking at her, thanking her or acknowledging her presence in any way because, as she kept insisting melodramatically, "This may be the most important moment in *my* life."

When Diana injected "the thoughts and meditations of Kahlil Gibran" into the show, she was armed with a large book of readings from *The Prophet*. Now she was ready to follow the lead of Stevie Wonder and become a visionary artist.

"And he spoke to us of love," Diana read in a high, piercing voice. "Know the secrets of your heart. Think not that you can direct the course of love."

The wind whipped her hair into her face and riffled the pages of the book and floated her words right over the heads of her audience. "What the hell is this?" someone up front asked.

"Who cares about this stuff?" a voice commanded.

"Sing 'Baby Love'!"

It might have happened even if she continued as energetically as she started, but early on her performance turned lackluster.

She pointed the microphone to the audience midway through songs, directing them to sing in the guise of conducting a sing-along when actually she was just being lazy. She kept asking the unseen conductor, "Where are we now?" as if she was unprepared. When she made her costume changes she seemed more interested in strutting about the stage than in her music. Certainly, this was not the Diana Ross her fans had admired for so many years. It was as if a self-indulgent impostor had somehow taken over.

"We have a few minutes left," she called out to people as they started to leave the park. "What do you want to hear? I don't have to disappear. I don't want to leave. You're wonderful. I love you. I love you," she cried out. "Bless you all. You've been so good to me."

Finally—and mercifully—it was over.

When exiting, Diana ran to associate producer Greg Sills. "Oh, thank you. Thank you so much for taking care of everything."

"My God, we're $500,000 over budget," Sills exclaimed.

By this time, Diana's fans were flocking around her. She may have given a poor performance, but she was still *the* Diana Ross and, up close, impossible to resist. "I love you all!" she exclaimed as she signed autographs and posed for pictures. "Bless you. You're so good to me. What a wonderful, wonderful day!"

After the Central Park show, marauding thugs stampeded from the park to Times Square, mugging tourists and New Yorkers alike and slashing anyone in their way with knives. Many victims were hospitalized. "Teeth were knocked out and heads cracked open," said one report. Thirty-eight were arrested. New York radio station WNEW referred to the concert as "the night New York was mugged."

The cost of the two Central Park concerts totalled $1.8 million. The City of New York paid $650,000 for police and cleanup services. And there turned out to be no money left for the playground, which was to cost $250,000. Nicholas Pileggi wrote an article for *New York* magazine (February 1982) entitled "Indecent Expenses." In it he tried to explain how Diana Ross' "humanitarian" effort went awry and how this fiasco "provides a rare and tantalizing peek into . . . the imperial style and spending habits of superstars like Diana Ross."

Diana spent $12,000 on limousines, though she had her own Rolls-Royce available. Catering, which Diana had estimated at $10,000 originally, cost $47,341. First class airline tickets came to $64,000. Security expenses jumped from an estimated $17,000 to an actual $55,969. It cost an incredible $431 to dry-clean the orange sequined jumpsuit Diana wore in the rain, which she didn't need for the second show. Two hundred sixty dollars was spent for her nails, one of which broke off during her performance.

"Miss Ross puts on a quality show, first and foremost," said John Frankenheimer, her chief attorney. "She puts quality ahead of everything. She wants the best cameramen, the best musicians, the best of everything."

"In this business, a star like Diana Ross knows what she wants, and there aren't too many people who are going to say no," observed Greg Sills, the associate producer. Sills also insisted that Diana's staff was stealing from her, submitting bills for services never rendered by people who weren't even involved in the show. He said that three sets of bills in identical handwriting for $20,000 each were submitted to him. Since he couldn't determine who they were from, he discarded them.

Diana Ross was not paid for her performance, but everyone else had to be: musicians, carpenters, dancers, two back-up singers, etc. "The concerts had raised hardly enough money to put up a seesaw," Pileggi wrote, "let alone a playground."

Now that the ego trip was over, Diana had to deal with the reality of what she had done. With the first concert, she had certainly accomplished a lot. She rectified a public relations problem by becoming a "humanitarian" and, in the process, got to be a brave trouper as well. She garnered enormous publicity and good will.

But rather than end it there so that there would be money left over for a children's park, she had to take it a step further because, for Diana Ross, worldwide attention is impossible to resist. She had to do another show "for my fans," thereby eating up any profit from the first concert. After the second show, her public image had become worse than it was before she had even started down the path of benevolence. Or, as an amused Berry Gordy told a friend, "Way to go, Diane."

Diana had to have been humiliated by the way all of this had turned out, especially when she was criticized in *People* magazine by New York City's Mayor Koch who said that he hoped she would recognize her "legal and moral responsibility. I don't believe it. My guts tell me there should be a profit."

Koch was angered by the fact that the accounting he had insisted upon from Diana Ross and Paramount took four months to prepare and, though it listed all of Diana's expenses, it didn't account for any money earned by the show. Diana insisted that she had spent $286,000 of her own on expenses no one even knew about, probably production costs.

"Of course it's a rip-off," Parks Commissioner Henry Stern told *The New York Times*. "These documents subject New York taxpayers to Hollywood economics. It's no way to treat the city."

If Diana hoped for support from her co-producer, Paramount, none was forthcoming. Paramount showed gross revenues in fiscal 1983 of roughly $4 billion and profits of $260 million. Gulf & Western, which at the time owned Paramount, also owned Madison Square Garden in New York. In 1982, in order to keep the Rangers hockey team and the Knickerbockers basketball team from moving to New Jersey, Koch granted Gulf & Western ten years of free taxes on the building and land. That was a gift of $50 million. Still, where the $250,000 children's park was concerned, Diana was on her own.

She promised to raise the money herself for what she must have privately been referring to by now as "that goddamn park." "I don't care if it takes a lifetime," she vowed with knuckles to forehead. "There's always tomorrow!"

This fiasco had become a serious image problem. Frantically, she complained to anyone who would listen that she had to find a way out as quickly as possible.

One of Diana's lawyers, Peter Tufo, decided to bring Howard Rubenstein into the picture. Rubenstein is a public relations man who, for the last 30 years, has been considered one of the best in the business. Because he primarily represents powerful builders, institutions and unions, he has strong connections in New York's City Hall.

Within a few hours, Rubenstein and Ross were in her RTC office discussing her image problems and how to solve them. He must have somehow convinced her that $250,000 is, to a woman who supposedly generates millions yearly in investment profits, just a drop in the bucket of big bucks. Would she be willing to hand over a check to put an end to her misery? She didn't have much choice. Either she would do so, or live with the media-established reputation of being the star who cheated New York out of a children's park.

A half hour after leaving Ross, Rubenstein met with Mayor Koch.

"I have something to tell you that's very important," he said. "I want that park for Diana Ross."

"It'll cost you," Rubenstein has remembered Koch replying. "How much?"

"A quarter of a million."

"You got it," said Rubenstein.

It was what they call in show business "a done deal." But it didn't make sense to have the transaction take place quietly between Diana and Koch, and then have her generosity announced subtly in a press release. It would end the way it started, with another major "media opportunity."

The next day, Diana held a press conference at City Hall and handed hizzoner a check for $250,000. He kissed her on the cheek and she glowed as photographers frantically snapped pictures and reporters asked her probing questions like "Where did the money come from, Miss Ross?" She said that the check "is from my own earnings. We all got rained on. But this is for the kids. It's not for anyone but the children of New York. All I wanted was the park."

With the press conference, Diana scored quite a few points with her public. Afterwards, Rubenstein rushed her to the park site where Diana graciously took more photos and also posed with her children.

Today, there is a small children's park on the corner of 81st Street and Central Park West in Manhattan. A tarnished gold-plated plaque on a block of wood states: "The restoration of this playground for the children of New York City has been made possible through the generosity of the Diana Ross Foundation."

Twelve feet away, on another block of wood, someone has carefully spray-painted in large blue letters one single word: "PEST."

Chapter
27

DIANA ROSS, WITH the pair of Central Park concerts behind her, embarked on a lengthy national tour from August 5 to November 16, 1983, mostly one-nighters. The park concerts were free, but now she was back on the road and making at least $100,000 per performance, and often close to twice that sum. "Miss Ross requires certain levels of compensation to entertain the idea of an appearance," her attorney John Frankenheimer would explain to potential promoters. She had been offered $500,000 for a 50-minute show in San Bernardino, California, as part of a three-day music festival. She declined because she does not appear on shows with other performers.

Diana Ross' accommodations were always first-class. Promised promoter Ronald Mayes, who was trying to book her for a San Francisco engagement, "The presidential suite in which Miss Ross will be booked will be stocked with whatever Miss Ross requests [VCR, stereo, records, spirits, food, etc.]. Her floor will have limited access and all charges outside of the incidentals will be billed to me."

Often, Diana Ross will ask that the dressing room be redecorated for her appearance. When she appeared at Five Seasons Center for a one-nighter in Cedar Rapids, Iowa, a waiting room and three adjoining dressing rooms had to be repainted and recarpeted for her. David Pisha, the manager of the facility, said that Miss Ross asked for "earth-tone colors" to be used in the new decorating scheme. "She asked that it be made to look like a star's dressing room."

Promoters were always required to provide at their own expense "a minimum of two security guards who will be available to guarantee Miss Ross' personal safety." Her personal appearance contracts reads, "All security people must wear BLACK CLOTHING. NO BLUE JEANS!"

Also in her standard one-night-only appearance contract, stipulated under the heading of "Miss Ross' Dressing Room":

1 bottle Hennessy XO (Cognac)
4 bottles Ruffino Classico Gold Label (Chianti)
Assorted sodas (Cola, 7-Up, Perrier)
Lemons and limes
Assorted fresh fruits
Cheese and crackers
Coffee and tea
Deli tray
Hot meal available
Chinese restaurant available for take-out, if requested
10 white towels, never before used

The tour reviews were mixed. "She acted like a haughty, spoiled diva, chiding the audience like a stern schoolmarm to stay in their seats . . . bitching about the electric piano," wrote Joel Selvin for the *San Francisco Chronicle*, "[but] the partisan crowd lapped it all up like kittens at a bowl of milk." It was reported by *Billboard* magazine that for the first 15 concerts of her tour, Diana played before 180,000 people and grossed $2.8 million.

During one show, she went into the audience, as she had customarily done for the past 15 years, to encourage people to sing with her and join hands. But when she extended her hand to one man, he refused to shake it. She made light of what she thought was his shyness, when suddenly the man snapped at her, "Hey! Get away from me! Go to hell!"

For a moment, Diana was speechless.

"Go to hell?" she repeated to herself, baffled. A hush fell over the entire showroom. Undaunted, Diana continued with her performance. By the time she finished, the man was on his feet and applauding with everyone else. But she was crushed. Nothing like this incident had ever happened to her during a performance.

When the show was over, Diana rushed to her dressing room, not anxious to meet well-wishers. "I just never thought that would happen to me," she told one friend. "I still cannot believe it."

Often, if Diana doesn't have the full attention of her audience, especially those closest to the stage, she becomes distracted and unnerved. During another show at Caesars, she noticed one ringsider who seemed utterly unimpressed with her performance, even though everyone else in the room was applauding wildly after each song. Diana was exasperated by his attitude and, looking down from the stage, said, "You don't want to be here, do you? Why don't you go out and gamble, or something?"

When the spotlight beamed down on the man, he began to squirm with embarrassment. Though he didn't seem to understand English, Diana persisted, "I mean, if you're gonna sit here like that, maybe you should get out of here."

Then she turned to the audience, some of whom appeared to be stunned by her words. "Well, he's *boring*," she explained simply.

She turned back to the man. "It's hard for me to work when you sit like that." Then she imitated his posture.

By this time, some of the audience was cheering her on, while others seemed shocked.

"Angelo, come and get him out of here," Diana hollered out to the maitre d'.

The maitre d' did not eject the paying customer; Diana continued with the show.

At another stop, a heckler refused to allow Diana to continue her performance unless she sang one of The Supremes' hit records that was not in her repertoire.

"Sing 'Baby Love,' " the woman kept shouting from the back of the showroom. Diana tried to ignore her, but this heckler was persistent. After every song, when the applause would die down, she would shout, "Sing 'Baby Love'!"

"I have a wonderful Billie Holiday song for you," Diana said later in the program. "And it means a lot to me." As she sat down on the edge of the stage, the lights were dimmed and one blue spotlight shone on her face. The room was so quiet you could hear the star breathing into the mike as she sang the first few bars of "My Man."

"It cost me a lot, but there's . . ."

Suddenly from the back of the theater: "Sing 'Baby Love,' goddamn it!"

Diana froze.

She got up and glared in the direction of where she thought the voice came from. Then she threw the microphone down. When it hit the floor, it made an eardrum-crushing, amplified thump.

Diana walked off the stage.

"Uh-oh."

"Is she coming back?" someone asked.

Finally, five minutes later, wearing a diaphanous white robe and holding a cup of hot tea to calm her nerves, Diana returned, the perfect picture of elegance and poise. Her hair was pulled severely back and she wore gardenias on one side. As the spotlight caught her sauntering back to center stage, a huge round of applause greeted her.

"I'm sorry," she began. "But this is *my* show. I have worked hard for many, *many* years. And I feel that I should be extended some courtesy. Don't you agree?"

Applause.

"I love to perform but I cannot do it if I am interrupted."

More applause. This crowd was hers now. She was back in control.

"I mean, really."

Big applause.

Diana sang a few more songs and then she left the stage to a thunderous standing ovation.

Three weeks into the post-Central Park tour, Diana Ross telephoned paralegal John Mackey, who was living at her Beverly Hills home, from Atlantic City where she was appearing at the Golden Nugget.

"Would you do something special for me?" she asked very coyly. "It seems that my sweet little brother 'T' had a big spat with his wife. She locked him out and I wonder if he can stay with you at the house for a few days until he and his little wife patch things up." At this time, T-Boy was married to a Jewish woman from the Los Angeles valley. Of course, Mackey agreed that T-Boy could stay at the house.

" 'T' tends to be a little wild and crazy sometimes," Diana explained. "If he gets rowdy, go ahead and lock him out."

John Mackey recalled, "From talking to T, a wonderful guy, I found that it was not easy to be Diana Ross' brother. There's no way he or the other kids could ever hope to measure up to her success. I would think that even Barbara, the doctor in the family, pretty much lived in the shadow of her sister. Like any young good-looking guy—he had dark brown hair and blue-green eyes—he wanted to be accepted by his friends as just one of the fellas and not because he was Diana Ross' brother. 'I am my own special person,' he used to say. But he adored and worshipped her. He thought she was the most wonderful, generous woman in the world.

" 'We love each other and have a family union most people

don't understand, or even have,' T-Boy said of his sister. 'One lesson I learned from her is how hard you have to work to succeed in this world as a black person.' "

Now and then, T-Boy would wax nostalgic about how most of the brothers and sisters and other relatives used to line up backstage after concerts and sister Diana would hand them all white envelopes containing money. "One for you, one for you and one for you," all the way down the line. She was generous with her family and enjoyed being able to give them these gifts. Eventually, T-Boy attended Morehouse College in Atlanta, and then the University of Washington, majoring in history and English. He was a junior high school teacher for a time.

In the '70s, Diana gave T-Boy an opportunity to prove himself at Motown as an artist and songwriter for Michael Jackson and The Miracles. He recorded one album for the label, which was a commercial disaster, selling 12,000 copies, partly because he didn't want his sister's name connected to the project. She wasn't even mentioned in his bio and his last name wasn't used on the record jacket. T-Boy went on to become an accomplished writer/producer, working with The Miracles and Marvin Gaye.

John Mackey said that in October of 1983, Diana's brother Chico was shocked to find that his brother T was staying at the Beverly Hills home. As it happened, Chico had pleaded with his sister many times to let him stay at the house. Diana, though, knew that Chico wouldn't be able to resist the temptation of hosting wild parties there. Ever since she moved into Beverly Hills in 1970, Diana had always been extremely anxious about making a positive impression on her mostly white neighbors, none of whom she ever socialized with. Black homeowners on her block were certainly in the minority, and she didn't want anything to happen at her home that would besmirch her reputation. Even in the '80s, she still felt she had reason to be concerned.

"She wasn't particularly concerned about Chico messing up the house, but she was very worried about the neighbors," Mackey said. "And she kept harping: 'What about my image?' She had gone to great lengths to keep a clean, upstanding reputation in the all white neighborhood because the last thing she ever wanted to hear was 'them blacks. Soon as they moved in we started having problems 'round here.' That was a major concern of hers. 'There goes the neighborhood!' So, as much as she loved Chico, she decided it would be best if he didn't move into the house if she wasn't able to supervise him."

At this time, Fred Ross, Sr., was working as a recording engineer. Margretia, a housewife married to Bryant Price, was the proprietor of La Mama, a resale boutique for maternity clothes in Berkley, Michigan. Prior to owning the store, Rita worked for Motown as a "talent scout." She planned to record her own album. "I sound like I'm white, not black," she said. "Like my sister, I was born with a voice." Publicity pictures were circulated of Rita in a Motown recording studio, but no album was ever released.

Diana's older sister, Dr. Barbara Lee (now married, with five children), had recently been inducted into the Naval Reserve as a Lieutenant Commander, MC (Medical Corps). It was the first such accomplishment for a black woman in the state of Michigan. Barbara, with whom Diana was always the most competitive, was now a doctor of osteopathic medicine.

"Oh, she's very proud," Barbara said of her famous sister. "She really wanted to come to the induction ceremonies, but had second thoughts about it causing too much commotion because the word was getting around that Diana Ross would be there."

Some of Diana's former employees, however, claimed that her relationship with her immediate family appeared to be rather distant by this time. Certainly, Diana no longer had much in common with her siblings and—since she is so obviously self-centered—some people have claimed that she has a difficult time being truly interested in the lives of her family members. Moreover, because of her full schedule and her own personal problems, Diana doesn't always have the time to keep tabs on what may be happening with the Ross brood, even though she will usually give them money if they ask for it.

Assistant road manager Michael Browne remembered when Diana and her staff flew to Detroit to spend a holiday with her mother and sisters. Diana had purchased a modest home for Ernestine and her second husband, John Jordan, in the Detroit suburb of Southfield. But, according to Browne, when the entourage arrived at the airport, Diana couldn't remember how to get to the house.

He recalled, "We drove through the snowy streets for an hour and a half, with her screaming all the way, 'Why doesn't anyone know where my mom's house is?' "

Browne claimed that Diana made the chauffeur pull the limousine over and ask people on the street, "Where does Diana Ross' mother live?"

He recalled, "Once she got there it was difficult to talk to her sisters because she couldn't relate to them. She sat at the end of a couch and acted completely bored with all of them. One of her sisters [Barbara] is a prominent doctor in Detroit but they couldn't seem to find anything in common to talk about.''

On October 17, 1983, following the post-Central Park concert tour, Diana Ross sat down to compose what has become known among her former employees as ''That Letter.'' On Diana Ross stationery (21 East 63rd Street, New York, New York), ''That Letter'' read:

To Whom It May Concern:
    The following people are no longer in my employment:
    [8 names were listed]
    If I let an employee go, it's because either their work or their personal habits are not acceptable to me. I do not recommend these people. In fact, if you hear from these people, and they use my name as a reference, I wish to be contacted.

Diana Ross

She signed her name in sprawling, determined letters.

It isn't uncommon in show business for an employer to use a press release to announce that an employee has left the company. But it is unusual for an employer to circulate a letter criticizing her former staff to practically everyone she knows in the entertainment business, none of whom asked for her opinion of these people.

One person close to RTC, who insisted on anonymity, explained, ''Apparently, a story about Miss Ross that she didn't like but which nonetheless was very true leaked out from the office. When she heard about this, she became very upset. She called every one of her employees into her office to try to determine who the snitch was. No luck. No one would 'fess up. So Miss Ross decided that they would all be punished. She canned everyone. Suddenly she had no staff.''

Another explanation from former RTC staff members has it that Diana Ross discovered that someone in her employ embezzled money from her and, since she couldn't figure out who the culprit was, she fired everyone.

Diana Ross is extremely sensitive about embezzlement because in February 1981, right after she left Motown, she discovered that Glen S. Kannry, a CPA employed by Price Waterhouse & Co. somehow managed to swindle Diana Ross and Diana Ross Enterprises, Inc., of at least $250,000, possibly much more. He admitted that he diverted funds from Ross' bank accounts for his own use without her authorization. He pleaded guilty and was sentenced.

"I signed the wrong papers because I wasn't knowledgeable," she said. "I was shocked. I began realizing that I was so vulnerable to people taking advantage of me because here I was, Diana Ross, so straight and honest and just knowing everyone else was good like me. Well, they're not. I thought, 'How could you be so stupid? Here you are from the projects in Detroit with somebody *else* handling your money.' "

Whatever the reasons for her actions, the way Diana Ross spread the written word about her former staff was particularly upsetting to Gail Davis. Davis, who had worked in the entertainment business for many years before becoming Diana Ross' administrative assistant, was one of the former employees listed in "That Letter." Davis explained that she usually worked seven days a week, without lunch and "often until eight or nine in the evening." She said that she wanted to resign her position in June of 1983, but Diana telephoned her from Paris and pleaded with her to reconsider, promising a lighter work load.

According to Davis' lawyer, Don Zakarin, Gail Davis was not "fired" by Diana Ross but had, in fact, resigned in November 1982, nearly a year before Ross circulated that letter. Gail Davis says she thought she had left on good terms.

Based on the reaction Davis got from the letter, Ross had sent out hundreds of copies. Zakarin said that he "had never heard of anything like this before in my life," and immediately sent a letter to Diana Ross' attorneys demanding a retraction. They refused. He filed a libel suit against her in the U.S. District Court for the Southern District of New York, seeking $1 million in compensatory damages and $1 million in punitive damages. Davis was working for David Bowie at the time.

Recalled Don Zakarin, "I took Diana's deposition over the course of two days. Her position was that the letter she sent was accurate, that it was true, that it was an opinion of hers and, as such, wasn't libelous. She also indicated that she had had a problem of some sort with the people listed in the letter, and that she sent the letter out in order to protect herself from these people, some of whom were purporting to act on her behalf. She said they were using her name in department stores without her permission.

"Obviously, she was attempting to defend her rationale for sending the letter. It was my job to establish that her rationale was nonexistent and that there was no reason to mention Gail in that letter because she had no objections to Gail's work, and had not fired Gail. Through various witnesses, I was able to establish that.

"I had heard that she was haughty, difficult and demanding," he continued. "That is certainly her reputation. But I found her to be level-headed, bright and not at all unpleasant. She was very responsive to my questions."

But again, Ross was in over her head. This kind of incident would never have happened at Motown under Berry Gordy's guidance. Diana allowed her volatile temper rather than her business sense determine her course of action. Infuriated by whatever happened in the inner sanctum of RTC, whether it was betrayal or theft, she probably shot off that letter in an impulsive, emotional moment and then, according to Zakarin, "mailed it off to everyone on her Rolodex."

After she had done this, she no doubt regretted it, especially when Davis, and then another employee listed in the letter (Carol Acquisto) both filed legal actions against her. By this time, though, she felt that it was too late for her to back off. To apologize for what she had done to her former staff would mean admitting that she was wrong. Most people who know her would agree that Diana Ross does not like to admit when she's wrong.

This case dragged on for two years.

In June 1986, just prior to going to trial, Ross and Davis reached a settlement. Don Zakarin said that the terms of the settlement prohibited him or his client, Davis, from disclosing them.

For obvious reasons, most of Diana Ross' former employees are not eager to discuss her or their work at RTC without a promise of anonymity. Ross asks staffers to sign a "secrecy agreement" which prevents them from discussing her if they should lose their jobs. Assistant road manager Michael Browne has said that in the five years he spent employed by Diana Ross, she hired and fired 42 secretaries.

"All you had to do was say one thing she didn't like or ask a question without her permission to speak," he said, "and you were out."

John Mackey, who worked closely with Diana during his tenure at Loeb and Loeb, explained that whenever Ross' employees felt they were establishing a warm rapport with her, they would often discover just the opposite. While he was living in Diana Ross' Beverly Hills home, Diana was scheduled to tape a television interview there. Because a crowd of neighbors had gathered in front of the house, Mackey stationed a limousine in the back to act as a decoy. As the swarm of people noticed the limousine and began to congregate around it in breathless anticipation, Diana could slip out the front door unnoticed. Since he was a longtime employee, he knew that, depending on her mood, Diana usually disliked crowds of fans descending upon her. She didn't seem in a good mood on this day.

Mackey then stationed a friend of his in the kitchen to act as a guard. The man had just finished a long day on his feet working as a store manager. He kicked off his shoes and sat on a chair, keeping watch to make sure no over-anxious fans interrupted the taping by knocking on the back door.

But when the interview was over, Diana's mood changed and so did the strategy: she decided she would delight her fans and leave through the back entrance. When she walked through the kitchen she discovered a flustered stranger in his stocking feet. Mackey's associate bolted up to shake her hand. Diana was gracious. Then she and Mackey discussed his sister who was at that time in a coma. Mackey remembered that Diana was warm and sympathetic; he had never felt closer to her as she tried to comfort him.

After she departed, Mackey put on a hanger the Galanos gown she left behind. He brought it into the Loeb and Loeb office the next day.

"Later," he recalled, "I discovered that she was telling everyone, 'John brought my expensive black dress to me on a wire hanger. The nerve! But worse than that,' she complained, 'he had this friend of his come over specifically just to meet me. And can you believe that this person had the poor manners to meet me with his shoes off? I had to go into that kitchen and shake his hand and smell his *stinking feet*!''

"It was almost a month before she would speak to me again," Mackey said, laughing.

Diana's employees are used to her mood swings, but often her petulance is confounding to outsiders. A backstage visitor during a Las Vegas engagement recalled, "I learned that when she wants to turn someone off, she will turn that person off and never give him a second thought. We were sitting together and the phone rang. One of Diana's staff came over and told her that so-and-so was on the line. " 'Hang up,' Diana said, very calmly.

" 'But Miss Ross, he wants to know if . . .'

" 'Hang up,' Diana repeated, this time curtly.

"So without saying another word, the aide went to the phone and hung it up. Diana then continued talking as if nothing strange happened. It was quite bizarre."

* * *

For Diana Ross, 1984 was an especially difficult year. Her mother Ernestine was desperately ill, battling cancer. Though Diana tried to continue her career into the year as best she could, her efforts were strained because of the personal crisis. Still, she had concert commitments to honor and also a new RCA album to promote. As much as she may have wanted to take time off because of her personal problems, her career wouldn't allow it.

That year she recorded her fourth RCA album, *Swept Away*. (The title track was produced by Darryl Hall.) The album was released with another ghastly cover photo: Diana with a spiked hairdo in a metallic pants outfit, which *People* magazine said made her look like "one of those West German postpunkers who do their hair with Krazy Glue." Again, Diana, at 40, was hell-bent on being perceived as youthful and contemporary, instead of looking like the mature, stylish woman she is. Certainly it must be insecurity that makes her feel a need to compete for a teen market against Madonna, Jodie Watley and other younger singers.

The album included the ballad "Missing You," written and co-produced by Lionel Richie, perhaps the best song Diana recorded while under contract to RCA. It's an impeccable performance. Still, Diana and Lionel apparently had their share of problems in the recording studio because the song was released before it was even finished—the vocals were incomplete at the end. "It's good enough as it is," Diana decided. "Just put it out there."

"Missing You" was dedicated to the late Marvin Gaye, which seemed odd to those Ross fans who always felt that there was no love lost between Ross and Gaye. Though this recorded tribute to Gaye may not have done much to rectify the public's perception of Ross as being somewhat insincere, "Missing You" was a Top 10 hit and became one of her most popular songs of the '80s.

In September 1984, Diana performed at Radio City Music Hall—her first appearance in Manhattan since Central Park a year earlier—and grossed a record-breaking $1.7 million for 11 performances, eclipsing Liberace's $1.6 million for 14. Following opening night, Diana, wearing a red silk sari, hosted a celebrity party on the USS *Intrepid*, now a museum permanently docked on the Hudson River.

Richard Gere, who always baffled Diana because of his unwillingness to be photographed in public, was an invited guest. As she went to his table to say hello, a group of photographers followed and Richard took off.

When Richard Gere opened on Broadway in *Bent*, Diana went to the show and then whisked him off in her limousine afterwards.

"I'm not used to this kind of treatment," he told her in the car.

"Well, you'd better get used to it, baby," she said, according to the chauffeur, "because this is how stars live!"

Diana was panned by critics and audience alike for her lackluster one-hour performance at the Music Hall. Her public did not realize that she was flying from New York to Detroit daily between shows to be with her cancer-stricken mother. Ernestine was much worse, and though Diana may have wanted to cancel the Radio City Music Hall engagement altogether, she, no doubt, felt she owed it to her public not to disappoint them. She was so exhausted that her voice was giving out on her and she required a doctor in attendance backstage for her throat.

"I got a little angry," she declared, "because I said if people really cared about you they'd stop and take the time to find out what's really going on in your life. At Radio City, I had other things going on that I thought were more important than standing up there and shaking my butt."

Ernestine Ross Jordan was 68 when she died of cancer at her suburban Southfield home near Detroit. Services were held the next day at St. Andrew's Catholic Church at Wayne State University. Diana's background singers, Sharon Wade and Robert Glenn, sang hymns. Rhonda wrote a touching biography of her grandmother that was handed out at the funeral.

One former employee remembered, "That was the only time I had ever seen Miss Ross break down. She tried to throw herself into her career, but she would dissolve into tears at any time. There was an older woman working in accounting whom Miss Ross seemed to like and, after Diana's mother died, she hired this woman to be a personal assistant. It was as if she wanted to be around an older woman who reminded her of Ernestine. It was very sad."

"I'm so sorry that she can't be here, and I truly miss her," Diana told *Essence* magazine. "I guess the best thing I can do is try to be like her and always make sure my children remember who she was and what she meant in my life. She was real special. And in a way, I am my mother. I look at myself in the mirror and I see her every day, all the time."

Diana didn't have many friends to turn to during this difficult time in her life. Surely it must be during these emotional crises when she fully realizes how much she has alienated herself from so many people over the years.

One person she was able to count on was Julio Iglesias. Her *Swept Away* album included a duet with Iglesias called "All of You." It was a Top 20 record for them, having also been included on *1100 Bel Air Place*, one of Julio's Columbia albums. At first, Diana was not going to allow "All of You" to be included on the Iglesias album. She said that Julio had promised that she would be his only duet partner on the album and when that turned out not to be true—the Beach Boys and Willie Nelson also make appearances on the record—she felt betrayed.

But Diana seemed to have a soft spot for this Latin lover who once told the press that he needed sex twice a day. It was reported in Hollywood gossip columns that the two of them had been romantically involved for a brief time, though that does not seem likely.

As the story went, and it was widely reported in gossip columns around the world, Diana telephoned Julio at his estate in Miami from her private jet to tell him that she was on her way to visit. When she got there, Julio was with Karen Baldwin, a former Miss Universe who was said to be his love interest. With Diana in the room, he supposedly told Karen that Diana was the woman he loved. But then, as soon as Diana left, he said to Karen, "It doesn't mean a thing. She's a business associate and I *have* to be nice to her."

Diana pleaded with Julio to accompany her to the island of St. Maarten, and he agreed. But then, the next day, he changed his mind and disappointed her.

Diana was infuriated by that story and said that none of it was true.

According to Diana, she and her children did indeed take her private jet to Julio's estate in Miami for a vacation, but he was out of town at the time. She said that she needed to collect herself during this emotional time in her life and that he generously offered his $5 million home as a refuge. "And then word of that got out and suddenly we're having an affair," she said. "But I'm used to gossip. It's part of what I do."

Neither the gossip column stories about the affair nor Diana's version of her rest time at Julio's seem to be true. Indeed, the genesis of a juicy Hollywood rumor can sometimes be quite sad. What really happened, according to Iglesias, is that Diana was appearing in Vegas when she confided in him that she had no friends with whom she could spend Christmas. Her mother was gone, she was depressed and lonely. Julio was astounded by Diana's confession.

"How can a popular woman like you be all alone at Christmas?" he asked incredulously. That's when Julio invited Diana to his home.

She was certainly in no mood to celebrate the holiday and couldn't decide whether to accept Julio's invitation. Apparently, it was a last-minute idea to take her private jet to Miami. According to Julio, Diana called him while airborne and told him that she would be arriving in two hours.

She and her children stayed with Julio and his children for three days. "I tell you this story so you can understand better about Diana Ross," he said in an interview. "She is a beautiful woman. She is a superstar. She is a great artist and she loves her children. But for that holiday, she was all alone."

Diana did have to admit that she found Julio tremendously appealing. The swarthy son of a prominent Spanish physician, and a former law student himself, Iglesias is intelligent and handsome. The video they taped and photos they took together looked amorous, the two embracing cheek-to-cheek, Diana with one bare leg straddling Julio's hip and the other locked sexily between his legs.

But at this time, Diana was so preoccupied with her mother's illness and then death that she probably had no time to consider a serious relationship.

After the holidays, it was time for Diana Ross to prepare another album, her fifth, for RCA. In February 1985, she began recording *Eaten Alive*, with Barry Gibb producing. Gibb co-produced the title track with Michael Jackson.

One day, Michael arrived at the recording studio in Los Angeles by himself, no security men at his side. Diana was very surprised. "Now, Michael, how can you do that?" she scolded the 26-year-old singer. "Don't you remember the last time you drove to the studio, when you got lost? And you were too afraid to stop and ask for directions? Now, you *know* you should have security, Michael. It's not safe."

"I just sneaked out, Diane, all by myself," he said with an impish grin. "I'm just having a good time."

At this point, Michael had recently had his second nose surgery. This was the first time Diana had seen the newly sculpted nose and, though she tried not to stare, it wasn't easy. Later, when Michael wasn't around, she turned to an associate and said, "My God! That boy has got to stop fooling with his face.

What is he doing?'' She became exasperated and asked again, "Someone please tell me, what he is doing to his face?''

The associate explained to her, "Miss Ross, they say he's trying to look like you.''

"I look like *that*?'' she asked incredulously.

The *Eaten Alive* album proved another commercial disaster. On the title track, she again ignored Berry Gordy's rule about the importance of understandable, meaningful lyrics and how they are reflected in record sales. Hardly a word of "Eaten Alive" made any sense at all.

One album cut, "Chain Reaction," was fun to listen to because it was masterfully crafted in the tradition of vintage Supremes. She never looked more exciting than she did in the video in which she contrasted a re-creation of herself as a '60s star on a TV dance show like "Hullabaloo" with color footage in contemporary Ross regalia. The song became Number One in England for weeks on the Capitol-EMI label, but in the United States there was no interest. "Eaten Alive" had sapped all of the enthusiasm for this project. "Chain Reaction" barely made the Top 100.

Other Diana Ross singles of late weren't making the charts at all.

Slowly, she was sabotaging her record career by trying to be trendy with her music rather than thoughtful about it. No one could reason with her because as she said, "I must have control.''

Since she insisted on regulating every aspect of her career, she had alienated most of the RCA executives who felt that she didn't trust them to do their jobs, including producers hired by her and the record company to work with her. Diana Ross was never savvy enough to understand record company politics, i.e., how to make people happy by having them do what you want them to do, only better (which is an art in which Berry Gordy excelled). So even when she wasn't officially producing a song, it was obvious from the results that Diana dominated and stifled whoever was in charge. She had never sounded so muffled and fuzzy-voiced on her records before. The days of crisp Motown productions were a thing of the past, and this fact reflected in her sales.

Because of her consistently weak showing in the record stores, RCA's promotion men—those responsible for convincing the radio stations to play her music—thought that she was no longer of any interest to a pop music audience. They continually undermined her efforts.

"We've got this silly Diana Ross record," one promo man told a radio station program director in Los Angeles. "You can play it if you want, but it sucks." Then he hurled the 45 across the room as if it were a Frisbee.

When "Telephone" was released from a previous album, RCA serviced it only to black radio stations and did not even try to generate pop airplay. They simply did not care enough about Diana Ross, or the music, which was really mediocre. This sort of marketing plan was unheard of where Ross was concerned at Motown. Even The Supremes' earliest records were serviced to all stations, though many did not want to play them at first. Oddly, considering her reputation as a "cross-over artist," Diana has enjoyed more success on black radio in the '80s than she has on pop stations.

The unthinkable had happened: Diana Ross was no longer a top pop recording artist. She had unwittingly trashed her own career as a pop music star—a career which had been so carefully orchestrated and nurtured by Berry Gordy and Motown over a 20-year period—and all because, "I must have control." To most observers, it all hardly seemed worth it.

But what could she do? She was sinking so fast, she never had the time to stop and try to figure out what was happening. She had alienated so many people along the way, no one seemed willing to assist her if she asked for a helping hand. Moreover, Diana would never ask because, to her, that would be an admission that she had made a mistake by leaving Motown. She could never do that.

During her Caesars Palace Vegas engagement early in 1984, she told all of her backstage visitors how unhappy she was with RCA.

"They don't listen to me," she complained. "They don't care about me."

She had said that she spent $50,000 of her own money preparing the Central Park concerts for release as a live album, but RCA wouldn't allow it to be issued. It just wasn't a strong enough concert to be put on record; it was barely good enough to put on television. Diana couldn't seem to understand that it was illogical to take a weak concert and put it on vinyl. Who would buy the record?

She told one visitor that she was going to try to have the Central Park LP released on the Motown label. When the guest asked how this would be possible, Diana grinned slyly, rubbed her index fingers and thumb together and said, "It's all in the bucks, baby.'' She had somehow deluded herself into thinking it was possible for Berry to release the album on a Motown label even though she was under contract to Robert Summers' RCA.

Whenever Diana is unhappy because of either business or personal problems, she usually becomes even more difficult. The engagement in Vegas started off on a sour note. According to her contract with Caesars Palace, the marquee must say ''DIANA ROSS''—and nothing else, not ''Presenting . . . ,'' not ''*Miss* Diana Ross,'' just ''DIANA ROSS.''

According to one of her drivers, it's become an opening-day ritual for her to drive by the entrance to the hotel to check that the marquee meets her requirements. She looks up at it, smiles to herself, then drives on. This time she drove by, looked up, and was horrified to see that the marquee proudly announced ''DIANA ROSS'' and then in smaller letters on the bottom of the sign, ''SHEENA EASTON APPEARING IN TWO WEEKS.''

''I put these things in my contract because they are my standards,'' she told the Caesars management. ''And I am not performing until the marquee is corrected.''

That night, fans packed Caesars waiting to see ''DIANA ROSS,'' who was back in her dressing room, dressed, made-up and ready to go on.

''Has it been changed yet?'' she asked an aide.

''Yes, Miss Ross.''

''Well, I want to see for myself.''

She and two security guards marched out of the dressing room, through the backstage area, through the casino, through the lobby and out the front door. With her arms crossed, she stood outside in her white sequined gown and fur wrap and looked up at the marquee.

''DIANA ROSS''

''There. Now that looks nice.''

Then she went back in and performed.

''Just because I have my standards,'' she complained, ''they think I'm a bitch.''

In Las Vegas, Diana, a concerned mother, confided that eight-year-old Chudney was having trouble in school and having difficulty adjusting to her mother's constant touring schedule.

''I know how important the family bond is to children,'' she told writer Tom Burke for *Good Housekeeping*. ''But I do believe that kids can be fine with a single parent. It's all about how much love they require, how much is given to them. Traveling is very hard when you're a single parent with three kids. I must organize my schedule carefully. When I plan a tour, I first find out how the girls *really* feel about my leaving home. We discuss choices—they can go with me if they're not in school, or they can stay with their dad. There's nothing wrong with having a successful mom, a mom who travels and sings and people like her. That feels good to them.''

The girls commuted to Dalton School in Manhattan from their home in Connecticut, a 45-minute ride by chauffeur-driven limousine. Dalton is one of the most exclusive of New York's private schools. Often, Diana would ride into town with them when she had to go to her New York offices. She also belonged to the PTA.

Once, Diana and the girls were riding along the Connecticut Turnpike in their white stretch limousine when Rhonda, 12, decided that the pretension was silly. ''Well, I'm just sick of it,'' she complained later in front of some of Diana's employees. ''Why can't we ride in a normal car like normal people?''

''Rhonda, I appreciate what you're trying to say,'' Mother said very patiently. ''But, please look at it this way. I worked really hard all of these years for this luxury. I'm sorry, but I don't like to drive. This is nice and comfortable and we should be very grateful that we're able to travel like this. Don't you agree?''

Rhonda nodded her head.

Usually, when not on the road, Diana had two security guards at her disposal: one for her and one for the children. Anytime the girls went out in public, they would be accompanied by a Ross employee and the security guard.

Of her children, Diana had said, ''If loving them means spoiling them, then that's just too bad.'' She apparently meant it. The girls became accustomed to receiving two of each gift for Christmas—two of the same outfits, two pairs of the same shoes. This way, Diana reasoned, if they lose any part of the ensemble, they would still have a matching pair. She would think nothing of buying the girls dozens of $300 to $500 sundresses—each designer outfit always in duplicate.

One Christmas, Diana chartered a DC-9 jet to fly herself and the three girls to Aspen for the holiday. Having completed her Christmas shopping for them, she came home with a limousine full of gifts; she had spent roughly $100,000 on presents for Rhonda, Tracee and Chudney.

Diana telephoned her assistant road manager, Michael

Browne, to ask him to help her wrap the presents, and when the two of them were finished, the pile totaled 55 boxes. The next morning, when it was time to leave, Ross' staff brought the gifts to the airport to have them loaded onto the DC-9, only to discover that all of them would not fit into the plane's cargo hold. Diana deliberated over this dilemma for a moment and decided that there was only one solution: charter a bigger jet just for the gifts. "Then there'll be one plane for us, and one for the presents!" she exclaimed. She truly enjoys these extravagant gestures.

Apparently at the last minute, she also decided to have a portable bowling alley installed in the aisle of the jet that she, Rhonda, Chudney and Tracee, and the staff would take. This way, her daughters would have something to do during the flight. It took three hours to install the bowling alley. Meanwhile, the jet sat on the runway and Diana was charged for what the airport called "runway time." Holding on the tarmac cost $1,100.

"Bill me," she told the officials when they added up the charges.

Once she was airborne, according to Michael Browne, she said, "They'll never see a cent of *that*."

The third week in March 1984, Michael Milken, the young junk bond impresario, hosted the annual Drexel High Yield Bond Conference—also called The Predator's Ball—at the Beverly Hilton Hotel in Beverly Hills. The ball was attended by every financial wizard in the country, including Ivan Boesky, Carl Lindner and Carl Icahn, all so-called "corporate raiders." Every stockbroker, analyst and money advisor in the country wanted to be invited to The Predator's Ball to be privy to take-over plans and new investment opportunities. In 1982, Frank Sinatra was the surprise entertainment. There was much speculation as to who would entertain this year, and some of the guests began speculating that it would be "either Michael Jackson or God." It was Diana Ross.

"She wanted to be in the company of all of these wheelers and dealers," said an associate of Diana's. "Michael Milken said there was three trillion dollars in that room. Diana was right in the middle of it all, soaking up all that money aura. She was becoming quite a wheeler-and-dealer, influenced. I think, by her attorney, John Frankenheimer, who is a brilliant man when it comes to finances. Above all, Diana likes to consider herself to be a powerful woman."

During her performance of "More and More," a song from her *Eaten Alive* album, she sat on the lap of billionaire Carl Lindner. Diana entertained in return for the chance to invest in one of Michael Milken's investment partnerships, Reliance Capital Group, L.P., a portfolio worth billions of dollars. It was said that she made "a killing" in the investment.

She may not have had a clue about what to do with her recording career, but Diana was apparently becoming quite shrewd in money matters. In 1982, when she purchased the brownstone in Manhattan at 21 East 63rd Street, between Fifth and Madison Avenues, where RTC was housed, it was against the advice of her financial advisors. She paid $4.25 million for the four-story building—$1.25 million in cash, and the rest borrowed from Chemical Bank in Manhattan on a five-year loan for one percent above prime. Within two-and-a-half years, she sold the building for a considerable profit. She told associates that she was prouder of that accomplishment than she was of anything she'd done recently.

In March 1984, another announcement was made regarding Ross' Josephine Baker project. Jean Briley, who wrote the screenplay for *Gandhi*, had been hired to do the script. François Lesterlin, president of Eurocom, announced plans to co-produce *The Life of Josephine Baker* with Diana Ross. But nothing happened.

Announcements of this nature where the Josephine Baker project was concerned were made almost every year, with many directors involved, including Sir Richard Attenborough, Franco Zeffirelli and Mark Rydell. But it has been very difficult for Diana to mount this project because, as she says, "I must have control."

Or, as her former Motown labelmates The Four Tops put it in one of their most popular recordings, "It's the Same Old Song."

Diana prefers independent financing for the film rather than to go through the normal channels of studio financing. When a movie studio backs a film, they take control of it, and Diana can't—won't—relinquish control.

She has certainly chosen a tough arena in which to flex her muscles because, although Diana showed great promise in her film portrayal of Billie Holiday in *Lady Sings the Blues*, good roles for women are rare—and for black women they are almost non-existent. Even though *The Wiz* hurt Diana's bankability as an actress, she still has had offers but, because of her ego, will apparently reject anything that is not a starring role. She also will not consider any film she cannot at least co-produce, and on which she would not have final say over the script.*

Even Cher had to work her way up to an Academy Award by first appearing in films in which she wasn't the female lead. In *Moonstruck*, the role for which she was awarded the Oscar, she was not even the center of attention but rather part of a talented ensemble. It's doubtful that Diana Ross would have accepted *Moonstruck* if it had been offered to her because it didn't meet her terms: she couldn't have produced it, she wouldn't have been permitted absolute script approval, and there were too many other actors in it with important roles.

Rob Cohen, who produced Diana in *Mahogany* and *The Wiz*, is sympathetic to Diana's problems in Hollywood. "Diana's position in movies is a no-win situation. For instance, she can't be in *Fatal Attraction*, can she? If she played the psychotic woman, the film would be accused of racism: 'Why is the black woman so crazy for this white man?' She can't play the man's wife because then it's a strange interracial-couple movie. And if you make it an all-black cast you have a movie you can't market.

"She also can't do black exploitation like Whoopi Goldberg has done recently. Diana won't be queen of the cocaine mamas or a black cop.

"And I'm sure that if I had convinced Warner Bros. to cast her opposite Cher in *The Witches of Eastwick*, she wouldn't have done it. She's not interested in ensemble.

"I read hundreds of scripts every year and Diana Ross is on my mind constantly, but I don't know what can be done with her. She's very rigid in what she will and won't do."

Another less tolerant Hollywood producer put it this way: "Diana wants it all. So she's getting nothing."

Indeed, after years of Berry Gordy's domination, Diana Ross was now a free woman. Where her recording and film careers were concerned, she finally had all of the control that she had dreamed about.

But at what cost?

---

*In January 1982, Liz Smith reported that Diana was asked to consider a movie remake of Carson McCullers' classic *The Member of the Wedding*. Smith said that the producers wanted Diana to portray a younger, more beautiful version of the household cook, originally played by Ethel Waters. But Diana would only play the role of Frankie. "The producers somehow didn't feel she was right for a 13-year-old white child of the South," wrote Smith.

Chapter

❦ 28 ❦

"THEY TELL ME that it will be hard to find a man strong enough to love my own strength and independence, and not worry about being Mr. Diana Ross," the lady had said in an interview. "But I disagree. I know absolutely that that man is somewhere out there."

In the summer of 1985, Diana vacationed in Lyford Cay in the Bahamas, enjoying a break before the demands of recording sessions for *Eaten Alive*. As she luxuriated under the hot rays of the Bahamian sun, her three daughters made a trio of new friends by the swimming pool. Through the children, Diana met Arne Naess (pronounced Ar-na Näs), who suggested that he and his two daughters and son have dinner with Diana and her girls. He would say on Norwegian television later, "The way to a woman's heart is definitely through her children."

Diana was fascinated with this balding, fiftyish, conservatively dressed man who was one of the most loquacious and charming men she had ever met. He was an avid sportsman who enjoyed deep-sea diving in the Philippines and skiing in Japan. Earlier in the year, he led a four-month Norwegian expedition to Mount Everest in Nepal, and retraced the steps of Sir Edmund Hillary's 1953 journey up the icy face of the world's highest peak.

"My ambitions are like a mountain without a summit," he said then. "When you have the top in sight, there's always another peak just over the rise, further on and higher up."

After the Mount Everest expedition, he became very popular in Norway, though he always acted as if he despised the publicity. He said that he preferred a private life and would often retreat to the three-story chalet he owns in the exclusive town of Verbier, Switzerland, surrounded by the Alps.

He also owns his own island, Taino, near Tahiti, a 370-acre paradise that he purchased in 1972 along with businessman Douglas Meyer, a friend from New Zealand. The island is near Marlon Brando's isle of Tetiaroa and was considered by Arne's friends to be, as one put it, "his folly—where he would go and have great fun with beautiful Tahitian girls."

Arne Naess, eight years older than Diana, was born in 1936, the only child of a German father, a doctor, and a Norwegian mother. He moved to Norway in 1945 at the age of nine with his mother, Kiki, when his parents were divorced. Kiki, who dedicated herself to raising her child alone, took her maiden name back when she left Germany. The name of Arne's father, who had practically no influence on his son's upbringing, has never been publicly revealed.

Norway was certainly not the ideal place to be for someone who spoke only German; most Norwegians were antagonistic toward Germans because World War II had just ended. As a child, Arne was taunted by the other youngsters, beaten up daily by his schoolmates and called a "Nazi pig" and "Hitler Youth." He became a loner.

"I didn't know what to do," said his mother. "If I went to talk to the other boys, he would be a momma's boy and never forgive me for that. I just had to tell him to fight back as much as he could. Fighting in school set the pace for the rest of his life. He always had a them-against-me attitude."

Arne's young life was complicated by dyslexia, a learning disability where letters and words are incorrectly perceived. Dyslexia frustrated him; he would say later that he knew he was intelligent but no one else did. Because of his childhood, Arne was always thought of by his friends and family as an angry young man fighting for attention and acceptance.

"Little Arne" was named after his mother's brother, a noted philosophy professor at the University of Oslo who was also a mountain climber. His Uncle Arne became the most influential male in his life and taught him to be strong, defiant and independent. The older man took his nephew on his first mountain-climbing expedition when the youngster was only eight years old. It's been said that Arne dropped out of high school after failing Norwegian language studies, which he blamed on his dyslexia. Others insist he graduated in 1956 when he was 18 and celebrated by climbing the tower of the National Theatre building in Oslo and placing his student's cap on top of the needle. Discrepancies are part of the mystery surrounding Arne Naess.

After a couple of years in the Norwegian military, Arne left Norway in 1960 and traveled abroad as a deckhand on a Liberian tanker. He then worked as a ski instructor in Japan, and in shipyards in England, Italy and Germany. Finally, in 1964, he started working for another of his mother's brothers, Earling Naess, in New York, known at the time as one of the three richest men in international shipping. When his uncle sold his enterprise, Arne left the business with $200 in his pocket and, he has recalled, "a lot of get up and go."

"Dreams are always bigger than what actually happens in a man's life, but I must say that I was never modest in my dreams," he once admitted. "I was very ambitious, much more than people around me even knew."

In 1968, Arne began working as a trainee for Haakon Fretheim, a shipping broker in New York. Later that year, he married Filippa Kumlin, 10 years his junior and a stunning, exotic woman who, with dark, penetrating eyes and brown hair, was a most unusual-looking Swede. It was her second marriage, the first being a short-lived union with a Brazilian playboy. Kumlin's father was the Swedish ambassador in Paris; her brother was also a diplomat. She attended the finest Swiss finishing schools, and Ingrid Bergman, her mother's best friend, was her unofficial godmother.

Filippa's mother, was, as the wife of the ambassador, considered one of the greatest Parisian hostesses of her time. She was not pleased that her only daughter had fallen in love with Arne, a man who had less than $200 to his name. When Filippa and Arne married, he didn't seem to have much of a future.

But Filippa was extremely devoted to her new husband and completely supported him and his aspirations for the next five years, boosting his ego and assuring him that he would one day be the success in shipping he dreamed of becoming. Arne promised her that one day he would be successful, and together they would share in his empire. Meanwhile, Filippa would pay the bills.

Too proud to ask for money from her parents—especially considering that they were not happy about her marriage to Arne—Filippa sold her personal possessions to pay for living expenses, including her jewelry which helped to subsidize the rent on their New York apartment.

Filippa's father decided that his daughter had sacrificed enough for her husband and purchased a fashionable three-bedroom, three-bathroom apartment on East 86th Street in New York for the couple, telling Arne that he expected him to one day pay him back. Marrying Filippa Kumlin was definitely a step up the social ladder for Arne Naess. He had been trying desperately to network into the established shipping community of New York, but was having difficulty doing so.

Filippa gave Arne social clout. She was instrumental in introducing him to the right people because his marriage to her gave him credibility in social, and also in royal, circles. Her friends Princess Christina of Sweden and her younger brother Prince Gustav—who would become king—would often visit, bringing other royals with them. "Having royalty come by the house was good for business," one friend of Arne's said, only half joking.

Around 1972, when Arne began to make a great deal of money in shipping as an independent businessman, he and his now-partner Fretheim had a disagreement over finances and separated.

(Years later, when Fretheim married, Arne sent him a telegram that was read aloud at the very conservative ceremony: "Dear Haakon, I wish you the very best. I'm sure this marriage will not interfere with our relationship. Much love, Xaviera Hollander." Fretheim and his bride were angry with Arne for embarrassing them at their wedding with a phony telegram from the "Happy Hooker." But Arne said in his defense that he never intended to humiliate them; he was just trying to be a good sport.)

In the '70s, Arne Naess made his fortune as a shipping broker. In just two business ventures, he made 100 to 200 million Norwegian *kroner*, roughly 30 million American dollars. "He makes his money by buying fast and selling fast," noted one Norwegian reporter. "He has amazing instincts and always has a hunch as to when to sell for a big profit."

"People used to say, 'After meeting with Arne, count your fingers before leaving the room,' " Arne observed. "But I have always been more concerned about collecting experiences than property and money." He and Filippa had three children: Cristoffer, Katrinka and Leona (16, 13 and 10, respectively, at the time their father met Diana Ross in 1985).

The Naesses eventually purchased a luxury apartment in Manhattan, the penthouse of a building on 79th Street. Filippa told her friends, though, that she had a difficult time convincing Arne to repay the money her father had spent when he purchased the apartment for them on East 86th Street. Finally, Arne relented and paid back the loan.

Filippa Naess, a talented interior decorator, furnished the

apartment in tasteful whites and pastels with exquisite works of art decorating the walls. She designed all of the furniture personally and had each piece custom-made. The apartment was featured in *Vogue* and *Architectural Digest*.

One morning, Filippa received a troublesome phone call from Arne saying that he was experiencing some sort of financial problem and that she had one week to sell the apartment, take the children out of school and move to London. She had no choice but to give up her career as an interior decorator and move. The furniture was put in storage.

Eventually, Filippa designed and built a home in Verbier, Switzerland, a very fashionable city two hours from Geneva. But then, in 1978, Arne and Filippa separated, divorcing three years later.

Apparently, according to close friends of Filippa's, the couple never had a formal divorce agreement. When she went to the Dominican Republic for a divorce, Filippa was left with the temporary separation agreement that provided her with what she considered just a small amount of money—the amount is unknown—and use of the guest house of the chalet she designed in Verbier. Arne promised her that one day he would provide her with more of a financial and property settlement, so she put her career on hold in order to devote her time and attention to raising their three children.

When Filippa asked Arne for the furniture she had designed for the New York apartment, he apparently refused to give it to her. Instead, he instructed his employees to take the pieces they wanted out of storage. Soon after, Filippa began hearing from members of Arne's staff—many of whom thought she simply didn't want the furniture—such comments as "I'm the one who got your couch and I just love it. Thank you so much."

As the years passed, Filippa Naess began to see that she was not going to get much more of a settlement from Arne. Hurt and disillusioned—considering the fact that she supported him in the early days of their marriage—in the next ten years Filippa would consult the best lawyers in New York and London, all of whom advised her not to waste her time and money attempting to track down her husband's investments. One attorney told her that it would cost $100,000 just to locate Arne's money because it is so well hidden. Even if she paid that amount, there was no telling how much of Arne's capital would be found.

By 1980, Arne Naess was an investor in nearly 25 companies registered in Liberia, Bermuda, Switzerland, the United States, the Canary Islands and Sweden. Although he is said to own 50 to 100 percent of the stock in these companies, none of them bears his name, so it is difficult to trace his interests. Naess invests his money in gold and other metals, oil, ships and oil rigs. He also stations his companies in places like Panama, countries called "tax paradises," because corporations located there are exempt from paying taxes. (The country benefits by the business entrepreneurs generate there.)

Naess remembered in 1980, "I don't pay taxes anywhere. When I moved to England, I had to document my fortune to prove that I wouldn't be a burden to the country. Since I don't pay taxes, there are many people here who regard me as a parasite. But my children go to private school and if they are sick we take care of them privately. So I feel that I pay my own way."

Arne continues to pay for the children's schooling, but Filippa's friends say that she has not gotten any money from her ex-husband in many years. "And if ever a woman deserves half of a husband's wealth, it is Filippa," says one longtime friend. But because of Arne's shrewd business dealings, his ex-wife has no hope of ever finding Naess' wealth. One lawyer she consulted apparently was impressed enough by Arne's savvy to go on to represent him in his marital negotiations with Diana Ross.

"If you're looking for my headquarters, they are where I am at any given moment," he said in 1980. "I know that some people think I'm hard-nosed, but when I do business with grown-up people, I expect that they can take care of their own interests."

Naess had been preparing to climb Mount Everest for seven years, finally attaining his goal just before meeting Diana. He said that the climb gave him new purpose in his life. "If one seeks the weak points in me," he says, "one can find them in my desire to risk life and limb."

When Diana appeared at Caesars Tahoe in Nevada, Arne flew in to surprise her. As she entertained, Arne turned to one of Diana's aides backstage and whispered, "I have never heard her sing before."

"You're kidding," said the aide.

Arne watched and listened. "You know, she's pretty good, isn't she?"

Soon, Arne began showing up in the front row at her concerts in London, Stockholm and Paris. Apparently, when he met Diana, he had been engaged to popular redheaded Norwegian state actress Mari Maurstad who was, at that time, in her late twenties. Maurstad comes from a prominent family of Norwegian actors and it is said she was very much in love with Arne. But when Diana came into his life, Arne was no longer interested in

Mari or any other woman. Naess owned an apartment in Oslo which he apparently gave Maurstad when he broke off with her.

The attraction between Arne Naess and Diana Ross was immediate. When the King of Norway offered Arne a knighthood, Arne asked Diana to be at his side. The press soon heard about the whirlwind romance, but Diana, who was under the mistaken impression that Arne valued his privacy, was terrified of scaring him off with the publicity she always seems to generate.

Actually, Arne Naess loves the glamour and glare of show business. To him, the media hoopla he causes in his home country of Norway when he climbs a mountain or makes a savvy business deal is just as important as any sense of personal achievement. Diana Ross could give Arne Naess what he did not have and what he was intrigued by, international fame and Hollywood glamour. By merely dating a show business star, he would be considered daring. Marrying a black diva would bring him instant notoriety.

In return, Arne seemed like the perfect catch for Diana. He is European, has a continental veneer that Diana found very attractive, and appeared to be tremendously rich. In other words, he isn't a ne'er-do-well Hollywood type like Ryan O'Neal or Gene Simmons. Naess had class, money and royal connections. Diana may well have thought she would gain immediate entree into the world of title, money and jet-set glamour. To marry him would be the ultimate fantasy, a Cinderella story come true.

The couple seemed to fall in love quickly.

Diana Ross had reached another turning point in her life. Her feelings for Arne were strong, and she must have known what they would lead to because she finally decided to sell the Beverly Hills house in the summer of 1985 for $1.75 million. The home was purchased by television producer-director James Burrows ["Cheers"] for $1.15 million less than Diana's original asking price. After Burrows bought the house, he posted two signs on the front lawn: "Diana Ross Does Not Live Here Anymore!" and "Please Do Not Disturb!"

She has said that selling the windowless fortress on Maple Avenue was more of an emotional experience for her than she thought it would be. Quite a lot had happened in that house in the seven years she lived there: Berry, Bob, the children, her new independence. Whenever Diana was in Los Angeles, she would have her driver take her there and she would sit in front of the house and think. There were many memories, but it was time to let them go.

Diana suddenly became very protective of her romance with

Arne, or, as one friend put it, "this was one man she didn't want to lose." She did not wish to answer questions about her new beau and did not like to have photographs of them appearing in newspapers and magazines, not until she could be sure of how he felt about her, and her fame.

The Oslo press reported that Diana and Arne would be engaged when she took time off from the Scandinavian leg of an upcoming European tour, so when the couple got to France in September 1985, the press was waiting for them.

Arne and Diana and her three daughters arrived at the Plaza Athenée Hotel in Paris in a black limousine accompanied by two bodyguards and a secretary. The bodyguards approached a waiting photographer, Erik Poppe, and warned him that he could not take pictures.

When Poppe ignored them and began shooting away, the photographer claimed, "They began kicking at me, throwing karate chops and chasing me. I ran through the cars to get away from them. While this was going on, Diana and the entourage ran into the hotel."

Poppe ran off to get reinforcements, and when he returned to the hotel, Diana, Arne, and the girls had already left for dinner at Maxim's restaurant.*

As they left the restaurant after dinner, Diana apparently told her children to hide their faces so that they could not be photographed. She and Arne did the same. Off they went in their limousine, with three more photographers in hot pursuit. When Diana's limousine stopped at a red light, one jumped out of his car, ran up to Diana's and quickly snapped a photo of her angry expression through the window.

At the next red light, the black limousine door flew open and Diana Ross jumped out. As Arne and the girls watched, Diana rushed to the startled photographer's car, reached into his open window and grabbed his camera. Then she smashed it to the ground.

"There! How do you like that?"

She scurried back to her limousine and it screeched off, headed back to the hotel.

Now the photographers felt challenged and followed her. Once the limousine pulled up to the hotel, the paparazzi tried again to take pictures of Diana and Arne.

---

*When Arne learned that Poppe was a photographer working for the Oslo press, he made a public apology, saying that both he and his ladyfriend were "extremely sorry."

"Diana just flipped out," recalled photographer Alain Masiero. "She took off her shoes and started beating the photographers with them. She was definitely trying to hurt someone, aiming for their heads with the pointed heels. She made one photographer's arm bleed as he tried to protect his face with his hand. She was yelling obscenities—shrieking and shouting as if she'd gone crazy, lashing out at the photographers."

Hiding their faces, Rhonda, 14, Tracee, 13, and Chudney, 11, ran inside the hotel. Seeing mother out of control must have frightened them. Said Masiero, "She didn't want to stop fighting. She suddenly ran after me to hit me but fell and lay sprawled on the ground."

As Diana tried to collect herself, Masiero snapped off a few shots of her lying in the parking lot in her stocking feet with her high heels in her hands.

"You just leave me alone," Diana shouted at her chauffeur as he tried to help her up. "Goddammit!"

She was still yelling at the photographers as Arne convinced her to retreat.

"It was amazing," Masiero recalled. "I'd always thought of Diana Ross as a great lady. But she's more like a street-fighter. I haven't photographed her since that night. She's too dangerous."

After so many years of being in show business, Diana must have known she could have just posed and gotten it over with. Perhaps she was trying to protect Arne and her children from the photographers. For years she had been cooperative with the paparazzi; now they had finally caught her in a weak moment. Whatever the case, the next day, photos of a wild-eyed Diana swinging her high heels at photographers were published in newspapers all over Europe.

Diana said later that she felt that she, Arne and the girls deserved one night of privacy together. When she couldn't get that, the reason why became a matter of principle to her.

It was said that Arne's reaction to all of this was both sympathy and amusement. "How have you been able to tolerate these leeches all of this time?" he asked.

"I have to," was her response. "It's my job, damn it."

Arne later told one friend, "It was rather exciting, I must admit." Naess may have been fascinated by all of the attention, but considering the fact that he personally apologized to the photographer from Oslo who had been hurt by one of Diana's bodyguards, he probably did not condone the fact that Diana had gone berserk in the hotel parking lot.

In October 1985, while Diana was on the European concert trail, some very sudden decisions were made.

On Monday, October 21, she performed in Rome and became very unpopular there when, according to the Italian press, she requested that no one attending her concert should wear blue jeans, but rather formal clothing, and she insisted that she be driven around in a white Rolls with a 24-hour chauffeur at her disposal. As far as the dress was concerned, Diana probably hoped to establish a "mood" in the theater, but the media considered hers a haughty request. The Rolls was just chalked up to being more diva-like excess.

When she learned that an October 24 concert in Paris had been canceled because of a labor strike, she decided to return to New York City. As soon as she got there, she and Arne applied for a marriage license.

The next evening, Wednesday, October 23, Diana and Arne were married at 8:00 P.M. at Blanche Etra's Madison Avenue office after all of the employees left. Etra, who was a witness to the ceremony, is one of Ross' many attorneys. Besides one other friend, there were no guests. Diana, who wore a short purple dress and held a bouquet, and Arne, in a conservative blue suit and white shirt, exchanged rings and drank champagne. The ceremony took three minutes and was reminiscent of Diana's first quickie wedding in Las Vegas to Robert Silberstein. After another ten minutes of toasting, Diana and Arne left for Gurney's Inn, a resort in Montauk, New York, the eastern tip of Long Island.

Diana's publicist, Gail Roberts, apparently was not informed of the wedding. Arne's office in London was also unaware of what had happened. Finally Arne made a statement: "We deny it. We're denying everything."

Diana and Arne continued to insist that the wedding never took place, even though *New York Post* columnist Cindy Adams broke the story. "I bumped into this judge, Theodore Kupferman," she reported. "I badgered Kupferman face-to-face. Reluctantly, he admitted it. 'They wanted this kept secret,' he said, 'but if you're asking me directly I have to answer honestly. Yes.' "

Diana and Arne had the secret wedding ceremony for business reasons that are still unclear, but since the couple seemed determined to marry before the end of the year, their decision probably had to do with taxes, likely Diana's, as Arne still insists he doesn't pay any. Since Diana did not have the sensational wedding she had always dreamed of, she immediately began to plan one. The date was set for February 1, 1986, in Switzerland. Arne decided to humor his new wife and go along with her idea for a second wedding, even though the fact that they were already married was not much of a secret anymore.

The wedding would be a spectacular affair, and first on Diana's guest list was Michael Jackson. Many have felt that Jackson's fame had long eclipsed Diana's, and she must have realized that having him at the ceremony would be a major coup and certainly help garner the kind of press she hoped the event would generate for her. She even considered asking Jackson to give her away.

Diana had noticed that Michael was acting particularly strange in recent years. She had extended many invitations to him to visit her at her home, but after *Thriller* became a major hit in 1984, he started to decline her offers and spend more time with Elizabeth Taylor, Sophia Loren, Liza Minnelli and other "competing" stars. In turn Diana began to distance herself from Michael.

"I think he's getting stranger and stranger," she told one confidante. "And, frankly, it scares me. I'm scared for him. What kind of life will he have? I really do care."

One evening, before the American Music Awards in January 1986, which Diana hosted, Michael visited her in Las Vegas where she was appearing at Caesars Palace. She later told Cindy Birdsong and John Whyman that she was sitting with Jackson in her dressing room when she was called away. When she returned, Michael wasn't in the sitting room where she had left him. Whyman recalled, "She told us that she looked around for him and eventually found him sitting in front of her make-up mirror carefully putting on her make-up."

Slowly, methodically, he was transforming himself into the very image of Miss Ross.

"Michael, now you get out of my make-up," Diana scolded him.

"But it's magic!" he insisted with a lip-glossed grin.

"Diana seemed very concerned about him," Whyman remembered. " 'I just wish he would be himself,' she told us in a confidential tone. 'I wish he would stop worrying about what people will think of him if he just got real. After all,' she said with a knowing look in her eye, 'He did write that song "Muscles" for me.' "

Michael Jackson was truly heartbroken that Diana Ross planned to marry Arne Naess, and would later say that he was particularly hurt that she hadn't even introduced him to Arne, especially since they were already man and wife. "I was jealous because I've always loved Diana Ross and always will," he claimed. Michael simply could not believe that Diana would actually marry this square-looking fellow. Jackson was apparently still obsessed with her, even though they were now living in entirely different worlds.

No matter how famous Michael Jackson becomes, he is still intrigued by the mystique of Diana Ross. When he was a youngster, he would study videotapes of her so that he could imitate the way she moved on stage. "He used to use his hands and arms like me," Diana once noted. She was very flattered by this imitation and wanted to influence Michael in any way she could. When Michael searched for his own style, the two spent endless hours talking about entertaining. He would ask Diana many questions about the way she performed, and it was often difficult for her to explain to him what she did on stage. Her art has always been instinctual. She rarely analyzed it.

"You just be you," she told Michael. "Don't be me. Don't be anyone else. Be Michael Jackson, and you'll be a star. I guarantee it."

"But I just want to be like you, Diane," he told her. "I want to thrill people the way you do."

Though Diana had been accused of feeling competitive where other top record artists are concerned, mutual friends of hers and Michael's insist that she has never been jealous of her protégé's fame. Rather she is proud of him and the influence she has had on him. Regardless of the fact that Michael Jackson has himself now influenced a whole generation of younger performers, he is still desperate for attention from the woman he had idolized as a youth. Letting Diana go is, to Michael, tantamount to growing up. Michael Jackson really does not want to grow up. He's said so many times.

Before Diana married Arne, Michael insisted that she was the one and only love of his life, something he seemed to believe. "Yes, I would like to marry her," he said. And when someone brought up the 14-year age difference, he said, "So what? What does age have to do with this. Look at it this way: how old would you be if you didn't even know how old you were?"

It must have been a difficult decision for him to make, but Michael Jackson would not go to Diana Ross' wedding, let alone give her away.

Things would never again be the same between them.

In addition to Michael, Berry Gordy felt sad over Diana's marriage. Diana had finally made a life for herself that did not include him. Moreover, she did so with a man everyone said was wealthier than Berry was. Somehow, say his friends, Berry always believed she would come back to him, especially after she appeared on the "Motown 25" program. Just a year before the wedding, Diana had said about Berry, "I love him desperately. I always have. He's my relative, my family. I don't think we can ever not love each other."

But despite his hurt feelings, Berry was a good loser. He hosted a party for Diana and Arne at his Bel Air home to celebrate the upcoming wedding, a generous gesture. He wanted Diana to be happy—that is really what he had always wanted for her through the years—and he had to admire Arne considering that the two of them are very much alike. Though they are from completely different backgrounds, they share common streaks of determination and ambition. Both men made something of themselves despite tremendous odds, Arne in industry, Berry in the record game. Both are self-promoters and staunch believers in the benefits of good public relations, that is what the public believes to be true is much more important than the truth.

Berry would not, however, attend the wedding. Suzanne dePasse would.

Diana had always said that she intended to marry a wealthy man, just as her idol, Jackie Onassis, had married Aristotle Onassis. By 1985, Arne Naess was said to be worth more than $100 million, but those reports of his wealth were exaggerated. He is a rich man, but not that rich. Of course, this discussion of finances is relative. Arne is a millionaire many times over, but close business associates estimate his liquid wealth to be about $25 million.

In Norway, reports of Arne Naess' finances have always been overblown, but never more so than when he and Diana began dating. It all seemed to be part of an unofficial campaign designed to infer that Ross had found the ideal tycoon she had often told people she was looking for. Arne apparently never denied the ridiculous reports of his great wealth, he just never commented, and neither did Diana. Rather, they let the rumor-mill churn because, in this case, the stories benefited their public images. Diana Ross had learned from the master, Berry Gordy (who inflated her record sales for public consumption), that image was everything.

Out of loyalty to Naess, a countryman, many reporters of the Norwegian press have not revealed the actual extent of Naess' wealth. In Norway, Arne is extremely wealthy even if that is not the case by American standards. Still, just as with his wife, it seems that most of Naess' friends and associates are reticent to discuss him without a guarantee of anonymity (even though Naess, unlike Ross, apparently does not request that the people with whom he does business sign secrecy agreements).

"I am absolutely sure that Diana Ross has a lot more money than Arne Naess," said one person who has known Naess for more than two decades and who, as a reporter, has covered Naess' exploits in the Norwegian press for many of those years. "Definitely. There's no doubt in my mind. My estimate is that Arne is worth somewhere around $15, maybe $20 million, no more. He is certainly not as they say one of the richest men in the world. Everyone in Norway who cares, knows."

Diana's total wealth has been estimated to be $500 million but that figure, too, has been exaggerated. She is actually worth about $75 million.* Diana was advanced $20 million when she signed with RCA in 1981. The money was wisely invested and the return for her has been enormous.

Since the early '80s, Diana Ross earns a minimum of $100,000 for a one-nighter; often she makes double that amount. It would be difficult to tally all of the one-nighters she has done since she left Motown, though the amount would be in the many hundreds. In 1989 alone, she would do at least 50 of them. No one but Diana and her accountants can be certain of what she made on record sales in the '80s because of her high-advance deal with RCA, and the fact that most of the records have not been successful. She is making a negligable $80,000 annually on royalties from records recorded at Motown in the '60s and '70s.

Certainly, it would appear that Diana has more money than Arne, and, in fact, so might Berry Gordy, Jr. Gordy's estimated worth was $75 million in 1981, and since he sold Motown for $65 million in 1988, even if half of that amount went for taxes and stocks to family members, which is extremely unlikely, he may still be worth more than Naess.

To put Naess' wealth into perspective, even if he is worth $50 million, *twice* as much as his friends and associates believe, that is really not much money in the world of high finance. According to *Forbes* magazine's list of Highest Paid Entertainers (September 1988), Michael Jackson made a total of $97 million in just two years, 1987 and 1988. Bill Cosby made $95 million in that two-year period. Sylvester Stallone, $63 million. If Naess' business associates have estimated his total wealth accurately at

---

*The richest entertainer in the world is said to be Paul McCartney, who has an estimated personal fortune of $560 million. His royalties alone come to a staggering $112,000 a day—$41 million a year.

$25 million—well, that's what Oprah Winfrey made in 1988 alone.

When *Forbes* and *Fortune* magazines publish their annual lists of the richest men in the world—most are billionaires, not millionaires—Arne Naess is never included. Perhaps he would say that the reason for his absence from such lists is because he does not want specifics of his wealth revealed, but it would seem that he really does not qualify.

Arne Naess was not eager to have another marriage ceremony, but he understood his wife's desire to have a big, highly publicized wedding. Arne enjoys high-profile publicity as much as Diana. But, still, Naess couldn't help but be embarrassed by the opulent spectacle planned by Diana. He told his former wife and his children that the upcoming grand wedding was Diana's idea and that he had ambivalent feelings about it. He would go along with it just to placate his new bride.

However, when he discovered that the wedding would cost about $500,000, he drew the line. According to Norwegian friends, he told her that he was not going to pay for it.

Arne has never completely understood Diana's extravagances. His mother, Kiki, had worked very hard to make sure her only son had everything he needed. She is still, in her late eighties, a totally selfless person who is Arne's ideal of the "perfect woman." Throughout his marriage to Filippa, Arne often complained that she spent too much money and chastised her by saying his mother never needed designer clothes, so why should she? He encouraged her to dress in cheap clothing, and because she was so devoted to him, she did what she was told. Still, Kiki had always felt that Filippa was a pretentious socialite. After Arne and Filippa divorced, Kiki told Arne that in order to be happy with a woman, he should find himself "a little field flower." Kiki wanted her son to marry an unpretentious waif. Instead he ended up with Diana Ross.

Norwegians, like Arne Naess, are traditionally embarrassed by conspicuous consumption. Since making his fortune, Naess has had the best, but he has been frugal, often even cheap. But Diana is influenced by Hollywood and the whole show business ethos, one in which rich stars spend their money carelessly because they are used to not only having the best, but *lots* of the best. Arne would have to make the necessary adjustments to Diana's lifestyle because she wasn't about to adjust to his. She had been far too independent for far too long. After Berry Gordy, Diana promised herself that she would never again let another man dictate to her how she should spend her money.

Today, even though Arne is often baffled by Diana's spending habits—her private jets ($25,000 a week), her limousines, the expensive homes she must rent whenever she is appearing somewhere for a long period of time ($20,000 a month)—he does not even dare to venture an opinion, especially since most of the money Diana spends is her own.

Friends of the couple predict that this difference is bound to cause conflict in the marriage. Just as it appears that Arne has tried to use his money to dominate Filippa, if Diana ever does the same to Arne the marriage won't last long. Whatever else he may be, Arne Naess is not the type to allow anyone to push him around. Also, according to people who know him well, if he ever begins to feel inferior because of Diana's greater wealth, that will not bode well for the relationship. After the way he was taunted in school, Arne vowed never again to allow himself to feel in any way inferior to anyone.

Certainly, Diana is accustomed to great extravagances in her private life, so the reason for this wedding seemed to be solely for *public* relations. Apparently, she did not want anyone to know that she and Arne had already been married because that would have sapped some of the important drama from the wedding ceremony. She was writing, producing and directing what she would later call "the biggest show of my life." But if she wanted a grand wedding to "one of the richest men in the world"—one that would make the cover of *People* magazine—Diana Ross would have to pay for it herself. She would do so, and gladly.

The second Ross/Naess ceremony was held on February 1, 1986, in a 10th-century Swiss Reformed church in Romainmotier, a small picturesque village in the foothills of the Jura mountains just outside of Geneva. Two hundred and forty people attended the service. The 45-member Norwegian *Soelvguttene* Boy's Choir sang. Diana was dressed in a white satin dress with a bodice of pearl embroidered lace. She flew a hairdresser from Los Angeles to Sweden first class ($15,000) just so that he could pull her long hair back in a chignon. Her white veil of antique, hand-made Belgian lace was crowned with a 250-year-old diamond tiara. Over each ear she wore white roses and baby's breath to match her bridal bouquet. The Bob Mackie-designed wedding ensemble reportedly cost about $50,000. The veil itself cost $12,000, the tiara about $10,000. Seven thousand dollars were spent on flowers, imported from London. Diana's smile was bright and electric. She never looked happier.

"Repeat after me," Graham Ferguson Leasy, a Baptist minister, instructed Arne. "I want you to be my wife because I love you."

According to press reports, Arne looked deep into his bride's eyes and repeated in his charming accented English, "I want you to be my wife because I love you." Then he added with a sly grin, "and because I desire you."

"We will respect each other's individuality and not change each other for our own gratification," Diana promised as her three children and Arne's two daughters, all bridesmaids, watched.

After they were pronounced husband and wife, Diana and Arne embraced and kissed passionately for several moments. For Diana Ross, a girl from the Brewster Projects of Detroit, this whole scene must have seemed surreal. Arne Naess certainly appeared to be the idealized, romantic catch of every woman, white, as well as every black. And he was hers. The fact that she really had more money than he did was inconsequential since no one knew about that. None of Diana's immediate family, other than her children, was in the wedding party and, indeed, from all reports, it doesn't seem that any of them even attended the wedding.

Rather, Diana Ross was surrounded by $70,000 worth of security men.

Following the hour-long ceremony, Diana donned a satin-lined white mink wrap before leaving for the reception. She and Arne emerged from the church and walked under a row of crossed ice axes used in mountain climbing. A lavish wedding reception followed at the Beau Rivage Palace Hotel in Lausanne. Fifty thousand dollars were spent on chauffeured limousines and buses which came complete with waiters, caviar and champagne. After a lunch of roast veal, waiters served a chocolate wedding cake (which was flown 6,655 miles from San Francisco) while Stevie Wonder sang "I Just Called to Say I Love You." Stevie performed gratis.

In its cover story, "Diana's Supreme Day," *People* magazine claimed that the wedding cost $1 million. "How could anyone think I would spend a million dollars on a wedding," she exclaimed to John Whyman. "They must think I'm crazy. Actually, it only cost me half that much." Diana confessed that she bought accessories for the bridesmaids' outfits at Montgomery Ward.

Diana and Arne had a disagreement as to who should pay for the guests' accommodations while they were in Switzerland. Arne felt that inviting people to a lavish wedding and then paying for their air-fare and their hotel suites was, as he put it to one friend, "a nouveau-riche thing to do." If these guests were friends, Arne reasoned, surely they could pay for their own accommodations. Among the European Establishment, it is not considered good taste to throw what Arne called "a wild, Arabic-type party" and then pay for everything. Naess has never been the type to host big, expensive parties to make himself look popular, mostly because he doesn't like to spend that kind of money. But Diana is from a world where a star wouldn't think of inviting her friends to a big affair and then not pay for everything. As often happens, husband and wife could not see eye-to-eye on the particulars of the wedding arrangements.

Eventually, it was agreed that the guests would pay for their own accommodations, even though Diana seemed to be embarrassed by this decision. Apparently, she didn't invite many friends of hers since so few were there. Those working for Diana in different capacities (her hairdresser, her gown mistress, her maid and other servants) would have their accommodations paid for by their lady-boss. Arne didn't need to pay for any assistance; he put on his own tux.

The newlyweds honeymooned on their private Pacific island on Taino. Though Arne had owned the island for 13 years, his first wife Filippa has never been to it, so Diana must have felt that this was a good sign.

Some of Arne's friends, family and business associates viewed Diana's union with Arne Naess not only with skepticism but cynicism. For instance, one of Arne's closest relatives had this comment to make about his new wife: "Well, okay, I admit it: she is not very deep. But she always seems so happy. Negroes are always happy, really. They're always laughing, smiling and playing music."

Another very close relative told Arne, "You have *affairs* with those kinds of women. You don't *marry* them."

A former girlfriend of Arne had this observation: "Oh, yes, Arne has gone off and married the big Negro mama with long, pink nails." That comment was published in the Norwegian press.

Arne Naess has apparently taken quite a bit of flak for marrying a black woman. Many people in the shipping community and in Arne's social circle do not care that Diana Ross is a star. They only care that she is black and that is a constant topic of conversation.

For instance, Arne and his ex-wife, Filippa, were members of the Maidstone Club in East Hampton on Long Island, New York, for many years. Filippa had friends on the Board and was able to influence them so that she and Arne could obtain a membership. Private clubs of this nature are traditionally very conservative. One such establishment in Southhampton called The Meadow Club would not allow Lee Radziwill to join because the board feared she would come to dinner with Andy Warhol and his wacky New York friends. Most members of The Meadow Club considered people like Warhol riffraff.

According to one report, the exclusive, very conservative Maidstone Club only allows three Jews to be members. But one member of the Maidstone Club for over 40 years said, "That's a pernicious lie. There are plenty of Jewish people who are members. Only someone who is not a member would spread a lie like that." As for blacks, he said, "How many blacks do you know who join expensive private clubs?"

Filippa enjoyed belonging to the Maidstone Club because of the youth activities it offered. After the separation, one of the few generosities Arne did extend to Filippa was to pay the rent on a home in East Hampton for her and the children so that they could use the facilities provided by the nearby Maidstone Club.

It's been said by friends in Naess' inner circle that Arne and Diana had dinner at the Maidstone Club one Sunday evening while a table filled with three generations of white grandparents, parents and children sat staring at them in disbelief because they were an interracial couple. Making matters even more "controversial," Diana and Arne were supposedly necking frantically at their table in between courses. Soon afterwards, Arne was kicked out of the Maidstone Club.

This story had been circulating among Naess' inner circle, even though it is apparently not true. According to the Maidstone Club's confidential records, Arne Naess did not renew his membership after divorcing Filippa, which he would be required to do under the club's by-laws if he intended to continue being a member. (So it would seem that the widely published reports that Naess was a current member of "the prestigious Maidstone Club" when he married Diana Ross was just more public relations hype to enhance his image.)

While it is true that the Naess children are no longer permitted to use the club's facilities, the reason that is so is not due to their father's marriage to Diana Ross but because the membership simply wasn't renewed. Moreover, according to the club's rules, Filippa Naess had the opportunity to re-apply for membership after the divorce had she chosen to do so.

Indeed, the fact that a popular rumor has it that Arne was

kicked out of this private club just because he was kissing his black wife in the dining room probably speaks volumes for whatever other kinds of problems the Naesses have experienced since marrying.

It's been said that Diana's children—Rhonda, Tracee and Chudney—did not have an easy adjustment when, six months after the wedding, Diana enrolled them in the same private Swiss prep school, Le Rosey, that Arne's children attended. The school is international in its student body—Arabs, English, Germans, French, Scandinavians, all in attendance—but blacks are definitely in the minority.

Just as in Norway, there are not many blacks in Verbier, Switzerland, where Arne and Diana share a chalet with the children. Switzerland is still a homogeneous country and people who are not northern European may appear more exotic than they would be in other countries. "Even if you are Diana Ross' children, if you go down the slopes or to a restaurant or out at night, unless you have a label on that says 'I am Diana Ross' child,' they don't know who you are and may be stand-offish," said one friend of Diana's.

Though Arne's children by his marriage to Filippa have many friends in Verbier and have been able to introduce Diana's offspring into their social circle, it is still not easy for her daughters. In what seems like a peculiar decision, Diana had her own children give up their father's name of Silberstein and enrolled them in Le Rosey under the surname of Ross. Diana has never explained her decision. It has been speculated perhaps she did so in order to insure that when her daughters are introduced they would be instantly identified as being children of a celebrity.

"In Scandinavia, now, they have gone totally matriarchal," explained a friend of Diana's. "The children there often get the mother's name unless you say otherwise. Personally, I'm all for it. If you want to be really practical about it, you always know who the mother of a child is but maybe not the father."

"Of course, I love my father," one of the girls reportedly said from Switzerland, explaining the name change. "But there was too much confusion."

A year later, when a photo taken by Rhonda Suzanne was used in a feature about her mother in *Us* magazine, the photo credit read "Rhonda Ross." (When she graduated from the exclusive Riverdale Country Day School outside of New York City in June 1989, Rhonda was also identified in the *New York Post* as "Rhonda Suzanne Ross.")

It is not known how Bob Silberstein feels about his children's new last name, though Silberstein has proved himself to be rather pliable over the years where Diana and her decisions are concerned. Not only that, he himself has decided to drop the Silberstein and is now using his middle name of Ellis as his last name.

Filippa Naess was having a particularly difficult time adjusting to Arne's new marriage. When she was invited to the fortieth birthday of King Gustav of Sweden, she decided not to go even though she and the King have been friends for many years. She knew that Arne would be in attendance with Diana, and that Diana would be the center of attention among Filippa's old friends. Though her friends urged her to attend—since she was the one who introduced Arne to the King in the first place—she felt uncomfortable about it.

She was also particularly upset whenever Diana Ross would bring her new stepchildren—Filippa's two daughters and one son—onto the stage during European dates, introduce them as her new family, and then later in press interviews say that all she was concerned about was the welfare of "all her children." Diana, in an obvious effort to be the ideal stepmother, was probably trying to be generous and loving. But according to Filippa's friends, she has always been a devoted, loving mother and Diana's informal "adoption" of her children hurt her deeply.

Arne Naess has, apparently, not had an easy time being a father. "Being with my kids is very important, and I spend a lot of time with them," he once said. But then he clarified, "That depends naturally on who you ask. My wife will say that's not the case." Filippa would agree.

In truth, friends of the Naesses claim that because of his business ventures, Arne spent little time with the children and often demonstrated a marked indifference to raising them. Arne never had a father to influence him when he was a youngster; he had no prior example of fatherhood. Once, one of his offspring had to be hospitalized for an operation. Filippa was told that the hospital bill would amount to $1,600, and that she would need this money before she would be able to admit the child to the New York hospital that specialized in the necessary treatment. She even had to borrow money from a friend to pay for the airline tickets from Europe to America, and once there, accepted the hospitality of another friend who put her up in her apartment. But then, when she told Arne—who was in Oslo at the time with Diana—that she needed $1,600, he sent her a check for $1,000.

Filippa has also told friends that when the children were young, Arne would often have his secretary forward a memo to them that would detail his itinerary so that they would know where their father was. Perhaps Arne was trying to be considerate, but it certainly seemed to family members that he was distancing himself. It was difficult for Arne to be fatherly because, for seven years, he was totally devoted to his ambition of climbing the Himalayas. His aspiration involved great dedication and practice. To practice, he climbed Mount McKinley, mountains in Argentina, and ranges around the world. Once, even Arne's secretary reported to Filippa that she hadn't spoken to him for over a year.

When Filippa and Arne separated, he told her that he was no longer interested in domestic life. Arne had been so preoccupied with his business affairs, he had not been an ideal father. So when he remarried and had two new children almost immediately, her friends say, Filippa found it difficult to reconcile all of this. When he was stingy with financial aid, she must have felt ever more bitter. He denied her emotional support as well. Once, Filippa was having a domestic problem with one of her teen-age children and asked Arne to step in and assist her. Friends say he mailed her an instructional audio tape he had apparently been given by Diana: "How to Deal With Your Teen-Agers."

"If Diana was smart, she would try to influence Arne into taking care of all of this unfinished business with his first wife," said a friend of Filippa's. "But she's not that smart. How can she have a happy marriage to Arne knowing that his first wife is so unhappy? Her position is that Filippa is not her problem. She has no patience for people who don't, in her opinion, have their lives together."

For the sake of her children's peace of mind, Filippa Kumlin Naess was determined to act civil toward her former husband and his present wife.

But Arne and Diana would not make it easy.

Chapter

❦ 29 ❦

DIANA ROSS WAS beginning an exciting new life with Arne Naess at the same time her former singing partner Mary Wilson was getting ready to rehash the old one. She was writing her memoirs, which promised to be a "tell-all," a Diana Ross exposé.

A month after the Naess/Ross wedding, Mary drove to Las Vegas with some friends to visit Diana backstage at Caesars Palace, hoping to corner her for an interview for her book. At this time, Diana was said to be the highest-paid performer in Las Vegas. She was reportedly earning $74,000 per show at Caesars during her two-week stint there (three years earlier, she received $37,000 per show, so her price was steadily rising).

After the show and drinks—to which Diana treated them—Mary Wilson and her entourage went backstage to Diana's dressing room where they found her with Suzanne dePasse, Diana's lawyer, John Frankenheimer, his wife and other friends. Everyone seemed to sense that something was going to happen, as it always did when these two women got together. Perhaps Diana wanted witnesses.

She mentioned to Mary and the others that Arne was on his way to Caesars from the Las Vegas airport, and that after the engagement the two of them would leave for Los Angeles before departing for Taino, their private island.

"Oh," said Mary, "when you get to L.A., call me because I want to talk to you for my book."

The room fell silent.

"What book is that, Mary?" Diana asked. "What's it about?"

"Well, no one wants to read about me," Mary said frankly. "It's about us, The Supremes."

"Is it a good book or a bad book?" Diana asked suspiciously. "I don't know anything about this other than what I've heard from others."

Everyone in the room quietly watched.

"If you call me when you get to L.A., we'll discuss it," Mary said with a frozen smile.

It was Diana's serve.

"Call you. Call you! Why should I call you?" she wanted to know.

"Well, *you're* the one who wants to know about the book," Mary shot back.

Diana then turned to someone else and started a conversation, thereby dismissing Mary and her book. "I was made to feel like I was writing something dirty about her," Mary complained later.

Mary, by now thoroughly agitated, was preparing to leave when Suzanne dePasse popped her head into the dressing room. "Arne's here," she said.

"How wonderful," Diana exclaimed as she bolted up, leaving the room.

Apparently, Arne didn't want to go into the lion's den. Instead, he stayed by the doorway in the hallway. As Arne and Diana kissed passionately in front of everyone, he came up for air long enough to ask, "Isn't that Mary Wilson in there?"

Mary, who had never met Diana's husband (and still hasn't), slipped out without saying good-bye. To date, that would be the last conversation she would have with Diana. Later that evening, she hosted a cocktail party in her suite and invited all of Ross' entourage, most of whom wouldn't dare show up.

Mary Wilson's literary agent, Bart Andrews, said that a mysterious caller offered him a five-figure amount for an advance copy of Wilson's manuscript months before it was published. "I'm pretty certain the caller was from Diana Ross' office," he said.

St. Martin's Press published Mary Wilson's autobiography, *Dreamgirl—My Life as a Supreme*, in October 1986. The book proved difficult to write because Mary could barely remember anything that had happened when she was with The Supremes. She had to have frequent sessions with a hypnotist to jog her memory. Still, all told, Mary would make nearly $1 million from the book, but in the process she would lose Diana Ross forever.

Diana is the godmother of Mary's first born—which she did not mention in the book—so Mary was reluctant to see the ties cut. On radio and TV talk shows, she stubbornly insisted that "I still love Diane, she's my sister," although the book did not show Diana in a good light. If anything, *Dreamgirl* showed that Mary had been harboring a great deal of bitterness and resentment toward Diana over the years.

Some of the questions asked of Mary on her tour concerned Diana's private life. While appearing on a San Francisco television program with Motown's former etiquette teacher, Maxine Powell, someone asked Mary directly whether Berry Gordy was the father of Diana Ross' first child, Rhonda Suzanne. This had been rumored for years. Wilson was at a loss for an answer. Powell began to fan herself with her hand as if she were about to faint.

Weighing her words, Mary Wilson said, "Many people have been whispering that and asking me. I haven't the slightest idea. I was not there. I don't know. Their relationship [Diana and Berry's], as far as I knew, ended before she married her first husband. I deliberately didn't touch those subjects [in my book]."

Publicly, Diana Ross didn't say much about *Dreamgirl*. To *Us* magazine she did imply that she felt that Mary had written the book as a last resort to salvage her failing post-Supremes career.

"I had a notion that there was some survival involved there," she said. "People don't remember. I've been away from The Supremes longer than I've been with The Supremes. And she's had time where, you know, if things aren't working . . .

"I'm godmother to one of her children. I don't see the girl very much anymore, because if your heart is broken, I find it really hard to be close. But I really don't bear ill will."

Mary neglected to mention in *Dreamgirl* that in the summer of 1981, she had called upon Diana for financial assistance. She was desperate to find a place to live for herself and her children. She needed to obtain the down payment for a house. After The Supremes broke up in 1977, she was dropped by Motown Records and then divorced shortly thereafter. Of all the people she knows, Diana was probably the last person in the world she wanted to ask to lend her money. It wasn't an easy decision, but her mother encouraged her to make it. Swallowing her pride, Mary made the phone call.

Diana, touched by her plight, happily lent Mary $30,000 and took back a promissory note drawn up by her business representatives at Loeb and Loeb. One of the four collaborators with whom Mary worked on *Dreamgirl* was distressed to discover that Mary planned to withhold the information about Diana's gener-

osity and the house Mary bought with the loan. The writer felt
uncomfortable writing about Diana under those circumstances.
But Mary told that journalist, and other friends, that she eventually did pay back the money (the note did not call for Mary to
have to pay interest on the loan, and she didn't) and that she
didn't feel it was necessary to mention it in the book. Despite
that, the ghostwriter quit the project.

"After what I did for her, why does she have to have such a
chip on her shoulder?" Diana angrily complained to mutual
friends when *Dreamgirl* was published. "Whenever she has
called on me for help, I have always given it." One former Mary
Wilson employee tried to secure employment in Diana's organization after he quit Mary's, but Ross would not hire him. She
didn't trust him, simply because he once worked for Mary. "And
I don't want that woman to know anything about my business."

That was not the only time Diana gave Mary money. Friends
say it happened more than once. "Sure, she's generous with her
money because she won't be generous with her time," Mary
once privately said of Diana Ross.

Mary Wilson has never discussed publicly any money she's
ever been given by Diana. While Diana's career has certainly
continued almost effortlessly after The Supremes, Mary's has
not. In the years since The Supremes, she has had to live out
her celebrity as a novelty star, a reminder of a glorious past
reclaimed now and then just as a whim. It's not that she doesn't
have the talent, she just hasn't had the luck. Also, Mary Wilson
has been known to make extremely foolish business decisions.

Still, Mary understands the value of public relations just as
well as Diana, because she, too, is a student of Berry Gordy's.
She is not about to reveal to her public that Diana Ross has lent
her money because that would surely indicate that she needed
it. She knows that her fans always want to think of her as they
have always thought of all The Supremes, rich and carefree.
Unfortunately, that fantasy was never true for any of the ladies,
except Diana Ross.

Many observers feel that Mary Wilson's book did great harm
to Diana's career, as well as to her reputation. Though the public
has always suspected that Diana was difficult and self-centered,
Mary's book was the first verification of those characteristics,
and from someone who should know. Unfortunately, Wilson
didn't even give credit to Diana for at least being a brilliant
entertainer who gave The Supremes a sense of commercial identity the other groups at Motown never had.

Diana Ross has not had a major hit record since Mary Wilson's book was published.*

By the spring of 1987, Diana was pregnant with Arne's child, and she was said to be thrilled. She was 43. She told someone that the baby was conceived on Valentine's Day in Paris. "It was her priority to have kids," said a friend. "When you marry a man who already has kids, you want to have your own children with him. It cements the bond."

"I hadn't really thought about being too old to have a baby until people kept saying I was," Diana said. "And I just screamed, 'I am *not* old.' Give me a break."

Diana had always wanted a son, and when medical tests revealed that the baby was a boy, she was so excited she telephoned many people who hadn't heard from her in years to tell them, "I'm finally going to have a son." Still, she was not eager to discuss her pregnancy with the press.

A reporter in London who interviewed Miss Ross wrote, "Diana Ross is—visibly—pregnant, but any reference to this condition will constitute grounds for instant termination of the interview. Similarly, questions relating to the contents of *Dreamgirl* are definitely not on the menu . . . it is crucial that she not be upset in any way."

The pregnancy was a difficult one. Diana called it "dreadful." Some have insisted that Diana said that if the baby was a girl she would name her Diana, and if it were a boy he would be named Ross.

Ross Arne Naess was born on October 7, 1987.

"I believe in children and family," she said later. "It just seems real important to me. Just having the first child was an unexpected pleasure."

Diana was extremely proud to be a mother again, and apparently she and Arne wanted the family to continue growing. When the tabloid *Star* first broke the news in early August 1988 that Diana was expecting *again*, most people were amazed. Not even those closest to Diana suspected she was even pregnant.

Diana's publicist, Elliot Mintz, insisted, "Diana is *not* preg-

---

*When The Supremes were inducted into the Rock and Roll Hall of Fame at the Waldorf-Astoria in New York in January 1987, Diana Ross failed to attend. The press speculated that Diana's absence was due to the fact that she knew Mary Wilson would be present. That night, Mary did bask in all of the media attention.

"Look, I'm a good person," Diana said later when asked about her absence. "But if people slap you and slap you, what are you supposed to do? Just smile?"

nant. I would know about it if she was. During her first pregnancy as Mrs. Naess, she let us know. I'm sure she would tell us now.''

Later that month, an official announcement was made. Diana had another boy, her second in ten months. Needless to say, a great deal of mystery and speculation has surrounded the birth of this eight pound, seven ounce child, Evan, born on August 26, 1988. The exact location of the birth remains a mystery, though it seems the child was born in America. No picture of Evan had ever been seen until Diana allowed both sons to appear on a Scandinavian television program with her and Arne in July 1989 under the condition that the show never be aired anywhere else in the world.

Diana Ross had become more of an enigma than ever. Gone were the days when she would discuss her children happily, or be photographed with them for women's magazines. She did say this much: ''Expecting again, it was exciting to me because I thought the two boys would be—well, I didn't know it was going to be a boy—well, the two babies would be companions. My mother had six children. And if you read back to early articles I did, I always wanted to have a lot of children. So, somehow it's happening.''

Diana and Arne asked Swedish Princess Christina, the sister of King Gustav, and her commoner husband, Tord Nagusson, to become Evan's godparents. Princess Christina and Filippa have been best friends since they were young girls. For Arne and Diana to ask Christina to be their child's godmother seemed rather insensitive to Filippa's feelings. But for whatever reason, Christina agreed to be Evan's godmother.

Most of the guests at the christening party, which took place at Diana's Connecticut home, were Swedish. Diana had only one personal acquaintance there. Apparently it was difficult for Filippa's friends to turn down such an invitation, no matter where their loyalties lie. Maybe they attended out of curiosity about Diana and to rub shoulders with Princess Christina. Guests' reports that the event, which was catered by Filippa's former caterer, gave the appearance of a Swedish party, odd considering the fact that the mother of the child is American and the father Norwegian. It seemed to most observers that Diana was desperately trying to fill the shoes of Arne's Swedish first wife or to outshine her.

Diana invited Michael Jackson to the christening. She certainly could have used another friend, but again he did not attend, much to her consternation.

At about this time, she was scheduled to host a salute to Michael Jackson on the Showtime cable network, which was being produced by Motown Productions. But when Michael didn't attend the christening party, Diana apparently felt very hurt. Perhaps that's why she decided not to host the Showtime special. In fact, say Motown staffers, she refused to be involved with it at all.

Michael was upset about this turn of events. He couldn't understand why Diana would be so hostile toward him. The more he thought about it, the angrier he got.

Since he had authority over the final edit of the program, Michael very artfully eliminated Diana from most of the "memory footage" of the two of them together, giving her perhaps 30 seconds of total airtime. He went so far as to have the script publicly deny for the first time the story Berry Gordy had told about Diana "discovering" Jackson 5. On the tape, Suzanne dePasse admitted that "it seemed like a good idea at the time" to say that Diana had found the group, but that it wasn't true. Then, in the next film clip, Ed Sullivan introduced Diana Ross from the audience as the person who discovered the Jackson Five, and she stood up and bowed graciously as everyone applauded. The way Michael Jackson had this version edited made Diana Ross look like a liar. She had to be insulted.

Perhaps Diana did not want to appear on the special because she knew how much power Michael now wielded—people in Hollywood now bow to him much the same way they do to her—and she does enjoy being the center of attention on any broadcast in which she's involved. This is why she rarely appears on TV anymore, unless it's a Motown special of some sort. Even then she usually requires that the program build up to a performance by her in which she is surrounded by all of the other guests. Rarely will Diana be seen on any kind of variety program that features other celebrities in as prominent a role as hers.

One of the staffers on that Motown special characterized Jackson as being "a quiet power," meaning he sometimes seemed duplicitous in his business dealings. For instance, he praised the show's producer Anson Williams (former "Happy Days" star) and claimed that he was extremely happy with his work. The next day, Williams was fired by someone else.

Unlike his former mentor, Diana, Michael Jackson really does not have the heart to lower the hatchet himself. He is much too sensitive to hurt anyone's feelings personally. But he can be just as demanding as Diana, if need be. For instance, he insisted that the tribute not include any photographs of him that were taken during the late '70s—before his three nose jobs.

Domestic turmoil for Diana continued because Arne still apparently refused to mend broken fences with his first wife, Filippa Kumlin Naess. Filippa has had more than a few disappointments along the way, just as any first wife does when the husband to whom she was totally devoted and dependent remarries.

For instance, Filippa had to surrender to Diana her home in Verbier, Switzerland, which she designed and had built, and in which she, Arne and their three children lived for many years. (It is not easy for foreigners to obtain permits to build a home in Switzerland—let alone buy one—but somehow Filippa was able to secure the proper papers and have the home built. Without her connections, it's possible that Arne would have had a difficult time owning a home in Switzerland.)

Chalets in Verbier all have names, which are used in place of street numbers for home addresses. The Naess home was called "Chalet Filippa." Diana Ross, as was her prerogative, had "Chalet Filippa" completely redecorated when she moved in. Whereas the chalet was once furnished with classic, hand-painted wood furniture, Swedish antiques, fur rugs and pillows, after Diana finished with it, it was turned into a contemporary home, refurnished in beige and earth tones. As Filippa cried to one friend, "Now it looks like an agent's office."

"Just be glad you got your antique brass candlesticks out of there when you did before *she* got a hold of them," was the friend's reaction.

As was her right, Diana very quickly took down the wooden sign that says "Chalet Filippa," which was posted on the front door. When Diana was away from the chalet during Easter 1985, Arne allowed Filippa to have a holiday dinner for some of her friends, and the children, in the main house. Filippa's friends, and one of her children, found the sign and put it back up. When Diana returned and found that the sign had reappeared above the door, she became exasperated. She had someone take the sign down, and it hasn't been seen since.

Because Arne and Diana rarely stay at the Verbier chalet, he allows his ex-wife and their three children to live in the guest house on the property. One Christmas, the newlyweds went on a holiday elsewhere and left Rhonda, Tracee and Chudney in the main house to fend for themselves. Filippa apparently felt sorry for them and, though she wasn't asked to, ended up entertaining the three children of her former husband's present wife in the guest house of the home she built.

Diana certainly sensed that Filippa had ambivalent feelings about her, but she has reasoned to friends, "The second wife always has these kinds of problems." Once, Filippa was in New York City on business when the telephone rang in her room. It was Diana's first husband, Bob Silberstein. He was calling to tell Filippa that he and Diana remained friends after their divorce and that she, too, should be friendly with Diana "for the sake of the children."

Filippa was stunned. Given the circumstances of her problems with Arne and the financial settlement she has never been able to get, she must have felt that Bob's advice was rather presumptuous. Whether the phone call was Diana's or Arne's idea is not clear. Certainly Bob Silberstein has always done practically anything Diana has asked of him.

But Arne also had a stake in this possible reconciliation since he has often told his children that Filippa's anger is unwarranted, and that it is *she* who is really responsible for the hurt feelings that exist. In order to try to be gracious "for the sake of the children," Filippa accepted an invitation from Diana to visit the home in Connecticut and "see the new babies."

Diana was, as always, the perfect hostess. Whereas this kind of multi-relationship socializing might be awkward for some people, it has never been for her. After all, she has always lived in what she perceives as an idyllic world, one in which her ex-husband Bob, former boyfriends Berry Gordy and Gene Simmons, their present mates and all of their children enjoy a happy life. All of these people, apparently, like to be in Diana Ross' company, no matter what personal complications are involved in maintaining a relationship with her. So Diana has been unable to understand that this kind of setup is not often realistic, nor is it always possible. Sometimes it can even engender hurt feelings and animosity. "I don't understand why Filippa is so distant," Diana kept saying. "I'm just not used to this. I simply must have alignment in my life."

When Filippa Naess was invited to the palatial Connecticut estate owned by the very rich second wife of her ex-husband just so that she could see "the new babies," it's not difficult to imagine that she might have felt a bit awkward, especially considering the unfinished business she has with Arne. But Diana said later that she thought Filippa had a fine time. Indeed, for her, the Naesses are "one big happy family."

* * *

After Ross and Evan were born, Diana was determined to jump back into the record-selling pop music world. In the last few years, other black divas had taken over, the most successful being Whitney Houston who is to today's generation what Diana Ross was to a '70s audience. Lynn Hirschberg wrote in *Vanity Fair* (March 1989) that Diana Ross gets irritated when anyone mentions the young singer's name in her presence because she is jealous of Whitney Houston's success. Hirschberg claimed that, after her wedding, Diana stopped worrying about Houston's fame, but then became concerned again, as if Whitney Houston's few years of fame can somehow threaten Diana Ross.

Ironically, one of Houston's producers is Michael Masser, the man responsible for many of Diana's most memorable records ("The Theme From 'Mahogany,' " "Touch Me in the Morning," "It's My Turn," among others). Masser has said that Diana refused to work with him in the '80s because he is so precise and controlling in the studio. So he turned his attention to Houston, and the results speak for themselves. Practically every song he has produced for her sounds as if it could have been tailor-made for Diana Ross. Three of them went to Number One on the charts. Whitney Houston has been guided every step of the way in her career by her record company's president, Arista's Clive Davis, much the way Berry Gordy masterminded Diana's original fame.

Whitney Houston was being considered for the starring role in the film version of *Dreamgirls* (the musical, not Mary Wilson's book). Houston would portray the character in *Dreamgirls* based on Diana Ross. Considering how Diana felt about the show, her reaction to this news was not surprising; she was not happy about it and reportedly had her attorneys look into the matter.

Whitney's spokeswoman, Jean Harvey, tried to calm everyone by insisting that Houston had not received a concrete offer to do the film. But Whitney was quoted as having said, "I'm very upset by Diana's actions. It's a great part and it's the one I want to be my acting debut. I don't want it ruined by anyone."

When Lynn Hirschberg mentioned Whitney's possible casting in *Dreamgirls*, Ross snapped at her. "I heard that isn't true. I heard that Whitney wasn't doing the movie." Hirschberg said that it took Diana a moment to calm herself while the subject was changed.

Houston continues to be a problem for Ross, especially given the fact that Hollywood producer Howard Rosenman is in the process of mounting a Josephine Baker film biography that does not include Diana but will, apparently, star Whitney. He said, "Whitney was a little concerned about the nudity involved, but she realizes it's absolutely necessary." Considering the fact that Diana has been attempting to launch her Josephine Baker project for well over 10 years, this news must certainly be disconcerting to her.

Diana Ross' feelings toward Whitney Houston echo the way she used to feel about Lola Falana, a protégée of Sammy Davis' who was popular in the '70s and signed to Motown. She actually resembled Diana Ross. But Falana never had a release the entire time she was under contract. She certainly was no real threat to Diana's career.

Dick Maurice, a leading columnist in Las Vegas and a friend of Falana's, recalled that Diana once rented his home during one of her Vegas visits. He wondered what her reaction would be to all of the photos of Lola on the coffee and end tables. When Diana surrendered the premises back to him, he discovered that the pictures were still there. But every one of them had been turned backwards.

In April 1988, Diana and Arne attended the Academy Awards in Los Angeles. Diana declined to be interviewed during the post-party at Spago because she felt that the mini-cam was placed too low on its tripod and wouldn't afford her a flattering TV picture. Her past came back to haunt her once again when, as she left Spago and was standing in its parking lot, someone in the crowd of spectators shouted at her, "Florence Ballard died for your sins." For a moment, Diana Ross looked as though she had been slapped.

The public's perception of Diana Ross' role as villainess in the story of Florence Ballard persists, and Mary Wilson's *Dreamgirl* memoirs certainly did nothing to exonerate Diana of any "guilt." Business associates, like Suzanne dePasse, have often encouraged Diana to write her own memoirs "and set the record straight," but she has always declined. Doubleday had been courting Diana for years, since the secret 1983 meeting with Jacqueline Onassis. In the spring of 1988, Diana and Arne met with Doubleday editor Paul Bresnick and his associates at their offices. Accompanying the Naesses, and representing Diana Ross, were two literary agents from the William Morris Agency.

In the meeting, Diana made it clear that she still wanted to write that "inspirational book with no personal details" that she had presented to Jackie Onassis. Though she maintained that she had not read Mary Wilson's memoirs, and had no intention of ever doing so, she said, "I will not write a *Dreamgirl*-type book. My story is too inspirational for *that*." After some discussion, Bresnick offered to assist in outlining the Diana Ross memoirs, hoping that in time she would become more candid about her life.

"Diana was all sweetness and light," said one Doubleday executive who attended the meeting. "Arne was grim and serious, extremely unfriendly. It was as if they had planned a strategy in advance. She would be personable while he would be menacing. He scowled a lot."

According to someone present, in the middle of the meeting, Arne suddenly turned to the Doubleday contingent and said, "Look, let's just get down to it. How much are we talking about here? How much are you going to pay? That's really what we want to know."

The William Morris agents both became red-faced and sank down in their chairs. Diana averted her eyes and bit her bottom lip. Arne's direct line of questioning wasn't the most tactful way to broach the subject of advance money. It certainly seems that he and Berry Gordy share similar philosophies in terms of the way they get to the bottom line.

A substantial advance, high in the six figures, was offered and the meeting was adjourned.

Doubleday employees were lined up in the hallway outside the conference room hoping to catch a glimpse of Diana and possibly secure an autograph as she exited. But after the door opened, Arne quickly whisked his wife away. Her head held high, Diana wore a somber expression on her face and looked at no one. Arne glared at the waiting crowd. His expression was intimidating enough so that no one dared approach his wife. The couple left quickly.

A few more weeks of discussion about the book with Doubleday ensued. When Michael Jackson heard that it seemed that Diana would be writing memoirs for the same house that published his best-selling *Moonwalk* autobiography, he had to laugh. He told his associate editor at Doubleday, Shaye Areheart, "Listen, if you think *I* was difficult, just wait."

Finally, much to Doubleday's consternation and without their knowledge, Diana and Arne went upstairs to Warner Books (in the same building) and consummated a deal with *that* house to publish the Ross memoirs. The advance was reported to be within the $1 to $2 million range. The deal was struck without giving Doubleday a chance to make any counter-offers, causing bad feelings at Doubleday where Diana Ross is concerned.

The announcement of Ross' signing with Warner Books was made in June 1988. But then, about six months later, Diana changed her mind. She would not write the book after all, much to Warner Books' chagrin. She returned the advance. Most people who know her were not surprised. At this point in her life, Diana Ross is not ready to be candid. It's much easier to be "inspirational."

In July 1988, Berry Gordy sold Motown Records to MCA Records and the investment group Boston Ventures, Ltd., for $61 million. Not included in the transactions were Berry Gordy's music publishing divisions—Jobete Music and Stone Diamond—and film and TV operations, Motown Productions, which scored in the television ratings game in 1989 with the critically acclaimed CBS mini-series *Lonesome Dove*.*

The last few years have not been good to Motown. It became more and more difficult to introduce new artists and get radio airplay for their records. Most of the major acts had defected to other labels, leaving Stevie Wonder, Smokey Robinson and Lionel Richie as its only major stars. All three had become erratic record sellers.

"The artists aren't like they used to be," Berry, who was 59 years old in 1988, said of Motown's younger set. "They're just a bunch of spoiled brats. It's not fun anymore. Besides, I've got high blood pressure now and I'm tired."

A 30-year anniversary special—in the tradition of "Motown 25"—that was to be taped in Detroit was canceled.

The last seven years found Berry Gordy bringing artists like The Four Tops and The Temptations back to the label with promises of career rejuvenation that would eventually be unfulfilled. It was reported in *The New York Times* that Motown's annual sales dropped from $100 million (in the '60s and '70s) to $20 million in the late '80s, and that more than half of that revenue was generated by the marketing of Motown oldies.

There were also unsuccessful TV ventures, including "Nightlife," a late-night talk show hosted by David Brenner. The ratings were so low that Suzanne dePasse begged Diana Ross to appear on the show to bolster interest. She refused. She felt Suzanne should not use her relationship with her to beef up the ratings of a failing Motown production.

---

*In May 1989, the *Los Angeles Herald-Examiner* reported that Jobete Music and Stone Diamond were for sale. The asking price was over $30 million. Michael Jackson was the most likely purchaser. If he is the buyer, Jackson will be owner of all of the Motown catalogue of hits including, of course, Diana Ross' songs.

The sale of the label to MCA became a poignant affair for many Motown fans because it, somehow, seemed to mark the end of an era. Motown had also been long considered important as a symbol of black business success. Berry Gordy had made an indelible mark by redefining American popular music. Now he is content to live his life with more leisure time and less chaos. If there had ever been any underworld connections to Motown Records and to Berry Gordy, Jr., it somehow doesn't seem to matter much anymore. The bodyguards that were always a part of the Berry Gordy mystique are still at his side, but now they seem to be there more for the sake of companionship than for protection.

Marvin Gaye, who had many heated battles with his former brother-in-law, once observed of Berry Gordy, "B.G. has survived in one of the toughest businesses around and to do that takes a lot of balls, a lot of hard work and a lot of risks. Believe me, he's given out a lot of shit in his time, but he's had to take a whole lot himself. Nobody, particularly a cocky black guy fresh from the assembly lines in Detroit, gets to make it that big without making a few enemies and taking a few cuts."

At the time of the Motown sale, Diana Ross found herself without a record deal. Her contract with RCA had expired and neither she nor the company was willing to renew it. "I'm in love with all the power at Motown," she had said toward the end of her RCA commitment. "I'm crazy about Suzanne dePasse and her entire staff. I'll always care about Berry. Going out on my own has made me value how good Motown was to me. It made me see that they did a whole lot."

In February 1989, Diana re-signed with Motown Records. "It's like the queen returning home," observed Jheryl Busby, the new company president. But without Berry Gordy at the helm of Motown, Diana Ross' return somehow seemed anti-climatic. Her fans yearn to have the two working together again, making the magic happen like they did in the '60s and '70s, but that's just not possible.

After signing, Diana then accompanied Arne on an expedition to Katmandu, Nepal. It was the couple's third expedition; they had already been to Africa and Chile.

"When you're out there, it is just the two of you together," Diana said to writer Rodney Tyler in an interview in May 1989. "These are the times when you are really and absolutely just the person you are. It's as though your skin is rolled off and you are right down to who you really are. You travel with little more than survival things. There are no phones, no make-up, no wigs, no long fingernails, no polish on your toenails. It's just you. It's a wonderful feeling to be able to let Nepal happen to you—rather than you happening to Nepal.

"The expeditions broaden my point of view about people and what is important in my life and give me a chance to think deeply about life, love and living and all the things that are important to me. They are part of the balancing in my life . . ."

Unlike the time she signed with RCA and her recording career was at a peak, when she re-signed with Motown she did not receive a multi-million-dollar check. Instead, she was given an unspecified amount of stock in Motown as an incentive to sign. By becoming a stockholder, she helped fulfill the 20 percent minority ownership specified by Berry Gordy in the sale to MCA.

She may be back at Motown again, but Diana Ross' life is very different from the way it was when she was Gordy's premiere artist living in an accessible home in Beverly Hills. Her mansion in Greenwich, Connecticut, is said to be very much like a fortress.

"You can't believe how fortified it is," one visitor has reported. "It's like the U.S. Embassy in Beirut, or as if she was living in exile."

But another visitor noted, "It's a wonderful, peaceful place to be. A sanctuary for her."

The New England home is Diana's responsibility—Arne has practically nothing to do with it—and she runs a tight ship. What goes on behind those walls is somewhat of a mystery since, as noted before, most of Diana's staff members are required to sign a secrecy agreement that discourages them from revealing anything about their employer during or after their period of employment.

As can be expected, Diana insists that all of the help—governesses, secretaries, cooks, gardeners—address her as Miss Ross. Also, all of the women in her employ are required to wear uniforms selected personally by Diana from a catalogue of discount clothes. The staff is always perfectly color-coordinated, and none of the ladies would ever think to wear anything other than the proper attire.

Apparently, Diana is still a bit petty and unreasonable where her household staff is concerned. Testament can be found in this story that has been circulating among Ross' former employees for the last few years:

Diana had a chef on the payroll whose job it was to bake pastries for her and the girls every morning. At dawn, Diana would come sweeping downstairs in her robe to inspect the tray of fresh pastries. She would taste one and, after a bite, quickly spit it out rather than risk gaining weight by actually swallowing it. Soon after, her daughters would descend to devour the warm goodies. Occasionally, there would be one or two pastries left. Diana had instructed the chef to throw away all leftovers into the garbage, but one morning, she caught the cook eating a couple of pastries.

"I paid for them and if I want them thrown into the garbage, they should be thrown into the garbage," Diana said angrily. The chef began to argue with her boss and, ultimately, she got herself fired, not only for eating leftover pastries but also for being obstreperous about it.

The pastry chef complained to another Ross employee—both of whom must remain anonymous because they signed secrecy agreements—that she had no money and no place to live because she had been discharged on such short notice. The employee offered to allow her to stay at his apartment for a few weeks while he was on the road with Diana. But Diana had warned him and the others in her employ not to ever socialize with people that had been fired from her organization. According to him, when she discovered that he was harboring the exiled pastry chef, she fired him too.

Diana and her husband seem happy in their marriage, even though they do not spend much time with each other because of their conflicting schedules. When she is not living in the Greenwich home, she is with Arne in the former "Chalet Filippa" in Switzerland, or in their London apartment.

"Our marriage is not an ordinary one," Arne has said. "We're too busy. It's more like an exciting and intense love affair."

Diana is still extremely protective of her relationship with Arne, especially where his former wife Filippa is concerned. Whereas Filippa and Arne used to meet privately on occasion to discuss family business, Diana now insists on being present at all of the meetings. She also insists that Filippa come escorted.

At one such family confab, Filippa tried to make her ex-husband understand that she wanted to move to Manhattan but could only afford a one-bedroom apartment for herself and the three children, when they would come to visit. (Christoffer was 20 and in school in Boston; Katrinka, 18, was in London; and Leona, 15, was enrolled at Le Rosay School in Switzerland.)

Diana listened for a moment before finally saying in an exasperated tone, "Filippa, I just don't know what the problem is.

You should work harder. That's what I do. I work hard and make my own money. So should you."

Filippa bit her lip rather than start a fracas. Perhaps Diana doesn't realize that when Filippa's father died, she gave her entire inheritance, a six-figure amount, to Arne to invest. Filippa has told friends that Arne made a poor investment and lost it all. She said that she has never seen a penny of it, and she is much too proud to ask her family for money.

"Yes, it was naïve of Filippa to think that Arne could handle this important investment just because he was her husband," observed one close friend. "But still, she probably can't help but feel that since he did lose the inheritance, he can be a little more sensitive to her financial needs."

It appears to be difficult to Diana Ross—a woman who came from a housing project in Detroit and worked hard for everything she has achieved—to feel sorry for Filippa Kumlin Naess, a woman who speaks seven languages fluently, who was born into Swedish society and was raised surrounded by the best of everything the world had to offer.

In some ways, Filippa must remind Diana of Florence Ballard. To Diana's way of thinking, both women had every opportunity to lead happy, wealthy lives: Filippa's by way of her privileged background and talent as an interior decorator and Florence's because of her talent and luck in becoming one of The Supremes. Diana has never been the type to let anything or anyone get in her way. She was determined to be a success, no matter what. She never really understood Florence's personal problems, just as she cannot relate to Filippa's.

Though Diana and Filippa have led entirely different lives—one pursued her career while the other had to give up hers for her husband and children—the two do share the belief that they were both dealt with unfairly by important men in their lives. Certainly the fact that Diana complained about having only "a few hundred thousand dollars" to her name after leaving Motown would indicate that she felt just as cheated by Berry as Filippa feels by Arne today.

But Diana Naess will never make the mistake Filippa Naess made. She will never allow Arne to be the center of attention in her life.

"He is not my focus," she has said of Naess. "He's my husband, my companion, my lover, my confidant. But not my focus. I wasn't lost—then found Arne. I was single and met a wonderful man and we enjoyed each other's company and enjoyed our times together. So it was not lost and found. That's crap.

"I have *never* been lost."

Some of her friends might disagree. Diana has lost touch with practically all of the people with whom she started. Now she is living the kind of life-style most of her former peers can only wonder about. Smokey Robinson has said that Diana telephones him occasionally. He wrote of her in his recent autobiography, *Smokey*, that "she's living in an opulent world where no one knows where she comes from and no one knows who she is.

"She sounds a little lost," he concluded.

When Suzanne dePasse appeared on "The Pat Sajak Show" in May 1989, Sajak asked her who "the biggest pain in the neck" was for her to work with.

"I was thinking about another part of the anatomy," dePasse quipped, "but as long as we're talking about pains, I'd have to say, pound for pound, Diana Ross."

"What's the biggest misconception about you?" Barbara Walters asked Diana two months earlier in a nationally televised interview.

"That I'm a bitch."

Barbara nodded her head. "Now why do they think that? Why do . . ."

Diana cut her off. She suddenly became defensive.

"Because I'm like you," she said, pointing at Walters and raising her voice just a little. "I have standards. You have a way you want to run your business. I have standards," she repeated. "I have a way that I think works. I request that in my presence."

Although Barbara did not ask Diana to elaborate on those "standards," business associates know some of them well. When she is visiting their offices, she usually enters the building by the freight elevator in order to avoid fans. Employees are instructed not to speak to her unless she speaks first and to "avert the eyes" if they see her. According to John Mackey, a former employee of Loeb and Loeb, the law firm representing Diana Ross, "avert the eyes" is a catch phrase to announce her arrival.

One temporary worker at Loeb and Loeb who was not fully aware of Diana's "standards," says that he was such a big fan of hers he could not help but approach her during office hours even though he was warned not to. He recalled that when he went up to her to tell her how much he liked her, she stared at him menacingly. He backed off.

When Lynn Hirschberg was doing her 1989 *Vanity Fair* cover story on Diana, a Ross acquaintance told the writer, "Diana's famous for insisting that people call her Miss Ross. I was with her once in Atlantic City, and a kid came into her dressing room with some food she had ordered. 'Oh Diana,' he said, 'I'm so happy to serve you.' She just glared at him and said, 'Please call me Miss Ross.' She is what she is. And what she is is a *star star star*."

Such behavior seems bizarre to a special group of fans who have followed her for years. Whenever some of these devotees are in the audience, she invites them backstage to her dressing room after the performance. There they will spend time discussing what has happened in their lives since they last met. She knows these people by name, and they are on a first-name basis with her. There is no "Miss Ross" formality in these relationships.

These fans of Diana's are always perplexed when told about her business "standards." Some of them simply cannot reconcile the "Diana" who welcomes them warmly and the "Miss Ross" they hear about. Others are intrigued by the "Miss Ross" personality and feel that such behavior is one of the prerogatives allowed a star of her caliber. Certainly Diana Ross isn't the only star who has a bitchy reputation. Some of her fans feel that women in Diana's position have no choice but to be temperamental in order to maintain their status. Or, as Bette Davis has said, "You don't know that you've made it until they call you 'difficult.' "

"I'm an insecure person, I really am," Diana has said in her defense. "I probably always will be, until the day I die." Some of her fans explain that her mercurial behavior obviously relates to deep insecurity, and they forgive everything in the name of vulnerability.

Naturally whenever there is royalty present, Diana is always on her best behavior. When she was enroute to London on the Concorde in May 1989, the Countess of Derby and the 18th Earl were sitting close by. The Countess couldn't help but walk over to Diana, who was in seat 1A, and ask for two autographs, one for the butler's children and one for the chauffeur's. Lady Derby was followed by a long line of fans, all asking for autographs. Diana was polite, generous and seemed happy to oblige. True to the contradictions of her nature, in the right circumstances, she is extremely approachable.

Of course, Diana Ross's availability depends entirely upon who is attempting to approach her. Mary Wilson is still strictly off limits.

In the years after her *Dreamgirl* memoirs, Wilson has been

fighting an uphill battle for recognition. First, she lost her legal battles against Berry Gordy and Motown Records; the court ruled that, indeed, Gordy—not Wilson—owned the name "Supremes."

Then, after losing the lawsuit, Mary had the poor judgment to impersonate Diana Ross in a Canadian Revue called *Beehive*. In the impression, she and two other women sang Supremes hits and wore the same gowns the group wore over 20 years ago. Mary popped her eyes and oozed phony sincerity all the while acting like a caricature Diana Ross puppet. Surely for Wilson, this was the ultimate career irony.

After *Beehive*, Mary attended Diana Ross' opening night performance at the Universal Amphitheatre in Los Angeles, accompanied by her 14-year-old daughter, Turkessa. Following the show, she went backstage to visit the star. Learning of Mary's presence there, Diana refused to come out of her dressing room; the message as relayed through her bodyguards: "I want her out of here!"

Mary asked one of Diana's representatives if Diana would at least see Turkessa, her own goddaughter? But godmother and -daughter have never been close; Diana could count the times she and the girl have seen each other on one hand. She must have thought that Mary was using this girl as bait, that she would go to any extreme to provoke an altercation with the other "Dreamgirl" just for the sake of the national publicity it would garner.

Is Mary Wilson so naïve that she actually believes she and Diana are friends, even after "that book"? Or is she really just a shrewd media manipulator who knows that the only way she can generate publicity is to exploit the fact that she used to have a relationship—albeit not a very good one—with "Diane." In a scene reminiscent of the last time the three original Supremes were seen together in 1968—when Berry Gordy demanded that Mary and Florence be thrown out of his home by a bodyguard— Diana insisted that Wilson and her daughter be escorted away from the backstage area by one of her henchmen.

Rather than just go back to the home she purchased with her *Dreamgirl* royalties, Mary decided to try to attend the private Diana Ross after-party at Spago restaurant in Hollywood. Unfortunately, her name had not magically appeared on Ross' guest list, and she was turned away at the door.

"I was so embarrassed," Mary later said. "Friends should be able to talk. I hope Diane will call me so we can work this thing out, *whatever* it is." With tears in her eyes, Mary Wilson and her daughter got into the back seat of a white Rolls-Royce with the license plate that says SUPRMES. After her chauffeur closed the passenger door, he took his position behind the wheel. Then he pulled away from the curb and drove the dejected Supreme into the night.

Indeed, fate has not always been kind to Mary Wilson. In fact, most of the artists who came out of Motown have had disappointing results when they attempted to handle their own careers. Berry Gordy and his staff managed all of his artists' career-planning and controlled their financial matters. Because the artists remember being manipulated—and some even think they were cheated—they are now determined to chart their own courses even though they are ill-equipped to do so. Too busy promoting themselves any way they can and searching in vain for record deals, former Motown stars, like Wilson, lack the business savvy and expertise needed to achieve financial success.

Today, Diana is in much the same situation. Though signing the multi-million dollar pact with RCA Records gave her the financial security she craved and deserved after leaving Motown with "a few hundred thousand dollars that I can actually put my hands on," Diana's new deal reaped few benefits for her commercially. She is a major star and dependable concert draw not because of any song she recorded at RCA but because of her stellar Motown past and the irresistible allure of her celebrity.

Diana Ross' 1989 return-to-Motown album, *Workin' Overtime*, is a typical example of the kind of self-imposed miscalculation of both image and musical style that has placed her recording career in jeopardy. Her attire for the jacket photograph was, for such an innately glamorous woman, quite unappealing: a black leather motorcycle jacket, shredded jeans with gaping holes in the knees, and clunky Wellington boots with bandanas wrapped around them. Obviously, this is not normal fashion fare for a woman who usually dresses to dazzle.

It could be argued that Diana Ross has never been one to follow fashion rules. She has always looked exactly as she pleased, dating back to the mid-'60s when she baffled the other Motown girls by combining Twiggy-like makeup with Annette Funicello hairstyles to create a new look for black women—the Diana Ross look. "She has the greatest eyes in show business," said Berry Gordy at that time. Indeed, those startling, heavy-lined and -lashed Diana Ross eyes, so expressive with a '60s innocence that belied her determination and experience, became an integral part of her Supremes' star persona.

Today, her look in repose—with that mad, tousled black mane of hair, the carefully madeup face that rarely smiles anymore but still seems a sculpted work of art, the expressive eyes that lost their "innocence" years ago and now peer out suspiciously from artfully air-brushed publicity photos—is a combination sexy and tough, but never tacky, as she portrayed herself as being on *Workin' Overtime*.

For many artists, album covers are not important considerations. But Diana Ross has built a career as much on image as on talent. To compound problems for her, not only was the *Workin' Overtime* packaging unattractive, the odd, herky-jerky youth-oriented music called "hip hop" was more suitable for a trendy artist half her age than for someone with Diana's pop music experience and preeminence. This career strategy is precisely the kind of madness Berry Gordy would never have considered for Diana. But Miss Ross insisted upon it and no one could—or would—talk her out of it.

The result? Diana's audience had the final word—they didn't buy it.

None of *Workin' Overtime*'s single releases cracked the Top Pop 100. The album was her poorest selling and lowest charting record of the last 21 years.

Chapter

❧ 30 ❧

Radio City Music Hall
Saturday, June 17, 1989
Midnight Show.

"Miss Ross does not want anyone to be seated during her first number," came the announcement. "If you do not sit now, you will miss the opening song."

Everyone took his seat obediently.

The lights dimmed. Suddenly, she materialized at the back of Radio City Music Hall to the strains of Michael Jackson's hit "Dirty Diana." Immediately, the cheering audience rose en masse. With two menacing-looking security guards flanking her, she rushed down the aisle of the theater, the bright spotlight following her. Running toward the stage, she adjusted the lavender coque-feathered cape to make certain that it billowed out behind her for just the right dramatic effect. Her smile was dazzling. Once on stage, she flung off the cape to reveal a sheer, pink quiana dress. She fluffed up her mane of wild ringlets, raised her arms in triumph, and beamed as waves of applause rushed over her.

Diana Ross was back in town.

It was easy to forget that she was 45 years old and the mother of five children. Banished were the tattered jeans and leather jacket she favored for her *Workin' Overtime* concept. Tonight at New York's Radio City Music Hall, whether mini-skirted or gowned, Diana was glamour personified.

From "I'm Coming Out" and "Upside Down" to "The Man I Love" and "Reach Out and Touch (Somebody's Hand)," the audience would be uncritical and adoring. Conspicuously missing was the elaborate staging of earlier days. The back-up was minimal and so were her introductions. The band members all seemed to lack last names. With 29 songs in less than two hours, it would be a breathless, generous performance. "I remember when I used to do these songs without sweating," she said with a self-deprecating grin.

Loyal fans, including now-traditional transvestites dressed to out-glitz the star herself, danced in the aisle to the sheer delight of the audience during Diana's costume changes. Were the impersonators hired by Ross? Or was it coincidence that they were there each night?

Each time Diana walked out with a new, stunning costume, the photographers down front went to work, angling their best shots and snapping away. As she posed, preened, and pouted, she never looked better, younger, more relaxed or self-confident. Like a prism in a spotlight, she filled the room with rainbows.

All of the photographers in the hall had dutifully signed a contract with her that restricts them from selling her smiling visage more than one time and to more than one publication. By enforcing this "standard," Miss Ross is able to control her own publicity. Photos of her at Radio City won't be published after the five-day engagement is over without her permission. If she learns that the contract has been broken, the offending photographer will hear from her battery of attorneys.

"It's a threat that hangs over your head for the rest of your life," one lensman put it.

"Spreadin' love," Diana cooed as she blew kisses to the photographers.

The way she tossed off a medley of Supremes hits, it was easy to forget that each song represents an important touchstone in the history of American pop and black music. It was obvious that Diana feels no emotional link to her past. In the program booklet hawked at lobby concession stands, there is a superficial Question and Answer section in which Diana "discusses" her days with The Supremes and somehow manages to do it without ever once mentioning the names Mary Wilson, Florence Ballard or Cindy Birdsong. She wrote of herself in relation to the group, "Our work had begun to be more than just fun. It was serious. If we were to continue to be successful someone needed to take charge." Actually, Ross has never been much for sentiment or nostalgia, anyway. Or, as she wrote in the booklet, she prefers "only touching on the past as it relates to where I am today."

But if it's "Stop! In the Name of Love" her audience wants, that's what they get. Her coy '60s-like girlish delivery, backed by rhythmic Motown arrangement, conjured up pleasant echoes of the past for her fans, if not for herself. She tries not to disappoint.

"*Spreadin' love!*"

Down front, two admirers showed a bit more enthusiasm than Diana deemed necessary. "Sing 'Endless Love,' " they kept demanding. Finally, she hissed at them through clenched teeth: "Will you sit down and be quiet!" She kept smiling as she did it, and people beyond the first two rows couldn't hear every word, but even if the entire audience had heard, it still wouldn't have mattered. Diana Ross is expected to be haughty. It's become part of her persona. "I told you to just wait. Sit down and wait," she scolded the two disruptive fans. "I mean it!"

"*Spreadin' love!*"

Whitney Houston was in the audience and Diana called her onto the stage. "I want to tell you all, don't you believe one word about what you have read about us," Diana said sincerely. "It's just not true. Not one word."

She was referring to the *Vanity Fair* feature about her in which Lynn Hirschberg reported she was "obsessed" and jealous of Houston's fame. The entire article—most of which was quite flattering—upset Diana. How is a star supposed to protect her mystique with reporters like Hirschberg running wild?

"They promised me a positive piece," she said, "and I get *this*?"

Through her attorneys, she reportedly demanded that the magazine apologize. She also asked for a complete list of the writer's anonymous sources, probably so that she could deal with each of them separately. After all, most probably signed the secrecy contract, and what good is such a pact if disgruntled former employees won't honor it?

Whitney Houston looked awed, almost stricken, as Diana embraced her. The applause was loud and full as the Queen kissed the Princess on the check and sent her back to her seat. The audience cheered its approval. Great singers like Whitney Houston are commonplace, but divas like Diana Ross are rare.

Finally, the pair of disobedient ringsiders got their wish. Diana sang "Endless Love." She struck the expected elegant note with her performance, which was flawless and assured, a vivid rendering of Lionel Richie's version. She sang the duet lovingly with a talented male vocalist, strategically placed 10 yards behind her.

"*Spreadin' love!*"

The show drew to a close. "I want to tell you, there are many audiences that warm themselves by the fire," she finally said to her adoring fans. "But you guys *light* the fire."

Applause.

Diana Ross's relationship with her audience is symbiotic. They need her for entertainment. She needs them for sustenance.

"I am telling you, you are the best!"

More applause, and then a standing ovation. She couldn't help but glow. Smiling broadly, she tilted her head back and extended her arms out to her devoted fans. "I am all yours," her body language seemed to say. Then she raised her arms again in triumph. There she posed, larger-than-life, the applause washing over her in waves, invigorating her and making her more dazzling still.

When Diana Ross now appears, people do not come to see a concert. They come to bask in the presence of a goddess. It's a quasi-religious experience. Over the last 30 years, Diana Ross has evolved into someone who is more illusion than substance. She seems to realize this, but rather than allow it to frighten her or concern her, she enjoys it. She knows that, she barely has To Do. Mostly she just has To Be.

When she performs, even the most critical observer has to marvel at the magnitude of her achievements: from the Brewster Projects to the top of the record charts, from sock hops and seedy Detroit beer joints to the Copacabana and Caesars Palace, from one-night stands in segregated theaters in the South to television and movie stardom.

Diana Ross Naess is a rich woman who could easily retire to her remote Tahitian island after three decades in the spotlight's glare. But despite the rigors of life on the road, a challenging marriage and raising five children, she continues to tour the world. More than anything, she loves to entertain. A consummate performer, she is also among the world's most glamorous women. It's easy to respect her accomplishments and enjoy her talents. Perhaps the real challenge—not only to the casual observer, but maybe even to the lady herself—lies in determining where the legend that is Miss Ross ends and the woman who is just Diana begins.

"I haven't changed," Diana Ross has insisted. "I am still the same person I was in 1964." Most people who knew her when The Supremes became famous and who know her now would agree. Now, as then, she is enormously talented and endlessly fascinating. And now, as then, she is unrelenting and unpredictable, temperamental and tough, vampish and vibrant, insecure, impetuous and confounding.

"You know, I've never asked anyone to call me Miss Ross," she said recently. "It started during The Supremes period. That's when I knew. I said, 'There's a difference here.' "

Once, a writer was making arrangements for an interview with Diana Ross when her publicist suddenly urged, "By the way, when you talk to her, call her Miss Ross."

"You're kidding, right?"

"No. She likes that," said the publicist.

"Sure. I'll call her Miss Ross. Why not? Quite the diva, isn't she?" observed the writer.

The publicist hesitated. "Well, let's just say little things mean a lot."

During the interview the next day, Diana couldn't have been more charming, gracious and cooperative. The journalist was quite impressed with her. But in his enthusiasm, he completely forgot about the publicist's odd request. He called her by her first name. Over and over again. She didn't seem to mind at all.

"A reporter once asked me if I ever cried," she confided during the interview. "I wonder if people think I'm just as hard as a rock and have no emotions at all." She paused to consider her statement, and then shuddered at the thought. "Could that be?" she asked, mystified.

The writer thought it best not to venture an opinion.

"I really just don't know," Diana concluded, sadly.

The next day, the publicist telephoned to find out how the interview went. The journalist raved about the experience, saying that Diana seemed candid and accessible. Then, just as the conversation was coming to a close, the publicist said, "Oh, by the way, why didn't you call her Miss Ross?" He sounded hurt, as if he had been somehow betrayed.

"I guess I forgot. How'd you know that?"

"I found out," he said. Then let out a weary, resigned sigh. "Miss Ross mentioned it."

🦋 Epilogue 🦋

On October 19, 1989, two weeks before publication of this book, Diana Ross commanded a press conference at the Intercontinental Hotel in Sydney, Australia, while on tour in that country. Though she did not mention *Call Her Miss Ross* by name, it seemed obvious to some reporters that the advance publicity about the book was on her mind.

"I am *not* a barracuda," she told the assembled reporters. "There's absolutely nothing that I won't answer."

Regarding Mary Wilson's *Dreamgirl* book, Diana said, "I'm unhappy because we were so close in the time that we were together. I didn't see our relationship in the way she did. There must have been a reason she decided to write this. I think maybe she needed the money." Then, Diana remarked dryly, "If I ever wrote a book, I would like to write something that was not quite so disposable. I won't write about any crap."

As for the much-publicized rivalry with Whitney Houston, Diana noted, "I love her. I think she's a tremendous artist and she knows that. If anybody plays the screen version of Diana Ross," she concluded with a smile, "it should be Whitney Houston."

Diana Ross required the Australian television crews to cap their camera lenses with diffuser filters and to photograph her from her left—and, she believes, better—side, and only for the first five minutes of the press conference. When asked about these demands, she unabashedly admitted, "Yes, I asked for those filters. Yes, I am worried about how I look. I'm forty-five and I'd like to look pretty on camera. Softer."

The press conference lasted about a half hour. Upon answering her last question, Diana stood up to leave, but stopped for a moment. She concluded, "I would just like to say that I have done nothing that I'm ashamed of. Absolutely nothing." Then, she was besieged by reporters, all scrambling to get her autograph.

After *Call Her Miss Ross* was originally published in November 1989, one associate asked Diana Ross about it. She cast him a withering look and said, "I don't want to talk about that book. Ever." She still seems—or at least *acts* as if she is—oblivious to the indignation she sometimes engenders. "I think most of the people who talked about me the way they did lied about their recollections," she would later say, "because that's not how I remember it at all."

A number of Motown-related books were published after *Call Her Miss Ross*. Two were worthwhile reading, both published in 1990: *Supreme Faith: Someday We'll Be Together* by Mary Wilson with Patricia Romanowski (published by HarperCollins and promoted as "the dramatic conclusion to the national bestseller, *Dreamgirl*") and *Berry, Me, and Motown* by Raynoma Gordy Singleton (Contemporary Books).

Wilson's book concentrated on her stormy personal life and career experiences as the only original member of The Supremes after Diana Ross left the group in January 1970. Unfortunately, since most of the public was apathetic about The Supremes during the years Mary wrote about, few people cared about what happened to Wilson or the group in retrospect. Unlike *Dreamgirl, Supreme Faith* was not a commercial success.

In her sequel, which was, surprisingly, more candid than her first book, Mary Wilson recounted the evening in early 1988 when The Supremes were inducted into The Rock and Roll Hall of Fame. Ross did not attend the ceremony; Wilson did. Mary wrote that she felt like "somebody's secretary sent to pick up an award in her boss's absence."

"As I stood at the podium giving my speech, I could see that many people in the room, even musicians and singers, probably didn't know who I was, or who Flo was," she observed. "And didn't care either. Literally and figuratively, we were history. In many people's minds, we were three people: the big star who made good, the one who died in poverty and me, the background singer. For so many years I had dreamed and hoped that I might one day change that, but it's probably impossible, and that's probably the one thing I've stopped dreaming about."

She also wrote that, in early 1990, she and Berry Gordy reached an agreement regarding The Supremes' name, and "I signed away my rights to the name—forever." She concluded, "I don't want anyone to cry for me, because I don't."

In Raynoma Gordy Singleton's well-written, often heartbreaking autobiography, she claimed that she and Berry Gordy started Tamla Records (and Motown) together in the late '50s and that she was never given proper credit or compensation. Gordy—who Raynoma claimed was a pimp when she met him—denied Singleton's claim, even though Singleton's name is listed on documents relating to the original incorporation of Motown Records, along with Gordy's and his sister Esther's. On talk shows promoting her book, Raynoma—who was married to Berry for a short time—said that even though Gordy sold Motown in 1988 for $65 million, "All I got was a plaque. I don't have a dime to my name."

Singleton also wrote of Diana's tumultuous love affair with Berry Gordy, much to Ross' consternation.

In mid-September 1990, Suzanne dePasse was attempting to launch Motown's thirtieth anniversary special for CBS (even though it had actually been seven years since NBC's "Motown 25" special). She had proposed the appearance of many major stars—including Michael Jackson and his sister, Janet—but when it came time to deliver the promised entertainment, she found that few celebrities were willing to appear. It's difficult for many artists to want to pay tribute to Motown's "family" spirit, especially after all that's been said and written about the company, and about Berry Gordy's ruthlessness. Finally, much to dePasse's relief and delight, Diana Ross agreed that she would be involved in the program, and possibly even host the festivities.

After committing to appear on the special, Diana was getting a pedicure in a New York salon when an interview with Raynoma Gordy Singleton, who was promoting her book, was broadcast on "The Joan Rivers Show." Back in the early seventies, when Raynoma worked for Diana as a manager, Diana had demanded that Raynoma call her Miss Ross, even though the two had known each other for twelve years. "I know that you have known me for some time," Diana explained, "but in my position I need to be treated with more respect."

"In the book you talk about Diana Ross's daughter being his [Gordy's] too," Joan said during her interview with Singleton. "That must have been a surprise for her husband [Robert Silberstein]."

"Yes, because Diana and Berry were lovers at the time they got married," Raynoma blithely explained. "What happened was that she and Berry were supposed to get married, but they didn't. So she married Bob, and she was pregnant at the time."

"So her first daughter was . . ."

"Was Berry's," Raynoma added.

"Does he know?"

"He does now," quipped Raynoma.

Diana could not believe her eyes and ears. To watch as Berry's former wife casually discussed Rhonda's paternity with Joan Rivers on national television was more than she could bear.

"She bolted out of that beauty shop like a bat out of hell, went straight to her office and called her attorney, John Frankenheimer," said an associate of Diana's. "The next day, Frankenheimer informed Motown Productions that Diana would not appear on the 'Motown 30' special. She was too humiliated to show her face on national television. And absolutely furious with Raynoma, Berry, Motown and anyone having to do with Motown. Instead of doing 'Motown 30,' she went to Europe and appeared in a fashion show with [her daughter] Tracey in France."

In her book, Raynoma claimed that Diana did not divulge to Rhonda the true identity of her father until the girl was seventeen. "How dare Raynoma discuss my private life," Diana said privately. "She has children of her own. She should understand how I have tried to protect mine from controversy. Yet, she does this. I simply cannot believe she would do this to me. What did I ever do to her?"

Diana Ross and Arne Naess are still married, and seem content. One waiter at Restaurant Aquavit in New York recalled, "They're always smoking, drinking, laughing, telling jokes and making enormous bets with each other. One night, they were here with another couple and betting thousands of dollars on magic tricks. Diana would do a magic trick with her dinner napkin and then bet everyone two thousand dollars that they couldn't figure out the trick. Then her husband would balance a glass on its side and bet everyone thousands of dollars that they couldn't do it. They're very fun people, but I'm always surprised at the wine they choose . . . they order very cheap red wine."

As of this writing, Diana Ross has not followed the poor-selling *Workin' Overtime* with any record, though she is working on a new Motown album. She also has been unable to successfully mount the Josephine Baker movie project, despite an announced production deal with Ted Turner's TNT cable network. (Another Baker bio-film, starring actress Lynn Whitfield, was produced by HBO and garnered excellent reviews when it was broadcast in March 1991.)

"It hasn't been an easy life," Diana Ross has admitted. "But it has been a good one, I think. I believe in my heart it will get even better. I'm looking forward to wonderful things."

In February 1991, Diana Ross was a presenter at the televised Grammy Awards ceremony in New York. Following the presentation, at a Grammy party, she was enveloped by enthusiastic reporters and enthralled fans.

"Miss Ross, would you answer a question?"

"Miss Ross, would you pose for a picture?"

"Miss Ross . . ."

"Please, stop it," Diana told the crowd, obviously irritated. "Don't call me Miss Ross. I'm sick of it. I really am."

"Well, what should we call you?" one reporter asked facetiously. "Miss Wilson?"

Even Diana had to laugh at that.

Notes and Sources

For about the last 10 years, Diana has required that most potential employees sign secrecy agreements as a condition of their employment. This contract not only prevents them from talking about her during their period of employment, but also guarantees their silence after their tenure. This secrecy agreement, along with a 1983 letter which Diana Ross sent out en masse to her friends in the entertainment industry (wherein she stated unflattering "opinions" of eight former employees), have caused many potential interview subjects to be extremely reluctant to go on record. Therefore, many of my sources who have worked closely with Ross would be interviewed only if guaranteed total anonymity. Additionally, some of Berry Gordy's and Arne Naess' former employees, business associates and friends also asked that their statements and observations not be attributed to them. Their wishes have been respected here.

I first met Diana Ross on July 24, 1966, in Atlantic City, New Jersey. I was 10 years old.

I began researching this book officially in October 1981 after an in-depth interview with Diana Ross. But prior to that, I was deeply immersed in the careers of Ross, The Supremes and Berry Gordy, Jr., as detailed in these notes and sources.

I secured many hundreds of interoffice Motown memos regarding Diana Ross' career for research purposes. Because of the confidential nature of these communications, and to protect those former Motown employees who made them available, these memos are not enumerated here though they were vital to the accuracy of the material in this book.

Voluminous Motown press department releases (and also releases from different public relations firms representing Diana Ross through the years) all were individually judged as to their validity and value, and utilized where appropriate.

Practically all of the interview sources listed here contributed to more than one subject area in the book, but, in most cases, they are listed only once. Most of the sources clearly identified within the text are not repeated here unless I decided to duplicate the mention for the sake of clarity. Whenever appropriate, a specific date on which the interview was conducted is provided.

Diana Ross' comments are culled from published sources that are listed in the bibliography, except when her comments were directly to me in an interview or during a press conference, which is noted.

As the former editor-in-chief of *Soul* magazine (1980) and then publisher (1981–1982), I had access to the complete *Soul* files. *Soul* was one of the first black entertainment publications (excluding *Jet* and *Ebony*, both general interest publications) and, as such, had a close association to Motown. Many of the Motown acts received their only national exposure through *Soul*. A great deal of the material in this book was culled from the extensive *Soul* files (1966–

1982), which includes previously confidential notes and memos regarding this material. I also drew heavily from notes and from rough drafts of stories about Diana Ross, The Supremes, Florence Ballard, Berry Gordy and Motown that were not published for one reason or another. (*Soul* was heavily supported by Motown advertising dollars in the '60s and '70s. Apparently, based on these notes and "killed" features, editorial compromises were made so as not to offend Motown.) Much of the material in this book was the subject of great Motown inner-office conflict and until now has never been revealed.

I have been researching this history in one form or another for 20 years. In 1985 and 1986, I published two related books, *Diana* and *Motown: Hot Wax, City Cool and Solid Gold* (both Doubleday), but most of the material I gathered in researching those books was not utilized until now. I also drew heavily from my unpublished 1986 manuscript, *The Supremes: Satin and Tears*.

Whenever practical, I have provided sources within the body of the text. The following chapter notes indicate some of the sources used by me in writing each chapter of the book, including some of the people interviewed and the documents examined. For some of the published sources consulted, see the bibliography. These notes and sources are by no means comprehensive, but are intended to give the reader a general overview of some of my research. Also included are occasional comments of an extraneous but informative nature.

I drew from a personal interview with Diana Ross on October 18, 1981, and a follow-up interview on October 19, 1981.

I also drew from 16 personal interviews with Mary Wilson on May 2, 1973; July 5, 1973; August 12, 1973; August 24, 1973; August 25, 1973; March 15, 1974; May 7, 1974; November 17, 1974; March 10, 1975; June 1, 1976; June 2, 1976; June 12, 1976; July 15, 1976; October 1, 1977; January 10, 1982; and November 24, 1983.

I conducted four interviews with Florence Ballard, dated August 31, 1973; September 2, 1973; January 13, 1975; and August 1975.

Twelve interviews with Cindy Birdsong were also conducted on April 7, 1974; April 23, 1974; September 18, 1974; November 8, 1974; November 15, 1974; November 16, 1974; January 23, 1975; March 10, 1976; March 11, 1976; August 25, 1983; August 26, 1983; and August 27, 1983.

Interviewed over the eight years of research were friends and associates of the Ross family, including Lillian Abbott, Walter Abbott, Walter Gaines, Barbara Abbott Gaines, Mavis Booker, Doris Jackson, Barbara Allison Simpson, McCluster Billups, Susan Burrows, Evelyn Daniels, Ann Brown Essien, Harold E. Baker, Carol Betch, Tremaine Hawk, Joseph Einhorn, Maria Gonzalez, Haywood Johnson, Lammii Allison, Charles Guy, Rita Griffin, Chester Logan, Tony Middleton, Levert Neyman, Mary Constance, Michelle Donate, Damian O'Brien, Davis Paris, Jr., Frances Hamburger, Thomas Perry, Mildred Browning Harris, Julia Cloteil Page, Robert Kraft, Joseph Payton, Levi Andrews, Andrew Popkin, Thomas Rork, Edward Gillis, Louella Jiles, James and Ellen Goldfarb, Gene Scrimpscher, Milton Ford, Ebie Herbert, and Tommy Gardner, Sr.

Researcher Reginald Wilson's visits to Detroit and the Brewster Projects in 1983 helped insure the accuracy of chapters regarding Ross' early years.

All of Fred Ross' quotes are culled from three interviews conducted with him in 1983. At that time, Diana Ross apparently requested that her family not speak to me or my researchers. Her mother, Ernestine, complied with her daughter's wishes. Fred's reaction to Diana's edict: "I love my daughter, but she doesn't tell me what to do. Historically, I think it's important that her story be told."

I have not interviewed Berry Gordy directly, but I have attended many press conferences over the years, in which I was able to direct questions to him.

I drew from interviews with the following people (such interviews were conducted for a variety of purposes, including this book): Taylor Cox (Motown's Multi-Media Management); Mickey Stevenson (A&R Department); Joe Shaffner (The Supremes' road manager); Wanda Rogers, Katherine Anderson Shaffner and Gladys Horton (The Marvelettes); Ardena Johnston (chaperone); Maxine Powell, Cholly Atkins and Maurice King (Artist Development, interviewed by author's associate, Reginald Wilson); Clarence Paul (producer); Mabel John (artist); Marc Gordon (producer); Gil Askey (musical conductor); Lamont Dozier (writer/producer); Freda Payne; Janie Bradford; Freddie Gorman; Jay Lasker; Mary Wells; Martha Reeves and Rosalind Ashford (The Vandellas); George Clinton; Mickey Shorr; Tom DiPierro; Aretha Franklin; Stevie Wonder; Marvin Gaye; Scherrie Payne; Susaye Greene; Phillippe Wynn; Billy Preston; Henry Fambrough, Bobbie Smith, Billy Henderson, Pervis Edwards and G.C. Cameron (The Spinners); Jerry Butler; Joe Harris; Willie Hutch; Billy Eckstine; Junior Walker; Edwin Starr; Bobby Taylor; William "Benny" Benjamin; Levi Stubbs, Lawrence Payton, Abdul "Duke" Fakir and Renaldo "Obie" Benson (The Four Tops); Smokey Robinson; Bobby Rodgers, Pete Moore and Ronnie White (The Miracles); Marlon Jackson, Tito Jackson, Jackie Jackson, Jermaine Jackson and Randy Jackson (The Jacksons); Eddie Kendricks, David Ruffin, Melvin Franklin, Otis Williams, Dennis Edwards, Richard Street, Damon Harris and Glenn Carl Leonard (The Temptations).

I drew from three personal interviews with Michael Jackson: at his home in Encino in July 1979, at the CBS Records offices on October 18, 1979, and a phone interview in June 1982.

Also vital to my research were copies of the recording contracts between Diana Ross, Mary Wilson and Florence Ballard and International Talent Management and Berry Gordy, Jr. Enterprises, dated April 23, 1965.

Also of assistance were many video tapes from my collection of Motown's artists in performance. I was the writer of *Motown on Showtime: The Temptations and Four Tops Starring Stevie Wonder*, and also the writer of The Supremes' segment featuring Mary Wilson on *Girl Groups: The Story of a Sound (MGM-UA)*.

I also drew from my interviews with Donald McKayle (choreographer) and Bob Mackie (costume designer). Also useful was a Western Union telegram sent to *Soul* Magazine dated October 3, 1968, in which Motown's legal positions regarding David Ruffin and Florence Ballard were conveyed. The nine-page telegram outlined Berry Gordy's strategy to the managing editor at the magazine with whom Berry was particularly friendly. Also interviewed: Gerald Davidoff, Walter Lawson, Thomas Freedman, Louis Henderson, Ari Marina, Kenneth Rain, Jane Elliot and Diana Thompson.

I maintained communication with Florence Ballard in the '70s. The principal source for Ms. Ballard's post-Supremes years are my and my researchers' interviews and telephone conversations with Ballard and husband Tommy Chapman (October 1984, Baton Rouge, Louisiana).

Also vital to my Florence Ballard research: "Supplemental Agreement" between Florence Ballard and Motown Record Corporation outlining the terms of her dismissal from The Supremes, dated July 26, 1967; "Authority to Represent" contract between Florence Ballard and the law firm Orkent, Baun & Vulpe to represent Ballard in her claim for damages against Motown Record Corporation, Berry Gordy, Jr., Enterprises, Inc. and Berry Gordy, Jr., dated August 24, 1967; legal documents pertaining to "Florence Ballard vs. Leonard A. Baun," civil action #166269 filed in Wayne County Circuit Court on October 1, 1970; Wayne County Circuit Court Civil Action 173–852: "Florence Ballard vs. Diana Ross, et al." (1970); miscellaneous press releases from Al Abrams Associates which represented Ballard in 1968, including "Florence Ballard Breaks Silence, Blasts Motown, Diana Ross"; ABC Records Special Information Bulletin about Florence Ballard (the only official record company biography released after Ballard left Motown); and transcripts from Ballard's appearance on "The Lou Gordon Show," February 1975.

Regarding Berry Gordy's legal problems with Holland-Dozier and Holland: I obtained copies of legal documents pertaining to the $4 million lawsuit filed in Wayne County Circuit Court on September 3, 1968, by Motown Record Corporation and Berry Gordy, Jr., against Holland-Dozier and Holland; and also the 31-page complaint and $22 million lawsuit filed in Wayne County Circuit Court on November 14, 1968, by Holland-Dozier and Holland against Motown Record Corporation, Jobete Music Company, Inc., Berry Gordy, Jr., Ralph Seltzer and Harold Noveck and Sidney Noveck. Also helpful was a detailed press release regarding the H-D-H vs. Gordy legal action, from Al Abrams Associates, representing H-D-H, dated November 15, 1968.

I was employed by The Supremes after Diana Ross left the group, making me privy to much of the internal conflict among the group, Ross, Gordy and Motown Records. Regarding Diana Ross' replacement in The Supremes, Jean Terrell: I had seven extensive interviews with Terrell, the first being on February 12, 1971, the last on March 5, 1980. Also helpful were two magazine articles: "Jean Terrell Going Up the Ladder" (*Black Stars*, December 1978) and "The Accidental Supreme" by Walter Burrell (*Soul*, March 9, 1970), in which Terrell discussed her relationship with Gordy and how she was discovered.

Also vital to my research: "Mary Wilson Ferrer vs. Motown Record Corporation Before the Labor Commissioner of the State of California" (filed September 30, 1977), which included, as a matter of public record, an agreement between Wilson and Motown Records pertaining to the right to and interest in the name "Supremes," dated April 22, 1974.

Primary sources for information regarding *Lady Sings the Blues* include my interviews with the film's producer Jay Weston, January 26, 1989; director Sidney Furie, January 1985; and assistant director, Charles Washburn, January 16, 1989. Also, material was gathered from the Motown-Weston-Furie Production contract with Joe Glaser Associated Booking representing Louis McKay, dated January 30, 1969. I also drew from an extensive interview I conducted with Billy Dee Williams in 1982, and with Richard Pryor in 1978, and from film production notes from Paramount Pictures Corporation.

Primary sources for information regarding *Mahogany* include my two interviews with the film's producer Rob Cohen in February 1989 and on April 24, 1989. Also interviewed were deposed director Tony Richardson on January 26, 1989; associate producer Neil Hartley on February 1, 1989; screenwriter John Byrum in February 1989; Marvin Whitney, Steven Redmond, Jerome Thomas, Thomas Hatfield, Steven Strickland, Elizabeth Van Buren and Michael Masser in 1985; and Billy Dee Williams in 1982.

Primary sources for information regarding *The Wiz* include my interviews with producer Rob Cohen in February 1989 and on April 25, 1989; tape recordings of a press conference in New York on the first day of rehearsal in September

1977 and on the first day of shooting, November 3, 1977; and the complete third-draft screenplay dated May 5, 1977, by Joel Schumacher (including many scenes that were eventually edited from the movie). Also, primary sources were Leonard Pitts' features, "Diana Ross—Dorothy" and "Sidney Lumet—Director" in *Soul* issue of October 30, 1978; and miscellaneous production notes for *The Wiz* from Universal Studios.

Much of the material about Diana Ross' letter of October 11, 1983, to the industry regarding her former employees was culled from an actual copy of the letter; legal documents obtained by the author pertaining to the $2 million libel suit brought against Ross by former employee Gail Davis, filed in U.S. District Court for the Southern District of New York on June 20, 1984; "To Whom It May Concern" by Patrick Goldstein, *Los Angeles Times*, July 15, 1984; and "The Revenge of the Fired," *Newsweek*, February 16, 1987. I also interviewed Gail Davis' attorney, Don Zakarin, in June 1989.

Observations and comments were also culled from my interviews and/or conversations with Carl Feuerbacher, January 4, 1989; John Whyman, January 7, 1989; Eddie Carroll, January 7, 1989; John Mackey, January 7, 1989 and January 15, 1989; Walter Burrell, January 10, 1989; Janet Charlton, January 11, 1989; Stephanie Thomas, January 14, 1989; Bill Geddie in June 1989; and Liz Smith, July 6, 1989.

Very special thanks to David McGough/DMI for his excellent photographs found within this book.

Chapter 1

I interviewed various people who attended the Florence Ballard funeral including Stacy Kimbell, Barbara Johnson, Frederick Alexander, Wanda Rogers and John Thompson. The dialogue at the beginning of the chapter among onlookers is recreated from actual conversations reported to me, and I also drew from news reports relating to Ballard's death and funeral.

"You know, you told me . . .": Ballard to Dave Diles (Lou Gordon's television show, Detroit), 1975.

"She wants out" and "That's when I started . . .": Ballard interview notes, 1975.

"You'll be sorry you messed with me . . .": Ibid. I also drew from an interview Ballard gave to the *Washington Post* published April 27, 1975, and a transcription of an interview with Ballard in the *Soul* files.

"Thin is in . . .": The Supremes at the Copa, 1965.

"Give me that gold . . .": The Supremes at the Copa, 1966.

The last time the three Supremes were seen together was dramatized using notes from Ballard interview, 1975. A slightly different version of this encounter appears in *Dreamgirl*, Mary Wilson's 1986 autobiography.

The anecdote re: Ballard's transportation dilemma: Ballard interview notes.

"Why did Diane have to act that way?": *Dreamgirl*.

Ross and Wilson at the casket: Mary Wilson from transcript of my interview for *Girl Groups: The Story of a Sound* video. Much of the material in this chapter was drawn from my interview with Wilson (November 24, 1983) for this home video; only 10 minutes of my 90-minute interview was used in the final product.

Diana knew how much Florence had depended . . . : Ross has never discussed the fact that she tried to prevent Florence Ballard's home from being foreclosed upon, but there are many Motown executives who recall this transaction and a copy of the voided check exists in Motown's accounting files.

"If I'd known how it was going to end . . .": Ross to Lynn Van Matre, *Chicago Tribune Magazine*, June 20, 1976.

"Florence was always . . .": Ibid.

"She was just one of those people . . .": Ibid.

Chapter 2

"Downstairs became headquarters . . .": Robinson in *Smokey*, his 1988 autobiography.

"They were four very . . .": Bradford in interview with me in 1983.

The re-creation of The Primettes' first audition at Motown was culled from an interview I conducted with Diana Ross at the Waldorf-Astoria in New York City, April 3, 1972; an interview with Florence Ballard, August 31, 1973; Mary Wilson's recollection from *Girl Groups*; and my interview with Janie Bradford. Diana Ross remembered a similar version of this story in an interview conducted by Andy Warhol, October 1981.

The re-creation of The Primettes' first recording session was culled from three interviews I conducted with Mabel John in 1984.

"tired of workin' for free . . .": The scene between The Primettes and Berry Gordy was re-created from Berry Gordy's memory in a press conference at the Shrine Auditorium, Fall 1982, and also from an interview I had with Florence Ballard, September 2, 1973.

"I wanted to be part of that . . .": Ross in interview with me, October 1981.

"Later, I remember walking . . .": Gorman in interview with me, 1983.

"I was still in high school . . .": Ross to Bill Harris on Showtime interview, July 1983.

"So man, what do you think . . .": Conversation between Robinson and Gordy was re-created by Robinson in interview with me in 1979.

"Look, if you want to manage . . .": *The Story of Motown* by Peter Benjaminson.

Berry decided to sign the girls . . . : The story of how The Supremes chose their name was re-created using notes from my interview with Janie Bradford, and also from memories of Florence Ballard and Mary Wilson in separate interviews. Although Bradford told me that she has no idea what the other names on the list were, in Mary Wilson's *Dreamgirl* memoir, she claims the other names under consideration were The Darlenes, The Sweet Peas, The Melodees, The Royaltones and The Jewelettes.

Fred and Ernestine Ross' family history was culled from an interview conducted by my researcher Reginald Wilson with Fred Ross, November 1983; my interview with Fred Ross, December 1983; and a detailed biography written by Diana Ross' daughter, Rhonda Suzanne Ross, and distributed to mourners at Ernestine Ross' funeral in Detroit, October 10, 1984.

"Not all of us kids . . .": "Diana Ross—The Big Event," NBC, March 6, 1977. "But you ain't a lead singer . . .": Conversation re-created using Ballard's quotes given during an interview on "The Jerry Blavat Show" in Philadelphia, 1968.

"Listen, Fred Ross was . . .": Ballard interview notes.

"Suppose they like her better . . .": Wilson interview notes.

"We always fought . . .": Ross to "L.E.," *Esquire*, November 1981.

Diana Ross remembered the meeting with Esther Edwards and her mother's reaction to Berry Gordy for the first time in an interview with Walter Burrell in *Soul Illustrated*, November 1970.

Chapter 3

Florence Ballard's rape is re-constructed using Mary Wilson's *Dreamgirl* as a primary source, and also my June 20, 1989, interview with Gladys Horton, in whom Ballard confided about the attack. Ballard also discussed events leading up to the attack in an interview in *Soul*, November 1968, and I utilized unpublished material from that interview.

"When am I going . . .": from *Smokey*.

Smokey Robinson's interest in women outside of his marriage to Claudette Robinson is verified by Robinson in his autobiography, *Smokey*. See p. 235: "Ever since Claudette and I had been married, she maintained a simple position: 'I can tolerate just about anything concerning you and another woman, long as you don't put it in my face, long as you don't disrespect me. There is, though, one thing that would make me leave you—if you ever had a baby with another woman.' "

"Soon, whenever The Miracles . . .": Horton in interview with me.

"You two will never guess . . .": Wilson interview notes. Mary Wilson also had similar recollections in *Dreamgirl* of the day Diana announced that she was dating Smokey Robinson. See p. 105: "Around this time Diane and Smokey's interest in each other was well known. Everyone knew he was married to Bobby Rogers' cousin, Claudette, so I was surprised when one day Diane said, 'Guess what? I went out with Smokey . . .' "

"Besides, you're doing this . . .": Ballard from *Soul* unpublished interview dates, November 18, 1968.

"an intimacy, a genuine love": Robinson in *Smokey*.

"There was only one reason . . .": Horton in interview with me.

"The gossip is upsetting me . . .": Ibid.

"See I told you . . .": Ballard, *Soul* files.

"If you really want to know . . .": Horton in interview with me.

"Berry's sister, Esther . . .": Ibid.

"I have to tell you one thing . . .": *Where Did Our Love Go?* by Nelson George.

"After singing, modeling was becoming . . .": Ross to Betty Thompson, *Top Teens*, April 1966.

"She wasn't a very . . .": Kraft in interview with me.

"You know, I'm going . . .": Constance in interview with me.

"I'd just smile in their faces . . .": Ross to *Philadelphia Bulletin*, November 1968.

"She used to call . . .": Griffin to my researcher Reginald Wilson.

"A lot of them she made . . .": Kron to Connie Berman, January 1979.

Chapter 4

"People kept coming in . . .": Gordy to Hershel Johnson, *Black Enterprise*, June 1974.

"You can understand every single . . .": Gordy to me during a press reception at the Shrine Auditorium, Fall 1982.

In 1957, Gordy was introduced . . . : Said Jackie Wilson of Berry Gordy in an interview in the '70s: "He was a little man with a big dream. I always said he was underrated as a songwriter and even at that time he could see what the future held." Wilson suffered a heart attack on stage at the Latin Casino in October 1975. He died eight years later on January 21, 1984.

"I was broke . . .": Gordy, *Soul* files.

"Why work for the man?": Robinson in interview with me. Berry was first interested in Erma Franklin . . . : Gordy's interest in Franklin was explained by Aretha Franklin in interview with me, October 18, 1980.

"I found Berry dashing . . .": Payne in interview with me, May 19, 1977.

"We try not to be overdressed . . .": Ross to Rita Griffin, *Michigan Chronicle*, June 1962.

"What makes you girls . . .": The scene at The Marvelettes' recording session was re-created by Gladys Horton in interview with me.

"Oh, she was mad . . .": Rogers in interview with me.

"Florence was a loner . . .": Horton in interview with me.

Chapter 5

"He thought I was like a baby . . .": Ross to "L.E.," *Esquire*, November 1981.

"I'm gonna get him . . .": John recollection in interview with me.

"Oh, please let me drive in the car . . .": Moore in interview with me, January 1983. Additional memories of the Motor Town Revue tour were culled from interviews I conducted over the years with various artists on the show.

Florence Ballard's father . . . : Ballard's family history was extracted from three interviews with Ballard conducted on August 31, 1973, September 2, 1973, and January 13, 1975, and also from the notes filed with *Soul* magazine for an interview with Ballard on November 21, 1968.

Though Mary and Florence bonded . . . : Wilson's family history was culled from an interview with her on Wilson, October 1, 1977, and also from notes taken by me during an interview on January 10, 1982, which were not utilized in a feature I wrote on Wilson ("I Wish They'd Let The Supremes Rest With Dignity") for *The Black American* newspaper, January 1982. Also utilized as a secondary source was Wilson's memoir, *Dreamgirl*.

This wasn't the first time . . . : That Ernestine Moten Ross suffered from tuberculosis was first revealed by Diana Ross in "From Real Rags . . ." *Look*, May 1966.

"I remember going in back doors . . .": Ross to interviewer on Motown promotion tape, July 1972.

"My first school was . . .": Ross in interview with me, October 18, 1981.

"But it was the smelliest tour . . .": Ibid.

"My first school was all-black . . .": Ibid.

"In practically every city . . .": Ibid.

"We all needed to go, *bad* . . .": Ballard in interview with me, August 1975.

"Eventually we made a deal . . .": Ibid.

"After the show in Birmingham . . .": Wilson in interview with me for *Girl Groups: The Story of a Sound*, November 1983.

"This kid would rehearse . . .": Stevenson in interview with me.

"She stole everybody's act . . .": Gordy to Michael Thomas, *Rolling Stone*, February 1, 1973.

"Find your own style . . .": Gordy interview notes, conducted by Leah Davis in 1973.

After the performance, Horton was accompanying . . . : Horton in interview with me.

"Once we were riding in the bus . . .": Ibid.

"The Apollo audiences just didn't . . .": Stevenson in interview with me.

During this engagement, a local . . . : The scene between The Supremes and Stu Gilliam was re-created using *Showtime at the Apollo* by Ted Fox as a primary source and my interviews with Mary Wilson, November 24, 1983; Stewart Richardson, February 1989; Harold Greenberg, February 1989; and Nancy Horne, March 1989.

Chapter 6

"Gordy had said that he wanted . . .": The details of this recording session were culled from interview I conducted with Clarence Paul.

Florence once remembered . . . : The song in question was "Makes No Difference Now" and all three Supremes sing leads on the record. It was the only recording on which all three had lead vocals.

"Then they would get together . . .": Reeves in interview with me, July 1977.

She began to pursue Brian Holland . . . : The fact that Ross had a relationship with Holland was also written about in Mary Wilson's *Dreamgirl*. See p. 139: "After Diana's relationship with Smokey ended, she set her sights on another married man—Brian Holland . . . Before long, everyone at Hitsville knew what was up and Brian's wife Sharon soon got wind of it, too."

"She didn't have to mess with Brian Holland . . .": Ballard interview, January 13, 1975.

"Berry Gordy was leading the way . . .": Gaye in interview with me, April 18, 1983.

As The Supremes walked out onto the stage . . . : The confrontation between The Supremes and Martha and The Vandellas at the Howard Theatre is recreated from an interview I conducted with Martha Reeves in 1976; John Whyman, January 1989; Mark Ulano, January 1989; Peter Taft, January 1989; and Norman Stern, February 1989.

"How dare you socialize . . .": Johnston in interview with me, 1983.

"I can talk to a fella if I want to . . .": Ross to Walter Burrell, 1970.

"It wasn't like I didn't . . .": Johnston in interview with me.

"Look, I don't care what nobody says . . .": Ross to Burrell, 1970.

Once, Mary was determined . . . : Ballard interview notes, and also notes of Ballard interview by Stewart Armstrong, transcription in *Soul* files.

"Girls, from now on . . .": Dozier in interview with me.

"I know you all sing lead . . .": Ibid.

"I can't say we minded . . .": Wilson in interview with me.

"One evening after a . . .": Dozier in interview with me.

"When my mother went out with us . . .": Ross to Walter Burrell, 1970.

"They even played tricks on her . . .": Ibid.

"We only had enough money for two rooms . . .": Ernestine Ross to Rona Jaffe, *Cosmopolitan*, September 1967.

"We'd go on stage . . .": Ross in interview with me.

"What happened? Who the hell . . .": Ballard, *Soul* files.

"I was very unhappy . . .": Ross to Burrell, 1970.

"To Berry, either a song . . .": Askey in interview with me.

". . . a dumb bunch of niggers": from *The Story of Motown* by Peter Benjaminson.

"You bet your ass . . .": Ibid.

"Berry is such a mentor . . .": Ross in interview with me.

"It was so corny and silly . . .": Dozier to *Rolling Stone*, September 8, 1988.

"In the early days . . .": Wilson in interview with me.

"At five o'clock, the phone rang . . .": Garland in *Heartbreaker* by John Meyer (Doubleday).

"We weren't even talking to each other . . .": Ross to Leonard Pitts, *Soul*, June 20, 1977.

"We need some choreography, quick . . .": Williams in interview with me, 1979.

"Berry could make you think . . .": Gaye in interview with me.

"I got him": Ballard interview notes.

Chapter 7

"The upstairs flat was for me . . .": Ross to Mary Ann Seawell, *The Washington Post*, 1968.

"two to three hundred dollars a week": Wilson in interview with me.

"I didn't know . . .": Reeves in interview with me, July 1977.

"They were taught . . .": Powell to Reginald Wilson, 1983.

"We were sitting in his . . .": Askey in interview with me, 1983.

"First the three of them . . .": Ibid.

"See, the whole thing . . .": Ibid.

"After that . . .": Ibid.

"It's important to remember . . .": Atkins to Reginald Wilson, 1983.

"There was plenty of dancing . . .": Ibid.

"Diane and I spent . . .": King to Reginald Wilson, 1983.

"If you think she learned . . .": Stevenson in interview with me.

"Why are we trying to make . . .": Ballard in interview with me, August 1975.

"We're stars now . . .": Ibid.

"Well, I'm no star . . .": Ibid.

"She wants to be somebody . . .": Gordy to Rona Jaffe, *Cosmopolitan*, September 1967.

"Berry made me talk to all . . .": Shaffner in interview with me.

"I wish I'd had . . .": Ross to Susan L. Taylor, *Essence*, December 1985.

"She had bought . . .": Horton in interview with me.

"You have no business selecting their gowns . . ." and subsequent dialogue: Wilson in interview with me, January 10, 1982.

"Diane, look who's here . . ." and "Berry, you . . .": Horton in interview with me.

"If these don't look stupid . . .": Florence Ballard, *Soul* files.

"Yeah, Diane . . .": Stevenson in interview with me.

"All right, girl . . .": Ballard interview notes, August 1975.

"She's always been like that . . .": Ibid.

"What did they say?": Stevenson in interview with me.

"Okay, everyone listen up . . .": Ibid.

Chapter 8

"Not bad, Blondie . . ." and subsequent conversation: from notes of interview conducted with Ballard by Karen Price for *Soul*, December 16, 1968. Anecdote was edited from published story and found in note form in *Soul* files.

"On the end is Florence Ballard . . .": Ibid.

"I have never offended . . .": Reeves in interview with me.

"I won't be Berry's idea . . .": Gaye in interview with me.

Footnote: "Berry never signed . . .": Wilson interview on "A.M. Los Angeles," 1986.

"It's just not true . . .": Ross in interview with me, October 1981.

"Don't you think . . .": King to Reginald Wilson.

"I think what stands out in my mind . . .": Ross in interview with me, October 1981.

"When I used to live in the Brewster Projects . . .": Ballard in *Look*, May 1966.

During this engagement, an interview was scheduled . . . : See *Dreamgirl* for a similar story, p. 169: "[In 1965], Flo, Diane and I were being interviewed for an important European magazine feature when we heard Diane announce that her real name was Diana. This was the first Flo and I had heard of this . . . Flo and I couldn't believe our ears. We just stared at each other."

"I pulled her aside . . .": Stories concerning Berry Gordy's sexual appetite have been told over the years by many Motown artists. See *Divided Soul*, a biography of Marvin Gaye by David Ritz, p. 71: "Same with women. [Berry] couldn't stay away from them, especially petite, light-skinned women. Berry was the horniest man in Detroit. He married blacks and fooled around with whites. You'd think he was working, but he might be freaking with some chick right up there in his office."

"Berry's such a hardcore . . .": Gaye to Ritz for *Divided Soul*. Also: See *Dreamgirl*, p. 191: "Gambling fever had always been rampant among the men at Motown, where there were probably as many all-night games upstairs at Hitsville as there were on the Strip. The stakes were also pretty outrageous—the keys to a brand new Cadillac, thousands of dollars, and once even the right to produce an up-and-coming female lead singer, bet by a producer and won by Berry. Sitting at a [gambling] table, Berry was in heaven."

"You would be surprised . . .": Ballard in interview with me.

A related note: David Ruffin, in an interview with me on August 23, 1979, said, "I think a lot of the Motown artists operated on a level of fear, but nobody knew what the hell they were afraid of. It got to the point, I think, where we were all sucked up in the intrigue of it all, but no one knew what we were intrigued with."

Regarding Gordy and the underworld: The charge concerning Gordy and Motown's involvement with organized crime has been leveled from several quarters over the years. See *Where Did Our Love Go?* by Nelson George, p. 57: "Undoubtedly, rumors linking Motown with organized crime coincided with [the] influx of whites into the company's management. According to legend, the Teamsters union loaned Motown money to pay some bills and never got out of the company . . . However, despite 25 years of innuendoes, there has never been any criminal investigation linking Motown to any segment of organized crime."

Regarding *Rock's* allegations in the fall of 1970, *International Times* reprinted them in 1971.

"That was one of the biggest . . .": Gordy to Herschel Johnson, *Black Enterprise*, June 1974.

"Those kinds of . . .": Robinson in interview with me, October 24, 1979.

"Bullshit . . .": Gaye in interview with me, San Diego, California, April 18, 1983.

"The Next Thing . . .": Barrow in interview with me, July 15, 1989.

"Basically, I never . . .": Ibid.

"He was impressed . . .": Ibid.

The plane carrying The Supremes . . . : The Supremes' visit to Chicago was documented in "The Supremes: 11 Frantic Hours, 50 Screaming Minutes," by Nancy Moss for *Chicago Tribune Magazine*, March 20, 1966. Information in these pages was culled from this very revealing article. It's said by many Motown historians that each of Gordy's artists had a frank story such as this one printed about them at one time or another before the publicity clamp came down from management. Then, no writer would be allowed such unsupervised access. Often—as in the case of reporter Rona Jaffe for *Cosmopolitan*—a reporter would manage to write an intriguing story despite Motown's efforts to whitewash.

"Just what do The Supremes dream about?": Ibid.

"Yeah, but even . . .": Ibid.

Chapter 9

"I am a student of Berry's . . .": Ross to Walter Burrell, November 1970.

"She has a very intelligent mind . . .": Gordy to Rona Jaffe, *Cosmopolitan*, September 1967.

"I was sick of hearing . . .": Gaye in interview with me, backstage at the Greek Theatre, Los Angeles, August 1983.

"Motown had a lot of people . . .": Stevenson in author's interview.

Details of the scene backstage at Blinstrub's in Boston were provided by many observers, but most valid were the June 1, 1972, memories of Sye MacArthur to me while The Supremes were appearing at the Copacabana in New York. Also helpful were Joe Shaffner's recollections. Florence Ballard's very specific memories of this night and her subsequent visit to Diana Ross in the Henry Ford Hospital are a part of the Florence Ballard file of *Soul*. Ballard remembered the conversation for a 1975 feature in *Soul* magazine entitled: "Florence Ballard: 'It Could Have Happened to Anyone.' " According to notes in the *Soul* files, after the interview, Ballard telephoned the publication and requested that the story not appear. "I think I may have said some things that are too personal," she said.

(Also, it should be mentioned that two sources have insisted to me that a conversation of this nature between Ross and Ballard actually took place a year later when Ross visited Ballard in the Henry Ford Hospital after Ballard was fired in 1967. It was my decision to stay true to Florence's own words and memories within the text. Though it may be possible that she was confused about time, she seemed certain during the tape recorded interview about the place and the emotions she and Diana shared.)

While in Tokyo . . . : Note—Ballard and Chapman actually met in 1965 in New Jersey.

"It was Flo who taught me the expression . . .": Williams in *Temptations* by Otis Williams.

"If you don't mind me . . .": Tommy Chapman interview notes, Fall 1980, unpublished *Soul* feature.

"What are *you* doing here . . .": Ibid.

"I told her to . . .": and subsequent argument: Ibid.

"Look, Blondie . . .": Ballard recounted the incidents in Boston, at Belle Island, and backstage at "The Ed Sullivan Show" in an unpublished interview for *Soul*, 1975. Also used as source material was *Dreamgirl* by Mary Wilson.

"You know somethin' ": Ibid.

"Oh, you think so . . .": Ibid.

"Do you see how bad . . .": Joe Shaffner's recollection to me in March 1984.

"I am an alcoholic . . .": Horton's recollection to me.

"Berry said there were problems . . .": Randolph in interview with me.

"Diane, I got . . .": Randolph's recollection to me.

"I *don't* want . . .": Ibid.

"She was not willing . . .": Ibid.

"She was ahead maybe . . .": Shaffner in interview with me. The scenes in Las Vegas were re-created from my interviews with Steven Strickland, January

3, 1989; John Simmons, January 22, 1989; Griffith Tomlin, March 1, 1989; and Abe Thomas, March 8, 1989. Details were also provided by author's interviews with Sye MacArthur, June 1, 1972; Joe Shaffner, March 1984; and Reginald Wilson's interviews with Cholly Atkins, March 1983; and Maurice King, March 1983.

The girls had been rehearsing daily . . . : The scene between Berry Gordy and Diana Ross while she was rehearsing for The Supremes' Las Vegas opening was reconstructed from interviews I had with Sye MacArthur, June 1972, and from Florence Ballard interview notes, January 13, 1975, and August 1975.

Addendum: Mary Wilson, in an interview with me on January 10, 1982, said: "Berry was toughest on Diane. He expected the most of her, made her life more difficult than I suppose ours were. Many times, people thought he was abusing her. I remember him shouting at her, accusing her of things that she hadn't done. Flo and I would just watch. What could we do? We were just girls; I think we were scared of Berry."

Later that day, a newspaper reporter . . . : Ballard interview notes. Also utilized, my interview with Gil Askey.

Note: Where Berry Gordy's transition to "Mr. Gordy" is concerned, see *Where Did Our Love Go?*, p. 140: "No more 'Berry, baby'—it was 'Mr. Gordy' for everyone. No more just walking into his office—make an appointment and talk to [lawyer] Ralph Seltzer first, the company's internal buffer. Berry, who once did all Motown-related interviews, cut down on his contact with the press. From 1965 on, Barney Ales and other white executives would do Motown's talking in industry publications."

Chapter 10

"And if I can't control her . . .": Ballard recollection, interview notes.

"I was going to give you girls . . .": Ibid.

"You could've had the time off . . .": Ibid.

"What do you think . . .": Conversation re-created from my interview with Joe Shaffner.

"I would rather . . .": Ballard interview notes.

"Mary has been . . .": Ross to Walter Burrell, 1970.

"At this time . . .": Ibid.

"It was nothing more than . . .": from *Doris Day, Her Own Story* by Doris Day with A. E. Hotchner.

"In those days . . ." and subsequent Ross/Birdsong meeting: Birdsong in interview with me.

"We told her that . . .": Ross to Walter Burrell, 1970.

On the way to Memphis . . . : Ballard's absence in Memphis was remembered by Shaffner and Askey in interviews with me. Also, Wilson's *Dreamgirl* was used as a source.

"Diana could see . . .": Shaffner in interview with me.

"Berry told me . . .": Ibid.

When Diana and Mary returned to Detroit . . . : Ballard interview notes, August 1975. Secondary source was "The Supremes Starring on Behalf of Our Torch Drive" by George Walker, *Detroit Magazine*, July 30, 1976.

On that day, Florence brought her mother . . . : Details of the meeting at Berry Gordy's home on April 23, 1967, were provided by many sources, including Ballard to researcher James Prichot, March 1975, and notes and transcripts in the *Soul* files; Ballard interview notes (January 13, 1975; August 1975); Mary Wilson interview notes, January 10, 1982. Also used as source material was Jacqueline Trescott's story on Ballard in the *Washington Post* on April 27, 1975.

"Diana was really gung-ho . . .": Birdsong in interview with me.

"We had a talk with Flo . . .": Ross to Walter Burrell, 1970.

"Mary worked with Cindy . . .": Ibid.

"Diana and Mary went tearing . . .": Birdsong in interview with me.

"Did you see that Cindy girl . . .": Ballard interview notes.

"We have, just like in a Broadway show . . .": "The Tonight Show" transcript, May 22, 1967.

Before the show that night, Florence confronted Berry . . . : The primary source for this confrontation is Florence Ballard in interviews conducted on January 13, 1975, and in August 1975. Also utilized: Jacqueline Trescott's *Washington Post* feature on Ballard; Tommy Chapman's secondhand report from his wife, Florence Ballard (transcripts and notes in *Soul* files); and previously unpublished notes and expurgated passages from "Flo: It's All Kind of Scary," *Soul*, December 16, 1968. Also vital were voluminous notes from an unpublished series on The Supremes in *Soul* titled "The Supremes Anniversary Spectacular," in June 1976, as well as legal correspondence between Ballard and Motown in the subsequent lawsuit [see Florence Ballard—post-Supremes sources]. Florence Ballard also discussed this night, though not in as much detail, with interviewer Dave Diles on "The Lou Gordy Show," 1974. Mary Wilson also wrote a slightly different version of this backstage drama in her memoirs, *Dreamgirl*. The author also utilized his interviews with Cindy Birdsong.

Chapter 11

"Motown will burn by Halloween": *The Story of Motown* by Peter Benjaminson.

"Now all of that was done . . .": Ross to Walter Burrell, 1970.

"Heavyset with thick hands . . .": description of Roshkind by writer Michael Aron for *Los Angeles* magazine, 1972.

"I've been called everything from the real boss . . .": Ibid.

"I was told I had no right . . .": Ballard to Jacqueline Trescott.

"You can take this paper . . .": Ballard interview notes.

"It wasn't like he was the king . . .": Birdsong in interview with me.

"It took me a long time . . .": Ibid.

But Cindy Birdsong remembers a very different . . . : Details of the day's events at the Mayfair Hotel were provided me by Birdsong in an interview and from Penny Singleton in her report in *Disc and Music Echo*.

Shortly after Florence Ballard was fired . . . : The conversation between Ballard and Chapman was re-created using previously unpublished material from the *Soul* files; from "Florence Ballard: 'It Could Have Happened to Anyone' " including notes and transcripts from interviews with Ballard and Chapman (October 1984).

Florence, her attorney Leonard Baun and Michael Roshkind . . . : Ibid.

Then the record company dropped her: Among the unreleased Florence Ballard masters owned by MCA Records (which has acquired the ABC catalogue): "Yesterday," "Yours Until Tomorrow," "It's Not Unusual," "The Impossible Dream," "Let's Stay in Love," "Walk on By," "My Heart," "You Love Me," "Sweetness," "Everything Wonderful" and "Like You Babe."

Details of the Gordys' wedding celebration were culled from a report in *Soul*, November 4, 1968.

"There's no truth to them at all . . .": Gordy to Bob Talbert and Lee Winfrey, *Detroit Free Press*, March 23, 1969.

"We all came up in the same area . . .": Ibid.

Right before the Carson show . . . : Askey in interview with me.

"Let our efforts be . . .": Transcript of "The Tonight Show," April 5, 1968. Also helpful in writing this section regarding Ross' appearance on the show were Sye MacArthur interview, June 1, 1972, and Maurice King to Reginald Wilson, 1983.

As Humphrey stood at the podium . . . : Details of the Hubert Humphrey/ Diana Ross press conference were culled from transcriptions and notes taken during the conference, provided by reporters Ivan Stewart, Alex Cortes and Alan Dale; also helpful was "Supremes Sure of Humphrey" by Mary McGrory, Associated Press; and "Supremes Perform . . . ," *Soul*, July 6, 1967, which covered The Supremes' first meeting with Humphrey.

"What are you gonna serve? Soul food?": *Tan* magazine, September 1968.

"Diana's always measured . . .": Gaye to David Ritz in *Divided Soul*.

"It was what you . . .": Askey in interview with me.

"I think we should . . .": Askey recollection in interview with me.

"But one thing that was always inevitable . . .": Richards in interview with me.

"I need a vacation . . .": Wilson in *Dreamgirl*.

"Hey Nigger!": The material regarding the racial slur directed at Diana Ross was culled from an in-studio interview with her that was conducted in Los Angeles at Motown in March 1971 as a promotional tool for *Lady Sings the Blues*. Ross told the story exactly as depicted in this prologue.

"It wasn't meant to shock people . . ." and the rest of the dialogue: Transcript of the press conference, November 12, 1968.

Chapter 12

"Why should it be Diana Ross and The Supremes?": Ruffin in interview with me.

"If it wasn't for me . . .": Williams to Judith Spiegleman, *Soul*.

"Though I don't think I saw Diana . . .": McKayle in interview with me.

"The others at Motown . . .": Ibid.

Berry was so smitten with Chris . . . : Berry's infatuation for Chris Clark was also written about by Rona Jaffe for *Cosmopolitan*, September 1967. It would be years later that I would discover that the blonde in question was Clark. Mary Wilson also wrote about Berry having arranged for Clark to be on the road with The Supremes, without Diana's knowledge, in her *Dreamgirl*.

Blues singer Mabel John . . . : All of the details regarding Diana Ross, Berry Gordy and Mabel John were provided by my interviews with John in 1985.

During this time, Berry brought a new . . . : Drawn from my interviews with Cindy Birdsong. Also helpful was dePasse's press release about her personal history, from Motown Records, November 1977.

[Note: In February 1989, Suzanne dePasse said to writer Darlene C. Donloe (*Rhythm and Business*), "Until you've had Berry Gordy assess your strengths and weaknesses, you haven't lived."] I requested an interview with dePasse in 1985, but she declined. I worked with dePasse on "Motown On Showtime: The Temptations and Four Tops" in 1986, which I wrote and dePasse produced.

Cindy must have known . . . : Birdsong in interview with me.

The first show went off without . . . : Details concerning the deaths of Ross' dogs backstage at the Latin Casino come from many sources including my first book about Diana Ross, *Diana* (published by Doubleday, 1985); my interviews with Wilson, Birdsong and Cox; transcript of Dave Dushoff press conference; and news reports from AP and UPI.

"Agents will not want . . .": Gordy to *Detroit Free Press*, March 23, 1969.

But life in Los Angeles was not without . . . : I interviewed Cindy Birdsong in 1974 and again in 1985 in which she discussed her kidnapping, and also Gordy's reaction to it. Also utilized: "Kidnap and Escape Reported" (AP wire story, November 1969) and "Supreme Kidnapped" (UPI wire story, December 1969).

Berry was in Los Angeles when Bobby Taylor . . . : I conducted interviews with The Jackson Five in July 1979 and August 18, 1979, from which much of this material was assembled. Also helpful were the October 1969 Rogers and Cowan press release, "Diana Ross Introduces Jackson 5," and the Motown Productions videotape, "Michael Jackson—The Legend Continues." I also utilized voluminous notes and features on The Jacksons from *Soul*'s files.

"You know, to be honest . . .": Birdsong in interview with me.

"To say we were anxious is an understatement . . .": Wilson in interview notes.

"The nights we were recording . . .": Birdsong in interview with me.

Diana Ross and The Supremes' final performance . . . : The material regarding the final performance was assembled from many eyewitness accounts, and also from my interviews with Cindy Birdsong and Mary Wilson. Also interviewed were Jean Terrell, June 1978; Willie Tyler, February 14, 1989; Steven Parish, February 11, 1989; Ace Fitzgerald, March 15, 1989; Gil Askey, January 1983; Monique Luttgen, June 4, 1989; Deke Richards, 1983; and Marvin Gaye, April 18, 1983.

[Note: Marvin Gaye also told me: "The night of her last show with The Supremes, that was the night I think I first realized what an actress Diane was."]

The dialogue from the performance was transcribed from recordings of the concert.

"It was all acting . . .": Birdsong in interview with me.

"I went along . . .": Ibid.

Berry headed for the house phone . . . : Wilson in interview with me, January 1982. Wilson remembered a slightly different version of this telephone conversation with Gordy in *Dreamgirl*.

Chapter 13

"I tried to marry her . . .": Gordy to Louie Robinson, *Ebony*, February 1970.

"I love Berry Gordy very much . . .": Ibid.

"I want to have a family . . .": Ross to Walter Burrell, 1970.

"Diana definitely wanted to get married . . .": Birdsong in interview with me.

"She's not really taking a big chance . . .": Gordy to Louie Robinson, *Ebony*, February 1970.

For instance, a month before . . . : The conversation between Ross and the fan, who will remain anonymous here, was recorded in December 1969. The tape has been circulating among Ross' fans since that time.

"Berry used to make her . . .": Langdon in interview with me.

"Berry used to come in on her sessions . . .": Ibid.

"He really is quite a creative person . . .": Ibid.

"But the people were coming . . .": Tyler in interview with me.

When Diana brought her new show . . . : Berry talked about tearing $20 bills in half to Robert Hillburn for an interview in the *Los Angeles Times*, March 22, 1983.

"I drove up to his huge mansion . . .": Langdon in interview with me.

"I want the biggest wedding of all . . .": Ross to *Teen* magazine, 1966.

"They were very secretive . . .": Langdon in interview with me.

"You see when I first met her . . .": Silberstein to Marin Scott Milam, April 1973.

"When she first started seeing Bob . . .": Birdsong in interview with me.

"I found Bob to be . . .": Ibid.

"I didn't even know who she was . . .": Rev. Frank Hutchinson to Judith Spiegelman for *Soul*.

"I'm proud to be her husband . . .": Silberstein to Rennie Walters, January 1973.

Within two weeks of the wedding . . . : Susan Stocking, *Detroit Free Press*, November 12, 1972.

"We had a tough first year . . .": Ross to Joseph Bell, *Good Housekeeping*, October 1978.

In May 1969, Weston and . . . : Conversations between Weston and Stulberg and Weston and Gordy are re-created from interview I conducted with Jay Weston.

Propitiously enough, *Look* magazine . . . : The *Look* magazine feature was published September 1969.

Chapter 14

I utilized an unedited shooting script of *Lady Sings the Blues* by Sidney Furie and Terence McCloy, dated February 1, 1972, in my research for this chapter.

The show's centerpiece . . . : The "Diana!" special aired on April 18, 1971.

After a few pleasantries . . . : The meeting among Weston, Furie, Gordy and Schoenfield was re-created using both a tape recording of it (Berry Gordy taped all of his business meetings at that time with the permission of all principals) and my interviews with Weston and Furie. The conversations between Diana Ross and Berry Gordy regarding her feelings about accepting the role of Billie Holiday, and her opinions about the original script, were re-created using a tape recording of the meeting as a source, and also my interview with Sidney Furie.

At this time, Diana received . . . : Ross remembered the episodes regarding brothers T-Boy and Arthur's scrapes with the law in "The Supreme Supreme" by Jack Hamilton, *Look*, September 23, 1969.

"There are times now when . . .": Ross to Walter Burrell, 1970.

"I saw a picture once . . .": Ross to Marin Scott Milam, *Photoplay*, April 1973.

Gordy sent his aides . . . : The story regarding the first time Diana Ross heard Billie Holiday sing "My Man" was re-created using my interview with Gil Askey as a source.

"Oh they moved . . .": Reeves in interview with me, January 1976.

[Note: Martha and The Vandellas had long been cast in The Supremes' shadow, almost to the point of public confusion over their identity. In 1967, at the Latin Casino in New Jersey, The Vandellas were handed three bottles of bourbon on stage with the accompanying note, "For The Supremes." Two years later, when Berry Gordy was planning an album for Reeves, he suggested that she record her voice over musical tracks that had been rejected by Diana Ross. Reeves was asked to sing over the tracks in Ross's key. "But my voice doesn't sound beautiful and sweet like Diana's because my life hasn't been beautiful and sweet, like hers," she said in March 1969 to reporter Rochelle Reed. Six years later, in an interview with Jay Grossman for *Rolling Stone* dated May 23, 1974, Martha said that when she complained to Gordy about her treatment at Motown, a loud argument ensued. "You can not run my record company," Berry told her. "No, and you can't either!" Martha retaliated. I worked as publicist for Reeves in the summer of 1978. Of Motown, she told me, "The company grew, the tree got weak and the limbs started fallin' off."]

Without Berry being around . . . : Wilson in interview with me. "Gladys Knight never got . . .": Jean Terrell to JTLA fan club newsletter, 1974.

It seemed that, for the most part . . . : Hazel Joy Gordy's 17th birthday party was attended and written about in detail by Judith Spiegelman for "Berry Honors Daughter," *Soul*, November 1, 1971. All of the observations about the party are from this published report.

Berry Gordy always had security . . . : The fact that a man was killed at the Gordy home was mentioned as a footnote in a Motown history published in 1979. See *The Story of Motown* by Peter Benjaminson, p. 115, footnote 4: "One of Gordy's security guards shot and killed a fellow guard at this house [Gordy Manor] in 1971. The surviving guard said his gun went off accidentally and indications were that the two men had been drinking."

"Whenever I did photo sessions . . .": Langdon in interview with me.

"But why, Flo?": Chapman interview notes (October 1984).

Chapter 15

"What the hell are you . . .": The argument between Gordy and Furie concerning the original script to *Lady Sings the Blues* was re-created using my interview with Furie.

"But they look crappy . . .": Ross to Karen Wenner, *Women's Wear Daily*, January 1973. Also, wrote Wenner: "Diana threw a temper tantrum over the initial wardrobe for the movie . . ."

"The producers felt she was a temperamental bitch . . .": Gordy to Michael Thomas, *Rolling Stone*, February 1, 1973.

"Diane is very shrewd . . .": Gordy to *Soul*, December 4, 1972.

"They want to butcher . . .": Ibid.

"Man, are you crazy?": Ibid.

"That woman has a fantastic mouth . . .": Williams in interview with me.

"Billy Dee tried to kiss . . .": Berry Gordy to *Soul*, December 4, 1972.

On Christmas Eve, the cast . . . : The story about Pryor and Ross on Christmas Eve was re-created using my interviews with Weston, Furie and Washburn.

Her doctor wouldn't allow her to . . . : Ross to *Los Angeles Times*, November 1, 1972—"My doctor won't let me take the pill . . ."

"I really don't have enough time . . .": Ross to Susan Stocking, *Detroit Free Press*.

"I don't know anything about . . .": Gordy to Will Tusher.

"Bob's being white has never been a problem . . .": Ross to Will Tusher.

"She used to come into . . .": Eddie Carroll in interview with me.

"The only thing . . .": Ibid.

Chapter 16

"I had heard that Motown . . .": Miller in interview with me.

"Well, I don't know . . .": Miller's recollections in interview with me.

"Would you like to . . .": Masser's recollections in interview with me.

"I didn't have the vaguest . . .": Miller in interview with me.

"It's okay . . .": Miller's recollections in interview with me.

"At this point . . .": Miller in interview with me.

"And she's got . . .": Ibid.

"That week, Ron Miller . . .": All of the details of the scene between Ross and Miller at Ross' home were provided from my interview with Miller who said, "I will never forget that morning as long as I live."

Finally she was stationed . . . : The recording session for "Touch Me in the Morning" was re-created using my interviews with both Miller and Masser.

"No way! I wouldn't go . . .": Marvin Gaye in interview with me.

"The chemistry was all wrong . . .": Art Stewart to David Ritz for *Divided Soul*.

Most people at Motown knew . . . : Details of the Diana Ross/Marvin Gaye recording session were provided by my interview with Marvin Gaye. I also interviewed the record's producer, Hal Davis, in 1983.

[Note: Gaye told the author: "One thing about Diane, she doesn't like it when I smoke dope. That was a problem between us. Diane, she's the squarest girl in the world, so clean. I admire that about her, being in show business all these years and still square and straight as an arrow. I have to have my dope or I cannot record, simple as that. I remember there being some run-ins with her in the studio because I wouldn't stop smoking. I was being difficult, just like she likes to be. Put me and Diane in the studio together and there's gonna be fireworks. I tried to tell B.G. that, but he wouldn't listen. So I guess you might say I went about the business of trying to prove I was right by making it extremely difficult for the little lady. I suppose I could have been nicer." He thought about his last statement for a moment and then added, *"Naaah!"*]

"During this album, she . . .": Marvin Gaye to David Ritz for *Divided Soul*.

Instead of going to New York . . . : Ross discussed the morning she and her husband waited for Gordy's call to Joseph Bell for *Good Housekeeping*. The conversation between her, Bob and Berry was re-created using quotes exactly as she gave them.

"Tonight everyone will know . . .": Mary Murphy, *Los Angeles Times*, October 30, 1972.

"I think she's a great wife . . .": Gordy to Will Tusher, interview in Las Vegas, 1972, which, he said, took place "backstage after Diana Ross finished a rousing dinner show." The rest of the quotes in this passage are from Tusher's interview with Gordy, Ross and Silberstein.

"It's a love story . . .": Gordy to Michael Thomas, *Rolling Stone*, February 1, 1973.

"Dear Jesus Christ . . .": Ross to Aljean Harmetz, *The New York Times*, April 3, 1973.

"I feel lost . . ." and the rest of the conversation: Diana Ross to Sasha Scott. [Note: Michael Thomas made a similar observation during an interview with Ross when she was complaining about feeling lost. "BG just smiled at her and says that's a lot of crap," he wrote in *Rolling Stone*.]

"She hates my guts . . ." and the rest of the interview: Roshkind and Ross to Joyce Haber, February 11, 1973.

"Oh creative one . . .": Miller, who attended the party, in interview with me.

"I'm not too crazy . . .": Fred Ross in interview with Reggie Wilson, 1983.

"When we left the ceremonies . . .": Ibid.

"I cried . . .": Ross in London press conference, April 1973.

"We'll be back . . .": Fred Ross' recollection to Reggie Wilson.

"White Hollywood is only . . .": Burrell in interview with me, February 1989.

Upon Diana's return . . . : Details of the second recording session for "Touch Me in the Morning" were provided by Miller and Masser in interviews with me.

"To my horror, I found . . .": Weston in interview with me.

For Diana Ross, this was a night . . .": Details of Ross' experience at the Cannes Film Festival were culled from "A Sensation at Cannes," Marvene Jones, *The Hollywood Reporter*, May 31, 1975.

"Honey, you sure showed them . . .": Ibid.

Chapter 18

"She was over-managed . . .": Weston in interview with me.

"Like a lot of white people . . .": Cohen in interview with me.

"When he heard . . .": Ibid.

"From age 24 to 29 . . .": Cohen to Chris Rigby, *California Living*, January 15, 1984.

"The work you got and the credit you got . . .": dePasse to Diane Haithman, *Los Angeles Times*, February 19, 1986.

"At my first meeting . . .": Cohen in interview with me.

One day, Rob Cohen got a call . . . : The meeting between Cohen and the William Morris Agency, and the follow-up meeting between Cohen and Gordy, are re-created using interviews I conducted with Rob Cohen.

"Bob and I thought . . .": Cohen in interview with me.

At Berry's mansion one evening . . . : The meeting at the Gordy mansion and subsequent conversation are re-created using my interview with Rob Cohen.

"He asked me to his house . . .": Richardson in interview with me.

"When I was in his home . . .": Ibid.

"The first thing to deal with . . .": Ibid.

"Berry and Tony were alike . . .": Byrum in interview with me.

"She was alone . . .": Ibid.

"I wondered if . . .": Ibid.

The matter of casting *Mahogany* . . . : Details of the meeting were provided by John Byrum in interview with me.

"The only point of contention . . .": Ibid.

"The whole point . . .": Ibid.

"She looked over to a picture . . .": Masser in interview with me, 1985.

"We got a problem . . ." and the rest of the conversation: Cohen in interview with me.

"If Rob is so goddamn stupid . . .": Ibid.

"She'd obviously been . . .": Richardson in interview with me.

"It looked like a goddamn . . .": Byrum in interview with me.

"The atmosphere on the set . . .": Richardson in interview with me.

"You could almost see the faces . . .": Ross to *Soul*, November 1975.

"What do you mean . . .": Williams in interview with me.

"I can't act with . . .": Richardson's recollection in interview with me.

"His whole thing . . .": Byrum in interview with me.

"Don't leave it up to me . . .": Byrum's recollection in interview with me.

One evening after a hectic day . . . : The details of the altercation between Gordy and the projectionist were provided in my interview with Richardson.

"There were stories . . .": Hartley in interview with me.

"I only remember . . .": Ibid.

"He blew up . . .": Richardson in interview with me.

"Diana wasn't very happy . . .": Richardson in interview with me.

"She had some legitimate . . .": Hartley in interview with me.

"When I reached him, he was flying . . .": Cohen in interview with me.

"Okay, let's get started . . ." and the rest of this scene: Reconstructed from Cohen's recollection during interview with me.

"Utter bullshit . . .": Richardson in interview with me.

"I could better relate . . .": Gordy to *Jet*, January 1975.

Chapter 19

"Oh, I was just tired of traveling . . .": Ballard to *Ebony*, February 1969.

A troubled history . . . : Threats against Florence and one of her producers are documented in *Forever Faithful* by Randall Wilson.

"You can't buck the boss . . .": Ballard to Al Abrams, press agent. [Note: A press statement entitled "Florence Ballard Breaks Silence, Blasts Motown, Diana Ross" is part of the *Soul* files and was apparently utilized for a feature written by Abrams in *The Michigan Chronicle*. According to handwritten notes on the printed statement: "The above comments were actually made by Florence." However, the *Chronicle* accredits them to "an associate of Florence— her brother—present at the interview." Also in this statement: "According to the interview, prior to their (she and Tommy Chapman's) Hawaiian honeymoon, a music executive was reported to have told Chapman, 'If you're marrying her for her money, forget it. I plan to break her.' " And: "Among Florence's greatest disappointments was the incident regarding a recording artist from whom Florence sought a loan in order to stop foreclosure on the $20,000 (sic) home she bought while a Supreme. The friend consented, and the money was waiting for her—at a business office, along with forms stating the method of repayment of the loan and interest charges, as well as blank papers to sign. A consulting lawyer held the pen ready. Disheartened and distrustful, Florence turned it down."]

"And you probably still workin' . . .": Ballard interview.

"Florence Ballard: 'It Could Have Happened to Anyone,' " *Soul* files.

"I put off going on welfare . . .": Ballard interview notes.

"No matter what happens now . . .": Ibid.

"All I knew . . .": Ibid.

"I remember thinking . . .": Ibid.

"Something good is bound . . .": Ibid.

"Enough is enough . . .": Rob Cohen's recollection in interview with me.

"Berry's a crapshooter . . .": Ibid.

"Goddamn, Berry, isn't that enough?" and the rest of the details of this confrontation between Ross and Gordy in Rome: reconstructed using interview I conducted with Cohen.

"I got this call . . .": Ibid.

"I don't think . . .": Ibid.

"That little blonde . . .": Ibid.

"I got a call from Berry . . .": Details of the telephone call between Cohen and Berry, ibid.

"The worst reviews in the history of the world . . .": Gordy to Robert Windeler, *People*, January 26, 1976.

"This would be much more accurate . . .": Roshkind letter to *The Hollywood Reporter*, November 17, 1975.

"I'll admit . . .": Ross in interview with me, 1981.

"No! Goddamn it . . .": Ross to Andy Warhol (interview conducted June 24, 1976, at the Carlyle Hotel, New York).

Chapter 20

"I talked to Diane just the other day . . .": Ballard interview notes.

"It was a very strange call . . .": Ross to Hans J. Massaquoi, *Ebony*, November 1981.

"Maybe it did come from . . .": Chapman interview notes.

"It didn't last too long . . .": Ballard to Barbara Holiday, *Detroit Magazine*, October 20, 1968.

"Did I cry? . . .": Ross to *People*, March 29, 1976.

"Why is my skin brown . . .": Ross to Joseph Bell, *McCall's*, October 1978.

"You guys are so beautiful . . .": Ross to Andy Warhol (interview conducted June 24, 1976).

"Who *is* Diana Ross . . .": Ibid.

"Open it!": Ross to O'Connell Driscoll, *Rolling Stone*, August 11, 1977.

"What a day . . .": Ibid.

"Emotionally, everything seemed out of whack . . .": Ross to Joseph Bell, *McCall's*, October 1978.

"It was the most . . .": Ibid.

"I'd certainly not considered him that . . .": Ibid.

"At first he was a dictator . . .": Ross interview notes.

"He's in charge of my life . . . not the director . . .": Ross to *Time*, 1977.

"We went through all kinds . . .": Layton in interview with me.

Footnote: Diana recounted Josephine Baker's offer and Berry's reaction in an interview with Tom Burke for *Cosmopolitan*, April 1979.

"When I walk onto the stage . . .": Ross to Andy Warhol.

"My audience . . .": Ross interview notes.

"I don't think he admitted to . . .": Ross to Barbara Walters, November 29, 1978.

Chapter 21

"Darn, I would love to be Dorothy . . .": Ross in interview with me, October 1981.

"I want to play Dorothy . . .": The telephone conversations between Diana Ross and Berry Gordy were re-created using "Diana Ross' Route to Oz Via Motown" by Joseph Bell, *Los Angeles Times*, September 25, 1977.

"Man, I was on the phone with Diane . . ." and the rest of the details of the telephone conversation between Cohen and Gordy: Re-constructed using my interview with Cohen.

"You can have her . . .": Ibid.

"I told him that I absolutely believed . . .": Ross to Bell.

"But you are just too old . . .": Ibid.

"The actual truth . . .": Ross in interview with me, October 1981.

"Even though she could be a real witch . . .": Mackey in interview with me.

"She was away from Berry . . .": Cohen in interview with me.

"For the first time . . .": Ross in interview with me, October 1981.

"What was happening to me . . .": Ibid.

"What the hell are you doing?": Ross to O'Connell Driscoll, *Rolling Stone*, August 11, 1977.

"I never even heard of him . . .": Ross in *The Wiz* press conference.

"I've never met a woman . . .": Lumet in *The Wiz* press conference.

"I remember that she had gotten herself . . .": Cohen in interview with me.

"We had some real emotional moments . . .": Ibid.

Soon after this *Wiz* incident . . . : *New York Post*, February 21, 1983.

"I had always been . . .": Cohen in interview with me.

"She was my mama . . .": Jackson in interview with me.

"Man, when I dream . . .": Ross to David Denby, "Like a Ton of Yellow Bricks," *New York*, November 6, 1978.

"It was just so important . . .": Ross interview notes.

"She loved success . . .": Cohen in interview with me.

"When I went in to tell . . .": Ibid.

"It was like losing a sister . . .": Ross to Hans J. Massaquoi, *Ebony*, November 1981.

During the interview . . . : I viewed the videotape of the Barbara Walters interview, broadcast November 29, 1978, as part of my research.

"He is an incredible lover . . .": Joanna Moore to Cynthia Fagen, *New York Post*, July 9, 1980.

It is not clear that Diana Ross . . . : See *Barbra Streisand—The Woman, The Myth, The Music* by Sean Considine, p. 270: "I gave the script to Sue Mengers," said [Howard] Rosenman. "We were developing it for Diana Ross, and we wanted Sue to get Ryan O'Neal interested—to costar with Diana . . ."

"People want so much out of me . . .": Ross to Pablo Guzman, *Sunday News Magazine*, January 13, 1980.

Chapter 22

"The man that she had picked . . .": Browne interview notes.

On March 26, 1979 . . . : Details of the birthday party were culled from "George Christy: The Great Life," *The Hollywood Reporter*, February 29, 1979.

At this time, Diana and her children . . . : from a report in *The National Enquirer*, May 29, 1979, by Jonathan Bernstein and Edward Tropeano.

On April 9, 1979 . . . : The scene at the Bonaventure Hotel was re-created using interviews I conducted with Jeffrey Wilson, March 29, 1989, and other Ross employees who requested anonymity.

"I never actually saw a script . . .": Diana Ross to Roderick Mann, *Los Angeles Times*, January 15, 1982.

"She would call him and pester . . .": Carroll in interview with me.

"She thought she had him tied down . . .": Browne in interview with Diane Albright.

"All of a sudden she didn't want . . .": O'Neal to Rex Reed, *New York Sunday News*, August 8, 1979.

"Bullshit!": Ross remembered the conversation with Suzanne dePasse to Susan Taylor, *Essence*, September 1985.

"I never had a girlfriend . . .": Ibid.

"I can be close with her . . .": Ross to Andy Warhol, June 1976.

"The people were pouring . . .": David Geffen in *Cher* by J. Randy Taraborrelli.

"All of these divas . . .": Ibid.

"Guess who got the biggest attention . . .": Ross to Andy Warhol, June 1976.

When Diana and Cher . . . : *Cher* by J. Randy Taraborrelli.

Diana and Cher would swap secrets . . . : Ibid.

"She's always complaining, that Cher . . .": Ross to Andy Warhol, June 1976.

"Diana needs her kids . . .": *Cher* by J. Randy Taraborrelli.

Some of the problems in Diana's relationship . . . : Ibid.

"My tongue is long enough . . .": Simmons to *Playboy*, 1988.

He is extremely sexist . . . : Gene Simmons' sexual antics have been well documented by Simmons himself in countless interviews he has given the media over the years. See Lisa Robinson, the *Boston Herald*, August 27, 1988: "What I did to relieve boredom and stay sane was bed down these girls, usually more than one a night or an afternoon—on the plane, anywhere—and it seemed like a good thing to do. And, like tourists do, I took pictures. So I have amassed something like 3,000 photos of where I have been."

"If one goes hunting . . .": Simmons to *Playboy*, 1988.

"What are you doing tonight?": Ibid.

"He is completely different in private life . . .": Ross to *Women's World*, 1979.

"I know that my fans want to know . . .": Ross to Hans Massaquoi, *Ebony*, November 1981.

"I was shocked . . .": Rodgers to *Billboard*, May 1980.

"I proceeded to make the record . . .": Ross in London press conference, reported by Danny Baker for *New Musical Express*, September 1980.

"Soon she wanted him by her side . . .": Browne to Diane Albright.

"A man can have a girlfriend and be devoted to her . . .": Simmons to *Playboy*, 1988.

Chapter 23

"The first time Diana . . .": Masser in interview with me.

"All of a sudden . . .": Ross in interview with me, October 1981.

"I got ripped off . . .": Ross to "L.E.," *Esquire*, November 1981.

"Diana said that Berry . . .": Whyman in interview with me.

"She had a woman . . .": Charlton in interview with me.

"In the scenario . . .": Masser in interview with me.

"In February 1981, Diana produced . . .": To demonstrate its indifference to the Diana Ross show at the Forum, Motown did not purchase tickets to give out as passes to employees and press. It was the first time the company had disassociated itself from a Ross concert.

"At first it wasn't a Motown . . .": Ross in interview with me, October 1981.

"But what about the money?": *Smokey*. [Note: In *Billboard* magazine, dated February 7, 1981, columnist Jean Williams reported: "Ross is asking for what Motown feels is astronomical dollars, and the company has not seen fit to meet her asking price. It is said that as far as Motown is concerned, based on her record sales, it will not be able to retrieve its investment. And if her asking price does not come down, Motown will be forced to wave goodbye to Ross."]

"I want a company . . .": Ross in interview with me, October 1981.

"It was the most important decision . . .": Ibid.

"I don't think that children . . .": Ibid.

"We'll always have communication . . .": Ibid.

"I know Berry loves me . . .": Ibid.

"It was a tragedy . . .": dePasse in BBC interview, 1982.

"I felt personally insulted . . .": Gordy to *Sunday Times Magazine*.

"But with Diane . . .": Ibid.

"the incredible sense of . . .": Ross to Maria Stassinopoulos, May 1983.

"I was like a kid . . .": Ibid.

"I feel that Diana . . .": Gordy to *Sunday Times Magazine*.

"My relationship with RCA . . .": Ross in interview with me, October 1981.

"but they wanted creative . . .": Ibid.

"Actually, I think my body . . .": Ibid.

"I was determined . . .": Ross to Hans J. Massaquoi.

"That's not true . . .": Ibid.

After she made that statement . . . : The incident in San Carlos was reported by the *Los Angeles Herald Examiner*, May 10, 1980.

"I want to help people . . .": Ross in interview with me.

Chapter 24

Diana turned 38 . . . : Details of the birthday party were culled from "George Christy: The Good Life," *The Hollywood Reporter*, March 29, 1979.

"I do know that I want . . .": Ross in interview with me, October 1981.

"I've ended a relationship . . .": Ross to Arianna Stassinopoulos.

"She said she'd didn't give a shit . . .": Delpit in interview with me.

"He's doing everything . . .": Gatlin to *Star* magazine.

"He spends a lot of time . . .": Ross to Gerri Hirshey.

"During the performance . . .": Concert reviewed by Moira Petty in *The Stage and Television Today*, June 10, 1982.

"I just love to read . . .": Ross to Rona Jaffe, *Cosmopolitan*, September 1967.

"People ask me, 'Whatever . . .' ": Ross at Caesars Palace, Home Box Office special, 1978.

"pull all kinds of . . .": Browne's comments in this chapter were to writer Diane Albright.

Then, on February 8, 1983, Diana . . . : The secret meeting between Ross and Onassis that took place at Doubleday's Manhattan office at 245 Park Avenue pertained to my first book about Diana Ross, entitled *Diana*. Also present at the meeting were Laura Van Wormer, a Doubleday associate editor; Irving "Swifty" Lazar, Ross' literary agent; and Sam Vaughan, editor-in-chief of Doubleday.

According to a correspondence from Mr. Vaughan to Jacqueline Onassis dated March 10, 1983, Lazar telephoned Vaughan to discern whether or not Doubleday was going to cancel my book and publish Miss Ross'. "I told him that [we] were going to make available the manuscript . . . for Diana Ross to go through—and that she would have about a month to do so," wrote Vaughan. The reason for this, according to Vaughan's correspondence, was "to keep up the goodwill between Diana Ross and us."

The manuscript for *Diana* was completed in June 1983. According to a memo from Laura Van Wormer to Karen Van Westerling, dated October 19, 1983, the author's manuscript "is particularly in need of TLC, since we have had such a runaround with Ross herself and Swifty as to whether she will do an autobiography for us. Ross is reading the ms [manuscript] quietly as a courtesy of the house."

I received my manuscript back from Doubleday on November 1, 1983, and was asked to delete anecdotes from friends and associates that did not paint Diana Ross in a favorable light. I was told that these anecdotes did not "suit the tone of the book."

I did not learn until January 1989 that Diana Ross received a copy of the manuscript prior to publication, nor am I certain that she requested the cuts that were made. [The deleted material does appear in *Call Her Miss Ross*.]

"This is my life; this is not a . . .": Ross to Gerri Hirshey.

"I wasn't even consulted . . ." and the rest of the paragraph pertaining to *Dreamgirls*: Ibid.

"If [only] there [was] . . .": Ibid.

"Once a reporter . . .": Ross in interview with me, October 1981.

Chapter 25

Regarding "Motown 25": In my research, I viewed both the broadcast version and an unedited four-and-a-half hour version. Also, most helpful were memories of some of The Supremes' loyal fans who attended the rehearsal and taping of the special in order to see the "reunion," and employees of Motown Productions who worked on the show and asked for anonymity rather than risk their jobs.

"I'm goin' out there!": DePasse's recollection to Steve Pond, *Rolling Stone*, May 26, 1983.

"When you get out there . . .": from *Dreamgirl*.

Chapter 26

"In the '60s . . .": Berry Gordy in NBC news footage, March 23, 1983.

"Did you see what that bitch . . .": John Whyman's recollection in interview with me.

"It was amazing . . .": Ross in Gail Roberts press release: "An Interview with Miss Diana Ross."

Though Birdsong and Whyman . . . : Whyman's recollections in interview with me.

"I had accumulated . . .": Birdsong to Jim Bakker during an appearance on "The PTL Club" in 1984.

"After I lost my apartment . . .": Ibid.

"There is only one person . . .": Mackey in interview with me.

It's not that she is a heartless person . . . : This story was reported in the *New York Post*, January 18, 1985.

"I really want to make a difference in my life . . .": Ross in interview with me, October 1981.

For her first number . . . : I studied videotapes of both Central Park performances as part of my research.

"Oh, thank you . . .": Greg Sills recollection to Nicholas Pileggi, *New York*, February 13, 1984.

"My God . . .": Ibid.

"Miss Ross puts on . . .": Frankenheimer to Pileggi, February 13, 1984.

"In this business . . .": Sills to Pileggi.

"Of course it's a rip-off . . .": Henry Stern to *The New York Times*, January 7, 1984.

One of Diana's lawyers, Peter Tufo . . . : *The New York Times*, September 3, 1984.

"I have something to tell you . . ." and the rest of this conversation: Ibid.

Chapter 27

"She asked that it be made . . .": David Pisha to *Rochester Democrat & Chronicle*, June 6, 1985.

"From talking to T . . .": Mackey in interview with me.

"We love each other . . .": T-Boy to *Soul* magazine, August 1975.

"She wasn't particularly . . .": Mackey in interview with me.

"Oh, she's very proud . . .": Barbara Jean Ross Lee to *Jet*, October 1982.

"We drove through the snowy . . .": Browne to Diane Albright.

"Once we got there . . .": Ibid.

"I signed the wrong papers . . .": Diana Ross in interview with me, October 1981.

"I took Diana's deposition . . .": Zakarin in interview with me.

"Obviously, she was attempting . . .": Ibid.

"I had heard . . .": Ibid.

"All you had to do . . .": Browne to Albright.

"Later, I discovered she was telling . . .": Mackey in interview with me.

"I got a little angry . . .": Ross to Miles White, *USA Today*, November 13, 1984.

"I'm so sorry she can't . . .": Ross to Susan Taylor.

"And then word got out . . .": Ross to Tom Burke.

"I tell you this story . . .": Julio Iglesias in interview notes.

"I know how important . . .": Ross to Burke.

The third week in March . . . : Some of the material regarding The Predators' Ball was culled from *The Predators' Ball—The Junk Bond Raiders and the Man Who Staked Them* by Connie Bruick.

"Diana's position in movies . . .": Cohen in interview with me.

Chapter 28

Arne Naess' background and quotes from Naess were culled primarily from Norwegian press reports. Particularly useful was "The Way You Become a Millionaire" (loose translation), *V.G.*, November 1, 1980, which supplied most of the information regarding his childhood; and also reports in issues of *V.G.* dated January 18, 1986, March 26, 1986 and April 7, 1987. Also helpful were copies of *Dagbladet*, dated April 16, 1984, and August 29, 1985. The author interviewed many friends of Filippa Kumlin, Arne Naess' first wife, who requested anonymity rather than jeopardize their relationship with Mr. Naess.

"They tell me that it will be hard to find a man . . .": Ross to Arianna Stassinopoulos.

Arne and Diana and her three daughters . . . : The confrontation between Ross and the photographers was documented in published and broadcast news reports around the world.

"Michael, now you get out of . . .": John Whyman's recollection to me.

"You just be you . . .": Jackson's recollection in interview with me.

"I would like to marry her . . .": Ibid.

"I love him desperately . . .": Ross to Susan Taylor, *Essence*, September 1985.

"the biggest show of my life . . .": "Diana's Supreme Day," *People*, February 17, 1986.

"Repeat after me . . ." and the rest of the wedding vows: Ibid.

"Of course I love my father . . .": *People*, October 6, 1986.

Chapter 29

"Oh," said Mary . . . : conversation re-enacted from eyewitness reports to me, particularly John Whyman's.

"I'm pretty certain . . .": Andrews in interview with me.

"Many people have been whispering . . .": Wilson on "A.M. San Francisco," November 4, 1986.

"I had a notion . . .": Ross to Christopher Connolly, *Us*, June 1, 1987.

"I'm godmother to one . . .": Ibid.

"Diana Ross is visibly pregnant . . .": Charles Shaar Murray.

"I believe in children and family . . .": Ross to Barbara Walters, March 29, 1989.

"Expecting again, it was exciting . . .": Ibid.

"Whitney was a little concerned . . .": Rosenman to *Los Angeles Times*, June 11, 1989.

Diana declined to be interviewed . . . : Frank Swertlow, *Daily News*, April 13, 1988.

"I say a lot of things . . .": Wilson on *"People"* magazine television program, March 1989.

"B.G. has survived in one of the toughest . . .": Gaye in *Motown* by Sharon Davis.

"I'm in love with all the power . . .": Ross to Susan Taylor, *Essence*, December 1985.

"When you're out there . . .": Ross to Rodney Tyler, *You Magazine*, April 16, 1989.

"The expeditions broaden . . .": Ibid.

"Our marriage is not an ordinary one . . .": Naess on Scandinavian television, June 1989.

"He is not my focus . . .": Ross to Rodney Tyler, *You Magazine*, April 16, 1989.

"She's living in an opulent world . . .": *Smokey.*

When Suzanne dePasse . . . : [Note: Sajak also asked dePasse, "If I were to ask Diana Ross who's the biggest pain in the butt she ever worked with, would she mention you? DePasse's answer: "She might. But I think she'd probably say Berry."]

"What's the biggest misconception . . . ?" [Note: The Barbara Walters interview was broadcast on March 29, 1989. Berry Gordy told friends that he was very disappointed in Ross' answer to Walters' question about the biggest misconception about her. "She should never have referred to herself as a bitch," Berry said. "She just opened the door wide open for more people to think of her like that. And then, from that point on in the interview, she acted like a bitch because she was still upset about the question." Also, many viewers felt that Ross must have had control over the questions asked of her, since Walters' interview was so extremely superficial. It was thought that if Walters had free reign, she would certainly have asked Diana to comment on Mary Wilson and the *Dreamgirl* book—a subject she does not like to discuss. However, Bill Geddie, producer of the special, denied that Ross had any say over what she would be asked. "That's not our policy and we don't allow it," he noted. Yet, in an interview with Barbara Walters in the July 4, 1987, issue of *TV Guide*, she said, "If I give my word that I'm not going to ask something, I don't. If I didn't keep my word, people would be saying, 'Don't trust her, don't do it.' "]

"I'm an insecure person . . .": Ross to Hirschberg, *Vanity Fair*, March 1989.

Her return-to-Motown album, *Workin' Overtime* . . . : [Note: Regarding the video for "Workin' Overtime," according to columnist Mitchell Fink in the *Los Angeles Herald Examiner*, March 8, 1989, the extras who danced with Diana Ross on the video "became upset when they received the grand sum of $25 for two 10-hour days. Apparently they thought they were getting $25 *a day*. But no. A representative of Ross claims it was a misunderstanding. The extras, according to the rep, were always supposed to get $25 for both days."]

Chapter 30

Chapter is drawn from eyewitness account of Ross' midnight performance at Radio City Music Hall, Saturday, June 17, 1989, and from press reviews of her show.

Bibliography

Many books and literally thousands of newspaper and magazine articles about this and related subjects were implemented as secondary sources to my own interviews. Often, what has been written about Diana Ross, The Supremes, Berry Gordy and Motown Records is considered suspect because of the manner in which features and articles were so carefully siphoned through Motown's image-making press department. Over the years, however, some writers have managed to break through the public relations facade. Listed here are books and features the author referred to in his research because he considers them valuable sources.

Abbey, John. "Supreme-acy." *Blues & Soul*, June 20, 1976.

Adams, Cindy. "How She Hitched." *New York Post*, November 19, 1985.

———. "She Do, He Do." *New York Post*, December 9, 1985.

Albright, Diane. "Diana Ross' New Marriage . . ." *National Enquirer*, November 25, 1986.

———. "Why Diana Ross Is Thrilled . . ." *National Enquirer*, April 21, 1987.

Allman, Kevin. "Mary Wilson—If I Wanted to Dish Some Dirt . . ." *Los Angeles Herald Examiner*, November 24, 1986.

Alterman, Lorraine. "Supremes, Flo Ballard: It's Said She's Leaving." *Detroit Free Press*, September 1, 1967.

Amory, Cleveland, ed. *Celebrity Registry: An Irreverent Compendium of American Quotable Notations*. New York: Simon and Schuster, 1973.

Archer, Leonard C. *Black Images in the American Theatre*. Brooklyn: Pageant-Poseidon Ltd., 1973.

Arrington, Chris Rigby. "DePasse—The Protege." *California Living*, January 15, 1984.

Bacon, James. "Diana Ross as Lady Day." *Los Angeles Herald Examiner*, October 22, 1972.

Baker, Danny. "Diana, Stop!" *New Musical Express*, September 30, 1980.

Balliet, Whitney. *American Singers—27 Portraits in Song*. New York: Oxford University Press, 1988.

Barrett, Charles. "Motown Industries Growth." *The Hollywood Reporter*, November 1, 1976.

———. "Wiz Leading Motown Down Path." *Daily Variety*, May 12, 1977.

Barol, Bill. "Motown's 25 Years of Soul." *Newsweek*, May 23, 1983.

Baskin, Wade, and Richard N. Runes. *Dictionary of Black Culture*. New York: Philosophical Library, 1973.

Bell, Joseph N. "I Love Being Diana Ross." *McCall's*, October 1978.

Beller, Miles. "Making Motown's Moves." *Harper's Bazaar*, September 1985.

Benjaminson, Peter. "One of Original Supremes Now Leads Forgotten Life." *Detroit Free Press*, January 17, 1975.

————. *The Story of Motown*. New York: Grove Press, 1979.

Bennett, Lerone, Jr. *What Manner of Man*. Chicago: Johnson Publications, 1964.

Bennetts, Leslie. "A Singer, A Throng in Central Park, A Deluge." *The New York Times*, July 22, 1983.

Berkowitz, Stan, and David Lees. "A Race for Fame and Money." *Los Angeles Times*, April 8, 1979.

Berman, Connie. "Young Diana Ross." *Sunday Woman*, January 7, 1979.

Bernstein, Carl. "Supremes Rolling in to Rock . . ." *Washington Post*, May 28, 1967.

Bernstein, Jonathan, and Edward Tropeano. "Ryan O'Neal and Diana Ross Secretly in Love." *National Enquirer*, May 29, 1979.

Betrock, Alan. *Girl Groups—The Story of a Sound*. New York: Delilah Publishing, 1982.

Black, Doris. "Diana Ross' Big Gamble." *Sepia*, December 1975.

Bogle, Donald. *Toms, Coons, Mulattoes, Mammies and Bucks*. New York: Viking, 1973.

Boyd, Blanche McCray. "Diana Ross' Stairway to Heaven." *Village Voice*, October 16, 1978.

Bronson, Fred. *The Billboard Books of Number One Hits*. New York: Billboard Publications, Inc., 1985.

Brown, Geoff. *Michael Jackson—Body and Soul*. New York: Beaufort Books, 1984.

Brown, Geoffrey. "Ghetto Experience Makes Mahogany . . ." *Jet*, October 9, 1978.

Brown, Len, and Gary Friedrich. *Encyclopedia of Rock and Roll*. New York: Tower Publications, 1970.

Brown, Peter, and Jim Pinkston. *Oscar Dearest*. New York: Harper & Row, 1987.

Brown, Stanley H. "The Motown Sound of Money." *Fortune*, September 1, 1967.

Bruick, Connie. *The Predator's Ball*. New York: Simon & Schuster, 1988.

Burrell, Walter. "What Turns Mary On." *Soul*, August 1969.

————. "Has Cindy Birdsong Been Overlooked?" *Soul*, February 9, 1969.

————. "Jean Terrell—The Accidental Supreme." *Soul*, March 9, 1970.

————. "How Diana Ross Got That Way." *Soul Illustrated*, November 1970.

————. "Gordy Scholarship Ball." *Soul*, June 7, 1971.

————. "New Supremes One Year Later." *Soul*, July 1, 1971.

————. "Mary Wilson and Her Fiancé." *Black Stars*, November 1973.

Burke, Tom. "Diana Ross—Delicious, Dynamic." *Cosmopolitan*, April 1979.

————. "Diana Ross, Supremely In Control." *Cosmopolitan*, December 1985.

Byrne, Bridget. "Michael Jackson." *Los Angeles Times Magazine*, November 11, 1987.

Cain, Pete. "The Motown Mob." *Rock*, July 6, 1970.

Canby, Vincent. "When Budgets Soar Over the Rainbow." *The New York Times*, November 26, 1978.

Carlson, Peter. "Diana Ross Promised a Playground." *People*, January 23, 1984.

Cash, Rita. "Jean Terrell—She's Going Solo." *Soul*, March 13, 1978.

Champlin, Charles. "Diana Ross in Her Last Date With Supremes." *Los Angeles Times*, January 19, 1970.

————. "Two Ladies Who Sing the Blues." *Los Angeles Times*, October 25, 1972.

Christy, George. "George Christy: The Good Life." *The Hollywood Reporter*, March 29, 1979.

Churcher, Sharon. "Diana Ross' Private Space." *New York*, January 2, 1984.

Clark, Dick, and Richard Robinson. *Rock, Roll and Remember*. New York: Thomas Y. Crowell Company, 1976.

Cleaver, James H. "Diana Gets $20 Million Deal." *Los Angeles Sentinel*, May 21, 1981.

Cobrun, Randy Sue. "Why They Split and Tell." *USA Today*, September 12, 1986.

Coleman, Stuart. *They Kept On Rockin'*. London: Blandford Press, 1982.

Collins, David. *Not Only Dreamers*. Elgin, Illinois: Brethren Press, 1986.

Connelly, Christopher. "Diana Ross—Frank Talk." *Us*, June 1, 1987.

Cook, Richard. "There's No Town Like Motown." *New Musical Express*, July 30, 1983.

Considine, Shaun. *Barbra Streisand*. New York: Delacorte Press, 1985.

Cruse, Harold. *The Crisis of the Negro Intellectual*. New York: William Morrow, 1967.

Culver, George Lincoln. "Supremes in L.A." *Soul*, September 15, 1966.

Curtis, Charlotte. "Billie Holiday Fans Turn Out." *The New York Times*, November 19, 1972.

Daley, Suzanne. "Youths Run Wild." *The New York Times*, July 24, 1983.

DaSilva, Benjamin. *The Afro-American in United States History*. New York: Globe Book Company, 1972.

David, Saul. *The Industry*. New York: Times Books, 1981.

Davis, Clive. *Clive: Inside the Recording Business*. New York: William Morrow & Company, 1975.

Davis, Daphne. "Diana Ross in Emerald City." *Cue*, September 29, 1976.

Davis, Leah. "Berry Gordy—King of the Mountain." *Soul*, October 6, 1969.

Davis, Sharon. *Motown—The History*. London: Guinness, 1988.

Day, Doris, with A.E. Hotchner. *Doris Day—Her Own Story*. New York: William Morrow, 1976.

DeLeon, Robert A. "Woman Behind the Stars." *Jet*, June 12, 1975.

deLisle, Tim. "Looking Back, Looking Good." *London Times*, May 4, 1989.

Delpit, Ron. "Cher: Even Out There On Her Own." *Vegas*, June 21, 1981.

Denby, David. "Like A Ton of Yellow Bricks." *New York*, November 6, 1978.

Deutsch, Linda. "Diana Ross' Acting Debut." *A/P*, October 5, 1972.

Diehl, Digby. "Diana." *TV Guide*, December 7, 1968.

Dragadze, Peter. "The Metamorphosis of a Black Galatea." *Los Angeles Times*, May 11, 1975.

Dreyfus, Joel. "Motown's $10 Million Gamble." *Black Enterprises*, July 1981.

Driscoll, O'Connell. "Diana: An Encounter in Three Scenes." *Rolling Stone*, August 11, 1977.

Ebony Editors. *The Negro Handbook*. Chicago: Johnson Publishing Company, 1966.

———. *The Ebony Handbook*. Chicago: Johnson Publishing Company, 1974.

Edelstein, Andrew. *The Pop Sixties*. New York: World Almanac Publications, 1985.

Eder, Shirley. *Not This Time, Cary Grant!* Garden City, New York: Doubleday, 1973.

Eisen, Jonathan, ed. *The Age of Rock*. New York: Vintage (paper), 1969.

Elsner, Constanze. *Stevie Wonder*. New York: Popular Library, 1977.

Engelmayer, Sheldon. *Hubert Humphrey*. New York: Methuen, 1978.

Everett, Todd. "Come See About Ex-Supreme . . ." *Los Angeles Herald Examiner*, May 9, 1986.

———. "Motown Records Spins Into MCA." *Los Angeles Herald Examiner*, June 29, 1988.

———. "Jackson, Manager . . . and Ross Reunites . . ." *Los Angeles Herald Examiner*, February 15, 1989.

———. "Ross No Longer Supreme." *Los Angeles Herald Examiner*, July 10, 1989.

Everette, Cheryl. "dePasse—The Boss." *Daily News*, December 20, 1986.

Ewen, David. *All the Years of American Popular Music*. Englewood Cliffs, New Jersey: Prentice Hall, 1977.

Farrell, Barry. "Farewell . . . to The Supremes." *Life*, February 1970.

Fearn, Kathi. "Sparkling, Superb, Soulful." *Soul Illustrated*, 1968.

Feather, Leonard. "Billie's Blues . . ." *Los Angeles Times*, October 29, 1972.

Feldman, Jim. "Miss Ross to You." *Village Voice*, August 2, 1983.

Ferris, Michael. "On Tour and Working Overtime." *Roland Users Group*, June 1989.

Flynt, Michael. "There's No Sweet Harmony . . ." *Star*, April 12, 1988.

Fong-Torres, Ben. "The Summer and Fall of Diana Ross." *Rolling Stone*, August 11, 1977.

———. *What's That Sound?* New York: Anchor Press, 1976.

Fornatale, Peter, and Joshua Mills. *Radio in the Television Age*. New York: Overlook Press, 1980.

Forsythe, William. "Diana Ross Walks Out . . ." *Philadelphia Bulletin*, June 1969.

Fox, Ted. *Showtime at the Apollo*. New York: Holt, Rinehart & Winston, 1983.

Franklin, John Hope. *From Slavery to Freedom: A History of Negro Americans*. New York: Knopf, 1980.

Freedberg, Michael. "Girl Groups—Soul From Baby Love." *Soul*, February 27, 1978.

Frost, Deborah. "Do You Know Where You're Going To?" *Record*, October 1983.

George, Nelson. "Diana Ross on Diana Ross." *Record World*, November 14, 1981.

———. *The Death of Rhythm and Blues*. New York: Pantheon Books, 1988.

Gertner, Richard, ed. *International Television Almanac*. New York: Quigley Publishing, 1975.

Giancana, Antoinette, with Thomas C. Renner. *Mafia Princess*. New York: William Morrow, 1984.

Gillet, Charlie. *The Sound of the City*. New York: Dell, 1970.

Gilmore, Mikal. "Motown's Showy, Soulful Anniversary." *Los Angeles Herald Examiner*, March 28, 1983.

Gitlin, Todd. *The Sixties: Years of Hope, Days of Rage*. New York: Bantam, 1987.

Goldstein, Patrick. "Hollywood Burning." *Los Angeles Times*, April 16, 1989.

Goldstein, Richard. "The Super Supremes . . ." *The New York Times*, July 23, 1967.

———. "Where Did Our Love Go?" *Village Voice*, August 9, 1983.

Goldsworthy, Jay. *Casey Kasem's American Top 40 Yearbook*. New York: Grosset & Dunlap, 1979.

Goodman, Mark. "Diana Ross." *Family Weekly*, October 24, 1982.

Gordy, Berry, Sr. *Movin' Up*. New York: Harper & Row, 1979.

Gormley, Mike. "A Musical Magician . . ." *Detroit Free Press*, February 8, 1970.

Gottlieb, Martin. "New York's Influential People Celebrate . . ." *The New York Times*, October 3, 1984.

Graham, Sheilah. *Confessions of a Hollywood Columnist*. New York: William Morrow and Company, 1969.

Greenberg, James. "Josephine on Eurocom." *Variety*, March 8, 1984.

Grein, Paul. "The Supreme Moments." *Los Angeles Times*, May 9, 1986.

———. "The End of an Era." *Los Angeles Times*, June 11, 1988.

Griffin, Junius. "A Biography of Mr. and Mrs. Berry Gordy, Sr." *Motown Records*, 1968.

Griffin, Rita. "Females Have It Tough." *Michigan Chronicle*, June 1962.

Grogam, David. "Stop! In the Name of Love." *People*, February 17, 1986.

Guzman, Pablo. "Diana." *Sunday News Magazine*, January 13, 1980.

Haber, Joyce. "She Doesn't Have To Sing Blues." *Los Angeles Times*, February 11, 1973.

———. "Berry: The Mentor From Motown." *Los Angeles Times*, January 20, 1975.

Haithman, Diane. "How Motown Corraled Lonesome Dove." *Los Angeles Times*, February 19, 1986.

Hall, Claude, and Barbara Hall. *This Business of Radio Programming*. New York: Billboard Publications, 1977.

Halliwell, Leslie. *The Filmgoer's Companion*. 4th ed. New York: Hill and Wang, 1974.

Hamilton, Jack. "The Supremes: From Real Rags to Real Riches." *Look*, May 3, 1966.

———. "The Supreme Supreme." *Look*, September 23, 1969.

Hanrahan, Thomas, and Larry Sutton. "Wind and Rain in Her Hair." *Daily News*, July 22, 1983.

Hans, Nathan. *Dan Emmet and the Rise of Early Negro Minstrelsy*. Oklahoma City: University of Oklahoma, 1962.

Haralambros, Michael. *Right On: From Blues to Soul in Black America*. New York: DeCapo Press, 1974.

Harmetz, Aljean. "How to Win an Oscar Nomination." *The New York Times*, April 3, 1973.

———. "Diana Ross: Lady Doesn't Sing the Blues." *The New York Times*, December 24, 1972.

Harris, Kathyrn. "Warner and PolyGram in Venture Talks." *Los Angeles Times*, June 30, 1983.

———. "MCA Reported in Talks to Buy Motown." *Los Angeles Times*, December 25, 1986.

Haskins, Jim. *Richard Pryor—A Man and His Madness*. New York: Beaufort Books, Inc., 1984.

Haskins, James, and Kathleen Benson. *The Stevie Wonder Scrapbook*. New York: Grosset & Dunlap, 1978.

Hilburn, Robert. "Diana Ross at the Ahmanson." *Los Angeles Times*, September 30, 1976.

———. "Motown's Berry Gordy Looks Back . . ." *Los Angeles Times*, March 22, 1983.

———. "Dramatic Motown Reunion." *Los Angeles Herald Examiner*, March 28, 1983.

Hill, Randall C. *Collectible Rock Records*. Orlando, Florida: The House of Collectibles, Inc., 1980.

Hinckley, David. "She Aims to Please." *Daily News*, July 21, 1983.

Hirschberg, Lynn. "The Re-Happening." *Vanity Fair*, March 1989.

Hirshey, Gerri. *Nowhere to Run*. New York: Times Books, 1984.

Hoare, Ian, ed. *The Soul Book*. New York: Delta, 1975.

Holden, Stephen. "Lionel Richie: King of the Pop Charts." *Rolling Stone*, October 15, 1981.

————. "Diana Ross Spreading Her Wings." *The New York Times*, July 4, 1984.

————. "Diana Ross Flirts With a Willing Audience." *The New York Times*, June 16, 1989.

Holiday, Billie, with William Dufty. *Lady Sings the Blues*. New York: Doubleday, 1956.

Holliday, Barbara. "De-Supremed Supreme Talks." *Detriot*, October 20, 1968.

Hughes, Langston. *Famous Negro Music Makers*. New York: Dodd, Mead, 1955.

Hughes, Langston, and Milton Meltzer. *Black Magic: A Pictorial History of the Negro in American Entertainment*. Englewood Cliffs, New Jersey: Prentice-Hall, 1967.

Hunt, Dennis. "Marvin Gaye Tells What's Been Goin' On." *Los Angeles Times*, November 28, 1982.

————. "Ross Takes the Safe Road." *Los Angeles Times*, July 10, 1989.

Ingrassia, Thomas. "Reflections of a Love Supreme." *Goldmine*, September 1983.

Jackson, Michael. *Moonwalk*. New York: Doubleday, 1988.

Jaffe, Rona. "The Supremes—They Make You Believe Again." *Cosmopolitan*, September 1967.

Jahn, Mike. *Rock*. New York: Quadrangle, 1973.

Jenkins, Flo. "Sneak Peek at *Mahogany*." *Right On!* November 1975.

Jewell, Derek. "Nod From the Beatles . . ." *London Sunday News*, April 4, 1965.

Johnson, Bonnie. "Ted Ross—The Lion." *Soul*, October 30, 1978.

Johnson, Connie. "An Evening on TV with Diana." *Soul*, March 14, 1977.

Johnson, Herschel. "Motown: The Sound of Success." *Black Stars*, June 1974.

Johnson, Richard. "Diana Making Sweet Music . . ." *New York Post*, September 11, 1985.

Jones, James T. "Diana Ross in Concert . . ." *USA Today*, June 16, 1989.

Jones, Marvene. "Diana—A Sensation at Cannes." *The Hollywood Reporter*, May 31, 1973.

Kalech, Marc. "Diana Tells All About the Supreme Man in Her Life." *New York Post*, September 12, 1980.

Kamien, Roger. *Music: An Appreciation*. New York: McGraw-Hill, 1976.

Kenon, Marci. "Diana." *Black Beat*, June 1983.

Kern, Dale. "Diana Ross, Designer Lacks Believability." *Los Angeles Herald Examiner*, November 4, 1976.

Kiersh, Edward. *Where Are You Now, Bo Diddley?* New York: Dolphin Books, 1986.

Kincaid, Jamaica. "Last of the Black White Girls." *Village Voice*, June 28, 1976.

Kisner, Ronald. "Ex-Supreme Fights . . ." *Jet*, February 20, 1975.

Kladney, Leonard. "Nudity Required." *Los Angeles Times*, June 11, 1989.

"L.E." "A Brief Encounter with Diana Ross." *Esquire*, November 1981.

Landay, Eileen. *Black Film Stars*. New York: Drake, 1974.

Lane, Jane F. "The Controlling Style of Diana Ross." *W*, November 19, 1984.

Larkin, Rochelle. *Soul Music*. New York: Lancer Books, 1972.

Lazell, Barry. *Rock Movers & Shakers*. New York: Billboard, 1989.

Leab, Daniel J. *The Black Experience in Motion Pictures*. New York: Houghton-Mifflin, 1975.

Leach, Robin. "Superstar Ryan Now Plays . . ." *Star*, September 11, 1979.

Lewis, Bobbi Jean. "The Truth Behind the Rumors . . ." *Soul*, November 13, 1967.

Lewis, Bobbi Jean, and Karen Price. "Could They Go It Alone?" *Soul*, May 6, 1968.

Lichter, Paul. *Elvis—The Boy Who Dared to Rock*. New York: Dolphin Books, 1978.

Lingeman, Richard. "The Big Happy Beating Heart of Motown." *New York Times Magazine*, 1967.

Litwak, Mark. *Reel Power*. New York: William Morrow & Company, 1986.

Lovell, John, Jr. *Black Song—The Forge and the Flame*. New York: Macmillan, 1972.

Lynn, Melda. "Supreme Happiness." *The Blade*, June 19, 1966.

MacMinn, Aleene. "Liza Minnelli, Falk Win." *Los Angeles Times*, December 12, 1972.

Mann, Roderick. "Diana Tries Again With Baker." *Los Angeles Times*, January 14, 1982.

Manning, Steve. *The Jacksons*. Indianapolis/New York: The Bobbs-Merrill Company, Inc., 1976.

Mapp, Edward. *Blacks in American Films*. Metuchen, New Jersey: Scarecrow Press, 1972.

———. *Directory of Blacks in the Performing Arts*. Metuchen, New Jersey: Scarecrow Press, 1978.

Marion, Frances. *Off With Their Heads*. New York: The Macmillan Company, 1972.

Martinez, M.R. "Motown: The Legend Loses Its Luster . . ." *Rhythm and Business*, July 1988.

Massaquoi, Hans J. "Ebony Interview With Diana Ross." *Ebony*, November 1981.

Matney, William C., ed. *Who's Who Among Black Americans*. v. 1 1975–1976. Northbrook, Illinois: W.W.A.B.A., Inc., 1976.

Maychick, Diana. "Reach Out But Don't Touch Diana Ross." *New York Post*, July 20, 1983.

McBridge, James. "Suzanne dePasse—Wonder Woman." *Us*, February 24, 1986.

McMurran, Kristen. "Showbiz Wiz Diana Ross." *People*, January 15, 1979.

Mellers, Wilfred. *Angels of the Night—Popular Singers of Our Time*. New York: Basil Blackwell, Inc., 1986.

Meyer, John. *Heartbreaker*. Garden City, New York: Doubleday, 1985.

Milam, Marin Scott. "I May Be Married . . ." *Photoplay*, April 1973.

Miller, Bill. "Echoes: Motown Origins." *Let It Rock*, November 1974.

Miller, Edwin. "Off the Record With The Supremes." *Seventeen*, August 1966.

Miller, Jim, ed. *Rolling Stone Illustrated History of Rock*. New York: Random House, 1980.

Morris, Chris. "Diana Ross Back at Motown." *Billboard*, February 25, 1989.

Morse, David. *Motown*. New York: Collier Books, 1971.

Moss, Nancy. "Supremes: 11 Frantic Hours . . ." *Chicago Tribune*, March 20, 1966.

Munden, Kenneth. *The American Film Institute Catalogue*. New York: Bowker, 1971.

Murphy, Mary. "An Intimate Glimpse of Diana Ross." *Los Angeles Times*, November 1, 1972.

Murray, James P. *To Find An Image: Black Films* . . . New York: Bobbs-Merrill, 1973.

Murrells, Joseph. *Million Selling Records*. New York: Arco, 1984.

Musto, Michael. "Musto La Dolce" (Review of Ross at Radio City Music Hall). *Village Voice*, June 27, 1989.

Nathan, David. "Talking With Diana Ross." *Blues & Soul*, September 1972.

Nickerson, Rhetta. "The Lady Sings the Blues." *Soul*, November 20, 1972.

Nite, Norm N. *Rock On: The Illustrated Encyclopedia of Rock 'N Roll* . . . New York: Crowell, 1974.

Norman, Barry. "Diana Ross Aims for the Top." *London Times*, April 3, 1973.

Null, Gary. *Black Hollywood*. Secaucus, New Jersey: Citadel, 1975.

O'Haire, Patricia. "Shining Lady Sings the Tunes." *Daily News*, June 16, 1989.

Orth, Maureen. "Boss Lady." *Newsweek*, June 28, 1976.

Osborne, Jerry, and Bruce Hamilton. *Blues/Rhythm & Blues/Soul*, Phoenix, Arizona: O'Sullivan, Woodside & Company, 1980.

Oviatt, Ray. "Hitsville U.S.A." *The Blade*, August 22, 1965.

Parales, Jon, and Patricia Romanowski. *Rolling Stone Encyclopedia of Rock & Roll*. New York: Summit, 1983.

Parker, Jerry. " '30s Scene Left Diana Stretched Musically." *Newsday*, February 4, 1973.

Pavelitch, Aida. *Rock-A-Bye Baby*. Garden City, New York: Doubleday, 1980.

Persky, Mort. "Supremes in Eight Easy Lessons." *Detroit*, January 30, 1966.

Peterson, Virgil W. *The Mob*. Ottawa, Illinois: Green Hill, 1983.

Petty, Moira. "Too Much Spitting and Snarling." *The Stage & Television Today*, June 10, 1982.

Pileggi, Nicholas. "Indecent Expenses." *New York*, February 13, 1984.

Pitts, Leonard, Jr. "Diana Ross." *Soul*, June 20, 1977.

———. "Mary Wilson Sues Motown." *Soul*, January 30, 1978.

———. "Eddie Kendricks—Still Fearful After All These Years." *Soul*, May 15, 1978.

———. "Diana Ross—Dorothy." *Soul*, October 30, 1978.

———. "Michael at 21." *Soul*, August 20, 1979.

Pond, Steve. "Lionel Richie: The Pot of Gold . . ." *Rolling Stone*, March 3, 1983.

———. "Former Motown Stars Return . . ." *Rolling Stone*, May 26, 1983.

Prial, Frank. "Diana Ross Performs an Encore." *The New York Times*, July 23, 1983.

Price, Karen. "The Supremes in Las Vegas." *Soul*, November 10, 1966.

———. "Flo: 'It's All Kind of Scary.' " *Soul*, December 16, 1968.

Propes, Steve. "Lamont Dozier." *Goldmine*, June 20, 1986.

Reed, Rochelle. "Supremes Team With Tempts." *Soul*, October 30, 1967.

Reeves, Martha. "What's In Her Heart?" *Soul*, July 1, 1968.

Regan, Stewart. *Michael Jackson*. London, England: Colour Library Books, 1984.

Ritz, David. *Divided Soul: The Life of Marvin Gaye*. New York: McGraw-Hill, 1985.

Roach, Hildred. *Black American Music: Past and Present*. Boston: Crescendo Publishing Company, 1973.

Robbins, Fred, and David Ragan. *Richard Pryor: This Cat's Got 9 Lives*. New York: Delilah, 1982.

Robins, Wayne. "The Disco-fication of Diana Ross." *New York Newsday*, June 16, 1989.

Robinson, Lisa. "The First Lady." *Disc*, April 14, 1973.

Robinson, Louie. "Why Diana Ross Left The Supremes." *Ebony*, February 1970.

————. "Lady Sings the Blues." *Ebony*, October 1972.

Robinson, Smokey, with David Ritz. *Smokey*. New York: McGraw-Hill, 1989.

Rolling Stone Editors. *Rolling Stone Rock Almanac*. New York: Macmillan, 1983.

Rollins, Charlemae. *Famous Negro Entertainers of Stage, Screen and TV*. New York: Dodd, 1967.

Rosenbaum, Helen. "Supremes—Frank Talk." *Record Beat*, May 24, 1966.

Rosenberg, Bernard, and Harry Silverstein. *The Real Tinsel*. New York: Macmillan, 1975.

Rubenstein, Hal. "Wigged Out." *New York Native*, November 17, 1986.

Ryan, Jack. *Recollections—The Detroit Years*. Detroit, Michigan: Whitlaker, 1982.

Ryon, Ruth. "Diana Ross Sells Home." *Los Angeles Times*, August 4, 1985.

Sampson, Henry T. *Blacks in Black and White*. Metuchen, New Jersey: Scarecrow Press, 1977.

Sauter, Van Gordon. "Motown Is Really Big." *Detroit Magazine*, March 21, 1965.

Shiffman, Jack. *Uptown: The Story of Harlem's Apollo Theatre*. New York: Cowles, 1971.

————. *Harlem Heyday*. Buffalo, New York: Prometheus, 1984.

Schoen, Elin. "The Lady Doesn't Sing the Blues." *Ladies Home Journal*, November 1978.

Seawell, Mary Ann. "The 'Nice Voice' of Diana Ross." *Washington Post*, July 7, 1968.

Shaw, Arnold. *Honkers and Shouters*. New York: Collier, 1978.

Shemel, Sidney, and William Krasilovsky. *This Business of Music*. New York: Billboard Publications, 1977.

Sheppard, Eugenia. "Coming Up Roses." *New York Post*, January 5, 1973.

Sky, Rick. "Whitney Gets Even in Ongoing Feud . . ." *Star*, May 17, 1988.

————. "The Babies Diana Ross Has Hidden . . ." *Star*, July 11, 1989.

Small, Michael. "Ain't No Storm Big Enough." *People*, August 8, 1983.

Smith, Bob. "Diana Ross Weds Billionaire . . ." *Star*, February 18, 1986.

Smythe, Mabel M. ed. *The Black American Reference Book*. Englewood Cliffs, New Jersey: Prentice-Hall, 1976.

Southern, Eileen. *The Music of Black Americans: A History*. New York: W. W. Norton, 1971.

Spada, James. *Streisand—The Woman and the Legend*. New York: Dolphin Books, 1981.

Spiegelman, Judy. "David Ruffin Answers the Big Question." *Soul*, May 19, 1969.

————. "Diana Ross Quits Supremes." *Soul*, December 1, 1969.

————. "Tears, Fears and Cheers at Diana's Last Performance . . ." *Soul*, February 23, 1970.

_____. "Diana Ross Now Mrs. Robert Silberstein." *Soul*, February 22, 1971.

_____. "Berry Gordy Honors Daughter." *Soul*, November 1, 1971.

_____. "The Spirit of Soul Music." *Soul*, May 1981.

Spiller, Nancy. "Motown Is Something Spiritual." *Los Angeles Herald Examiner*. August 9, 1985.

Spitz, Robert S. *The Making of Superstars*. Garden City, New York: Doubleday, 1978.

Stassinopoulos, Maria. "Diana Ross." *Town & Country*, May 1983.

Stearns, Dave. "Will It Be Sequins . . . ?" *Rochester Times Union*, October 19, 1982.

Stein, Jeannine. "Suzanne dePasse: My Style." *Los Angeles Herald Examiner*, August 26, 1985.

Steinberg, Cobbett. *Reel Facts: The Movie Book of Records*. New York: Vintage Books, 1978.

Sternfield, Aaron. "An Act for All Ages." *Billboard*, August 7, 1965.

Stevenson, Richard. "Can Motown Be Supreme Again?" *The New York Times*, February 19, 1989.

Stinton, Michael. "Diana Ross' Secret Wedding . . ." *Star*, December 10, 1985.

Stocking, Susan. "Diana Lifts the Curtain . . ." *Detroit Free Press*, November 12, 1972.

Stokes, Geoffrey. *Star Making Machinery: The Odyssey of an Album*. New York: The Bobbs-Merrill Company, 1976.

Suzy. "One Romance Blazes . . ." *Daily News*, June 6, 1979.

Talbert, Bob, and Lee Winfrey. "A Talk With Berry Gordy." *Detroit Free Press*, March 23, 1969.

Tannenbaum, Rob. "Diva Diana Proves Irresistible." *New York Post*, June 16, 1989.

Taraborrelli, J. Randy. "Hollywood Is Talking About Diana Ross." *Black American*, March 10, 1976.

_____. "An Intimate Chat With Martha Reeves." *Right On!* July, 1977.

_____. "Temptations and Four Tops Retrospective." Part One. *Black American*, February 23, 1978.

_____. "Temptations and Four Tops Retrospective." Part Two. *Black American*, March 1, 1978.

_____. "The Four Tops—25 Years of Soulin'." *Hip*, July 1978.

_____. "Richard Pryor—The Wiz." *Soul*, October 30, 1978.

_____. "Jean Terrell—Show Business Is Not Her Life." *Inside Gossip*, December 1978.

_____. "A Look at Eddie James Kendricks." *Black American*, April 1979.

_____. "The Jacksons—After Ten Years." *Black American*, May 1979.

_____. "Interview With Michael Jackson." *Soul Teen*, December 1979.

_____. "Smokey Robinson—He's Still Cruisin'." *Soul*, January 1980.

_____. "The Spinners Back in Focus Again." *Hip*, March 1980.

_____. "Billy Dee Williams: Sex Appeal With a Purpose." *Soul*, November 1980.

_____. "Diana Ross Leaves Motown." *Soul*, August 1981.

_____. "Ross: What Does It Mean?" *Soul*, August 1981.

_____. "Diana: The Untold Story—The Complete Series." *Soul*, Winter 1981.

_____. "What Does RCA Have Planned for Diana Ross?" *Soul*, Winter 1981.

_____. "Q and A With Diana Ross." *Soul*, Winter 1981.

_____. "Interview With Diana Ross: 'I'm Willing to Make a Fool of Myself.'" *Soul*, January 1982.

———. "The Continuing Saga of The Supremes." *Black American*, January 1982.

———. "Mary Wilson: 'I Wish They'd Let The Supremes Rest in Dignity.' " *Black American*, January 1982.

———. "Does Broadway's Salute to The Supremes Mean New Deal for Wilson?" *Soul*, January 1982.

———. "It's My Turn." *Class*, January 1984.

———. *Diana*. New York: Dolphin/Doubleday, 1985.

———. *Motown: Hot Wax, City Cool & Solid Gold*. New York: Dolphin/Doubleday, 1986.

———. *Cher*. New York: St. Martin's Press, 1987.

Taylor, Susan. "Diana!" *Essence*, September 1985.

Thomas, Michael. "From Rags to Riches." *Rolling Stone*, February 1, 1973.

Tiegel, Eliot. "Motown Expansion in High With Broadway, TV, Movies." *Billboard*, June 11, 1966.

———. "New Diana Ross Show." *Billboard*, September 30, 1978.

Tosches, Nick. *Unsung Heroes of Rock 'n' Roll*. New York: Charles Scribner & Sons, 1984.

Townsend, Richard. "Diana Did It Berry's Way." *New York Sunday News*, August 8, 1976.

Trescott, Jacqueline. "When Everything Was Perfect." *Washington Post*, April 27, 1975.

Tucker, Ken. "The Mystique of Diana Ross." *Philadelphia Inquirer*, March 13, 1983.

Tyler, Rodney. "Ain't No Mountain High Enough." *You Magazine*, April 16, 1989.

Tyler, Tim. "At Home With the Jackson Five." *Creem*, August 1971.

Valentine, Penny. "Supreme Supremes." *Disc and Music Echo*, February 3, 1968.

Van Matre, Lynn. "Having It Her Way." *Chicago Tribune Magazine*, June 20, 1976.

Wahls, Robert. "The Lady Sings the Blues." *Sunday News*, February 4, 1973.

———. "Diana Reigns Supreme." *Sunday News*, June 20, 1976.

Walker, George. "The Supremes Starring on Behalf of Our Torch Drive." *Detroit Magazine*, July 30, 1967.

Waller, Don. *The Motown Story*. New York: Charles Scribner & Sons, 1985.

Warhol, Andy. "Diana Ross by Andy Warhol." *Interview*, October 1981.

Weinstein, Steve. "It's Prime Time for '60s Music." *Los Angeles Times*. February 21, 1989.

Wenner, Jan, ed. *The Rolling Stone Interviews, vol. 2*. New York: Warner Books, 1973.

Wenner, Karen. "On Holiday." *Women's Wear Daily*, January 1973.

Werba, Hank. "Motown's Berry Gordy Emerges." *Variety*, January 27, 1975.

Whitburn, Joel. *Top Pop Records 1955–1970*. Detroit, Michigan: Gale Research Company, 1971.

Whitcomb, Ian. *Pop Music: From Rag to Rock*. New York: Simon & Schuster, 1972.

White, John. *Billie Holiday*. New York: Universe Books, 1987.

White, Miles. "No More Blues for Diana Ross." *USA Today*, November 13, 1984.

Wickham, P.J. "Michael Jackson—The Scarecrow." *Soul*, October 30, 1978.

Williams, Jean. "New Diana Album All Mixed Up." *Billboard*, May 1980.

Williams, Otis, with Patricia Romanowski. *Temptations*. New York: G.P. Putnam's Sons, 1988.

Williams, Ted. "The Supremes at N.Y.'s Copa . . ." *Soul*, June 8, 1967.

Wilson, Barbara. "Diana Kicking Up Her Heels . . ." *Philadelphia Inquirer*, January 1973.

Wilson, Earl. *The Show Business Nobody Knows.* New York: Cowles Book Company, 1971.

———. "Diana Ross Sings the Oscar Blues." *New York Post*, December 16, 1972.

Wilson, Jeffrey. "Exclusive Interview With Mary Wilson, Pts. 1 and 2." *California Voice*, July 1983.

———. "Mary Wilson—Dreamgirl." *Edge*, October 16, 1986.

Wilson, Mary. *Dreamgirl—My Life as a Supreme.* New York: St. Martin's Press, 1986.

Wilson, Randall. *Florence Ballard—Forever Faithful.* San Francisco: Renaissance Sound & Publications, 1987.

———. "Florence Ballard: You Control My Destiny." *Goldmine*, September, 1983.

Windeler, Robert. "Mr. and Mrs. Diana Ross?" *People*, January 26, 1976.

Witherspoon, William Roger. *Martin Luther King, Jr. . . . To the Mountain Top.* New York: Doubleday, 1985.

Wofford, Harris. *Of Kennedys & Kings.* New York: Farrar-Straus-Giroux, 1980.

Wolf, William. "The Many Faces of Diana Ross." *Cue*, January 13, 1973.

The following features, which were also valuable secondary source materials, were not credited with bylines:

"Supremes Swing at Philharmonic." *Variety*, September 15, 1965.

"Toting For Tamla." *Melody Maker*, September 16, 1965.

"Motown Sets Expansion." *Soul*, June 23, 1966.

"Motown Artists Booked . . ." *Soul*, July 1966.

"Supremes Storm Japan." *Soul*, September 13, 1966.

"Another Hit, Award and TV Show for The Supremes." *Soul*, February 16, 1967.

"Motown Closed by Rioting in Detroit." *Soul*, August 21, 1967.

"Florence Asks Out." *Soul*, September 4, 1967.

"Diana Performs for Poor March." *Soul*, July 1, 1968.

"New Looks for The Tempts." *Soul*, July 1968.

"What's Happening to Motown." *Scope*. September 14, 1968.

"Motown Sues Top Songwriting Team." *Soul*, October 21, 1968.

"Ruffin Sues Motown." *Soul*, October 21, 1968.

"Salute to a Fifty Year Marriage." *Soul*, November 4, 1968.

"Taking Care of Business." *Soul*, January 6, 1969.

"Former Supreme Talks a Little." *Ebony*, February 1969.

"Diana Ross Sings the Blues for Her Dogs." *New York Post*, June 9, 1969.

"Motown Now Planning Move . . ." *The Hollywood Reporter*, September 2, 1969.

"Baby, Baby, Where Did Diana Go?" *Time*, August 17, 1970.

"What's It Like to Be Michael Jackson." *Soul*, August 1970.

"Motown: The Uptight, Outasight." *Let It Rock*, November 1970.

"Supreme Sacrifice for Ballard." *Michigan Chronicle*, November 14, 1970.

"Hit Factory." *Sunday Times Magazine*, February 14, 1971.

"Lady Sings the Blues." *Soul*, November 20, 1972.

"Berry Gordy Raps on His Lady." *Soul*, December 4, 1972.

"New Day for Diana." *Life*, December 8, 1972.

"Temptations' Paul Williams Dead." *Rolling Stone*, September 27, 1973.

"Ewart Abner on Motown." *Record World*, October 3, 1973.

"Gordy to Direct *Mahogany*." *Los Angeles Times*, January 17, 1975.

"Mrs. Berry Gordy, Loved By All." *Soul*, March 17, 1975.

"Ballard: Finding Her Way." *Black Stars*, May 1975.

"*Mahogany*." *Ebony*, October 1975.

"*Mahogany* Reveals Diana." *Soul*, November 10, 1975.

"Sad Song for Florence." *Jet*, March 18, 1976.

"Original Supremes Mourn Florence." *Soul*, April 12, 1976.

"*Mahogany* Fails to Win." *Soul*, May 10, 1976.

"Diana Ross Files for Divorce." *Soul*, August 1, 1976.

"Guru-ving With Diana in Ind-ya." *Daily News*, July 12, 1977.

"*The Wiz* and How It Was Filmed." *American Cinematographer*, November 1978.

"Diana Ross' Medic Sister." *Jet*, October 1982.

"Motown at 25." *Detroit Free Press*, May 5, 1983.

"Stop In the Name of Love." *Us*, May 23, 1983.

"Motown Sale: Supreme $61 Million." *Variety*, June 28, 1988.

"Stop! In The Name of Love, The Top 100," *Rolling Stone*, September 8, 1988.

Also vital to the author's research were the following documents:

U.S. Congress. Senator Philip A. Hart. Testimony to Berry Gordy, Jr. before the Senate. 92nd Cong. 1st sess. April 19, 1971. Congressional Record, vol. 117.

Official Motown Statement: David Ruffin Firing. Motown Records, August 1968.

David Ruffin vs. Motown Record Corporation. Wayne County Court. October 3, 1968.

"Why I Am Fighting Motown by David Ruffin." Dave Hepburn Enterprises. October 22, 1968.

"Diana Ross and The Supremes Fan Club Newsletter #1" August 1969.

"Singer Pleads For Racial Harmony." AP, 1969.

"The Motown Story" booklet. Motown Record Corporation, 1971.

"Diana Ross Has to Pay Latin Casino." UPI, January 1971.

"Supremes & Diana Ross Newsletter: Supremes Promotion & Information." April 1973.

"Roundtable Discussion with Diana Ross." Paramount Pictures Q&A, October 7, 1975.

Transcript of *Soul* interview with Art Sarno, public relations representative of Academy of Motion Pictures Arts and Sciences. January 20, 1976.

"Berry Gordy, Sr.—Celebration of Life." Funeral Program, November 27, 1978.

"An Interview with Miss Diana Ross." Gail Roberts Public Relations, 1983.

"Diana Ross: A Woman in Business." RCA Records, 1983.

"Motown 25—Yesterday, Today & Forever" program booklet, Motown Record Corporation, 1983.

The Diana Ross
Discography 1959–89

THE SUPREMES Singles 1959–67

**Denotes single was released to disc jockeys only,
#Denotes availability on compact disc*

(As The Primettes)
3/59   "Tears of Sorrow"/"Pretty Baby" (Lu-Pine)

(As The Supremes)
3/61   "I Want a Guy"/"Never Again" (Tamla)
7/61   "Buttered Popcorn"/"Who's Lovin' You" (Tamla)

(All singles are Motown releases except where noted.)
5/62   "Your Heart Belongs to Me"/"(He's) Seventeen"
11/62 "Let Me Go the Right Way"/"Time Changes Things"
2/63   "My Heart Can't Take It No More"/"You Bring Back Memories"
6/63   "A Breathtaking, First Sight Soul Shaking, One Night Love Making, Next Day Heartbreaking Guy" (*Later shortened to* "A Breathtaking Guy.")/"(The Man with the) Rock and Roll Banjo Band"
10/63 "When the Lovelight Starts Shining Through His Eyes"/"Standing at the Crossroads of Love"
2/64   "Run, Run, Run"/"I'm Giving You Your Freedom"
6/64   "Where Did Our Love Go"/"He Means the World to Me"
9/64   "Baby Love"/"Ask Any Girl"
-/64   "A Hard Day's Night"/"A Hard Day's Night"*
10/64 "Come See About Me"/"(You're Gone But) Always in My Heart"
2/65   "Stop! In the Name of Love"/"I'm in Love Again"
-/65   "Funny How Time Slips Away"/"Funny How Time Slips Away"*
-/65   "You Send Me"/"You Send Me"*
4/65   "Back in My Arms Again"/"Whisper You Love Me Boy"
6/65   "The Only Time I'm Happy"/"Supremes Interview" (*A promotional record on the George Alexander label but with a Motown catalog number.*)*
6/65   "Things Are Changing"/"Things Are Changing" (*Issued to disc jockeys by the United States Congress in a 1965 Equal Employment Opportunity campaign.*)*
7/65   "Nothing But Heartaches"/"He Holds His Own"
10/65 "I Hear a Symphony"/"Who Could Ever Doubt My Love"

11/65   "Children's Christmas Song"/"Twinkle, Twinkle, Little Me" ("Twin-
        kle, Twinkle, Little Me" *also issued to disc jockeys on red vinyl.*)*
12/65   "My World Is Empty Without You"/"Everything Is Good About You"
 4/66   "Love Is Like an Itching in My Heart"/"He's All I Got"
 7/66   "You Can't Hurry Love"/"Put Yourself in My Place"
10/66   "You Keep Me Hangin' On"/"Remove This Doubt"
 1/67   "Love Is Here and Now You're Gone"/"There's No Stopping Us Now"
 3/67   "The Happening"/"All I Know About You"
 -/67   "Falling in Love with Love"/"Falling in Love with Love"*

DIANA ROSS AND THE SUPREMES Singles (1967–81)

 7/67   "Reflections"/"Going Down for the Third Time"
 9/67   "Baby Love" (*Novelty item—one-sided cardboard picture disc distrib-
        uted by Motown in one-stop grocery stores.*)
 9/67   "Stop! In the Name of Love" (*Same as above*)
 9/67   "Where Did Our Love Go" (*Same as above*)
10/67   "In and Out of Love"/"I Guess I'll Always Love You"
 2/68   "Forever Came Today"/"Time Changes Things"
 4/68   "What the World Needs Now Is Love"/"Your Kiss of Fire"*
 5/68   "Some Things You Never Get Used To"/"You've Been So Wonderful
        to Me"
 9/68   "Love Child"/"Will This Be the Day" (*Also issued to disc jockeys on
        red vinyl.*)*
 1/69   "I'm Livin' in Shame"/"I'm So Glad I Got Somebody (Like You
        Around)" (*Also issued to disc jockeys on red vinyl.*)
 3/69   "The Composer"/"The Beginning of the End"
 5/69   "No Matter What Sign You Are"/"The Young Folks"
 7/69   "The Young Folks"/"No Matter What Sign You Are" (NOTE: "The
        Young Folks" *charted on* Billboard *listings in July 1969, even though
        the record was not commercially reissued. It was, however, issued to
        disc jockeys on red vinyl, with* "The Young Folks" *on both sides of the
        record.*)
10/69   "Someday We'll Be Together"/"He's My Sunny Boy"
 -/81   Medley of Hits: "Stop! In the Name of Love"; "Back in My Arms
        Again"; "Come See About Me"; "Love Is Like an Itching in My
        Heart"/(*Same*)*
 -/81   Medley of Hits: (*Same as above*)/"Where Did We Go Wrong"

DIANA ROSS AND THE SUPREMES WITH THE TEMPTATIONS
Singles (1968–69)

12/68   "I'm Gonna Make You Love Me"/"A Place in the Sun"
 2/69   "I'll Try Something New"/"The Way You Do the Things You Do"
        (*Also issued to disc jockeys on red vinyl.*)
 7/69   "Stubborn Kind of Fellow"/"Try It Baby"*
 8/69   "The Weight"/"For Better or Worse"

548   *J. Randy Taraborrelli*

DIANA ROSS Singles (1970–89)
MOTOWN RECORDS

4/70   "Reach Out and Touch (Somebody's Hand)"/"Dark Side of the World"

7/70   "Ain't No Mountain High Enough"/"Can't It Wait Until Tomorrow"

12/70 "Remember Me"/"How About You" (*Issued to disc jockeys on red vinyl.*)*

4/71   "Feelin' Alright" (*Diana Ross with the Jackson 5*)/"Love Story" (*Diana Ross and Bill Cosby*)*

4/71   "Reach Out, I'll Be There"/"They Long to Be Close to You" (*Issued to disc jockeys on red vinyl.*)

7/71   "Surrender"/"I'm a Winner"

10/71 "I'm Still Waiting"/"A Simple Thing Like Cry"

11/72 Sneak Preview of *Lady Sings the Blues:* "T'Ain't Nobody's Bizness If I Do"; "Good Morning Heartache"/"My Man"; "You've Changed" (*45 r.p.m. extended play promotional item.*)

12/72 "Good Morning Heartache"/"God Bless the Child"

5/73   "Touch Me in the Morning"/"I Won't Last a Day Without You"

12/73 "Last Time I Saw Him"/"Save the Children"

4/74   "Sleepin' "/"You"

2/75   "Sorry Doesn't Always Make It Right"/"Together"

9/75   "The Theme from 'Mahogany' (Do You Know Where You're Going To)"/"No One's Gonna Be a Fool Forever" (*Issued to disc jockeys on yellow vinyl.*)*

2/76   "I Thought It Took a Little Time (But Today I Fell in Love)"/"After You"

3/76   "Love Hangover"/"Kiss Me Now"

7/76   "One Love in My Lifetime"/"Smile"

10/77 "Gettin' Ready for Love"/"Confide in Me"

1/78   "Your Love Is So Good for Me"/"Baby It's Me"

7/78   "You Got It"/"Too Shy to Say"

9/78   "Top of the World"/"Top of the World"*

10/78 "Lovin', Livin', Givin' "/"Lovin', Livin', Givin' "*

12/78 "What You Gave Me"/"Together"

5/79   "The Boss"/"I'm in the World"

10/79 "It's My House"/"Sparkle"

3/80   "Diana Ross—An Interview with an Artist, Featuring Some of Her Hit Recordings, with Bill Huiy/Randy Van Wormer—An Interview with an Artist . . ." (*Special promotional item*)

6/80   "Upside Down"/"Friend to Friend"

8/80   "I'm Coming Out"/"Give Up"

8/80   "I'm Coming Out"/"Friend to Friend" (*Reissued with new B-side.*)

9/80   "It's My Turn"/"Together"

2/81   "One More Chance"/"After You"

5/81   "Cryin' My Heart Out for You"/"To Love Again"

12/81 "My Old Piano"/"Now That You're Gone"

8/82   "We Can Never Light That Flame Again"/"Old Funky Rolls"

3/89   "Love Hangover '89" (12x only)

4/89   "Workin' Overtime"/"Workin' Overtime" (instrumental)

7/89   "This House"/"Paradise"

RCA RECORDS (1981–87)

9/81   "Why Do Fools Fall in Love"/"Think I'm in Love"
9/81   "Endless Love" (long version)/"Endless Love" (short version) (Issued to disc jockeys on white vinyl.)*
12/81   "Mirror, Mirror"/"Sweet Nothings"
4/82   "Work That Body"/"Two Can Make It"
9/82   "Muscles"/"I Am Me"
2/83   "So Close"/"Fool for Your Love"
6/83   "Pieces of Ice"/"Still in Love"
9/83   "Up Front"/"Love or Loneliness"
2/84   "Let's Go Up"/"Girls"
8/84   "Swept Away"/"Fight For It"
11/84   "Missing You"/"We Are the Children of the World"
5/85   "Telephone"/"Fool For Your Love"
8/85   "Eaten Alive"/"I'm Watching You"
11/85   "Chain Reaction"/"More and More"
2/86   "Chain Reaction" (re-mix)/"More and More"
4/86   "Dirty Looks"/"So Close"
7/87   "Tell Me Again"/"I Am Me"

DIANA ROSS AND MARVIN GAYE
Singles (1973–74) Motown

9/73   "You're a Special Part of Me"/"I'm Falling in Love"
1/74   "My Mistake (Was to Love You)"/"Include Me in Your Life"
6/74   "Don't Knock My Love"/"Just Say, Just Say"

DIANA ROSS, MARVIN GAYE, STEVIE WONDER, AND
SMOKEY ROBINSON Single (1978) Motown

12/78   "Pops, We Love You"/"Pops, We Love You" (Instrumental) (Issued to disc jockeys on green vinyl and also commercially on red vinyl in a die-cut heart-shaped disc.)

DIANA ROSS AND MICHAEL JACKSON
Single (1978) MCA Records

8/78   "Ease on Down the Road"/"Poppy Girls" (B-side by Quincy Jones.)

DIANA ROSS AND LIONEL RICHIE
Singles (1981) Motown

5/81   "Endless Love"/"Endless Love" (Instrumental)

DIANA ROSS AND LIONEL RICHIE
Single (1981) PolyGram

9/81   "Dreaming of You"/"Dreaming of You"*

DIANA ROSS AND JULIO IGLESIAS
Single (1984) Columbia

6/84 "All of You"/"The Last Time" (*B-sided Iglesias only*)

MCA RECORDS

11/88 "If We Hold on Together"/"If We Hold on Together" (instrumental)

THE SUPREMES Albums (1963–67)
† *Denotes album was canceled shortly before scheduled release.*

(As The Primettes)

-/72 *Looking Back with The Primettes and Eddie Floyd* (*United Kingdom release featuring* "Tears of Sorrow" *and* "Pretty Baby") (Ember)

(As The Supremes)

(All albums are Motown releases except where noted.)

3/63 *Meet The Supremes*
—— *The Supremes Sing Ballads and Blues*†
8/64 *Where Did Our Love Go*†
9/64 *Where Did Our Love Go* (*Special 33¹/₃ r.p.m. jukebox issue of:* "He Means the World to Me"; "Baby Love"; "Ask Any Girl"/"Where Did Our Love Go"; "Come See About Me"; "Run, Run, Run.")
12/64 *A Bit of Liverpool*
1/65 *A Bit of Liverpool* (*Special 33¹/₃ r.p.m. jukebox issue of:* "You Can't Do That"; "Can't Buy Me Love"; "Bits and Pieces"/"You've Really Got a Hold on Me"; "Because"; "How Do You Do It.")
2/65 *Meet The Supremes* (Reissued with new cover art.)
3/65 *The Supremes Sing Country, Western & Pop*
—— *The Supremes Live! Live! Live!*†
4/65 *We Remember Sam Cooke*
7/65 *More Hits by The Supremes*†
7/65 *More Hits by The Supremes* (*Special 33¹/₃ r.p.m. jukebox issue of:* "Stop! In the Name of Love"; "Back in My Arms Again"; "Ask Any Girl"/"Nothing But Heartaches"; "Mother Dear"; "Whisper You Love Me Boy.")
—— *There's a Place for Us*†
11/65 *The Supremes at the Copa*
—— *A Tribute to the Girls*†
11/65 *Merry Christmas*#
2/66 *I Hear a Symphony*#
3/66 *I Hear a Symphony* (*Special 33¹/₃ r.p.m. jukebox issue of:* "I Hear a Symphony"; "Yesterday"; "My World Is Empty Without You"/"Everything's Good About You"; "He's All I Got"; "A Lovers' Concerto.")
—— *The Supremes Pure Gold*†
8/66 *The Supremes A-Go-Go*†
8/66 *The Supremes A-Go-Go* (*Special 33¹/₃ r.p.m. jukebox issue of:* "You

Can't Hurry Love''; ''Love Is Like an Itching in My Heart''; ''This Old
Heart of Mine''/''I Can't Help Myself''; ''Come and Get These Memories''; ''Money [That's What I Want].''*)

1/67   *The Supremes Sing Holland, Dozier and Holland*#
2/67   *The Supremes Sing Holland, Dozier and Holland (Special 33⅓ r.p.m.
       jukebox issue of:* ''You Keep Me Hangin' On''; ''Love Is Here and Now
       You're Gone''; ''Mother You, Smother You''/''It's the Same Old Song'';
       ''Going Down for the Third Time''; ''There's No Stopping Us Now.''*)
3/67   *The Supremes from Broadway to Hollywood*†
5/67   *The Supremes Sing Rodgers and Hart*

DIANA ROSS AND THE SUPREMES
Albums (1967–86)

7/67   *Diana Ross and The Supremes Sing and Perform Disney Classics*†
8/67   *Diana Ross and The Supremes Greatest Hits, Volumes 1 and 2*†
12/67 *Diana Ross and The Supremes On Stage*†
3/68   *Reflections*
8/68   *Diana Ross and The Supremes Sing and Perform "Funny Girl"*
8/68   *Diana Ross and The Supremes Live at London's Talk of the Town*
1/69   *Love Child (Original title: Some Things You Never Get Used To)*#
5/69   *Let the Sunshine In (Original title: No Matter What Sign You Are)*#
11/69 *Cream of the Crop*#
12/69 *Diana Ross and The Supremes Greatest Hits, Volume 3*
4/70   *Farewell*
7/74   *Anthology (# w/alternate tracks)*
9/79   *Superstar Series, Volume 1*
7/82   *Diana Ross and The Supremes Captured Live On Stage (Originally re-
       leased as Farewell, 4/70.)*
8/83   *Great Songs and Performances That Inspired the Motown 25th Anniver-
       sary TV Special*
2/84   *21 Greatest Hits Compact Command Performances (Motown Compact
       Disc)*
3/86   *25th Anniversary (# w/alternate tracks)*

DIANA ROSS AND THE SUPREMES WITH THE TEMPTATIONS
Albums (1968–69)

9/68   *. . . Join The Temptations*#
12/68 *T.C.B. (Original TV Soundtrack)*#
9/69   *Together*#
9/69   *On Broadway*

DIANA ROSS AND THE SUPREMES
also appear on . . .

-/62   *The Motortown Revue Recorded Live at the Apollo*
4/63   *The Motortown Revue in Paris (Tamla)*
8/66   *The Temptations Gettin' Ready (Vocals on* ''Not Now, I'll Tell You
       Later.'') *(Gordy)*
11/66 *The Four Tops Live (Guest appearance on* ''I Can't Help Myself.'')
8/68   *In Loving Memory*

6/69   *It's Happening Neil Diamond/Diana Ross and The Supremes* (One side each) (MCA-MT)

12/69   *Motown at the Hollywood Palace*

——   *The Andrews Sisters Live* (European bootleg issue includes Andrews Sisters/Supremes hits medley recorded from the Sammy Davis, Jr., television program, 3/4/66.) (Andros/Ands)

1/79   *From the Vaults* (Originally released on Motown's Natural Resources label.)

1/82   *From the Vaults* (Reissued on the Motown label.)

Diana Ross and The Supremes also appear on various Pickwick, Ronco, and K-Tel multi-artist packages and reissues, not to mention many Motown compilation albums.

DIANA ROSS Albums (1970–89)

(All albums are Motown releases unless otherwise noted.)
†Denotes album was canceled shortly before scheduled release.

5/70   *Diana Ross#*

10/70   *Everything Is Everything*

10/70   *Everything Is Everything (Special 33⅓ r.p.m. jukebox issue of:* "My Place"; "Baby It's You"; "The Long and Winding Road"/"How About You"; "I'm Still Waiting"; "Everything Is Everything.")

3/71   *Diana! (Original TV Special Soundtrack)*

7/71   *Surrender#*

12/71   *Lady Sings the Blues (Original Motion Picture Soundtrack)#*

12/71   *Lady Sings the Blues 10x interview (Limited edition promotional disc.)* (MRA-Paramount/Motown 181)

6/73   *Touch Me in the Morning#*

12/73   *Last Time I Saw Him*

12/73   *"Sleepin' ";* "Love Me"/"No One's Gonna Be a Fool Forever"; "Stone Liberty" *(Limited edition four-song promotional 33⅓ r.p.m. disc.)*

5/74   *Live! At Caesars Palace*

10/75   *Mahogany (Original Motion Picture Soundtrack)*

2/76   *Diana Ross#*

7/76   *Greatest Hits*

1/77   *An Evening With Diana Ross*

9/77   *Baby It's Me#*

9/78   *Ross*

12/78   *Diana Ross Sings Songs from The Wiz†*

-/79   *Bobby DJ Spotlights Diana Ross (12x disco release) Medley:* "Love Hangover *(re-mixed)*/"Going Down for the Third Time"/"Love Is Like an Itching in My Heart"/"What You Gave Me"/"Where Did Our Love Go" *(Disconet)*

5/79   *The Boss#*

5/80   *diana#*

——   *diana* (Half-speed mastered superdisc.) (Nautilus)

2/81   *To Love Again*

9/81   *All the Great Hits*

9/81   *Diana's Duets#*

10/81   *It's My Turn (Original Motown Picture Soundtrack)*

9/81   *Why Do Fools Fall in Love* (RCA) *(# U.K. only)*
9/82   *Silk Electric* (RCA)
5/83   *Anthology* (# w/alternate tracks)
6/83   *Ross* (RCA)#
2/84   *14 Greatest Hits Compact Command Performances* (Motown Compact Disc)
9/84   *Swept Away* (RCA)#
8/85   *Eaten Alive* (RCA)#
5/87   *Red Hot Rhythm and Blues* (RCA)#
6/89   *Workin' Overtime#*

DIANA ROSS AND MARVIN GAYE Album (1973)

10/73 *Diana Ross and Marvin Gaye#*

DIANA ROSS AND LIONEL RICHIE Album (1981)

6/81   *Endless Love (Original Motion Picture Soundtrack)* (Mercury)

DIANA ROSS also appears on . . .

-/72   *Marlo Thomas and Friends, Free to Be You and Me* (Song: "When We Grow Up.") (Bell)
3/78   *Pops, We Love You . . . The Album*
9/78   *The Wiz (Original Motion Picture Soundtrack)* (MCA)
5/83   *Motown Superstars Sing Motown Superstars*

Index

Abbott, Lillian, 24
Abernathy, Ralph (Reverend),
    182–83
Acquisto, Carol, 437
Adam Ant, 409
Adams, Cindy, 459
Aghayan, Ray, 259
"Ain't No Mountain High
    Enough," 407, 409
Alabama, 248
Albright, Diane, 346, 399
Ales, Barney, 253
"American Bandstand," 56
Anderson, Edna, 290, 308, 325
Andrews, Bart, 473
Anna Records, 49, 51
Ant, Adam, 409
Apollo Theatre (N.Y.), 71–73
Areheart Shaye, 483
Askey, Gil, 93, 111, 144, 150,
    153, 187, 250–51, 252, 260,
    278, 410, 421
Atkins, Cholly, 111, 142, 185–
    86
Atkins, Mae, 118
Avildsen, John, 291

Bacon, Jim, 156
Badham, John, 324, 326, 327
Baker, Josephine, 285, 319n, 323,
    363, 371, 372, 406, 448, 482
Baldwin, Karen, 441
Ball, Lucille, 205
Ballard, Cornell, 34
Ballard, Florence, 3–4, 488
  absence from recording dates,
    130–31

background, 62
and birth of Ross's first child,
    256
and Chapman, 140–41, 164–65,
    176–77, 303, 314
at Copacabana, 120–22, 132
death, 314
drinking, 141–42, 144, 145,
    158–59, 312
at end of life, 9
finances, 148, 170, 177,
    314
funeral, 4–5, 8, 9–10, 12
and Gordy, 128, 130, 143, 153–
    55, 162, 165–66, 167
health, 142–43
and Marvelettes, 56–57, 62
new home, 101–2
in Primettes, 13–21, 26–27, 28,
    29
rape, 34–35, 40–41, 57
replacement of, 131–32, 145–
    46, 155, 159, 162, 164–65,
    167
and Robinson, Smokey, 36–37,
    38
and Roshkind, 170
and Ross, 5–8, 10–11, 115, 136–
    38, 141–43, 144, 155, 160,
    177–78, 313–14, 482
on Ross's father, 30
in South, 66
after Supremes, 10–12, 302–5,
    312–14
training, 112–13
voice, 28, 29
weight, 145, 304

555

and Wilson, 143, 155, 160, 162, 312, 313
See also Supremes, The
Ballard, Lurlee, 9, 34, 161, 162, 304, 314
Barnes, Billy, 209
Barr, Oda, 124
Barrett, Rona, 335
Barrow, Marlene, 130, 131–32, 159, 165
Bateman, Robert, 14, 15, 20
Baun, Leonard, 177
Beatles, The, 91*n*, 97, 107
Beatty, Warren, 266
Bell, Joseph, 265, 278
Benjaminson, Peter, 49
Bennett, Michael, 401
Benson, Obie, 140
Berger, Shelly, 180, 191, 192, 208, 311, 316, 352
Berry, Chuck, 90
"Billie Jean," 408
Billups, McCluster, 25
Binder, Steve, 372
Birdsong, Cindy, 156–58, 162–65, 167, 171, 174, 175, 190–92, 203–5, 207, 210–12, 214, 220, 225–26, 236, 254, 375, 405, 407, 408, 410–11, 415–18
See also Supremes, The
Birmingham (Ala.), 66
Black and White Minstrels, The, 193, 195–96
Black films, 246–47
Black music, 90–92, 96, 123
See also Motown Sound; Rock 'n' roll
Bland, James, 91
Bluebells, The, 156–57, 164, 191
Bo Diddley, 90
Bodyguard, The, 336, 337, 345, 353
Bogart, Neil, 375
Boorman, John, 336, 345, 353
Born Yesterday, 288
Boss, The, 351, 352
Bowles, Beans, 67, 69

Bradford, Janie, 13, 14, 16, 21, 49, 52, 77, 161, 405, 418
Brenner, David, 484
Bresnick, Paul, 482
Brewster Projects (Detroit), 25–26, 33, 40, 160–61, 227–28
Briley, Jean, 448
Brown, Earl, 209
Brown, James, 196, 202
Brown, Jim, 205
Browne, Michael, 346, 354, 399, 434, 437, 446–47
Burke, Tom, 344, 445
Burkes, Jackie, 16
Burrell, Walter, 230, 280, 281
Busby, Jheryl, 485
Byrum, John, 293, 294, 296, 298

Caesars Palace (Las Vegas), 1–2, 415, 445
Calley, John, 336, 353
Campbell, Choker, 67, 69, 79
Campbell, Roger, 192
Cannes Film Festival, 284
Carmichael, Stokely, 196
Carroll, Diahann, 240, 242
Carroll, Eddie, 264, 354
Carson, Johnny, 165, 179, 180, 181
Cass Technical High School (Detroit), 42–45
"Cavalcade of Stars," 84–87
"Chain Reaction," 443
Chaka Khan, 382
Champlin, Charles, 258*n*, 310
Chantels, The, 28
Chapman, Tommy, 8, 11, 140–41, 164–65, 176–78, 303, 314
Charlton, Janet, 370–71
Cher, 355, 356, 357, 359, 392, 393, 449
Chess Records, 49
Christina, Princess, 477
Christy, George, 391
Civil Rights movement, 179–80, 183, 194–96
Clark, Chris, 126, 200, 201, 257
Clark, Dick, 56, 84, 85, 86

Cohen, Rob, 287–91, 293, 295, 297, 299, 300, 307–9, 324–28, 330–32, 334, 449
Cole, Natalie, 341, 342
Cole, Nat "King," 54n
Collier, Charles, 211
Commodores, The, 374, 375
Constance, Mary, 43–44
Contours, The, 57, 61, 72
Cooke, Sam, 107
Copacabana nightclub, (N.Y.), 108, 110–12, 115–21, 130–32, 164
Cosby, Bill, 324, 463
Costello, Frank, 116
Cox, Taylor, 35, 85, 151, 208, 389
Crosby, Bing, 205
Crudup, Arthur "Big Boy," 91

Dangard, Colin, 392
Darin, Bobby, 205
Davis, Billy, 49–53
Davis, Gail, 436–37
Davis, Hal, 272, 319
Davis, Sammy, Jr., 205
Day, Doris, 48, 51, 52, 83, 155–56
Dells, The, 80
Delpit, Ron, 393
dePasse, Suzanne, 192, 203–5, 233, 237, 256, 257, 261, 268, 281, 287, 288, 290, 324, 340, 343, 352, 355, 377, 384, 393, 402, 404–6, 408, 409, 411, 413, 414, 417, 462, 472, 473, 478, 482, 484, 489
Detroit (Mich.), 13, 23–24, 50, 124–25, 168
Detroit/Windsor Freedom Festival, 15, 29
diana, 359, 360, 363
Diana and Marvin, 272–73
Diana Ross Foundation, 422
Diddley, Bo, 90
Disco music, 318–19, 359
Doubleday Books, 482–83

Dozier, Lamont, 75–76, 77, 78, 84, 87, 92, 95, 172–73
Dreamgirl—My Life as a Supreme, 12, 21n, 65, 115, 473–84, 482, 490
Dreamgirls, 401–2, 481
Drifters, The, 14
Dudak, Les, 357
Dufty, William, 262
Dushoff, Dave, 207–8

Eaten Alive, 442, 443
Edwards, Bernard, 359, 360, 381
Edwards, Dennis, 199
Edwards, Esther, 31, 40, 51, 63, 69, 70, 81–82, 85, 106, 129, 209
Ellington, Duke, 91
"Endless Love," 373–74, 496
Erhard, Werner, 317–18, 323, 327, 342
Etra, Blanche, 459
Evans, Bob, 284, 290

Factor, Donald, L., 227
Fakir, Duke, 140
Falana, Lola, 482
Fawcett, Farrah, 354
Feather, Leonard, 275–76
Ferrer, Pedro, 254
Fisher, John, 160
Fonda, Jane, 283
"For Once in My Lifetime," 267
Fosse, Bob, 327
Four Tops, The, 189
Fox, Ted, 71
Frankenheimer, John, 390, 426, 429, 447, 472
Franklin, Aretha, 53
Franklin, C.L. (Reverend), 8, 9, 53
Franklin, Erma, 53
Franklin, Melvin, 169
Freed, Alan, 91
Fretheim, Haakon, 452, 453
Friendly, Ed, 200
Funny Girl, 187

Fuqua, Harvey, 108, 131
Furie, Sidney, J., 242–47, 257–59, 261, 262, 264, 267, 284

Gaines, Barbara, 40
Gardner, Tommy, 300
Garfein, Jack, 156
Garland, Judy, 98, 283
Garrett, Lee, 61
Gatlin, June, 394
Gaye, Marvin, 3, 18, 78, 99, 104, 123, 126–27, 130, 135, 187, 219, 253–54, 261, 271–73, 439, 485
Geffen, David, 355, 356, 375, 401
George, Nelson, 43, 129
Gere, Richard, 439
Gibb, Andy, 358–59
Gibb, Barry, 442
Gilliam, Stu, 72–73
Giraldi, Bob, 420
Gleason, Ralph, 276
Glickman-Marks Management, 380, 381–87, 388
Goffin, Gerry, 295
Gordy, Anna, 48–49, 51, 219
Gordy, Berry I, 46
Gordy, Berry II, 46–47
Gordy, Berry, Jr.
    artist development, 123–24
    background, 46–47
    and Ballard, 128, 129–30, 144, 145, 153–55, 162, 165–66, 167
    bodyguards, 255–56
    chauvinism, 383–84
    and Clark, Chris, 200–201
    Cohen, Rob, on, 287, 334
    Copacabana bookings, 108, 110–12, 115–22, 130–32
    and crime, 210, 211
    "cross-over" hits, 54–55, 58, 71–72
    and dePasse, 204
    desire for respect, 149–51
    early career, 47–48
    finances, 457

gambling, 126–29, 147–48
    and Gaye, 271–72, 485
    Hitsville headquarters, 13, 168
        homes, 209
    and Jackson Five, 212–13
    and John, Mabel, 201–2
    and *Lady Sings the Blues*, 239–47, 249–53, 257–64, 267, 273–74, 275
    and *Look* interview, 139
    and *Mahogany*, 290–301, 305–11
    Motor Town Revue, 59
    and Motown Sound, 90, 91*n*, 92
    and Motown's 25th anniversary reunion, 404–12
    and Primettes, 14–21, 31–32
    in Puerto Rico, 126–29
    and Robinson, Smokey, 36, 49, 50
    and Ross, 5–8, 51, 60, 74–75, 81–82, 99–100, 106–7, 113–15, 126, 135, 138, 151, 173, 174, 176, 199–204, 205, 223–25, 262, 317–19, 352, 366–69, 377–79
    and Ross' Academy Award nomination, 279–81
    and Ross' album covers, 232–34
    and Ross' last performance with Supremes, 220–22
    and Ross' marriage to Naess, 462
    running of Motown, 91–95, 103, 253, 365–66
    search for female star, 51–54
    and Silberstein, 274–75, 316–17
    songwriting, 49–50
    and Streisand, 187–88
    and Supremes, 74–75, 82–84, 87–88, 102–5, 107–8, 139, 171, 182–83, 214–15, 225–26, 254
    and Temptations, 197, 199
    underworld connections, 116, 129, 169, 178–79
    and Wilson, 189, 220, 224, 405
    and *The Wiz* 325–27, 333

See also Motown Records
Gordy, Bertha, Ida Fuller, 46–47, 306
Gordy, Fuller, 7
Gordy, Gwen, 48–49, 51, 117, 118, 119, 167, 219
Gordy, Hazel Joy, 255
Gordy, Louyce, 51, 119
Gordy, Raynoma Liles, 49
Gordy, Thelma Louise Coleman, 47–48
Gorman, Freddie, 19
Greene, Al, 49
Griffin, Rita, 44

Haber, Joyce, 279
Hackett, Joan, 347
Haddad-Garcia, George, 357
Hamilton, Jack, 241
Harper, Ken, 324
Harris, Richard, 289
Hartley, Neil, 298, 302, 307
Harvey, Jean, 481
Hendryx, Nona, 158, 164
Hewlett, Charles, 210
Hewlett, David, 415
Hilburn, Robert, 320
Hirschberg, Lynn, 481, 489–90, 496
Hirshey, Gerri, 331, 396, 402–3
Hold, Peter, 397
Holden, Stephen, 402
Holiday, Billie, 51, 52n, 239–43, 245–46, 247, 249–52, 257, 259, 260, 261, 275–76, 323
Holiday, Jennifer, 402
Holland, Brian, 19, 20, 75–78, 83–84, 87, 172–73
Holland, Eddie, 75–76, 77, 78, 84, 172–73
Holland, Sharon, 77–78
Holliday, Judy, 288
Holloway, Brenda, 84–85
Holly, Buddy, 91
Horne, Lena, 52, 89, 246, 327, 330

Horton, Gladys, 37, 38, 39–40, 55, 56, 57, 68–69, 117–18, 145–46
Houston, Thelma, 295
Houston, Whitney, 481–82, 496
Humphrey, Hubert, 183–85
Hutchinson, Frank (Reverend), 237

Iglesias, Julio, 440–42
"I'm Coming Out," 360
Isley Brothers, 90
"It's My Turn," 366–69
"I Want a Guy," 19–20, 35

Jackson, Doris, 42–43
Jackson, Joe, 212–13, 394, 395
Jackson, Katherine, 394
Jackson, Mahalia, 51n
Jackson, Michael, 212–13, 329, 331–32, 346, 393–96, 401, 402, 408, 412, 420, 421, 442, 460–61, 464, 477, 478, 483
Jackson, 5, The, 213–14, 478
Jaffe, Rona, 113, 201
Jagger, Mick and Bianca, 266
Jenkins, Milton, 27, 28
"Jimmy Mack," 92
J.L. Hudson's (department store), 44
John, Little Willie, 202
John, Mabel, 17, 18, 53, 201–3
John Robert Powers School for Social Grace (Detroit), 109
Johnson, Louis, 332
Johnson, Marv, 49
Johnston, Ardena, 80–81, 85
Jones, Quincy, 332

Kannry, Glen S., 435
Katz, Gary, 420
Kendricks, Eddie, 26, 27, 198
Khan, Chaka, 382
King, Coretta, 182
King, Martin Luther, Jr., 179–81, 193, 194, 195

King, Maurice, 112, 124, 148, 149, 197, 198
Kirk, Andy, 71
Kirkland, Douglas, 381
Koch, Edward, 422, 423, 426–28
Kraft, Robert, 43
Kron, Aimee, 45
Kumlin, Filippa, 452–55, 464, 467–68, 470–71, 477, 479–81, 487–88
Kupferman, Theodore, 459

LaBelle, Patti, 156, 158
Lady Sings the Blues, 239–47, 249–53, 257–64, 267, 273–74, 275–76, 279–80, 281, 284, 286, 291
Langdon, Harry, 232–34, 236, 255
Las Vegas (Nev.), 147–48
Latin Casino (Cherry Hill, N.J.), 205–8
Lawrence, Lynda Tucker, 254
Layton, Joe, 319
Lazar, Irving "Swifty," 400
Leasy, Graham Ferguson, 465–66
Leiviska, Nancy, 299, 306
Lemmon, Jack, 287
Lennon, John, 387
Lesterlin, François, 448
Linder, Carl, 447
Loeb and Loeb, 389
Look magazine, 138–39, 240–41
"Love Child," 189, 190
"Love Hangover," 319
Lumet, Sidney, 327, 330, 331

MacArthur, Sye, 136, 137, 148, 149, 150
MacCrae, Joyce, 331
Mackey, John, 328, 359, 392, 419, 420, 432, 433, 437–38, 489
Mackie, Bob, 209, 259, 284, 320, 356, 419, 465
Macon (Ga.), 65, 69
Mafia, 116, 129, 169, 178–79
Mahogany, 290–301, 306, 311
Maidstone Club, 467–68

Main Event, The, 337, 338
Malcolm, Derek, 195
Mann, Roderick, 353
Marks, Howard, 380–81, 385–87
Martha and the Vandellas, 61, 64, 76, 78–79, 93, 198
Martin, Barbara, 17, 31, 55
Martin, Jeannie, 199
Marvelettes, The, 40, 55–57, 61, 62, 72, 76, 83
Masiero, Alain, 458
Massaquoi, Hans J., 382
Masser, Michael, 268, 270, 271, 295, 309, 366, 367, 371–72, 481
Matadors, The, 49
Maurice, Dick, 482
Maurstad, Mari, 455, 456
Maxwell, Larry, 156, 158
Mayes, Ronald, 429
McAlpern, Nate, 161, 162
McCartney, Paul, 463n
McCloy, Terence, 258
McFarland, Eddie, 69
McGlown, Betty, 13, 16, 27
McGuire Sisters, The, 89, 90
McKay, Louis, 246, 249, 257, 260
McKayle, Donald, 199
McRae, Carmen, 251
Mengers, Sue, 338
Merrill, Bob, 289, 290
Milken, Michael, 447, 448
Miller, Ron, 267–71, 282–83
Mills, Stephanie, 324
Minnelli, Liza, 279, 280, 282, 283
Mintz, Elliot, 477
Miracles, The, 19, 40, 49, 54, 57, 61–62, 65–66, 104
Mischer, Don, 406, 408
"Missing You," 439
Moonwalk, 483
Moore, Joanna, 338
Morris, Richard, 14, 17, 30, 33
Moten, Ernestine. See Ross, Ernestine
Moten, Isabel, 22
Moten, William (Reverend), 22

Motor Town Revue, 59–73, 98–99
Motown Records, 55, 57, 89, 91–
    95, 102–6, 168–69, 177–79,
    210, 252–53, 365–66, 369,
    379, 384, 404, 484–85
Motown Sound, 5, 75, 88, 90,
    91n, 92, 318
"Motown 25—Yesterday, Today,
    Forever," 404–14
Mount, Tom, 326
Muktananda, Swami, 323
"Muscles," 395, 396, 397

Naess, Arne, 450–73, 479–81,
    483, 486–88
Naess, Earling, 452
Naess, Evan, 477
Naess, Filippa. See Kumlin,
    Filippa
Naess, Kiki, 451, 464
Naess, Ross Arne, 476
Newman, Barry, 282
Nicholson, Jack, 293
"Nothing but Heartaches," 105

Onassis, Jacqueline, 399–401, 462
O'Neal, Ryan, 336–39, 345–54
O'Neal, Tatum, 347–48

Page, Julia, 24
Paramount Pictures, 261, 264, 426
Parker, Alan, 327
Paul, Clarence, 74–75, 94
Payne, Freda, 53
Perkins, Anthony, 293, 296, 305
Perry, Richard, 323
Petty, Moira, 396–97
"Pieces of Ice," 420
Pileggi, Nicholas, 425
Pisha, David, 429
"Please Mr. Postman," 55, 68
Podell, Jules, 132, 164
Poor People's March, 182
Poppe, Erik, 457
Powell, Maxine, 110–11, 118, 119,
    123, 320, 474
Predator's Ball, 447

Presley, Elvis, 91
Primes, The, 26, 27, 28
Primettes, The, 13–20, 26, 27, 29,
    30, 41
Principal, Victoria, 358–59
Pryor, Richard, 260, 262–64, 327,
    409, 411

Queen Mother (Great Britain),
    194, 195

Racism, 64–66, 70, 190–92, 281,
    297
    See also Civil Rights movement
Radio City Music Hall, 439, 440,
    494
Ralph, Sheryl Lee, 401–2
Randolph, Barbara, 128–29, 146–
    47
Rayber Voices, The, 49
RCA Records, 376–81, 389, 404,
    443, 444, 445, 485, 492
"Reach Out and Touch," 227,
    229–30, 388
Recording Industry Association of
    America (R.I.A.A.), 103
Record sales charts, 54
Reed, Rex, 310
Reeves, Martha, 76–80, 117, 123,
    168, 253, 390
    See also Martha and the
    Vandellas
Revlon, 384–85
Rhythm and blues, 90
Richards, Deke, 188
Richardson, Tony, 291–92, 295–
    301
Richie, Lionel, 373, 439, 484
Ritz, David, 253
Roberts, Gail, 459
Robinson, Claudette, 36–37, 38–
    39, 218–19
Robinson, Lisa, 282
Robinson, Smokey, 13, 14, 20, 25,
    35–39, 49, 50, 94, 107, 123,
    130, 178, 218–19, 376, 411,
    484, 489

Rock 'n' roll, 26, 90
Rodgers, Bobby, 66, 67, 140
Rodgers, Nile, 359–60, 380
Rogers, Wanda, 57, 84
Roosevelt, Franklin Delano, 329
Rosenman, Howard, 338, 481
Roshkind, Michael, 170, 177, 230, 233, 242, 256, 279, 310, 311, 351, 352
Ross, 420
Ross, Arthur (T-Boy; brother), 230, 247–48, 432–33
Ross, Barbara Jean (sister), 23, 24, 28, 30, 42, 71, 230, 434
Ross, Chico. *See* Ross, Wilbert Alex
Ross, Diana
  Academy Award nomination, 278–80, 282–83
  album covers, 232–34, 272, 351, 381, 420, 439
  at Apollo Theatre, 71–72
  and Ballard, 6–8, 10–12, 117, 136–38, 141–43, 144, 155, 160, 185–86, 303, 313–14, 335, 482
  on Ballard's dismissal, 163
  at Ballard's funeral, 3–5, 8, 9–11, 12
  biography, 400–401
  and Birdsong, 416–18
  birth, 23
  birth of first child, 256
  birth of second child, 274
  and black causes, 386, 398
  and *The Bodyguard*, 336–37, 345, 353
  boyfriends, 80–81
  break with Motown, 367–69, 376–79, 380
  business ventures, 388–90
  at Caesars Palace, 1–2, 415, 444–45, 472
  at Cannes Film Festival, 284
  Central Park concerts, 420, 422–28, 444
  and Cher, 355–57, 393

  childhood, 25–26
  at Copacabana, 117–22
  current persona, 497–98
  decision to leave Supremes, 147, 213–14
  desire for respect, 340–41, 388
  desire for social acceptance, 397–98
  dogs, 206–8
  downturn in career, 442–44, 493
  education, 42–45
  employees, 341–44, 435–38, 486–87
  in England, 174–75, 192–94
  fans' opinions, 3–5, 490
  and father, 27–28, 29–30, 42, 231
  final performance with Supremes, 216–21
  finances, 226–27, 370–71, 386–87, 418, 447–49, 463, 492
  first solo TV special, 242
  flirting, 38–39
  friendships, 354–55
  gambling, 147–48
  and Gaye, 271–73
  good side, 228–29
  and Gordy, 5–8, 51, 60, 74–75, 99–100, 106–7, 113–15, 126, 135, 138, 151, 173, 174, 176, 199–206, 223–25, 262, 317–19, 352, 366–69, 377–79, 383–84
  health, 136–38, 330, 415
  and Holland, Brian, 77–78
  homes, 101–2, 213, 227, 229, 379, 420, 456, 487
  and Horton, Gladys, 117, 118
  and Houston, Whitney, 481–82, 496
  and Humphrey endorsement, 183–85
  insecurity, 341–42, 490
  isolation from others, 198–99, 386–88, 440
  and Jackson, Michael, 393–96, 442, 460–61, 477–78

and Jackson Five, 213
and John, Mabel, 202–3
on Johnny Carson show, 179–82
and *Lady Sings the Blues*, 239–
    47, 249–53, 257–64, 267–76,
    281, 284, 286
Look interviews, 139, 240–41
at Los Angeles Forum, 372–73
and *Mahogany*, 290–301, 305–11
and Marvelettes, 55–56
motherhood, 315–17, 381–82,
    445–47, 476–77
mother's death, 440, 441–42
at Motown's 25th anniversary
    show, 404–14
mystique, 321, 344
and Naess, 450, 455–72, 479–
    80, 487
name change, 125
1983 national tour, 429–32
and O'Neal, 345, 355
philanthropy, 422, 428
physical appearance, 109–10,
    172, 492–93
in Primettes, 13–21, 26, 29, 31–
    32
and racism, 64–67, 70, 190–92,
    249
at Radio City Music Hall, 439–
    40, 494–97
at RCA, 379–81
and Reeves, Martha, 76, 117
and Robinson, Smokey, 35–39
sibling relationships, 432–34
and Silberstein, 235–39, 264–
    66, 274, 316, 322, 361,
    382
and Simmons, Gene, 356–59,
    360–64, 379, 382, 383, 391–
    93
solo career, 226–27, 231–34
as star of Supremes, 5, 89, 146–
    47, 151–52, 192
and Streisand, 186–87, 188, 245,
    250, 252, 268, 337, 354–55,
    420–21
teen years, 33–45

tour accommodations, 429–30
training, 109–13
voice, 19–20, 28, 29, 83
Walters interview, 334–36, 489
and Wilson, 11–12, 115, 167,
    214, 406, 413, 472–76, 490,
    491, 492
and *The Wiz*, 324–34, 448
See also Supremes, The; specific
    albums, movies, and records
Ross, Edward (grandfather), 22
Ross, Ernestine (mother), 231,
    274, 280, 434
background, 22–23
at Ballard's funeral, 4–5
death, 440
illness, 64, 439, 440
and *Look* interview, 139
marriage and young family, 23–
    24, 25
and Primettes, 27, 28, 31–32
as Supremes chaperone, 85–86
Ross, Fred (father), 231, 280,
    433
background, 22–23
and daughter's career, 21–22,
    27–28, 29–31, 33, 231
marriage and young family, 23–
    26
and Primettes, 27
Ross, Fred Earl (brother), 230,
    248–49
Ross, Herb, 327
Ross, Ida (grandmother), 22
Ross, Margretia (sister), 70, 230,
    318, 331, 433–34
Ross, Rhonda Suzanne. *See*
    Silberstein, Rhonda
Ross, Rita, *See* Ross, Margretia
Ross, T-Boy. *See* Ross, Arthur
Ross, Ted, 324, 327
Ross, Wilbert Alex (Chico;
    brother), 230–31, 433
RTC Management Corporation,
    382, 388–89, 394
Rubenstein, Howard, 427–28
Ruby and the Romantics, 21*n*

Ruffin, David, 197, 199
Russell, Nipsey, 327

Schlatter, George, 200, 209
Schoen, Elin, 345
Schoenfeld, Joe, 243
Schumaker, Joel, 327
Seltzer, Ralph, 126, 253
Selvin, Joel, 430
Shaffner, Joe, 36, 56, 113–148,
    160, 167, 207, 208
Shore, Dinah, 52n, 205
Short, Don, 195
Showtime at the Apollo, 71
Siegel, Benjamin "Bugsy," 116
Silberstein, Chudney Lane, 315,
    317, 445, 458, 469
Silberstein, Rhonda Suzanne, 315,
    316, 318, 321, 382, 447, 458,
    469, 470, 474
Silberstein, Robert, 235–39, 264–
    65, 274–75, 307, 315, 317,
    318, 321, 361, 382, 388, 398,
    470, 480
Silberstein, Tracee Joy, 274, 316,
    318, 458, 469
Silk Electric, 393, 396, 397,
    418
Sills, Greg, 425, 426
Simmons, Gene, 356–59, 360–64,
    379, 382, 383, 391, 393
Simpson, Valerie, 351
Slavery, 96
Smith, Bessie, 323
Smith, Liz, 321
Smokey, 489
"Someday We'll Be Together,"
    215
South (U.S.), 64–67, 69–70
South Carolina, 65, 67
Spiegelman, Judy, 255
Springfield, Dusty, 99
Stassinopoulos, Arianna, 392
Stern, Henry, 423, 427
Stevenson, Mickey, 67, 71, 72,
    108, 112, 119, 135
Stewart, Art, 271

"Stop! In the Name of Love," 95,
    99
Story of Motown, The, 49
Streisand, Barbra, 187, 188, 245,
    250, 252, 268, 289, 338, 345,
    354–55, 405, 420, 421
Stulberg, Gordon, 239, 240
Styne, Jule, 187
Sullivan, Ed, 88–89, 139, 143,
    144, 197, 215
Summers, Robert, 378, 405, 445
Supersonic Attractions, 59
Supremes, The
  at Apollo Theatre, 71–72
  Ballard's dismissal, 162–63, 165,
    167
  in Chicago, 133–34
  at Copacabana, 115–22, 124,
    130–32
  in Detroit, 124–25
  Dick Clark tour, 85–87
  Dreamgirls, 401–2
  early engagements, 55
  on Ed Sullivan show, 88–89,
    144, 197, 215
  in England, 174–76, 192–96
  European tour, 98–99
  final performance with Ross,
    216–21
  finances, 98n, 102–5, 254
  and Gordy, 74–75, 82–84, 85,
    87–88, 102–5, 107–8, 139
  hit songs, 95–96
  and Holland-Dozier-Holland,
    77–78, 88, 131, 158, 173, 188
  Humphrey endorsement, 183–85
  last reunion, 7
  in Las Vegas, 147–52, 165–66
  and Martha and Vandellas, 78–80
  meeting with Beatles, 97
  Motor Town Revue, 59–73, 98–99
  Motown's 25th anniversary
    show, 404–14
  name, 21, 405
  in 1965, 95–101
  in 1966, 124–53
  in 1967, 153–73

in 1968, 173–205
in 1969, 205–15
in 1970, 215–22
rise to fame, 5, 86–90
without Ross, 225–26, 254
in Tokyo, 139–40
training, 108, 110–13
See also individual members
Suzy, 354
Swept Away, 439, 441

Tamla Records, 13, 32, 35, 50, 54
Tarplin, Marv, 36, 62
Taylor, Bobby, 212, 213
"T.C.B.—Taking Care of Business," 197–200
Temptations, The, 3, 88, 99, 140, 179, 197–99, 209
Terrana, Russ, 359
Terrell, Jean, 208–9, 220, 221, 226, 254
Terrell, Tammi, 168
Thomas, Michael, 262
Tomlin, Lily, 414*n*
"Touch Me in the Morning," 268–71, 282, 283–84
Trudeau, Margaret, 353
Tufo, Peter, 427
Tyler, Rodney, 485
Tyler, Willie, 216, 231
Tyson, Cicely, 280, 281

Vandellas. *See* Martha and the Vandellas
Vietnam War, 184–85
Vonyillius, Alun, 351

Walker, George, 160
Walker, Jimmy, 331
Walters, Barbara, 335, 489
Walters, Rennie, 238
Warhol, Andy, 399
Warner Books, 484
Waters, Ethel, 205
Wells, Mary, 53–54, 57, 66–67, 68, 365, 407

Weston, Jay, 239–47, 249, 252, 253, 257, 258, 259, 261, 264, 281, 284, 286
Weston, Kim, 88
"Where Did Our Love Go," 83–84, 85, 86, 87, 103, 104, 105
Where Did Our Love Go, 88
Why Do Fools Fall in Love?, 381
Whyman, John, 370, 372, 373, 415, 416, 418, 460, 466
William Morris Agency, 288–89, 483
Williams, Anson, 478
Williams, Billy Dee, 253, 257, 258, 260, 261–62, 279, 289, 290, 293, 294, 297, 300
Williams, Otis, 140
Williams, Paul, 26, 27, 199, 408
Wilson, Jackie, 49
Wilson, Jeffrey, 348, 349, 350
Wilson, Johnnie Mae, 4, 63, 161, 406
Wilson, Mary, 4
  background, 62–63
  and Ballard, 143–44, 155, 160, 162, 312, 313, 335, 409
  at Ballard's funeral, 4, 5, 8, 10, 12
  book, 12, 21, 65, 115, 476, 482, 490
  boyfriends, 39, 41–42, 81–82
  finances, 102–3, 190*n*, 474–75
  and Gordy, 189–90, 220, 223, 226, 254, 405
  at Los Angeles Forum, 372–73
  marriage to Ferrer, 254
  and Marvelettes, 57
  at Motown's 25th anniversary show, 404–9, 411–14
  new homes, 101–2, 189
  and press, 192
  in Primettes, 13–15, 27–28
  and Ross, 5–8, 11, 115, 169, 214, 406, 413–14, 472–76, 491–92
  on Ross' future, 375
  on Ross' voice, 29

Wilson, Mary, *(continued)*
  in South, 65
  after Supremes, 10, 491–92
  and Supremes' name, 21n
  training, 112
  See also Supremes, The
Wilson, Sam, 63
Wilson, Turkessa, 491
Winston, Stan, 323
Wiz, The, 324–28, 331–34, 353, 448

Wonder, Stevie, 421, 424, 484
Workin' Overtime, 492, 493
Wright, Syreeta, 221, 225
Wynne, Henry, 59

Yablans, Frank, 247, 261
"You Can't Hurry Love," 103, 105

Zakarin, Don, 436–37
Zeffirelli, Franco, 374

ABOUT THE AUTHOR

J. Randy Taraborrelli was born in Philadelphia in 1956. At the age of sixteen, he conducted his first interview with Diana on the day of her opening at the Waldorf-Astoria in New York City. Eventually, he moved to California to work for The Supremes.

For five years he served as the editor-in-chief and publisher of *Soul* magazine, a popular entertainment publication.

He subsequently wrote five books: *Motown; Cher; Laughing Till it Hurts: The Complete Life and Career of Carol Burnett; Call Her Miss Ross;* and the bestselling *Michael Jackson: The Magic and the Myth.*

An American Cable Excellence Award nominee for writing "Motown on Showtime," J. Randy Taraborrelli resides in Los Angeles.